# European Private Law

**Droit privé européen**
**Europäisches Privatrecht**
**European private law**

Fondé par
Begründet von
Founded by

**Andreas Furrer**
**Thomas Probst**
**Franz Werro**

Edité par
Herausgegeben von
Edited by

**Andreas Furrer**
Professor an der Universität Luzern

**Pascal Pichonnaz**
Professeur à l'Université de Fribourg

**Thomas Probst**
Professor an der Universität Freiburg

**Franz Werro**
Professeur à l'Université de Fribourg et au
Georgetown Univrsity Law Center

Stämpfli Publishers Ltd. Berne · 2009

# European Private Law

## *A Handbook*

Edited by
**Mauro Bussani**
and
**Franz Werro**

Bruylant Brussels

Carolina Academic Press

Ant. N. Sakkoulas Publishers Athens

Stämpfli Publishers Ltd. Berne · 2009

Library of Congress Cataloging-in-Publication Data
European private law : a handbook / edited by Mauro Bussani and Franz Werro.
p. cm.
Includes bibliographical references and index.
ISBN 978-1-59460-555-0 (alk. paper)
1. Civil law--Europe. 2. Contracts--Europe. 3. Liability (Law)--Europe. 4. Torts--Europe. 5. Commercial law--Europe. I. Bussani, Mauro. II. Werro, Franz. III. Title.
KJC985.E97 2009
346.4--dc22
2009009020

Bibliographic information published by the Deutsche Nationalbibliothek
The Deutsche Nationalbibliothek lists this publication in the Deutsche Nationalbibliografie; detailed bibliographic data are available on the Internet at http://dnb.d-nb.de.



ISBN 978-3-7272-2646-5 (Stämpfli)
ISBN 978-2-8027-2534-3 (Bruylant)
ISBN 978-960-15-1990-6 (Sakkoulas)

Carolina Academic Press
700 Kent Street
Durham, North Carolina 27701
Telephone (919) 489-7486
Fax (919) 493-5668
www.cap-press.com

Printed in the United States of America

# Contents

# European Private Law

1

# Foreword

Mauro Bussani & Franz Werro

Overcoming the national dimension of the law is the focus of an array of initiatives, meetings, seminars and books, not only in Europe and in the Western world. What usually underpins these efforts is the idea that the law has to be harmonized, integrated or uniformed in order to match social and economic needs. Besides being controversial, these ideas bear different meanings and are often bred by a variety of perspectives on the future of the law. At the outset, we do want to stress that 'changing the law' is not the primary goal of the present enterprise. This two volume book is simply devoted to producing reliable information on private law in an increasingly integrated Europe.

With few exceptions, such as the publications of "The Common Core of European Private Law" Project, there is little literature available for any lawyer, scholar or student interested in understanding a law in Europe different from her/his own. Often, indigenous presentations consist of contributions, which due to open or hidden assumptions of municipal lawyers contain misleading information. At times, articles and monographs are grounded on deep comparative knowledge, but often limited to models considered paradigmatic (i.e. the ones provided by German, French and English law). Thus even this learned scholarship ends up leaving an important part of European law in a penumbra and contributes to a parochial attitude, often blamed by the Europeans to be that of their American colleagues. The aim of this handbook is to correct culturally misleading and/or biased information.

We certainly do not claim that each European legal culture is an absolute unique cultural product that is incommensurable and untranslatable. We believe, however, that one can understand another country's law only through an accurate comprehension of its context, a 'context' that lies beyond the positive law in which lawyers are trained. To avoid ethnocentricity and superficiality, the researcher is always bound to delve beyond judicial decisions, doctrinal writings and the black-letter law of code and statute and reach into the region of 'deeper structures' where law meets cultural, political, socio-economic factors and actors. This is the overall approach this handbook should provide the reader with.

As far as method is concerned, this handbook does not aim to promote the merits of one technique of comparing laws over the others. In particular, the goal is not to dredge up an opposition between the 'functionalist' (à la Zweigert & Kötz) vs. the 'structuralist' (à la Sacco) comparative law methods. In our opinion, this opposition, at least as currently perceived, might at most convey the idea of an integrative comparativism (emphasizing analogies) as opposed to a contrastive comparativism (emphasizing differences)—with all the possible limits already underlined by a great number of comparativists. Furthermore, the functionalism vs. stucturalism debate has presently assumed a very intense normative flavour, linked, as it is, with the idea of comparative law research as ultimately conducive to an 'ought to be' catalogue of changes. This is not what this handbook is looking for. What appears much more important to understand, indeed, is not which side should prevail but how these distinctions are presently and actually used in approaching the legal issues.

On these premises, the overall rationale and goals of the book can be described in the following terms: the handbook is a collection of specially commissioned essays with a set of references to further readings. In addition to the entries the reader will find in this volume, the second one will include contributions on: Corporation Law, Trusts, Law of Sales, (fair and unfair) Competition Law, Liability for Services, Environmental Liability, Personal Injuries Law, Products Liability, Limitation Periods, European Constitutional Order and Private Law, an Economic Analysis of the Harmonization of European Private Law, and the Social Dimension of the Harmonization of European Private Law.

The essays are original and not previously published elsewhere. They are designed not only to offer a comprehensive overview of the different topics, but also to display and provoke lively and controversial debate. The handbook aims at meeting some needs that appear to be both of great momentum and largely overlooked by contemporary literature, namely a) the need to examine current and possible future developments in European private law institutions and issues affecting legal life of private, business and public actors; b) the opportunity to fill a gap in the comparative literature through a concise reference book, which should offer a quick and easy access to the most relevant legal issues; and c) to mark a point in the cultural debate through the presentation of what the European private law is and could be, rather than what it 'ought to' be. It follows that the handbook is not meant to simply describe substantive law, but instead to "compare" private law institutions and cultures.

Ideally, there are two types of books: Those that provide a 'definitive' word in a widely researched area and those that open new areas and raise more questions than they provide answers. This handbook is intended to be much more of the second than of the first type. Our goal is to show how legal comparativism can be used to study the evolution of European supranational rules as well as national ones. The actual dynamics of rule implementation and living life is complex and it may involve several interactions of variables and effects—due to technical and cultural traditions, as well as mentalities and access barrier to knowledge—that are difficult or even impossible to capture in a simplified framework such as a handbook. This doesn't preclude, however, finding driving forces behind the transformation of national and supranational rules.

Rules matter and rules change. At critical junctures of history, the redrafting of rules has involved political issues. For instance, in the 19th century, the combined movements of nationalism and liberalism fixed their sight on building nation states and redrawing the legal map of Europe. The colonial empires did the same out of context and many think that inefficient rules superimposed on local communities heavily contributed to the social and economic failures of the former colonies. The collapse of the Soviet Union in the late 1980s led to the rebirth of a number of nations in Eastern and central Europe, but also to the enfeeblement of legal relationships between individuals, grounded such as they were on a set of formal and informal assumptions that disappeared nearly at once. The process of deep economic integration in Europe as a whole accompanied by pressure for political decentralization, calls into question the role and function of national rules that municipal lawyers keep instrumentalizing as protective shields, competitive factors, offspring of tradition, as well as actual grounds for future developments. We hope the contributions presented in the two volumes of this book can shed some light on these important issues relating to those complex events, while keeping the reading as simple as possible.

As sometimes happens in collective enterprises such as this one, not each and every contributor has perfectly abided by the guidelines that we established at the outset of the project. Nevertheless there is, we believe, broad enough compliance in most cases to produce the advantages that we had wished for.

Trieste & Fribourg, August 2008

# 2

# Fundamental Rights and European Private Law

SAMANTHA BESSON*

## Summary



* PD (Bern), Dr.iur. (Fribourg), M.Jur. (Oxon.), lic.iur. (Fribourg and Vienna). Professor of Public International Law and European Law, University of Fribourg. I would like to thank Ms Verena Seiler, LLM, FNS research assistant at the University of Fribourg, for her assistance with the formal lay-out of the present chapter. The present chapter was finalized in December 2005.

## Introduction

Questioning the place of fundamental rights in *private law* is *en vogue.* There is hardly a serious study of private law nowadays that does not refer to the thinning of the public/private law divide and more specifically to the paradoxical relationship between a branch of law dominated by individual autonomy and economic freedom, on the one hand, and the duties of equal concern and due respect generated by fundamental rights in all areas of human life, on the other.[1] The decreasing role of the State and the corresponding privatization of those entities owing services to the public has increased the power some individuals[2] have over others, thus enhancing the possibility of fundamental rights' violations in horizontal and intersubjective relationships which have traditionally been regulated according to the principle of equality before the law and cut off from constitutional law and the protection of fundamental rights.[3] The mere vertical effect of fundamental rights in a vertical relationship between the State and its citizens no longer suffices to protect these very citizens from private violations of their fundamental rights. Hence the idea of the horizontal or third-party effect ('*Drittwirkung*', '*effet horizontal*') of fundamental rights in private relationships, whether direct or indirect, or at least that of the State's positive duties of protection of fundamental rights among individuals. While all horizontal relationships among individuals potentially concern these more or less direct horizontal effects of fundamental rights, the impact is particularly clear and unprecedented in private law. It is difficult to find an area of private law that has been left untouched by fundamental rights; this may be ascertained in areas as diverse as contract law, commercial law, family law or even property law.

1. See e.g. Besson, Egalité horizontale; Besson, Discrimination; Barak.
2. The term 'individuals' is understood in a broad sense to refer to physical, as well as to legal persons. See on legal persons' duties stemming from international human rights law, Alston; Reinisch; and De Schutter.
3. See Friedmann/Barak-Erez, 1.

Of course, the issue is far from being entirely new in Europe. Fundamental rights' effects in private law have been discussed in Germany[4] and Switzerland[5] since the 1970s. More recently, the adoption of the Human Rights Act (HRA) in the United Kingdom has drawn attention to the quasi-constitutional nature of fundamental rights and to the question of their potential horizontal effect in private relationships, an issue which previously had hardly been addressed in English law.[6] The potential horizontal effect of fundamental rights guarantees has also long been an object of controversy in international law, although with very little success in practice until recently.[7] It is the emergence and development of positive duties of protection of fundamental rights in the European Court of Human Rights' (ECtHR) case-law in the early 1990s that launched the current Europe-wide debate on the relationship between European fundamental rights and national private law.[8] The European Convention on Human Rights (ECHR) is an international instrument that only binds States[9] and as such, for a long time, it did not have any impact whatsoever on intersubjective relationships and private law in particular. The Court's development of States' positive duties as an alternative to the lacking third-party effect of the ECHR is, however, currently reshaping the private law landscape in Europe. This has been discussed in numerous recent studies on the impact of the ECHR in private law.[10]

It should come as no surprise, therefore, that the question also arises with renewed intensity in the context of the development of what is now commonly referred to as *European private law*, that is to say, private law norms that result from the comparison of national legal orders in Europe or from European Union (EU) law *stricto sensu*.[11] In fact, the issue emerges with even more acuity in a European legal context that gives rise not only to norms that provide greater protection (e.g. four freedoms and the principles of Article 3 of the European Community Treaty (ECT)) and scope for private exchanges and

4. See Scheuner, 253; Starck, 97.

5. See Egli; Besson, Egalité horizontale, 982.

6. See Hunt, Horizontal Effect; Phillipson; Leigh; Wade; Buxton; Beale/Pittam; Bamforth; Hunt, Moving; Beyleveld/Pattinson. For the situation before the HRA, see Mitchell.

7. See Clapham, Private law; Hangartner. See, however, on the international legal duties and responsibility of non-state actors, Alston; Reinisch; and De Schutter.

8. Cf. Sudre. See more generally, Wildhaber/Breitenmoser, passim; Frowein/Peukert, passim; Harris/O'Boyle/Warbrick, 19.

9. See e.g. De Schutter.

10. See e.g. the essays in Werro and Ziegler.

11. In the present chapter, the terms 'European law' or 'EU law' refer to the law of the Treaties on the European Union, including the law of the European Community.

transnational economic efficiency (e.g. European directives in the field of company law,[12] product liability law[13] and consumer protection law[14]), but also to norms that ensure greater protection of fundamental rights in national legal orders (e.g. European Charter of Fundamental Rights [ECFR] or Equality directives[15]). This increases, therefore, the possibility of clashes between European private law and national fundamental rights, between national private law and European fundamental rights and, finally, between European private law and European fundamental rights. Moreover, the Europeanization of private law has triggered a reaction on the part of national public law that is gradually reduced to being the only sovereign area of national law, thus giving rise to a renewed interest for the relationship between public and private law[16] and for the impact of fundamental rights on private law. This reaction may be compared to that of the German and Italian constitutional courts in the 1970s[17] and explains how the national and European agendas on fundamental rights are suddenly quite unified on the importance of the impact of fundamental rights on European private law, even if they diverge on the modalities, as we will see.

Finally, this increase in potential violations of fundamental rights through private law norms in Europe also means that, due to the multi-level institutional arrangement in Europe, different jurisdictions might give different answers based on the same fundamental rights regarding the invalidity of the same private law norms. Thus, while national legal orders and jurisdictions

12. See e.g. Directive 90/314/EEC of 13 June 1990 on package travel, package holidays and package tours (OJ L 158 23/06/1990 p. 59); Directive 2004/25/EC of 21 April 2004 on takeover bids (OJ L 142 30/04/2004 p. 12).

13. See e.g. Directive 85/374/EEC of 25 July 1985 on the approximation of the laws, regulations and administrative provisions of the Member States concerning liability for defective products (OJ L 076, 22/03/1991 p. 0035-0041).

14. See e.g. Directive 2002/58/EC of 12 July 2002 concerning the processing of personal data and the protection of privacy in the electronic communications sector (Directive on privacy and electronic communications) (OJ L 201 31/07/2002 p. 37); Directive 2000/13/EC of 20 March 2000 on the approximation of the laws of the Member States relating to the labelling, presentation and advertising of foodstuffs (OJ L 109 06/05/2000 p. 29).

15. See Directive 2000/78/EC of 27 November 2000, establishing a general framework for equal treatment in employment and occupation and Directive 2000/43/EC of 29 June 2000, implementing the principle of equal treatment between persons irrespective of racial or ethnic origin. See Coester-Waltjen on the impact of these directives in German private law.

16. See e.g. Caruso.

17. See e.g. the German decisions BVerfGE 37, 271—*Solange I*, BVerfGE 73, 339—*Solange II*, and BVerfGE 89, 155—*Brunner*.

have addressed the ways to reconcile the often conflicting requirements of national private law and national fundamental rights each in their own way since the 1970s, the European Court of Justice (ECJ) now needs to have a clear line on third-party effect and so do all the national and European jurisdictions currently contributing to the development of European private law. Besides providing grounds to examine an old issue in the new light of European law, the impact of fundamental rights on European private law also reveals therefore the pluralist and multi-level nature of the European fundamental rights protection framework. I will argue that this in turn constitutes an argument for fostering a pluralistic European private law developed at different levels and in different jurisdictions, rather than as a codified state-like private law.

Just like the older issue of the horizontal effect of fundamental rights in national private law, the impact of fundamental rights on European private law has found its share of academic interest[18] and has even led to a revival of interest in third-party effect issues that had long been neglected in some countries.[19] However, few of these studies and publications look at the issue from a constitutional perspective, and most of them focus on the private law dimension of the question with the dangers this presents.[20] Of course, this article's scope precludes addressing every detail of the constitutional dimension. I shall focus, therefore, on the *conceptual* delineations of the different ways in which fundamental rights may influence private law in Europe, rather than on a case study of the occurrences of the problem in Europe. Scope also precludes exploring the way in which the issue is addressed in all European countries.[21] A choice had to be made therefore with respect to the *legal examples*; the conceptual delineation of the impact of fundamental rights on European private law will consider cases where (a) *fundamental rights* stemming from the ECHR and EU law, as well as from Swiss, German and English law conflict with (b) *European private law* understood *qua* Europeanized private law of European countries such as Switzerland, Germany and the United Kingdom.

The present chapter is structured as follows: its first section defines the key concepts in its title and delineates the boundaries of the chapter's topic (1.).

18. See e.g. http://www.fundamentalrights.uni-bremen.de/.

19. See e.g. Coester-Waltjen on the renewed interest for those issues in Germany that was triggered by the new Equality directives.

20. See e.g. Hesselink; Brüggemeier; Joerges, Challenges; Joerges, Process; Joerges, Conflict. See on the dangers of commodification of human rights, Besson, Commodification; Gerstenberg, Constitutions; Besson, Social goods.

21. For national reports, see http://www.fundamentalrights.uni-bremen.de/. See also the essays in Friedmann/Barak-Erez.

In the second section, I argue for the applicability of fundamental rights in private law in general and distinguish the issue from other similar ones (2.). The third section provides a detailed overview of the different modalities of the application of fundamental rights to European private law in different European jurisdictions and of their comparative advantages (3.). Finally, the last section presents the main implications of the growing impact of fundamental rights in European private law for the development of a form of constitutional patriotism in Europe and the future of the Europeanization of private law (4.).

# 1. Some Delimitations

Before turning to the question of the application of fundamental rights in European private law and to its different modalities, it is important to set the scene and define the scope of three relevant concepts besides the two basic concepts of Private Law and Fundamental Rights (see 1.1): European private law (see 1.2), European fundamental rights (see 1.3), and European jurisdictional control (see 1.4). As we will see, the different components of these three elements may indeed be combined to produce a variety of conflicting cases between European private law and fundamental rights.

## *1.1. Two Basic Concepts*

The two concepts of private law and fundamental rights interlinked in the present chapter's title call for a brief clarification, before we look at their European counterparts.

### 1.1.1. Private Law

Private law is a distinct legal domain whose norms govern horizontal relationships among individuals.[22] It entails sub-domains like property law, family law, contract law and tort law. Besides this descriptive definition of private law, there is also a more historical or almost ideological one that relies on the *laissez-faire* conception of private law *qua* area of law that is completely free from public intervention and regulation and that puts private autonomy first.[23]

22. The tie-break element lies therefore in the nature of the norms applied, rather than in the private nature of the actors (who may be bound by public law norms and hence for self-evident reasons by fundamental rights). On the difficulties raised by the definition of non-state actors in the human rights context, see Alston.

23. See Hesselink, n. 3.

Private law has traditionally been a national issue, as confirmed by the development of private international law in case of conflicts of private laws. With the development of trade and, in particular, of the European Economic Community, private law has quickly become an object of legal harmonization and most recently of potential unification. The four basic freedoms, together with the other principles related to the establishment of the European common market, have contributed to create a reinforced European core of private law principles.

### 1.1.2. Fundamental Rights

Although fundamental rights constitute an incontestable part of contemporary law and politics, their positive guarantees are largely general and vague and their exact nature and consequences remain as a result largely controversial. In a nutshell, fundamental rights are rights human beings have simply by virtue of being humans. As such, they are rights which protect fundamental universal and general interests. This definition explains why the term 'human rights' is often used interchangeably with that of 'fundamental rights'.

Strictly speaking, 'human rights' are often said to have a larger scope than 'fundamental rights'. This has to do, first of all, with the *prima facie moral* nature of human rights as opposed to the alleged *legal* nature of fundamental rights. This distinction has no real grounding in moral theory, however, since all legal rights are also generally moral rights. A second alleged reason is that human rights have usually been regarded as those basic rights guaranteed in *international* instruments, whereas fundamental rights were regarded as national basic rights whether guaranteed in constitution or legislation. This distinction too has become moot due to the development of international human rights guarantees and their increasing reception in national legal orders, as exemplified, for instance, by the place of the ECHR in national law. Moreover, the development of 'fundamental rights' in the EU, which gather fundamental rights stemming from national constitutional traditions and human rights from the ECHR, has also led to the growing irrelevance of the distinction between international human rights and national fundamental rights. In this chapter, it is accordingly the concept of fundamental rights that will be preferred.

## *1.2. European Private Law*

European private law encompasses private law norms from European national legal orders, but also private law norms from the European legal order *stricto sensu*. Given that the rest of the book is dedicated to drawing the boundaries of European private law, I will be brief in my exposition.

### 1.2.1. National Private Law

National private laws constitute together the first constitutive element of European private law. Their convergences and divergences are best captured through comparative private law and their inescapable conflicts due to the Europeanization of private exchanges and relationships are solved through a branch of international private law dedicated to European conflicts of laws.[24]

### 1.2.2. European Private Law Stricto Sensu

European private law *stricto sensu* currently encompasses incremental and piecemeal private law norms (1.2.2.1.), but a systematization of European private law has been discussed for some time now (1.2.2.2.).

#### *1.2.2.1. Sector-Specific European Private Law*

Current European private law norms are piecemeal and are specific to sectors of private law, such as contract law, product liability law, and consumer protection law. The full measure of the diversity of the areas concerned may be drawn from the table of contents of the present commentary. European private law, moreover, has the specificity of consisting mostly in directives and as such is to be implemented through national private law. European private law *stricto sensu* in its current state is therefore integrated into national private law. In this chapter, I shall focus on the first sense of European private law *qua* ensemble of national private laws integrated through transnational norms of private law.

#### *1.2.2.2. Systematic European Private Law*

Ever since the beginning of the Europeanization of private law, there have been discussions in academic circles, but also since the late 1980s in the European Parliament[25] and since 2001 in the European Commission, of the possibility of drafting a European civil code that would codify the patchwork of existing sector-specific norms of European private law.[26]

This project of unification of European private law has taken different shapes. Some academic circles have suggested a common core of European

24. On these two constitutive elements of European private law, see Joerges, Challenges.
25. 1989 OJ (C 158) 400; 1994 OJ (C 205) 518.
26. See e.g. Kötz.

legal principles,[27] while others have proposed a full-blown European civil code either as a traditional continental civil code[28] or as a new kind of socially oriented code.[29] In 2001, the European Commission published a Communication on the future of European contract law and reaffirmed its call for coherence in European contract law in its 2003 Action Plan.[30] This project of codification and research of a common core of European legal principles and rules is not entirely uncontested, however. Most critiques rely on the elusive divide between public and private law and on the intensifying links between private law and other areas in *national law*, as well as on the diversity of national private law traditions, on the one hand.[31] They also focus, on the other hand, on the *sui generis* and multi-level nature of the Europeanization of law and of the legitimation mechanisms of European law, as well as on the constitutional dimension of the new *European* private law.[32]

## *1.3. Fundamental Rights in Europe*

Fundamental rights in Europe are those fundamental rights protected by European national legal orders, by the ECHR and by EU law. For reasons of clarity and scope, I am excluding the further international layer of fundamental rights applying to private actors,[33] although it also applies to European private law.[34]

### 1.3.1. National Fundamental Rights

Fundamental rights are regarded as more fundamental than other legal rights because they often also protect common goods and not only individual interests. Besides, even when they protect fundamental interests, they do so in a way that pays more attention to people's fundamental status and in-

27. See the Common Core of European Private Law, University of Trento, http://www.jus.unitn.it/dsg/common-core/home.html. See also the Lando Commission's European Principles of Contract Law (Lando/Beale).

28. See Von Bar. See also the work of the Study Group on a European Civil Code, www.sgecc.net and most recently the edited Principles of European Law, Brussels/Oxford/Stämpfli 2005.

29. See Mattei. See also the Social Justice Group in ELJ.

30. Communication on the Future of European Contract Law, COM(01)398 final and A More Coherent European Contract Law—An Action Plan, COM(03)68 final.

31. See e.g. Hesselink.

32. See e.g. Joerges, Challenges; Joerges, Process; Gerstenberg, European private law.

33. On the horizontal effect of international human rights, see Clapham, Private law. See also most recently, Alston; and Reinisch.

34. See e.g. De Schutter.

violability than ordinary legal rights. National fundamental rights are therefore usually entrenched and protected from ordinary legislative revisions through constitutional protection or at least through higher forms of legislation.[35] Thus, they usually differ both *formally* and *substantively* from ordinary legal rights.

### 1.3.2. European Fundamental Rights

European fundamental rights are all the rights protected by the European Convention on Human Rights that entered into force in 1950. Most of these rights are already formally guaranteed as national fundamental rights, but the ECHR makes a difference with its specific Protocols and, most importantly, the ECtHR's case-law.

There are a number of questions to assess before getting to the issue of the impact of the ECHR in private law: these questions pertain to the effect, rank and scope of the rights protected by the ECHR. Primarily, the ECHR can only have a direct horizontal effect in private law, if its *immediate validity* is recognized in national law in the first place, whether *per se* like in Switzerland or France, or by incorporation in dualist countries like the UK or Germany.[36] Secondly, the ECHR's *rank* over national law should also be examined if it is to take priority over national private law; in some countries, the ECHR has legislative rank and takes priority only over prior laws like in Germany,[37] while in others it has quasi-constitutional or constitutional rank and takes priority over all laws whether prior or ulterior like in Switzerland.[38] There is a favour clause in Article 53 ECHR, however, that tempers the ECHR's primacy and limits its application to cases where it protects fundamental rights better than national guarantees. Finally, the *scope* of ECHR rights extends in principle to the entirety of national law whether public or private. As such, ECHR rights could pre-empt any norms of European private law.

### 1.3.3. EU Fundamental Rights

Besides fundamental freedoms whose aim is the creation of the European internal market, EU law also protects fundamental rights. True, this was not the

35. This is the case, for instance, in French law where fundamental rights are to be found in the Preamble to the 1958 Constitution and in organic laws. Similarly, the British 1998 Human Rights Act does not technically have constitutional rank in the a-constitutional English legal system.

36. See Ellger, 163–164.

37. See Ellger, 164–165.

38. See ATF 125 II 417.

case from the beginning of European integration.[39] Fundamental rights were first recognized by the ECJ's case-law as unwritten general principles of EU law,[40] but are now mentioned in the Treaties through Article 6 of the European Union Treaty (EUT). They encompass those rights stemming from national constitutional traditions and from the ECHR, as well as further rights and principles.[41] In 2000, the European Charter of Fundamental Rights was adopted in Nice, guaranteeing all the rights previously recognized by the ECJ as well as others. The Charter remains non-binding, although it is readily used by General Advocates and the Tribunal of First Instance in Luxembourg.[42] In 2007, the Charter was included in the Lisbon Treaty that, if adopted, would make it binding. It now shares, however, the same uncertainty as to its future fate as the Treaty itself. EU fundamental rights remain, however, binding as general principles of EU law and through Article 6 EUT. In the present chapter, European fundamental rights refer therefore to all the fundamental rights guaranteed in national constitutional law, the ECHR and the Charter, as well as the general principles of EU law.

As with the ECHR, there are a number of questions to assess before getting to the question of the impact of the ECHR in private law: these questions pertain to the general effect, rank and scope of the rights protected by EU law. With respect to the *effect* of EU fundamental rights, they clearly benefit from the same effect as the rest of EU law, which is ensured either directly in monist countries or through incorporation as in the case of the UK. The *direct effect* of EU fundamental rights is given when those provisions are sufficiently clear and precise like for the rest of EU law. While the Charter is considered as soft law and as such cannot have direct effect,[43] EU fundamental rights *qua* general principles of EU law and through Article 6 EUT belong to primary EU law and have direct effect when they are sufficiently clear and precise. As to the *rank* of EU fundamental rights, it follows from the principle of the primacy of EU law that those rights should in principle take priority over national ones. It was the whole gist of the ECJ's case-law on fundamental rights to take up the challenge of the German Federal Constitutional Court and to ensure the primacy of EU law in protecting fundamental rights to the same

39. On their relationship, see ECJ, Case C-112/00 *Schmidberger* [2003] ECR I-5659.

40. See e.g. ECJ, Case 29/69, *Stauder* [1969] ECR 419.

41. See ECJ, Case 11/70 *Internationale Handelsgesellschaft* [1970] ECR 1125 and ECJ, Case 36/75 *Rutili* [1975] ECR 1291.

42. See TFI, Case 54/99 *Max. Mobil* [2001] ECR II-313; Tizzano AG in Case 173/99 *BECTU* [2001] ECR I-4881; Mischo AG in Cases 122P&125/99P *D v. Council* [2000] ECR I-4319.

43. See ECJ, Case 322/88 *Grimaldi* [1989] ECR 4707.

extent as national constitutional law. As such, EU fundamental rights take clear priority over national constitutions and national fundamental rights.[44] If one refers to the Charter's horizontal clauses, and Article 53 in particular, however, it is clear that EU fundamental rights are not meant to diminish European fundamental rights protection overall; these articles establish a principle of favour in cases where national or ECHR rights are more extensive than EU fundamental rights. Finally, the *scope* of EU fundamental rights extends to all activities covered by EU law, whether at the level of EU law *stricto sensu* or in national law provided they are activities where national law implements or derogates to EU law.[45] This is clearly the case of European private law, since national private law is Europeanized through implementing European private law directives.

## *1.4. Jurisdictional Control in Europe*

A third layer of the question of the impact of fundamental rights on European private law and of its modalities is given by the institutional level at which this impact is judged in Europe[46] and whether it is the competence of national jurisdictions, of the ECtHR or of the ECJ. Not only is the horizontal effect of fundamental rights in European private law a difficult question *per se* because of the diversity of norms of European private law and of fundamental rights in Europe, but it is made even more difficult by the diversity of views of the institutions in charge of settling this question.

### 1.4.1. National Jurisdictions

National jurisdictions are all those in charge of judging the violation of fundamental rights in private law and the means to guarantee a certain effect of those rights in private law. In countries where the jurisdiction is divided between private and public law, they encompass mostly private law courts, but when the horizontal effect of fundamental rights and positive duties are granted in a certain legal order, the issue may also be addressed by constitutional courts. National jurisdictions apply national fundamental rights and the ECHR, but

44. See ECJ, Case *Internationale Handelsgesellschaft* [1970] ECR 1125.

45. See e.g. ECJ, Case 5/88 *Wachauf* [1989] ECR 2609; ECJ, Case 260/89 *ERT* [1991] ECR I-2925.

46. This does not exclude legislative and executive positive duties of protection of fundamental rights in private law (see below), but simply shows that European jurisdictions often have the final word on *how* this horizontal effect is implemented.

also EU fundamental rights when they have to review national decisions implementing or derogating to EU law, as it is the case with European private law.

### 1.4.2. The European Court of Human Rights

As I hinted earlier, the ECtHR has been developing a new approach to the impact of fundamental rights in private law aiming at palliating the lack of horizontal effect of the rights guaranteed in the ECHR: European States' positive duties of protection of fundamental rights. The ECtHR's case-law has been applying these duties to private law in an increasing number of cases, thus leading to fundamental changes in European private law. Decisions of the ECtHR take priority over national decisions, whether they have applied national, ECHR or EU fundamental rights.[47]

### 1.4.3. The European Court of Justice

Finally, having recognized the existence of fundamental rights *qua* general principles of European law, the ECJ has considerably extended the scope of its control over European institutions' violations of fundamental rights in private law, but also—and most importantly—over those of national institutions in the context of the implementation of or derogation to EU law. This is clearly the case of European private law, where national private law is Europeanized through implementing European private law directives. Because EU fundamental rights encompass the ECtHR, the ECJ may sometimes constitute a second layer of control of the impact of the same fundamental rights over European private law. This makes the diversity of views regarding the horizontal effect of fundamental rights in European jurisdictional control even more disturbing. While ECJ decisions on fundamental rights are now considered as having primacy over national ones,[48] their status vis-à-vis ECtHR decisions is not entirely clear and this puts national jurisdictions in a difficult situation.[49]

---

47. See, however, on the authority of its case law, the recent German decision, BVerfGE, 2 BvR 1481/04 [14/10/2004]. This decision was rendered as a countermeasure to the European Court of Human Rights decision, ECtHR, Case 59320/00 *Hannover v. Germany* [24/06/2004].

48. This is not entirely clear to all national courts, however. See e.g. *Bananenurteil* BVerfGE 102, 147, 2 BvR 1/97 [07/06/2000] and most recently BVerfGE, 2 BvR 2236/04 [18/07/2005].

49. Both courts regard themselves as independent; see e.g. the ECJ, Case 17/98 *Emesa Sugar and Aruba* [2000] ECR I-665 and the ECtHR, Case 24833/94 *Matthews v. UK* [18/02/1999].

Recent decisions, however, reveal an intensification of the coordination between courts.[50]

## 2. The Applicability of Fundamental Rights in Private Law in General

Before looking into the modalities of the impact of fundamental rights over European private law, it is important to isolate the problem set by the horizontal effect of fundamental rights in private law *per se* (see 2.1), present different justifications for this effect (see 2.2) and, finally, distinguish it from other kinds of effects of fundamental rights in private law (see 2.3).

### *2.1. The Problem*

The problem with the horizontal effect of fundamental rights in private relationships, and private law in particular, lies in the conflict between traditional private law values of autonomy and freedom whether from state intervention or any other individuals' intervention, on the one hand, and the protection of certain other values that are deemed superior to these values, i.e. fundamental rights and the duties they give rise to on the part of the State but also of individuals, on the other. True, private relationships may be the source of growing violations of fundamental rights, but these relationships are allegedly governed by equality before the law as unique principle of distribution and non-legal imbalances of power are not regarded as anomalies.[51]

This approach to private law is not entirely flawless, however. To start with, the *laissez-faire* approach to private law is not uncontroversial and might not have always been there historically.[52] Moreover, the public/private law divide is currently collapsing with increasing delegations of public duties to the private sphere and, hence, growing private power.[53] This evolution is even more striking in the case of European private law that is characterized by new models of regulation and legitimation.[54] The Europeanization of private law is in-

---

50. See e.g. the ECJ, Case 94/00 *Roquette Frères* [2002] ECR I-9011 and the ECtHR decision, Case 45036/98 *Bosphorus v. Ireland* [30/06/2005].

51. See Friedmann/Barak-Erez, 1.

52. See e.g. Besson, Egalité horizontale; Müller, Kunst.

53. See e.g. Besson, Egalité horizontale; Besson, Discrimination.

54. See e.g. Hesselink; Joerges, Challenges; Joerges, Process.

deed piecemeal and based on types of regulation inspired by public law regulation. This inclusive approach to the fundamental market freedoms in EU law has been confirmed in the ECJ's recent case-law and in particular in the *Schmidberger* case, where the Court not only accepted fundamental rights-based restrictions to fundamental freedoms, but emphasized the need for the weighing and balancing of the interests at stake on both sides.[55]

## 2.2. Some Justifications

Besides the shortcomings of the *laissez-faire* approach to private law, there are important positive arguments for an effect of fundamental rights in the entire legal order and hence also in private law. Scope precludes, however, providing a complete justification of horizontal effect.[56] It suffices to refer to the material primacy of constitutional law in the whole legal order, and accordingly to the fundamental role of human rights.[57] Once the role of fundamental rights is acknowledged, this also implies seeing them as an objective value order that underlies, like a thin red line, all legal domains and in particular private law. These domains are indeed concretizations of fundamental rights in different social contexts, where different interests and values are balanced against one another. It is crucial, therefore, to bear in mind the image of private law under the umbrella of constitutional law whenever private law is to be interpreted and applied.[58] Private law should be interpreted and applied so as to accommodate the values which underlie it, such as human dignity or moral autonomy. It would be a mistake to think that private law can be kept alive artificially on the basis of the sole basic values it expressly guarantees such as personality rights or '*bonnes moeurs*'.[59] Rather than undermining private law's specificities, such a coherent approach to shared values and fundamental rights underlying the whole legal order will, on the contrary, reinforce the deontological basis of private autonomy.[60]

The role of fundamental rights in the whole legal order is even clearer at the European level. Built as a form of externalization of human rights duties and

55. See ECJ, C-112/00 *Schmidberger* [2003] ECR I-5659.

56. See Barak, 14.

57. This is what follows, for instance, from Article 1 par. 3 of the German Constitution, and has now penetrated other constitutional traditions in Europe, as, for instance, Article 35 par. 1 of the Swiss Constitution. See Müller, Allgemeine, §39, 30.

58. See Besson, Commodification.

59. See, however, the Swiss case: ATF 129 III 35, 40, cons. 5.2.

60. See Gerstenberg, European private law, 767; Tushnet, Judicial review.

responsibilities to all Europeans across national borders, the EU, and the Member States through the EU also have further global human rights duties to non-Europeans,[61] which European national states do not yet have *per se*.[62] As such, its internal fundamental rights agenda cannot but adapt to these external duties and become more inclusive of individuals and situations.[63] This means, in turn, that fundamental rights are even more closely linked to other areas of law in the EU than at the national level. Moreover, the multi-level institutional framework of governance and legitimation of EU law makes it the case that fundamental rights penetrate private law even deeper through the different levels of control. Finally, the EU law principle of coherence ensures unity in diversity in the Europeanization of law through a normative use of comparative constitutional law and this leads to a certain levelling-up effect.[64] This has recently been illustrated in the context of EU fundamental rights by the *Omega* case, where the ECJ has recognized as a EU fundamental right a principle of human dignity equivalent to that guaranteed by the German Basic Law, thus gradually levelling up European fundamental rights protection in all Member States while also respecting the diversity of national fundamental rights traditions.[65] This levelling-up effect can only reinforce the position of fundamental rights in European private law.

## *2.3. Delimitations*

Not all European constitutional traditions recognize the same horizontal effect of fundamental rights. Before distinguishing between these different conceptions, the horizontal effect of fundamental rights needs to be distinguished from other effects of fundamental rights with which it might be conflated: fundamental rights' purely vertical effect and their half-way vertical-horizontal effect.

### 2.3.1. Vertical Effect and Its Impact on Private Law

The horizontal effect of fundamental rights in private relationships must be distinguished from the traditional vertical effect of fundamental rights between the State and its legal subjects.

61. See e.g. De Schutter on multinational corporations' duties in the context of ACP-EC association agreements.

62. See Nicolaïdis/Lacroix; Besson.

63. See Alston/Weiler; Williams.

64. See Besson, Integrity; Besson.

65. See ECJ, Case 36/02, *Omega Spielhallen-und Automatenaufstellungs-GmbH* [2004]. See also the dialogue between Besselink and Weiler.

Things are not always that clear, however. This vertical effect may also have consequences in private law. For instance, the relationship between individuals and State organs in family law has to be addressed by private law in a way that respects the vertical effect of fundamental rights. It is important, however, on the one hand, to distinguish this vertical effect in private law-making from fundamental rights' *horizontal effect* in private law. An example of the latter may be given in private relationships regulated by private law in family matters such as the relationship between a natural child and his father. On the other hand, the negative dimension of the vertical effect of fundamental rights in private law should not be conflated with *positive duties* of protection of the State to implement fundamental rights through private law, although there are obvious links between the two, as we will see.

### 2.3.2. Vertical-Horizontal Effect and Its Impact on Private Law

Another important distinction is that between the horizontal effect of fundamental rights in private law and their vertical-horizontal effect. The latter concerns cases where it is not the State that ought to respect fundamental rights, but private entities acting in its place through a delegation of public duties. This effect may not, therefore, be deemed purely vertical. The effect of fundamental rights on the relationship between these entities and individuals is not purely horizontal either—these entities, even if they are private, do not act as individuals. They have to respect fundamental rights just as the State would have to in the same situation.[66]

## 3. The Modalities of Application of Fundamental Rights in European Private Law

Even though most European jurisdictions now accept a certain horizontal effect of fundamental rights, they diverge as to its extent. Given the diversity of sources of fundamental rights in Europe and of jurisdictions controlling their respect, the diversity of forms of horizontal effect should come as no surprise. For reasons of space, I have decided against taking up a complete *horizontal* analysis of the variety of cases of horizontal effect of different types of fundamental rights in different types of European private law and in different

---

66. See e.g. Article 35 par. 2 of the Swiss Constitution which assimilates the State and private entities acting in its place in their duties to respect fundamental rights. See Schefer, Schutzpflichten, 113; Häner, 1144; Müller, Allgemeine, n. 34-35.

types of European jurisdiction.[67] What I propose to do in this section is rather to take up *vertically* the different conceptual categories of horizontal effect one encounters in practice, linking them in each case to the different fundamental rights instruments *and* jurisdictions I have mentioned before.[68] The increasing connections between fundamental rights jurisdictions in Europe makes it the case indeed that their views on the issue of horizontal effect will inescapably reflect each other[69] or at least, as it is this chapter's argument, should do so to ensure a greater coherence in fundamental rights protection in Europe.[70] In what follows, I shall distinguish between two groups of horizontal effect according to the *addressee* of the duties at stake and more precisely between the positive and negative duties of individuals (see 3.1) and the positive duties of the State (see 3.2).[71]

## *3.1. Individual Negative and Positive Duties*

Individuals may be given both negative and positive duties as a result of the horizontal effect of negative and positive fundamental rights in private law. Among these negative and positive duties, one should distinguish between those that give fundamental rights a direct horizontal effect and those that only recognize their indirect horizontal effect.

### 3.1.1. Direct Horizontal Effect

Fundamental rights' direct horizontal effect implies that individuals may directly invoke their rights against other individuals without having to wait for an interpretation of private law that conforms with fundamental rights. This direct horizontal effect may be general (3.1.1.1.) or specific (3.1.1.2.).

---

67. Scope precludes going beyond a brief reminder. For further details, see Barak, 14; Tushnet, State action.

68. Fundamental rights' horizontal effect is indeed a product of *both* fundamental rights guarantees themselves (see e.g. Article 35 of the Swiss Constitution) and the jurisdictions applying them (e.g. a national jurisdiction granting ECHR rights a horizontal effect the ECtHR cannot grant to them).

69. See Clapham, Private law, 347; Frowein, 302.

70. See on the importance of coherence in EU law, Besson, Integrity.

71. For obvious reasons, States' duties that may have a horizontal effect can only be positive.

### *3.1.1.1. General Direct Horizontal Effect*

Fundamental rights' direct horizontal effect is general when it depends neither on a specific context nor on a specific right. It may be granted by fundamental rights guarantees or a general jurisprudential principle.

Very few national *fundamental rights' instruments* recognize a general direct horizontal effect in private law. Article 35 of the Swiss Constitution acknowledges such a general direct horizontal effect, but qualifies this acknowledgement by adding that this only applies to those rights which are such that they can apply to inter-individual relationships. This form of horizontal effect relies therefore on the assessment of the authorities in charge of the control of the private measures at stake. The ECHR does not recognize a general direct horizontal effect to fundamental rights either. This is a consequence of its conventional nature and the fact that it only binds States as this is confirmed by Article 1 ECHR. In fact, Article 34 ECHR emphasizes the procedural impossibility of making an ECHR claim against an individual. Nor do, finally, EU fundamental rights expressly foresee a general direct horizontal effect; their addressees are mainly EU institutions (Article 6 EUT) and Member States in the context of the implementation of or derogation to EU law. This is confirmed by Article 51 of the Charter which does not mention individuals in the list of potential perpetrators of Charter's violations.

In the absence of a legal provision stipulating fundamental rights' general direct horizontal effect, the latter may derive all the same from a *jurisprudential principle*. Most national jurisdictions exclude the general direct horizontal effect of fundamental rights.[72] As to the ECtHR, the State-oriented scope of its jurisdiction intrinsically limits the list of those it can regard as responsible of a fundamental rights' violation. This has raised an important controversy among internationalists. Whereas a minority of authors defend the possibility of granting horizontal effect to ECHR rights jurisprudentially, the majority and the Court itself do not share that opinion.[73] Of course, a direct horizontal effect may be given to ECHR rights by national jurisdictions if they recognize such an effect to national fundamental rights guarantees.

---

72. See in Switzerland: ATF 118 Ia 46 *Scientology*; and in Germany: BVerfGE 7, 198—*Lüth*.

73. See Alkema, 36; Drzemczewski; Kohl; Eissen, Droits; Eissen, Obligations; De Fontbressin; Hahne. See also Clapham, Drittwirkung; Clapham, Private law, 163; Besson, Discrimination, 1045; Spielmann.

The situation is not as negative in the EU case-law, however. True, the direct horizontal effect of EU fundamental rights is still largely an open question. There are, however, important areas of EU primary law whose purpose is to have a direct horizontal effect in private relationships and hence in private law. It suffices to think, for instance, of *fundamental freedoms*, such as the free movement of workers. Article 39 ECT can indeed be opposed to private associations[74] or even to contractual price agreements.[75] Recently, its direct horizontal effect has even been extended to all private labour relationships.[76] This has been illustrated in the field of the prohibition of discrimination, for instance.[77] The case-law has, however, left some questions open such as that of the horizontal effect vis-à-vis restrictions to the free movement of workers and not only the freedom itself or that of the justifications individuals may produce to excuse an inter-individual restriction to Article 39 ECT given that Article 39 par. 3 and 4 ECT foresee state-oriented justifications only. There are exceptions, of course, among fundamental freedoms. This is the case of the free movement of goods and of Article 28 ECT whose direct horizontal effect has clearly been rejected by the ECJ.[78] The problem lies in the potential conflict between EU competition law, whose function is precisely to settle private conflicts, and direct horizontal effect. It remains, however, that the increasing convergence of fundamental freedoms[79] and the development of the direct horizontal effect of Article 39 ECT may justify extending this horizontal effect to all fundamental freedoms.[80]

Given the increasing number of cases where the direct horizontal effect of fundamental freedoms is acknowledged, it would be surprising not to extend this effect to EU *fundamental rights* themselves.[81] The question has, however,

---

74. See ECJ, Case 36/74 *Walrave* [1974] ECR 1405; ECJ, Case 415/93 *Bosman* [1995] ECR I-4921.

75. See ECJ, Case 15/96 *Kalliope Schöning-Kougebetopoulou* [1998] ECR I-47.

76. See ECJ, Case 281/98 *Angonese* [2000] ECR I-4139.

77. See ECJ, Case 36/74 *Walrave* [1974] ECR 1405; ECJ, Case 13/76 *Donà* [1976] ECR 1333. See also Besson, Droit communautaire.

78. See ECJ, Case 249/81 *Commission v. Ireland* [1982] ECR 4005.

79. See Steinberg.

80. See e.g. Canaris; Ganten.

81. One may also argue that the direct horizontal effect of fundamental freedoms merely increases individuals' freedom and autonomy and cannot therefore be considered an argument for a horizontal effect of fundamental rights which may precisely restrict that freedom. The problem with this argument is that, besides not seeing the justifications for horizontal effect *per se*, it draws boundaries among fundamental rights and freedoms which cannot be drawn in such a clear way given their mutual reinforcement.

always been left open by the ECJ's case-law. Fundamental rights are clearly capable of being invoked in legal disputes between individuals. This would also be the case of the rights guaranteed in the Charter, when it becomes binding.[82] True, Article 51 of the Charter foresees a list of potential violators of fundamental rights that excludes individuals. It would not, however, be the first time individuals fall outside the scope of application of fundamental rights provisions, although these rights are then recognized a direct horizontal effect. Finally, a direct horizontal effect could in any case be granted to EU fundamental rights by national jurisdictions if they recognize such an effect to national fundamental rights guarantees.

#### *3.1.1.2. Specific Direct Horizontal Effect*

Specific direct horizontal effect can be recognized in the case of a specific right or in a specific context. This may derive from fundamental rights' guarantees themselves or from the case-law. Very few national *fundamental rights' instruments* foresee a specific direct horizontal effect. There are exceptions, however. This is the case, for instance, of Article 8 par. 3 of the Swiss Constitution, which guarantees the equality of remuneration between men and women. For the reasons evoked before, this is impossible, however, in the context of the ECHR's guarantees and case-law, although this may be done through national case-law. In the EU, on the contrary, a case of specific direct horizontal effect may be found: that of the equality of remuneration between men and women according to Article 141 par. 1 EUT.[83] The 2000 Equality Directives mentioned previously also foresee the direct horizontal effect of the equality principle in private relationships.[84] Some have even proposed to extend this specific direct horizontal effect to the general anti-discrimination clause of Article 12 EUT through the ECJ's *case-law*.[85]

### 3.1.2. Indirect Horizontal Effect

The horizontal effect of fundamental rights may also be ensured indirectly when it happens through the mediation of private law and hence through the intervention of an authority. Individuals remain the addressees of these fundamental duties, but their horizontal effect is *indirect* because it only takes

82. See Curtin/Van Ooik, 112.

83. See ECJ, Case 43/75 *Defrenne II* [1976] ECR 455; ECJ, Case 381/99 *Brunner* [2001] ECR I-4961; ECJ, Case 320/00 *AG Lawrence* [2002] ECR I-7325.

84. See Coester-Waltjen.

85. See Bieber/Epiney/Haag, §6, 68.

place once the case is examined by an authority which creates or interprets private law so as to grant fundamental rights a horizontal effect. As such, fundamental rights' indirect horizontal effect and the duties they give rise to for individuals should not be confused with the State's positive duties to protect those rights. Of course, as we will see, before indirect horizontal effect can be granted, there will usually be a positive duty for the legislator or the judge to make sure fundamental rights are protected even among individuals.

Because indirect horizontal effect is only granted through the creation or interpretation of private law, it is generally accepted more easily; it does not threaten private autonomy and freedom directly and as such is deemed to respect the values of private law.[86] It is recognized as a jurisprudential principle in most European countries, as in Germany[87] and Switzerland.[88] It is also applied to ECHR rights by national jurisdictions applying them, when they grant the same effect to national fundamental rights as in Switzerland or Germany.[89] Finally, it is a principle one finds in the ECJ's case-law as well as in national decisions applying EU law.[90] One distinguishes between moderate indirect horizontal effect (3.1.2.1.) and reinforced indirect horizontal effect (3.1.2.2.).

### *3.1.2.1. Moderate Indirect Horizontal Effect*

Moderate indirect horizontal effect is very limited and implies at the most the diffusion of constitutional values in private law. It is useful to distinguish between fundamental rights' mere radiation in the whole legal order (3.1.2.1.1.) and their stronger effect through general private law clauses (3.1.2.1.2.).

#### 3.1.2.1.1. Fundamental Rights' Radiation in Private Law

If fundamental rights constitute an objective value order that underlies the whole legal order, their radiation in that legal order implies granting them an indirect horizontal effect in private law. This can be done, for instance, by creating and interpreting private law norms in conformity with fundamental rights. This is something which all European legal orders recognize either expressly or tacitly. Article 35 par. 1 of the Swiss Constitution foresees this radiation expressly, while it has long been recognized as a jurisprudential prin-

---

86. See Barak.

87. See e.g. 1 BvR 1962/01 vom 7/3/2002; BVerfGE 86, 122—*Brokdorf.*

88. See e.g. ATF 123 IV 211 *Rinderwahnsinn*; ATF 61 II 95.

89. See Ellger, 167. See also BVerfGE 74, 370.

90. See ECJ, Case 333/94P *Tetra Pak* [1996] ECR I-5951; ECJ, Case 62/86 *Akzo* [1991] ECR I-3359; ECJ, Case 6-7/73 *Commercial Solvents* [1974] ECR 223; ECJ, Case 260/89 *ERT* [1991] ECR I-2925.

ciple in German law.[91] This first form of indirect horizontal effect is also granted to ECHR rights when they are applied by national jurisdictions.

#### 3.1.2.1.2. General Private Law Clauses

A stronger form of indirect horizontal effect is granted through the application and interpretation of general private law clauses such as the good faith principle or the '*bonnes moeurs*'. These principles are indeed interpreted so as to ensure the respect of fundamental rights in private law.[92]

This is something which all European legal orders recognize either expressly or tacitly. It is the case, for instance, of Article 28 of the Swiss Civil Code that protects personality rights in private law.[93] Another typical example is provided by Article 138 of the German Civil Code which protects individuals against immoral actions on the part of others ('*Sittenwidrigkeit*') and has been used by the German Federal Constitutional Court to declare invalid the extensive personal securities provided for the debts of close relatives.[94] A further example may be found in Articles 1366, 1374 and 1375 of the Italian Civil Code which protect the good faith principle and have been said to translate the constitutional obligation of solidarity ('*solidarietà sociale*') in horizontal relationships.[95] National jurisdictions also recognize this effect to ECHR and EU fundamental rights through general private law clauses.

### *3.1.2.2. Reinforced Indirect Horizontal Effect*

Fundamental rights' indirect horizontal effect may also be reinforced in granting a horizontal effect with respect to specific private law norms themselves and not only to general clauses.[96] This reinforced horizontal effect remains indirect, however, in that it requires the intervention of an authority. There are two kinds of reinforced indirect horizontal effect: conform interpretation of private law and revision of private law.

#### 3.1.2.2.1. Conform Interpretation of Private Law

The interpretation of specific private law norms in conformity to fundamental rights ensures their indirect horizontal effect. It is recognized in almost

91. BVerfGE 7, 198—*Lüth*.
92. See Besson, Egalité horizontale.
93. See ATF 129 III 35, 42, cons. 6.
94. BVerfGE 89, 214—*Bürgschaftsbeschluss*. See Heldrich/Rehm.
95. See Cass., 20/04/1994, 3775, Corr. giur. 1994, 566.
96. See Barak, 28.

all European legal orders either expressly or tacitly. This is, for instance, what Article 35 par. 3 of the Swiss Constitution foresees expressly. It is also what was established by the German jurisprudential principle developed in the famous *Lüth* case in the 1950s.[97] Although ECHR rights cannot be granted an indirect horizontal effect by the ECtHR, they may be given one in national decisions. Similarly, EU fundamental rights may be given an indirect horizontal effect in the interpretation of European private law norms by national jurisdictions and the ECJ.

#### 3.1.2.2.2. Revision of Private Law

A final degree of reinforced indirect horizontal effect may be reached when private law norms are not only interpreted so as to conform to fundamental rights, but are actually revised accordingly. This is a very incisive model of indirect horizontal effect that is recommended by some authors like Judge Aharon Barak.[98] It is not, however, recognized by national jurisdictions nor by the ECJ, whether they apply national, ECHR or EU fundamental rights.

## *3.2. State Positive Duties*

Besides the horizontal effect granted to some individual positive and negative fundamental duties in private law, fundamental rights may also have an impact in private law through the positive duties of States to protect fundamental rights. After a short introduction to the notion, I will present different types of positive duties depending on their addressees.

### 3.2.1. Notion

In view of the difficulties of granting fundamental rights a horizontal effect in private law, which are due mainly to the resistance of traditional private law values such as private autonomy and freedom, an alternative has been developed to grant these rights a certain effect in private relationships: positive duties of protection of fundamental rights in the public sphere, but also in the private sphere and among individuals. These duties are States' duties unlike those that derive from the indirect horizontal effect of fundamental rights, even if the latter are mediated by an authority's intervention and interpretation of private law and are usually based on that authority's positive

97. BVerfGE 7, 198—*Lüth*.

98. See Barak, 29, 31.

duties.[99] Positive duties correspond, in other words, to the *vertical* effect of fundamental rights, but are *positive* and require as such more than the mere abstention of the State and an intervention in the private sphere.

Positive duties to protect fundamental rights in the private sphere have been known within national jurisdictions for a long time. It is, however, their emergence in the case-law of the ECtHR, whose only instrument of horizontal effect it is, that has reinforced the role of positive duties for the horizontal effect of fundamental rights in Europe.[100] Positive duties first appeared in the ECtHR's case-law in the *Marckx*[101] case in 1979, but have been strongly developed since the 1990s.[102] Finally, positive duties are also known to EU law. The ECJ has long recognized the existence of positive duties of protection of fundamental rights. These duties may actually be derived from Article 10 ECT. As in the context of the ECHR positive duties,[103] positive duties based on EU fundamental rights leave a large scope of appreciation to Member States.[104] In fact, some authors claim the horizontal effect of EU fundamental freedoms should in fact be ensured through positive duties and not through a direct horizontal effect.[105] *A fortiori*, therefore, this would make the argument for a direct horizontal effect of EU fundamental rights I alluded to earlier even thinner.

Positive duties complement all fundamental rights, whether positive or negative. They may have many objects.[106] They can be duties to ensure certain material positive services, duties to provide certain procedural and institutional instruments of protection of fundamental rights, duties to adopt certain legal norms and especially criminal laws to protect fundamental rights[107] or, finally, duties to take concrete measures to guarantee individuals' security

99. Contra: dissenting opinion of Judge Kriegler in the South African Constitutional Court's decision *Du Plessis v. De Klerk*, (1996) 3 S.A. 850, 914H-915D, who regards positive duties as an indirect horizontal effect of fundamental rights. See also Hunt, Horizontal effect, 438. Contra: Phillipson, 830–831; Leigh, 840.

100. See Besson, Obligations positives, 49.

101. ECtHR, Case 6833/74 *Marckx v. Belgium* [13/06/1979].

102. See ECtHR, Case 23452/94 *Osman v. UK*, [28/10/1998]; ECtHR, Case 16798/90 *López Ostra v. Spain*, [9/12/1994]; ECtHR, Case 14967/89 *Guerra and others v. Italy*, [19/02/1998].

103. See e.g. ECtHR Case 44306/98 *Appleby and others v. United Kingdom*, 2003-VI [06/05/2003].

104. See ECJ, Case C-265/95 *Commission v. France* [1997] ECR I-6959. See also the *Schmidberger* case.

105. See Bieber/Epiney/Haag.

106. See Schefer, Kerngehalte, 276; Besson, Obligations positives, 73.

107. See ECtHR, Case 8978/80 *X. et Y. v. The Netherlands*, [26/03/1985]; see also BVerfGE 39, 1—*Schwangerschaftsabbruch I* and BVerfGE 88, 203—*Schwangerschaftsabbruch II.*

against risks generated by third parties or even natural risks. In all jurisdictions which recognize positive duties, they are deemed to give rise to *subjective and justiciable claims* to positive protection on the part of all authorities.[108] Given the increasing scope and importance of these duties, authors and judges are more and more divided about their legal justifications, their implementation modalities or their restriction criteria.[109] Scope precludes, however, addressing these difficulties here.

### 3.2.2. Types of Positive Duties

Positive duties of protection of fundamental rights differ not only in content and scope, but also with respect to the *institutions* they oblige. Most legal orders foresee positive duties for all State's institutions. This is the case, for instance, of Article 35 par. 3 of the Swiss Constitution which establishes a duty for all authorities as far as possible to ensure the respect of fundamental rights among individuals.[110] The same applies to ECHR rights which bind all national authorities,[111] and even all EU authorities through the intermediary of EU fundamental rights. Finally, Article 10 ECT also foresees positive duties of implementation of EU law for all national and EU authorities in charge of the latter. Some legal orders, however, only recognize some institutions' positive duties, usually judicial positive duties. One should distinguish therefore between judicial, legislative and executive positive duties.

#### *3.2.2.1. Judicial Positive Duties*

The judge is clearly the primary addressee of positive obligations of protection of fundamental rights among individuals. She is indeed the first to interpret and apply positive law in such a way as to protect individuals' fundamental rights against others. In fact, fundamental rights' indirect horizontal effect necessarily implies respecting judicial positive duties.[112] Even though indirect horizontal effect creates individual as opposed to institutional duties, it requires the judge's active participation. The reverse is not necessarily true, however: a judge's positive duties to protect fundamental rights do not necessarily give rise to giving the latter an indirect horizontal effect.

---

108. See in German law, Unruh, 58; Bleckmann, 219; Hesse, 350. See in Swiss law, Schefer, Kerngehalte, 266. See in the ECHR context, Wildhaber/Breitenmoser, 74; Frowein/Peukert, Articles 8, 9.

109. See Besson, Obligations positives; Schefer, Kerngehalte, Ch. C.

110. See ATF 126 II 300.

111. See the ECtHR, Case 23452/94 *Osman v. UK* [28/10/1998].

112. See Unruh, 71.

In fact, in some legal orders, judicial positive duties are the only positive duties one may think of, as in the United States or in Canada, whereas in most European countries, these duties complement other institutions' positive duties. It is useful in this respect to distinguish between vertical and horizontal judicial duties.

#### 3.2.2.1.1. Vertical Judicial Duties

In the United States and in Canada, the effect of fundamental rights in private law is only recognized in presence of a '*state action*'.[113] While a purely private relationship in which a fundamental rights' violation takes place may not be submitted to fundamental rights' protection, the judge's intervention in this private law matter suffices to constitute a state action and hence to be submitted to the respect of fundamental rights. This effect is purely *vertical* as its addressee is a judge and no horizontal albeit indirect effect of fundamental rights in private law may be derived from it.[114]

#### 3.2.2.1.2. Horizontal Judicial Duties

In most European legal orders, judicial positive duties almost always imply giving fundamental rights' indirect horizontal effect in private law. The judge's positive duty usually consists indeed in interpreting and implementing private law in conformity with fundamental rights.

Judicial positive duties usually complement legislative and executive positive duties. There may be cases, however, where horizontal judicial duties stand on their own independently of a violation of legislative or executive positive duties. This is the case in the ECtHR's recent decision *Pla* which states that, even in the absence of a violation of legislative or executive duties, a certain indirect horizontal effect may be granted to the ECHR in private law through the judge's positive duty to interpret private law in the light of the ECHR.[115]

### *3.2.2.2. Legislative Positive Duties*

In most European legal orders, and in the context of the ECHR, positive duties also extend to the legislature which has the obligation to protect fun-

---

113. See the American Supreme Court decision *Shelley v. Kraemer* 334 US 1 (1948) and the Canadian Supreme Court decision *R.W.D.S.U., Local 580 v. Dolphin Delivery Ltd*, [1986] 2 S.C.R, 573 revised in 2002 by *R.W.D.S.U., Local 558 v. Pepsi-Cola Canada Beverages (West) Ltd.*, 2002 S.C.C. 8. See also Nowak/Rotunda, Ch. 12; Tribe, 246.

114. See on recent evolutions, Tushnet, State action; Sunstein.

115. ECtHR, Case 69498/01 *Pla and Puncernau v. Andorra* [13 juillet 2004], §59.

damental rights in private relationships in drafting private laws which concretize the latter.[116]

It is important not to conflate legislative positive duties with the legislator's negative duties in virtue of fundamental rights' afore-mentioned *vertical* effect. Although these two types of duties are distinct, there could be cases where the legislator's vertical duties have an effect in private law. Moreover, legislative positive duties should be distinguished from fundamental rights' *indirect horizontal effect*. True, the latter may imply drafting new private legislation or revising the latter to extend fundamental rights' protection to individuals. Even though this indirect horizontal effect primarily aims at creating individual obligations, it implies the existence of positive duties for the legislator to make sure this indirect horizontal effect can take place through legislation.[117] The reverse is not necessarily true, however: legislative positive duties may not necessarily give rise to an indirect horizontal effect.

#### *3.2.2.3. Executive Positive Duties*

In most European legal orders, and in the context of the ECHR, positive duties also extend to the executive who has the duty to take all necessary measures to protect fundamental rights among individuals. In fact, most of the case-law concerns the implementation of executive positive duties, such as insufficient police measures or environment protection measures.[118]

### *3.3. Comparative Advantages*

After this presentation of the different types of horizontal effects of fundamental rights in private law one encounters in Europe, depending on the origins of these rights and on the jurisdictions in charge of implementing them, it is important to assess their advantages and disadvantages. One should note, before doing so, that very often the type of horizontal effect chosen does not only depend on its substantive merit, but also on the historical, social and political context behind a legal order,[119] as well as other legal constraints such as the absence of judicial review of legislation or the respect of the margin of ap-

116. See Besson, Integrity.

117. See Tushnet, Judicial review.

118. See ECtHR, Case 23452/94 *Osman v. UK*, [28/10/1998]; ECtHR, Case 16798/90 *López Ostra v. Spain*, [9/12/1994]; ECtHR, Case 14967/89 *Guerra and others v. Italy*, [19/02/1998].

119. See Tushnet, State action, 84. See in Germany, Starck, 111.

preciation of national courts at European level, etc.[120] This has clearly been illustrated by the diversity of views on the subject in Europe depending on whether we are looking at the horizontal effect of fundamental rights in European private law from a national perspective, from that of the ECtHR or of the European Court of Justice. Some comparative advantages may be usefully delineated, however, even though scope precludes mentioning all the dimensions in which the implications of horizontal effect may be criticized and improved.[121]

To start with fundamental rights' *direct horizontal effect*, it is clearly the most contested form of horizontal effect. This has to do primarily with its impact on private law and the principle of private autonomy.[122] Provided, however, by reference to the argument I made earlier, that this traditional approach to private law is abandoned and fundamental rights are given the place they deserve at the heart of private law norms, this critique is no longer valid. On the contrary, direct horizontal effect presents the advantage of being an uncompromised recognition of individual fundamental duties in private law.[123] Moreover, direct horizontal effect avoids translating fundamental rights into private law, either through blanket norms or in concrete norms, and hence circumvents the dangers of commodification that are linked to the privatization of fundamental rights.[124] These dangers may occur, for instance, through the type of legal reasoning used in private law, the justifications one may oppose to a restriction in private law and, finally, the type of proportionality test used in private law.[125] Finally, direct horizontal effect does not overburden authorities with the mediation of fundamental rights' horizontal effect, either indirectly like in the case of indirect horizontal effect or directly as in the case of positive duties.

It is precisely the difficulty often encountered with *indirect horizontal effect* that it submits individual duties to the intervention of an authority, most usually the judge, but also the legislator in the case of reinforced indirect horizontal effect. This gives rise in turn to a further difficulty, that of a breach of the separation of powers in that it is usually the judge who grants indirect horizontal effect. The latter problem is in fact solved by *positive duties* which apply across the board to all institutions. As such, positive duties limit judicial

120. See Besson, Obligations positives.

121. See Besson, Commodification. See also Barak.

122. See Bleckmann, 220–221.

123. See Barak, 15.

124. See Besson, Commodification; Besson, Social goods. See also Somek, Antidiscrimination; Tushnet, Judicial review.

125. See e.g. Ellger, 175–178.

power[126] and maintain a certain institutional balance.[127] Moreover, positive duties emphasize the importance of measures of implementation and concretization of general and abstract fundamental rights. The problem remains, however, that of the mediation of the horizontal effect, with addressees of positive duties being institutions only. Moreover, as I hinted earlier, positive duties generate as yet unsolved implementation problems. For instance, since positive duties can only be violated by omission, the margin of appreciation of authorities is broad and a justification for restrictions is easy to provide. Another problem lies in the type of economic justifications that may be put forward to account for the non-respect of a positive duty. Finally, the test of proportionality applied to restrictions to positive duties does not abide by the strict standards that apply to the violation of other fundamental rights. In sum, therefore, the solution seems to lie in the combination of direct horizontal effect and positive duties, which both present advantages and can complement each other effectively.

## 4. Implications for the Respect of Fundamental Rights in European Private Law

The complexity of these different approaches to the effect of fundamental rights in European private law has many implications, and in particular, first of all, implications for the future reinforcement of a *sui generis* regime of fundamental rights protection in Europe (see 4.1) and, second, implications for the future of the Europeanization of private law (see 4.2).

### *4.1. Towards European Constitutional Patriotism*

What the presentation of the different types of horizontal effect of fundamental rights in European private law has shown is that there is a diversity of approaches to the same problem depending on the origins of the fundamental rights and the jurisdictions concerned. This diversity of approaches, together with the growing number of sources of fundamental rights and private law norms that may conflict in Europe, increases the risk of diverging solutions to the same cases when some of these jurisdictions function as appellate jurisdictions, but also over different cases. This calls for a more coherent ap-

126. See on the importance of separation of powers in the constitutionalization of private law, Tushnet, State action, 98.

127. See Besson, Integrity, 63–64.

proach to the issue of horizontal effect in Europe. As I have explained elsewhere, coherence is a central principle to European integration; it ensures unity in diversity through dialogue, mutual learning and a constant levelling-up of guarantees in Europe, rather than through uniformisation *stricto sensu*.[128]

This very *dialogue* among jurisdictions as to what this horizontal effect should be, is already at work in an embryonic form in the different forms of horizontal effect I have presented. For a long time, the multitude of jurisdictions and hence of views about horizontal effect led to a levelling-down of the overall fundamental rights protection potential in Europe.[129] Each national court decided on horizontal effect without any regard for other European jurisdictions' approaches. Recently, national decisions have started to borrow models of horizontal effect from other legal orders.[130] Similarly, the ECtHR's position respected, as an international court applying an international convention,[131] the national margin of appreciation in matters of horizontal effect. Its recent case-law over positive duties has shown, however, the potential for a real dialogue and levelling-up in fundamental rights protection in Europe.[132] This tendency is also confirmed by the ECJ's recent case-law on fundamental rights and in particular by the *Omega* case, where the ECJ recognized the German principle of human dignity as a EU fundamental right, thus gradually levelling up European fundamental rights protection despite respecting the diversity of national fundamental rights traditions.[133] Finally, the relationship between the ECtHR and the ECJ is as before deeply uncertain. There are signs, however, of a growing willingness to collaborate in the protection of shared values.[134] One may therefore have faith in the development of a European '*constitutional patriotism*' to borrow Jürgen Habermas' expression,[135] which has since then been used by Oliver Gerstenberg in the European fundamental rights context.[136]

Of course, the EU needs to have a clearer line on third-party effect, especially when applied to fundamental rights and not only to fundamental freedoms. This European dialogue over fundamental rights should therefore be

128. See Besson, Integrity.

129. See Clapham, Private law, 347; Frowein, 302.

130. See ATF 126 II 300 for a comparative approach.

131. See Clapham, Private law, 343.

132. See, however, Besson, Reception; Gerstenberg, Constitutions, for some reservations on the *Appleby* case.

133. See the *Omega* case. See the dialogue between Besselink and Weiler, 1999.

134. See the ECHR decision *Bosphorus* and the ECJ decision *Emesa Sugar*.

135. See Habermas, 156.

136. See Gerstenberg, Constitutions.

reinforced. This could occur through an increased use of comparative constitutional law across Europe.[137] One may also suggest adopting a clear constitutional arrangement on horizontal effect of fundamental rights in Europe.[138] This could be done through a revision of Article 51 of the Charter for fundamental rights, although this is very unlikely, given that the Charter was not at all revised before being inserted in the Lisbon Treaty in 2007.

## *4.2. Future Europeanization of Private Law*

Besides providing new hopes for constitutional patriotism in Europe, the issue of the impact of fundamental rights on European private law has revealed the pluralist and multi-level nature of the European legal order. This constitutes an argument for fostering a pluralistic European private law developing at different levels and in different jurisdictions through dialogue and mutual learning, rather than as a codified state-like private law imposed from above.

Moreover, if fundamental rights are to be understood, as I have argued before, as even more central to European law than to national law, European private law cannot afford to develop without reference to them.[139] Since EU fundamental rights are clearly developing in a pluralistic way, it would be counterproductive to isolate European private law from them in a way even national private law no longer is, given the penetration of multi-level fundamental rights protection in national law. In fact, this would be even more counterproductive as national and European fundamental rights agendas with regard to private law seem to have come in line with one another, as was illustrated in the Charter drafting process. This tendency may also be explained by reference to the loss of sovereignty that goes together with the Europeanization of private law.[140] We might therefore soon be watching a replica of the *Solange I* and *II* challenge, if the ECJ does not find a clear line on issues pertaining to the Europeanization of private law and the impact of fundamental rights on the latter. In sum, the way fundamental rights impact on European private law may be said to plead against a unified European civil

---

137. See on the authority of comparative constitutional law in Europe, Besson/Pfersmann. See also Möllers, 41; Gerstenberg, Constitutions.

138. See at the national level, Barak, 42.

139. See e.g. Hesselink; Joerges, Challenges; Gerstenberg, European private law; Joerges, Conflict.

140. See Caruso.

code. All this confirms, albeit on other grounds, the very conclusion others have reached on the basis of the failure of the European Constitutional Treaty.[141]

## Conclusions

The now well-known question of the horizontal effect of fundamental rights has recently re-arisen with a renewed intensity in the context of the development of European private law. Rather than pouring old wine into new casks, the issue emerges with more acuity in a European legal context. Not only does EU law give rise to norms that provide greater scope for private exchanges and transnational economic efficiency, but it also generate norms that ensure greater protection of fundamental rights in national legal orders. This increases, as this chapter has demonstrated, the possibility of clashes between European private law and national fundamental rights, between national private law and European fundamental rights and, finally, between European private law and European fundamental rights. Moreover, this increase in potential violations of fundamental rights through private law norms in Europe also explains how, combined with the multi-level institutional arrangement, different jurisdictions develop the different approaches to the horizontal effect of fundamental rights in European private law this chapter has presented and how they may therefore give different answers, albeit based on the same fundamental rights, to the question of the invalidity of the same private law norms. Thus, while national jurisdictions have addressed this issue each in their own way since the 1970s and the ECtHR has too often resisted imposing a European levelling-up out of respect for the national margin of appreciation, the ECJ now needs to have a clear line on third-party effect in European private law and so do the ECtHR and all the national jurisdictions currently contributing to the development of European private law.

Besides providing grounds to examine an old issue in the new light of European law and to propose coherent solutions to a common question across Europe, the impact of fundamental rights on European private law has also revealed the pluralist and multi-level nature of the European fundamental rights protection framework and emphasized the need for the development of a true constitutional patriotism in Europe. Finally, the diversity of horizontal effects in Europe provides an argument for fostering a pluralistic European

141. See Joerges, Conflict; Gerstenberg, European private law, 786.

private law developing at different levels and in different jurisdictions, rather than as a codified state-like private law. At a time when national public law is gradually being reduced by the Europeanization of private law to being the only sovereign area of national law left, thus giving rise to a renewed interest for the relationship between public and private law and for the impact of fundamental rights on private law across Europe, it would be counterproductive to suppress the very means we have to develop a living European private law based on the fundamental values shared by all Europeans.

## References

Alkema Albert, The third-party applicability or 'Drittwirkung' of the European Convention on Human Rights, in Matscher Franz/Petzold Herbert (eds), Protecting Human Rights: The European Dimension, Studies in Honour of G.J. Wiarda, Cologne 1988, 33.

Alston Philip, The 'Not-a-Cat' Syndrome: Can the International Human Rights Regime Accommodate Non-State Actors?, in Non-State Actors and Human Rights, Oxford 2005, 3.

Alston Philip/Weiler Joseph, An 'Ever Closer Union' in Need of a Human Rights Policy: The European Union and Human Rights, in Alston/Bustelo/Heenan (eds), The EU and Human Rights, Oxford 1999, 1.

Bamforth Nicholas, The True Horizontal Effect of the Human Rights Act 1998, Law Quarterly Review (2001) 117, 34.

von Bar Christian, From Principles to Codification: Prospects for European Private Law, Columbia Law Journal (2002) 8, 379.

Barak Aharon, Constitutional Human Rights and Private Law, in Friedmann Daniel/Barak-Erez Daphné (eds), Human Rights in Private Law, Oxford 2001, 13.

Beale Hugh/Pittam Nicola, The Impact of the Human Rights Act 1998 on English Tort and Contract Law, in Friedmann Daniel/Barak-Erez Daphné (eds), Human Rights in Private Law, Oxford 2001, 131.

Besselink Leonard, Entrapped by the Maximum Standard: on Fundamental Rights, Pluralism and Subsidiarity in the European Union, Common Market Law Review (1998) 35, 629.

Besson Samantha, L'égalité de traitement entre particuliers en droit communautaire, in Werro Franz (ed), L'Européanisation du droit privé, Vers un Code Civil européen?, Fribourg 1998, 51 (Droit communautaire).

Besson Samantha, Discrimination and Freedom of Contract, International Journal of Discrimination and the Law (1999) 3, 269 (Discrimination).

Besson Samantha, L'égalité horizontale—l'égalité de traitement entre particuliers. Des fondements théoriques au droit privé suisse, Fribourg 1999 (Egalité horizontale).

Besson Samantha, Les obligations positives de protection des droits fondamentaux—Un essai en dogmatique comparative, Revue de droit suisse (2003) 1, 49 (Obligations positives).

Besson Samantha, From European Integration to European Integrity. Should European Law Speak with Just One Voice?, European Law Journal (2004) 10:3, 257 (Integrity).

Besson Samantha, Social Goods, Market Forces and Anti-Discrimination Laws, Comment on "Antidiscrimination and Decommodification", in Cinar Dilek (ed), Doing Justice to Diversity, Aldershot 2006 (Social goods).

Besson Samantha, Comment humaniser le droit privé sans commodifier les droits de l'homme, in F. Werro (ed.), La Convention européenne des droits de l'homme et le droit civil, Ståmpfli: Bern 2006, 1. [How to humanize private law tihout commodifying human rights].

Besson Samantha, The Reception of the ECHR in the United Kingdom and Ireland, in Keller, H./Stone Sweet, A. (eds), A Europe of Rights. The Reception of the European Convention on Human Rights, Oxford: Oxford University Press 2008, 31.

Besson Samantha, The European Union *qua* Agent of Global Justice, (2006) [on file with author].

Besson Samantha, L'autorité du droit constitutionnel comparé dans l'UE, (2009) [on file with author].

Beyleveld Deryck/Pattinson Shaun, Horizontal Applicability and Direct Effect, Law Quarterly Review (2002) 118, 623.

Bieber Roland/Epiney Astrid/Haag Marcel, Die Europäische Union, Basel 2005.

Bleckmann Albert, Staatsrecht II: Grundrechte, 4th edn, Cologne 1997.

Brüggemeier Gert, Horizontal Effect of Fundamental Rights—A Critical View from the German Cathedral and Beyond, Law Yearbook, University of Coimbra, Coimbra 2004.

Buxton Richard, The Human Rights Act and Private Law, Law Quarterly Review (2000) 116, 57.

Canaris Claus-Wilhelm, Drittwirkung der gemeinschaftlichen Grundfreiheiten, in Bauer Harmut et al. (eds), Umwelt, Wirtschaft und Recht: Wissenschaftliches Symposium aus Anlass des 65. Geburtstages von Reiner Schmidt, Tübingen 2002, 29.

Caruso Daniela, Private Law and Public Stakes in European Integration: the Case of Property, European Law Journal (2004) 10:6, 751.

Clapham Andrew, Human Rights in the Private Sphere, Oxford 1993 (Private law).

Clapham Andrew, The "Drittwirkung" of the Convention, in McDonald Ronald/Matscher Franz/Petzold Herbert (eds), The European System for the Protection of Human Rights, Dordrecht/Boston 1993, 163 (Drittwirkung).

Coester-Waltjen Dagmar, Discrimination in Private Law—New European Principles and Freedom of Contract, in Ziegler Katja et al. (eds), Human Rights and Private Law: Privacy, Oxford 2007 [on file with author].

Curtin Deirdre/Van Oijk Roger, The Sting is Always in the Tail: The Personal Scope of Application of the EU Charter of Fundamental Rights, Maastricht Journal of European Law (2001) 8, 102.

Drzemczewski Andrew, The European Convention on Human Rights and Relations between Private Parties, Netherlands International Law Review (1979) 26, 163.

Egli Patrizia, Drittwirkung von Grundrechten. Zugleich ein Beitrag zur Dogmatik der grundrechtlichen Schutzpflichten im Schweizer Recht, Zürich 2002.

Eissen Marc-André, La Convention européenne des droits de l'homme et les obligations de l'individu, in René Cassin Amicorum Discipulorumque Liber III, Paris 1971, 151 (Obligations).

Eissen Marc-André, La Convention et les droits de l'individu, in La protection des droits de l'homme dans le cadre européen, 1. Int. Kolloquium über die EMRK in Strassburg, Paris 1961, 167 (Droits).

Ellger Reinhard, The European Convention of Human Rights and Fundamental Freedoms and German Private Law, in Friedmann Daniel/Barak-Erez Daphné (eds), Human Rights in Private Law, Oxford 2001, 161.

De Fontbressin Patrick, L'effet horizontal de la Convention européenne des droits de l'homme et l'avenir du droit des obligations, in Mél. M.A. Eissen, La Haye 1993, 157.

Friedmann Daniel/Barak-Erez Daphné (eds), Introduction, in Human Rights in Private Law, Oxford 2001, 1.

Frowein Jochen, Fundamental Human Rights as a Vehicle of Legal Integration in Europe, in Cappelletti Mauro/Seccombe Monica/Weiler Joseph (eds), Integration through Law: Europe and the American Federal Experience, Berlin 1986, Vol. I:3, 300.

Frowein Jochen/Peukert Wolfgang, EMRK Kommentar, 2nd edn, Kehl 1996.

Ganten Ted Oliver, Die Drittwirkung der Grundfreiheiten, Berlin 2000.

Gerstenberg Oliver, What Constitutions Can Do (but Courts Sometimes Don't): Property, Speech, and the Influence of Constitutional Norms on Private Law, Canadian Journal of Law and Jurisprudence (2004) 17:1, 61 (Constitutions).

Gerstenberg Oliver, European Private Law and the New European Constitutional Settlement, European Law Journal (2004) 10:6, 766 (European private law).

Habermas Jürgen, Die postnationale Konstellation und die Zukunft der Demokratie, in Die postnationale Konstellation. Politische Essays, Frankfurt am Main 1998, 156.

Hahne Méo-Micaela, Das Drittwirkungsproblem in der EMRK, Heidelberg 1973.

Häner Isabelle, Grundrechtsgeltung bei der Wahrnehmung staatlicher Aufgaben durch Private, Pratique Juridique Actuelle (2002) 10, 1144.

Hangartner Yvo, Völkerrechtliche Grundpflichten Privater, in Völkerrecht im Dienste des Menschen, Mél. H. Haug, Bern 1986, 120.

Harris David/O'Boyle Michael/Warbrick Colin, Law of the European Convention on Human Rights, Londres 1995.

Heldrich Andreas/Rehm Gebhard, Importing Constitutional Values through Blanket Clauses, in Friedmann Daniel/Barak-Erez Daphné (eds), Human Rights in Private Law, Oxford 2001, 113.

Hesse Konrad, Grundzüge des Verfassungsrechts der Bundesrepublik Deutschland, 20th edn, Heidelberg 1995.

Hesselink Martijn, The Structure of the New European Private Law, Electronic Journal of Comparative Law (2002) 6:4 http://www.ecjl.org/64/art64-2.html.

Hunt Murray, The "Horizontal Effect" of the Human Rights Act, Public Law (1998), 435 (Horizontal effect).

Hunt Murray, The "horizontal effect" of the Human Rights Act: Moving beyond the public-private distinction, in Jowell Jeffrey/Cooper Jonathan (eds), Understanding Human Rights Principles, Oxford 2001, 161 (Moving).

Jaensch Michael, Die unmittelbare Drittwirkung der Grundfreiheiten, Untersuchung der Verpflichtung von Privatpersonen durch Articles 30, 48, 52, 59, 73b EGV, Baden-Baden 1997.

Joerges Christian, The Challenges of Europeanization in the Realm of Private Law: A Plea for a New Legal Discipline, Duke Journal of Comparative & International Law, (2004) 14, 149 (Challenges).

Joerges Christian, Europeanization as Process: Thoughts on the Europeanization of Private Law, European Public Law, (2005) 11:1, 62 (Process).

Joerges Christian, Why a European Code would be Unconstitutional and Irreconcilable with the Patterns within which Europe is Constituted: A Plea for a Supranational Conflict of Laws, 2006 forthcoming [on file with author] (Conflict).

Kohl Alphonse, The Protection of Human Rights in Relationships between Private Individuals: The Austrian Situation, in René Cassin Amicorum Discipulorumque Liber III, Paris 1971, 195.

Kötz Heinz, The Trento Project and its Contribution to the Europeanization of Private Law, in Bussani Mauro/Mattei Ugo (eds), Making European Law. Essays on the 'Common Core' Project, Universita degli Studi di Trento 2000, 117.

Lando Ole/Beale Hugh (eds), Principles of European Contract Law, Parts I and II, Prepared by the Commission on European Contract Law, The Hague 2000.

Leigh Ian, Horizontal Rights, the Human Rights Act and Privacy: Lessons from the Commonwealth?, International and Comparative Law Quarterly (1999) 48, 840.

Mattei Ugo, Hard Code Now!, Global Jurist Frontiers (2002) 2:1, Article 1.

Mitchell John, Some aspects of the Protection of Individuals against Private Power in the United Kingdom, in René Cassin Amicorum Discipulorumque Liber III, Paris 1971, 234.

Möllers Christoph, Globalisierte Jurisprudenz: Einflüsse relativierter Nationalstaatlichkeit auf das Konzept des Rechts und die Funktion seiner Theorie, Archiv für Rechts-und Sozialphilosophie Beiheft (2001) 79, 41.

Müller Jörg Paul, Allgemeine Bemerkungen zu den Grundrechten, in Thürer Daniel/Aubert Jean-François/Müller Jörg Paul (eds), Verfassungsrecht der Schweiz, Zürich 2001 (Allgemeine).

Müller Jörg Paul, Kunst des juristischen Urteils: Impulse von Kant und Savigny, recht (2003) 21:4, 125 (Kunst).

Von Münch Ingo/Salvador Coderch Pablo/Ferrer I Riba Josep (eds), Zur Drittwirkung der Grundrechte, Frankfurt am Main 1998.

Nicolaïdis Kalypso/Lacroix Justine, Order and Justice Beyond the Nation State: Europe's Competing Paradigms, in Foot Rosemary et al. (eds), Order and Justice in International Relations, Oxford 2003, 136.

Nowak John/Rotunda Ronald, Constitutional Law, 5th edn, St Paul Minn. 1995.

Phillipson Gavin, The Human Rights Act, 'Horizontal Effect' and the Common Law: a Bang or a Whimper?, Modern Law Review (1999) 62, 825.

Reinisch August, The Changing International Legal Framework for Dealing with Non-State Actors, in Alston Philip (ed.), Non-State Actors and Human Rights, Oxford 2005, 37.

Schefer Markus, Die Kerngehalte der Grundrechte, Bern 2001 (Kerngehalte).

Schefer Markus, Grundrechtliche Schutzpflichten und die Auslagerung staatlicher Aufgaben, Pratique Juridique Actuelle (2002) 10, 1131 (Schutzpflichten).

Scheuner Ulrich, Fundamental Rights and the Protection of the Individual against Social Groups and Powers in the Constitutional System of the Federal Republic of Germany, in René Cassin Amicorum Discipulorumque Liber III, Paris 1971, 253.

De Schutter Olivier, The Accountability of Multinationals for Human Rights Violations in European Law, in Alston Philip (ed.), Non-State Actors and Human Rights, Oxford 2005, 227.
Social Justice Group, Social Justice in European Contract Law. A Manifesto, European Law Journal (2004) 10, 653.
Somek Alexander, Antidiscrimination and Decommodification, in Cinar Dilek (ed), Doing Justice to Diversity, Aldershot 2006.
Spielmann Dean, L'effet potentiel de la Convention européenne des droits de l'homme entre personnes privées, Bruxelles 1995.
Starck Christian, Human Rights and Private Law in German Constitutional Development and in the Jurisdiction of the Federal Constitutional Court, in Friedmann Daniel/Barak-Erez Daphné (eds), Human Rights in Private Law, Oxford 2001, 97.
Steinberg Philipp, Zur Konvergenz der Grundfreiheiten auf der Tatbestands- und Rechtfertigungsebene, Europäische Grundrechtszeitschrift (2002), 13.
Study Group on a European Civil Code, Principles of European Law, Brussels/Oxford/Stämpfli 2005 etc.
Sudre François, Les "obligations positives" dans la jurisprudence européenne des droits de l'homme, in Mélanges Rolv Ryssdal, Cologne 2000, 1359.
Sunstein Cass, State Action is Always Present, Chicago Journal of International Law (2002) 3, 465.
Tribe Lawrence, Refocusing the 'State Action' Inquiry: Separating State Acts from State Actors, in Constitutional Choices, Cambridge Mass. 1985, 246.
Tushnet Mark, The issue of state action/horizontal effect in comparative constitutional law, International Journal of Constitutional Law (2003) 1, 79 (State action).
Tushnet Mark, The Relationship Between Judicial Review of Legislation and the Interpretation of Non-Constitutional Law, with Reference to Third-party effect, Manuscript prepared for presentation at 12th Annual Conference on "The Individual versus the State", Central European University, Budapest, June 18–19, 2004 (Judicial review).
Unruh Peter, Zur Dogmatik der grundrechtlichen Schutzpflichten, Berlin 1996.
Wade William, Horizons of Horizontality, Law Quarterly Review (2000) 116, 220.
Werro Franz (ed), La Convention européenne des droits de l'homme et le droit civil, Bern 2006.
Weiler Joseph, Fundamental Rights and Fundamental Boundaries: On the Conflict of Standards and Values in the Protection of Human Rights in the European Legal Space, in The Constitution of Europe: "Do the new

clothes have an emperor?" and other essays on European integration, Cambridge 1999, 102.
Wildhaber Luzius/Breitenmoser Stephan, Internationaler Kommentar der EMRK, Cologne 1992.
Williams Andrew, EU Human Rights Policies: A Study in Irony, Oxford 2004.
Ziegler, Katja et al. (eds), Human Rights and Private Law: Privacy, Oxford 2007p.

# 3

# Western Property Law

Antonio Gambaro

## Summary



## 1. Discussions of Property and Their Present Meaning

In the history of Western thought, property law has been the subject of impassioned debate for centuries. All the disciplines which come under the umbrella of the social sciences or humanities have devoted close attention to studying the question of property. In general, the aim of such research is to shed light on the fundamental justification for the existence of private property, or to negate that such justification could exist.

In general, every discipline represents a distinct tradition of research, which distinguishes itself from others because, during the course of its evolution, it defined a certain set of issues as boundaries for its scope. However, the modern age has witnessed a convergence of various research traditions into the question of property, in the fields of law, politics, moral philosophy and economics. Thus, on the one hand, debate which has been generated within the scope of one or other of these traditions seems to represent a single train of thought; on the other, it seems as if the institution of private property is the epicentre of the entire legal, economic, philosophical and moral systems.

In the eighteenth and nineteenth centuries, property law seemed to account for the entire accumulation of thought which had been developing in the Western world since the seventeenth century.[1] The 20th century view, beginning with the early analyses dedicated to the separation of property and the control of wealth within corporate structures,[2] has revived all the complexity of the debate on property, which derives from its range of possible subject-matter and the technical variety of its forms. The result is that, at the beginning of the 21st Century, while on the political philosophy front the old debate proceeds wearily along the classic lines,[3] the two most current and most-cited theories go by the names of 'the tragedy of the commons'[4] and 'the tragedy of the anticommons'.[5]

The first takes as background such resources—treated in legal terms as *res communes omnium,* or things which abound in nature—to which everyone may freely help themselves. Jurists in antiquity were accustomed to cite as examples of *res communes* such things as the air we breathe, water, and wildlife

1. See. *e multis*, J. Locke, *Two Treaties on Government*, Vol. II, 1690, Ch 94; J. Nedelsky, *Private Property and the Limits of American Constitutionalism. The Madisonian Framework and Its Legacy*, Chicago, 1990. Madison's problem was to reconcile democracy, understood as government by the majority, with the safeguarding of property, which concerned only a minority. This idea was, and has remained, very widespread throughout the whole period of the convergence of the various traditions of research; however, if one accepts the marginal utility theory, it would be more logical to consider that those who possess a few essential things consider safeguarding them as essential; K.R. Minogue, *The Concept of Property and its Contemporary Significance,* in J.K. Pennock and J.W. Chapman, *Property* (Nomos, XXII), New York, 1980, p. 3 *ff.* Ch Reich, *The New Property,* 73 *Yale Law J.* 733 (1964); W. Van Alstyne, *Cracks in "The New Property", Adjudicative Due process in the Administrative State,* 62 *Cornell L. Rev.* 445 (1977); F. Cohen, *Dialogue on Private Property*, 9 *Rutgers L. Rev.* 357 (1954).

2. A.A. Bearle Jr. and G.C. Means, *The Modern Corporation and Private Property*, New York, 1932.

3. S.R. Munzer, *A Theory of Property*, Cambridge, 1990; J. Waldron, *The Right to Private Property*, Oxford, 1988; M. Xifaras, *La propriété. Étude de Philosophie du droit*, Paris, 2004.

4. G. Hardin, *The Tragedy of the Commons,* 162 *Science* 1243 (1968).

5. M.A. Heller, *The Tragedy of the Anticommons*, 111 *Harv. L. R.* 625 (1998).

from both the sea and the land. The tragedy of the commons, therefore, puts in correct perspective the fact that the free appropriation of the *res communes omnium* is only possible in conditions of environmental equilibrium between the resources themselves and those who may take possession of them, and secondly emphasizes that the interruption of such equilibrium causes an increasingly desperate race to exploit these resources, which become more and more scarce—a race to the bottom which can only come to a ruinous, and tragic end. The theory suggests that no alternative to property exists in our crowded planet, and that discussion of this type was probably the result of an optical illusion caused by the wide open spaces which western man came to dominate through certain historical contingencies. Freed of such illusions, the scarce resources should be made over to individuals or organized groups or to the State,[6] so that they have an interest in conserving them.

The second theory, the tragedy of the anticommons, assumes that assets which are subject to rights of property belonging to different persons, each of whom therefore has a right of veto regarding the transformation of the assets or to their transfer in unitary form. It can be shown that this leads to a less than optimal use of the resources, since efficient innovations, whether material in nature or by way of legal transfer, have to deal with practically prohibitive transactional costs whenever it is necessary to obtain unanimity of consent. The anticommons theory, therefore, demonstrates that the way in which property rights are sorted and shaped by the legal system remains the fundamental basis which activates many social and economic mechanisms. The word 'tragedy' recalls Greek tragedy, in which a series of events were made inevitable by Fate. Both theories highlight how, starting with property rights, automatic mechanisms are set off which do not require the intervention of regulatory bodies. For example, the tragedy of the anticommons may paradoxically suggest that if there is a wish to conserve a forest in ecological balance, it would suffice to assign common ownership to the land on which the forest stands and ownership of each tree to different individuals belonging to a widespread community, and then establish as a binding condition that every human intervention in the forest required unanimous consent by the individual owners of the trees, who would have an injunction to prevent any other action. It would be reasonable to assume that no human action would disturb the forest's eco-system,[7] with no need to use public resources.

6. C. Rose, *The Comedy of the Commons: Customs, Commerce and Inherently Public Property*, 53 *U.of Chi. L.R.* 711 (1986).

7. The intensely irrational feelings which have been stirred up by the age of convergence around the word property, that potent verbal symbol, could lead to the belief that if

From differing perspectives, both theories highlight the relationship between property and market forces as a means of ensuring optimum use of the resources and which, taken together, demonstrate that no single form of ownership exists which is universally efficient in every situation that the market can create.

The field of property therefore has to refer to a multiplicity of disciplines, which contemplate differing forms of ownership.

## 2. Property in the Framework of EC Legal System

So far as positive law is concerned, it should be recalled that Art. 296 of the EC Treaty states that the existent laws in the Member States concerning property remain untouched. Strictly speaking, therefore, it would appear that property lies outside the competence of the Community and, consequently, beyond the tendency to harmonization of national laws which lies at the basis of a renewed common law for Europe.

One should not forget, however, that the following areas come within the competence of the Community: the environment, industrial property rights, the free movement of goods, agriculture. Besides this, the European Convention on Human Rights acts as a monitor on the exercise of all Community powers,[8]—therefore the protection of property rights laid down by the first additional Protocol to this Convention constituted a common European principle, even before equal protection was inserted into Article 17 of the Nice Charter.

The reality is that it is futile to think of governing a complex system such as Community law omitting the notion of property rights. However, we cannot expect that a common concept of property will gradually take shape in the form of Community legislation, as has happened with regard to the law of contracts. An '*acquis communautaire*' in the field of property rights hardly exists and what there is, is certainly unsuitable for the purpose of establishing the elements of a common framework. There is, therefore, an inevitable task to undertake, of delineating the convergent and divergent features in order to forge connections between the concepts of property in the various European legal systems.

---

property in individual trees were assigned to single individuals, they would rush to give common consent to cut the forest down so as to be able to capitalize on their property. Although such an idea could originate in some of the paradigms illustrated by scholars of economic science, it remains an unrealistic notion.

8. See OJ C 103 of 27 April 1977.

The first issue which presents itself is obviously that of language, in the sense that it is necessary to clarify what meaning is to be assigned when referring to the term 'property' in the various European languages. The law which Europe shares in common is first and foremost a dense network of dialogues, and it is an indispensable premise of dialogue that the speakers clarify reciprocally what they intend to talk about.

## 3. Constitutional Protection of Property Rights

It is easier to understand the issue of property when it is put in the context of constitutional/administrative law.

To this end, it does not matter if the constitution is written or unwritten, or whether it is rigid or flexible. What matters is that, from a cultural viewpoint, the whole history of European legal experience has evolved across historical periods which have had to contend with similar problems, even though they have been resolved in very different ways at different moments in history.

In the ambit of constitutional law, the notion of property refers to private property and guarantees offered by the State's legal system, with particular reference to powers of expropriation of private property. Since such powers essentially concern immovable property, this is the type of private property which comes to mind when considering constitutional principles. From a constitutional perspective, the question of guarantees offered in respect to private property is a technical one, which is nonetheless connected to those very general views about social organization which have been so passionately debated in the past.

Since property was the greatest economic right which an individual citizen could possess over tangible things, the entire problem of taking private property was a matter of establishing the limits on what the owner could do, without harming others or the collective interest. And, conversely, what actions State power could prevent an owner from doing, without contravening constitutional safeguards against expropriation without just compensation. The argument does not, however, concern any specific content of property but reflects only the legality principle, and in particular the corollary of equality of treatment before the public, because what is prevented to one must be prevented to all. This does not imply that problems of identifying the limits of regulatory activity and expropriation, or taking, do not exist. Indeed, these problems, when taken to extremes, are practically insoluble, as the American experience demonstrates. However, it should be noted on the one hand that a problem is not posed whenever an individual has been deprived of his property rights for reasons of public utility;[9] on the other hand, in complex cases[10] the problems that have to be faced are independent of the language in the various constitutional texts. Whether or not such texts connect the property with some social function, or, more precisely for a conceptual viewpoint, whether they establish that the right of property implies obligations, or whether they are silent on the point, the constitutional language is quite irrelevant when it comes to deciding whether a certain public course of action involves expropriation, or whether it is merely regulatory.

In fact, all constitutional texts leave open too many questions on the identification of property rights—by consequence the resolution of the issue depends on what notion of property the adjudicator in question has in contemplation,[11] on the basis of which s/he decides whether the regulation went too far. The latter evaluation is largely connected with individual ideology, but, even when it is tacit, the notion of property is a cultural idea that developed in a social context throughout history and can be appreciated through the comparative study of history. In addition, the legal mentalities that are at work in the adjudication process of constitutional law have been shaped for centuries in the province of private law, and property rights are considered to be at the core of private law. Therefore, some attention will have to be devoted to this aspect.

## 4. Corporeal and Incorporeal Property: Basic Conceptual Definitions

Looking at the European manuals, it would seem that two concepts dominate: Property may be thought of as a right over a tangible object, which confers an open range of rights and options upon the owner.

Property may be thought of as a collection of rights and options, which do not immediately refer to a tangible object.

---

9. In such cases, the only problematic aspect concerns the methods for calculating compensatory payments and whether they reflect true market value.

10. See, e.g., F. Biglione, La notion de privation de propriété, Aix-Marseille, 1999.

11. There is little help in this regard in the case-law of the European Court of Human Rights, which has, up to now, been called upon to deal with cases on a purely commonsense basis, without having to reckon with issues that require a rather more far-reaching vision.

The difference between the two lies precisely in the tangible nature of the object which is the subject-matter of the property right.

If one accepts the concept of tangibility/corporality, and fixes the proprietary right directly onto the object in question, the fact that the list of rights and options is indefinite is justified, because it can be left to the physical characteristics of the specific corporeal object to define the range of possible uses and there will always be room for more to be invented. Property therefore becomes a subjective right with a structure unique in the field of economic rights, or rather, it has a content which the legal system leaves undefined but not unlimited, with a view to legitimizing conduct which has not been anticipated by the law and is not foreseeable by the social practices, and indeed may be idiosyncratic and altogether strange. That is, the owner's personality is left to reveal itself, so far as the exercise of property rights is concerned and it is protected by the law against the social constraints that force the individual into path dependency.

If the position is adopted which states that property is simply a collection of rights and options, its unique character becomes blurred, because in the bundle of rights[12] called property, some of them have their content predetermined by law and acquire their identity from the very fact that their content is fixed; some others are rights of undefined content. This is what John Austin meant when he said, criticizing the distinction made between things corporeal and incorporeal, "Things incorporeal are rights and duties themselves, and yet the distinction is utterly useless: inasmuch as rights and duties, having names of their own, need not to be styled as incorporeal things".[13]

In fact, the logic underlying the viewpoint that reduces the idea of property to a catalogue of rights is quite distinct from that which makes specific room for idiosyncratic, innovative and risky behavior. This tends to widen the circle of rights which are valid *erga omnes*—against the world—in the sense that being universally protected, they can only be removed from their owner with his consent[14] and therefore necessarily become the object of exchange because whoever wants to acquire them must do so from their current owner. In other words, the incorporeal notion of property rights extends the number of individual rights that can be exchanged or traded.

---

12. I adopt the vocabulary of Hohfeld, who is unrivalled in modern American legal literature.

13. See J. Austin, *Lectures on Jurisprudence or the Philosophy of Positive Law* (1863), 5a ed., London, 1885, 777.

14. See G. Calabresi and D. Melamed, *Property Rules, Liability Rules, Inalienability: One View of the Cathedral*, 85 *Harv. L. Rev.* 1089 (1972).

The two fundamental concepts which have just been emphasized are both present in the European legal tradition, and are represented on the one hand by the Roman law tradition, codified today in German law and in the systems which follow the BGB model, and on the other hand in the English common law tradition; although obviously all the systems in their positive expressions depart to some extent from the general model.

In this scheme, French law occupies a middle, complex position with regard to these two opposing models. Other European models have been further hybridized.

The above fundamental difference remained obscure until immovable property came to dominate the scene. Indeed, in the case of immovable property, the operative differences between the two concepts become somewhat blurred. However, when movable property emerged as dominant and became the essential means for the acquisition of and access to wealth, those fundamental differences came to the forefront in relation both to circulatory mechanisms and the protection of property rights, as well as to the framework of new forms of intangible movable chattels. That is to say that it is on the modern trend toward commodization that differences came afloat, being understood that property rights have no competitors to smooth out difficulties in the exchange process.

These differences are to be found in reference to the basic concepts of the law of property present in each national model. Therefore, in order to understand them, it is necessary to briefly describe the nature of property rights in the three main European legal systems, namely that of English and Irish common law and the French and German systems, with the proviso that each owes its basic structure to historical evolution rather than planned reforms.[15]

## 5. The Property System in the Common Law Legal Traditions

### *5.1. Real Property*

The fundamental distinction made by English law in the field of property lies between real and personal property.

15. Not that quite extensive law reform has not taken place—take, for example, the English 1925 Law of Property Act.

This distinction was based on the nature of the remedies which could safeguard various aspects of property and it disappeared a long time ago. Nowadays, the subject-matter of real property is immovable property, and therefore concerns land law; but, in the intervening time, the two categories of property became fixed since each was the subject of refined development, based on the nature of each type.

Initially, the subject matter of real property concerned feudal possessions. Feudal ownership conferred the right to exercise certain rights and exact certain dues, traditionally owed by the local population to the lord of the manor: for example, the right to appoint the parish priest (Advowsons), to levy a toll for crossing a ford, to administer local justice, and so on. However, the granting of a feudal title by the sovereign did not usually involve giving over potential riches underground, not yet discovered; this right was retained by the Crown. In the same way, hunting rights might be kept by the overlord, and so on. In this way, the same feudal property could provide rights for different individuals, each of whom owned certain rights and not others. Initially, therefore, a feudal grant was territorial in nature, but not pertaining to the actual ground itself. The granting of a feudal property did not involve the ground as such being made over to the vassal; the object of the grant were just the various benefits which came with investiture. In the same way nowadays, the territory belonging to the local municipality is the geographical area over which the municipality exercises its powers, but it would be inaccurate to say that such land *belongs* to the town council, whereas it would be natural to say that although the extent of the territory can be identified as lying within the boundaries of the municipality etc., there is an exercise of municipal, provincial, regional or State power over it, as the case may be.

The strongly dematerialized nature of ownership, which applies to precise rights of use, has remained one of the cornerstones of the concept of real property. For this reason it has to be emphasized that, in a similar context, the concept of ownership does not coincide with the one understood by the Roman law tradition, and instead becomes more of a synonym for the concept of title.

By a slow process of transformation, the feudal possessions became estates on (or in) land. The so-called doctrine of estates is found at the heart of common law, and therefore is the result of centuries of development, over which the evolution and passage of all the historical phases of English law can be perceived.

In the beginning, there were various ways in which estates could be held, since each vassal (tenant) fixed the rights which belonged to his feudal holding, but, since these derived from an individual pact, the situation with regard to them varied. The first stage was therefore to bring each situation within a certain type. Later on, however, the variety of types favored the subdivision of the benefits, providing the necessary material for legal techniques which, by calculating the value of the estate, took the place of many of the functions of contract under the Roman law tradition.

Briefly this technique was based on a grant, reproducing the original investiture, which, due to the disappearance of the feudal relationship had become quite unilateral—coupled with a careful process of division of the granted right. Broadly speaking it could be said that whereas in the Roman tradition the contract was adjusted to calibrate the title according to the needs of the particular case—in the common law tradition this function was superseded by the definition of the type of interest in the property being granted. For example, suppose Titus wants to transfer title in building X to Caius, on condition that Caius uses the said building for cultural meetings; the lawyer trained in the Roman law tradition will tend to interpret the parties' wish in terms of a conditional contract. A common lawyer would, conversely, prefer to consider the property right as being conditional, therefore defining it by means of the insertion of a conditional clause to the grant. This may appear to be merely a semantic difference, but it is not so. As a general rule, where the condition is inherent in the contract, it will affect the parties only, with the consequence that it becomes necessary to set up a system of registration to allow Titus to put the condition up against possible third parties bringing an action against Caius. Otherwise the claim out of the condition is *in personam*, affecting only the transferee. On the other hand, if the condition directly affects the acquired property, the claim is *in rem*, good against the world independently by a system of registration that may or may not exist. Of course the creation of these rights *in rem* requires that the transfer system be strictly based on the idea that no transferee can acquire more rights than those of the transferor (*nemo dat quod non habet*).

The costs of the system are therefore economic and social in kind, because, cumulative effects of the various divisions and subdivisions of rights over immovable property develop with the passage of time, making the circumstances of land property holding rather intricate, paving the way to legislative reforms of the law of property.

It is therefore not surprising in this regard that there has been a tendency in modern times to simplify matters. In England there are now only two types of estate holding which are valid at common law: fee simple absolute and leasehold; other types can only be protected in equity. Nevertheless, if one wants to understand the mentality arising from the common law legal tradition, some familiarity with the concept of estate is required.

## *5.2. The Estates*

The concept of the estate is three-dimensional.

The first part of the concept relates to time, and measures the duration of the holding; the second measures the extent of the right of alienation; the third part measures the enjoyment of the asset involved.

If the maximum value is assigned to each of the three dimensions, the highest type of estate is obtained, which is known as 'fee simple absolute'.

Fee simple absolute is the basis of the calculation of the estate, since it contemplates a form of holding in which the duration is unlimited, the power of disposal (in the sense of transferring title to someone else) seems unfettered and enjoyment is the maximum permitted by law. It follows that below this, other minor interests can be carved out. However, these minor interests, when taken together, still amount to a fee simple absolute.

The simile which is often adopted to begin explaining the mechanism behind the calculation of an estate is that of a stick. The whole stick represents the fee simple absolute. When smaller portions are cut off, some part of the original stick necessarily remains. Thus, for example, if A, the holder of a fee simple absolute, grants B a fee for life, that is, an interest in the estate which lasts for B's lifetime, A still retains the right to be entitled to the estate for an unlimited period, less B's lifetime. A estate is thus considered an estate in reversion because when the particular estate that has been subtracted from the original fee simple is extinguished on B's death, the land is said to revert to A or his successors.

However, what is conveyed to B is a right which, aside from the shorter duration, has the same characteristics as the previous fee simple absolute; the right of alienation is therefore unfettered. Naturally, however, if B alienates his right, or mortgages it, what he alienates or mortgages can only be what he received—in other words a right whose length is determined by his lifespan. When B dies, the life interest is extinguished, independently of whoever is the holder of it at that particular time.

Considered from this perspective, it is not difficult to see how both interests can exist simultaneously. If a fee for life is created out of a fee simple absolute, this means that two estates exist at the same time, based on the same piece of land. Of these, the fee for life is an estate in possession, since the holder of the life interest has the immediate use and enjoyment of the estate; the fee simple will be an estate in expectancy, since its enjoyment will be postponed to the expiry of the life interest. However, both can be alienated, divided or mortgaged. In the same way, in civil law systems bare ownership and the right of use and enjoyment subsist simultaneously, and are likewise contemporaneously capable of being alienated or used as collateral for a loan.

If both interests subsist simultaneously in relation to the same estate, this implies that the one who is in actual possession of it must behave in such a way as not to damage the rights of the one who has the estate in expectancy. These obligations are contained in the notion of waste and are quite obvious.

To this point, the doctrine of estates would not seem to hold any particular surprises. The fee simple absolute closely resembles immovable property in all the civil law systems, and the fee for life is analogous to the concept of a Roman law usufruct. The surprising features appear when conditions begin to be attached to the grant. It has already been pointed out that conditions are inherent to the property right because it shapes the estate but this technique deserves some further explanation.

We can start with the assumption that a fee simple absolute is unconditional—therefore if A, holder of a fee simple absolute, wants to assign his right to B, but also wants the estate to be used for a certain purpose, such as for a university campus, he assigns to B a fee simple determined, where the determination is the fact that the estate must be used as a university campus. In this example, the principle outlined above, which states that the estate must amount to a fee simple absolute, means that some part must remain to A and his heirs because B's estate is something less that a fee simple absolute. In fact, A and his heirs retain the possibility of reverter, that is, that B's estate returns to A should the estate not be used as a university campus. Since the determination of the use is attached to B's estate, its extinction in the case of a change of use is automatic. Then a variant can be introduced by formulating the wording of the grant in a different way, specifying that the grant is in fee simple absolute, but with a condition subsequent that, should the land cease to be used as a university campus, the holder of the original fee simple absolute can exercise a right of entry. In this case, if the conditional event occurs and there is a change of use, B's interest in the estate is not automatically extinguished, but only when A or his heirs exercise their right of entry.[16] It is clear that the range of possible conditions increases the facets of ownership where they apply, and it is this range which complicates the field of real property and makes the drawing up and interpretation of estate grants a delicate procedure.

The focal point lies in the fact that the original notion of investiture made the grant compatible with any type of condition subsequent, and incompatible conceptually with any kind of condition precedent. This can be better understood if one examines the original logic of the vassal relationship. In this

16. Once the right of entry implied precisely a literal re-entry onto the estate. Nowadays, the right of entry is obtained through legal action.

context, the phrase "I give you this estate in feud, on condition that you remain faithful to me" was binding despite the fact that the second part, though an integral condition of the relationship, was never even enunciated. Whereas the phrase "I give you this estate in feud on condition that you find the Holy Grail first" was not valid as a grant. In fact, while waiting to discover the Grail, the knight had no feudal estate at all. Equally, following the same logic, a feudal estate could not be granted to someone not yet born, because in that case no personal lord/vassal relationship could be created.

Once the feudal estates were fixed and their transformation into estates was achieved, the primitive logic was substantially preserved.

It follows that if A, the holder of a fee simple absolute, leaves a will in the following terms: "To B, my wife, for life and on B's death to C (my son, a bachelor) if, but only, if C marries" the result is an incomplete grant of the original estate. The calculation which has to be made in this case is the following: when his wife dies, her life interest in the estate is automatically extinguished and if at that moment C is not yet married he cannot expect to inherit anything. However, A's fee simple absolute remains, because it was vested and cannot be extinguished, therefore the fee simple already held by A will pass on his death to his heirs and not just to son C. In the last analysis, in this example, what will be granted to C, since it is subject to a condition precedent, cannot be described as an estate, but merely the possibility that what he will be granted will become an estate.

This is the origin of the fundamental distinction between vested and contingent remainders. A could make the following dispositions in his will: 'to James, but if he fails to graduate in Law within ten years, all to Josephine'. Such a term in the will would have the effect of the estate in expectancy vesting immediately in James, save for the condition subsequent of his not graduating.

The puzzling nature of this neat opposition comes from the fact that the practical effects of the two conditions may be perfectly analogous, but the legal position is formally quite different. Once a remainder-man is vested, he may freely dispose of his estate, he is certainly protected by the rules against waste, and cannot lose his title by operation of the rule against perpetuities. If the grant is contingent, however, the estate cannot be alienated, it is less protected by the waste rules and is vulnerable to invalidity under the rule against perpetuities.

In the latter case, the level of complexity becomes very contorted. The rule against perpetuities has not been very clearly formulated, by reason of contingencies. The rule essentially states that it is not possible, either at law or in equity, to create a valid future interest if it is not certain that the interest can become vested within 25 years of the death of a person now living. The great uncertainty of the rule is for the most part attributable to the fact that it invalidates the grant and therefore the calculation has to be made *ex ante*.[17] In other words, it is necessary to evaluate whether there are sufficient reasons for believing that the interest in question will vest within the stated time, with reference to the moment that the future interest is created. The complexity and difficulty of the rule creates pressure to simplify or abolish it by means of legislation.

Beyond all these considerations, it should be recalled that the opposition between vested and contingent interests arises from three factors which are powerful crypto-types within the logic of the law of property, which may be summarized as follows: the need that the transfer of a freehold estate should be operated by a deed, called a conveyance, which is a unilateral act; the concept of property as a certain measure of the rights in which it consists; and the idea that while the deed can define the measure and extent of the property, it cannot define the extent of its effects. For this reason the opposition of vested and contingent interests has a range of application which goes well beyond the position of the remainder-man, to become one of the most important categories of the entire sector of forms of ownership.

What remains of all this, however, is essentially a legal mentality grown up with constructing forms of ownership, which nowadays finds its main application in the financial sector.

In the field of land law in England, the old system based on legal estates and the investigation of the chain of titles is disappearing and, since the 1990s the system of land registration has become the normal method of transferring landed property. The advantages of registration are indeed enormous, especially since the modern technologies of electronic information and data retrieval can be exploited.

## *5.3. The Leasehold*

Alongside the estates of feudal origin, known as freehold estates, there is another type of estate relating to land with a commercial character, which by way of contrast are known as non freehold estates.

In medieval times, if a lord was in need of liquidity he could borrow cash, giving over his feudal estate to the lender to enjoy for a certain number of years (a term of years) sufficient to repay the debt, or he could give him the use of it in exchange for a rent.

---

17. For this reason, many American States have introduced the opposite criterion, known as wait and see, which establishes that the grant is presumed to be valid unless there is evidence that once the term has run no one is become vested.

This was a functional arrangement, analogous to the Roman "locatio". Whoever took the land under lease was in no sense vested with a right, since investiture was only for relationships of vassalage; therefore his position was not protected as that of a freeholder was. However, the development of remedies has eliminated the difference. The dichotomy between freehold and non-freehold estates was rooted in the technical advances in the concept of *seisin*, which was granted to the holders of freehold estates but absent in the non-freehold estates.

This made it difficult to classify the position conferred on these estates, particularly on the term of years (also known as *leasehold*). Traditional classification puts leasehold among personal property, although the trend now is to consider it as part of land law. The assimilation of leasehold into real property is a modern tendency which seems more and more widespread, whereas the traditional classification is just a historical remnant without much justification for continuing.

Having said this, it should be noted that the term of years, or leasehold, is very widespread in common law countries. Indeed, from one point of view, its precise duration in terms, or fractions or multiples of years, allows for very reliable business planning. In addition to this, all the requirements for living or uses of the building which are consonant with the needs of modern life may be satisfied by the grant of a long lease. From another point of view, it should be recalled that, unlike the case of freehold estates, the creation of a leasehold leaves a lot more room for the contract and its effects. The difference lies in the fact that, with regard to freeholds, no obligation on the seller can be conceived beyond transferring title when promised and for that reason, once the conveyance has taken place, the seller remains liable only for breach of contract if the title is defective, and he will avoid even that liability if the transfer has been the execution of a gift. In the case of leaseholds, the landlord agrees in the contract to allow the leaseholder free enjoyment of the estate, which is identified in the contract. This duty survives execution[18] and may be amplified by the addition of various kinds of express or implied contractual terms. In recent times, the social requirement to regulate the market in relation to urban dwellings has led to a large increase in landlords' obligations, by including among them clauses concerning the maintenance of the property in a suitable state for habitation and so on. From this perspective, the greater flexibility and amplitude of contractual terms, in comparison to the unilateral act defining the property right granted, is advantageous to the leaseholder.

18. Traditional common law denied this consequence, in that the courts reduced the landlord's obligations to the transfer of title and the undertaking not to evict the leaseholder during the term of years.

## 5.4. Personal Property

The organized grant of leaseholds forms a bridge between real and personal property. As regards personal property, it should be noted for accuracy that its internal distinctions make a differentiation between *chattels real* and *chattels personal.* The category of chattels real contains only leaseholds, and therefore it only exists in reference to the traditional classification. Chattels personal cover all items of personal property in the strict sense. The category of chattels personal is further subdivided into *choses in action* and *choses in possession*; the latter class includes goods and money.

The supporting structure underpinning the whole subject of personal property is the distinction between choses in action and possession.

Choses in possession are those material, movable goods which can be enjoyed directly; the further subdivision between goods and money partly derives from the fact that, under English law, the definition of goods is to be found in the Sale of Goods Act, and naturally in the scheme of sales, money is the item given over by one party in exchange for the goods, and so is distinct. To a large extent, therefore, it is worth making the distinction between money and other goods because of the differing regulatory scheme which applies in terms of circulation and safeguards. In fact, the rule that a person acquiring *a non domino* in good faith and for value undoubtedly becomes the owner applies only to money, whereas in the case of other movable goods, the fundamental principle is *nemo dat quod not habet*, namely that one cannot acquire good title from someone who does not possess it in the first place.

The expression *chose in action* derives from the position of debt. If one makes a contract with another person in which the other makes him a promise, that promise has a value, but it can be regarded as a thing only if that value can be transferred from the promisee to a third person. To be transferable a promise must satisfy two conditions: to be assignable and to be of such kind that it will not change its content upon transfer to another person. This happens in the case of a promise to pay fixed sums of money or to deliver fixed quantities of goods. The right to receive such sums of money or quantity of goods is a debt and it can be enforced and protected only by way of a legal action. The category of choses in action has gradually increased to include a range of intangible movables, from copyright to goodwill and know how. This category is never closed, since the only requirement is that it concerns a defined benefit which can be ceded to others without changing its characteristics.

The breadth of the category of choses in action and, consequently, of the law of property and its capacity to include new non-material benefits is an immediate consequence of the very wide range of the law of property, as extended to intangible movables.

But above all, it is in considering choses in action that one grasps the basic idea that a property right means the ownership of a right which is valid *erga omnes*. It follows from this that the common law systems seem to be property oriented, while the civil law systems, particularly the German one, tend to be oriented towards dealing with issues of patrimonial law by referring to the relationship of duty and are therefore obligation-oriented. Proof of this lies in the fact that, in common law systems, all the new rights that were introduced in the 19th Century as a result of the industrial revolution and in the 20th Century by the information technology revolution, may be conveniently classified as belonging to the law of property, whereas they cannot be classified that way in the German system and only partially in the French one.

The institution of trusts, which has an increased scope concerning property rights, basically supports this orientation since, through the system of holding property for the benefit of third parties, the rights are doubled by the inclusion both of the trustee's formal ownership and the beneficiary's equitable interest. The important aspect of this field is that the beneficiary's title is good for all purposes (*erga omnes*) and is protected from claims by the trustee's other creditors.

For a long time it was an undisputed principle of the law of property that the doctrine of estates does not apply to choses in action or in possession. Today, however, it is thought that by having recourse to trusts, it is possible to subdivide the benefits under a trust fund according to models that are quite similar to those of estates, including the creation of future interests. From this, the widespread technique of subdividing trust funds has been much appreciated in the financial markets, since it combines the extreme flexibility of these schemes with the *erga omnes* safeguards typical of the law of property.

If in the past the division of property rights has been confined to the real property sector, it should nonetheless be recalled that co-ownership has always been admissible in universal form, that is with regard to all the types of things which can be owned. The reason behind this is that it concerns a state of affairs that is always with us. Take, for example, the case of co-heirs. In this situation the common law systems recognise two forms of co-ownership, called respectively joint ownership and ownership in common.[19] The difference, apart from the historical origins, lies in the fact that ownership in common is a hold-

---

19. If one is referring to a freehold the following expressions are also used: joint tenancy and tenancy in common.

ing by share in which the individual's share can be passed on also by succession, while joint ownership is a holding in common where on death the co-owner's share is divided proportionally among the others.

In comparison with civil law systems, the law of property has an important characteristic in that possession is marginalized. Obviously, possession is a legal concept which figures largely in English common law too, but it does not play the fundamental role in ownership mechanisms which it does in civil law systems.

This point will emerge more clearly when these latter systems have been considered. For the moment, we need only recall certain aspects. Possession, understood as *de facto* power over an object, has a positive role in allowing its transformation into good title in the case of adverse possession, which is analogous to possession *ad usucapionem*. It is still the most important feature in protection from trespass and its numerous derivative actions under the law of torts; but, in this case, the possessor must also prove good title for possession. The rule is not unfair, since it is sufficient to show better title than the trespasser. In many cases this means that proof of title does not even feature in the case. But the bare fact of possession does not create any presumptions, and thus does not limit safeguards on the property right, nor does it adversely affect the burden of proof, which is borne by the owner. Where there are two contenders for possession of an object, it is always a case of evaluating the proof offered by both sides in order to establish who has the better title. As a result, even when the property is in circulation, possession of the object has no special significance. The fundamental rule remains the one which is typical of a system oriented towards the protection of property, which states that "*nemo plus juris trasferre potest quam ipse habet*". The exceptions, which permitted the acquisition of ownership even from someone who was not the owner, have recently been abolished. What remains is that in the sale of goods, if the buyer leaves the goods in the possession of the seller and the latter fraudulently sells and delivers the goods to a second buyer, who purchases them in good faith, the seller can be seen to have had the authority of the first buyer to sell the goods to the second, and therefore the property is acquired by the latter. The same result can be explained considering that the sale of goods without delivery has the effect of transferring property only between the parties but not for all purposes.

The reality is that it is inevitable in a system whose fundamental orientation is to consider the rights of property as a bundle of rights that possession, in the sense of physical control over an object, should be marginalized. The general consequence of this trend is that legal remedies are afforded to those able to show a better title than their opponents and so, when others element are balanced, possession can play a role at the margin of the main rule.

### 5.5. *Ownership*

In contrast with the trends in practice, particularly financial ones, the current legal literature in England tends to stress the notion of ownership as the framework for property matters. It should be recalled that the term 'ownership' is of relatively recent origin. In fact, it has come about as the result of Continental influence, through schools of thought aimed at constructing a general theory of law, whose originator was John Austin and which took the name Jurisprudence. Austin favoured the idea that the notion of ownership should apply only to corporeal things, but clearly this type of teaching, belonging more to logic and philosophy than to legal technique, would have little chance of being accepted in an English legal environment. However, it undoubtedly possessed logical coherence and can be presented in a more moderate form today, embodying the notion that links ownership to property in corporeal things, but allows the rules designed for that situation to be extended by analogy to include incorporeal things as well.[20] As distinct from what happens in American common law, where Hohfeld's teachings reign supreme,[21] this proposal for a balanced compromise enjoys wide consensus in England, at least in academic circles. The notion of ownership is thus constructed around the following elements: the right to use, the right to manage, the right to security, the rights or incidents of transmissibility and absence of terms, the prohibition of harmful use, liability to execution.[22] In several circumstances the notion of ownership is easily comparable to the concept of *propriété* or *Eigentum*. Although it concerns a concept which is still more popular in academic debate than in the legal profession, it can serve to mediate the different conceptions present in Europe, so performing a useful service to dialogue between jurists.

## 6. Historical Background of Property in the Civil Law Traditions

In the civil law tradition, the notion designated by the term *propriété, Eigentum, proprietà*, or *proprietad* indicates a real right, which will be inserted in this last and broadest category.

20. See A.M. Honorè, *Ownership*, in A.G. Guest (ed.) *Oxford Essays in Jurisprudence*, Oxford, 1961, 108.

21. See *Fundamental Legal Conceptions as applied in Legal Reasoning, and Other Legal Essays*, New Haven, 1919.

22. See A.M. Honorè, *Ownership*, cit., p. 113.

The concept of 'real' rights (*droits reél, sachenrechts, zakelijke recthten, diritti reali, derechos reais*) is normally identified by reference to the law of property/rules governing the right of property (ownership). This is almost always given a definition in the civil codes.

Such is the case with the French civil code, which defines ownership in Article 544 as the right to enjoy and dispose of things in the most absolute manner, provided that it is not used in a manner prohibited by laws or regulations. The same situation applies in the German civil code, where, under §903, the owner of an object may use it as he likes and exclude others from any interference, so long as such use is not contrary to law or the rights of third parties. To take the new Dutch civil code as a further example, which devotes Title 5 to the *Zakelijke Rechten*, but opens at 5.1.1 with the definition of ownership, it defines as "the most comprehensive right which a person can have in a thing. To the exclusion of everybody else, the owner is free to use the thing provided that this use not be in violation of the rights of others and that it respect the limitations based upon statutory rules and rules of unwritten law". This circularity, where the broadest category—'real' rights—is defined by reference to the definition of one of its constituents—namely the right of ownership—is surely a peculiarity which is explicable by the history of the civil law tradition.

Taking the definition of the right of property in the codes, academic writers in the civil law systems have constructed the concept of a 'real right' which, although not free from dispute and contradicting viewpoints, boasts the most widespread support.

In this context, the 'real' right comes within the broadest category of economic rights and it is a right *in rem* because it gives title to the direct enjoyment of the thing. The problem is that the word 'thing' is ambiguous, except under German and Greek law where it is clear that something which is the subject of a real or property right can only be a corporeal thing.

The semantic ambiguity of the term can be realized by noticing that a 'thing' can be both a corporeal object and an incorporeal one, and hence a right; This is an ambiguity that is emphasized as soon as the more technical term "bien-bene" replaces the word 'thing', as occurs in French and to some extent in Italian legal language.

The same ambiguity can also be appreciated, and even more forcefully, by reference to the past.

As has been seen in relation to England, where it was Real Property which set the whole tone of property law, in civil law systems the core concept to which the *jura in re* refers was originally set up by the political-legal organization of the ways of owning real property, in whose logical and systematic construction generations of jurists have taken part.

Europe, home of the Western legal tradition, was one vast agricultural land, engaged in intensive cultivation,[23] from Charles the Great until the 19th–20th centuries. A piece of land was the most important form of ownership upon which lawyers focused their attention, thus creating a watershed between all the other relationships of commercial activity, which did not require a contextualized and immediate form of exchange. This consequently was the origin of relationships of obligation. This classic configuration is the arrival point of an evolution stretching from the glossators down to Pothier,[24] both elaborated Roman sources handed down from the Justinian laws and created a new category *ex novo* to suit a context which did not exist in the time of ancient Rome.

The *summa divisio* separating the law of obligations and contracts from the law of property is, as always happens in the case of great categories in the legal system, the result of setting down the organized systems of a material culture. But such forms of systematic legal organization do not aspire to universal truth and are legitimized only by reference to a tradition, although they are fairly long-lasting as regards the material civilization which produced them, and in effect, as Holmes[25] noted, they endure by adapting to new requirements when those which gave rise to them have disappeared. In order to discover the logic behind them, it is therefore necessary to deconstruct the meaning they have gradually accumulated, albeit on the basis of formal identity.

In this regard it is worth noting that the link between the piece of land and the rights that one can have over it, like the one between the land and its products, is a link which identifies a right in relation to a geographical area. In medieval Europe, the ford, the parish, the squire's jurisdiction, were always identified by place-names. The long-term social organization and the general mind-set deriving from it, once translated into legal dogma, therefore resulted

23. The ground-breaking work of H. Pirenne is relevant to this aspect; see, among other works, *Mahomet et Charlemagne* (various editions), also *Histoire de l'Europe, des invasions au XVIe siècle*, Paris, 1936.

24. G. Pugliese, *Diritto, VII, Diritti soggettivi, b) Diritti reali*, in *Enc. Dir.*, vol. XII, (1964) at 756.

25. O.W. Holmes Jr, *The Common Law*, 1881, p. 8 (Boston, Little Brown &Co, 1923): "A very common phenomenon, and a very familiar to the student of history, is this. The customs, beliefs, or needs of a primitive time establish a rule or a formula. In the course of centuries the customs, belief, or necessity disappears, but the rule remains. The reason which gave rise to the rule has been forgotten, and ingenious minds set themselves to inquire how it is to be accounted for. Some grounds of policy is thought of, which seems to explain it and reconcile it with the present state of things; and then the rule adapts itself to the new reasons which have been found for it, and enters on a new career."

in a divergent development, neither of whose paths was in conflict with the underlying mentality.

On the one hand, the simplest organizational solution could be imposed, namely the transformation of all feudal rights pertaining to the lord into absolute rights over property, making the distinction between corporeal and incorporeal things secondary. As we have seen, this was the solution adopted by the common law, and subsequently transferred to all common-law jurisdictions.

On the other hand, a more sophisticated arrangement could be adopted, deriving from the idea that protection *erga omnes* is linked to and derives from another way of thinking, namely that *dominium* can only consist in the approach to and confrontation of man and the cosmos[26] and hence the *proprium* in this context is located in the right directly to use and dispose of a *res corporalis*. Seen from this perspective, rights in land are only a part of property as a whole. This provides the reason why the entire matter of real rights derives its own essential connotations from the notion of property itself.

This is a concept which gains strength from the recognition of the plural nature of "*dominia*", which are, however, often "*dominia juris*"[27] whose subject-matter is therefore incorporeal things, connected to the land only in a spatial sense.

The reason for this overturning of a realistic perspective connecting property rights to the physical reality of the land, in favor of rights over things, a notion conceptualized by logical argument, can be appreciated by considering that Roman law passed on a system of legal taxonomy to medieval law which is difficult to understand. This difficulty arises because, according to the reading of it which the interpreters were able to undertake, it placed real property rights within the *res incorporales*, together with *hereditas* and *obligatio*, while it placed other forms of property among the *res corporales*.

This taxonomy originated in the desire to organize all the rights which represented an individual's wealth in the most simple and elegant manner,[28] and was based on the observation that property includes and represents all the economic potentiality of the corporeal thing. Therefore when a corporeal is

26. On this, see: P. Grossi, *Domina e Servitutes—Invenzioni sistematiche del diritto comune in tema di servitù*, in 18 Quad. Fiorentini per la storia del pensiero giuridico moderno, 1989, 364.

27. See, e.g., P. Grossi, *Le situazioni reali nell'esperienza giuridica medioevale—Corso di Storia del diritto*, Padova, 1968.

28. Simplicity, precision and elegance are aspirations which legal science has long shared with mathematics, which the latter has maintained, while the former has lost these qualities.

owned, the value of the right is equal to the value of the thing itself. However, so long as the evaluation of the economic worth is undertaken in relation to the thing (the horse, the ship, the piece of land) and to its specific features, it is natural to elide the mechanism of property law and consider the economic value of the thing itself directly. To the contrary, when a limited property right is to be counted, the language was unable to elide the reference to the type of rights involved, since only a part of the value of the things was credited to the owner. Hence there arose the distinction between *res corporales* and *res incorporales*, which represented the entirety of a person's wealth or assets. The result of this taxonomy was to consider on one side (*res corporales*) things corporeal as the only things capable of being the object of ownership, and on the other side (*res incorporales*) all the other assets: usufruct and other real rights, property of a fund (*universitas rerum*) and also the right to receive a corporeal thing or services.

Such a distinction suited a culture based on trade, which existed in the Roman empire at the time of Gaius, who made the distinction originally, but put the medieval interpreters of law in serious difficulty. Not only did they have to deal with a largely agricultural economy, but also a society which made a clear distinction between wealth in landed property, particularly in relation to the aristocracy, and wealth in movable property and trade. They therefore found it artificial to start with a *summa divisio* of patrimonial rights, which immediately distinguished (allodial) property—free from encumbrances—(quite rare) from other rights in land, which were seen as conferring social status, and consequently subject to the same rules of inheritance under local customary law. Above all, however, the law provided protection of possession of these limited property rights in the same form as protection of ownership, and both were object of *seisin*. In this sense the legal system was in harmony with the social way of thinking, reflecting the world view proper to medieval man. From another viewpoint, connecting things with their natural ontology made the distinction between things and rights quite logical and persuasive and as a result, the efforts made by legal scholars were almost always devoted to keeping property rights distinct from other rights over things.

The insoluble problem called for a radical reworking. Pothier[29] cut the Gordian knot by making reference to positive law. Since wealth under French cus-

29. R.J. Pothier, *Traité des personnes et de choses*, in *Oevres de R.J. Pothier contennat les traités de droit français*, par M. Dupin Ainé, Tome V, Bruxelles, 1831, 204 (Seconde partie—Des Choses, §II): «Les choses incorporelles n'étant point des être réels, mais des être intellectuels, quae in jure consistunt, quae solo intellectu percipiuntur, ne sont point proprement par elles—mêmes susceptibles de la qualité de meubles, ni de celle d'Immeubles. Néanmoins, comme, selon notre droit français, toutes le choses que nous avons in bonis,

tomary law was divided into immovable and movable goods, and given that *res incorporales* were neither definable as movable or immovable, he abolished the distinction *de facto* by indicating what operations were required to reclassify every economic right either as movable or immovable property.[30] The French civil code accepted and broadcast this instruction.[31] The unfortunate consequences of this will be examined later.

## 7. The German Model of Property

### *7.1. Historical Background*

The evolution of the *jus commune* and its fundamental issues are crucial to understanding the present German system.

In the German context, the opposition between property rights and rights of credit, which the sources passed down via the (albeit different) opposition between *actiones in rem* and *in personam*, is anchored to the distinction between human and inanimate, namely objects extrinsic to man which can be devised by him (*Ding*), or those which are seen as part of the impersonal material world (*Sache*). This allowed development in two opposite directions.

From one point of view, all objects which are extrinsic to man, either devised or already existing in the world independent of thought, were conceivable as the subject-matter of rights attributable to human beings by the law. This was the solution enshrined in the Austrian *Allgemeines Bürgerliches Gesetzbuch* (ABGB). From another, the ambit of property rights could be confined only to those objects which exist independent of man, therefore excluding those whose contents are determined by human conduct. This alternative involves not only the notion of property, but also the concept of possession.

Since the 18th Century, possession could imply both possession of rights as well as things. This solution, present both in the Prussian *Allgemeines Lan-*

---

sont distribuées en deux classes, des meubles ou immeubles, les choses incorporelles, ainsi que les autres, doivent être assignées à l'une ou à l'autre de ces classes.»

30. R.J. Pothier, op loc cit.: «Les choses incorporelles sont, ou des droits réels, jus in jure, ou des créances, jura ad rem. Les droit réels, que nous avons sur les héritages, tel que les droits de fief, de censive, de champart, de rentes foncière, les droit de justice, les droit d'usufruit, d'usage, doivent sans doute appartenir à la classe des immeubles; car ces droits ne sont autre chose que l'héritage même sur lequel nous les avons à prendre, considéré comme nous appartenant à certains égards.»

31. This is in fact surprising, since this code was careful to abolish the reasons why French customary law stressed the distinction between movables and immovables.

*drecht* (ALR) and the Austrian ABGB,[32] was furnished through historical reasons, since the word 'possession' *(Besitz)* derived from Latin, the language in which laws were drawn up in the period mentioned above, but it often translated the concept of *gewere* (*seisin*). The notion of *gewere* has been an extremely vague and controversial legal conundrum in the history of European law, and certainly innumerable meanings have been attributed to it;[33] nonetheless, it is certain that *gewere* also included the possession of rights.[34] In practice, *gewere* took effect both as a result of *de facto* circumstances, where (the subject-matter of the right) had remained undisturbed for at least a year and a day,[35] and legal vesting in possession, understood as a form of ritual which was clearly witnessed by onlookers, as has been seen in the English system. In circumstances such as this, German customary law assured protection which could readily be taken for the protection of possession by the possessory actions under Roman law. But an abyss remains, not only because the *gewere* also concerned rights belonging to a certain territory, but also because it included all circumstances of protected ownership and therefore was not in contradistinction to property. Such opposition however was present in the concepts of Roman law, in that possession was actual enjoyment, located in the sphere of perceptible experience, in that it exists effectively in relation to the object; conversely, property implies absolute sovereignty over the object, which belongs to the individual by virtue of a title which is recognized by the law.

The conjugation of *gewere* and the binomial notion of possession/property is a phenomenon which runs throughout the whole period of the *jus commune*.

Under English common law, as we have seen, *seisin*, which was the local equivalent of the Germanic *gewere*, generated property rights, and was extin-

32. B. Pozzo, *Eigentum*, in A. Candian, A. Gambaro, B. Pozzo, *Property, propriété, eigentum*, Padova, 1992, 318.

33. A survey of sources collected by the end of the long drawn out debate in the 19th Century can be read in Heusler, *Institutionen des deutschen Privatrechts*, vol. II, Weimar, 1886, 20 *ff.*

34. In this regard, Bruns' research is definitive: *Das Recht des Besitzes im Mittelalter und in der Gegenwart*, Tübingen, 1848.

35. As Frazer states (*The Golden Bough*, London, 1922, vol. III, 873), in many cultures, including all the Indo-European ones, there was a rite repeated at 5-yearly intervals, which took place very often at the time of the spring equinox, involving the ritual expulsion of all the evils of the village by material, vehicular means. The evil was therefore symbolised by either a human or an animal. The period of a year and a day could therefore prove that on that occasion s/he had remained undisturbed within the circle of those who were part of the right and the just, in contrast to the evil which had been expelled.

guished by them. In France, gewere (*seisine*) disappeared with the Revolution but possession remained for the purposes of the possessory actions in the case of immovable property, and as a form of ownership for the purpose of the circulation of movable property.

In Germany, the new direction carries the stamp of Savigny, and came to pass in the name of a revived form of legal science, which coupled the logical rigour of legal rationalism with the wholesale revival of Roman law, seen as a cultured tradition in comparison to customary law. This led to *Besitz* being viewed once more as the unique *de facto* form of holding based on the control over a corporeal thing, with the radical exclusion of the possibility of acquiring possession over a mere right. Because ownership must be symmetrical to possession, ownership also suffers the same limitation and thus only concerns things which are capable of being possessed and which therefore may form the subject-matter of a claim, when it is in the possession of someone who does not have title to it. In a singular way, this configuration served to distinguish the matter of property rights very clearly from that which merely concerned a personal relationship. The theoretical organization of the concept of possession therefore became definitive for the purposes of constructing a logically coherent system of patrimonial rights.

This was enshrined in the *Bürgerliches Gesetzbuch* (BGB), leading the German model to confine the category of property rights to the *Sachenrecht*, namely the possession of and real rights over corporeal things. But in this way, from an exclusively logical perspective, one goes back to the beginning in considering the irreducible differences between *res corporalis* (ownership) and all other patrimonial rights. This distinction is logically incompatible with the opposition between real rights, on one side, and personal rights, or relationships involving obligations, on the other side. From this arises one of the very few logical contradictions encountered in the BGB, namely that *Sachenrecht* refers to corporeal things, but then, in the third Book, also includes pledges for credit (*Pfandrecht an einer Forderung* § 1279-1290) and Usufruct on rights (*Nießbrauch an Rechten* § 1068-1084). This aside, the German codification of the law of property rights can be seen as an extremely compact system.

## 7.2. Property in the BGB

The third Book of the BGB, containing the laws governing property rights and other real rights is called *Sachenrecht*, literally 'the law of things', but in the first Book, dedicated to the General Part of private law, § 90 BGB concretely sets out the fundamental principle that, according to the law, a thing can only be corporeal.[36] Unlike the common law, which makes an immediate distinction between real and personal property, and the French codified system which makes movable property quite different from immovable property, the German system considers property as a unitary concept which includes both movable and immovable property, although obviously the regime governing their enjoyment and circulation is necessarily very different.

The regime governing immovable property is marked by the *Grundbuch*, setting out the founding principles, which lists all the rights of property whose subject-matter is immovable. The constitution, transfer or amendment of a real property right must be transcribed into the *Grundbuch*. Without such transcription the constitution, transfer or amendment of a real property right does not exist. For a working point of view, immovable property is therefore a wholly documentary part of private law. The *de facto* opposing circumstances which are in conflict with the reality as documented are therefore marginalized. This is comparable to the marginalization of bare possession in English common law, which stands as a symbol of a strong legal system that recognizes and protects title, but not mere factual situations; thus the German system with its *Grundbuch* symbolises a strong state which guarantees a precise and accurate system of title registration, capable of conferring absolute certainty on legal transactions in immovable property.[37]

So far as movable property is concerned, the rules of circulation hinge upon delivery of the goods in such a way that the party acquiring them is in a position of complete sovereignty over them. Even if the notion of *constitutum possessorium* is admitted, as we shall see later on, the two rules just mentioned already imply a rejection of the consent principle, that is to say, the principle that a contractual act automatically operates as a conveyance of ownership.[38] This rejection becomes really apparent if one considers that, under the German system, the will to change a legally regulated situation concerning real property can only be achieved by executing a special deed (*dingliches Rechtsgeschäft*), which differs from the legal act under the law of obligations.[39] The latter has no power to create or amend a right of property. The legal act re-

36. See also the Dutch NB, Art. 3.1.1.1 "Things are corporeal objects susceptible of human control."

37. This is not the exclusive prerogative of systems on the German model. A comparable solution is to be found in the so-called Thorens system which has spread from its origins in Australia to many countries throughout the common law world, although the feature of absolute certainty is not perfect due to the immovable presence of equitable interests.

38. See §.8.4 on the French system.

39. See L.P.W. van Vliet, *Transfer of movables in German, French, English and Dutch law*, Nijmigen, 2000.

lating to property (*dingliches Rechtsgeschäft*) is constituted by a demonstration of will and a deed of execution, which could be the registration of the name of the acquiring party in the *Grundbuch*, or the delivery of the goods or thing in question. It does not express the reason for the amendment of the property right, which makes it abstract. Juridical real acts (*dingliches Rechtsgeschäfts*) are abstract in this sense, and therefore reference is made to the principle of abstraction (*Abstraktionsprinzip*). If the contract creating an obligation to transfer is set aside for some reason, this does not affect the transfer of the property. However, if the contract creating the obligation to transfer is set aside, this does give rise to an obligation to make restitution, by virtue of the rules on unjust enrichment, rules which therefore have a wide application under the German legal system. The *Abstraktionsprinzip* provides great security for buyers, since the accuracy of entries in the *Grundbuch* can only rarely be challenged.

The *Grundbuch* is an official register kept by a public authority and is based on the identification of each individual piece of land. This is in conformity with the principle of specificity (*Spezialitätsgrundsatz*) and for this reason property rights refer to individually identified corporeal things and never to a disparate collection of property, such as occurs with a trust fund or the 'universality' of movable goods under Roman law. A three-part inscription corresponds to each parcel of land. The first part recites the name of the owner and the origin of his/her title to the property. In the second and third parts there are the real property rights affecting the property. In particular, charges/mortgages are registered in the third part. An obvious corollary of the registration system in the *Grundbuch* is that there is a strictly closed number of property rights. In fact, by looking at the type of property right registered, it should be immediately apparent what sort of charge is attached to the real property.

Limited real rights are divided into the rights of enjoyment, security and acquisition.

Rights of enjoyment in this context are the following: usufruct (*Nutzungsrechte*); the right of superficies (*Erbbaurecht*); and servitudes and limited personal servitudes (*Beschränke Persönlische Dienstbarkeiten*), which are rights or benefits over a servient tenement in favour of certain individuals, including also a right of habitation (*Wohnungsrecht*).[40] Finally the BGB also establishes burdens in relation to land (*Reallasten*), upon the basis of which

40. See § 1093 BGB, A limited personal right in relation to the property could be the use of a building or part of a building as a dwelling.

an immovable property may have certain burdens attached to it, such as services which may have to be carried out periodically for the person in whose favor the right has been created. The special law on town apartment ownership has also introduced a right of use which may be ceded and passed on to heirs and successors.

Security rights, in addition to using the property as security (*Sicherungseigentum*) or creating a mortgage (*Hypothek*), are land debts (*Grundschuld*)[41] and rent from the property (*Rentenschuld*),[42] and pledges over movables. A right of acquisition is the right of preference (*Vorkaufrecht*).[43]

In general, then, these types of rights under the German system, although limited in number, cover a vast range and are capable of satisfying almost every need.

## *7.3. The Besitz*

The *Sachenrecht* includes the regime governing possession (*Besitz*). Possession is considered as *de facto* control over a particular corporeal thing. The functions of possession are limited to protection for the possessor and the right of acquisition by prescription (*Ersitzung*), which is achieved on uninterrupted possession in good faith for 10 years. In the case of real property, *Buchersitzung* (prescriptive possession capable of Land Registry registration) is achieved after 30 years' registration in the *Grundbuch,* thus confirming the documentary nature of real property rights.

The importance of possession can be gauged better in the area of personal (movable) property. It has already been noted that the transfer of personal property requires delivery (*Übergabe*) of the thing. But the possession of movable property gives rise to a presumption of ownership.[44] This is a simple presumption, which is not valid in the case of loss or theft of the property, except in the case of cash or bearer bonds. In reality, delivery and the related presumption favors the circulation of goods because it acknowledges *constitutum*

---

41. See §1191 BGB, A burden may be created in relation to a property in such a way that the person in whose favour the benefit has been created must be paid a certain sum of money from the property.

42. See §1199 BGH A debt due in relation to the property may be created in such a way that a certain sum of money from the property has to be paid at regular intervals.

43. See §1094 BGB A burden may be created on the property in such a way that the person in whose favour the right has been created can legitimately exercise this right against the owner of the property.

44. See §106 sect. 1 BGB.

*possessorium*,[45] which means that although ownership is transferred, physical control remains with the transferor, but s/he changes her attitude and possesses the thing in the interest of the transferee, having certain obligations towards the latter. For this reason, it is sufficient that at the moment ownership ceases, the seller in possession of the thing acknowledges that from that moment on, s/he no longer possesses the thing as owner but as the buyer's bailee. From then on the buyer is the possessor and the owner, because delivery of the thing has taken place (*i.e.* ownership of the thing has passed) without it having to be physically moved. This possibility, widely used in commercial practice, has also given rise to a system of security on movable property without possession being given up. As such, the BGB recognized the pledge as the only form of security concerning movables, but a pledge requires dispossession of the debtor of the item of property constituting the security, and for that reason has ceased to be used, and transfer of property as security has replaced it. In this regard, property is naturally transferred under the rules relating to *constituto possessorio*, together with a deed of security specifying that the transfer is by way of security and governs the event of the security being called upon. This is normally accompanied by another document in which the owner authorizes the debtor to dispose of the things under certain conditions.

Protection of property in the German system occurs by way of the traditional Roman law actions of vindication, by which the owner of a thing is entitled to revendicate it from any person who detains it without right; and actions against troubles and nuisance (*Beseitigung-und Unterlassungsanspruch*).[46]

Proof of ownership can be given by any means, and the principle stating that ownership can only be proved by written documents of certain date, one of the most tedious corollary aspects of the consent principle, is likewise unknown.

In civil law jurisdictions, protection of property depends on the way in which the relationship between protection of property and protection of possession is conceived. Unlike the common law, and ancient German law in general, Roman law made a clear-cut difference between property and possession (*nihil commune habet proprietas cum possessione*).[47] Canon law transposed the same distinction into the field of procedure: where possession was the matter in issue, title was immaterial. The defendant could not set it up in defence. French law, as we shall see, has preserved this arrangement. The common law always prefers the one who can show the better title; this solution, however, implies the exclusion of the defence of *jus tertii*, for a defen-

45. See §930 BGB.
46. See §1004 BGB.
47. D.41.2.12.1

dant cannot set up the better title of a third party against a plaintiff who is claiming a right from him based on prior possession; the defendant can succeed only upon the basis of his better right. German law is somewhere in the middle. Defence of *jus tertii* is excluded, but defences on the basis of a better right are admitted to the extent that they can show that the defendant's behavior is not unlawful.

## 8. The French Model of Property

The two systems considered so far—the English common law and the modern German system—are both, from opposite standpoints, internally coherent. The same thing cannot be said for the system which was brought about by the codification of civil law in France. This view may seem surprising, because it has become customary to regard Napoleon's civil code on property as the code *par excellence* of its kind. However, it is important to distinguish between its use as rhetoric and the normative provisions of the text of the code. From the first viewpoint, the dense, epigrammatic phraseology in the code lent themselves to raising the law of property to dizzy heights. From the second, it is demonstrable that the code is not completely on the side of the property owner, to which it offers less protection than other systems.

### *8.1. The Concept of Property in the Civil Code*

The civil code was drawn up in the wake of a social revolution which had changed the face of landed property. One of its aims was to enshrine the new arrangements for landholding and make them irreversible. To this end, it was said that a return had been made to Roman principles of property—meaning the classic form of *dominium* which had been handed down in the Justinian laws. This was only partially true. Indeed, the notion of property was designed on the paradigm of individual ownership which confers complete power over the thing to its owner.[48] Limited property rights were kept to an absolute, indispensable minimum.

Since the right of ownership is the absolute dominion that a person can exercise over a thing, it gives a right over everything which the thing produces and over that which unites with it accessorily, either naturally or artificially.[49]

48. See the well-know definition in Art. 544 of the civil code, above §6.
49. See Art. 546 civil code.

This is an absolute right which includes the option of using or not using the thing; consequently this is perpetual in the sense that it is not extinguished by reason of the owner not exercising rights of ownership. Because ownership confers upon the owner all the uses and benefits which the thing can generate, the right of ownership is naturally exclusive since nothing is left over for others, unless a specific right is detached from it (*demembrements de la propriété*).

An absolute nature, perpetuity and exclusiveness are therefore the essential characteristics sanctified by the civil code.

Property therefore fulfils the same function as the fee simple absolute, forming the basis of all the other real property rights, conceived as fractions of the property, to which they are reunited automatically, as soon as they are extinguished.

## *8.2. The System of Property Rights*

Under the French system, limited property rights are derived from the traditional ones under ordinary Roman law: usufruct, right of use and habitation, servitudes, pledges and mortgages. Apart from usufruct, which may have as subject-matter any real or personal property, and, obviously, the pledge, the function of limited property rights is to systemize title to a piece of land. Co-ownership also serves primarily the same function, which in France is governed by collection of laws outside the code.

From an objective viewpoint, a piece of land is governed by rules dealing with legal distances: those concerning common walls and access roads, including the regime governing easements, which plays a leading role.

From a subjective point of view, the rules of property govern the way in which the use of the thing is shared between people.[50] Various techniques may be adopted in relation to this. The oldest form was concurrent attribution. One particular piece of land can generate uses or benefits which are attributed to different people. This may happen in relation to time, as in the case of usufruct, use and habitation; or else, from the point of view of the simultaneous co-existence of different benefits, such as occurs in the case of mortgages, which provide security for the mortgage lender, but do not interfere with the owner's possession. Attribution of co-ownership is a time-honored technique, which, however, the code treats as a negative, in its enunciation of the principle "*nul ne peut être contraint à demeurer dans l'indivision*", in Art. 815. Each person who has a share in common therefore has title to a fraction

---

50. Ch. Atias, *Droit Civil—Les biens*, 5eme ed., Paris, 2000.

of the property which s/he can assign or mortgage. Although the code's perspective has been reduced by subsequent laws, the general provision under which co-ownership can be dissolved at the will of one co-owner explains the reason why there is another widespread method for dividing property, which makes use of the technique of setting up a legal person as the formal owner of the property. This method is very common in the building industry, where frequent use is made of property companies for building new developments and allotting the individual apartments to company shareholders.

In a certain sense, this trend fully demonstrates the faith which the French system places in the dogma of individual property and which therefore prefers to have recourse to creating legal fictions rather than spoil the integrity of the holding by dividing it up. From another perspective, the same trend indicates quite clearly that the differences between the system of property rights and the laws of obligations are getting slimmer. In order to become an owner, one is required to become a shareholder, that is to say, to place oneself within a network of obligations. The dividing line may be crossed in another sense as well: in order to encourage the granting of loans by banks, a special law has introduced a fairly simple system for making the assignments of credit valid against the creditors of the transferee.[51] The regime is modelled on rules governing registered goods, but formalities are reduced to a minimum order to reduce transaction costs. In doing so, the law-makers themselves have used the terminology of personal property, and refer to *propriété de la créance*—a characterization that would be inconceivable in Germany.

From the point of view of the object of property rights and the consequent distinction between rights *in rem* and *in personam*, the French system seems to be evolving towards a model which is similar to the English one, and conversely, away from the German system, which is based on the clear and radical distinction between 'real' rights (*Sachenrecht*) on the one hand and obligations on the other hand.

The reasons for this trend are complex. It must be remembered that the French civil code, following Pothier's suggestion, has made reference to the distinction between movables and immovables, and it is silent on the crucial distinction between *res corporales* and *incorporales*. Unlike the BGB, and the Dutch NBW, the code does not provide that the law of property and possession be reserved to specific kinds of things. This explains the success of the

51. The reason for this is that normally business people assign their credits to the bank, in order to receive an advance, but the civil code rules make this assignment good against the businessman's other creditors only if there is a written document with a certain date (see infra, §8.4).

(originally German[52]) theory, enjoyed in France more than in other countries in continental Europe, which holds that a property right is merely one aspect of the relationships between people, based on a universal passive obligation to avoid interference with an owner's enjoyment of his possessions.[53]

However, the code's ambiguity as to what constitutes property is linked to more profound legal mechanisms that are at the root of the present trends in the French legal system. When landed property was regarded as property *par excellence*, the law of property tended to be identified with the thing itself,[54] and by consequence the law of property was considered to be internally coherent. The reality is that the codifiers, immersed as they were in the intellectual atmosphere of the time of the convergence of differing traditions of research, considered that land was *par excellence* that thing that constituted property and that movable property was corporeal, even though they did not want to exclude *la propriété littéraire,* which, at a constitutional level, was considered the most sacred of things which could be owned. They failed to set out a comprehensive system for the law of property in general. The two tests of this failure are the so-called consent principle that governs the transfer of property and protection of possession, which for many years was regulated outside the code but has always been an important part of the system.

### *8.3. The Transfer of Property*

It is well known that the French civil code has adopted the so-called consent principle by which in order for A to transfer property to B, the consent of both parties is sufficient, and it is not necessary for the thing to be handed over to the transferee or the price to be paid.[55]

The French codifiers were impelled to do this because of two convergent pressures. The first one was that the principle of transfer of title by consent corresponded to one of the teachings of the school of natural law, whose ad-

52. Ch. Atias, *Droit Civil-Les biens*, 5eme ed., Paris, 2000.

53. E. Roguin, *La règle de droit. Etude de science juridique pure*, Lausanne, 1889; S. Ginossar, *Droit réel, propriété, créance*, Paris, 1960; F. Zenati, *La nature juridique de la propriété. Contribution à la théorie du droit subjectif*, Thèse, Lyon, 1981; Id., *Les biens*, Paris, 1988.

54. See below, recalling Demolombe's cry, *Cours de Code Napoléon,* T. 9, De la propriété, n° 540, «le droit de propriété c'est le bien lui-même, le bien corporel, meuble ou immeuble».

55. See Art. 1583: «(La vente) est parfaite entre le parties, et la propriété est acquise de droit à l'acheteur à l'égard du vendeur, dès qu'on est convenue de la chose et du prix, quoique que la chose n'ait pas encore été livrée ni le prix payé».

herents started with the assumption that the owner's will regarding the destination of the property was sovereign, and consequently his consent alone was sufficient to effect the transfer. Moreover, in France the practice of *constitutum possessorium* was well established, which meant delivery was, in effect, notional and was substituted by a formulaic phrase in a document by which the seller stated that he was assuming the role of bailee of the property for the buyer, to whom property in (but not actual possession of) the goods then passed. It was then resolved to eliminate this useless fiction by simplifying the system of property transfer. However, doing this created the possibility of setting up a system for the circulation of property rights (not only goods, as in England) without any form of publicity. This was a particular problem so far as mortgages were concerned, where the possibility of setting up hidden mortgages, far from favoring the granting of credit, hindered both this and the market in real property, given the understandable diffidence on the part of lending institutions and buyers. The lacuna in the law was filled about 50 years after the code, with the creation of a system of registration of real property transactions. The obvious function of this form of publicity, achieved through the use of public registers, is to keep potential buyers and potential mortgage lenders informed about the ownership situation in relation to the property. The inevitable corollary of this information supplied by public registries is that all unregistered rights are not valid against those already registered. Otherwise, setting up a public registry of property rights would be worthless. However, there was no wish to abandon the principle of transfer of title by mere consent which was therefore maintained, although somewhat devoid of effect, given that whoever buys before registering acquires a right in property which is not valid against the world, which rather contradicts the essence of a property right.

The system of registration was extended to include other property interests, including those outside the context of immovable property. There are numerous registries in France today.

Besides the area of real property and other registered interests, the French codified system has introduced numerous checks and balances of the consent principle. The conflict between two different buyers of the same thing is resolved by making possession the criterion for resolving disputes. Art. 1141 states that in the case of double assignment of movable property, the person able to demonstrate actual possession of the property in good faith[56] will be

56. «Si la chose qu'on s'est obligé de donner ou de livrer à deux personnes successivement, est purement mobilière, celle des deux qui en été mise en possession réelle est préférée

treated as the owner; the criterion of good faith is repeated and amplified so far as a subsequent disposal of movable property is concerned under Art. 2279, which sets out the famous principle that "*en fait de meubles, la possession vaut titre*".[57] This creates an obvious contradiction with the consent principle because, once again, the title acquired on the basis of consensual agreement is not good against the world. In fact, the lack of such universal protection is augmented, in the case of acquisition of property or other property rights unaccompanied by actual possession, by the rule enshrined in Art. 1328 of the civil code, which lays down that written documents of uncertain date are not valid against third parties.[58] Consequently, the creditor of the person retaining them can take executive action to recover them, without the owner being able to defend himself, unless he is able to produce a written document of certain date preceding the date of execution, proving acquisition of the goods. This criterion is specifically repeated concerning pledges under Art. 2074, which sets out that a pledge is not valid against third parties unless it was set up by public deed or private written document, duly registered. This indicates a clear rupture in the system of property rights.

In this connection, the divergence between declarations of principle and operational rules is very marked in the French codified model. At a declaratory level, the consent principle conveys into the system of positive private law the natural law school's notion that the owner's will is *per se* the only form of sovereignty over the thing.[59] For this reason, it would seem to elevate the status of the owner, who enjoys the power to change the legal position of things, by a pure act of will. At a practical level, however, the consent principle is able to transfer property only between the parties and not for all purposes. This

---

et en demeure propriétaire, encore que son titre soit postérieur en date, pourvu toutefois que la possession soit de bonne foi».

57. This principle, however, does not apply to lost or stolen goods, unless they have been acquired in public places of sale (market overt), because in such a case there is a right of retention until reimbursement of the price paid by the one bringing an action for restitution of the property.

58. Les actes sous seing privé n'ont date contre les tiers que du jour où ils ont été enregistrés, du jour de la mort de celui ou de l'un de ceux qui les ont souscrites, ou du jour où leur substance est constatée dans les actes dressées par des officiers publics, tel que procès-verbaux de scellé ou d'inventaire.

59. See G. Blanluet, *Le moment du trasfert de la propriété*, in *Université Panthéon-Assas (Paris II), 1804–2004 Le Code Civil. Un passè, un present, un avenir*, Paris, 2004, p. 410: «cette unité et cette cohérence découlent largement, il est vrai, de la conception que les ouvriers du Code civil se faisaient du pouvoir de la volonté individuelle. La volonté peut tout, non seulement dans les rapports entre les hommes, mais également dans les relations qu'ils entretiennent avec les choses».

introduces two forms of ownership, the first with the effect of transferring the risk to the transferee, but without exclusivity. The second is traditional ownership, but agreement alone is insufficient to acquire it. Far from decreasing transaction costs, the consent principle increases them. What is more, it increases them substantially, since the written form of registration is a very rarely used procedure in commercial trading in movable goods. The final result is diminished security for movable property rights. Diminished security—which is principally noticeable when the unregistered goods are consigned to other people—is an ever more frequent practice a in modern economy. Here we are seeing the emergence of a crypto-type of the French model: the hidden principle, which states that property rights that together represent a person's wealth are only those which are outwardly visible to his creditors. Consequently it follows that, beyond the relationship between the parties, a dissociation of apparent and actual property is not admitted. Whoever is an owner on the basis of rules relating to the circulation of goods and essentially on the basis of the consent principle has no valid title against third parties unless on the basis of further elements of publicity previously codified by the legislators. Only the tax authorities, by special dispensation, can (sometimes) make reality prevail over appearances, to the owner's disadvantage.

The consensual transfer system that the civil code has introduced into French law is thus subject to very important exceptions. The ideology of the natural law school seems to be turned upside down, if transaction costs are taken into account.

The so called "*effet translatif des contrats*" requires a valid contract with a *justa causa traditionis*. The will of the parties is not enough: this opens the doors for monitoring the transfer of property in a way that has no parallel in other systems. For instance, despite the efforts of some authors,[60] the trust (*fiducie*) is not recognized as a sufficient "cause" for transfer of property. *Constitutum posserorium* has been deleted because transfer of possession is not required. This implies that it is impossible to acquire property in the full sense of the word without physical possession or some form of registration.

## *8.4. Property and Possession*

The French codified system is generally described as being one which is very favorable to the property sector, but, from a technical point of view, the most effective safeguards concern owners who are also in possession. If the owner

60. See C. Witz, *La fiducie en droit privé français*, Paris, 1981.

is not also in possession, his right receives only slim protection. Certainly, he may bring an action for *vindicatio*, the usual way for an owner to recover possession. However, under the French system, the burden of proof which the owner must discharge is quite heavy, because he has to prove a right which is good against the world and not just against the possessor he is suing. Although French case law has reduced this burden and adopted a criterion which is nearer to the common law—the one with the better title wins in an action for possession—the one with the better title wins, the principle nevertheless continues to be proclaimed. To make things worse, the French system has preserved the old distinction between possessory and proprietary remedies. It should be recalled in this context that the civil code did not regulate possession or protection of possession. This derived from the fear that, via possession, all the ancient customary and feudal rights would migrate into the new regime for real property brought about by the Revolution and enshrined in the Code. However, actions for possession were immediately reintroduced by case law into the area of real property, giving rise to dual forms of protection.[61] Having existed outside the code for a long time, this procedure inherited forms from the past, and in particular, inherited the rule from canon law whereby a ruling on possession preceded a ruling on the merits of the property right. Hence in the proceedings to consider the protection of possession, the law of property may not be invoked, and an action for (re)possession (*i.e.* on the merits of the property right) cannot be started until there is a ruling in relation to the issue of possession (*le possessoire tient le petitoire en état*). This is a rule which shows some elements of conflict with any constitutional guarantee relating to property.

## 9. Property in European Legal Systems Today

The models presented here have been hybridized in various ways by each system of positive law which, so far as detailed rules are concerned, is constantly evolving. The world of property is too variegated and complex to be enclosed within artificial formulas. The other European systems are further hybridizations of the main models. Each has tried to find a balanced position between differing needs.

From a constitutional perspective, property rights within the European legal traditions serve to ensure an independent space to individuals and to legit-

---

61. The *actions possessoires* were introduced into the French civil code in 1975. They are now considered under Articles 2282 and 2283 Code civil.

imize idiosyncratic behavior. From this point of view the law of property is at the foundation of an important part of European civilization. In this perspective, private property is to be evaluated from the standpoint of political, social and economical organization. Normally from this perspective, it is hard to see any significant difference between European legal systems. Taken together, they are all considered to be the expression of a liberal system of justice, and distinguishing those which are more concerned with issues of distribution is just a matter of degree.

It is astonishing how many variations of the same principle of political organization exist, developed by the technicalities of private law.

This does not mean that these technicalities do not really matter; on the contrary, the identification of property rights serves various regulatory purposes. In short, reference can be made to the fact that the localization of property rights is used as a criterion for separating jurisdictions between judges of differing states, and for the division of competences between judges within the same state. Moreover, the exclusivity of property rights allows property to be consigned to others' keeping without competing with other creditors when the property is in the hands of some person who becomes insolvent.

The last point is the crucial one in many private law commercial arrangements. In all the European legal systems, principles governing bankruptcy seems to be strictly similar; variations are in the identification of property rights. At this regards the certainty and security which goes with title to property rights, facilitates the economic calculus, and essentially decreases the risk of the unforeseen. This explains the modern-day trend to multiply property rights. The heart of the matter is that, in European law there are no common principles in the law of property, making it probably the most fragmented part of European private law.

## References

W. Van Alstyne, *Cracks in "The New Property", Adjudicative Due process in the Administrative State*, 62 *Cornell L. Rev.* 445 (1977).

Ch Atias, *Droit Civil—Les biens*, 5eme ed., Paris, 2000.

J Austin, *Lectures on Jurisprudence or the Philosophy of Positive Law* (1863), 5a ed., London, 1885.

A.A. Bearle Jr. e G.C. Means, *The Modern Corporation and Private Property*, New York, 1932.

F. Biglione, *La notion de privation de propriété*, Aix-Marseille, 1999.

G. Blanluet, *Le moment du trasfert de la propriété*, in *Université Panthéon-Assas (Paris II), 1804–2004 Le Code Civil. Un passè, un present, un avenir*, Paris, 2004, 410.

C.G. Bruns, *Das Recht des Besitzes im Mittelalter und in der Gegenwart*, Tübingen, 1848.

G. Calabresi and D. Melamed, *Property Rules, Liability Rules, Inalienability: One View of the Cathedral*, 85 *Harv. L. Rev.* 1089 (1972).

A. Candian, A. Gambaro, B. Pozzo, *Property, propriété, eigentum*, Padova, 1992

F. Cohen, *Dialogue on Private Property*, 9 *Rutgers L. Rev.* 357 (1954).

J.G. Frazer, *The Golden Bough*, London, 1922, III.

S. Ginossar, *Droit réel, propriété, créance*, Paris, 1960.

P. Grossi, *Domina e Servitutes—Invenzioni sistematiche del diritto comune in tema di servitù*, in 18 *Quad. Fiorentini per la storia del pensiero giuridico moderno*, 1989, 364.

P. Grossi, *Le situazioni reali nell'esperienza giuridica medioevale—Corso di Storia del diritto*, Padova, 1968.

G. Hardin, *The Tragedy of the Commons*, 162 *Science* 1243 (1968).

M.A. Heller, *The Tragedy of the Anticommons*, 111 *Harv. L. R.* 625 (1998).

W.N. Hohfeld, *Fundamental Legal Conceptions as applied in Legal Reasoning, and Other Legal Essays*, New Haven, 1919.

O.W. Holmes Jr, *The Common Law* (1881), Boston, Little Brown &Co, 1923.

A.M. Honorè, *Ownership*, in A.G. Guest (ed.) *Oxford Essays in Jurisprudence*, Oxford, 1961, 108.

K.R. Minogue, *The Concept of Property and its Contemporary Significance*, in J.K. Pennock e J.W. Chapman, *Property* (Nomos, XXII), New York, 1980.

S.R. Munzer, *A Theory of Property*, Cambridge, 1990

J. Nedelsky, *Private Property and the Limits of American Constitutionalism. The Madisonian Framework and Its Legacy*, Chicago, 1990.

H. Pirenne, *Histoire de l'Europe, des invasions au XVIe siècle*, Paris, 1936.

R.J. Pothier, *Traité des personnes et de choses*, in *Oevres de R.J. Pothier contennat les traités de droit français*, par M. Dupin Ainé, Tome V, Bruxelles, 1831.

G. Pugliese, *Diritto, VII, Diritti soggettivi, b) Diritti reali*, in *Enc. Dir.*, vol. XII, (1964), 756.

Ch. Reich, *The New Property*, 73 *Yale Law J.* 733 (1964).

E. Roguin, *La règle de droit. Etude de science juridique pure*, Lausanne, 1889.

C. Rose, *The Comedy of the Commons: Customs, Commerce and Inherently Public Property*, 53 *U.of Chi. L.R.* 711 (1986).

L.P.W. van Vliet, *Transfer of movables in German, French, English and Dutch law*, Nimijgen, 2000.

J. Waldron, *The Right to Private Property*, Oxford, 1988.

C. Witz, *La fiducie en droit privé français*, Paris, 1981.
M. Xifaras, *La propriété. Étude de Philosophie du droit*, Paris, 2004.
F. Zenati, *Les biens*, Paris, 1988.
F. Zenati, *La nature juridique de la propriété. Contribution à la théorie du droit subjectif, Thèse*, Lyon, 1981.

# 4

# A Comparative Analysis: The Contractual Transfer of Ownership of Movable Property

Rodolfo Sacco*

## Summary



* Professor Emeritus, University of Turin.

# 1. Introduction

## *1.1. Scope of the Chapter*

*The notion of transfer.* There is a fundamental debate involving the notion of property transfer. Certain jurists reject the idea of the literal transfer of a right: in their view, the replacement of one owner with a new one means that the old interest is extinguished and a new interest is created. Other jurists insist that certain properly facts of disposition by a non-owner may renew the right of ownership (termination-creation), which is technically neither a succession nor a transfer. However, the debate over whether ownership can be transferred does not impede a comparative analysis. Our comparison encompasses both the applicable operational rules, and classifications, dogmatic schemas, and definitions with which any jurist must necessarily be familiar per her national legal system. For instance, the dissimilar expressions "renewal of ownership" and "transfer of ownership" reference empirically similar events. Any inconsistencies between the two are perhaps best analyzed by comparativists. Thus, the value of comparative analysis does not depend on the value and logical coherence of the rules and definitions emphasized by some observers.

*The notion of ownership.* The sheer breadth of the notion of ownership is daunting—it is not uniform across the globe. In certain systems it affords an absolute protection while elsewhere it protects the claimant with the clearer title to possession of the object. In romanist legal systems, ownership of an object is weighed against other more limited rights over the object. Yet, the common law legal vocabulary does not adequately differentiate the exclusive, absolute, superior, and general right that may be had over an object. "Ownership" in English refers a broader notion than does "*propriété*" in French. Furthermore, French law and its progeny are set apart from other legal systems in conceiving of authors' rights as a form of *propriété (littéraire)*. The words ownership, *propriété*, *Eigentum*, and *sobstvennost* may not be perfectly interchangeable; however, this does not prevent our use of the term *ownership* as a conventional reference to the broadest and most general right over a material thing.

*The transfer of ownership.* Despite the nearly worldwide use by lawyers of the phrase "transfer of ownership", difficulties arise from the fact that some legal systems distinguish "transfer of ownership between parties" from "transfer of ownership for all purposes", while others do not. This asymmetry makes our comparison more delicate. We will use "transfer of ownership" as a theme; it will encompass each phase of the process by which legal title passes to a new owner from the former. Of course, within each legal system these phases differ and are worthy of comparative analysis.

One final potential source of confusion is rooted in linguistic asymmetry. The words *propriété* and *Eigentum* and *sobstvennost* are typically said to correspond to the English word *ownership*, whereas the French expression *transfert de propriété* can be translated as *transfer of property*, incorporating the idea of the transferred tangible object as opposed to the rights in that object. Almost everywhere we encounter the tendency to confuse the idea of ownership with the more tangible idea of property.

## *1.2. Simplifications*

In German law, "the handing-over transfers the ownership of movable objects" whereas in Italian law, "the handing-over effectively transfers the ownership of negotiable instruments but not of other movable objects." When comparing the two rules, we have first to establish whether the expression "handing over" has the same meaning in both contexts. However, a thorough study of such an elementary notion would entail an analysis of the entire private law systems of relevant countries. In the interest of succinctness, we consciously overlook certain nuances and subtleties of domestic laws.

*Agreements.* We will avoid equivocating the terms *agreement*, *contract*, *contrat*, *Vertrag*, *dogovor*, contract, etc. The difference between contracts conceived of as mere agreements versus as agreements based on *cause* or form are much too important to ignore. However, we will ignore differences such as those relating to the conclusion of agreements, the capacities of the subjects, defects of agreement, the effects of a retraction of an offer, and discrepancies between an individual's mental and declared wills. Finally, the meaning of "*accord, Einigung, agreement*" is the mutual declaration of the two parties. But, the same word is often used to refer to the combination of mutual declaration with *cause*.

Likewise, there is a similar ambivalence concerning the transfer of ownership. Two expressions so dear to the French—"the transfer of ownership can only take place through a meeting of the minds of the transferor and the transferee" and "the act of transferring ownership arises from the will of the parties"—are undermined by the reality that an agreement will have no effect where it is not accompanied by *cause*. We will speak of consent and agreement in reference to the hypothesis whereby the parties want nothing more or less than "for ownership of a specified object to pass from the transferor to the transferee." When we speak of a contract, the term will reflect what values are given to it by the relevant legal system.

*Cause, Consideration.* Quite frequently a simple agreement is not enough to produce the effects intended by the parties if it is not anchored by the element that justifies it or makes it binding: *cause, Grund,* consideration, etc. This ulterior element varies from one system to the next, but herein we are forced to reduce it to something the different legal systems have in common, and apply it as if it were invariable. Consideration perhaps more closely corresponds to the idea of "*cause autre que libérale*" (not gratuitous causa) than to the general idea of *cause*. It is thus more practical to use the notion "*cause autre que libérale*" or consideration without making distinctions within this category thereby neglecting any differences between the notions of *cause, Grund,* consideration, etc.

*Notice.* The goal of notice can be pursued in ways that are not the same everywhere: registers, records, etc. There is no way to keep in account these differences.

*Written Documents.* Private agreements have different characteristics in different countries (for example, in France the number of copies issued depends on the number of parties to the agreement). The same thing could be said for notarized agreements. We must speak of "private deeds" and "notarized agreements" without being too precise. The deed instrument employed in common law systems will be treated separately.

*Livraison, remise, traditio, Übergabe,* delivery, *peredača, consegna.* The transfer of possession holds a primordial position in the theory of the transfer of ownership. As the notion of possession is not conceived of in the same way everywhere (possession, *Besitz, possesso, vladenie, possession*), the transfer of that power can depend on the importance that the relevant legal system places on agreement between the parties, as well as on the extent to which physical delivery can be replaced by a symbolic delivery, by intent alone, etc. To make this observation does not prevent the emphasis, wherever necessary, on the opposition between actual delivery and presumed or symbolic delivery.

*Third party good faith transferee.* The definition of a good faith third party—a third party who in good faith claims ownership of the object or concludes the corresponding contract for dispossession—is subject to variation by virtue of where the line is drawn between negligence and bad faith, or by reason of linking bad faith to an understanding of the rights of one's counterpart or to the intent to harm or to defraud. We will ignore these differences.

*Moveable Property.* Transfer of ownership doctrine largely deals with the opposition between chattels (*choses mobilières; bewegliche Sachen*; etc.) and land (*choses immobilières; unbewegliche Sachen*; etc.). It is beyond the scope of this study to account for where the dividing line is drawn in the various legal systems.

# 2. The Fundamentals[1]

## *2.1. Major Historic Models*

In no legal system does a mere agreement between seller and buyer suffice (without *cause*, consideration, or some kind of further justifying element) for the effective transfer of ownership.[2] Here, we will survey different adaptations of this rule which have been adopted at one time or another throughout history. Historically, we find two primordial models, which multiplied into four in the age of codified law.

To begin with, the *ius commune* model, lasting until the Savigny era, founded the transfer of ownership upon two essential elements: the *titulus* and the *modus*. The *titulus*—for example, a sale contract—justified the transfer, but was not its direct cause. The *modus*—normally represented by the delivery of the item sold—was the direct act of transfer, but could not justify it. Initially, this was the model subscribed to by the writers of the ABGB (*Allgemeines Bürgerliches Gesetzbuch*, Austrian civil code). Then, an evolutionary process that began in Italy and ended in France resulted in its simplification: delivery was first replaced by a *constitut possessoire*; later the *constitut possessoire* came to be considered as an implied term of the sale; at last, the will of the law replaced the mutual will of the contracting parties. So the *titulus* became sufficient alone for the transfer of ownership. France's *Code Napoléon* accepted this conclusion.

Savigny proposed a third and conceptually inverted simplification. The *modus* would no longer need a *titulus* to justify it; it would carry its own autonomous justification. The BGB (*Bürgerliches Gesetzbuch*, German civil code) ultimately took on the Savigny conclusions as its own.

As for the spread of these three models to other legal systems, the French solution transplanted itself in Italy, Belgium,[3] and Romania, Poland, Bulgaria,

---

1. Our study does not address negotiable and quasi-negotiable instruments; nor does it deal with aircraft, boats, and automobiles.

2. Certain systems, such as the Swedish one, ignore the notion of *cause* and assume that the agreement is enough for the effective transfer of ownership. But in these systems we find that a donation produces the effect only if the will is accompanied by certain solemnities or by the delivery of the object. Form, delivery, and non-gratuitous title are the alternatively necessary elements for determining the transfer of ownership.

3. On the resistance to this principle in Italy see GAMBARO, *cit*. The principle was misinterpreted *de lege lata* (BORSARI), a return to the former system was hoped *de lege ferenda* (FADDA, BENSA, BETTI). On the reservations about this principle in Belgium, see DAVID-CONSTANT, *cit*.

and Louisiana without posing many problems. Swiss cantons and German states temporarily incorporated it until the adoption of their respective Swiss civil code and BGB. This solution was found in the *Svod Zakonov* (for personal property), in the Russian GK of 1922, and in the Czechoslovakian OZ of 1948. This solution also exerted influence on Spanish law. Certain Spanish-speaking American countries, ever faithful to the *droit commun*, have preserved the original Spanish solutions (as in Argentina for example[4]). Others have accepted the French model as having passed through the Spanish code (project) of 1851 (as in Mexico[5] for example). The Swedish system, quite foreign to the *ius commune* tradition, adopts a solution identical at its core to certain French rules: a contract for sale suffices for the transfer of ownership, or at least for certain prerogatives tied to ownership.

A solution offered by the Austrian model is found in Hungary and elsewhere. Austria is not the only country whose solution is rooted in the *ius commune* tradition. Despite the wording of the *Svod Zakonov*, the Russian scholars of the last century were very sensitive to the German models and added to the (legal) notion of the necessity of contract the necessity of delivery. In this way, they reintroduced the rule of the *ius commune*. In the era of the GK of 1922, the Russian doctrine again started to express its preference for this idea which prevailed in the *Osnovy* of 1961 and again in the Russian GK, I P., of 1995, Arts. 218 (necessity of the contract) and 223 (necessity of the transfer). Similarly, it took over in Czechoslovakia (OZ of 1964).

The rediffusion of the *ius commune* system is attributable to somewhat of a decline of the Savigny system. It appears that the drafters of the Swiss civil code were more in tune with German legal thought than with the drafters of the Austrian code. However, they did not settle the question of the need for a *titulus* in the transfer of property. In recent times, interpreters have opted for the idea of the *ius commune*,[6] and the Swiss interpretation prevails in Turkey.

The Savigny solution (with its autonomous *modus*) does not contemplate the control that public powers exert over the circulation of goods and wealth. Therefore, in the era of socialism the abstraction principle was considered to be incompatible with a socialist law and economy. The jurists of the D.D.R.

4. ALTERINI and COGHLAN, *cit.*

5. GARFLAS, *cit.*

6. The *Code civil* is not explicit; the *Code Fédéral des obligations* could suggest that the delivery suffices. See article 63 which denies a right to claim back the payment of an undue payment if performed without error. This position was shared by the Supreme Court when in 1929 it expressed a preference for causality over abstraction.

interpreted the BGB accordingly,[7] and in 1975, the ZGB (*Zivilgesetzbuch*) of the DDR formally arrived at a solution which served as both the *ius commune* and the Soviet solutions.

While the Savigny solution has retreated from central and eastern Europe, it is not only in Germany that the *titulus* retains its superfluous nature. If in principle the *ius commune* lies at the very core of Scottish law, however the *titulus* serves no purpose other than to prove that the parties did indeed want the transfer. Its invalidity does not undermine the effectiveness of the *traditio*.[8]

A fourth solution comes from outside of the *ius commune* systems: the English system and its common law progeny. A fundamental tenet of the common law—that a contract for sale transfers ownership of personal property[9]—is clearly enunciated in an English Statute of 1893 (The Sale of Goods Act) as well as in the American *Uniform Commercial Code* of 1952 which incorporated the rules of the *Uniform Sales Act* of 1906. A second tenet lies at the very foundation of the system: a delivery is sufficient when carried out with the intention of transferring ownership.[10] Thus, English law, as relates to the transfer of ownership of personal property, provides a choice between the Napoleon Code solution (centered on the contract) and the German one (centered on the delivery). The contract reminds us of the *titulus* of *ius commune*, while the delivery reminds us of the *modus*. We would describe the interaction between the English rules by saying that *titulus* and *modus* are alternatively necessary; that each suffices individually to transfer ownership. The independence of the delivery with respect to the contract, which seemed dangerous to European continental jurists, is considered normal in common law countries.[11]

---

7. KLEINE, in the collective work *Das Zivilrecht der DDR. Sachenrecht*, 1956, p. 102; KLINKERT, "Die Regelung des sozialistischen und des persönlichen Eigentumrechts im ZGB", *Neue Justiz*, 1975, p. 628.

8. The illegal character of the contract implies, however, the illegal character and consequential nullity of the *traditio* (SMITH, *cit.*): such was already the case in imperial Roman law.

9. The rule did not originate in the common law. It is of French origin. Not surprisingly, the French consensualist rule took root in Louisiana. J. P. Benjamin, a Louisiana-trained lawyer who later became a law professor in England, taught this rule (CHIANALE, *Obbligazione di dare e dissociazione della proprietà*, 1990, pp. 369 ff.).

10. Stock v. Wilson, 1913, 2 K.B. 235, 246 and CHESHIRE a. FIFOOT, *Cases in the Law of Contract*, 1977; the possessor had delivered the object in performance of a contract that was null.

11. We see here an abstraction of the *modus* with respect to the *titulus*. But the notion of abstraction does not exist for practitioners of the common law. Only in the area of real property do we find within the common law a "doctrine of merger of the contract in the

As a final note, in Scottish law the same *Sale of Goods Act* applies as in English law.

In conclusion, legal transfers of ownership are rooted in a *titulus* and/or a *modus*. In certain countries the two elements are both required. Elsewhere the *titulus* is both necessary and sufficient (as in the French legal system); elsewhere it is the *modus* that is sufficient and necessary (the German system); still elsewhere the subjects can choose one or the other (the English system). One should not consider the four solutions (*titulus*, *modus*, *titulus* + *modus*, *titulus* or *modus*) as having equal weight. The solutions "*titulus*", "*modus*" and "*titulus* plus *modus*" directly correspond to ideas and scholarly expressions which prevail, respectively, in France, Germany, and Austria (and elsewhere). By contrast, the "*titulus* or *modus*" solution does not correspond to any expression used by the English; it is entirely my creation which I use to classify a legal system foreign to my own. In spite of this, I will rely on these four expressions for the purposes of juxtaposition and comparison.

## 2.2. Difficulties in Defining the Elements That Transfer Ownership in Different Legal Systems

The competing French and the German systems offer an empirical starting point for our comparison. In France, the *contrat* (the sale, the exchange, and the gift) produces the transfer of ownership. In Germany the *Vertrag* of sale (of exchange or of gift) does not produce an obligation to deliver; a second act is necessary to transfer ownership. This opposition is not as simple to describe as it seems at a first look. Because the process that in Germany transfers ownership includes the *Vertrag*,[12] one cannot simply state, "In France ownership is transferred by the *contrat*; in Germany it is not transferred by the *Vertrag*." Ignoring the detailed preconditions for the obligation and more simply referring to "the act which normally suffices to create an obligation," we could pose the following question: "would the same act also suffice to transfer ownership, where the parties have a common intent?" But to approach the

deed" which is comparable to the doctrine of abstraction (MERRYMAN, note 78 to the *cit.*).

12. Legal scholars prefer to attribute a contractual nature to the physical act which executes the contract in Germany, Switzerland, etc. (SCHLECHTRIEM, POSCH, *cit.*). The notion seems better established for certain forms of the executing act where the importance of consent is paramount (*traditio brevi manu*). The contractual theory is probably stronger where it underscores the "voluntary" nature of the transfer: the English emphasize the existence of an agreement in a simple delivery where the delivery was not preceded by a contract (LAWTON, *op. cit.*).

problem this way presupposes the presence of conditions that may not always exist. For example, according to the text of Article 894 of the *Code Napoléon* a mutual agreement based on the solemn form is enough to transfer ownership by free title but would not suffice to create the obligation to transfer the ownership by free title.

So, it is helpful to introduce a distinction between the notion of "contract based on a nongratuitous intention" and the more general notion of "a contract creating an obligation". This distinction allows us to coherently explain the rules bearing on the transfer of ownership as a matter of comparative law. Since the expression "mutual contract based on nongratuitous intention for the purpose of transfer of ownership" is quite verbose, it is more convenient to replace the general category with an example, and to speak concisely of a sale (*vente*; *Kauf*; *prodaža*). The factors that are pertinent to the sale must be equally pertinent (except in Scottish law) to the exchange (for specifics, cf. *infra*, n. 3.4). In this manner of speaking, we can temporarily say that the transfer of ownership can be the effect of any of the following elements: the sale (*Code Napoléon*), the delivery (Germany), the sale followed by delivery (*ius commune*), and the sale or the delivery (England).

## 3. Intent (to Transfer) and Delivery

### *3.1. Agreement: An Ambiguous Concept*

Given the focus of our research on the voluntary transfer of ownership, it is no surprise to learn that virtually all legal systems place some value on the meeting of the minds, or at least on the will of the seller. It is not so easy to state what constitutes this agreement. Everything would be much simpler if the immediate object of the agreement was always the transfer of ownership. But it is not always and necessarily so.

We have already seen that the technique adopted for assessing intent relies largely on presumption if not fiction. The German jurist tells us that when a seller hands over the object sold to the buyer, at that moment the seller intends to transmit ownership and possession. Jurists in a country where the handing over is less conclusive will say that at the very moment of sale the seller intended to transfer, and that this intent suffices to produce (at the moment of delivery) the intended effect.[13] The legal importance of this question

13. For Hungary, CSANÁDI, *cit.*, p. 5. The Swiss jurist is also familiar with this concept.

is obvious whenever the intent to transfer is vitiated at the moment of delivery. However, it cannot be taken for granted that the psychological fact (intent to alienate) which is assumed in the different theories is the same in Germany and elsewhere.

It is without a doubt the French who place the most emphasis on the voluntary nature of property alienation. In French law, ownership is transferred at the moment of sale because the individual intent is the sole condition, both necessary and sufficient, of the transmission.[14] But the law as written does not at all encourage this reduction of French law to schemas of natural law. The letter of the Napoleon Code refers to a seller who wishes to oblige himself to transfer; it recognizes his right to bind himself and to exercise the authority that the obligation gives him as creditor-owner of the object.[15] In principle, the intent to self-oblige suffices for the transfer of ownership; the consequences owing thereto being mere legal details. The solution is inverted when it comes to donations where the intent to bind oneself, if it excludes the intent to transfer, vitiates the act.[16]

Academics have replaced the rule of the Napoleon Code with its opposite, that is, with the principle of intent. We are thus able to distinguish the sale from the promise to sell. But we still do not require the buyer asserting ownership to prove that the intent of the parties encompassed not only the obligation but also the subsequent transfer of ownership.[17] The specificity of the French system becomes more evident if we consider Article 2, Part 4, Section 2.401 of the American Uniform Commercial Code, in addition to the Napoleon Code, where rights over the merchandise pass from seller to buyer "in any manner and under any conditions explicitly agreed on by the parties".

What we find is that there are some systems in which the agreement to transfer must clearly derive from the circumstances, other systems where the right and intent to bind oneself is practically inherent, and still others where

14. Cf. TERRÉ, SIMLER and LEQUETTE, *Droit civil, Les obligations*, 6th ed., 1996, p. 820, m. 2014: "*L'effet translatif de la propriété résulte en principe ( ... ) du seul échange des consentements: solo consensu*".

15. *Code Napoléon*, article 1138: "*L'obligation de livrer la chose est parfaite par le seul consentement des parties contractantes. Elle rend le créancier propriétaire et met la chose à ses risques dès l'instant où elle a dû être livrée, encore que la tradition n'en ait point été faite*".

16. *Code Napoléon*, article 894.

17. History explains the formula adopted by the French legislature. The sale became sufficient for the transfer of ownership as soon as the law assumed that the contracting parties add a *constitut possessoire* to their contract: the transfer of ownership thus became the legal consequence of a contract that creates an obligation.

it is the delivery that indicates this presumption.[18] Only where the act is subject to formal requirements do we require the parties to formally declare their intentions to transfer property. In all other cases, the intent to transfer hinges on some other element that explains and executes it.[19] More clearly stated, intent is not necessary if that other element exists, and where there is no proof of contrary intent to undermine the other element.

### *3.2. The Obligation to Transfer versus the Transfer of Ownership (An Uncertain Symmetry)*

Legislators and scholars articulate rules intended to emphasize a symmetry between the act which obliges and the very act of alienation. For example, "the obligation to give transfers ownership" and "the creation of an obligation and the transfer of ownership require nothing more than the agreement of the parties." Yet, this symmetry deserves an analysis that has never been done.

"*L'accord des parties*" is necessary to give rise to an obligation and is defined quite pertinently by the Napoleon Code as "*le consentement de la partie qui s'oblige*"(the consent of the party who binds himself) (Art. 1108). Interpreters of the Napoleon Code view as sacrilegious any departure from the construction of contract as the product of a bilateral agreement. But the courts continue to profess a certain reverence for such formulas while evading them through legal fiction and practically gravitating back to the code.[20]

In other countries, the code even more fervently affirm that the consent of the self-obliging party suffices to give rise to an obligation (so long as the as-

---

18. When it comes to making presumptions, the English have a real talent. If a husband transfers an object to his wife, it is thought to have done so out of an obligation to support her. If the wife does the same, she is presumed to have intended to create a trust.

19. Naturally, the existence of an element (E) which presumes the will to alienate (V) could lie at the very core of apparent conflicts between different legal systems. Jurists of different systems may state a rule subordinating the transfer to the presence of V (the will to alienate) or alternatively to the presence of E+V. They could also anchor the transfer on the presence of E alone. The Scottish system, in which it is the *iusta causa traditionis* that recognizes the existence of the will, leaves this ambivalence clearly intact.

20. Req. March 29, 1938, *Dalloz*, 1939, I, p.5 (including the VOIRIN note); Civ. December 1, 1969, *Dalloz* 1970, 422, obs. PUECH; *JCP* 1970, II, 6445, obs. AUBERT, *Rev. trim. dr. priv.* 1971, 164, obs. DURRY; Soc. December 15, 1970, *Bull. Civ.* V, n.722, 590. We have applied a more in depth analysis of the problem: "Définitions savants et droit appliqué dans les systèmes romanistes", *Rev. intern. de droit comparé*, 1965, p. 827.

signee of the offer raises no objections); and the interpreters have gradually ceased looking to natural law and have accepted the will of the legislature.[21]

The existence of such unilateral contractual declarations can be problematic.[22] Can these contracts transfer ownership? The legal obligation to transfer would center primarily on the presumption that the parties desired a *constitut possessoire*. Ironically, the *constitut possessoire* is technically the product of a mutual agreement such that it would be counterintuitive to consider it a mere accessory to a unilateral declaration. In countries that do not require the consent of the third party (and where the contract is all that is needed for the transfer of ownership) we encounter the same problem in the case of contractual stipulations benefiting third parties. An examination of the case law of those countries reveals consistency only as far as land easements and mortgaged properties are concerned, where acquisition of the land is conditioned upon the consent of the third party.

### *3.3. The Role of Contract (and the Too General Nature of the Notion of Contract)*

Thus far we have spoken of contracts, or of contracts with a *cause* (causa), or of contracts for value. Such contracts are vital to the transfer of ownership in legal systems modeled after the French and English systems, and to the obligation justifying delivery in the Austrian and German model. We now add that the notion of a contract—even the contract for value—is too general a notion when it comes to the transfer of goods.

In England, the parity of the sale contract with respect to other kinds of contracts is not above debate. In Scotland, the application of the statute that governs sales draws a fundamental distinction between the effects of a sale and those of other kinds of contracts. (We frequently find that where a distinction is maintained between the *titulus* and the *modus*, the voluntary circulation between co-owners of the object's different components takes place without de-

---

21. Art. 1333 of the *Codice civile, "Contratto con obbligazioni del solo proponente":* "La proposta diretta a concludere un contratto da cui derivino obbligazioni solo per il propenente è irrevocabile ( … ). Il destinatario può rifiutare la proposta ( … ). In mancanza di tale rifiuto il contratto è concluso". On this article, SACCO (et DE NOVA), *Il contratto*, 3rd ed., Turin, 2004, I, p. 243 ff.

22. I write to a friend promising to give him my copy of the *Lois* of Domat if he does a certain favor for me. The friend does not respond to me but goes ahead and performs the favor. Does ownership automatically transfer? In England this problem arises in the context of offers calling for an act, but since the execution of the favor in this scenario is considered an acceptance of the offer, the desire to acquire can justifiably be presumed.

livery.[23] So, those contracts are subject to special legal rules.) The French were able to codify the obligation to make the transfer of ownership independently sufficient. Historically, this rule was only supported in the case of a sale; certain legal systems owing to the *Code Napoléon* have adopted a less consent-based solution for contracts other than sale contracts. This is often true in three scenarios:

1. with the supply and construction contract in which the transfer of ownership can take place at the moment of the delivery, at the acceptance, or at the receipt of the object;
2. with the partnership agreement in which the contribution of ownership in a good is distinct from the partnership agreement itself;
3. with the agency contract without power of attorney in which the agent may find himself the owner of the goods acquired and is obliged to relinquish them to his principal.[24]

Elsewhere, distinctions could be necessary within the contract of sale. From the perspective that the elements necessary for an obligation to hand over an object are also sufficient for the transferal of that object, it follows that the sale of future items vests the buyer with ownership in them as soon as they come into existence (at least insofar as the purchased objects are readily identifiable). But this logic is not always upheld. A different view is that the transfer of future goods—of fruits—is the normal consequence of the rental contract. Surely, the rental contract represents the *titulus* justifying the lessee's ownership of the fruits. But legal systems that require both the *titulus* and the *modus* can find the *modus* in the delivery of the fruit-bearing good to the lessee, in the lessee's taking of the fruits, or could possibly make an exception so as to consider the *titulus* sufficient for all purposes.

In short, in order to pinpoint the contract's role in the transfer of ownership we must first isolate the role of each contractual norm in the transfer of ownership, and then conduct some sort of comparison across legal systems.

## *3.4. The Ambiguous Notion of Delivery*

When we say that certain legal systems require delivery we are saying nothing precise. We must further explain whether we are using this word in reference to the delivery of the object into the physical possession of the acquirer,

---

23. For Germany, Schlechtriem, *cit.*, p. 58.

24. In Italy, articles 1705 ff. of the *Codice civile* regulate on this basis the standing of an agent who has acquired real estate property without power of attorney.

or whether we are speaking of delivery in a more general and liberal sense. For example, it is possible virtually everywhere to replace physical delivery with the handing over of that which is necessary and sufficient to exert control over the object (e.g. the keys of a building).

Furthermore, the descendants of the Roman legal system have inherited the assimilation to the delivery with the *constitutum possessorium*, the *traditio brevi manu*, and the surrendering of any right of reversion in the object[25] (except for certain limits that are tied to the legal devices adopted for the transfer of ownership). Indeed, where the transfer of ownership is generally subordinate to the delivery, the latter can be replaced by a *constitutum possessorium*, a *traditio brevi manu*, and a surrendering of any right of reversion of the object. This is the case with Austria, Hungary, Germany, Switzerland, Turkey, and Argentina (and also for Poland with regard to fungible goods). Similarly, Louisiana law hinges the effects of transfer with respect to third parties upon delivery, and has merged effective and constructive delivery.

The assimilation does not come into play where the delivery that transfers of ownership serves to remedy the absence of valuable consideration (*don manuel* in France and in Louisiana),[26] or in the case where the transferor is not the owner (Germany). In Sweden, where the delivery is only imposed in the event of an *a non domino* acquisition or an alienation (in exchange for nothing), the *constitut possessoire* does not exist. Similarly, the *constitute possessoire* is unknown in English law where the delivery is sufficient but not necessary for the transfer of ownership.

The rule conditioning the legal transfer of ownership upon delivery is thus a rule of indulgence. If the formation of a pledge is subordinate to the handing over of the object in countries where the sale produces the transfer, then the rights anchored in the delivery (or some equivalent thereto) suggest that the *constitut possessoire* can suffice for the formation of a pledge or of fiduciary ownership. The jurists must be fully conscious of the fact that the legal relationship created thereby corresponds to a pledge without dispossession.[27] Thus, the *constitut possessoire* is no longer seen as a special form of delivery,

25. This assimilation is unknown in Swedish law. It is also unknown in English law where the intent to alienate and simultaneously conserve possession in the interest of the acquirer would give rise to a trust. In Scotland, it is accepted much more cautiously than on the continent.

26. Other systems bring into play here the assimilation. For example, Germany, cf. ENNECCERUS and LEHMANN, *Recht der Schuldverhältnisse*, 15th ed., 1958 (in ENNECCERUS, KIPP and M. WOLFF, *Lehrbuch des Bürg Rechts*), § 120, III.

27. For Germany, SCHLECHTRIEM, *cit*, p. 51.

but as an alternative to it.[28] The alternative nature of the *constitut possessoire* has perhaps influenced the auxiliary nature of certain rules that impose delivery "where the parties do not stipulate otherwise".[29]

# 4. Abstraction and Causality (A Fundamental Rivalry)

## *4.1. The Problem*

The BGB, in anchoring the transfer of ownership to the delivery, has chosen the abstraction principle according to which the transfer does not depend on the more fundamental act that caused the obligation. The common law system has adopted the same principle without giving it a name or definition. Other systems seem to refuse this abstraction, their jurists critiquing it harshly. The problem is figuring out what truly defines the opposition between abstraction and causality. To that end, let us examine the systems of Austria, France, Italy, and Germany.

## *4.2. The Austrian System*[30]

The writers of the Austrian code conceived of transfer that presupposes the *titulus* as well as the *modus*, and cites the *titulus* among the necessary elements to create an obligation to hand over. Taken to its logical ends, this means that the absence of legal title allows the one who delivered the object (if he was the owner before the delivery) to reclaim ownership and recover the thing. Yet § 1432 ABGB disallows a cause of action for reclaiming what was not owed where one has executed a prescribed obligation, a null obligation due to lack of form, or an obligation with no corresponding cause of action. Relief is also denied to one who has made payment knowing that he was not debtor.

---

28. This alternative character is what allowed KRUSE to conclude that virtually every sale transfers ownership between parties (*op. cit.*, p. 500 ff.).

29. KNAPP, *cit.*

30. The operational rules of the ABGB gave rise to various doctrinal systematizations, the first of which (loyal to the ideas of the original writers) was anchored in the necessity of the both *titulus* and the *modus*; the second of which, open to the ideas of Savigny, reduced the importance of the *titulus* and considered the delivery to be a veritable contract founded upon a subjective consideration; the third of which reestablished the importance of the *titulus* as an objective consideration for the delivery.

Scholars interpret the intent of this provision as a removal of not only the action for unjustified enrichment, but also of the claim to repossess the object.[31] It originates from the idea that a handing over performed without error and without prior obligation is a donation, as stated by the ABGB and the first interpreters of the code.[32] More recently, the equation of a donation to an unowed payment (made consciously) ceased to be upheld, and the will of the transfer who waived his legal protection is considered sufficient to explain the effects of the handing over.[33]

As for a handing over done in honor of a natural obligation, it is that natural obligation that the Austrian system considers to be the *titulus.*[34] The delivery that follows an otherwise null contract is presented as a confirmation of the contract.[35] This means that the *titulus* that justifies the handing over is the necessary and sufficient element to create an obligation (since a null contract does not create any obligation). More importantly, it means that the delivery needs no other justification than the unerring will of the transferor. If we define a normal delivery as one that is not the result of an error, then we find that in Austria the delivery independently produces the transfer of ownership.

We find an analogous situation in Switzerland, where the reclaiming of what was not owed (and any associated recovery) is prohibited if the delivery was not the result of error. (Art. 63 *code féd. obl.*)[36] The scholars accept this autonomy of payment with respect to its purpose; they find the cause of payment in the will of him who is paying, in a donation, in the settling of a debt, in the purpose of avoiding litigation, or in the absence of interest to reclaim the thing.[37] In other words, the purposeful handing over, performed without error and with the intent of transferring ownership, is itself sufficient to that end.

---

31. WILBURG, *Die Lehre von der ungerechtfertigten Bereicherung nach österreichischem und deutschem Recht*, 1934, p. 11; Id., in KLANG, cur., *Kommentar zum ABGB*, VI Bd., 2nd edition, 952 pp. 458–489.

32. §59 of the *Codex theresianus*, chap. XIX; §404 of the *Galician Code;* §1411 of the revised project. Cf. D. 50, 17, 53.

33. PFERSCHE, *Die Irrtumslehre des öst. Privatrechts*, 1891, p. 307 f.; SWOBODA, in KLANG, cur., *Kommentar zum ABGB*, VI Bd., 1935 p. 474 ff. (the alienator could not invoke the revocation allowed for donations).

34. WILBURG, in KLANG (cur.), *Kommentar*, cit., VI Bd., 2nd ed., 1951, p. 460.

35. STANZL, in KLANG (cur.), *Kommentar*, cit., VI Bd., 2nd ed., 1968.

36. CARRY, *Les conditions générales de l'action en enrichissement*, 1927, pp. 168–169; OSER-SCHOENENBERGER, *Obligationenrecht, Kommentar ad art. 63 OR.*, n.11.

37. CARRY, *loc. cit.*: GUHL, *Das Schweizerische Obligationenrecht*, 4th ed., 1948, p. 153; THUR, *Schw. Obligationenrecht, Allgemeiner Teil*, I, 2nd ed., 1964, p. 409; VON BÜREN, *SCHWEIZ, Obligationenrecht, Allgemeiner Teil*, 1964, pp. 298–299.

The situation appears the same in Poland. Polish law requires a cause to justify acts of transfer. It is perhaps the only system that emphasizes that the validity of the contractual transfer performed *solvendi causa* depends on the existence of this obligation (Art. 156 *kod. cyw.*).[38] But an enrichment resulting from an undue payment or service does not give rise to a right of restitution "when he who effectuated the payment or services knew that he would not be protected" (Art. 411, no.1). Here again, a handing over performed with the intent (to pay, which is to say) to transfer produces its effect independently of *causa*.

## *4.3. The French and Belgian Systems*

The French solution, resulting from both a small number of exceptional legal rules and a large number of praetorian rules, has systematically reversed the Napoleonic legal model to arrive at a position half way between abstraction and causality. It places the delivery on par with the contract for value as an alternative procedure for transferring the ownership of movable property.[39] What then are the operational rules practiced in France and Belgium allowing us to arrive at this conclusion, which does not correspond to the definitions we find in French and Belgian scholarly works? We have three rules in mind:

1. the *don manuel* rule;
2. the rule of natural obligation;
3. the rule of restitution for undue payment.

A donation, as established by the *Code Napoléon*, usually refers to the conventional donation concluded by a notarized deed. However, in the case of moveable property, the practice of French law let survive the old practice of handing over things with a donative intent. The *Code Napoléon* denies the right to reclaim what was not owed where one has voluntarily fulfilled a natural obligation (art. 1235, 2° al.). It remains to be clarified who is the owner of moveable objects delivered pursuant to the natural obligation. Did the legislator intend to prohibit a right to reclaim, or did they intend to make the

38. CZACHÓRSKI, *cit.*, p.65.

39. WINDSCHEID deemed that delivery was removed by the *Code Napoléon* as a mean of transfer: *Zur Lehre des Code Napoléon von der Ungültigkeit der Rechtsgeschäfte*, 1847.

On this problem, SACCO, *Un cryptotype en droit français: la remise abstraite, dans Études pour Rodière*, 1981, 273.

payment irreversible by ruling out not only any personal right of action but also any recovery of the object? There are multiple indications in French law to suggest that the performance of a natural obligation effectuates the transfer of ownership (at least where moveable property is concerned).

The French jurist imposes a natural obligation not only where there exists a rule broadly accepted and enforced by the social morals, but also where the subject is stimulated by his own subjective conscience.[40] In France, each time that an individual delivers the object to enrich his counterpart or to satisfy his own conscience, ownership is transmitted. If a nonlegal duty to one's conscience is enough to justify the delivery, then this suggests that delivery continues to play a role in the transfer of ownership in France and Belgium even outside of the context of a donation, and that the delivery is not itself justified by some preexisting obligation. However, one must not overvalue the systematic importance of article 1235, 2° al. French and Belgian interpreters consider the promise to fulfill a natural obligation as giving rise to a civil obligation. Under these conditions it is normal for a natural obligation—the admitted cause for a civil obligation—to cause the transfer of ownership. The symmetry between the elements forming an obligation and those necessary for the transfer of ownership is therefore partially reestablished.[41]

Outside of gifts and civil or moral obligations, every delivery intended to fulfill a nonexistent obligation gives rise to a right of restitution. "*Tout payement suppose une dette. Ce qui a été payé sans être du, est sujet à répétition*" (any payment supposes a debt. What has been payed without being owed is subject to restitution), according to Article 1235. The French practice has long reduced the breadth of Article 1235, and has subordinated such an action to the error of the paying party. The solution, as difficult as it was to reconcile with the black-letter code,[42] falls much more comfortably in line with the rules of *don manuel* and natural obligation. Only cases of error, violence, or insanity can explain the *animo solvendi* delivery of an object in the absence of any moral

40. For all, MARTY and RAYNAUD, *Droit civil*, 1961, I, 272, 2.

41. Why "partially"? This is because we still view a natural obligation as sufficient consideration for a promise; we do not yet view a natural obligation as justifying a consensual transfer of ownership (independent of any handing over of the object). We cannot say whether this nuance was intended.

42. The interpreters superimpose upon article 1235 the rules regarding the payment of another's debt. Belgian interpreters looked less kindly upon such superimposition than the French. De PAGE (*Traité élément de droit civ. belge*, 3a ed., III, 18, n.13) clearly states that error is not a prerequisite for the claiming back of what was not owed, except in cases regulated by article 1377.

duty or intent to enrich one's counterpart. At present, the enounced rule in France is different and proof of error is no longer necessary for the recovery. It remains to be seen if he who makes a full payment, while conscious that there is no debt, will be allowed by the French courts to exert a right of restitution.

We also note that French law indirectly separates the cause of action for recovery of unjust enrichment from that brought by one who performed a defective contract: it conditions the latter on an action for invalidity, thereby relieving it of the more rigorous elements required for claims under Article 1235.[43]

To conclude, in France and Belgium, the handing over of an object with the intent to transmit ownership, performed freely and without error by one who is mentally competent, transfers ownership in the majority of cases involving moveable property even where the handing over does not follow a prior obligation. The Austrian and Swiss systems on the one hand, and the French and Belgian systems on the other (in practice, as markedly opposed to in theory), largely accept the delivery as an autonomous mode of ownership transfer;[44] however, that autonomy never fully equates to the complete abstraction characteristic of the English and German systems, where an error in the reason for payment does not hinder the transfer of ownership.

## *4.4. Remarks on the Italian, Turkish and Hungarian Systems*

Though the conclusion above may come as a surprise to French, Belgian, Austrian, or Swiss, it is supported by comparison. Italian law as applied has elaborated a *cause* based solution on legal bases borrowed from France. In

43. This has to do with one of the most obscure provisions in French law. AUBRY and RAU introduced a distinction between the claiming back of what was unduly paid (article 1235) and *condictio sine causa* (§§442, 442 bis). The presence of two distinct recourses, as well as the difference between payment of what was not owed and payment without *causa* are neither mentioned nor rejected by more recent jurists. Yet, they seem to fall among the ideas underlying the French solutions. And the recovery of payment made without cause seems to have been absorbed into the nullity action.

44. Is it possible that no French jurist has ever pointed out this circumstance? We think not. In fact, we find that in composing the list of ways to acquire property DEMOLOMBE adds "*Il en est de même de la tradition, qui, bien que n'étant pas mentionnée non plus dans l'énumeration faite par le code, n'est pas moins aussi, dans beaucoup de cas encore, une manière d'acquérir la propriété. C'est ainsi ( ... ) dans les obligations de genre ( ... ), dans ( ... ) la tradition d'un objet mobilier corporel ( ... ) reçu* a non domino. *On peut remarquer aussi que la transmission de propriété des meubles, dans le don manuel, admise sans contestation par la doctrine, ne peut également s'expliquer que par l'effet translatif de propriété résultant de la tradition, lorsqu'elle a eu lieu, en effet,* animo trasferendi domini."

Italy, the *don manuel* is only permitted for objects of little value. The natural obligation only covers limited circumstances, and the strictly objective concept of recovery of unowed payment is divorced from the condition of error on the part of the paying party. Thus, the transfer of ownership by method of handing over—possible in certain cases in Italy—is exceptional in nature. The solution adopted by the French code, which in France has never succeeded at uprooting the Roman system, is thus found in force in Italy.

The Turks reject the liberal ideas adopted by the Swiss on the basis of Article 63 CO. The Turks interpret Article 63 CO—denying restitution for unjust enrichment where one has paid without error—to come into play where a valuable transfer of property has occurred and where such a transfer presumes the presence of consideration.[45] The Hungarians, insofar as their system grew out of the Austrian system, grant a claim to one who has delivered without cause and draw no distinction between intent and error.[46]

## *4.5. The German System*

German law considers that a transfer of ownership is abstract and independent of the fundamental relationship between the parties. Whereas the law expressly prohibits subjugating the alienation of (immoveable) property to any condition (§925, al. 2) BGB), its silence on the transfer of moveable property makes clear that such transactions can be conditioned. So, there is nothing to prevent the transferor and the transferee from conditioning the legal effect of their delivery upon the validity of the underlying *fundamental* contract, which is to say upon the existence of a *causa solvendi*. Further, nothing prevents such a condition from being tacitly incorporated in a contract.[47] Perhaps there is nothing at all to stop the parties from reducing the fundamental contract and the delivery to a single complex act.[48] Naturally, the subjugation of the act of transfer to such a condition practiçally negates the difference between the system of abstraction and that anchored in the *titulus + modus* combination. In those systems that link the transfer of ownership to the handing over, he who has received the object is its rightful owner, with the caveat of a right of restitution reserved to him who delivered the object through an action *in personam*.

---

45. OGUSMAN, *cit.*

46. CSANÁDI, *cit.*, p. 120.

47. Which normally happens if the tradition and the sale happen simultaneously: cf. STAUDINGER, *Kommentar zum BGB*, III, 1935, ad §929, Anm. IV, 3, b (by ROBER).

48. BAUR, *Sachenrecht*, 9te Aufl., 1977, §5, IV, 3 c., p. 43; WESTERMANN, *Sachenrecht*, 5te Aufl., 1966, 74, IV; SCHLECHTRIEM, *cit.*, p. 61.

In German law we find unexpected data. He who has delivered the object may only pursue a personal action on grounds of unjust enrichment. However, if he who received the object has handed it over to a third party free of compensation, then that third party is in turn considered to have been unjustly enriched and may be subject to a claim of restitution by the damaged party. If the transferor gives the object to a third party in bad faith, then the third party will be required, based on his extra-contractual obligations, to return the object to the victim. As a result, in Germany, only the third party acting in good faith and armed with valuable consideration is sheltered from action initiated by him who carried out the delivery without consideration.

## 5. Comparative Remarks

### *5.1. A Graphical Illustration of the Data*

The rule of abstract delivery[49] is opposed to the rule of consent with cause. The cumulative rule requiring both the contract and the delivery is opposed to the alternative rule, which provides a choice between the contract and the delivery. The rule of abstract delivery has at least in common with the alternative rule a point—both recognize the delivery as sufficient; and it has a point in common with the cumulative rule—both necessitate the delivery. The rule of consent plus cause has a point in common with the alternative rule—both consider as sufficient the sole contract (with cause)—and a point in common with the cumulative rule—both necessitate the consent plus cause.

It is possible to graphically illustrate the relationship between these rules—each solution is represented by a letter and located next to the other solutions with which it has something in common. If we call M(odus) the rule of delivery in itself sufficient, T(itulus) the rule of consent with consideration, the other two rules A(lternative) and C(umulative), and if we place the letters A and C in the east and west positions, then we can place M and T respectively

49. This is of the utmost importance—that the *modus*, the exterior act, is the delivery everywhere and always. The study of the transfer of ownership of real estate helps us to appreciate the simplicity of the rules regarding moveable property.

in the north and south positions. We then have a circle where the four equidistant letters are positioned as such:

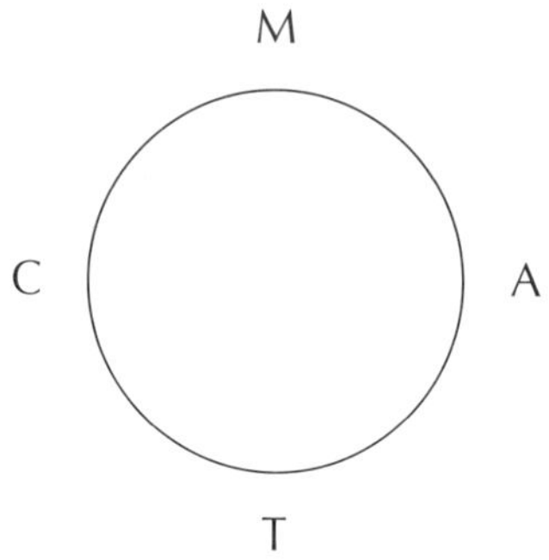


We can now fill in the rules that occupy intermediate positions between the letters already depicted. The semi-abstract handing over characteristic of the French and Austrian systems produces rules which occupy intermediate positions in our figure. Austrian law is found halfway between points M and the C, and we represent this with a new letter: E. French law (as distinguished from Italian law) is found halfway between points T and A, so we place there the new letter I. To be clear, the arcs that join the four cardinal points are not unoccupied. In fact in those positions we may place many systems, intermediary or pluralist (which we will deal with more directly in the next chapter).

Is there some solution equidistant from all the solutions represented thus far? If it exists, it will be positioned at the center of the circle. It exists in the consciences of jurists who use it to better orient themselves, and who sometimes inappropriately conceptualize it as superimposed upon solution T. It consists of considering the pure will of the parties to be sufficient for the transfer of ownership. Every legal system dreads this solution. If every legal system does its best to establish that this element (which we will call V) is necessary for the transfer, then every system supports the conclusion that V must be accompanied either by an exterior element (M), by a cause, (T), by them both, or by either one (A).

German law, which allows for replacing the delivery with the *constitut*, has started down a path that will ultimately lead it to position V. But we know that another movement is taking place in Germany that will restore the *causa*. The German system today occupies the space between M and V (which we coin as F), or better yet, the intermediate position between F and A.

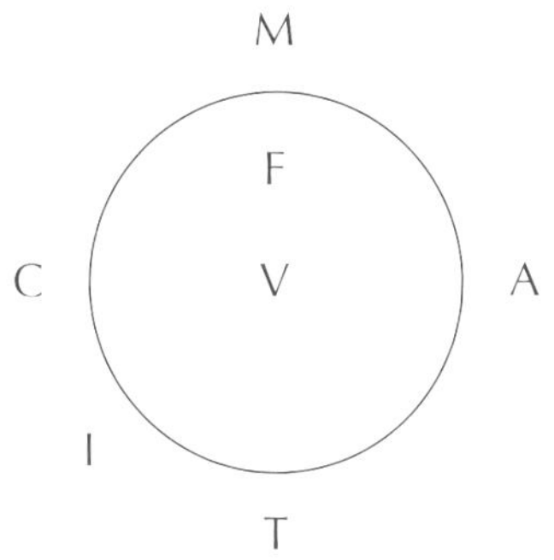


The transformation of legal systems normally occurs with respect to the figure that we have provided: in a clockwise motion (from the *ius commune* to the *Code Napoléon*) and sometimes in a counter clockwise motion (from the *ius commune* to the BGB).

## *5.2. Dislocations in the Law*

History would prefer to replace one legal system with the next without interruption. The *ius commune* solution succeeded at spawning several variations, the traces of which can be found today in the Scottish and Austrian systems, among others. However, the present study only addresses modern history. Thus, the dislocations that come within our scope are those that exist synchronically within a given legal system and are due to the plurality of its constituent elements: dislocations between written and applied law for example, or between an operational rule of a given country and how that country's jurists conceptualize it.

The ambition of the comparativist is to determine whether such dislocations are predictable and rationally explicable. The three oppositions which we find most interesting are {written law vs. applied law}, {written law vs. the law as understood} and {what the law considers to be normal vs. what is sociologically normal}. These three oppositions give rise to dislocations in France, Germany, Switzerland, and Hungary.

In France, the purely legal system is linked to a variation of system T in that it anchors the transfer in the will *to oblige oneself* (the only exception being in the context of donations). By contrast, legal scholars view the system as though it were inspired by a perfect symmetry between the contractual will and its effects; it views the will to transfer and to acquire as if it were the unique element of the transferal contract. The law in action juxtaposes the semi-abstract handing over to the contract, the latter being sufficient for the transfer of ownership. So, the dislocations happen in two directions: from written to practical law the displacement is from T → I; and from written (and applied) law to the concepts of the French jurist the displacement is from I → T and from T → V. Since French law (both as written and applied) makes modest concession to the C systems (see n° 18 ff.), the French jurist is fully aware of the presence of model C (as the minority model) in his system.

History provides us with situations where the instability of the contractual model (T) is due to dislocations favoring the cumulative system (C). In the era of Italy's *codice civile* of 1865 interpreters exhibited two tendencies: 1) to follow the French in their march toward the alternative regime, and 2) to return to the former regime of withholding legal transfer of ownership until the moment of delivery (the cumulative regime). In the old Russia of the *Svod Zakonov*, the French inspired law which was attached to model T was displaced by interpreters in the direction of regime C. The GK RSFSR of 1922, closely tied to model T, was followed by the *Osnovy* of 1961 which, under the pressure of interpreters, returned definitively back to the cumulative model.

Austrian law, a legal system positioned half between the cumulative and abstract regimes (and therefore positioned at point E in the illustration), managed to give way to doctrinal formulations anchored in regime models C or M. As is to be expected, here too the (scholarly) formulations progress toward less nuanced solutions. Germany remains faithful to the abstract delivery. However, two tendencies appear to juxtapose to legal texts certain practices which the code has perhaps made possible but certainly did not foresee: the practice that embeds *cause* in the delivery thereby subjecting the effects thereof to the validity of the obligatory contract (M → C); and the practice that nullifies the delivery when replacing it with a possessory *constitut* which can be reduced to the agreement for the change of ownership (M → V).

## *5.3. Doctrinal Qualifications*

In the legal systems that require both the *titulus* and the *modus* for a transfer of ownership, the relationship between these two elements is the subject of variable definitions. Whereas Austrians formerly held that the transfer of ownership was determined by the binding contract in conjunction with the delivery, they prefer today that the transfer of ownership be determined by the physical contract (that is by the agreement between the transferor and transferee concluded at the moment of delivery), and that the contract forming the obligation itself be the cause for the physical contract. The Swiss prefer to bring the transfer of ownership back to the agreement that the parties concluded at the moment of the binding contract. Thus, the delivery is not in and of itself a contract but merely a material act. It is not easy to say whether these conceptual differences correspond to specific variations in positive law, or if they simply reflect systematizations preferred by theoreticians of different countries, the latter tending to correspond to an unnecessary multiplicity of qualifications. If a handing over without a preexisting obligation effectively transfers ownership, then that rule does not appear to be an explanation as far as theoreticians are concerned, but rather an empirical observation which must be reconciled with principles of the law through appropriate qualifications.

The search for the appropriate way to qualify such principles of law could lead to multiple results. In certain instances, the idea of abstraction resolves the qualification problem: the handing over is a sufficient act because it is "abstract". We have already seen that the Savigny noble doctrine handed down this explanation into German law. A second explanation is rooted in the donation: if the transferor delivered the object with absolutely no obligation to do so, then he must have wanted to donate it. This explanation has an official character, so to speak, in English law. It enjoyed some support in Austria. It is not contested in France within the limits of the French system, and is used (albeit alternatively to other explanations) in Switzerland. A third explanation is anchored in the nullity of the acts and on the possibility of validating them. If someone delivers an object, though not obliged to do so, then this can mean that the delivering party had intended to validate the (null) act generating the obligation. So, we find that three theoretical explanations may correspond to a single phenomenon.

Here, again, legal scholars have missed out on a few opportunities. It could have elaborated on the conceptual categories capable of overcoming the boundaries of separate legal systems. Quite to the contrary, instead it adds to the boundaries of operational rules in the form of new qualifications and explanations. Furthermore, it systematically favors general definitions reflecting rules of great breadth (the rules M, C, T, A, if not also rule V, borrowed from rational law). The comparison must begin with the operational rule most limited in reach. Then it can take on progressively broader generalizations and groups of rules.

## 6. The Transfer and the Attributions of Ownership

### 6.1. The Problem

So far we have dealt with the transfer of ownership. We have mentioned in passing the distinction between a transfer of ownership between parties, and a transfer of ownership with respect to third parties, or transfer of ownership to all purposes. We have also discussed the general Scandinavian mistrust of the expression "transfer of ownership". However, we have not yet drawn up the list of elements that are affected by broad references to "ownership". It would be impossible to create a definitive list of the normal attributions of ownership. We can, however, mention the most important ones:

- The transferee is entitled to possession of the object.
- The owner may prohibit possession of the object by a third party.
- The owner may restrict any encroachment by third parties.
- Since the transferee is the owner, the transferor no longer has control of the object.
- The owner appropriates any fruit thereof.
- Loss of the object is wholly the risk of the owner.
- The object guarantees the creditors of its owner.
- It is the owner who receives indemnification in case of the expropriation of the object.
- The owner is liable for any harm that the object may cause to others.

The power to transfer must be analyzed further: the transfer of ownership to a good faith third party is not the same as the transfer to a third party who is aware of the true situation; the title of transfer—gratuitous, or for value—requires a further distinction. The creditors may enjoy heigthened protection, in the event of the debtor's bankruptcy. It remains to be seen to what extent expressions like "the sale transfers ownership in France", "the sale does not transfer ownership in Germany and Austria", and "the delivery not supported by *cause* transfers ownership in Germany" can be interpreted in the sense that all the attributes of ownership are (or are not) transferred at the moment of the sale or the delivery.

## *6.2. The Right to Possession*

The right to possession is not the mere consequence of ownership. In every system where delivery is necessary for a complete transfer, the right of possession is the immediate effect of the sale and precedes the delivery. There is quite a marked conceptual difference on this point between those systems anchored in the consent (where the right to a handing over flows from the ownership that the contract has transferred to the buyer) and the systems anchored on the delivery (where the right to a handing over is a personal contractual right). From an operational point of view however, the end results are the same.

At times we find that a right to the handing over only exists after the payment. Such is the case in English law by virtue of the right of stoppage in transit.[50] In other systems, the seller's reserved right to refuse the handing over before receiving payment stands as an exception to the contractual action (*exceptio inadimpleti contractus*), or as a personal right of guarantee (*ius ritentionis*) that has no bearing on the ownership regime. Here, operational rules which are identical in practice give rise to different theoretical explanations. At the same time, payment of the contract price, upon which the parties are free to condition the effects of the contract, can become a legal condition for the transfer of ownership on the basis of the presumption of the law. Such is the case with retail sales where the removal of merchandise without paying constitutes theft.

The right to possession can be transferred even before ownership has changed hands. This anomaly arises in the context of the 'consensus' system as well as within systems anchored in the delivery, if the delivery is not preceded by a valid contract: *don manuel*, execution of a natural obligation, conscious payment of what is not owed, etc. The new owner has no right—neither personal nor real—before the handing over. If it is linked to the retention of title clause, this mechanism prevents the acquisition of ownership by the buyer, but does not limit his right to receive the object.

### 6.3. Action against a Third Party Possessor without Title

In principle, only the owner can bring a suit against the third party who retains possession of the object without title, or who in some other way infringes upon the ownership. The buyer in France and England will be able to act against the third party as soon as the sale is accomplished, while the opposing rule takes hold in Germany, Austria, and elsewhere.

There are numerous exceptions to these rules. In England, the buyer who has become the owner cannot bring actions of conversion or detinue unless he also has the right to possession. In Hungary, the buyer may sue for the object, although he is not yet the owner. In Germany, although the buyer is not yet the owner, he may proceed against the third party (at least if that party is in bad faith) by a tort action for intentional wrongdoing under Section 826 of the German Civil Code, and his remedy in specific performance can include recovery of the object.

In some countries, property can be recovered by two different actions. One, known as *petitory* can be brought when a third party possesses an object with-

---

50. LAWTON, *cit.*, p. 1 (sec. 28,44 f. of the *Sale of Goods Act*). Cf., in the same sense, the uniform Scandinavian law on the sale of merchandise, sec. 41.

out title. The other, known as *possessory*, can be brought when the third party has obtained possession of the object unlawfully. A possessory action can be brought by a person who had obtained the object by delivery. Thus, again, it makes little difference whether ownership is said to pass at the moment of delivery or at the moment a contract is made. The buyer who has become owner but has never taken delivery cannot bring a possessory action. We find such a situation in Italy where a person can become owner without taking delivery. We do not find it in Germany where the buyer normally becomes owner upon delivery. We do not find it in France where possessory actions for personal property do not exist. In Italy, in Germany, and in Austria, a person who has taken delivery pursuant to a contract can bring the possessory actions, and thus the rules are similar, even though the right to bring these actions is not said to be an attribute of 'ownership'.

In England and in the United Stated, at common law, ownership is transferred in one way, while an equitable interest that amounts to a proprietary right is transferred in equity in an entirely different way. The buyer's right to obtain a thing from a third party does not always depend, therefore, on his becoming the owner at common law.

### *6.4. The Right to Alienate*

All legal systems are in agreement on at least two fundamental rules:

1. If a person sells an object to a first buyer, and then subsequently sells and hands over the same object to a second good faith buyer, then the second buyer becomes the owner of the object.
2. If a person has sold the object to one party, then he cannot transfer it to a bad faith third party except under several restrictive conditions.

The first rule is perfectly consistent with legal systems where the delivery effectively transfers the ownership. Up until the moment of delivery, the seller is the object's owner. Thus, he may transfer it. But this rule takes on a special systematic importance in the countries that favor the consent rule—France, Belgium, Italy, Romania, Bulgaria, Mexico,[51] Sweden, England etc. Of course, certain details of the rule may vary. It may be that objects which have been stolen or lost are excluded from this anomalous fluidity, or that only the possessor who has acquired title through valuable consideration is protected against the

51. The countries listed so far are all Romanist countries. Their solution is remarkable considering that Roman law knows no such anomaly, which is due to an influence of Germanic law.

first acquirer. Nonetheless, the broad contours of this rule are found everywhere. The right of the possessor to relinquish the object to a second good faith acquirer plays a role even where the ownership is transferred by the delivery. In effect this means that the transferor who has concluded a *constitut possessoire* with the transferee may subsequently transfer the object yet again.

Conversely, almost everywhere one may transfer the object after having obtained possession without complete ownership of it. In the Romanist countries, these rules constitute special applications of the principle that "*possession vaut titre chez les tiers*". In Louisiana, the effect of a consent which transfers ownership "between the parties" with no opposable effects to third parties, but which is not followed by a delivery, explains this conclusion.[52] By contrast, in England and in America, the law presumes the rightful owner to have granted this power to the seller (the *Sale of Goods Act*, §21). Swedish jurists do not engage in the search for an explanation.

Here, as before, we observe both an unvarying operational rule and a multiplicity of explanations. The seller who has not yet delivered the object must be the owner in countries where the transfer depends on the handing over; it follows that he must have the power to transfer the object, and that he who receives it must conclude a most secure operation. The solution to the problem is not so simple.

The German system of tort liability implies the illicit nature of an intentional immoral act (§826 of BGB). The bad faith infringement upon the personal right of another is an example of such an act. The liability of the second buyer is tied to the contractual obligation of the bad faith seller, and the prescribed sanction for the tortious act is the handing over of the object to the first buyer. Austria and Switzerland have adopted this same solution. In Hungary, the second sale is considered null if there is bad faith on the part of the second buyer and the nullity of the sale prohibits the transfer of ownership. Where ownership is in dispute, the first buyer can claim ownership of the object if it is in his possession.[53] This is where the opposition between seller-owner and seller-non-owner becomes blurry and gives way to the category of seller-possessor who may always transfer to a good faith buyer by handing over the object, and who can never effectively transfer to a second acquirer in fraud or bad faith.

---

52. JOHNSON, *cit.*, p. 121. Louisiana law does not know the expression "*possession vaut titre*"; it must therefore explain the power of the transferor. So, it takes recourse to the idea of "transfer of ownership between the parties", and rigorously upholds this idea which we do not find in England.

53. CSANÁDI, *cit.*, p. 126.

The following four formulas result in uniform operational rules thanks to the interaction of the rule "*possession vaut titre*" with tortious liability:

1. Obligatory effect of the sale and tortious liability in case of fraud.
2. Power to dispose of the object granted by the transferee to the transferor.
3. Transfer of ownership between the parties.
4. Effectiveness of the sale, and protection of the good faith third party.

Problems concerning the nonowner/seller-possessor's power to transfer do not exist where the delivery that transfers ownership is not preceded by an obligation to transfer (i.e. the *don manuel* and analogous cases).

## *6.5. The Risks*

The transferred object is vulnerable to certain risks. Of course, the owner is the one who bears the risk of losing all rights in that object if it is perishable. However, a second question lingers between the buyer and seller: at what moment does the buyer become obliged to pay for the object despite the loss or destruction of the object? In other words, since the owner is the party bearing all the risks, then the transfer of ownership could (should?) transfer all risks from the seller to the buyer. Until then, the seller-owner is responsible to the buyer as guardian of the object. The risks could even be placed in the hands of him who is charged with the safe-keeping of the object—him who is practically the possessor of the object. Finally, insofar as the parties' contractual relationship adds to their ownership relationship, the influence of the *casum sentit debitor* principle could be interpreted to support imposing the risks upon the buyer. The parties can contract for this detail as they see fit; the legal rules are merely supplemental in nature combining with whatever local rules apply to the buyer and seller. We find a symmetry between ownership and risk that does not exist, e.g. regarding the rights of disposal and possession.

To begin with, the common law is loyal to the notion of symmetry. It upholds the will of the parties and views this solution as the best reflection of their will (sections 30, and following of the *Sale of Goods Act*). French law and its progeny also owe their solutions to symmetry. While interpreters of the *Code Napoléon* reproach Article 1138 for its awkward construction, they have no difficulty attributing its significance to adage *res perit domino*.[54] In any case, the rule so readily proclaimed by interpreters is vulnerable to breach. There

54. The text of the code transfers the risk at the moment when the thing "should have been delivered". Here, French law draws more from the ideas of the interpreters rather than from the code itself.

are no retroactive effects of the condition with respect to risks for events that take place before the happening of the condition (Art. 1182 *Code Napoléon*, art. 1465 *codice civile*). In Italy, the buyer under a retention of title clause assumes all risks at the moment of delivery. Alternatively, one can imagine the solution whereby the seller who ceases to be the owner but retains possession of the object would be liable to the buyer. The Swedish rule is similar to this solution: according to § 17 of the law of 1905 on the sale of moveable property, the seller bears all risks up to the moment at which he has performed all obligations allowing the buyer to assume possession of the object or, where differentiated objects are involved, up to the moment when the buyer has the right of possession though the seller still has it at his disposal. In short, it is the offer—the placement of the object at one's disposal—that transfers the risks. The solution is similar to that which links risk and possession.

As is to be expected, those systems that prioritize delivery delay the transfer of risk until the moment of the handing over. We find this solution in Germany (§ 446 and foll. BGB),[55] Austria (§ 1048 and foll. ABGB), Russia, and Hungary. In cases where, in spite of the conditions of ownership, the transfer of risk occurs at the moment of the delivery, it must be said that the risks more closely follow possession rather than ownership. Moreover, a group of countries have held on to a solution deriving from Roman law that delays the transfer of ownership until the *traditio* phase, but advances the displacement of risks up to the moment of the sale (*casum sentit creditor*): Swiss and Spanish law have accepted this asymmetry.

The Vienna Convention on international sale has regulated the transfer of risks without linking it to the more general notion of the transfer of ownership. The solution it adopted is anchored on the delivery. Many countries thereafter adopted a double regime of risk transfer in domestic and international transactions. The problems examined heretofore do not appear where a transfer of ownership (due solely to delivery) does not follow an obligation to hand over (*don manuel*, etc.).

## *6.6. The Parties' Creditors: Undelivered Property*

A third party may have an interest in the transfer of ownership not only as potential transferee, but also as a creditor whose guarantee of repayment lies

55. In German law, where the place of execution of the handing over is the domicile of the seller, the risks are in principle transferred in the same moment that the object is delivered to the carrier. But if the contract prescribes the buyer's domicile as the place of execution (and not merely the place of destination) then the seller bears all risks during transportation.

in the debtor's new wealth. In principle, the good that secures the creditor is the good that potentially belongs to the debtor. The transfer of ownership must therefore be opposable as against the transferor's creditor, and the transferee's creditor must be allowed to claim against it. In practice, this is not always the case. The symmetry between the ownership of the object and the security of the credit can in fact be thrown off balance. This imbalance occurs frequently in three hypotheses:

1. if the sale is not followed by the handing over of the object;
2. if, once the object has been delivered, a contractual clause impedes the transfer of ownership;
3. if, once the handing over has occurred, the contract price has not been paid.

The sale which is not followed by delivery causes significant upsets in legal systems that subordinate the transfer of ownership to the delivery of the object. The buyer in this instance is no different than any other creditor. These systems see to it that up until the delivery, only the creditors of the seller can subject the object to legal action, and that after the delivery this same power rests exclusively with the creditors of the buyer. This solution is in effect in Germany, Hungary, Scotland, Russia, Argentina, etc. Their jurists derive this solution from the symmetry that exists between the ownership of the debtor and the security of the creditor. However, since ownership and possession in this case are reunited in the hands of the transferee, it is not clear whether the element that justifies subjecting the object to the power of creditors is the ownership or the possession. To answer this question, one must consider the case of a debtor who has appropriated the object by mechanism of a *constitut possessoire*. Here, German law permits the transferee to defend his title against the creditors of the transferor; it accepts this consequence even if the transfer has served security purposes, and if the transferor is bankrupt.[56]

In systems that have adopted the consent rule, the guarantee of the transferor's creditors becomes the guarantee of the transferee's creditors at the moment of the sale, independently of any delivery. English law sees nothing wrong

56. On the transfer of ownership intended as security in Germany, see cf. Reichsgericht, November 8, 1904 (*Entsch. d. Reichsger. Zivils*, 59—N.F.9.—, 46): what is not clear is the extent to which § 1205 of BGB, which anchors the lien upon dispossession, is applicable to the *Sicherungsübereignung*, cf. ENNECCERUS, KIPP, M. WOLFF, *Lehrbuch des Bürg. Recht*, III (*Sachenrecht*, by WOLFF and RAISER), 10th ed., 1957, p. 746; STAUDINGER, *op. cit.*, 11th ed., 1956, ad § 929, Anm. VIII, 2, a). If the goal of the transaction is contrary to *boni mores*, the transfer is void.

with this result; the effects of the contract are opposable as against creditors of the seller who no longer has possession of the object; most notably, they are opposable as against a trustee in bankruptcy nominated pursuant to the seller's bankruptcy filing[57] if the seller-possessor has received the contract price.[58] The same solution is found in France where the non-possessing buyer claims rights as against the seller's creditors even if the seller has gone bankrupt.[59] However, the problem of protecting the creditors in the case of a transfer without delivery does not exist in France if the transfer is done for security purposes: such a transfer is null and thought to undermine Article 2076 of the code which subjects the constitution of a pledge to dispossession. Thus, in France and in Italy the transferor' act of dispossession plays a more important role than in Germany so as to reassure the transferee of the effect of the act with respect to his contract counterpart and to third parties.

Sweden does not reject the consent-based notion, but affords no protection to the transferee's creditors until the moment of the handing over.[60] In Italy, the buyer or transferee who has not received the object can only defend his title as against the transferor's creditors if such title is the result of a written act having a specific date (Art. 621 *codice di procedura civile*, Art. 2704 *codice civile*).

## *6.7. The Parties' Creditors: Property Delivered but Not Alienated*

If the object is delivered and some contractual provision prevents the transfer of ownership, the problem to be resolved concerns the protection of the seller-owner as against the buyer's creditors. Will the seller under a retention of title clause or under condition precedent be allowed to defend his title against the buyer's creditors especially where the latter has gone bankrupt? Of course, the act of dispossession weakens the owner's position. However, in France, Germany, and Italy we find that in the two hypotheses where the owner has transferred possession and where the seller has not yet been paid, the seller is not considered to have disposed of the object until it is under buyer's phys-

57. LAWSON, *Introduction to the Law of Property*, 2nd ed., 1975, p. 52.

58. Scottish Commission Memorandum n.25, §44, concerning the *Sale of Goods Act* (cited in the SMITH report, p. 171).

59. Civ., 24 June 1845, *D.*, 1845, I, 309; Civ., 1 June 1874, *D.*, 1876, I, 473; Civ. 27 February 1846, *D.*, 1896, I, 15.

60. UNDEN, *Svensk sakrätt*, I, 4th ed., 1961, p. 97.

ical control. Only the presence of the object in the physical control of the buyer (the *Gewahrsam* of the buyer) threatens the seller's protection (the *Besitz* of the buyer would not have this effect).

Almost everywhere we find that the seller under condition precedent, or retention of title, can defend his title as against the buyer's creditors. But in Sweden, the dispossession renders the seller's ownership unprotected from creditors of the buyer.[61] In Italy, the seller's title must result from a written act on a specified prior date (in certain cases subject to notice as established by Art. 1524 *codice civile*). In France and Belgium, the seller's action for recovery is not allowed where the buyer is bankrupt.[62] It bears repeating that the act of dispossession is better protected under German law than under French law.

## 6.8. The Creditors of the Parties and the Default of the Buyer

If the seller has delivered the object without being paid and has not granted the buyer a delay in payment, then French law affords the seller a right of recovery (Art. 2102, 4 al., *Code Napoléon*), which the authors interpret as a right to recover possession of the object (regulated in Articles 1612 and 1613 of the same code). Moreover, if the buyer does not perform his obligations, the code authorizes any seller to exert privilege over the object sold or to rescind the contract. These remedies are opposable as against the creditors of the buyer so long as the buyer is not in bankruptcy.

In Belgium, the protection afforded to the buyer's creditors is again more rigid than in France, because the right to demand the resolution of the contract is subject to restrictions established in the interest of the creditors (Art. 20, L. December 16, 1851). In Italy, the resolution is not sheltered to third parties (Art. 1458 *codice civile*), and the right to reclaim possession of the object is not sheltered from good faith third parties. Protection of the dispossessing transferor is more energetic under German law. In Germany, the resolution of the transferring act (not to be confused with the resolution of the sale) is opposable as against third party creditors.

---

61. UNDEN, *op. loc. Cit.*

62. The breadth of the rule does not derive from the text of articles 534 and 549 of the commercial code. Yet the law did pull from these two articles the general principle that strengthens the importance of possession (Civ. 22 October 1934, *S.*, 1935, I, 337; Civ., 23 March 1934, *ibidem*). For Belgium, Cass. 9 February 1933, *Pas.* 1933, I, 103; Cass., 23 May 1946, *Pas.*, 1946, I, 204 (cited in the DAVID CONSTANT report, p. 137).

# 7. Comparative Remarks

## *7.1. The Ownership of an Object Sold but Not-Delivered*

The ownership, with its many attributes at the transferor's disposal, gets somewhat deconstructed in transition from the conclusion of the contract to the delivery. The sale, the delivery, the payment of the contract price, the formalities, all conspire to transfer different attributes of ownership.

*The ability to transfer in favor of third parties* in bad faith is forfeited in all legal systems as soon as the object is sold.

*The ability to transfer in favor of good faith third parties* is not forfeited anywhere so long as one has not relinquished the object.

*The seller's right to recover possession* of the object depends everywhere on the sale (if the parties have not conditioned it upon payment) or on the payment (if the parties have not chosen some form of sale on credit).

Thus far, we have dealt with a uniform (or almost uniform) law. This uniform law already involves a basic separation of the elements of ownership. Moreover, this uniformity only shows up in operational rules: the concepts elaborated by scholars take pleasure in masking it.

*The right to challenge a third party's possession without title* could extend from the right to demand delivery, and can depend on the sale or the delivery (which will represent a transfer of the action whenever possession precedes the transfer of property).

*The transfer of risk* can depend on the sale or on the possession of the object. As a substantive matter, the uniformity is lost. We are trying to relocate it, at least for international transactions, on the basis of the Vienna Convention.

An object guarantees the creditors of a subject, and a second subject may take the place of the first either at the moment of the sale or the delivery. Here, the importance of the delivery is more acknowledged than in the areas of risk and rights of action. In addition to the importance of the delivery, what is to be considered is the payment of the price, before which the seller can maintain a right (opposable as against third party claimants) to retain the thing.

{Ownership is transferred at the moment of sale/Ownership of the object sold is transferred at the moment of delivery}.

Here are two legal propositions employed alternatively in various countries. What is their significance? In the first place, they distort the domestic laws of the relevant countries by giving the impression that each legal system is coherent; that it sustains a "transfer of ownership" that is solid and indivisible. They tend to hide the dismemberment that ownership undergoes as it changes hands. In the second place, they distort comparisons of law by giving the impression that different legal systems adopt extremely antithetical solutions, with nothing in common, while all legal systems are in effect located between opposing extremes and are thus in condition to perform uniform operational rules.[63]

A comparison of laws allows us to view the transfer of ownership as yet another chapter of private law in which jurists' concepts exaggerate the differences between various systems to the effect of depicting each national law as a simple and extreme concept. A transfer of ownership accomplished in a single act is only possible where the handing over was not attached to any prior obligation (*don manuel*, and analogous cases).

There is nothing revolutionary about our solution. Since the beginning, German jurists studying French law have observed that remarkable similarities existed between French and Prussian law,[64] and that Article 2279 introduces an important correction of the consent principle.[65] The tradition of *ius commune* had instituted the notion of *ius ad rem* as a situation stronger than a simple credit and yet weaker than a 'real' right. The common law distinguishes the transfer between the parties from the transfer to all purposes.

Our solution develops the notions set forth by Kruse,[66] and evokes suggestions from Scandinavian jurists. It corresponds to the commentary found in many works emphasizing that what interests us the most is not the moment of transfer of that which, from a nominal point of view, corresponds to the ownership, but rather the moment when all risks, rights, and other situations change hands.

## *7.2. Doctrinal Qualifications*

We have observed (n. 6.5) that the seller's alienation to a third party is presented in certain countries as the product of four different ideas: the contractual obligation, the power granted by the transferee to the transferor, the rule "*possession vaut titre*", and the personal and intangible character of the transferred ownership. We saw (n. 6.5) that the transfer of risk, if it occurs at the

---

63. KRUSE, *op. cit.*, claims that a common ground shared by all legal systems can be constructed around two basic principles: the contract produces effects "between the parties"; certain exterior factors produce effects "with regard to third parties".

64. CROME, *Parte gen. del dir. priv. francese* (tr. It.), 1906, p. 228.

65. FERID, *Das französische Zivilrecht*, I, 1971, p. 589.

66. Not every problem is resolved by distinguishing the effects concerning the contracting parties from the effects concerning third parties. The risks and the right to the delivery concern the relations "between the parties" but are transferred separately.

moment of the sale, represents at times a consequence of the transfer of ownership, and at other times an application of the principle of *casum sentit creditor*. We would find multiple explanations founded upon material and procedural law had we asked why the object changing hands is burdened with the debts of the seller or the buyer. A myriad of explanations does not always appeal to a sense of sound logic, and causes trouble where unnecessary. It prevents us from seeing the elements which are uniform across different legal systems and tends to falsify the terms of comparison.

## References

Comparative law studies on property do not adequately address the topic of property transfer. It is as if in the eyes of comparativists, the transfer of property is not worthy of its own chapter within the broader theory of property. Similarly, scholarly works on contract law do not offer chapters focusing on the effects of contracts on ownership. Of course, it would be impossible to list herein the numerous works of general private law, or those dealing with property, contracts, or the sale of property (we will make certain exceptions). So, we refer to general bibliographies on different national legal systems and single out the works that deal specifically with the transfer of property.

On the *usus modernus pandectarum*: FELGENTRAGER, *Friedrich Carl von Savignys Einfluss auf die Übereignungslehre*, 1927; RANIERI, "Brevi note sull'origine della nozione di negozio reale e astratto", *Tijdschrift voor Rechtsgeschiedenis*, XXXVIII, 1970.

On French, Belgian, and Italian legal systems: BUFNOIR, *Propriété et contrat*, 2nd ed., 1924; SALEILLES, *De la possession des meubles*, 1907; GORLA, «L'atto di disposizione di diritti», dans *Annali Università di Perugia*, 1936; GORE, «Le moment du transfert de la propriété dans les ventes à livrer», *Rev. trim. dr. civ.*, 1947, p. 161; id., «Le transfert de propriété des choses de genre», *Dalloz, chronique*, 1954, p. 175; FRIEDEL, «*Le* déplacement volontaire du moment du transfert de la propriété», in HAMEL, *La vente commerciale de marchandises*, 1951; TALLON, «Le transfert de propriété des marchandises vendues en dehors de la convention des parties», in HAMEL, *La vente*, cit.; CARBONNIER, «L'influence du payement du prix sur le transfert de propriété dans la vente», in *Travaux et conférences de la Faculté de droit de l'Université de Bruxelles*, VIII, 1960, p. 127; DEMEESTER et DE MORTIER, *De la réserve de propriété et de la vente à tempérament*, 1931; PIRET, «La revendication du vendeur à tempérament», *Belg. Jud.*, 1937, c. 321; id., *Le droit au prix du vendeur de meubles corporels et ses garanties*, 1941; De NYS, «Le transfert de propriété des choses de genre», *Journ. Trip.*, 1949; VAN HECKE, «La spécification comme condition du transfert des risques dans la vente», *Rev. crit. jur. belge*, 1952, p. 255; MENGONI, *Acquisto a non domino*, several editions beginning in 1949; BIANCA, «Riflessioni sul principio del consenso traslativo», *Riv. dir. civ.*, 1969, I, p. 535; CAMPAGNA, «La posizione del mandatario nel mandato ad acquistare beni mobili», *Riv. dir. civ.*, 1974 I, p. 7; SACCO (and DE NOVA), *Il contratto*, in *Trattato di dir. civile diretto da Sacco*, 3rd ed., 2004, I, pp. 878; AMADIO, "Proprietà e consegna nella vendita dei beni di consumo", *Riv dir. civ.*, 2004, I, 127.

On German, Austrian, Swiss, and Dutch legal systems: EXNER, *Die Lehre vom Rechtserwerb durch Tradition*, 1867; STROHAL, "Rechtsübertragung und Kausalgeschäft im Hinblick auf den Entwurf eines BG", *Jher. Jahrb*, 27, p. 135 ff.; BREYHAN, *Abstrakte Übereignung und Parteiwille in der Rechtsprechung*, 1929; HECK, *Das abstrakte dingliche Rechtsgeschäft*, 1937; KADEN, "Zum Problem der Fahrnisübereignung im schweizerischen Recht", in *Festschr. Hedemann*, 1938; BRANDT, *Eigentumserwerb und Austauschgeschäft*, 1940; PITLO, *Het verbintenissenrecht naar het Nederlands Burgerlijk Wetboek*, 5th ed., 1957; id., *Het Zakenrecht naar het Nederlands Burgerlijk Wetoek*, 4th ed., 1958; NOLTE, *Zur Reform der Eigentumsübertragung*, 1941; BEYERLE, "Der dingliche Vertrag", in *Festchr. Boehmer*, 1954; SCHWEIGER, "Die Sittenwidrigkeit der Sicherungsübereignungen", in *Monat. F. Deutsches Recht*, 1953, p. 707; WACKE, *Das Besitzkonstitut als Übergabesurrogat in Rechtsgeschichte und Rechtsdogmatik*, 1974.

On Scandinavian law: LAGERGREN, *Deliver of the Goods and Transfer of Property and Risk in the Law of Sale*, 1954; USSING, "Le transfert de la propriété en droit danois", *Rev. intern. dr. comp.*, 1952 (IV), p. 1; STRÖMHOLM, "*Bona fides* in the Swedish Law of Property", *Amer. Journ. Comp. Law.* 1963, p. 42; HESSLER, "Property and third Party Protection", in *Academiae Regiae Scientiarum Upsaliensis*, 18, 1974.

On socialist legal systems of the past: EÖRSI, *A tulajdonátszállás kérdéséről* (On the questions of the transfer of property), 1974; CZACHÓRSKI, *Czynnoci prawne przyczynowe i oderwane w polskim praxie cywilnym* (Legal acts with cause and without cause in Polish civil law), 1952; DROZD, *Przeniesienie wlasnosci nieruchomosci* (The transfer of ownership of immovable property), 1974; BEKIE, "Kategorija predača v graždanskom prave" (The handing over category in civil law), in *Vestnik Moskavskogo Universitetu*, 1978.

On English and American law: CHALMERS, *Sale of Goods Act*, 17th ed., by MARK, 1975; BURNETT, *Elements of conveyancing*, 8th ed., 1952; FRIEDMAN, *Contracts and conveyances of Real Property*, 2nd ed., 1963; WILLISTON,

*The Law governing Sales of Goods at Common Law and under the Uniform Sales Act*, ed. Rev., 1948; CROSSLEY VAINES, *Personal property*, 3rd ed., 1962.

On the problems of comparison and unification of legal systems: VON CAEMMERER, "Rechtsvergleichung und Reform der Fahrnisübereignung", *Rabelsz.* 12 (1938–39), p. 675 ff.; BAGGE, "Quelques réflexions à propos du règlement du transfert du risqué dans le projet de loi internationale sur la vente ( ... )", in *Etudes Capitant*, 1939; POROY, *Le transfert des risques* ( ... ) thèse, Genève, 1950; Institut intern. pour l'unification de droit privé (Unidroit), *Draft of a uniform law on international sales of goods*, ed. Rev., 1951; GOTTHEINER, "Zum Eigentumsübergang bein Kauf beweglicher Sachen. Eine rechtvergleichende ... Betrachtung ...", *Rabelsz.*, 19 (1953), p. 356 ff.; SOVILLA, *Eigentumsübergang an beweglichen körperlichen Gegenständen bei internatinoalen Käufen*, 1954; SCHULTSZ, *Eigendomsverkrijging bij Koop van roerende goederen in het Westeuropees international privaatrecht*, 1955; RABEL, "Die Haager-Konferenz für die Vereinheitlichung des Kaufrechts", *Rabelsz.* 17 (1952), p. 212; HEENEN, "Le transfert des risques ( ... )", *Rev. dr. int. et dr. comp.*, 1954, n. sp., p. 109; KRUSE, "What does transfer of Property mean with regard to Chattels? A study in Comparative Law", *Am. Journ. Comp. Law*, 1958, p. 500; WAELBROECK, *Le transfert de la propriété dans la vente d'objets mobiliers corporels en droit comparé*, 1961: SAUVEPLANNE, "The protection of the bona fide purchaser of corporeal movables in comparative law", *Rabelsz.* 29 (1965), p. 651; van VLIET, *Transfer of Movables in German, French, English, and Dutch Law*, Nijmegen, 2000; NICOLUSSI, "Diritto europeo della vendita dei beni di consumo e categorie dogmatiche", *Eur. dir. priv.*, 2003, p. 525; DROBNIG, "Transfer of Property", in Aa. Vv., *Towards a European Civil Code*, 3rd ed., Nijmegen, 2004, p. 725; STAGL, "Der Eigentumsübergang beim Kauf beweglicher Sachen", *Jahrb. Jung. Zivilrechtswissenschaftler*, 2004, p. 369; MONATERI, *Contratto e trasferimento della proprietà. I sistemi romanisti*, Milan, 2008.

In 1978, the International Academy of Comparative Law hosted a conference in Budapest addressing the subject. Several national reports were subsequently published: for England, LAWTON, in *U.K. National reports submitted to the Congress, Budapest, 1978*, 11 A 3; for the German Democratic Republic, POSCH, in Nationales Komitte für Rechtswissenschaft der DDR, *Berichte zum X internationalen Kongress für Rechtsvergleichung, Budapest 1978*, 2, pp. 44–71; for Belgium, DAVID-CONSTANT in Centre Interuniversitaire de Droit Comparé *Rapports belges au X° Congrès international de droit comparé*, 1978, pp. 133–145; for Scotland, SMITS, in *U.K. reports*, cit., 11 A 3/S; for the United States of America, MERRYMAN, in HAZARD and WAGNER (ed.), "Law in the Bicentennial Era", *Amer. Journal of Comp. Law*, vol. 26, 1978, suppl., pp. 91–108; for Hungary, CSANÀDI, in SZABÓ and PÉTÉRI (ed.), *Comparative law*, 1978, pp. 119–129; for Italy, GAMBARO, in Associazione italiana di diritto comparato, *Rapports nationaux italiens au X° Congrès International de Droit Comparé, Budapest* 1978, pp. 199–220; for Louisiana, JOHNSON, in HAZARD and WAGNER, "Law", cit. pp. 109–122; for the Pays-Bas, WILLELMS in JESSURUN D'OLIVEIRA, ed., *Rapports Néerlandais pour le X° Congrès International de Droit Comparé, Budapest 1978*, pp. 103–115; for Poland, CZACHÓRSKI, in Polska Akademia Nauk, *Rapports polonais présentés au dixième congrès international de droit comparé*, 1978, pp. 55–70; for Romania, BÎRSAN and BELCIU, in "Les rapports nationaux roumains pour le X Congrès International de Droit Comparé", *Rev. roumaine des sciences sociales, Séries de sciences juridiques*, 1978, n.1; for Tcheckoslovakia, KNAPP, in *Travaux de droit comparé*, n.4, 1978. The general report, by SACCO, is partially published in Akadémiai Kiadó, Budapest, *General Reports to the 10th International Congress of comparative law*, 1980, pp. 247 ff.

In 1990 ARISTEC held a Congress in Pisa focusing on the theme "*Vendita e trasferimento della proprietà nella prospettiva storico-comparatistica*". The acts were published in two volumes by Giuffré in Milan under the direction of L. VACCA, 1991 (reports edited by PUGLIESE, P. GROSSI, PETRONIO, SAINT-ALARY HOUIN, LUIG, WIEACKER, MAYER-MALY, KNÜTEL, SCHMIDLIN, RAINTER, WOLDKIEWICZ, GARCÍA GARRIDO, SCHRAGE, CANNATA, KUPISCH, GAMBARO, CHIANALE, SACCO and others).

In 1995, the *Semaine Juridique* published Supplement n.5 of *Cahiers de droit de l'entreprise* edited by C. MOULY on the theme *Faut-il retarder le transfer de la propriété?* (articles by MOULY, DURAND, GARDNER DE BÉVILLE, REVET, LAPASSE, SACCO, BRICCHI, PÉROCHON, ULLMO, PASQUALINI, DEBRUYNE, ROBINE, ATIAS, MALAURIE).

# 5

# Western Law of Obligations

Geoffrey Samuel

## Summary



An obligation is defined in Justinian's *Institutes* as a "legal bond (*vinculum juris*) whereby we are bound by the need to perform something according to the laws of our city."[1] The *Institutes* go on to state that this division "sees a subdivision into four *species*: they arise from contract (*ex contractu*), quasi contract (*quasi ex contractu*), delict (*ex maleficio*) or quasi delict (*quasi ex maleficio*)."[2] Behind this definition, both conceptual and metaphorical in nature, lies a model of legal thought so powerful that it has now seemingly conquered a legal tradition that knew, and cared little for, during much of its history the *Corpus Juris Civilis*. The result is that the law of obligations is a category that

1. J.3.13pr.
2. J.3.13.2.

is universal throughout the countries of the European Union. This handbook contribution will, accordingly, largely focus on this conceptual model. However, the category is not without its difficulties. In addition, the division 'obligations' cannot be understood in isolation from other aspects of legal knowledge. Something will need to be said, therefore, about the contexts within which the *divisio* is to be understood and the reasoning methods associated with the category.

# 1. Introduction

The law of obligations occupies a central part of what a jurist from the Romano-Germanic tradition would call private law (itself to be distinguished from public law).[3] The first task of any *handbook entry* would, therefore, appear to be to examine exactly what is meant by the notion of a 'law of obligations'.

## *1.1. Epistemological Considerations*

Yet, as obvious as this assertion might appear, defining what is meant by the law of obligations—or indeed any other domain of the law—is dependent upon the epistemological model deemed appropriate. Defining it from, for example, a functional viewpoint is likely to lead to a rather different analysis than defining it from, a structural perspective.[4] The epistemological dilemma does not stop with this dichotomy; there are further questions about whether one is describing a set of linguistic propositions (rules and principles) or various legal relations or a structure of concepts (rights, duties, interests) or whether one is relating one category to another, or others, within a self-referencing system. Or, again, is one simply trying to make sense of facts?

These dilemmas matter to the comparatist because it cannot be assumed that all legal systems share the same epistemological starting point. For example, at the beginning of the 19th century, the expression 'law of obligations' would probably have meant little to an English lawyer, because the categories of legal thought used within the common law were not at that time taken from Roman law. Indeed even today the idea of a 'private law' is by no means with-

3. HF Jolowicz, *Roman Foundations of Modern Law* (Oxford, Oxford University Press, 1957), pp. 49–53.

4. For a brief discussion of these different schemes of intelligibility see G-G Granger, *La science et les sciences* (Paris, Presses Universitaires de France, 2nd ed., 1995), pp. 90–92.

out its problems.[5] Thus, while it is possible to assert that the law of obligations is part of a coherent *system* of legal institutions and relations whose foundation is to be found in Roman legal thought, such an assertion is always contingent and relative. There are other *grilles de lecture*. And so when one talks of a 'law of obligations' it has to be remembered that one is likely to be appealing—indeed conceptually one can only appeal—to a Roman model of law and to the epistemological implications, fashioned and refined over many subsequent centuries, lying behind the model. Now this model is extremely powerful—so powerful, in fact, that some are calling for a European Code of Obligations[6]—that an approach other than one that starts with Roman legal thought is almost unthinkable. This contribution will be no exception. Yet, it must always be borne in mind that the notion of a law of obligations is a relatively new idea for common lawyers. One might reflect, also, on whether it will still have validity in a century from now.

### *1.2. Definitional and Contextual Considerations*

The law of obligations is a civil law creation; it comes, as was stated at the outset, from Roman law where it acted as a substantive category for a particular kind of remedy called an *actio in personam*. These personal actions were to be contrasted with *actiones in rem*, which were property claims and formed part of the law of property.[7] In modern civilian legal thought the law of obligations is part of a highly systematic structure of legal rights (*droits subjectifs*) which rigidly distinguishes rights *in rem* from rights *in personam*.[8] In very general terms, *owing* (*devoir*) is kept quite distinct from *owning* (*la propriété*). This conceptual model within which the law of obligations is located is known as the 'institutional system' and it holds the key to a proper understanding of the *divisio obligationum*.[9]

---

5. See G Samuel, The Impact of European Integration on Private Law—A Comment (1998) 18 *Legal Studies* 167.

6. See generally A Hartkamp *et al* (eds), *Towards a European Civil Code* (Nijmegen/International, Ars Aequi Libri/Kluwer Law, 3rd ed, 2004).

7. Gaius, *Institutes*, 4. 1–5 (herein after cited G).

8. The Romans did not of course think in terms of rights in the modern sense of the term and thus the distinction was expressed at the level of actions: see G.4.1-4. Nevertheless it would appear that the classical jurists appreciated a substantive distinction between the law of property and the law of obligations: see *Digest* 44.7.3pr (herein after cited D). For an historical discussion see P Ourliac & J De Malafosse, *Histoire du droit privé 2/Les Biens* (Paris, Presses Universitaires de France, 2nd ed., 1971), pp. 47–59.

9. P Stein, *Legal Institutions: The Development of Dispute Settlement* (London, Butterworths, 1984), pp. 125–129.

However, it is important to distinguish between the law of obligations in the early civil law period (Roman classical law, later Roman law, medieval Roman law) and obligations in the later civil law (Humanist and Enlightenment influences, codification and post-codification). One factor which underpins the early and later periods is the style of reasoning. Roman and medieval Roman law were uncodified systems in the modern sense of the term and thus the techniques were case-orientated.[10] Modern civil law, thanks to the influence of the Enlightenment, is traditionally founded on an inference model (codes) where solutions are deduced via syllogistic logic from a major (code provision) and minor (facts of a case) premise.[11] French cases in particular have a very distinctive formal style. Of course beneath this style, other factors may well be at work.[12]

### *1.3. Common Law Methods*

In addition to this difference of method within the civil law tradition, method in the common law must equally be distinguished. For a start, private law (if such a category exists in the common law) is rarely expressed through general principles. This is partly due to the fact that the basis of civil liability has grown up around different types or forms of action and different species of remedy.[13] Certainly, there are generalities; all contracts are governed by a general theory of contract and one can probably say now that there is a general principle of fault liability.[14] But the forms (causes) of action can still exert an influence with the result that the alphabet remains one way of classifying the common law.[15]

Secondly, the idea of symmetry and classification is much less important to the common lawyer.[16] Law, thanks to the forms of action, is seen as being

---

10. A Wijffels, European Private Law: A New Software-Package for an Outdated Operating System?, in M Van Hoecke & F Ost (eds), *The Harmonisation of European Private Law* (Oxford, Hart Publishing, 2000) 101.

11. The change is usually associated with the 16th century humanist school: P Stein, *Roman Law in European History* (Cambridge, Cambridge University Press, 1999), pp. 79–82.

12. M de S-O-L'E Lasser, *Judicial Deliberations: A Comparative Analysis of Judicial Transparency and Legitimacy* (Oxford, Oxford University Press, 2004).

13. For a general discussion of common law reasoning methods in the 18th and 19th centuries, see M Lobban, *The Common Law and English Jurisprudence 1760–1850* (Oxford, Oxford University Press, 1991).

14. *Letang* v *Cooper* [1965] 1 QB 232.

15. B Rudden, Torticles (1991–92) 6/7 *Tulane Civil Law Forum* 105.

16. P Legrand & G Samuel, Brèves épistémologiques sur le droit anglais tel qu'en lui-même [2005.54] *Revue Interdisciplinaire d'Études Juridiques*, 1

located as much in fact as in any notion of an abstract rule and this has resulted in reasoning methods that are much more rooted in analogy and policy than in deduction.[17] Common law methods are, in some respects, much closer to those of the old Roman jurists, although the common law judicial habit of emphasising policy (functionalism) would probably not have appealed to the likes of Ulpian.[18]

Thirdly, there are formal differences of method. Precedent is said to be central to the common law while *la jurisprudence* is not a formal source of law in France. Precedent, in turn, requires knowledge about what binds and what court decisions are authoritative. Indeed, precedent is characteristic of a methodology that is more casuistic than axiomatic which implies that the idea that there are natural or abstract propositions that can be detached from the precedents ought to be treated with scepticism.[19]

Fourthly, there are the methodological issues surrounding interpretation of texts (especially legislation and written contracts). Common law interpretation is often said to be more literal than in France, the judges frequently refusing to look beyond the text itself; it must be said, however, that many judges and academics like to think that the gap is closing.[20]

These differences of method may not as such directly affect the scope and meaning of the law of obligations, but they can impact on the way litigation problems are resolved. Care must be taken, then, not to become entrapped within a scientific definition of obligations; it is a domain of law with huge practical implications. The problem with empiricism, however, is that it can often tell a very different story to the one found in textbooks on, say, contract or delict (tort). For example, textbooks on the law of tort in England and Wales give the impression that the subject is rich in its diversity; yet, statistically, most tort cases are personal injury claims arising out of accidents on the road or in the factory.[21] One might reflect, accordingly, whether the subject ought to be relabelled 'personal injury'. Contract, equally, appears from the casebooks to be about claims for compensation against those who have failed to perform their promises or agreements; in reality, in England at any rate,

17. Lobban, *op.cit.*

18. See generally G Samuel, *The Foundations of Legal Reasoning* (Antwerp, Maklu, 1994).

19. G Samuel, Methodology and Sources of Law: English Report, in J-L Bergel (ed), *La méthodologie de l'étude des sources du droit* (Aix-en-Provence, Presses Universitaires d'Aix-Marseille, 2001), 29, 34–42.

20. *Ibid*, pp. 42–47.

21. P Cane, *Atiyah's Accidents, Compensation and the Law* (Cambridge, Cambridge University Press, 7th ed, 2006).

the great majority of contract cases begun in the lower courts are claims in debt by unpaid suppliers of goods or services. Beneath the category of 'obligations', and beneath the various sub-categories that act as their conceptual sources, there is, then, another world of economic, social, moral and political theory.[22] In many civilian law schools these economic and philosophical aspects may well be excluded, or marginalized, on the basis that such knowledge does not constitute *legal* knowledge.[23] However, this is much less true of Anglo-American law faculties whose courses and doctrine display a range of titles such as the 'philosophy of tort', the 'theory of contract' and so on.[24] Indeed, it is now possible to teach whole courses devoted entirely to contract or tort theory.

## 2. Institutional System and the Law of Obligations

Personal injury and debt, however relevant they might be empirically speaking, are not the scientific categories of *le droit savant*.[25] However, the law of obligations is not merely a category; it is part of a system of legal thought whose roots are to be found in Roman law. The law of obligations can be understood only in relation to this system.

### *2.1. Private Law*

The structure of all the modern codes is largely based upon what Peter Stein has called the institutional system of Roman law.[26] This system takes its name from the Institutes (*institutiones*) of Gaius (published around 160AD) and of Justinian (533AD) and these books were elementary teaching manuals that differed from other texts on Roman law in that they treated law in a systematic and relatively abstract way. The system developed by Gaius, and adopted

---

22. See J Coleman Theories of Tort Law, The Stanford Encyclopedia of Philosophy (Winter 2003 Edition), Edward N. Zalta (ed.), URL = <http://plato.stanford.edu/archives/win2003/entries/tort-theories/>. See also SA Smith, *Contract Theory* (Oxford, Oxford University Press, 2004).

23. T Kirat, *Économie du droit* (Paris, Éditions La Découverte,1999), p. 3.

24. See Colman, *op.cit.*

25. However note *Principles of European Contract Law* art 9:101(1) (herein after cited PECL); *Principles of European Tort Law* (European Group on Tort Law) art 2:102 (herein after cited PETL).

26. *Legal Institutions*, *op.cit*, pp. 125–9.

by Justinian,[27] is founded upon three 'institutions'—that is to say upon three elements that exist at one and the same time in the world of social fact and in the world of law—namely, *persona*, *res*, and *actio*. "All our law", said Gaius, "relates either to persons, to things or to actions."[28] In the later civil law, thanks to the work of jurists such as Hugo Donellus, the *actio* was removed from the scheme and replaced by *obligatio*.[29] In a sense, this was both rational, after the subjective right had become the main focal point of legal thought in the civil law world, and founded on authority in as much as actions and obligations are found together in the *Digest*.[30] The modern codes are thus framed around *persona*, *res*, and *obligatio*, although *res* here has a more restricted meaning; it is a category dealing with *owning* and its associated relationships (possession, real rights). Obligations deal with the relationship of *owing*.

## 2.2. Classification of Rights

As for the law of persons, this became the category encapsulating all rights that were non-patrimonial in nature, that is to say rights which "are devoid of any monetary value, at least in principle."[31] They are not, in other words, treated as property rights in the broad sense of the term 'property'; they are rights which depend strictly on the person and are thus referred to as rights of personality. Perhaps the two most striking personality rights—at least if one takes the *Code Civil* as the paradigm map of private law—are privacy and dignity. These rights would appear by definition to be outside of the law of obligations, a point seemingly confirmed by their location within the law of persons in French private law.[32] However, they cannot be ignored by the obligations lawyer for several reasons: first, despite being extra-patrimonial in nature, they tend to be protected by the law of obligations and thus each time there is an actionable invasion of dignity or privacy the victim may well receive damages founded upon extra-contractual liability.[33] Secondly, personality rights can be the object of a contract; a sports personality may contract

27. Justinian, *Institutes*, 1.2.12 (herein after cited J); D.1.5.1.

28. G.1.8.

29. P Stein, *The Character and Influence of the Roman Civil Law* (London, Hambledon Press, 1988), pp. 73–82.

30. D.44.7

31. B Beignier, Droits (Classification), in D Alland & S Rials (eds), *Dictionnaire de la culture juridique* (Paris, Presses Universitaires de France, 2003), p. 533.

32. *Code civil* arts 9, 16 (herein after cited CC).

33. CC art 1382.

with a commercial enterprise to exploit his or her image. Thirdly, in English law, many 'personality rights' are defined and protected—as far as they are protected—only by the law of tort. Even ownership itself can be dependent upon status, that is to say, upon a rule belonging to the law of persons.[34]

The distinction between patrimonial and non patrimonial rights is not the only fundamental distinction to be made by civil lawyers. As has already been mentioned, rights *in rem* have to be distinguished from *rights in personam*.[35] The distinction is said to have come from Roman law, but a close reading of the sources will soon reveal that the dichotomy was one that found expression, as has been mentioned, at the level of actions rather than *iura*. Even the *Institutes* do not clearly assert that the law of property is quite separate from the law of obligations, although it is fair to say that this can be implied.[36] Nevertheless, from a structuralist viewpoint,[37] the Romans created the foundation for the distinction in suggesting that there were two kinds of legal relations: one flowing between *persona* and *res* (*in rem*) and one flowing between person and person (*in personam*). A right *in rem* attaches to a thing, while a right *in personam* lies only against another named person.

## *2.3. Rights* in personam *(Obligations)*

The law of obligations is thus concerned with personal (not *personality*) rights. In Roman law the sources of such 'rights' (*iura*) were originally contracts and delicts,[38] but this was extended to quasi-contracts and quasi-delicts by Justinian.[39] These four categories are to be found in *Code Civil*, although quasi-delict is not distinguished from delict. In the BGB, however, quasi-delict was rejected as "defunct and useless"[40] and the label of quasi-contract was equally abandoned, unjust enrichment, a principle equally to be found in the Roman sources,[41] being adopted instead.[42] All the modern codes tend to treat, to a greater or lesser extent, contract as the paradigm obligation and thus the

34. See eg *Stevenson* v *Beverley Bentinck Ltd* [1976] 1 WLR 483.

35. Beignier, *op.cit*.

36. See eg D.44.7.3pr.

37. See Granger, *op.cit*, p. 91.

38. G.3.88.

39. J.3.13.2.

40. R Zimmermann, *The Law of Obligations* (Oxford, Oxford University Press, 1996), p. 1130.

41. D.12.6.14; D.50.17.206.

42. Zimmermann, *op.cit*, pp. 20–22; R-M Rampelberg, *Repères romains pour le droit européen des contrats* (Paris, LGDJ, 2005), pp. 39–42.

majority of the paragraphs are devoted to contractual rules.[43] However the case-law tells a rather different story. The industrial revolution created a social situation in which the empirical source of non-contractual obligations (road and industrial accidents) grew to such a proportion that it changed the litigation symmetry that formerly existed between contractual and extra-contractual liability. What is different is that there seems to be far fewer 'rules' in the area of non-contractual obligations, although this perhaps is being modified by an ever-increasing body of EU law.[44]

In Gaius the law of obligations was part of the 'law of things' because an obligation was a form of property.[45] Thus, despite the fundamental distinction made by later civilians between real and personal rights, it has to be remembered that an obligation is a *res incorporalis*. Property and obligations, in other words, merge once one thinks in terms of patrimonial rights.[46] One might note, also, that in the *Code Civil* the law of obligations still forms part of the law of property in that obligations are classified alongside succession and gifts in Book III entitled *Des différentes manières dont on acquiert la propriété*. In the *Código civil* obligations are elevated into their own Book IV under the title of *De las obligaciones y contractos*. The BGB makes a fundamental distinction between property and obligations.[47]

## 2.4. Classification of Things

This property point needs to be developed because it is the source of both the strength and the weakness of the whole institutional scheme.[48] It is a source of strength in as much as the idea of a legal relation, or right, attaching to a thing allows the system to construct a conceptual foundation both for secure property rights and for real security; the owner or secured creditor simply follows the thing. There is a weakness, however, in that once one treats a debt as a 'thing' it would seems to follow that the debt itself can be 'owned.'[49] Indeed,

---

43. As Stephen Waddams points out, 573 pages out of 578 of the Evans' translation of Pothier's *Traité des obligations* are devoted to contract: S Waddams, *Dimensions of Private Law: Categories and Concepts in Anglo-American Legal Reasoning* (Cambridge, Cambridge University Press, 2003), p. 6.

44. See eg the new CC art 1386-1-18.

45. G.2.14.

46. Jolowicz, *Roman Foundations*, *op.cit*, pp. 61–62.

47. Obligations are in Book 2 while property is in Book 3.

48. Jolowicz, *op.cit*, p. 61.

49. S Ginossar, *Droit réel, propriété et créance* (Paris, Librairie Générale de Droit et de Jurisprudence, 1960).

the moment that the subjective right became the key concept in legal thought one had gone far in introducing into the institutional system a paradox. Is a right something that is 'owned'? And if so, can one 'own' an obligation right? If a debtor's assets are there to support the debtor's obligations,[50] why distinguish between real and personal rights? Perhaps, in the civil law system, these paradoxes do not really matter since the institutional systems seems to work well enough in commercial practice, although the point has been made many times that contract is a new form of property.[51] However, in the common law world, the concepts of owning and owing—that is to say property rights and obligation rights—can and do become confused on occasions, especially in the area of the law of restitution. Claimants can sometimes recover a sum of money in another's bank account on the basis that the owner has a property right in the money itself.[52]

Such reasoning can cause confusion in comparative law in that money is normally treated as a consumable item like flour, bread or wine. Thus where one 'lends' such items to another ownership in the goods passes on transfer and the only remedy that the lender has against the borrower is an *actio in personam* arising out of a contract of loan.[53] In other words the legal right is personal not real. Such thinking must on the whole be true of the common law simply because it is seemingly unthinkable in practice that the lender of a loaf of bread retains title to the *res* even after it has been consumed by the borrower; indeed the lender of a five pound note, who subsequently physically recovers his 'property' by entering the borrower's room and re-possessing the item, will probably be guilty of theft. Yet with money, there is nothing physical about asserting that it has been 'digested' once it has been 'consumed' by the payee, that is to say, spent or put into his bank account. It is possible to imagine a notional 'thing' remaining within the payee's patrimony since money is actually different from other consumable items; it is not the money that is important in a patrimony, but its value. This is a point that seems always to have been recognised by the Court of Chancery.[54] Moreover, one can go further; even the consumed loaf of bread can leave a juridical 'image', analogous

50. CC art 2092.

51. See eg W Friedmann, *Law in a Changing Society* (Harmondsworth, Penguin Books, 2nd ed, 1972), pp. 96–97; P Atiyah, *The Rise and Fall of Freedom of Contract* (Oxford, Oxford University Press, 1979), p. 102.

52. See eg *Lipkin Gorman* v *Karpnale Ltd* [1991] 2 AC 548.

53. G.3.90.

54. FH Lawson, *Remedies of English Law* (London, Butterworths, 2nd ed., 1980), pp. 147–160.

to the smile of the Cheshire cat in Alice's Wonderland, and this image can act as the basis for a legal *res*, thus allowing property rules to remain in play.[55] Chancery and common lawyers could be highly conceptual when it suited them, even if the concepts they employed transgressed the authority of Roman *scientia iuris*.

### *2.5. Public and Private Law*

The *persona*, *res* and *actio* structure was a model of private law, that is to say, it was a structure primarily concerned with the interests of private individuals. The Romanist tradition has also recognised a category of public law (*ius publicum*) which, according to the Roman sources, was concerned with the interests of the state.[56] This division between public and private law is one of the distinctive features of the civil law tradition and, in France, it is so fundamental that there are two sets of courts each with its own jurisdiction.[57] Public law matters are heard in public law courts, while private law matters are dealt with in the private system. The law of obligations is not generally seen as having a place in public law (at least in the French tradition), save to the extent that a public authority is permitted to enter into private law contracts or sue and be sued for acts or facts giving rise to a private law liability. However, at the level of liability, the *Conseil d'État* has not been insensitive to developments and ideas in private law.[58] In the common law systems the distinction has no role at the formal level and thus the ordinary law of contract, tort and restitution applies indifferently to all individuals and to public and private entities alike.[59]

## 3. Sub-Divisions and Sources of the Civilian Law of Obligations

It has already been observed that the *divisio obligationum* consists of the four sub-categories of contract, quasi-contract, delict and quasi-delict and it

55. *Foskett v McKeown* [2001] 1 AC 102.

56. D.1.1.1.2.

57. For a comparative reflection from the point of view of the liability of public bodies see D Fairgrieve, *State Liability in Tort* (Oxford, Oxford University Press, 2003).

58. R Chapus, *Responsabilité publique et responsabilité privée: Les influences réciproques des jurisprudences administratives et judiciaire* (Paris, LGDJ, 1954).

59. JWF Allison, *A Continental Distinction in the Common Law: A Historical and Comparative Perspective on English Public Law* (Oxford, Oxford University Press, 1996).

is these categories that actually make up the substance of the whole domain. Each of these sub-divisions has its own independent history. However, this history is twofold depending upon the scheme of analysis applied; there is a conceptual history attaching to the form of each category and there is an empirical history reflecting social and economic change over the centuries.[60] A work on the 'Western law of obligations' needs to focus on the conceptual history since law as a discipline is governed not by a paradigm of social science enquiry but by the paradigm of authority. The subcategories of the law of obligations are the authoritative sources of an obligation.

### *3.1. Contract*

The subcategory of a law of contract is Roman in origin in the sense of a *vinculum iuris* based upon agreement, but the fashioning of a general theory of contract is post-Roman.[61] The Romans themselves developed a detailed set of contractual ideas around a range of transactions such as sale, hire, partnership, loan and deposit; and each of these transactions had their own particular *actiones*.[62] The Romans did not stop with these transactional forms, for they equally developed some more general ideas of contracting. For example, formal promises (stipulations) were enforceable at law provided they were spoken in a particular form and pacts and innominate (unnamed) contracts were also given legal enforceability where justice required.[63] What the Romans did not do was to fashion a general theory of contract based upon promise or agreement. Indeed, Ulpian famously asserted that *nuda pacta obligationem non parit*.[64] This said they nevertheless recognised that all the different contracts shared the common denominator of agreement (*conventio*) and they were accordingly able to categorise them within the single classification of actions *ex contractu*.[65] Ulpian suggests that if there was a sufficient ground (*causa*) this might be the basis for a 'synallagmatic' obligation,[66] because contracts arise

60. For example, the growth of delictual and quasi-delictual liability during the 19th and 20th centuries can be directly linked to industrial and road traffic accidents: Zimmermann, *op.cit*, pp. 1130–1131. For a social and economic view of public and private law, see Friedmann, *Law in a Changing Society*, *op.cit*.

61. See generally Rampelberg, *op.cit*, pp. 64–71.

62. See T Weir, Contracts in Rome and England (1992) 66 *Tulane Law Review* 1615.

63. D.19.5.1.

64. D.2.14.7.4; Zimmermann, *op.cit*, p. 508.

65. D.2.14.1.3.

66. D.2.14.7.2.

out of agreements.[67] In the later civil law the medieval doctors of law and the canon lawyers started to develop the common denominator of *conventio* and *consensus* (also found in Roman law) into a general theory of contract, a process that came to fruition with the humanists and natural lawyers.[68] *Consensus*, in other words, became the normative foundation of the contractual obligation and there was no longer a need for a law of contracts based on a set of empirical transactions and associated legal actions. There was a general theory of contract which was to find its most perfect expression in article 1134 of the French *Code Civil* (CC) of 1804: "Les conventions légalement formées tiennent lieu de loi à ceux qui les ont faits."

### 3.2. Delict

A similar story is to be found in the history of delictual liability. In Roman law a number of legal actions had been developed to deal with harm arising outside of contractual transactions and the general foundational idea, according to Gaius, was the notion of wrongfulness (*ex maleficio*).[69] Thus obligations arose from theft (*ex furto*), damage (*ex damno*), robbery (*ex rapina*) and insult (*ex injuria*). In order to be actionable, the harm suffered had to fall within one of these categories and although Gaius tells us that they share the common denominator of wrongfulness the Romans did not fashion any general theory of delictual liability at the level of the generic category itself. What the Romans did do, however, was to lay the foundations for a claim for wrongful damage based upon fault (*culpa*). It was the jurists and practitioners of the later *jus commune* who undertook the work of extending and adapting the Aquilian action.[70] The key concept was that of *culpa* and these jurists gradually managed to detach this notion not just from its foundation in actions for wrongful damage to property but from the Aquilian category itself. Thus by the 17th century Grotius (1583–1645) recognised the general principle that any person who does culpable damage ought to make good such harm.[71] And, later in the century, Domat (1625–96) asserted that: "Toutes les pertes, tous les dommages qui peuvent arriver par le fait de quelque personne doivent être réparées par celui dont la faute y a donné lieu."[72] This formula was taken to

67. D.16.3.1.6.
68. Rampelberg, *op.cit*, pp. 68–69.
69. D.44.7.4.
70. See generally Zimmermann, *op.cit*, pp. 1017–1049.
71. Zimmermann, *op.cit*, p. 1032.
72. Quoted in J-P Lévy & A Castaldo, *Histoire du droit civil* (Paris, Dalloz, 2002), p. 915.

an even higher level of abstraction by the drafters of the *Code Civil* with the result that Article 1382 declares, simply, that any act which causes damage must be compensated by the person at fault for the damage.

Now there is no doubt that this French code provision reflected what was to become an axiomatic truth during the 19th century: there could be liability for damage only if there was fault. As Zimmermann observes, this principle had a number of very real advantages—moral, economic and historical—which can be summed up in the idea that "it was seen to provide adequate protection without unduly restricting the freedom of the individual will or hampering entrepreneurial activities."[73] However, such a wide liability, which encompassed all types of physical and economic harm, did not appeal to the Pandectists and thus the provision in paragraph 823 of the BGB is more limited. Whereas the French provision requires only damage, fault and causation, the German text adds a list of particular interests that must be invaded before there can be liability (life, body, health, freedom, property, or other right).

### *3.3. Quasi-Delict (and Liability without Fault)*

One reason why the fault principle can give the impression of being trapped within 19th century thinking is that it has to some extent been outflanked by developments in non-fault liability. The foundations of such liability are once again Roman in origin in that the *Corpus Iuris* contains examples of certain actions based on ideas other than fault. Some of these actions were said to arise *quasi ex maleficio*.[74] The occupier of a house, for example, was liable without proof of fault for things thrown or falling from his house onto the public way[75] and innkeepers and certain others were strictly liable for property lost or stolen while in their custody. Other actions such as the liability for harm done by animals suggest the notion of a liability for damage done by things.[76] These latter claims were not actually classified under quasi-delict, but even if they had been, it would still be difficult to determine what the common-denominator of this category was and thus it cannot be asserted with any certainty that quasi-delict is a term that gives expression to no-fault liability.

The result is that the category of quasi-delict was never properly developed in the later civil law, although it did not disappear completely. French legal

73. Zimmermann, *op.cit*, p. 1035.
74. J.3.13.2.
75. See D.9.3.1.
76. D.9.1.1pr.

theorists used the term to give expression to non-intentional harm and thus in the *Code civil* the dichotomy between delict and quasi-delict reflects the distinction between intention and negligence.[77] Of course, this thesis had no basis whatsoever in Roman law itself. Yet given that in Rome the category did contain certain actions that could be described as no-fault claims, it is permissible, if only for the sake of symmetry, to use this category as a space for explaining that the French jurists, in respect of non-contractual liability claims, went further than the induction of a single principle based on *culpa*. They also continued to develop the forms of stricter liability established by the Romans with respect to slaves, buildings and animals. For example, Pothier (1699–1772) declared that a master was generally liable for delicts committed by his servant.[78] Now, before the 19th century, it would be misleading to state that these forms of stricter liability were seen as harbouring some general principle of strict (no fault) liability, if only because *culpa* carried with it such a moral force leading in turn to the principle of justice, especially in Germany, that there should be no liability without fault.[79] Nevertheless in CC Article 1384 there is the opening declaration that "On est responsable non seulement du dommage que l'on cause par son propre fait, mais encore de celui qui est causé par le fait des personnes dont on doit répondre, ou des choses que l'on a sous sa garde".

This statement in the code was originally regarded only as an article of transition linking the general fault liability with various specific liabilities placed on one person for damage caused by another (in particular employers and parents) and for damage resulting from dangerous things (notably buildings and animals).[80] Indeed, these specific liabilities were themselves originally seen as forms of *culpa in vigilando* and *culpa in custodiendo*. However, at the end of the 19th century, the *Cour de cassation* elevated the transitional article into a general principle with its own independent normative force thus opening up the way for an area of strict liability to rival that of fault.[81] *Ubi emolumentum ibi onus* became the basis for making the employer liable for the delicts of his employees and 'collective solidarity' based upon the idea of risk and insurance ensured an ever-increasing liability without fault for damage done by things.[82]

77. Lévy & Castaldo, *op.cit*, n° 627.
78. Zimmermann, *op.cit*, p. 1124.
79. Zimmermann, *op.cit*, p. 1034–1035.
80. Lévy & Castaldo, *op.cit*, n° 642.
81. Cass.civ. 16 juin 1896; D.1897.1.433.
82. J-L Gazzaniga, *Introduction historique au droit des obligations* (Paris, Presses Universitaires de France, 1992), n° 220.

These developments prompted the legislator to intervene with specific statutes to ameliorate the position of victims from the two main empirical sources of personal injury, namely work and traffic accidents.[83] Germany, by contrast, never developed a general non-contractual principle of strict liability for things or for persons and even liability in respect of animals and buildings has a certain fault dimension.[84] However, legislation outside the code has gone further and there are special regimes covering traffic accidents, dangerous products,[85] railways, and the environment.[86]

## *3.4. Quasi-Contract (and Unjust Enrichment)*

Quasi-delict itself may not have had much of a history in the later civil law, but the same cannot be said of the other Justinian category of quasi-contract, even if the expression itself has been increasingly avoided. In substance, the need for such a category was recognised by Gaius who dealt with a number of claims, classed under 'various causes', which could not actually be treated as arising out of a contract nor could they be seen as delicts. They could be regarded as being founded only upon an obligation 'as if there had been a contract' (*quasi ex contractu teneri*).[87] These remedies had been developed to deal, for example, with situations where money had been paid under a contract that turned out to be defective or where there never had been such a relationship in the first place. As we have seen, these cases were logically problematic in Roman law because money was treated as a consumable item and thus ownership passed with the payment of the money. This meant that the payer could not reclaim the sum using an *actio in rem*.

Perhaps the two most important actions within the quasi-contract category were the *condictio*, an *actio in personam* for a sum of money, and the *actio negotiorum gestorum contraria* which was a means by which someone who had reasonably intervened into the affairs of another in the sole interests of that other could recover his expenses.[88] These two actions, as has been stated, were independent of any contractual relationship between the parties and thus the question arose as to what the normative basis of the remedies might be. It

83. Lévy & Castaldo, *op.cit*, nº 642.

84. BGB §§833, 836–838.

85. And see also CC art 1386-1ff.

86. See generally F Stone, Liability for Damage Caused by Things, *International Encyclopedia of Comparative Law*, Volume XI, Chapter 5 (JCB Mohr, 1970).

87. D.44.7.5.1; Lévy & Castaldo, *op.cit*, nº 439.

88. J.3.27.1.

could not be *conventio* and *consenus* because there was no such agreement and consent; equally it could not be a wrong because there was no wrong. The Romans suggested that these claims might be motivated by the principle that no one should be allowed unjustly to enrich himself at the expense of another.[89] However, they never really developed this idea and as a result the category of quasi-contract on the one hand and the principle of unjust enrichment on the other remained rather separate conceptual focal points.

This separation was largely maintained in the early part of the second life of Roman law with the result that, until recent times, the two notions have attracted their own interpretation and developments. Thus in the *Code civil* there is no reference to the principle of unjust enrichment as a source of obligations but there is a section on quasi-contracts (Arts. 1371–1381). In the BGB, by contrast, there is no section on quasi-contracts but the unjust enrichment principle finds expression in paragraph 812(1). French jurisprudence has, however, modified the position in as much as unjust enrichment was recognised as a general principle of law lying behind the action *de in rem verso* (Art. 1371) and thus, to this extent, it is a normative force which is independent of the code.[90] In addition, the whole notion of a 'quasi-contract' came in for criticism, above all on the basis that it was a contradiction in terms; either there is agreement (*conventio* and *consensus*), and thus contract, or there is no agreement and thus no (not even an 'as if') contract.[91] The result is that the unjust enrichment principle has largely become the starting point for analysing problems where money, property or services have been transferred to another in situations where the facts disclose neither a contractual nor a delictual obligation. Despite the criticisms, the category of quasi-contract has by no means been suppressed: it remains not just as a formal category within the *Code Civil* but as a practical starting point for the remedies available for reversing enrichments.

As for the principle itself, it does give expression to a certain symmetry in the law of obligations. Whereas delictual liability arises from physical or patrimonial damage and thus tends to generate the compensatory remedy of damages, unjust enrichment liability looks to patrimonial benefit and asks whether

89. D.12.6.14; D.50.17.206.

90. Arrêt *Boudier*: Cas.req.15 juin 1892, Dalloz.1892.1.596.

91. Zimmermann, *op.cit*, pp. 20–24. In Roman law itself it has to be remembered that there was no general theory of contract based upon *conventio* and *consensus*; liability was a matter of established transactions. Accordingly, the idea of a 'quasi-contract' made sense since one was not looking for agreement but for a transactional analogy. In French law the term 'quasi-contract' continued to attract criticism in the two centuries following codification: Lévy & Castaldo, *op.cit*, n° 550.

a cause for it exists in law. If no such legal cause can be established the person whose patrimony has diminished because of the other's enrichment might well have a remedy. There is therefore a dichotomy between liability *ex delicto* and liability *quasi ex contractu* that does make sense at the level both of fact and of law.[92] Furthermore the principle itself contains the conditions of liability in as much as there must be (i) an enrichment (ii) at the expense of another which is (iii) unjust, that is to say *sans cause*.[93] Of course each of these three conditions have given rise to difficulty—there are several celebrated real and hypothetical examples that generate pages of discussion—but at least they provide a structural starting point and will undoubtedly be used as the basis for a European code.[94]

### *3.5. General Theory of Obligations*

The notion of 'obligations' is not just a generic category but also an independent concept in itself. As such, it has attracted its own rules and theories that deserve some, if limited (because of space), attention.[95] In addition, the relationship between obligations (*iura*) and liability is something that has given rise to its own tension, a tension mediated by the *actio* (remedy).

Logically the formation, content and extinction of an obligation are matters that can be treated at a general theory level. However, with the exception of the distinction between legal acts (contract) and legal facts (delict, quasi-contract), in practice they are dealt with as part of the substantive knowledge of contract, delict and unjust enrichment. Perhaps the only formation point, therefore, that space permits to be made at this general level is that the Romans recognised that an obligation could be created by 'nature', as opposed to the *ius civile*, and this notion of a natural obligation still has a role in the modern civil law.[96] For example, one who knowingly pays a statute barred debt cannot recover the payment.

With respect to the content of an obligation, one aspect that is of interest at a general theory level is the role of fault in the determination of liability.[97]

---

92. F Terré, P Simler & Y Lequette, *Droit civil: Les Obligation* (Paris, Dalloz, 8th ed, 2002), nº 1029.

93. *Ibid*, nºs 1066–1071.

94. J Beatson & E Schrage (eds), *Cases, Materials and Texts on Unjustified Enrichment* (Oxford, Hart Publishing, 2003).

95. Terré, Simler & Lequette, *op. cit*, nº 1075.

96. Lévy & Castaldo, *op.cit*, nºs 656–658.

97. G Treitel, *Remedies for Breach of Contract* (Oxford, Oxford University Press, 1988), pp. 7–42.

This has general importance in that when the Roman jurists discussed liability they did so in very similar terms irrespective of whether the obligation breached was delictual or contractual. In both Alfenus' discussion of the Capitoline Hill accident[98] and Ulpian's analysis of liability arising from a contract of hire,[99] the search for responsibility is effectively a search for *culpa*.[100] This central role of fault in obligational liability cases has been carried over into, first, the *Code civil* and, now, the *Unidroit* Principles and the *Principles of European Contract Law*.[101] According to these codes, a non-performing party is not to be liable in damages if he can prove he was not at fault. This does not mean, however, that liability without fault has no place in contract. French doctrine distinguished between means and ends.[102] Some obligations are undertakings to achieve a particular result while others are undertakings only to use one's best efforts. Thus the doctor does not undertake to cure the patient, only to apply her reasonable skill and care. From a liability point of view, this translates into liability without fault (strict liability) and liability for fault, the doctor being liable to the patient only if she was negligent. The carrier of goods or persons, in contrast, will be strictly liable if the person or property does not reach the promised destination.[103] This distinction between *obligation de moyens* and *obligation de résultat* now finds textual expression in Article 5.1.4 of the *Unidroit Principles*. One should add that the dichotomy between fault and no fault liability is equally to be found in extra-contractual obligations and so it could be said for example that the distinction between articles 1382 and 1384 of the *Code Civil* is one of content or level of the duty imposed by these provisions.[104] More difficult, of course, is the role of fault in the area of unjust enrichment since this area of the law of obligations has something of a proprietary flavour.[105]

The final aspect of an obligation is the way it can be extinguished. The Romans regarded the extinction of the *vinculum iuris* as a matter of form analogous to the formation of the obligation. Thus, if a contractual obligation has been created by the delivery of a thing then its extinction will occur only on redelivery. If it has been created by words, then its extinction will be either by

98. D.9.2.52.2.
99. D.13.6.5.7.
100. D.13.6.5.4.
101. CC art 1147; PECL arts 8:101, 8:108; Unidroit art 7.4.1.
102. Treitel, *op.cit*, p. 33; Terré, Simler & Lequette, *op.cit*, n° 577.
103. Terré, Simler & Lequette, *op.cit*, n° 590.
104. *Ibid*, n°s 682 etc.
105. See eg Terré, Simler & Lequette, *op.cit*, n° 1058.

performance of what was promised or by words.[106] Equally, contracts formed by bare agreement can be ended by agreement.[107] Two particular means of extinction emerge from this formality: an obligation can be extinguished either by performance or by agreement. However, Roman law recognized that an obligation could also be extinguished indirectly through rules that attach to the *actio*; a creditor who failed to enforce a claim at law would after a certain period of time lose the right to sue through a device known as prescription. The flow of time presumed the extinction of the debt.[108] In situations where the *actio* has not been extinguished by time, the effect of legal proceedings is to put an end to an obligation either through enforced performance or through the payment of damages. Of course it may be that a defendant will be able to resist a claim for damages on the basis of a *force majeure*, in which case it could be said that an obligation is extinguished as a result of an outside event.[109] However, one traditional explanation of such an extinction is through the notion of a condition and thus it could be said that the obligation is ended by implied agreement.[110] Assignment and transfer are yet other means of putting an end to an obligation as far as one of the parties is concerned. Perhaps, then, one comes back to Roman law: obligations are ended either by performance (prescription being a negative form of performance) or by agreement (defined widely).

## 4. Law of Obligations in the Common Law Tradition

When one turns to the common law one finds, until relatively recently, a quite different structure of thinking. Roman learning was largely absent and in its place were forms of thought that had been fashioned by institutions and procedures that were the product of the social and political conditions existing in England and Wales during the late Middle Ages. Of course, the same was true elsewhere in Europe, and thus the common law is in one sense simply a *droit coutumier*;[111] but the continental European customary systems gradually became Romanized as a result of the influence of the university profes-

106. D.46.3.80.
107. D.50.17.35.
108. Lévy & Castaldo, *op.cit*, n°s 732 etc.
109. Terré, Simler & Lequette, *op.cit*, n°s 581 etc.
110. Lévy & Castaldo, *op.cit*, n° 648.
111. RC van Caenegem, *Judges, Legislators and Professors: Chapters in European Legal History* (Cambridge, Cambridge University Press, 1987), pp. 114–119.

sors of law and their graduates. In England and Wales, there were no faculties of common law to speak of before the late 19th century and thus there was no *droit savant*; the common law was, for most of its history, almost exclusively in the hands of its practitioners.[112] None of this is to say that the idea of a law of obligations is completely alien to the contemporary English lawyer. It is not, and there are indeed textbooks published using this title.[113] However, the expression is a recent import and to some extent sits uneasily both with the traditional forms of legal thought and with the inherited structural basis of the common law.[114]

### *4.1. Personal Actions at Common Law*

The main formal distinction to be found in the early days of the common law was the one between real and personal actions. Real actions were those brought for the specific recovery of land, tenements or hereditaments, whereas personal actions were those brought for the specific recovery of moveable goods, of a debt, of damages or for other redress. By the end of the 14th century real actions had largely fallen into disuse as a result not just of the decline of feudalism but also of unpopularity owing to their excessive procedural technicalities.[115] The history of common law remedies is, therefore, largely a history of personal actions. In the early days of the common law courts, the court which supposedly had exclusive jurisdiction over personal actions was the Court of Common Pleas. However this arrangement "was departed from at the expense of the Court of Common Pleas, for the other two courts, while retaining each its own exclusive jurisdiction, succeeded in encroaching upon the jurisdiction of the Common Pleas over personal actions, with the result that in modern times any personal action could be brought in any one of the three Courts of Common Law."[116]

The personal actions at common law were very different from the *actiones* to be found in Roman law and were based on the system of writs. The original formulation of each action was a response to an empirical problem that

---

112. *Ibid*, pp. 53–65.

113. See eg J Cooke & D Oughton, *The Common Law of Obligations* (Oxford, Oxford University Press, 3rd ed., 2000).

114. See generally G Samuel, *Understanding Contractual and Tortious Obligations* (Exeter, Law Matters, 2005).

115. JH Baker, *An Introduction to English Legal History* (London, Butterworths, 4th ed., 2002), pp. 235–237.

116. R Sutton, *Personal Actions at Common Law* (London, Butterworth & Co, 1929), p. 36. The other two common law courts were King's Bench and Exchequer.

existed in English society at the time of formulation.[117] However, some of the actions subsequently became enlarged, if not deformed, through development by lawyers and courts, often as a result of the use of fictions. The main actions of relevance to the law of obligations which were to survive into the 19th century (if not later) are account, assumpsit, debt, detinue, trespass, trespass on the case, and trover.

### *4.2. Abolition of the Forms of Action*

Even after many centuries of personal actions, it was still not easy to conceive of the common law as a coherent system of abstract rules or principles. "At the beginning of the eighteenth century," notes Lobban, "most common lawyers did not seek to put their law into a rational form" because "they saw the law as a form of reasoning working within a set of remedies" and so "most legal texts were written not in a systematic way, but as lists."[118] The law was still, in other words, a matter of plea precedents in which the emphasis was on procedural form; the job of the lawyer was to make sure that the right form had been chosen and to present correctly the case to the jury. As the century progressed, more substantive ideas began to emerge with the result that during the 19th century, in the grip of course of the industrial revolution, the old system was seen to be quite inadequate and in need of fundamental reform. When this reform was undertaken, however, it was not at the level of substantive law: it was almost exclusively procedural.[119] Nevertheless, these reforms were to impact on the law in general and one in particular, the abolition of the forms of action, was to free the 'law of obligations' from its procedural straightjacket.

Reform came with the *Common law Procedure Act* of 1852, which did away with having to name the form of the action. This was subsequently followed by a more wholesale reform of the English legal system in 1873–1875. A plaintiff was, according to this new legislation, only required to state the material facts of his case.[120] The effect was momentous in that the common law, freed from the procedural grip of the old personal actions, could now give expression to a theory of contract which had been slowly taking shape over the previous century.[121] This theory had been partly shaped by the influence of the

117. Baker, *op.cit*, p. 55.

118. M Lobban, *op.cit*, p. 9.

119. Baker, *op.cit*, pp. 67–69.

120. See Baker, *op.cit*, pp. 67–69.

121. D Ibbetson, *A Historical Introduction to the Law of Obligations* (Oxford, Oxford University Press, 1999), p. 215.

civil lawyers, in particular Pothier; partly by the fact that the role of the judge in moulding the law was becoming more prominent as the emphasis began to shift away from the jury; and partly by the development of a body of doctrinal works on contract during the 19th century.[122] Indeed, six years before the abolition, a Parliamentary commission investigating the state of legal education reported that there was little or no such education to be had in England and recommended amongst other things that legal science—in effect Roman law—be introduced into the training.[123] Gradually, as a body of legal academics began to establish itself, the law came to be seen in quite a different light; the common law was to be regarded no longer as a mass of facts, procedures and remedies but, as in the civilian tradition, as a coherent body of rules.[124]

### *4.3. Contract and Tort*

One of the more immediate effects of the abolition of the forms of action was that the common law stopped thinking in terms of remedies and adopted the Roman law categories of contract and tort. Indeed, during the latter half of the 19th century there is a distinct Romanization of thinking in as much as one finds the judges not only referring to civilian doctrine but also employing terms such as *ex contractu* and *ex delicto*.[125] The transformation was not without its complexities in that the old common law was suffused with many non-Roman terms and ideas[126] and even a judge such as Blackburn J, who was an authority on Pothier and Roman law, still employed on occasions 'assumpsit' rather than contract.[127] However, the basic principle that people could make promises enforceable as substantive contracts was well established by 1850. Thus, one finds a judge in 1861 asserting that there "can be no contract until there is a final and mutual assent; an agreement of the minds of the parties, upon the same terms." And when "that assent has taken place … there is a contract; and a cause of action on that contract then and there arises."[128] All

---

122. See generally Ibbetson, *op.cit*, pp. 215–244.

123. P Stein, *Legal Evolution: The Story of an Idea* (Cambridge, Cambridge University Press, 1980), pp. 78–79.

124. See S Hedley, How has the Common Law Survived the 20th Century? (1999) 50 *Northern Ireland Legal Quarterly* 283.

125. G Samuel, Civil Codes and the Restructuring of the Common Law in D Fairgrieve (ed), *The Influence of the French Civil Code on the Common Law and Beyond* (London, British Institute of International & Comparative Law, 2007), 11).

126. See eg *Denton v GNR* (1856) 25 LJQB 129 especially Crompton J.

127. See *Tweddle v Atkinson* (1861) 30 LJQB 265, 268.

128. *Aris v Orchard* (1861) 30 LJ Exch 21, 23 per Wilde J.

that remained was for the courts, aided by the growing textbook tradition, to refine the theory in terms of a model of rules regarding formation (offer, acceptance, consideration and intention to create legal relations), content (condition, warranties and implied terms), and discharge (performance, agreement, breach and frustration).[129]

One might note, however, that contract was enforceable at common law not as a form of private legislation, despite the consistent emphasis during the 19th century of the doctrine of freedom of contract.[130] A failure to perform a contractual obligation was actionable as a 'cause of action'. This notion of a cause of action remains fundamental to liability: when the forms of action were abolished the categories of facts which constituted them did not disappear nor, indeed, did the actual names of the forms of action. Thus, both the categories of fact which would entitle one person to obtain a remedy from another and the name of the action survived as causes of action. "But it is essential to realise," said a judge a century later, "that when, since 1873, the name of a form of action is used to identify a cause of action, it is used as a convenient and succinct description of a particular category of factual situation which entitles one person to obtain from the court a remedy against another person."[131]

The cause of action foundation to liability is much less evident in contract because the breach of a contractual promise—and one should note that English contract law is based on the notion of promise rather than *conventio*[132]—is a cause of action in itself. In tort, however, the individual causes of action remain fundamental because the common law has never developed a general principle of wrongful liability. Indeed, such an approach was specifically rejected in the famous case of *Bradford Corporation v Pickles*[133] and the requirement of a cause of action has not, as such, been affected by the incorporation of the European Convention of Human Rights and Fundamental Freedoms into United Kingdom law.[134] Thus, in order to establish liability in tort one must still have recourse to a list of actions. A claimant is obliged to show that the facts pleaded constitute trespass, public nuisance, private nuisance, negligence, misfeasance in public office, defamation or some other tort and fail-

---

129. Ibbetson, *op.cit*, pp. 220–244.

130. *Printing and Numerical Registering Co.* v *Sampson* (1875) LR 19 Eq 462, 465.

131. Diplock LJ in *Letang v Cooper* [1965] 1 QB 232, 243.

132. Samuel, *Understanding*, *op.cit*, pp. 37–41.

133. [1895] AC 587. This case is now the subject of a whole book: M Taggart, *Private Property and Abuse of Rights in Victorian England: The Story of Edward Pickles and the Bradford Water Supply* (Oxford, Oxford University Press, 2002).

134. See *Wainwright v Home Office* [2004] 2 AC 406.

ure to plead such a cause of action might jeopardise the whole action.[135] As one leading tort lawyer asserted, tort "is what is in the tort books, and the only thing holding it together is the binding."[136] This said, such fragmentation at the level of causes of action has not prevented more theory-orientated minds from advancing taxonomical possibilities other than the alphabetic list. And it is possible to discern a shift towards general principle since 1873.[137] In particular, the tort of negligence, established as an independent cause of action in 1932,[138] has grown so rapidly that it is encroaching upon other, older established causes of action.[139] One result of this expansion is that the areas of liability without fault are becoming increasingly restricted.[140]

## *4.4. Restitution*

The terms 'contract' and 'tort' were not restricted to the case-law but were equally employed by the legislature with the result that they became formally embedded in legal thinking.[141] As a judge at the time observed, "there is no middle term; the statute supposes all actions are founded either on contract or on tort" and so "that it is tort, if not contract, contract if not tort."[142] Of course, the judges could have developed a third category of liability after 1875, but a rigid adherence to the doctrine of precedent resulted in the contract and tort dichotomy being reconfirmed by the House of Lords in 1914 as a matter of law.[143]

This duality was, of course, to prove problematic for common lawyers just as it had done for Gaius, in that there were a number of claims that could not easily be accommodated either under wrongs (tort) or under agreements (contracts). The most difficult of these claims, taxonomically speaking, were several debt actions, which were allowed where a defendant had received money from the plaintiff to which he was not entitled in situations where there was no actual contract. As Lord Atkin pointed out in 1941, "it was necessary to

---

135. *Esso Petroleum Ltd* v *Southport Corporation* [1956] AC 218. However a court now has more discretion under procedural rules than it did in 1956.

136. T Weir, *An Introduction to Tort Law* (Oxford, Oxford University Press, 2nd ed, 2006), p ix.

137. See eg *Wilkinson v Downton* [1897] 2 QB 57; *Donoghue* v *Stevenson* [1932] AC 562.

138. *Donoghue* v *Stevenson* [1932] AC 562.

139. T Weir, The Staggering March of Negligence, in P Cane & J Stapleton (eds), *The Law of Obligations: Essays in Celebration of John Fleming* (Oxford, Oxford University Press, 1998), 97.

140. See eg *Transco plc v Stockport MBC* [2004] 2 AC 1.

141. See *County Courts Act 1984* s 15(1).

142. Bramwell LJ in *Bryant v Herbert* (1877) 3 CPD 389, 390.

143. *Sinclair* v *Brougham* [1914] AC 398.

create a fictitious contract: for there was no action possible other than debt or assumpsit on the one side and action for damages for tort on the other."[144] In short, these quasi-contractual debt claims were rationalised under the principle of an implied contract. This rationalisation was, however, to prove logically problematic where money had been paid under a supposed contract that subsequently proved to be non-existent for reasons of *ultra-vires*; quasi-contractual debt claims could not be used to recover the money because all contracts, express or implied, were void.[145] In addition, it was clear that the implied contract theory was a fiction. As a result, both doctrine and the case-law in the second half of the 20th century gradually moved towards a re-conceptualisation of these quasi-contractual claims under a third category generally called 'restitution' whose indirect normative basis was the principle of unjust enrichment.[146]

The independence of restitution, however, comes with a price. First, although it is independent of contract and tort, there are many contract and tort cases that seem equally to belong to restitution. For example, contract textbooks and casebooks contain a range of cases dealing with the recovery of money, either as debts or as damages, in situations where contracts have proved to be defective for misrepresentation, duress, illegality, frustration, or whatever.[147] Equally, in the law of tort, there are cases where damages have been measured less by the claimant's loss and more by the defendant's enrichment; indeed, the property torts—in particular trespass to goods and conversion—are almost by definition 'restitutionary' in that the gist of the claim is the restoring of a benefit.[148] Secondly, the category of restitution, together with the principle of unjust enrichment, is wider than the old category of quasi-contract; there are a number of equitable (and common law) claims whose basis is more proprietary than obligational with the result that the category of restitution belongs just as much within the law of property as within the law of obligations.[149] Thirdly, it would probably be wrong to think that there is as yet a general unjust enrichment action in English law. In order to succeed a claimant must establish a cause of action and thus the rules attaching to the old quasi-contractual debt claims—and of course any equitable principles attaching to the various tracing, account or trust actions—remain of relevance. Finally,

144. *United Australia Ltd* v *Barclays Bank Ltd* [1941] AC 1, 27.
145. *Sinclair* v *Brougham* [1914] AC 398.
146. Waddams, *Dimensions*, *op.cit*, pp. 10–12.
147. *Whittaker v Campbell* [1984] QB 318, 326–327.
148. See eg *Inverugie Investments Ltd v Hackett* [1995] 1 WLR 713.
149. Waddams, *op.cit*, pp. 11, 13–14.

the law of restitution has generated a mass of doctrinal literature far out of proportion to the social importance of the subject. This has resulted not just in wasted energy but also in the production of theories, with regard both to restitution itself and to taxonomy in general,[150] that have little connection with practical reality.[151] As several sceptics have pointed out, one does not need an elaborate theory of unjust enrichment, or even an independent category of restitution, to know that a fraudster must return his ill-gotten gains.[152] A more realistic dividing line would be a remedial one between debt (including account)[153] and damages; and thus an independent category of quasi-contractual remedies (minus the implied contract theory), together of course with equitable remedies, would probably have been more suitable for the common law mind.[154] But 'contract', 'tort' and 'other remedies' are an anathema to those who think that legal categories should be scientific and that legal solutions should have logic rather than the complexities of social reality as their source.

## *4.5. Law of Obligations*

The development of an independent category of restitution seems to have been accompanied by a movement towards the generic category of a 'law of obligations.' As Stephen Waddams reminds us, when Pothier was translated into English at the beginning of the 19th century, the English readers were so unfamiliar with the idea of a law of obligations "that the translator found it necessary to add to the title, calling it *A Treatise on the Law of Obligations or Contracts*."[155] Nevertheless as a university tradition began to establish itself towards the end of the 19th century—a tradition in which Roman law was compulsory as a Bar requirement until around 1970—the generic category became increasingly familiar to English lawyers, finally receiving modern judicial

150. On this taxonomy question, see further G Samuel, English Private Law: Old and New Thinking in the Taxonomy Debate (2004) 24 *Oxford Journal of Legal Studies* 335.

151. For example, restitution lawyers have suggested that the claimant in *Bolton v Mahadeva* [1972] 1 WLR 1009, who failed to perform his contract, ought to have had an unjust enrichment claim for the partial benefit he had conferred on the defendant: see Law Commission Report No 121 (1983). Yet the rule that a contractor who fails to perform is entitled to nothing provides some real protection to consumers against 'cowboy' builders and the like. Happily, the government did not act on the Report.

152. The tort of deceit is perfectly adequate: see *Smith New Court Securities Ltd v Scrimgeour Vickers Ltd* [1997] AC 254.

153. On which see *Attorney-General v Blake* [2001] 1 AC 268.

154. On which see, generally, Waddams, *op.cit.*

155. Waddams, *op.cit*, pp. 5–6.

approval in a judgment by Lord Diplock reported in 1973.[156] The term was then taken up by several academic writers with the result that the expression finally became incorporated within professional thinking. Liability is no longer divided into contract and tort (at least in form), but into Obligations I and Obligations II.

However, the category must be treated with a great deal of caution with regard to the common law. In civilian legal science, as we have seen, the category forms part of a coherent structure in which real rights are separated from personal rights and patrimonial rights in general are distinguished from personality rights. Such a coherent scientific plan is not to be found in the common law. Indeed much of personal property law is contained in contract, tort and restitution—one need look only at the *Torts (Interference with Goods) Act 1977*—with the result that if there is an English 'law of obligations' it is not a law consisting strictly of *iura in personam*. 'Owning,' in other words, is not always distinguished from 'owing.' In addition, the law of tort contains causes of action that a civil lawyer might consider to be claims which belong more properly to the law of persons rather than the law of obligations.[157] Thus privacy and dignity, as far as they are protected in common law jurisdictions, do not enjoy some special status that distinguishes them clearly from patrimonial rights. All law, it might be said, is a matter of 'property,' using this term in its wider sense. Furthermore the actual reasoning of lawyers and judges does little to inspire taxonomical confidence. "The evidence tends to show," notes Professor Waddams after an exhaustive analysis of the case-law, "that the conclusions were not reached in either Chancery or the Queen's Bench by allocating the facts to pre-existing categories, or by reference to anything like a pre-existing map or scheme."[158] Legal concepts, legal facts and legal reasoning are much too complex for a 'law of obligations' to have much meaning for the common law.[159]

## 5. Western Law of Obligations: Comparative Conclusions

It would be idle to say that, at one level, a 'Western law of obligations' is a myth. The three main sub-categories of contract, delict (tort), and unjust en-

156. *Moschi* v *Lep Air Services Ltd* [1973] AC 331, 346.

157. For an interesting case see *Stevenson* v *Beverley Bentinck Ltd* [1976] 1 WLR 483.

158. Waddams, *op.cit*, p. 38.

159. See also G Samuel, Can the Common Law be Mapped? (2005) 55 *University of Toronto Law Journal* 271.

richment find expression across the national systems and it is proving possible to draft international codes in respect of all three. At an empirical source level, the kind of factual situations giving rise to these three forms of legal obligation are encountered in all Western states. And while one such factual situation might be conceptualised, for example, as contract in one jurisdiction and in delict in another, this merely indicates that the boundaries between the different types of obligation are fluid. Of course, this very existence of the possibility of a law of obligations across the civil and common law divide is the result of the influence, especially during the last two centuries, of Roman thinking and civilian legal science and there is little doubt that this was helped by the establishment of university law schools. This influence is probably set to continue at a doctrinal level as academics from across the EU meet to discuss various harmonising projects.[160]

Yet, as we have seen, there are also problems with trying to re-conceptualize the common law along Roman scientific lines.[161] At another level, therefore, it might be misleading to talk in terms of a law of obligations in the common law world: for it might give the impression that there is a coherent (in the civilian sense) structure underpinning English law. As Tony Weir has pointed out, "the law tends to seem seamless" because the rules of the common law have been created ad hoc and form and symmetry have been of little concern to practitioners.[162] This lack of interest in logic and maps has been re-confirmed recently by one of the common law's leading exponents, Stephen Waddams, who also makes the point, quoting Maitland, that famous distinctions from Justinian's *Institutes* have from time to time attracted English lawyers but attempts to impose them have not been very successful.[163] It is usually equity that undermines these plans, although the general methodology of common law judicial reasoning can equally ensure that conformity to some academic scheme comes to nothing. As a Law lord once pointed out, the task of the House of Lords "is to decide particular cases between litigants and your Lordships are not called upon to rationalise the law of England." Such an "attractive if perilous field may well be left to other hands to cultivate." But arguments "based on legal consistency are apt to mislead for the common law

160. See generally Hartkamp *et al* (eds), *op.cit.*

161. See further on this point G Samuel, Property and Obligations: Continental and Comparative Aspects, in A Hudson (ed), *New Perspectives on Property Law, Human Rights and the Home* (Cavendish Publishing, 2004), 295.

162. T Weir, The Common Law System, *International Encyclopedia of Comparative Law*, Volume II, Chapter 2, Part III (JCB Mohr) (Completed 1971), n° 82.

163. Waddams, *op.cit*, p. 190.

is a practical code adapted to deal with the manifold diversities of human life, and as a great American judge has reminded us, 'the life of the law has not been logic; it has been experience.'"[164] Some may well feel that these comments belong to the past, but a close reading of many recent judgments from the United Kingdom's highest court will soon indicate that academics who make such claims are possibly out-of-touch with the mentality of the common law.[165]

## References

Atiyah, P, *The Rise and Fall of Freedom of Contract* (Oxford, Oxford University Press, 1979).

Cane, P, & Stapleton, J (eds), *The Law of Obligations: Essays in Celebration of John Fleming* (Oxford, Oxford University Press, 1998).

Gordley, J, *The Philosophical Origins of Modern Contract Doctrine* (Oxford, Oxford University Press, 1991).

Gordley, J, Contract in Pre-Commercial Societies and in Western History, *International Encyclopedia of Comparative Law*, Volume VII, Chapter 2 (JCB Mohr, 1997).

Ibbetson, D, *A Historical Introduction to the Law of Obligations* (Oxford, Oxford University Press, 1999).

Jolowicz, H, *Roman Foundations of Modern Law* (Oxford, Oxford University Press, 1957).

Kaser, M, *Divisio Obligationum*, in P Stein & A Lewis, *Studies in Justinian's Institutes in memory of J A C Thomas* (London, Sweet & Maxwell, 1983), 73.

Legrand, P, & Samuel, G, *Introduction au common law* (Paris, La Découverte, 2008).

Lévy, J-P, *Histoire des obligations* (Paris, Montchrestien, 1978).

Lévy, J-P & Castaldo, A, *Histoire du droit civil* (Paris, Dalloz, 2002).

Lobban, M, *The Common Law and English Jurisprudence 1760–1850* (Oxford, Oxford University Press, 1991).

Ourliac, P & De Malafosse, J, *Histoire du droit privé 1/Les Obligations* (Paris, Presses Universitaires de France, 2nd ed., 1969).

Ourliac, P & De Malafosse, J, *Histoire du droit privé 2/Les Biens* (Paris, Presses Universitaires de France, 2nd ed., 1971).

164. Lord Macmillan in *Read* v *J Lyons & Co* [1947] AC 156, 175.

165. See for example Lord Steyn in *Att-Gen v Blake* [2001] 1 AC 268, 292.

Rampelberg, R-M, *Repères romains pour le droit européen des contrats* (Paris, LGDJ, 2005).

Rudden, B, The Domain of Contract: English Report, in Harris, D & Tallon, D (eds), *Contract Law Today: Anglo-French Comparisons* (Oxford, Oxford University Press, 1989), 81.

Rudden, B, Torticles (1991–92) 6/7 *Tulane Civil Law Forum* 105.

Samuel, G, *Contract Law: Cases and Materials* (London, Sweet & Maxwell, 2007).

Samuel, G, *Tort: Cases and Materials* (London, Sweet & Maxwell, 2nd ed, 2008).

Samuel, G, Property and Obligations: continental and comparative perspectives, in Hudson, A (ed), *New Perspectives on Property Law, Human Rights and the Home* (London, Cavendish, 2003), 295.

Samuel, G, *Understanding Contractual and Tortious Obligations* (Exeter, Law Matters Publishing, 2005).

Stein, P The Development of the Institutional System, in P Stein & A Lewis, *Studies in Justinian's Institutes in memory of J A C Thomas* (London, Sweet & Maxwell, 1983), 151.

Stein, P, *Legal Institutions: The Development of Dispute Settlement* (London, Butterworths, 1984).

Terré, F, Simler, P & Lequette, Y, *Droit civil: Les Obligations* (Paris, Dalloz, 8th ed., 2002).

Waddams, S (2003), *Dimensions of Private Law: Categories and Concepts in Anglo-American Legal Reasoning* (Cambridge, Cambridge University press, 2003).

Weir, T, Contracts in Rome and England (1992) 66 *Tulane Law Review* 1615.

Weir, T, The Staggering March of Negligence, in Cane & Stapleton (*supra*), 97.

Weir, T, *An Introduction to Tort Law* (Oxford, Oxford University Press, 2nd ed, 2006).

Weir, T, *A Casebook on Tort* (Sweet & Maxwell, 10th ed., 2004).

Zimmermann, R, *The Law of Obligations* (Oxford, Oxford University Press, 1996).

Zweigert, K, & Kötz, H, *An Introduction to Comparative Law* (Oxford, Oxford University Press, 3rd ed., 1998; trans T Weir).

6

# Western Law of Contract

Carla Sieburgh[1]


## Summary

1. Introduction, 1.1. Life of Contract—2. General Remarks, 2.1. Contracts and the Public Order of the European Union, 2.2. Five Principles, 2.3. The Purpose of Principles, 2.4. Shift of Emphasis—3. Freedom of Contract, 3.1. Substantive Freedom of Contract, 3.2. Freedom of Contract and Contractual Altruism, 3.3. Inequality in Exchange, Iustum Pretium, Causa, Consideration, Unconscionability, 3.4. Formalities, 3.5. Enforceability of Promises, 3.6. Discussion, 3.7. Freedom of Contract and Other Principles—4. Reliance Principle—5. Pacta Sunt Servanda—6. Societal Justice, 6.1. Good Faith, 6.2. Good Faith as a Combination of Principles, 6.3. Equality in Exchange 6.4. Societal Justice and Other Principles—7. Social Conformity, 7.1. Unenforceability, Restitution and Damages, 7.2. Discussion—8. Epilogue—References


## 1. Introduction

Law is a product of mankind and its object is mankind. Its close relation to society is a strong point of the law. However, the fact that law is, like its object, relatively unpredictable has often been regarded as its weak point. To control uncertainty, lawyers have been looking for save harbours—embodied either as firm, overriding principles or as fundamental doubts with regard to whatever principle.

1. Professor of Private Law, University of Nijmegen.

The path of Contract Law can be regarded as a distinctive expression of this tendency. After the practical approach of Roman law and, in the beginning, common law,[2] several theoretical directions have been and are being chosen. Many of these theories aim at explaining the law of contract in terms of one underpinning principle or paradigm.

In the sixteenth century, contract law was explained in terms of liberality (giving resources away sensibly) and commutative justice (exchanging resources of equivalent value, so that neither party was enriched at the expense of the other).[3] The liberal approach in the nineteenth century stressed the will theory, framed into the principle of contractual freedom. Since these principles and concepts have not been and still are not able to explain contract law in its entirety, other principles have been put forward. Sometimes presented as brand new, many of these theories go back to ideas found in Greek philosophy and/or to the approach chosen by scholastics and natural lawyers.[4] Examples of these are the objective theory that focuses on the factual consequences of making promises, the reliance theory, and the ideas of fairness and distributive justice amongst citizens.

The interrelationship between these theories emerges when one realises that in order to uphold the aim of any of these single theories it is necessary to uphold others. Nobody is able to act freely in a world that does not recognize the need of parties to be able to rely on the conduct of others. Freedom of contract is a vain concept when parties to a contract cannot rely on each other's actions. For comparable reasons, the idea of freedom of contract relates the law of contract to the law in general and to society as a whole. Without a stable society that is founded upon fundamental values, freedom of contract cannot be exercised. This shows that principles like societal justice and social conformity are of equal importance for a healthy law of contract.[5]

History has brought us several principles of contract law. None of them is able to explain and underpin the entire body of contract law. On the contrary, often a certain solution can be explained by reference to apparently contradictory doctrines. On the other hand, a specific doctrine can be the foundation for two different, contradictory solutions. The aim of a theory of con-

---

2. See *retro*, Chapter n. 2, par. 4, by G. Samuel.

3. J. Gordley, *The Enforceability of Promises in European Contract Law* (Cambridge 2001), 4.

4. J. Gordley, *The Philosophical Origins of Modern Contract Doctrine* (Oxford 1991) pass., by example 231, 232.

5. The interrelationship of several principles of contract law and the effect thereof for various parts of contract law has been extensively elaborated by E.M. Belser, *Freiheit und Gerechtigkeit im Vertragsrecht* (Fribourg 2000). See for a general discussion on weighing principles R. Alexy, *Theorie der Grundrechte*, (Baden-Baden 1985), 342.

tract law is to find the most important principles and to use them as a means to analyze a legal problem and to reach solutions that approach contractual justice (in German "*Vertragsgerechtigkeit*"), taking into account circumstances of time and society.[6] Trying to reach contractual justice enables contract law to both support and control agreements.

The aim of modern contract theories is not to press every solution found in legal practice into a theory. A theory should be of help for practice, to come to solutions that connect with other solutions and with the actual situation in society. Theories provide us with a common ground of thought and explanations rather than with logically compelling solutions and answers. Consequently, contractual justice ("*Vertragsgerechtigkeit*") is in my view not another principle of contract law, but an aim that can be strived for. To achieve that goal, knowledge about principles of contract law can be of assistance. Like law in general, contract law is an open and dynamic system. Contractual justice is the "preliminary" result of a discursive process that, given ever-changing societal circumstances, will remain uncompleted.[7]

## *1.1. Life of Contract*

During the last decade, contract law has been subject to quintessential debates. In 1974, Gilmore proclaimed the Death of Contract.[8] In 1979, Atiyah described the Rise and, according to his opinion today more importantly, the Fall of Contract Law.[9] In 1991, Gordley made a comprehensive summary: "In the twentieth century, will theories fell from favour and courts were more explicitly concerned with fairness. Nevertheless, we have not seen another great rethinking of the principles behind the civil law, as happened in the sixteenth/seventeenth and nineteenth centuries. It is not surprising, then, that when problems of fairness arise that the old doctrines do not address, there are two alternatives: to have recourse to blurry doctrines that say little more than that a contract should be fair, or to turn the problem over to draftsmen who can frame particular rules to deal with a specific situation. So it will re-

6. H. Kötz, *Europäisches Vertragsrecht I* (Tübingen 1996), 15

7. Compare in general wording H.L.A. Hart, *The Concept of Law* (Oxford 1961), 124; K. Larenz, *Methodenlehre der Rechtswissenschaft* (Berlin 1975), 161; R. Alexy, *Begriff und Geltung des Rechts* (Freiburg 1992), 117–120; Asser-Scholten, *Algemeen deel* 2nd ed. (Zwolle 1934), 102–103; Asser-Vranken, *Algemeen Deel* ** (Zwolle 1995), 141. Compare in relation to contracts J. Gordley, *Enforcing Promises, California Law Review* 2 (1995), 614.

8. G. Gilmore, *The Death of Contract* (Columbus, Ohio 1974), 3: "We are told that Contract, like God, is death. And so it is."

9. P. Atiyah, *The Rise and Fall of Freedom of Contract* (Oxford 1979).

main, perhaps, until the next time a systematic effort is made to bring theoretical coherence to private law."[10]

Gordley's description implies that contract is still alive. At the same time, it draws contract theory as degenerated into a lamentable potpourri of old and dusty, incoherent principles. Gordley may be right with respect to the situation in the twentieth century. Scholars were busy to overcome the pressure of the will doctrine and to sort out an appropriate equilibrium. At the beginning of the twenty-first century, however, the situation in Europe is changing. Private law scholars, particularly contract law scholars, are confronted with new developments. As will be seen the influence of the European Union on private law is gaining importance. Provisions originally regarded as being of a public law nature penetrate the private sphere. The task of today's private law doctrine is to gear contract law towards this changing situation.

The integration of public and private law is not unique to Europe,[11] but for the European contract law debate it will be the main issue in the nearest future.[12] It is in this light that twenty-first century contract law (and private law) needs fundamental rethinking. On the one hand, because the focus of private law will change, on the other because private law will only survive the development towards integration with public law if it is able to combine the preservation of its essential features with adjustments to the requirements of society in general. The emphasis must shift from a continuation of the discussion on principles of contract law which concern the internal relationship of parties to the development of the principle of contract law that concerns the external relationship between parties and society: the principle of social conformity (see hereafter par. 7).

# 2. General Remarks

## *2.1. Contracts and the Public Order of the European Union*

The most general and common shared basis of present (Western) European contract law is to be found in the European Community Treaty (TEC) and the

10. Gordley, *Enforceability of Promises*, 374.

11. Atiyah, *Rise and Fall*, 726; C. Dalton, *Deconstructing Contract Doctrine*, *Yale Law Journal* 94 (1985), passim.

12. See A.S. Hartkamp and C.H. Sieburgh, *De invloed van het Europese recht op het Nederlandse privaatrecht: een korte verkenning*, in A.S. Hartkamp, C.H. Sieburgh and L.A.D. Keus (eds.), *De invloed van het Europese recht op het Nederlandse privaatrecht* (Deventer 2007). See for European Consumer Law *infra* Chapter 19 par. 2, by T. Wilhelmsson, G. Howells and H. W. Micklitz.

European Union Treaty (TEU). This is not only true for the provisions that directly concern contract law, e.g. Articles 81 and 82 TEC. At least as important is the common legal background created by TEC and TEU.[13] In its Article 2, TEC promotes the establishment of a common market and an economic and monetary union. According to Article 3, one of the ways to achieve that goal is to abolish obstacles to the free movement of goods, persons, services, and capital. Establishing a common market is one of the means to promote even more ambitious aims such as a harmonious, balanced and sustainable development of economic activities, a high level of employment and of social protection, equality between men and women, sustainable and non-inflationary growth, a high degree of competitiveness and convergence of economic performance, a high level of protection and improvement of the quality of life, and economic and social cohesion and solidarity among Member States. The other means to attain these aims are the implementation of common policies or activities referred to in Articles 3 and 4 TEC. Amongst these policies and activities are, besides those that refer specifically to the common market, 1) the strengthening of economic and social cohesion, 2) a policy in the sphere of the environment (see also Article 6 TEC), 3) the promotion of research and technological development, 4) a contribution to the attainment of a high level of health protection, 5) a contribution to quality education and training and to the flowering of the cultures of the Member States, 6) a policy in the sphere of development cooperation, 7) a contribution to the strengthening of consumer protection (see also Article 153), and 8) measures within the sphere of energy, civil protection and tourism.

It is clear that bringing about free competition in accordance with Articles 81 and 82 TEC and the policies and activities referred to in Articles 3 and 4 TEC require measures emanating from public authorities. It is this public background that inevitably has effects on the law of contract. Even though Articles 3 and 4 do not produce direct effect, they invade private law. The requirements set by the treaties can only be met if Member States control contracts concluded within their borders in conformity with these requirements. For instance, it is not possible to meet the ideal of environmental protection if acts of private parties, including contracts concluded between them, are not controlled as to their compliance with these ideals.[14] In other words,

---

13. See S. Vogenauer, *Eine gemeineuropäische Methodenlehre des Recht—Plädoyer und Programm*, *Zeitschrift für Europäisches Privatrecht* 2 (2005), 253, 254; R. Schulze, *European Private Law and Existing EC Law*, *European Review of Private Law* (2005), 9,10.

14. See C.H. Sieburgh, *Het Europese gemeenschapsrecht en het Nederlandse buiten-contractuele aansprakelijkheidsrecht*, in A.S. Hartkamp, C.H. Sieburgh and L.A.D. Keus (eds.), *De invloed van het Europese recht op het Nederlandse privaatrecht* (Deventer 2007).

the provisions of TEC and TEU are determinative for the public order of the Member States. According to the precautionary principle, Member States are required to take appropriate measures to prevent specific potential risks to public health, safety and the environment.[15] Moreover, the provisions of the TEC and TEU have effects on open norms of national private law like public policy, good faith, and duty of care. Even if a controlling doctrine uses these instruments of private law, the substantive ground for the exercised control depends on the public background against which it is carried out. Due to both mechanisms the provisions of TEC and TEU set prerequisites for the contents of contracts.[16]

Whereas the influence of public law on contract law in this area is very clear, it is not unique for contracts that fall within the scope of the influence of European law. Controlling contracts within the Member States has always had public aspects. As Kötz has put it: "All legal systems reserve the right to declare a contract void if it is legally or morally offensive, contrary to public policy or "*ordre public*" or involves the commission of an unlawful act."[17] An example of a field in which we have already become used to the effects of public values on the framework of private law is fundamental rights. A contract that has been concluded in mutual freedom but which endangers a fundamental right can, according to the different national laws for instance, be avoidable, null and void, unenforceable, or it can be of no effect (hereafter I use "unenforceable" and "unenforceability" as general terms referring also to more specific doctrines like voidness, voidableness, nullity, invalidity and being of no effect). Often, unenforceability is based on open norms of private law like good faith and public policy. In its Pla decision,[18] the ECHR held that the interpretation by a national court of a testamentary disposition was discriminatory pursuant to Articles 14 and 8 ECHR. The interpretation by the national court had been made in the light of the social conditions which existed at the time when the will was made (1939) and at the time of the testatrix's death (1949). According to the ECHR, a national court cannot ignore the profound

---

15. See K. Lenaerts and P. Van Nuffel, *Constitutional Law of the European Union*, 2nd ed., (London 2005), no. 17-070.

16. See Hartkamp and Sieburgh, *De invloed van het Europese recht op het Nederlandse privaatrecht*.

17. Kötz, in H. Beale, A. Hartkamp, H. Kötz and D. Tallon, (eds.), *Contract Law. Cases, Materials and Text* (Oxford 2002), 295. See also Kötz, *Europäisches Vertragsrecht*, 235 and Lando, O., *CISG and Its Followers: A Proposal to Adopt Some International Principles of Contract Law, American Journal of Comparative Law* 2 (2005), 387 who refers to PECL Article 1:102 and 1:103, UPICC Article 1.4.

18. ECJ 13 July 2004, Case of Pla and Puncernau vs Andorra, no. 69498/01. Compare ECJ 12 June 2004, Case of Van Kück vs Germany, no. 35968/97.

social, economic, and legal changes that have occurred when it interprets the will in 1996, when the estate of the testatrix passed to the heirs. Even though the Court stressed that the testatrix's free will was not at issue, the method of interpretation prescribed by the ECHR results in an interpretation of the will that, taking into consideration the realities of 1939 and 1949, most probably never has been intended by the testatrix. Even though this decision did not concern a contract but a unilateral juridical act, it results in policing the free will of a party according to the present approach toward fundamental rights. The fundamental rights as a common background[19] to today's Western contract law are to be found in Article 6 TEU,[20] the Charter of Fundamental Rights of the European Union (the Nice Charter)[21] and the Draft Treaty amending the Treaty on European Union and the Treaty establishing the European Community[22] (hereafter the Draft Reform Treaty) and

---

19. Even though it is subject to debate whether these provisions provide citizens (and so contracting parties) directly and/or indirectly with rights towards each other, it is clear that at least through the general concepts of private law the principles laid down in these provisions permeate private law. See *infra* Chapter 7 par. 1 by N. Reich and N. Reich, *The tripartite function of modern contract law in Europe: Enablement, regulation, information*, in F. Werro and Th. Probst, *Le droit privé Suisse face au droit communautaire européen* (Berne 2004), 153 ff and D. Coester-Waltjes, *Constitutional Aspects of Party Autonomy and Its Limits—The Perspective of Law*, in: S. Grundmann, W. Kerber & S. Weatherill (eds.), *Party Autonomy and the Role of Information in the internal Market* (Berlin 2001), 43, 45; P. C. Müller-Graff, *EC Directives as a Means of Private Law Unification*, in A. Hartkamp et. al. (eds.), *Towards a European Civil Code*, 3rd rev. ed. (Nijmegen 2004), 77 ff.

20. Article 6 TEU: 1.The Union is founded on the principles of liberty, democracy, respect for human rights and fundamental freedoms, and the rule of law, principles which are common to the Member States.

2. The Union shall respect fundamental rights, as guaranteed by the European Convention for the Protection of Human Rights and Fundamental Freedoms signed in Rome on 4 November 1950 and as they result from the constitutional traditions common to the Member States, as general principles of Community law.

3. The Union shall respect the national identities of its Member States.

4. The Union shall provide itself with the means necessary to attain its objectives and carry through its policies.

21. Preambule: "Conscious of its spiritual and moral heritage, the Union is founded on the indivisible, universal values of human dignity, freedom, equality and solidarity; it is based on the principles of democracy and the rule of law. It places the individual at the heart of its activities, by establishing the citizenship of the Union and by creating an area of freedom, security and justice."

22. The importance for relations governed by private law of the Draft Treaty establishing a Constitution for Europe that has not become effective is shown by T. Tridimas, *The General Principles of EU Law*, 2nd ed. (Oxford 2006), 15: "These values (the values reflected in Article 2 Constitution) have declaratory character and represent the EU legal order as it

the European Convention for the Protection of Human Rights and Fundamental Freedoms (ECHR).[23]

It will be clear that a reference to notions like protection of the weaker party, solidarity, altruism, welfarism, and/or regard and fairness is not sufficient to meet the goals set by the TEC, the TEU, the Nice Charter, and the Draft Reform Treaty and the ECHR. The spirit of these treaties is not only to regulate relations between parties but, in my opinion at least as important, also to regulate the interrelationship of parties and the society in which they conclude their contracts. This aspect of contract law is not concerned with the question whether the relationship between parties meets standards of party-bound solidarity. It concerns the question whether the relationship complies with the general rules and values of society. Therefore it is a means to check how parties to a contract relate to society in general. It creates the possibility to uphold overarching values that relate to the characteristics and fundamental values of society rather than to the characteristics of the contracting parties.[24] For example, the ECJ held in the cases Courage vs Crehan and Manfredi vs Lloyd Adriatico[25] that agreements which are prohibited pursuant to Article 81 TEC are automatically void and that "the principle of automatic nullity can be relied on by anyone", both the parties to the contract and others. The purpose of this remedy of Community law is to uphold the full effectiveness of a fundamental Treaty provision like Article 81 TEC and the maintenance of effective competition in the Community.

## *2.2. Five Principles*

In this chapter, the aims set by the TEC and TEU, the Nice Charter, and the Draft Reform Treaty, and the ECHR and the underlying grounds for many

---

currently stands." and 16: "A concept which is of particular relevance in this context is the concept of 'solidarity'. This transcends the relations between the individual and the State and refers to a sense of community. According to Bogdandy, it embodies an aspiration to make life better, 'to create new bonds' and 'the social basis for a broader polity in which the individual acts as a responsible social being'." See also M. Hesselink, *The Horizontal Effect of Social Rights in European Contract Law*, in M.W. Hesselink et. al. (eds.), *Privaatrecht tussen autonomie en solidariteit* (The Hague 2003), 120.

23. Compare PECL Article 15:101, TEU Article 6.

24. H. Collins, *A Workers'Civil Code? Principles of European Contract Law Evolving in EU Social and Economy Policy*, in: M. Hesselink (ed.), *The Politics of a European Civil Code* (The Hague 2006), 55 ff. emphasizes the possibility for a Civil Code that provides citizens with social, economic and cultural rights. He does not, however, discuss the attitude of citizens towards a society that provides them with those rights and is supposed to uphold the possibility to keep on providing all citizens with those rights.

25. ECJ 20 September 2001, C-453/99 (Courage/Crehan), *Jurispr.* I-6297; ECJ 13 July 2006, C-295/04-C-298/04 (Manfredi/Lloyd Adriatico), not yet published.

of the contractual theories and practices in the Member States are expressed by five guiding principles:[26] the principle of contractual freedom, the reliance principle, the principle of *pacta sunt servanda* (binding force of promises), the principle of societal justice, and the principle of social conformity.

It must be noted that both the European Commission[27] and the European Parliament (in its report of 23 February 2006)[28] highlight the principle of freedom of contract as the starting point and red thread for the entire discussion on a Common Frame of Reference for contract law. Nevertheless, it is debatable how literally this statement should be taken. Taking the principle of freedom of contract as the first and main principle of contract law does not comply with the taxonomy of Community and Union law; not only because the principle of freedom of contract is not able to cover the entire relationship between parties,[29] but also because it does not sufficiently cover the relationship between parties and society.[30] Not all the aims set by the European Union would be covered under the primacy of contractual freedom.[31] Moreover, fo-

26. Lando, *CISG and Its Followers*, distinguishes 8 principles: 1. substantive freedom of contract, 2. you shall keep your bargain (pacta sunt servanda), 3. informality, 4. the unilateral promise should be binding, 5. good faith and fair dealing, 6. reliance, 7. the "reasonably foreseeable" test, 8. proportionality, whereas K. P. Berger, *The Creeping Codification of the Lex Mercatoria* (The Hague 1999), distinguishes 78 principles and Kötz, *Europäisches Vertragsrecht*, 11 distinghuishes 4 principles: Autonomie, Fairnessgebot, Vertrauensschutzprinzip, Risikoverteilung. See also M.J. Bonell, *An International Restatement of Contract Law. The UNIDROIT Principles of International Commercial Contracts* (Artsley, 2005), 87 ff, who distinguishes with regard to the Unidroit Principles five "Basic Ideas": Freedom of Contract, Openness to usages, *Favor contractus*, Observance of good faith and fair dealing in international trade, Policing against unfairness.

27. Action Plan on Contract Law (COM (2003) 68), Communication of 11 October 2004 (COM (2004) 651), First Annual Progress report of 23 September 2005 (COM (2005) 456).

28. Report on European contract law and the revision of the acquis: the way forward (2005/2022(INI), A6-0055/2006 of 23 March 2006).

29. Which is the main critique produced by the Study Group on Social Justice in European Private Law, *Social Justice in a European Contract Law: a Manifesto, European Law Journal* 10 (2004), p. 653-674. The Manifesto emphasizes that principles which respect other equally important demands for social solidarity, which prohibit individuals from taking advantage of superior economic strength or from ignoring the claims of justified reliance upon others have to be balanced with the weight attached to individual private autonomy as expressed in the idea of freedom of contract. See 656, 661.

30. See Atiyah, *Rise and Fall*, 736.

31. See also B. Heiderhoff, *Vertrauen versus Vertragsfreiheit im europäischen Verbrauchervertragsrecht, Zeitschrift für Europäisches Privatrecht* (2003), 769 ff and Manifesto, 665 ff.

cusing on just this principle would run counter to all efforts by scholars in the past and to a widely shared common understanding that contract law cannot be founded on just one principle.[32] It would unacceptably simplify private law reasoning.[33]

Even the fact that (national) codifications usually work with general rules and exceptions to those rules, is not a convincing argument to put forward the proposition that such a codification, when regarded in its entire context, heralds just the principle that underpins the general rule. The combination of general rule and exception is a drafting necessity rather than that it shows an ideological preference for one single principle. Especially legal practice supports this view. Solutions that are in line with the needs of parties and of society result from balancing several principles that underpin both the general rule and its exception. This leads many times to the (equally fruitless) theoretical proposition that the exception is or should be the general rule.

## *2.3. The Purpose of Principles*

In order to understand differences in contract laws of Western European countries, it is useful to know which concerns are shared and which are the principles that have given birth to several different doctrines. I realize that the quest for commonalities can be dangerous. In the end, it might enable us to diagnose every difference as a similarity. However, without a recognisable framework the uniqueness of a single difference gets lost in a morass of incomprehension. Moreover, several comparative studies show that the importance of differences should not be exaggerated. Phrased by Beale: "... it is remarkable to what extent the civil law systems do in fact reach similar results to the common law. Perhaps this should not surprise us: the needs of an effective legal framework for the use of resources in producing goods and services will be essentially the same in every society of a given type."[34]

---

32. Gordley, *Philosophical Origins*, 230, 244; F. Kessler, G. Gilmore, A.T. Kronman, *Contracts. Cases and Materials*, 3rd ed. (Boston 1986), 14–15; Atiyah, *Rise and Fall*, 5; Kötz, *Europäisches Vertragsrecht*, 11; F. Bydlinski, *Fundamentale Rechtsgrundsätze. Zur rechtsethischen Verfassung der Societät* (Wien 1988), 320.

33. F. Bydlinski, *System und Principien des Privatrechts* (Wien 1996), 95, 96.

34. H.G. Beale, W.D. Bishop, and M.P. Furmston, *Contract. Cases and Materials*, 3rd ed. (London 1995), 9; A.S. Hartkamp, *Modernisation and Harmonisation of Contract Law: Objectives, Methods and Scope, Uniform Law Review* 1/2 (2003), 83. See also B. Fages, *Einige neuere Entwicklungen des französischen algemeinen Vertragsrecht im Lichte der Grundregeln der Lado-Kommision, Zeitschrift für Europäisches Privatrecht* (2003), 517.

When doctrines differ, solutions can still be the same. When solutions differ, they can go back to the same doctrines and the same concerns. In that case the difference is rather a matter of choice than of principle. This is the reason why this chapter takes as starting point five principles of contract law that in history have been and still are regarded as the devices that enable us to balance different circumstances from different viewpoints in order to reach a result that is regarded in the relevant society and circumstances as contractual justice (*Vertragsgerechtigkeit*).

The five guiding principles represent the different aspects of a contract: a contract as a means to develop oneself according to one's own wishes and possibilities, a contract as a way to communicate with other people resulting in a binding agreement, a contract as a responsibility between parties, a contract as a possibility and a need for two or more people to relate to society as a whole and reciprocally as a necessity for society to control the exercise of the possibility to conclude contracts.

Although it is inevitable to discuss these principles separately, they can only give constructive insights when we consider their interrelationship. The function of these principles can be traced back to the two main functions of the law of contract: support and control.[35]

## 2.4. Shift of Emphasis

During the discussion of these principles sometimes reference will be made to several concepts used in the national laws of contract. However, I merely intend to provide some input for a shift in the doctrinal debate. Rather than arguing about the utmost refinement of the equilibrium between contractual freedom, reliance and societal justice, private lawyers should be prepared for the century to come. The important issues are where public and private meet. Contract doctrine should consider how it should be dealt with in a discussion not confined to private law. What are the elements and aspects that are crucial and should be retained, and which require special care and attention? What concepts and techniques can be used to integrate private and public law? What are the legal consequences of using private law techniques in a field that is not

35. Beale, Hartkamp, Kotz and Tallon (eds.), *Contract Law. Cases, Materials and Text*, 6, 7. Reich, *The tripartite function of modern contract law in Europe*, 145 ff. recognises three functions: enablement, regulation and information. The subjects that are discussed by Reich under the heading "information" do have aspects of enablement and/or regulation. For that reason, I do not mention "information" as a separate function of the law of contract.

merely governed by private law? How can an approach be developed that provides for well-integrated legal consequences?

## 3. Freedom of Contract

The importance of the principle of freedom of contract is not a subject of discussion, neither in contract law practice nor in theory. The principle of contractual freedom is logically related to the ideas of free will and of self responsibility that are necessary prerequisites for the structure of (modern) Western society.[36] Core points of discussion are whether the principle of contractual freedom requires parties to be formally or substantively free and whether next to the principle of freedom of contract other (partially) contradicting principles have to be distinguished, and, if so, whether these principles are equally important as the principle of freedom of contract. Roughly, two lines of thought can be distinguished. The first considers the principle of contractual autonomy as dominant. Often this approach goes together with a formal interpretation of the principle of contractual freedom. Contract law supports the freedom of parties if it is treated as a means to enforce their agreements, irrespective of the substance of those agreements. It stresses the right of the party who wants to have the contract enforced. The principle of societal justice is the ground for exceptions. The second considers the principles of contractual freedom and of societal justice (also phrased as altruism, contractual solidarity, social contract law, welfarist contract law, and principle of regard and fairness)[37] as equally important. Often this approach goes together with a substantive interpretation of the principle of contractual freedom. Contract law supports the mutual freedom of parties if it substantively policies their agreements in accordance with fairness and reasonableness. It stresses the interest of parties to be only bound to a contract that (objectively) can be regarded as a fair result of negotiations. The party who wants to have the contract enforced can only invoke his expectations if they are objectively justified.

36. N. Reich, *Understanding EU Law* (Antwerp 2003), 255, 263, 264 shows that freedom of contract is a fundamental right in the sense of Article 6 TEU.

37. B. Lurger, *The "Social" Side of Contract Law and the New Principle of Regard and Fairness*, in A. Hartkamp et. al. (eds.), *Towards a European Civil Code*, 3rd rev. ed. (Nijmegen 2004), 285, 286; T. Wilhelmsson, *Literatur, Lurger, Brigitta: Grundfragen der Vereinheitlichung des Vertragsrechts in der Europäischen Union*, Wien, New York: Springer 2002, *RabelsZeitung* 70 (2006), 612.

To be protected, reliance on performance has to be substantial and not just formal.

It is striking that discussions about the place and substance of the principle of freedom of contract focus time and again on the nineteenth century approach that emphasized, as a continuation of the will theory, the need for formal freedom. Less attention is paid to the fact that before, after, and even during the nineteenth century,[38] always counterbalancing doctrines have been employed to ensure substantive freedom of contract. To understand modern contract law, it is important to realise that both legal practice and doctrine strive for substantive freedom. Differences in place and time are to be explained by differences in valuation of various principles rather than by ignoring their existence.[39]

Substantive freedom can be reached by construing the principle of contractual freedom in a substantive way, putting this principle into perspective by reference to other principles, or a combination of both.

### *3.1. Substantive Freedom of Contract*

Substantive freedom of contract presupposes that a party who concludes a contract is aware of the situation it enters into and is able to choose on the basis of this knowledge to enter into the contract. Lack of awareness or knowledge (information) or ability to choose (either due to internal factors such as minority and mental disturbance or due to external factors like duress, fraud, threats, abuse of circumstances) can create circumstances in which a party is not able to act in substantive freedom.[40] With regard to this, Gordley distinguishes between two kinds of autonomy: the party's decision to exchange or not at a given price because he believes he will receive something of greater value to him than what he is to give in return (a minimum condition for the exchange to occur) and the decision of a party whether he can receive a better deal.[41] Deciding about the conditions on which one wants to exchange presupposes the ability to decide. Ignorance or necessity block the last aspect of autonomy.

---

38. Gordley, *Enforceability of Promises*, 9.

39. That differences in valuation of principles nevertheless have important consequences is pointed out by T. Wilhelmson, *Varieties of Welfarism in European Contract Law*, *European Law Journal* 6 (2004), 712–733.

40. See *infra*, Chapter n. 19, par. 6.1, by T. Wilhemsson; Reich, *The tripartite function of modern contract law*, 163, 164.

41. J. Gordley, *Equality in Exchange*, *California Law Review* 6 (1981), 1617, 1618, 1622.

In order to guarantee that the basic right to freedom retains its significance, both inside and outside the principle of contractual freedom, some guiding concepts have been proposed in practice and legal literature.

A party who, due to incapacity, is not internally free to enter into a contract is entitled to invoke this incapacity. This part of substantive freedom of contract is hardly subject to debate.[42] It is subject to more discussion whether a party should take care of its own substantive freedom (*caveat emptor*) or whether he may expect the other party to (partially) take into consideration its need for substantive freedom. In this context, status and capacity of parties play an important role. When one party has more relevant knowledge, it can be expected to inform the other party especially when that party is less able to collect relevant information.

Moreover a party must have a real choice whether or not to enter into the contract (with regard to entering into the contract, with regard to the other party and with regard to the substance of the contract). Freedom of choice is questionable if a party is dependent on the other party or on the performance to be rendered by the other party. Due to inequality of bargaining power, substantive freedom of contract comes into question.

It should be mentioned that civil law systems are more willing to construe the principle of contractual freedom substantively than the common law is. This is caused by significant differences between (the purpose of) common law and civil law systems, and by a different conception of the role of the judge toward the law and the role of the judge towards the parties. Whereas a judge in civil law systems will not hesitate to construe a contract according to what is supposed to be objectively reasonable to create just solutions and to avoid "unjust" solutions, a common law judge avoids to interfere with the literal interpretation of contracts. Due to its important position in business relations, according to the common law of contracts the principles of certainty and predictability prevail over the principle of good faith and fair dealing.[43]

---

42. M. Fabre-Magnan and R. Sefton-Green, *Defects on Consent in Contract Law*, in A. Hartkamp et. al. (eds.), *Towards a European Civil Code*, 3rd rev. ed. (Nijmegen 2004), 399–414; Beale, Hartkamp, Kötz and Tallon (eds.), *Contract Law. Cases, Materials and Text*, Chapter 3.2 (fraud, mistake, misrepresentation) and Chapter 3.3 (threats, abuse of circumstances).

43. G. Cordero Moss, *International Contracts between Common Law and Civil Law: Is Non-state Law to Be Preferred? The Difficulty of Interpreting Legal Standards Such as Good Faith, Global Jurist* 7 (2007), 1–13, 35–38; B. Fauvarque-Cosson, *La confiance légitime et l'estoppel*, in K. Boele Woelki & S. van Erp, *General Reports of the XVIIth Congress of the International Academy of Comparative Law* (Utrecht 2007), 139.

### 3.2. Freedom of Contract and Contractual Altruism

Apart from protection of freedom of contract in cases of inequality of informational power or bargaining power between parties, contract law has a long history as a means to interfere in cases that are characterized by inequality in exchange. Several concepts, doctrines, and theories presuppose a lack of substantive contractual freedom behind the inequality in exchange.

Many theories (inequality of bargain, *causa*, consideration, unconscionability, *laesio enormis*, *iustum pretium*, formalities), which have been developed in a number of countries and seem to be an obstacle to regard national contract laws as interchangeable, are concerned with situations in which one party promises to perform towards the other without getting something in return or in which no objective balance exists in the exchange between parties. The common idea behind these theories seems to be that in private law[44] it is less probable that parties who are able to decide in full freedom relate to each other in a sphere of altruism. Liberality does not mean "merely giving recourses away, but giving them away sensibly."[45] As soon as a contract is not understandable from an economic point of view, it is liable to be tested against one of these theories. The deeper rationale appears to be that a party, when concluding a contract to its own detriment, lacks autonomy.

It is not surprising that theories like inequality of bargain, *causa*, consideration, unconscionability, *laesio enormis*, *iustum pretium* and formalities have created considerable problems, both theoretical and practical. This is not due to the fact that they try to police an unbalanced exchange[46] but rather to the fact that they try to explain the interference with the contract by referring to an underlying lack of contractual freedom.

It is, for instance, not clear why a party that in substantive freedom decides to enter into a contract that for him is economically detrimental and accordingly makes its promise towards the receiver does not bind itself. Why should it be entitled, when asked to perform, to factually come back on its (deliberately made) promise? Equally unclear is why parties should be precluded from the certainty of being legally bound. Since theories that presuppose a lack of contractual freedom for reasons of economic inequality in exchange are able to undermine substantive contractual freedom, they have been heavily criti-

44. Hesitations towards altruism as a source for obligations exist also outside contract law. See on altruism, negotiorum gestio and negligence J. Kortmann, *Altruism in Private Law. Liability for Nonfeasance and Negotiorum Gestio* (Oxford 2004).

45. Gordley, *Enforceability of Promises*, 4.

46. See par. 6 (the principle of societal justice).

cized. As far as a contract is concerned, which is concluded in a situation of inequality of bargaining power, it is understandable and even necessary that the law recognises concepts and theories to protect the weaker party against abuse by the stronger party.[47] However, the theories relate to contracts in general. They hide an ambivalence. Their rationale is the lack of contractual freedom but their mechanism works via the substance of the contract, rather than by reference to the aspect of the contract that matters in fact: status and/or capacity of (one of) the parties.[48] This might be the reason why these theories are felt to be an obstacle, why they received heavy criticism and why they got eroded because the exceptions to them gained more importance than the theories themselves. As will be explained hereafter in par. 3.5, social survival of people depends on more than just the economic balance of their exchange.

The main problems dealt with by theories that focus on the inequality of the exchange are whether a mere promise is enforceable, whether a gift is a valid contract/enforceable promise, and whether a valid contract may come into existence in spite of an unequal bargain. In broad outline, there are two ways to solve these problems. According to the first approach, an objective judgement is given about the (lack of) exchange. According to the second approach, the judgement does not regard the (lack of) exchange as such, but considers substantially the freedom of the party who has been objectively disadvantaged. At first sight these two ways of thinking seem to represent the difference between neutral, formal arguments and assessing, substantive arguments. However, the application of each theory shows that in the end each judgement has substantive aspects. Every interference with a contract has its specific background valuations.[49] For example, the theory of *cause* can be used in a purely formal way but also substantively by avoiding enforcement of an unequal bargain.[50] The theory of consideration seems to require an substantive evaluation of the exchange. However, in practice it is most of the times a purely formal standard.

---

47. See par. 3.1, 3.2, 3.3.

48. See on the interrelationship between contractual freedom, reliance and equality in exchange Belser, *Freiheit und Gerechtigkeit im Vertragsrecht*, 129, 155, 278–280.

49. See Dalton, *Deconstructing Contract Doctrine*, pass.; Belser, *Freiheit und Gerechtigkeit im Vertragsrecht*, 111, 163–169, 397

50. Fages, *Einige neuere Entwicklungen des französischen algemeinen Vertragsrecht*, 524.

### *3.3. Inequality in Exchange,* Iustum Pretium, Causa, *Consideration, Unconscionability*

An important concern of the law of contracts is the exchange of performances that are not in (economic) balance. Such unequal bargains are objected to several policing theories like fraud, duress and unconscionability, inequality in exchange, *iustum pretium*, *causa* and consideration.

The rationale behind the theory of inequality in exchange in its purest form is according to my opinion not to be found in the (lack of) contractual freedom of the parties but in the straightforward need to police the substance of the concluded contract.[51] For that reason this theory will be dealt with in par. 6.

Today, the doctrine of "just price" gets some revaluation.[52] It is invoked by several scholars to emphasize the need for a more social contract law. Although it is clear that in some distinct cases the doctrine can serve as a means to protect the weaker party who has been abused by a stronger party who unjustifiably profited from the weakness, the theory as such is not specifically focused on the capacity of parties but on the substance of the contract. It attacks contracts for a reason, which is not the real problem. It is highly debatable whether *iustum pretium* is a convincing theory to be adopted in general contract law doctrine.[53]

Like the theory of *iustum pretium*, the techniques of *causa*, consideration and unconscionability try to police contracts that have been concluded between unequally equipped parties.[54] Their starting point, however, is not the inequality of capacity but the inequality of the bargain. For the introduction

51. Compare Gordley, *Equality in Exchange*, pass., who argues that the doctrine of inequality of exchange is a separate doctrine (at 1639) and who finds the rationale of this doctrine in the principle that neither party to an exchange should be enriched at the other's expense (at 1625). Via the enrichment argument he links the doctrine with a concrete idea of freedom of contract (also at 1625).

52. M.W. Hesselink, *Capacity and Capability in European Contract Law, European Review of Private Law* 4 (2005), 501, 507.

53. Contra *iustum pretium*: R. Zimmermann, *The Law of Obligations* (Oxford 1996), 296. 270; Lando, *CISG and Its Followers*, 398. Compare Fages, *Einige neuere Entwicklungen des französischen algemeinen Vertragsrecht*, 522, who describes the case law of the Court de Cassation who abandoned the requirement of a certain price.

54. Zimmermann, *The Law of Obligations*, 507, 549, 554; Dalton, *Deconstructing Contract Doctrine*, 1066 ff, Atiyah, *Rise and Fall*, 453; Belser, *Freiheit und Gerechtigkeit im Vertragsrecht*, 512, 513; J. Ghestin, *Traité de Droit Civil, Les Obligations, Le Contrat: Formation*, 3rd. ed. (Paris, 1993), no. 629-705.

of these doctrines in earlier days is an explanation. Consideration, for instance, was introduced as a means to make a difference between actionable and non-actionable promises, e.g. between promises that were seriously made and promises that were not seriously made, between promises that comply with and promises that do not comply with public order or between promises that led to an equal or unequal bargain. Without having clear content, it was a notion to express whether a contract was enforceable.[55] In modern terms, it was a way to make policy as a means to distinguish promises that are of importance for society and should be legally binding from promises that are not.[56] In the course of time, the notion of consideration gained substance.[57] It has for instance been influenced by the idea of reciprocity of exchange and by the free will theory.[58] As a result, consideration in itself is an unclear and inconsistent mixture of underlying ideas.[59] For each of them today we have separate principles and tools available which are more relevant, clear and flexible. It is for these reasons that the Unidroit-Principles do not contain any reference to *causa* or consideration.[60]

As already discussed in par. 3.2, the problem with these theories is their ambivalence. Whereas they seem to focus on the inequality of the bargain (the substance of the contract) the theoretical background of these theories is the supposed lack of freedom of one party rather than the substance of the unequal exchange. The theories police the contract via the abstraction of free will rather than admitting that it is the unfairness of the exchange as such that matters.[61] The consequence of this ambiguity is that these theories do not provide for clear and sufficient guidance to decide whether or not a contract is valid or whether it should be enforceable.

Next to the dogmatic concerns relating to these constructions, case law has shown that in cases of inequality in exchange without abuse of inequality of capacity, application of these theories leads to undesirable solutions. As a consequence judges are compelled to evade a technique by using another artifice or by making exceptions.[62]

---

55. Zimmermann, *The Law of Obligations*, 556.

56. Compare with regard to *causa* M. Bussani, *Libertà Contrattuale e Diritto Europeo* (Torino 2005), 18–27.

57. G.H. Treitel, *The Law of Contract*, 8th. ed. (London, 1991), 63–148.

58. Atiyah, *Rise and Fall*, 745.

59. Gordley, *Equality in Exchange*, 1595–1598.

60. U. Drobnig, *Substantive Validity*, *The American Journal of Comparative Law* 40 (1992), 639.

61. See about policing a contract according to fairness par. 7.

62. See on exceptions to consideration: Gordley, *Enforceability of Promises*, 376.

Today, scholars argue that the concepts of *causa* and consideration do not add to the debate and should not be part of common (European) private law.[63] Even though these theories are deeply rooted in the legal culture of the countries concerned, they are not even fully understandable for lawyers of those particular legal systems. Therefore, it is in my opinion for good reasons that they get excluded form today's supranational debate.

### *3.4. Formalities*

Protection of a weak party against the supremacy of the other party is not only the purpose of the theories that focus on the inequality of the bargain but also of rules prescribing a formality. The arguments that apply to the theories mentioned above apply in the same way to formalities required for promises which purport to enrich the promisee at the promisor's expense. Whereas the purpose of formalities is to protect someone from making a promise without sufficient deliberation, formalities do not straightforwardly do so. A formality as such does not guarantee that the promise has been made deliberately. Absence of a required formality does not correspond with absence of deliberation. Therefore, formalities are not proper means to reach the purpose and to replace the substantive considerations with regard to concerns about deliberation and reliance.[64]

### *3.5. Enforceability of Promises*

The problem of the binding force of promises is closely connected to the way in which a contract is concluded.[65] Especially the binding force of unilateral promises has been questioned. According to many national private law systems, a contract can only be concluded if (two or more) parties to the contract exchange a promise and if the promise is followed by an agreement. While this approach can be understood as a way to frame contracts into the ideas of

63. Lando, *CISG and Its Followers*, 390, M. Storme, *The Binding character of Contracts—Causa and Consideration*, in A. Hartkamp et. al. (eds.), *Towards a European Civil Code*, 2nd rev. ed. (Nijmegen 1998), 245. Contrast with R. Hyland, *The American Experience: Restatements, the UCC, Uniform Laws, and Transnational Coordination*, in A. Hartkamp et. al. (eds.), *Towards a European Civil Code*, 3rd. rev. ed. (Nijmegen 2004), 71–73; Bonell, *An International Restatement of Contract Law*, 113, 114.

64. Gordley, *Enforceability of Promises*, 379 ff.

65. H. Beale, A. Hartkamp, H. Kötz and D. Tallon, (eds.), *Contract Law. Cases, Materials and Text*, Chapter 1.1.

equality in exchange and mutual consent, it is not necessarily in line with every-day practice. Modern contracts are frequently long-term relationships. In such a relationship, it often happens that one party to the contract makes a unilateral promise without receiving something in return. Agreement by the other party is not required.[66]

As Gordley has made it clear, a variety of reasons may be advanced to hold a unilateral promise unenforceable. These concerns, however, do not justify the general unenforceability of unilateral promises. As he put it, we should straightforwardly render a unilateral promise enforceable. It goes without saying that this principle is open to exceptions, but it is undesirable to make out of these exceptions general rules that hold a unilateral promise unenforceable.[67]

One of the concrete issues with regard to enforceability of promises is the approach of several national private law systems towards gifts. Since a gift is characterised by the absence of an exchange of performances, doctrinal suspicion towards a gift can be easily explained. Nevertheless, making gifts is a vivid part of daily life. As already mentioned, it has to be kept in mind that economic balance is not the only reason for parties to enter into a contract. To survive it is of equal importance to have social power. For example, research has shown that a gift or an economic unequal bargain is not merely an act of altruism. It is also a way to establish and maintain a moral binding with the donee, to expose one's wealth and to gain social power.[68] It is not convincing to refuse to recognise a gift as a part of contract law and by doing so to withhold judicial protection to the beneficiary of a gift.

Another aspect of enforceability of promises is the question whether the promise must be accepted to be enforceable. However, acceptance as a requirement for enforcement has been rejected by many scholars.[69] What matters is not acceptance but reliance upon the promise and actions based upon such reliance. A promise is binding if a party who does not keep its promise acts "inconsistently with an understanding it has caused the other party to

---

66. Lando, *CISG and Its Followers*, 391.

67. See also R. Sacco, *Formation of Contracts*, in A. Hartkamp et. al. (eds.), *Towards a European Civil Code*, 3rd rev. ed. (Nijmegen 2004), 354, 358.

68. See for example D. Lancianese, A. Bianchi and V. Hunter, Vicki, *Gifts and Social Status: On-Going Experimental Tests of Behavior-Status and Social Exchange Theories*, Paper presented at the annual meeting of the American Sociological Association (Montreal and Quebec, 2006), http://www.allacademic.com/meta/p104220_index.html.

69. Lando, *CISG and Its Followers*, 391; Sacco, *Formation of Contracts*, 357; Storme, *Binding Character of Contracts*.

have and upon which that other party reasonably has acted in reliance to his or her detriment."[70]

## 3.6. Discussion

The problem with theories like *iustum pretium*, *causa*, consideration and unconscionability is that their rationale goes back to the principle of contractual freedom but that they do not control substantive freedom of contract. Instead, they assess the bargain. People are essentially free to make unequal bargains, to make gifts and to make unilateral promises. In order to control the mutual freedom of parties the controlling doctrine must focus on the substantive freedom of both parties. It is not the effect (the bargain) of the contract that should be decisive for this kind of protection—rather, the characteristics such as ignorance, incompetence and inexperience of the party to the contract are. The most direct and, therefore, convincing approach is to police the situation of the party concerned. Inevitably, the character of the exchange is a relevant part of the evidence in assessing the (in)validity of the contract.[71] Moreover, it is an element of the principle of societal justice. This, however, is not the same as the prima facie protection that emanates from the several theories that focus on the quality of exchange as a criterion for contractual freedom rather than on the parties' characteristics.

From this brief description of several theories that function as a means to protect one of the parties to the contract, it emerges that the main difficulty that they raise is their disregarding the real freedom of parties. Parties who want to conclude a contract obliging to an objectively unequal exchange lack the certainty that in the end their contract remains valid. Generally, there is no justification for this lack of certainty. It is only justified if one of the parties is not allowed to rely on the bargain. The reasons can be that a party had a responsibility towards the other party to protect him from concluding the contract or that he unlawfully influenced the other party to conclude the contract. However, in the absence of such circumstances, there is no remaining justification for the uncertainty. To arrive at a general acceptable balance of protection and certainty, the first step to take is to construct a device that has been geared towards the specific interest to be protected.

This is why several scholars propose to abolish these specific theories. They prefer to use theories developed more recently like informational freedom of

70. Lando, *CISG and Its Followers*, 394.

71. See J. Cartwright, *Unequal Bargaining. A Study of Vitiating Factors in the Formation of Contracts*, (Oxford 1991), 215.

contract, equality of bargaining power and reliance, which address more directly the circumstances that characterise parties instead of the exchange.[72] Others however emphasize that the obligation to inform the other party is too soft a way of protection of the weaker party. Referring to the re-distributionist function of contract law, they argue to police the content of a contract directly.[73] In that case, the inequality of the exchange is not regarded to be an element of contractual freedom but as an aspect of contract law theory that will be dealt with under societal justice (see par. 7).

### *3.7. Freedom of Contract and Other Principles*

The discussion of the several theories that I subsumed under substantial freedom of contract makes clear that people think differently about what to understand as contractual freedom. The more we consider it to be a substantive criterion, the more we get involved with principles that are regarded by others as values that go beyond contractual freedom.

It would require a lengthy discussion, to go into details about the way people understand various principles differently. Even if it were possible to do so, in the end the conclusion will be that principles of contract law are not isolated. They got developed in relation to each other. Whereas this is true for all five principles distinguished above, it probably is most clear with regard to the relation between the principle of contractual freedom and the reliance principle.

## 4. Reliance Principle

Traditionally considered to be a counter principle to the freedom of contract[74] and derived from contractual freedom as a means to overcome lack of

---

72. See Lando, *CISG and Its Followers*, 390 with regard to *causa* and consideration.

73. See Gordley, *Equality in Exchange*, 1637: "... the disparity in price is itself a reason for giving relief"; Lurger, *The "Social" Side of Contract*, 281 ff.;Hesselink, *Horizontal Effect of Social Rights in European Contract Law*, 128; Reich, *The tripartite function of modern contract law in Europe* and *Understanding EU Law*, 278, 286.

74. Especially Common Law regards the reliance principle as a counter principle to freedom of contract. Continental systems regard this principle as implied in the principle of contractual freedom. Nevertheless, in the laws of Continental European countries, the reliance principle is considered as a principle that is opposed to freedom of contract as it has been understood in the 19th century. This might be one of the reasons that it continues to be discussed as a separate principle. See, for example T. Wilhemsson, *Questions for a Critical Contract Law—and a Contradictory Answer: Contract as Social Cooperation*, in T. Wilhemsson (ed.), *Perspectives of Criticial Contract Law* (Aldersot 1993), 16 footnote 13.

consideration,[75] the reliance principle is more than that. It is also a principle that ensures the freedom of each possible (future) party to a contract. The reliance principle purports maximization of mutual freedom. Contract law is not merely interested in the freedom of one single party. Of equal importance is the effect of the use of freedom by one party for the position of others. Only if others are allowed to rely on the created position, they remain free to create circumstances according to their own free will. As described above, substantive contractual freedom implies a social order in which parties can rely on the legal consequences of freely made choices and therefore on the free acts of other persons. In a society in which one cannot rely upon the acts of other people, one's substantial freedom becomes illusory.[76]

After the will dogma played a key role in the nineteenth century, ideas of reliance have received renewed attention. Due to the fact that each party theoretically could insist that whatever he did it was not its will to do so, the need for an equilibrating principle was considerable. This has been found in the notion of reliance. What matters is not the subjective will of a party but what a reasonable person is allowed to derive from its acts. This theory has also been described as the objective theory. What objectively can be derived from the acts of a party is of importance, rather than the subjective thoughts of a party.

## 5. Pacta Sunt Servanda

In line with both the freedom of contract and the reliance principle is the principle of *pacta sunt servanda*.[77] This principle can be explained to mean that the mere contract is enough to bind oneself (*pacta nuda sunt servanda*). It implies that in general no form is needed to come to a binding contract based on the will of both parties (consensuality). As far as form prescriptions relating to unequal bargains are concerned, this aspect of the principle of *pacta sunt servanda* has been described under the principle of contractual freedom.

Another aspect of *pacta sunt servanda* is that it expresses the existence of societal circumstances according to which one is allowed to rely on the binding force of a promise.[78] This situation is crucial for a person to enable him to

---

75. Dalton, *Deconstructing Contract Doctrine*, 1083, 1084, argues that there is not necessarily a huge difference between consideration and reliance.

76. See par. 5.

77. See, for example Reich, *Understanding EU Law*, 254.

78. See Beale, Hartkamp, Kötz and Tallon (eds.), *Contract Law. Cases, Materials and Text*, Chapter 1.3, 127; Atiyah, *Rise and Fall*, 655.

make up his own considered and deliberate will. It is the basis people must be able to rely upon—otherwise they will be paralysed and withheld from whatever exchange or relationship with other people. The fact that their existence depends on this very idea characterizes human beings as social animals. Not every exchange or relationship is relevant for law. Every legal relationship presupposes that people must in a minimum degree be able to trust one another. It could be seen as an aspect of civilization, as a minimum moral standard,[79] or as a prerequisite for social life.[80]

Even though many scholars and philosophers recognize the importance of the principle of *pacta sunt servanda*, they have not yet fathomed the very reason why contracts are binding.[81] The source of the obligation to perform one's promise continues to be unelaborated.

It is most probable that more interplaying rationales have to be distinguished. For example, the binding force of a contract can be the result of agreement, of exchange/benefit and of reliance.[82] Since these rationales do not necessarily have the same result, the main problems arise where different rationales point to contrasting results.

## 6. Societal Justice

The principle of societal justice regards objectively the (contractual) relationship established by parties. Like *iustum pretium*, *causa*, consideration and unconscionability, the purpose of this principle is to substantively assess the relationship between parties. Unlike these theories, however, it does so more evidently and openly. Moreover, thanks to its vagueness and openness, the principle of societal justice does not need to hide behind concepts that go back to presumed (un)freedom of will. The principle of societal justice controls contracts not for reasons of a lacking will. It polices a contract in a way that is thought to be suitable for parties concerned. This principle is a means to build a contract system that fits with the economic, political, cultural and historical circumstances of society. Parties to a contract (are supposed to) know

79. See Gordley, *Enforceability of Promises*, 4 ff. on the ideas of Aristotle and Aquinas. See Zimmermann, *Law of Obligations*, 576.

80. Kessler, Gilmore & Kronman, *Contracts. Cases and Materials*, 2nd. ed. (1970), 117: "All contracts, even express ones, are implied: that express contracts are possible only through "a regulation which is originally social". Compare with Dalton, *Deconstructing Contract Doctrine*, 1022, 1023 and Atiyah, *Rise and Fall*, 652 ff.

81. Atiyah, *Rise and Fall*, 653.

82. Atiyah, *Rise and Fall*, 654, 655, 716, 731; Sacco, *Formation of Contracts*, 357.

more or less how their relationship will be regarded and so they can take into account these aspects of the principle of societal justice.

As a matter of fact, the principle of societal justice is a means to assess a contract normatively. Both the weight attributed to it in relation to the principles of freedom of contract and reliance and its substantive development determine the final result. Which position one supports depends on economic, political, cultural, and historical choices. As mentioned earlier, one can roughly distinguish the approach that takes the freedom of contract as starting point and red thread and the approach that puts these two principles on the same level of importance. Taking into consideration the system, taxonomy, and effect of prevailing law, to me it seems not to be tenable that freedom of contract is the predominant principle.[83]

Less easy to answer is the question in which way the principle of societal justice should be developed. The methods that are chosen to advance social aspects of contractual relationships determine the substantive effects thereof. For example the autonomy of the weaker party can be supplemented by adequate information obligations or by mandatory rules. Since consumers do not always feel the danger behind even drastic warning clauses, for consumers to be really protected against unfair exemption clauses it is preferable to control these clauses by mandatory rules.[84]

## *6.1. Good Faith*

The concept of good faith is an element of the principle of societal justice. Its content is decisive for the way a society expects parties to relate to each other. It does not (only) regard the legal consequences of their mutual freedom of will or reliance. Based on the societal circumstances it supplements or restricts the legal consequences of the relationship created by parties. Good faith is a means to assess which other legal consequences such as informational duties, duties of care and guarantees belong to the relationship of parties. Consequently, unlike the principle of contractual freedom and the theories following from that, the principle of good faith also operates in situations in which a contract has not yet or not validly been concluded.

A remarkable effect is the possibility to accept liability for breaking off negotiations.[85] Liability for breaking off negotiations is either framed as con-

---

83. See par. 2.1.

84. Reich, *Tripartite function of modern contract law in Europe*, 169, 170.

85. See Beale, Hartkamp, Kötz and Tallon (eds.), *Contract Law. Cases, Materials and Text*, Chapter 2.2; M.W. Hesselink, *The Concept of Good Faith*, in A. Hartkamp et. al. (eds.),

tractual liability or liability in tort. Both solutions are based upon open clauses: good faith and negligence. What is according to or against good faith or what is negligent depends on all kinds of considerations. Whether or not negotiations are broken off in good faith depends on the relationship between parties. But the valuation of this relationship as being close enough to render walking away from negotiations bad faith or negligence is an assessment of what society regards to be proper and effective in that situation rather than an assessment of the relationship between parties.[86]

A substantial freedom to break off advanced negotiations recognises the possibility for parties to find out in detail whether or not a contract is attractive enough to be concluded. On the other hand, it does not recognise reliance that might be created amongst parties during long, detailed, far-reaching and costly negotiations.

For parties that are aware of the choices made by the legal system according to which they conclude their contract, each chosen balance between these extremes can be taken into account when they start to negotiate. They can, for instance, conclude a preformation contract. The chosen approach towards walking away from negotiations in a society particularly polices cases in which at least one of the parties is not aware of the rules of the governing law. Especially for those cases, it matters whether reliance is protected or rather the freedom to walk away from negotiations.[87]

The approach towards precontractual duties should be regarded in relation to other devices that can serve as grounds for liability. Reluctance towards accepting liability for breaking off negotiations can be counterbalanced and be understood in a system that accepts liability for unilateral promises and/or that recognizes the possibility to base liability in cases of breaking off negations on unlawfulness, misrepresentation and/or unjust enrichment.[88]

Besides this, during the twentieth century the notions of good faith and fairness have gained importance for the entire assessment of contractual relationships.[89]

---

*Towards a European Civil Code*, 3rd. rev. ed. (Nijmegen 2004), 479; Fages, *Einige neuere Entwicklungen des französischen algemeinen Vertragsrecht*, 518–521.

86. See Dalton, *Deconstructing Contract Doctrine*, 1024, 1029, who argues that the doctrines of duress and unconscionability are public insofar as they are designed to police the limits of fair bargain.

87. Compare Cordero Moss, *International Contracts between Common Law and Civil Law*, 20.

88. E.A. Farnsworth, *Contracts*, 2nd ed. (Boston 1990), 116–118 and 202–208; Cordero Moss, *International Contracts between Common Law and Civil Law*, 9.

89. Hesselink, *The Concept of Good Faith*, 478–484.

## 6.2. Good Faith as a Combination of Principles

Following from the above, good faith as a yardstick for the way parties are supposed to behave towards each other is a combination of various principles. It is influenced by ideas of reliance and contractual freedom, and also by the societal situation concerning the relationship between parties including allocation of risk[90] and, as will be explained under the principle of social conformity, also by the societal situation in general.[91] Good faith is modelled differently in a society that heralds predictability rather than trying to do justice to the (presumed) will of contracting parties.

## 6.3. Equality in Exchange

An important concern of the law of contract is an unequal exchange.[92] There are good reasons for policing a contract that obliges to disproportionate exchange. These reasons depend on the societal climate in which a contract is concluded. A society makes a choice in respect to what kind of contractual freedom it protects. Does it protect the freedom of parties to make exchange to the detriment of other parties or does it rather protect the freedom to come to a more balanced exchange. In other words, does it take as a starting point that citizens may not rely right away on a clear enrichment? If the aim of the governing contract law system is to protect against enrichment, it will police unequal bargains straightforwardly. This policing activity does not go back to the lacking freedom of the particular contracting party but to a presupposed standard that heralds a certain balance in exchange. As Gordley has put it: "Yet to explain relief by a flaw in the contracting process is unsatisfactory, since one would not care about the flaw, or even be able to describe it, unless one were concerned about the disproportionate exchange that the process produced."[93]

The fact that the theory of equality in exchange concerns a choice of society results in the fact that parties cannot freely decide to set aside the rationale of the policy. They can still make unequal bargains. However, whenever one of them invokes the policy of equality in exchange, the bargain will be tested against that standard. In a society that does not recognise the idea of

90. Kötz, *Europäisches Vertragsrecht*, 17, 18.

91. See, for example Lando, *CISG and Its Followers*, 393 who argues that the reliance principle, the reasonably forseeability test and the principle of proportionality can be seen as specific applications of the good faith principle.

92. See par. 3.1, 3.2, 3.3.

93. Gordley, *Equality in Exchange*, 1637.

equality in exchange, the bargain cannot be tested against that standard. In that case the remedy has to be found in the lacking contractual freedom.

### *6.4. Societal Justice and Other Principles*

The first three principles of contract law, contractual freedom, reliance, and *pacta sunt servanda*, can be regarded as principles that dictate the relationship between parties in a way that is geared towards the parties concerned. The principle of societal justice adds an assessment that is not necessarily taken into consideration by (one of) the parties concerned. The assessment depends on the economic, political, cultural and historical background and choices of a certain society. Still, the principle of societal justice also concerns the relationship between parties.[94] Accordingly, these four principles are not concerned with the relationship between parties and society. However, concluding a contract is a way in which parties relate to society as a whole. This particular aspect of the law of contract can be explained by a principle that specifically focuses on the relationship between parties and society: the principle of social conformity. I will deal with this principle in the next paragraph.

## 7. Social Conformity

The debates on Western (and) European contract law largely focus on issues that concern the relationship between parties. In this debate, less attention has been paid to the fact that contracting parties do not merely create a relationship between each other, but by concluding a contract, also relate to society. The conditions provided by a certain society enable parties to conclude contracts. Conversely, the contract, once concluded, should not undermine fundamental values of the society that enable parties to conclude contracts in freedom. Moreover, society should uphold these values, amongst other things by controlling contracts.

The relationship between parties and society is controlled by concepts such as illegality and immorality. According to those theories a contract is null, annullable, void, voidable, invalid, unenforceable or of no effect if it is legally

94. See also H. MacQueen, *Illegality and Immorality in Contracts: Towards European Principles*, in A. Hartkamp et. al. (eds.), *Towards a European Civil Code*, 3rd rev. ed. (Nijmegen 2004), 419.

or morally offensive, *contra bonos mores*, if it undermines *l'ordre public*, if it is contrary to public policy or involves the commission of an unlawful act.

Several important studies on contract do not pay much attention to this aspect of contract law.[95] This can probably be explained by the fact that private lawyers do not recognise the reasons for illegality as belonging to private law. They regard these reasons as something outside private law that comes like a stranger in the dark and invades private law from outside. It is against public law provisions to dump polluted soil without having a permit or outside specially designated areas for dumping polluted soil. Parties, however, can agree to dump polluted soil without having a permit or at the wrong place. Additionally, they can agree that the owner of the polluted soil merely has to pay for the costs of dumping unpolluted soil. In the relationship between parties no values are undermined that specifically protect the parties concerned. The contract between parties, however, undermines the health and safety of society as a whole. Of course, this problem has to be dealt with by public law (penal law). That, however, does not mean that it is not also a part of private law. Private law does not only cover the freedom of individual parties. At least as important is its covering the general possibility of making choices in freedom. To provide for that freedom, within the law of contract there has to be room for respecting common goods that advance the possibility to determine one's free will. The general idea of contractual freedom includes values that citizens share, for example, respect for human rights. If these general values are not regarded as elements of private law, the result is that the very function of private law is limited to the protection of merely concrete, individual freedom. The consequence thereof would be that it only matters that one party can do what it likes. It would not matter whether mutual contractual freedom is being maximalized. However, that is not what is generally thought to be the purpose of private law.

Moreover, the fact that the above-mentioned polluted soil problem has to be dealt with by public law (penal law), should not withhold private law from taking a position concerning the contract. Private law has done so but not entirely. A lively debate continues as to whether or not a contract that infringes general societal values or public policy should be rendered unenforceable and even more difficulties arise with regard to the legal consequences of unenforceability. One of the issues in this respect is the difference in approach be-

95. Gordley, *Philosophical Origins*, does not discuss this part of contract law theory. But see Belser, *Freiheit und Gerechtigkeit im Vertragsrecht*, who does at 391–437; Bussani, *Libertà Contrattuale e Diritto Europeo*, 18–26; Ghestin, *Le Contrat: Formation*, no. 93-146.

tween contracts that have been performed (executed contracts) and contracts that will be performed in the future (executory contracts). If in practice only executory contracts are subject to avoidance,[96] the very aim of the rule whose infringement requires unenforceability will be only partially materialized.

The lack of attention given to the relationship between parties and society is inconsistent with the fact that concepts considered to be a typical part of private law, like freedom of contract and party autonomy, cannot be materialized without a society-related framework. Therefore this society-related framework that has been built on commonly shared values is one of the essential parts of the law of contract. Parties who use the freedom to conclude contracts are obliged to frame their contract within the bounds set by society as a whole. Taking the fundamental values of society into account is necessary to ensure that the principle of freedom of contract does not only support the freedom of the party concerned, but supports freedom as a general, fundamental right of all citizens.[97] Only in that case can the idea of contractual freedom remain meaningful for more than one person. Consequently, the fundamental values of society are also part of private law. Parties to a contract as the users of a functional contract law and as members of this society have a duty to respect these values and to take care of them.[98]

Regardless of its importance in history, this part of contract law will gain in importance due to European integration.[99] Whereas Article 81 EC explicitly renders a contract automatically void if it breaches antitrust law, an infringement of other, already mentioned provisions of the TEC, TEU and the ECHR might also require unenforceability if the contract is contrary to the purposes of the European Community or contrary to the shared fundamental values. As already mentioned in par. 2.1 in its Pla decision the ECHR regarded the interpretation of a will by the national court of Andorra as "blatantly inconsistent with the prohibition of discrimination established by Article 14 and more broadly with the principles underlying the Convention."[100] For this reason, Andorra had infringed the relevant provisions of the ECHR and was held liable under the Convention to pay damages. If Andorra has to com-

96. As argued by Atiyah, *Rise and Fall*, 755.

97. Alexy, *Theory der Grundrechte*, 342, 343.

98. See C.H. Sieburgh, *Tertium datur. De niet uitgesloten derde in het burgerlijk recht* (Deventer 2004), 15–34.

99. Compare W. van Gerven, *Mutual Permeation of Public and Private Law at the National and Supranational Level, Maastricht Journal of European and Comparative Law* 5 (1998), 7–24; Bussani, *Libertà Contrattuale e Diritto Europeo*, 64–82.

100. ECJ 13 July 2004, Case of Pla and Puncernau vs Andorra, no. 69498/01.

pensate Pla's damages entirely, the material effect is the same as when the will would have been rendered null and void.

Citizens can invoke the European provisions and fundamental human rights either directly (Article 39, 43, 49, 81, 82, 12 and 141 TEC) or via open concepts and general clauses of private law like public policy, good faith and the duty of care or negligence.

The importance of the social conformity of contracts concerning competition as regulated in Articles 81 and 82 TEC is also illustrated by the development that citizens are entitled and supposed to enforce these rules of Community law privately.[101] Also with regard to Art. 43 and Art. 49 the ECJ accepted the possibility of private enforcement.[102] At least with regard to other provisions of Community law producing a direct horizontal effect it is reasonable to expect that the possibility of private enforcement will be supported by the ECJ.[103]

Another implication of the new common background for today's private law is that national values that are not shared by the Member States can be enforced less easily in national legal systems. The enforcement of values that are not of importance to the European Union as a whole might be an infringement of Community law. The over all result for the theory of illegality and immorality will be a shift from the enforcement of national values towards the enforcement of values shared by the Member States. If it is for example contrary to national or local provisions to smoke sausages on wood since tradition and the law prescribe that sausages must be smoked on peat, the conclusion of a contract obliging a butcher to smoke sausages on wood is unenforceable according to national law. This unenforceability might however interfere with the freedom to provide services.[104] In that case the national value

---

101. Commission of the European Communities, Brussels 19.12.2005, COM (2005) 672 final, Green Paper, Damages actions for breach of the EC antitrust rules. See on private enforcement: W. van Gerven, *Privaatrecht handhaaft mededingingsrecht: 'Alice in Wonderland?'*, D.C. Buijs et. al. (eds.), *Mok-aria* (Deventer 2002), 63–76.

102. ECJ 11 December 2007, C-438/05 (ITWF/Viking); ECJ 18 December 2007, C-341/05 (Laval/SvB).

103. W. van Gerven, *The ECJ Case-law as a Means of Unification of Private Law?*, in A. Hartkamp et. al. (eds.), *Towards a European Civil Code*, 3rd rev. ed. (Nijmegen 2004), 111 footnote 48, 114.

104. See on the (im)possibilities for Member States to uphold national measures of market regulation which restrict commercial freedom A.S. Hartkamp, *Het Europese recht en het Nederlandse contractenrecht*, in A.S. Hartkamp, C.H. Sieburgh and L.A.D. Keus (eds.), *De invloed van het Europese recht op het Nederlandse privaatrecht* (Deventer 2007), no 8; S. Weatherill, *Recent developments in the law governing the free movement of goods in the EC's*

will be overruled by the Community value. Consequently, according to Community law the contract that obliges the butcher to smoke sausages on wood has to be upheld.

The same spirit pervades the PECL system of unenforceability for reasons of illegality and immorality. The PECL system implies that the unenforceability of a contract should not be easily invoked. The fact that other principles of contract law, like freedom of contract and the parties' reliance on the contract and on its binding force should not be endangered on unimportant grounds, requires a certain degree of reluctance towards unenforceability for reasons of illegality and immorality. Only the (endangerment of) breach of values that really matter justifies the unenforceability of a contract. Once such values are endangered, the device of unenforceability is necessary and (sometimes) useful.

The EU and EC values are commonly shared and are moreover important to establish the aims of the Union and the Member States. Since European law has for a long time focused on public law and, since the EC institutions demonstrate a reluctance to tread on the private law field, it is unclear what the private law effects should be if a contract does not comply with provisions or general principles of European law. As far as absolute voidness following from Art. 81 TEC is concerned, the implications of this invalidity are dictated by the ECJ. The ECJ approach to the concept of invalidity is functional. Consequently, it does not necessarily comply with the current concepts of invalidity in the national systems.[105] Even less elaborated are cases of infringements of other provisions which produce a direct horizontal effect. Although citizens can invoke these provisions vis-à-vis other citizens, it is unclear whether the legal effect should be unenforceability. Moreover, if unenforceability would be the appropriate solution, it remains unclear which legal effects this would have, whether absolute unenforceability is required or whether other, less stringent, types of unenforceability might be an adequate alternative and whether restitution or damages should or should not be granted.[106] In order to gear private law towards the background set by public law, the legal effects of un-

---

*internal market*, *ERCL* 2 (2006), 91 ff; O. Remien, *Zwingendes Vertragsrecht und Grundfreiheiten des EG-Vertrags* (Tübingen, 2003), 363 ff.

105. Compare in general Weatherill, *Recent developments in the law governing the free movement of goods*, 90.

106. See M.W. Hesselink, *The European Commission's Action Plan: Towards a More Coherent European Contract Law?*, *European Review of Private Law* 4 (2004), 408 ff., who discusses the Courage/Crehan case (ECJ Case C-453/99, [2001] ECR I-6297); Van Gerven, *ECJ Case-law as a Means of Unification of Private Law?*, 109–112, 114, 115.

enforceability have to be in line with the aims of the infringed provisions. This process requires detailed knowledge of the aims and context of the EC provisions and of the devices provided by private law like unenforceability, restitution and damages.

On the European level, the influence of public law on the enforceability of contracts also emanates from the grounds of justification, respectively the exceptions provided by the TEC provisions on fundamental freedoms (Articles 30, 39 para. 3, 46, 55, 58, concerning grounds of derogation in case of discrimination according to nationality) and by the European Court of Justice (exceptions based on fundamental human rights and the mandatory requirements or, as the case may be, the rule of reason concerning grounds of derogation for non-discriminatory restrictions).[107] These justifications and exceptions refer to general values and aims like public morality, public policy, public security, public health, the protection of the health and life of humans, animals or plants, the protection of national treasures possessing artistic, historic or archaeological value, the protection of industrial and commercial property, the protection of consumers, the environment, language and culture, diversity of the media, spatial planning and the coherence of the tax system.[108]

Where general provisions of the Treaty themselves lead to private enforceability, the justifications for breaching those provisions can also be invoked by private persons.[109]

With regard to the grounds of justification and exceptions given by the TEC provisions and by the European Court of Justice, one more remark must be made. These justifications and exceptions concern public values. They can be invoked directly by private parties. However, private parties are not allowed to invoke more private law-oriented grounds of justification. That can be a reason to consider these justifications in a private law relationship as being too limited.

These remarks make it clear that contracts between parties are embedded in a legal framework of private law values and public law values. Consequently, contracts are affected by the general principles underlying or laid down in Community law. Their enforceability is influenced by their compatibility with those principles, aims and provisions.

---

107. ECJ Rewe v. Bundesmonopol, Case 120/78.

108. See Lenaerts & Van Nuffel, *Constitutional Law of the European Union*, no. 5-102-114.

109. ECJ Omega Spielhallen v. Oberbürgermeisterin der Bundesstadt Bonn, Case C-36/02; ECJ Schmidberger v. Republik Österreich, Case C-112/00; ECJ Bosman v. UEFA, Case C-415/93; ECJ Walrave and Koch v. Association Union cycliste internationale, Case C-36/74.

To uphold the aims of Community law the absolute or other, less stringent, types of unenforceability should be combined with an appropriate restitutional effect.

## *7.1. Unenforceability, Restitution and Damages*

In a modern society, the grounds for unenforceability which are derived from EU law will gain in importance. Consequently, questions concerning damages and restitution will arise. While these issues are problematic in the systems of the Member States, they lead to even more questions in the Community context. It has to be considered which restitutionary approach must be followed if a contract is found to violate fundamental provisions and values. A common approach towards questions of restitution and damages must be developed just as a common approach towards questions of validity.[110]

The main systems of national law do not share a common approach towards restitution and damages.[111] Some systems do not in general allow for restitution. Cases in which restitution is allowed are considered an exception. Other systems do generally allow for restitution and consider situations in which restitution is not allowed as the exception. Since the reasons for unenforceability can be far-reaching, in practice both approaches meet severe problems.[112]

As far as contracts covered by Community law are concerned, the system of (in)validity, restitution and damages has to comply with the approach of Community law. Community law uses a functional approach that focuses on results which comply with its aims rather than on the techniques to achieve those aims and to come to those results. This requires private law scholars to develop an approach that meets the needs of contract law and at the same time the needs of Community law.[113]

The best way to attain pragmatic results that comply with the aims of Community law and with the reasons for (un)enforceability appears to be a system that avoids sharply distinguishing between arguments relating to (un)enforceability and to restitution or damages. The question whether or not restitution or damages should be allowed must be answered in association with

---

110. See in general Sieburgh, *Tertium datur*, 35–57.

111. See *infra*, Chapter n. 10, by A.C. Hahn.

112. H.J. van Kooten, *Illegality and restitution as a matter of policy considerations, Restitution Law Review* 9 (2001), 67–75.

113. Compare Van Gerven, *ECJ Case-law as a Means of Unification of Private Law?*, 115.

the question whether the contract should be enforceable or not.[114] This system has been chosen in the PECL, Chapter 15, Articles 15:104 sub 2 and 15:105 sub 2.[115]

### *7.2. Discussion*

The elements and aspects of contract law that should be maintained in a confrontation between contract law and public law have been established during a long history. Freedom of contract, party autonomy, reliance, fidelity, trust, and fairness are the most characteristic and important concepts of Western contract law. In the course of history, each of these concepts has received variable emphasis. Moreover, each of these concepts has been given variable contents and accents. Yet, again and again the concerns and discussions went along the lines of these concepts.

In a confrontation with public law, these concepts are the starting point for private law. At the same time, it is clear that the content of these private law concepts depends on general choices of society concerning e.g. the protection of human rights, risk allocation, social standards, distributive justice and the protection of weaker parties. When public law provisions come into play, the way of gearing private and public law towards each other is to recognize the interrelationship of the concepts of unenforceability and restitution or damages. This approach leads to legal consequences that as far as possible meet the requirements set by public law. At the same time, due to this flexible approach, contracts will remain useful tools.

## 8. Epilogue

Contract law cannot be explained by reference to just one overarching principle. It is difficult to understand Contract law because it is difficult to understand human beings and their interaction towards each other and their social environment. According to Aristotle and the alchemistic approach (human) life can be reduced to the interaction of five elements: earth, water, fire, air and ether (quintessence). In this chapter about Western contract law I tried to envision the law of contract by discussing it from five interrelated points of

114. Compare *infra*, Chapter n. 10, par. 3.1.1.1, by A.C. Hahn.
115. MacQueen, *Illegality and Immorality in Contracts*, 424.

view: the principles of contractual freedom, reliance, *pacta sunt servanda*, societal justice and social conformity.

It follows from the above discussion that the five principles of contract law cover 1) the aspects of the relationship between parties that concern those parties, 2) the aspects of the relationship between parties that depend on economic, political, cultural and historical choices and circumstances of the society concerned with respect to the relationship of parties, and 3) the aspects of the relationship between parties and society.

Throughout history the first and second aspects have been subject to vast doctrinal and theoretical debates. These discussions have ended in a morass of concepts, theories and dogmas that repeat in other words what has been said before. It is clear that a due consideration of the subtleties in this field remains of great importance. Yet, at the beginning of the twenty-first century the real challenge for Western, particularly European contract law is to deal with its relation to public law. The importance of the contractual principle of social conformity has to be stressed.

Under the influence of globalisation the importance of public morals and customs on the local level declines, whereas the importance of commonly shared public values increases. For the Member States of the European Union and their citizens, an important source for a common public background is to be found in the TEC and TEU, in the general principles of Community law recognised by the ECJ and in fundamental human rights. This common background of public values influences private law. In the field of contracts, it influences the contents of contracts to be concluded, both by public bodies and by private parties. Consequently, it influences the enforceability of contracts that are concluded and that do not comply with these public values; and, if a contract is rendered unenforceable, it also influences the regime of restitution and damages. Moreover, it influences the balance to be found between values concerning general interests requiring the unenforceability of a contract and values concerning individual interests which rather support the enforceability of the contract.

This layer of interplaying values interweaves the very aims of the European Community and the Member States with the legal background of contracts. These values can be invoked either directly (horizontal direct effect) or by means of open clauses and general provisions of private law.

Public law aspects of today's contract law have barely been discussed. Even in the arena of European Community private law, the debates have been mainly along the lines of the principles of freedom of contract, reliance, the binding force of contracts, and societal justice. It is of great importance to shift the contract law discussion towards hard-core themes of European Union law.

Even though it is hard to think of creating a new coherent theory of contract,[116] this aspect has to be incorporated in current contract theory. The discussion of private law and fundamental rights is only a part of this task. It is at least as important to develop a private law approach towards cases in which private law tools are confronted with tools of public law. This part of contract law is covered by the principle of social conformity.

Only by developing a branch of contract law theory that deals with how to gear contracts as a private law device towards the prescripts given by public law, particularly the law emanating from the general principles of Community law, the Treaty provisions and the case law of the European Union, will contracts remain useful and workable tools.

## References


Alexy, R., *Begriff und Geltung des Rechts* (Freiburg 1992).

Alexy, R., *Theorie der Grundrechte* (Baden-Baden 1985).

Arnull, A., *The European Union and its Court of Justice* (Oxford 2006).

Atiyah, P., *The Rise and Fall of Freedom of Contract* (Oxford 1979).

Beale, H.G., Bishop, W.D and Furmston, M.P., *Contract. Cases and Materials*, 3rd ed. (London 1995).

Beale, H., Hartkamp, A., Kötz, H., Tallon, D., (eds.) *Contract Law. Cases, Materials and Text* (Oxford 2002).

Belser, E.M., *Freiheit und Gerechtigkeit im Vertragsrecht* (Fribourg 2000).

Berger, K.P., *The Creeping Codification of the Lex Mercatoria* (The Hague 1999).

Bonell, M.J., *An International Restatement of Contract Law. The UNIDROIT Principles of International Commercial Contracts* (Artsley, 2005).

Bussani, M,. *Before and Beyond a European Civil Code*, in G. Barrett and L. Bernardeau (eds.), *Towards a European Civil Code* (Trier 2002), 109–120.

Bussani, M., *Libertà Contrattuale e Diritto Europeo* (Torino 2005).

Bydlinski, F., *Fundamentale Rechtsgrundsätze. Zur rechtsethischen Verfassung der Societät* (Wien 1988).

Bydlinski, F., *System und Principien des Privatrechts* (Wien 1996).

Cartwright, J., *Unequal Bargaining. A Study of Vitiating Factors in the Formation of Contracts*, (Oxford 1991).

Coester-Waltjes, D., *Constitutional Aspects of Party Autonomy and Its Limits—The Perspective of Law*, in: S. Grundmann, W. Kerber & S. Weatherill


116. See M. Bussani, *Before and Beyond a European Civil Code*, in G. Barrett and L. Bernardeau (eds.), *Towards a European Civil Code* (Trier 2002), p. 109-120.

(eds.), *Party Autonomy and the Role of Information in the internal Market* (Berlin 2001).

Collins, H., *A Workers'Civil Code? Principles of European Contract Law Evolving in EU Social and Economy Policy*, in: M. Hesselink (ed.), *The Politics of a European Civil Code* (The Hague 2006), 55–70.

Cordero Moss, G., *International Contracts between Common Law and Civil Law: Is Non-state Law to Be Preferred? The Difficulty of Interpreting Legal Standards Such as Good Faith, Global Jurist* 7 (2007), 1–38.

Dalton, C., *Deconstructing Contract Doctrine, Yale Law Journal* 94 (1985), 997–1114.

Drobnig, U., *Substantive Validity, The American Journal of Comparative Law* 40 (1992), 635–644.

Eisenberg, M.A., *The Nature of the Common Law* (Cambridge (Mass.) 1991).

Fabre-Magnan, M. and Sefton-Green, R., *Defects on Consent in Contract Law*, in A. Hartkamp et. al. (eds.), *Towards a European Civil Code*, 3rd rev. ed. (Nijmegen 2004), 399–414.

Fages, B., *Einige neuere Entwicklungen des französischen algemeinen Vertragsrecht im Lichte der Grundregeln der Lado-Kommision, Zeitschrift für Europäisches Privatrecht* (2003), 514–524.

Farnsworth, E.A., *Contracts*, 2nd ed. (Boston 1990).

Fauvarque-Cosson, B., *La confiance légitime et l'estoppel*, in K. Boele Woelki & S. van Erp, *General Reports of the XVIIth Congress of the International Academy of Comparative Law* (Utrecht 2007), 137–188.

Gerven, W. van, *Bridging (Private) Laws Closer tot Each Other at the European Level*, Florence-paper (www.law.kuleuven.ac.be/ccle/pdf/2005-01-18_WvG_.Impact_courts_on_private_law.pdf), 1–47.

Gerven, W. van, *Mutual Permeation of Public and Private Law at the National and Supranational Level, Maastricht Journal of European and Comparative Law* 5 (1998), 7–24.

Gerven, W. van, *Privaatrecht handhaaft mededingingsrecht: 'Alice in Wonderland?'*, D.C. Buijs et. al., *Mok-aria* (Deventer 2002), 63–76.

Gerven, W. van, *Private Enforcement of EU Competion Rules*, EU/IBA Conference March 2005 (www.ibanet.org/images/downloads/Walter%20Van%20Gerven%20-%20Paper.pdf).

Gerven, W. van, *The ECJ Case-law as a Means of Unification of Private Law?*, in A. Hartkamp et. al. (eds.), *Towards a European Civil Code*, 3rd rev. ed. (Nijmegen 2004), 101–124.

Ghestin, J., *Traité de Droit Civil, Les Obligations, Le Contrat: Formation*, 3rd. ed. (Paris, 1993).

Ghestin, J., *Traité de Droit Civil, Les Obligations, Les Effets du Contrat* (Paris, 1991).

Gilmore, G., *The Death of contract* (Columbus, Ohio 1974).

Gordley, J., *Enforcing Promises, California Law Review* 2 (1995), 547–614.

Gordley, J., *Equality in Exchange, California Law Review* 6 (1981), 1587–1656.

Gordley, J., *The Philosophical Origins of Modern Contract Doctrine* (Oxford 1991)

Gordley, J. (ed.), *The Enforceability of Promises in European Contract Law*, (Cambridge 2001).

Hart, H.L.A., *The Concept of Law* (Oxford 1961).

Hartkamp, A.S., *Modernisation and Harmonisation of Contract Law: Objectives, Methods and Scope, Uniform Law Review* 1/2 (2003).

Hartkamp, A.S., *Het Europese recht en het Nederlandse contractenrecht*, in A.S. Hartkamp, C.H. Sieburgh and L.A.D. Keus (eds.), *De invloed van het Europese recht op het Nederlandse privaatrecht* (Deventer 2007).

Hartkamp, A.S., and Sieburgh, C.H., *De invloed van het Europese recht op het Nederlandse privaatrecht: een korte verkenning*, in A.S. Hartkamp, C.H. Sieburgh and L.A.D. Keus (eds.), *De invloed van het Europese recht op het Nederlandse privaatrecht* (Deventer 2007).

Heiderhoff, B., *Vertrauen versus Vertragsfreiheit im europäischen Verbrauchervertragsrecht, Zeitschrift für Europäisches Privatrecht* (2003), 769–788.

Hesselink, M.W., *Capacity and Capability in European Contract Law, European Review of Private Law* 4 (2005), 491–507.

Hesselink, M.W., *The Concept of Good Faith*, in A. Hartkamp et. al. (eds.), *Towards a European Civil Code*, 3rd. rev. ed. (Nijmegen 2004), 471–498.

Hesselink, M.W., *The European Commission's Action Plan: Towards a More Coherent European Contract Law?, European Review of Private Law* 4 (2004), 397–419.

Hesselink, M., *The Horizontal Effect of Social Rights in European Contract Law*, in M.W. Hesselink et. al. (eds.), *Privaatrecht tussen autonomie en solidariteit* (Den Haag 2003), 119–132.

Ibbetson, D., *A Historical Introduction to the Law of Obligations* (Oxford 1999).

Kessler, F., Gilmore, G., Kronman, A.T., *Contracts. Cases and Materials*, 3rd ed. (Boston 1986).

Kooten, H.J. van, *Illegality and restitution as a matter of policy considerations, Restitution Law Review* 9 (2001), 67–75.

Kortmann, J., *Altruism in Private Law. Liability for Nonfeasance and Negotiorum Gestio* (Oxford 2004).

Kötz, H., *Europäisches Vertragsrecht I* (Tübingen 1996).

Lando, O., *CISG and Its Followers: A Proposal to Adopt Some International Principles of Contract Law, American Journal of Comparative Law* 2 (2005).

Larenz, K., *Methodenlehre der Rechtswissenschaft* (Berlin 1975).
Lehne, K.H., *European Contract Law—The European Parliament's Prospective, ERA-Forum*, Special Issue European Contract Law (2006), 12–15.
Lenaerts, K and Van Nuffel, P, *Constitutional Law of the European Union*, 2nd ed., (London 2005)
Lurger, B., *The "Social" Side of Contract Law and the New Principle of Regard and Fairness*, in A. Hartkamp et. al. (eds.), *Towards a European Civil Code*, 3rd rev. ed. (Nijmegen 2004), 273–296.
MacQueen, H., *Illegality and Immorality in Contracts: Towards European Principles*, in A. Hartkamp et. al. (eds.), *Towards a European Civil Code*, 3rd rev. ed. (Nijmegen 2004), 415–430.
Müller-Graff, P.C., *Basic Freedoms—Extending Party Autonomy across Borders*, in S. Grundmann, W. Kerber & S. Weatherill (eds.), *Party Autonomy and the Role of Information in the internal Market* (Berlin 2001).
Müller-Graff, P.C., *EC Directives as a Means of Private Law Unification*, in A. Hartkamp et. al. (eds.), *Towards a European Civil Code*, 3rd rev. ed. (Nijmegen 2004), 77–100.
Pfeiffer, T., *Good Faith, ERA-Forum*, Special Issue European Contract Law (2006), 67–75.
Poillot, E., *Consumer and Contract Law, ERA-Forum*, Special Issue European Contract Law (2006), 36–44.
Reich, N., *The tripartite function of modern contract law in Europe: Enablement, regulation, information*, in F. Werro and Th. Probst, *Le droit privé Suisse face au droit communautaire européen* (Berne 2004), 145–172.
Reich, N., *Understanding EU Law* (Antwerp 2003).
Remien, O., *Zwingendes Vertragsrecht und Grundfreiheiten des EG-Vertrags* (Tübingen, 2003).
Sacco, R., *Formation of Contracts*, in A. Hartkamp et. al. (eds.), *Towards a European Civil Code*, 3rd rev. ed. (Nijmegen 2004), 353–362.
Scholten, P., *Asser-Scholten. Algemeen Deel* (Zwolle 1934).
Schulze, R., *Conclusion of Contract, ERA-Forum*, Special Issue European Contract Law (2006), 26–36.
Schulze, R., *European Private Law and Existing EC Law, European Review of Private Law* 1 (2005), 3–19.
Sieburgh, C.H., *Het Europese gemeenschapsrecht en het Nederlandse buitencontractuele aansprakelijkheidsrecht*, in A.S. Hartkamp, C.H. Sieburgh and L.A.D. Keus (eds.), *De invloed van het Europese recht op het Nederlandse privaatrecht* (Deventer 2007).
Sieburgh, C.H., *Tertium datur. De niet uitgesloten derde in het burgerlijk recht* (Deventer 2004).

Storme, M., *The Binding character of Contracts—Causa and Consideration*, in A. Hartkamp et. al. (eds.), *Towards a European Civil Code*, 2nd rev. ed. (Nijmegen 1998), 239–254.

Study Group on Social Justice in European Private Law, *Social Justice in a European Contract Law: a Manifesto*, *European Law Journal* 10 (2004), 653–674.

Trebilcock, M.J., *The Limits of Freedom of Contract* (Cambridge (Mass.) 1993).

Treitel, G.H., *The Law of Contract*, 8th. ed. (London, 1991).

Tridimas, T., *The General Principles of European Law*, 2nd. ed. (Oxford 2006).

Vogenauer, S., *Eine gemeineuropäische Methodenlehre des Recht—Plädoyer und Programm*, *Zeitschrift für Europäisches Privatrecht* 2 (2005), 253, 254.

Vranken, J.B.M., *Asser-Vranken. Algemeen Deel* ** (Zwolle 1995).

Weatherill, S., *Recent developments in the law governing the free movement of goods in the EC's internal market*, *European Review of Contract Law* 2 (2006), 90–111.

Wilhelmsson, T., *Critical Studies in Private Law* (Dordrecht 1992).

Wilhelmsson, T,. *European Rules on Pre-contractual Information Duties?*, *ERA-Forum*, Special Issue European Contract Law (2006), 16–25.

Wilhelmsson, T., *Literatur, Lurger, Brigitta: Grundfragen der Vereinheitlichung des Vertragsrechts in der Europäischen Union*, Wien, New York: Springer 2002, *RabelsZeitung* 70 (2006).

Wilhemsson, T., *Questions for a Critical Contract Law—and a Contradictory Answer: Contract as Social Cooperation*, in T. Wilhemsson (ed.), *Perspectives of Criticial Contract Law* (Aldersot 1993), 9–54.

Wilhelmson, T., *Varieties of Welfarism in European Contract Law*, *European Law Journal* 10/6 (2004), 712–733.

Zimmermann, R., *The Law of Obligations* (Oxford 1996).

Zweigert, K., & Kötz, H., *Einführung in die Rechtsvergleichung*, 3rd ed. (Tübingen 1996).

7

# "Eastern Contract Law" or Transformation of Contract Law and Civil Justice in New EU Member Countries: The Example of the Baltic States, Hungary and Poland*

NORBERT REICH**

## Summary



* An earlier version had been published in (23) PennStateIntLawRev 2005, 587–623 and F. Cafaggi (ed.), The Institutional Framework of European Private Law, Academy of European Law, European University Institute, Florence, 2005, 271–302. For more recent developments see Chr. V. Bar/N. Reich/P.Varul, European Initiatives and Reform of Civil Law in New Member States, Juridica Int. Tartu 2008.

** University of Bremen, Faculty of Law (em.). Visiting professor, University of Tartu.

the Starting Point, 4.2. Information Requirements in Contract Legislation of New Member States, 4.2.1. Estonia, 4.2.2. Latvia, 4.2.3. Lithuania, 4.2.4. Hungary, 4.2.5. Poland—5. Contract Law 'in the Books' and 'in Action': 'New' Rules for 'Old' Mechanisms of Civil Justice?, 5.1. A Summary of the 'New' Contract Law of 'New' Member States, 5.2. 'Law in Action': Deficits in Civil Justice?

# Introduction

## *Functions of European Contract Law as the Theoretical Starting Point*

This chapter is entitled "Eastern Contract Law." Since there is really no such concept, I will analyse the transformation of contract law in new "Eastern" EU Member countries which must be linked to the general contract law *acquis* in the EU. This again must be seen as part of an overall discussion on European contract law.

My concept of European contract law is a functional one and has been described elsewhere.[1] I will distinguish between three main functions of modern European contract law, namely:

- Autonomy
- Regulation
- Information

By *autonomy* I understand the fundamental function of any contract law in a market economy like the one enshrined in the EC and EU Treaties, namely the making of economic transactions by subjects of private laws (natural persons including consumers, business entities, the state acting in its 'dominium' function) as securely and efficiently as possible, and to enforce them effectively under the *pacta sunt servanda* rule, once the conditions of a 'free meeting of minds' are met. At the same time I am convinced that, even in a liberal economic and legal context, autonomy is not without borders; therefore, its inherent restrictions have to be made the subject of reflection, most notably by the principle of 'good faith' and third party interests.[2]

---

1. See Reich, 'The Tripartite Function of Modern Contract Law in Europe: Enablement, Regulation, Information', in F. Werro and T. Probst (eds.), *Le droit privé suisse face au droit communautaire européen* (2004), at 145–172.

2. For a comparative overview (excluding however standard form contracts) see R. Zimmermann/S. Whittacker (eds.), *Good Faith in European Contract Law*, 2000.

The *regulatory function* of contract law may be the subject of doubt by many, notably liberal authors; they may fear a return to 'socialism.' I do not share this scepticism, but am convinced that this regulatory function has always been present in contract law, sometimes hidden in general clauses like those concerning 'good morals,' 'public policy,' and '*ordre public*,' and later more openly in the deliberate protection of the weaker party in labour and consumer transactions. National[3] and European constitutional law also invades contract law, for example in the theory of the 'direct horizontal effect' of fundamental freedoms and of the non-discrimination principle.[4] Regulation may come from outside contract law, for example by way of restrictions on certain types of gambling contracts or lotteries,[5] but in recent times it has been introduced into contract law itself, for example by consumer law becoming part of contract law.[6] I will not go into the details of this protracted discussion, but simply take 'consumer law' as part of the European *acquis* which has therefore greatly contributed to the transformation of contract. But consumer law may inspire a completely new orientation of traditional civil law principles.

*Information* is itself a rather vague concept, because it can already be found in traditional rules on fraud and misrepresentation as part of contract formation. These rules have been extensively studied elsewhere and will not be subject to my reflections. I am concerned with more subtle and differentiated rules on information provision by one of the parties to the (future) contract who either is in possession of this information or is required by law to provide this information, and the other party who needs this information for rational decision-making. Again, consumer law is a good example of this new principle which departs from the classical rule of *caveat emptor*, but it is not limited to this area. Transaction cost economics may help to define the conditions and limits of this information paradigm in modern contract law.[7] I am

3. See Canaris, 'Wandlungen des Schuldvertragsrechts—Tendenzen zu seiner Materialisierung', 200 *Archiv für die civilistische Praxis* (2000) 1.

4. See N. Reich, *Understanding EU Law—Objectives, Principles and Methods of Community Law* (2nd edition 2005), at 17–18 referring to the case law of the ECJ.

5. As an example see Case C-275/92 *HM Customs and Excise Services v Schindler* [1994] ECR I-1039, subject, however to control by EC law principles on freedom to provide services, case C-243/01 *Piergorgio Gambelli* [2003] ECR I-13031.

6. See Rott, 'German Sales Law Two Years after Implementation of Dir. 1999/44/EC', 5 *German LJ* (2004) 237.

7. See S. Grundmann, 'Information, Party Autonomy and Economic Agents in European Contract Law', 39 *CMLRev* (2002) 269; Kerber/Vanberg, 'Constitutional Aspects of Party Autonomy and Its Limits', in St. Grundmann al (eds), *Party Autonomy and the Role of Information in the Internal market* (2001) at 49–79.

interested not so much in looking at the highly specific and technical rules on information provision, but rather at the emergence of general principles and rules for its effective enforcement[8] without endangering the *pacta sunt servanda* principle.

## *The Enlargement Process*

The enlargement process is mainly concerned with the new Member States coming from the 'former socialist' block. I deliberately choose the Baltic States, particularly Latvia where I lived from 2001 to 2004, and Estonia where I was visiting professor at the University of Tartu from 2006 to 2008. Thus I had convenient access to information. I also extended my research to Hungary and Poland which had enacted Civil Codes, while still under the socialist regime: in 1959 and 1964 respectively, that were substantially modified but not completely abolished after the demise of socialism, though new codifications are on the agenda.[9] I will explain the differences in their contribution to modern contract law, as compared to that of the Baltic States. Again, I have had to rely on secondary sources which, however, seem to be better elaborated because these countries, in contrast to the Baltic republics which lost their independence in 1940 and again in 1944, never had to abandon their academic and professional contacts with the 'Western' world even during the darkest days of socialism.

After the 1990s, all of these countries became politically and legally linked to the European '*acquis*' by the so-called Europe Agreements (*infra* at 1.4), which exercised a deep influence on their contract law before accession. This will be shown by looking at the transformation (not: implementation) of two important, so-called 'horizontal' European directives, namely 93/13/EEC of 5 April 1993 on unfair terms in consumer contracts and 99/44/EC of 25 May 1999 on the sale of consumer goods and associated guarantees.[10]

The enlargement process cannot, however, be understood without at least referring briefly to the prior legal system under socialist principles and its transformation under the rules of market economy. This was an autonomous legal revolution which the countries under scrutiny had undertaken before their

8. See T. Wilhelmsson, 'Private Law Remedies against the Breach of Information Requirements of EC Law', in R. Schulze, M. Ebers, and H. C.Grigoleit (eds.), *Informationspflichten und Vertragsschluss im Acquis communautaire* (2002), at 245–265.

9. For Hungary cf. the paper by Vékas, 'Die Vorbereitungsarbeiten zu einem ungar. Zivilgesetzbuch', 13 *Wirtschaft und Recht in Osteuropa (WIRO)* (2001).

10. OJ 1993 L 95/29 and OJ 1999 L 171/12.

membership of the EU was ever discussed. This revolution has a truly constitutional character[11]—the abolition of socialist elements of property, of legal personality, and of restrictions of autonomy by a complex (some say: corrupt) licensing and regulation system, and its replacement by liberal principles of market economy which cannot be studied here in great detail, but must be remembered as a precondition to the now existing contract law and its tripartite function as described here.

## *'Relative Autonomy' of Contract Law and Civil Justice*

This chapter aims at a legal-theoretical analysis of the transformation process of contract law in the jurisdictions studied. Therefore, attention will be paid to the integration of these modern functions of contract law into the relevant legal systems. It may be a surprise to many observers that, despite similar political-economic principles, their implementation in the transformation process has been very different. There is clearly no 'European' model of private, or even only of contract, law, while there are indeed several models, traditions, and systems, and they vary greatly among the new Member States.

Among Marxist authors in the heyday of socialism this was known as the 'relative autonomy' of law[12] to explain why, despite the social and political revolution which had taken place in the countries studied, their legal systems still contained elements of 'traditionalism', particularly under the influence of the continental codification idea.

It can be shown that this ideological paradigm also worked the other way round: even under principles of market economy, the old socialist codes were not immediately replaced by new ones which reflected the imperatives of the transformation process. Sometimes only incremental changes were introduced into prior existing codes, but there is an inherent tendency to reshape legal reality by codification. The legal staff itself whose older members were trained under the socialist regime did not immediately convert to liberal ideas of market economy and government of laws (Rechtsstaatlichkeit).

Within this systemic transformation process, another question becomes crucial: how to integrate specific protective laws into the more general, and to some extent abstract and formal, codification principles? This is not specific to the contract law of the new Member States, but has been debated with equal

11. See A. Fogelklou and F. Sterzel (eds.), *Consolidating Legal Reform in Central and Eastern Europe—An Anthology*. (2003).

12. See N. Reich, *Sozialismus und Zivilrecht* (1972), at 33–37.

passion in 'old' Member States like Germany, France, and Italy.[13] Labour law had been completely separated from general contract law and will therefore not be studied here. With regard to consumer law, the debate is still open, and we must thus study the different legal mechanisms for integrating this new, still rather unsystematic, area of law into the more general principles of contract law. This is not a merely theoretical debate. It also has great importance for the understanding and application of contract law itself: how far can 'specific private laws' (*Sonderprivatrechte*) inspire or, for its critics, undermine general contract law? Should an integrationist or a separatist approach be used? The debate has not ended, with some countries like Germany choosing an integrationist approach in its *Schuldrechtsmodernisierungs-Gesetz* (Act modernizing the German law of obligations) of 2001.[14]

The solutions found in the countries studied here are particularly relevant for the future of European contract law. Indeed, they form a wide field of legal and systematic experimentation, the results of which are slowly emerging. Can they contribute to answering the central question of 'codification' of European contract law, namely either to systematise the existing *acquis* in consumer law or to favour an integrationist approach?[15]

## 1. Contract Law: From Socialism to Market Economy

### *1.1. Overview*

The Baltic countries, on the one hand, and Poland and Hungary, on the other, had been forced into a socialist system of economy which obviously had a decisive influence on their respective contract law systems and principles. Owing to substantial political differences in the realization of this process, the impact on the legal system was quite different and will be mentioned below.

---

13. References by Vékás, 'Privatrecht des Verbraucherschutzes in der EU', in L. Vékás and M. Paschke (eds.), *Europäisches Recht im ungarischen Privat-und Wirtschaftsrecht* (2004), at 19–24.

14. See Micklitz, 'The New German Sales Law: Changing Patterns in the Regulation of Product Quality', 25 *J Consumer Policy* (2002) 379; Rott, *supra* note 4.

15. See the different answers in the contributions to S. Grundmann and J. Stuyck (eds.), *An Academic Green Paper on European Contract Law* (2002). For a codification of European consumer law, cf. H. Rösler, *Europäisches Konsumentenvertragsrecht* (2004), at 250–288; Reich, 'A European Contract Law: Ghost or Host for Integration?', *Wisconsin Int. LJ* 2006, 425 at 458–463.

The politico-economic specifics are, however, quite similar, even if their intensity has varied over time and place.

The socialist economy, in its conflict with market economy, is based on a completely different concept of property and the legal relations emerging from it. We will refer to them very briefly without intending to go into details or to repeat the century-long debate on their ideological origin and truth.

Since, according to Marxist theory, the system of private property in capitalist economies permits the extortion of the fruits of production by the owner and thus establishes a system of "class-dominance," a socialist system which aims to overcome this process of unjust dominance and distribution of economic resources must and will at first radically modify the system of property ownership. Instead of a prevalence of private property over land and the means of production, a mechanism of socialist property is introduced. In the Soviet model of socialism, the state becomes the main owner of property, which is allocated to economic unities (state enterprises etc.) only for management, not for full use and disposal. Alongside this state property, certain forms of collective, co-operative, or communal property are installed, the extent of which has varied greatly over time. There is no autonomous contract regime on the use and transfer of this type of socialist property. It underlies state supervision and disposal. In the interest of socialist economy, a certain transactional autonomy relating to the proceeds out of running production (*Umlaufvermögen*), not to the stock of property itself, will be guaranteed to socialist entities, and in this context contract law plays a certain, yet limited, role. The *pacta sunt servanda* rule exists, but subject to the imperatives of the socialist economy, and therefore litigated before a special type of court, the so-called '*gosarbitrage*', a state agency with quasi-judicial functions which could impose contract conditions on socialist enterprises. Contract law was not governed by the principle of autonomy, but by regulation of planning institutions and a rather restrictive licensing system, depending on the type of economic activity.[16]

Whether elements of private property, mainly small businesses, were allowed to exist in parallel to socialist economic entities was subject to intense debate and conflict in the socialist economies before their own complete abolition, and there have been substantial changes in the countries studied to which I will refer later (*infra* 1.2.1.3). Also with regard to foreign investment and trade different rules were imposed, always subject to state control and revocation.

16. Reich, *supra* note 12, at 275–303, referring to the Soviet debate; D. Loeber, *Der hoheitlich gestaltete Vertrag*, 1964.

*Personal* property—in striking difference from 'private' property—was allowed in all socialist countries and formed part of the civil law, but was restricted to items for personal and family use to a varying degree. It should not be used to create private property. Contractual relations with the latter objective were regarded as against the principle of socialist economy, and therefore void.

Parallel to this concept of property law, the law of persons systematically distinguished between those subjects who were managing state socialist property, namely socialist production and distribution entities, so-called socialist enterprises with a certain margin of discretion concerning the retention of profits for investment purposes, and other entities like communes, branches of allowed political parties (mostly relating to the governing Communist parties and their auxiliary organizations), labour unions, recreation associations, etc. Other entities in the economic and social sphere were subject to a strict licensing system.[17] There was obviously no freedom of association, only a gradual alleviation of existing restrictions subject to the discretion of the ruling party.

In this system of socialist property and legal persons, a rather elaborate, but to some extent irrelevant, contract law system existed, playing a limited role in legal practice. Between 'socialized entities' this was not conceptualized as an expression of 'party autonomy', but as the transmission of the will of the ruling class (the Communist party and its state and societal organs) and the socialist five year plans into the economy. This was clearly expressed in Article 159 of the Civil Code of the Russian Socialist Soviet Republic (RSFSR) which was similar in the then "socialist republics' of Estonia, Latvia and Lithuania. According to this article, socialist entities had to conclude contracts according to the plan; in case of dispute, the "gosarbitrage" had competence to impose a binding contract (*Kontrahierungszwang*).

Limited autonomy was granted only in transactions regarding 'personal property.' Therefore, many transactions, even though quite common in socialist countries, were regarded as illegal, and therefore became part of an ever growing black market—a phenomenon that explains to some extent the priority that is still given to criminal law over private law in legal practice, and the fundamental problems in the process of transformation to civil justice. Contract law operated more in the 'shadow of the law,' instead of being a central part of the law itself as in market economies.

---

17. See Kordasiewicz and Wierzbowski, 'Polish Civil and Commercial Law', in A. Frankowski and B. P. Stephan (eds.), *Legal Reform in Post-Communist Europe* (1995), at 163, 184–188.

After the fall of socialism—a truly fundamental revolution—both the system of socialist property and that of licensing of legal entities and specific types of contracts were abolished. At the same time, a process of privatization and restoration of formerly nationalized property was initiated.[18]

## *1.2. The 'Baltic Revolution'*

The formerly independent Baltic states came under Soviet dominance in 1940, and then again in 1944 after the retreat of the German occupation forces. For these formerly independent countries, this implied a 'double negative revolution':

- A *political revolution,* since they became part of the Soviet Union as Soviet Republics, which implied loss, not only of sovereignty, but also of independent legislative functions. In civil law matters, this led to a separation of the Union competence to lay down 'fundamentals' of civil law, from that of the republics, to implement them in separate codes.[19]
- An *economic and social revolution,* which consisted in taking over the abovementioned principles concerning ownership, legal personality, and restricted autonomy.

It is obvious that this double revolution brought to a halt the already quite advanced codification work taking place in the three republics:[20]

- Latvia had enacted its Civil Code in 1937. This came into force in 1939 and could not survive the Soviet take-over. It was immediately replaced by the RSFSR Code of 1924 in 1940.
- The Estonian codification was nearly finished before the Soviet take-over, but the draft Code of 1939 was never formally enacted. It did not play any role later.[21]
- The Lithuanian codification work proved to be particularly difficult and protracted because of the several civil law systems which existed in this country, namely German law in the Klaipeda (Memel) region, Polish law (modelled on the *Code Napoléon*) in Wilna (Vilnius), (pre-revolutionary) Russian law in Kaunas, and Baltic law in Palanga. The merging of

18. A typology of privatization is given by Brunner, 'Privatisierung in Osteuropa', 45 *Osteuroparecht* (1999) 2.

19. Reich, *supra* note 12, at 311–326.

20. See Loeber, 'Kontinuität im Zivilrecht nach Wiederherstellung staatlicher Unabhängigkeit', in J. Basedow *et al.* (eds.), *Aufbruch nach Europa—75 Jahre Max Planck Institut für Privatrecht* (2001), at 943–954.

21. *Ibid.*, at 948.

these different system was not successful before the war.[22] A draft Code was prepared in 1940 but lost after Soviet occupation.[23]

After the Baltic Revolution in 1990–1991, which re-established the three formerly independent republics as sovereign states,[24] it was obvious that the law stemming from Soviet times had to be abolished and replaced by new civil legislation. However, this process happened differently in the three Baltic states, which explains the divergence of civil jurisdictions in this region:

- Latvia decided to re-enact the Civil Code of 1937 in 1992–1993, and to amend it mostly with regard to family and inheritance law. A draft commercial code including the regulation of certain transactions was prepared but never enacted. The existing commercial law is limited to company law and to formal questions on registration and the like. A separate Consumer Rights Act was enacted in 1999. It served to enact the relevant EU consumer law directives into Latvian law, and has been amended with the coming of new directives, for example, in 2001, to implement the Sales Directive 99/44. This dual system will be analysed in more detail below.[25]
- Estonia decided on a step-by-step codification of its civil law, starting with the most urgent subjects in property law.[26] By Act of 28 June 1994, General Principles of the Civil Code were enacted. Finally, in 2002 a comprehensive Law of Obligations was enacted to take effect from 1st of July 2002. It closely followed the Swiss and Dutch models, thereby including both commercial and consumer transactions. It is based on a 'comparative approach', taking over important parts of the CISG.[27] EU

22. *Ibid.*, at 951.

23. Schulze, 'Das litauische Zivilrecht', WGO 2001, at 332.

24. See A. Lieven, *The Baltic Revolution* (1994), at 194. International and constitutional law aspects have been treated by Baltic authors, namely L. Malksoo, *Illegal Annexation and State Continuity: The Case of the Incorporation of the Baltic States by the USSR*, 2003; I. Ziemele, 'State continuity, succession and responsibility: Reparations to the Baltic Stats and their üeoples'? *Baltic Yearbook of International Law*, vol. 3.

25. See Broka, 'Topical Issues of Protection of Consumer Rights', in University of Latvia (ed.), *Problems of Transformation of Law in Connection with European integration. Current Topics in Latvian Law* (2002-3), at 345–355.

26. See Kaërdi, 'Estonia and the New Civil Law', in H. McQueen, A. Vaquer, and S. Espiau (eds.), *Regional Private Laws and Codification in Europe* (2003), at 250, 253–255; Paju, 'Basic Features of Estonia Property Law' [2000] *ZEuP* 87.

27. Kaerdi, *supra* note 26, at 257; Varul, CISG: a Source of Inspiration for the Estonian Law of Obligations, Uniform Law Review 2003, 209; Sein/Kull, Die Bedeutung des UN-Kaufrechts im estnischen Recht', *Internationales Handelsrecht (IHR)* 2005, 138.

consumer directives have been included in the Code. This monist system is important from a legal-theoretical point of view.

- Lithuania decided first to 'de-socialize' the existing (socialist) civil law and at the same time to prepare a new comprehensive codification which was enacted on 18 July 2000.[28] This came into force on 1 June 2001. Its contract law closely follows the UNIROIT principles.[29] Its part 6 contains the general principles as well as detailed rules of contract law, including consumer contracts. A separate Consumer Protection Law (CPL) of 2000 exists, but the Code provisions will take priority over special laws: Article 1.3(2). This has led to a parallel regulation of consumer contracts, notably those determined by EC directives, while conflicts are solved not by the *lex specialis* principle, but by the *lex superior* rule.[30] This may change in the future when the CPL will be limited to institutional questions.

The different contract law systems in the Baltic states enable us to look at contract regulation as an experimental field, and to draw some conclusions for the future European contract law model.

### 1.3. Hungary and Poland

The 'revolution' which took place under Soviet dominance in these countries was a social and economic, more than a political, one. It meant the—however incomplete—take-over of the Soviet system of socialist property and legal persons, but left formal jurisdiction with the constitutional authorities of these countries and gave them at least some margin of 'relative autonomy.' The solutions and techniques used in contract law are therefore to some extent different from those used in the Soviet Union and its republics like the Baltic states before their revolution. Both countries enacted their Civil Codes, Hungary in 1959 and Poland in 1964, which show some specifics and which are still in force today, even though the underlying economic systems have been substantially changed. Both countries work on new codifications.

---

28. See Mikelenas, 'Unification and Harmonisation of Law at the Turn of the Millennium: the Lithuanian Experience', 5 *Uniform L Rev* (2000) 243–261; Schulze, supra note 23 at 339–353.

29. Mikelenas, *supra* note 28, at 252–254.

30. See Schulze, *supra* note 23, at 340; for new tendencies see E. Matulionyte, 'Towards a New Reform of Lithuanian Consumer Protection Law', in: Y. Goldammer (ed.), *The Long Road of Smaller Countries inot the Enlarged European Union*, 2006, 130.

### 1.3.1. Hungary

The Hungarian Civil Code of 1959 deviated from the Soviet model to the extent that it recognized private property rights, though to a limited extent.[31] The Code was elaborated in the reform period—liquidated by the Soviet occupation in 1956—and was adopted briefly after the execution of the leader of the reform government, Imre Nagy. It allowed the acquisition of ownership rights in land and anything else that could be taken into possession. Ownership rights could be acquired by transfer, manufacture, separation, accretion, adverse possession, and inheritance. Ownership was defined in the traditional sense, but it did not include using the property in a manner that would needlessly disturb others or jeopardize another's property rights. In parallel to this limited regime of 'private' property, the Code recognized socialist property and provided that it enjoyed 'increased legal protection.' It authorized private ownership of land, in contrast to the Soviet Union, but did not stop or reverse collectivization.[32] Full privatization occurred only after 1991.[33]

The introduction of the 'New Economic Mechanism'[34] allowing the introduction of some market elements into the economy, increased the need for consumer protection. The first moderate rules were included in the Civil Code in 1977 by Act IV, allowing challenge to unfair contract terms. In section 209 the concept of general contract terms was, however, not defined. This was done only in 1997.[35]

Later reform concentrated on enacting a separate Consumer Protection Act. As a forerunner, in 1984 the Act to Prohibit Unfair Business Practices was enacted. This was substantially amended by Act LXXXVI of 1990 on the prohibition of Unfair Market Practices.[36] Finally, in 1997 Act No. CLV on Consumer Protection was adopted, and it came into force in 1998. It implemented several EC Directives, including the one on consumer credit.[37]

Directive 93/13 was transposed as Act CXIX of 1997 and amended sections 205(3), (5), (6), 207(2), and 209-209(d) of the Civil Code (*infra* 2.2.4). The

---

31. See Spall, 'The Development of Private Property Rights in Communist Hungary and the Theory of Path Dependent Institutional Change' *Global Jurist Topics* [2004] 1.

32. See Vékás, *supra* note 13, at 25.

33. See Gobert, 'Eigentumsordnung und Privatisierung in Ungarn' [1997] *WIRO* 361.

34. See Cseres, 'The Hungarian Cocktail of Competition Law and Consumer Protection: Should it be Dissolved?', 27 *J Consumer Policy* (2004) 43, at 46.

35. Vékás, *supra* note 13 at 27.

36. Cseres, *supra* note 34, at 51.

37. Cf. the critique of Vékás, *supra* note 13 at 9.

Sales Directive, 99/44 was introduced into the Civil Code by Act XXXVI of 2002 (*infra* 3.2.4).

Hungary therefore can be said to have a *modified uniform system*, but with a clear preference for putting consumer protection directives, as far as they relate to contract law, into the Code as general legislation, and not into the special legislation on consumer protection (with the exception of consumer credit) or other separate acts (for example, package holidays).

Hungary is working on a new Civil Code which, according to one of its proponents, will be comprehensive legislation including commercial and consumer contracts.[38]

### 1.3.2. Poland

Polish civil law was codified by the Civil Code of 25 April 1964 which is still in force today. Naturally, its provisions bear characteristics of the earlier political system, the most salient having been the excessively privileged position of so-called 'social property.'[39] On the other hand, its system and rules are reminiscent of traditional continental codes. Socialist economy was ruled by decrees of the Council of Ministers which was empowered to regulate commerce between 'the units of the socialised economy' (Article 2). This was done to a great extent, but stayed completely outside civil law. Economic activities by private persons, including the founding of legal persons, were based on a system of licences.

Surprisingly, the imposition of martial law on Poland in 1981 led to a further liberalization of the economy and therefore a re-establishment of civil law relations. 'The idea began to be advanced that "socialism" did not rule out the adoption of certain elements of a market economy'.[40] State enterprises gained more autonomy, the founding of small businesses was eased, and consumer protection inserted into the Code. By the Act of 23 December 1988 the state endorsed the freedom to engage in economic activity and the replacement of the almost universal system of licensing.[41]

The political changes after the demise of the communist regime introduced traditional elements of property into the emerging (somewhat chaotic) market economy. The Civil Code underwent a first stage of reform on 28 July

---

38. See Vékás, *supra* note 8; ibid, 'Die Grundzue der ungarischen Privatrechtsreform', in: Liber amicorumTugrul Ansay, 2006, 437; ibid, Hungary, ERCL 2006, 112.

39. See Kordasiewicz and Wierzbowski, *supra* note 17, at 165.

40. *Ibid.*, at 166.

41. See Gralla, 'Polen—Gesetz über die Wirtschaftstätigkeit' [1992] *WIRO* 215.

1990.[42] The concept of property was unified as a legal category. Privatization began, but was not completely implemented. Privatization through liquidation was used more frequently than commercial privatization—a sign of the bad state of the Polish economy which left little room for consumer protection.[43] Foreign investment was allowed almost without restriction.

Contractual autonomy was secured by abolishing the rules that pertained to the socialized elements of the economy, for example, the influence of the bureaucracy on engaging in and shaping of contractual relations. Article 353(1) of the Civil Code restored the principle of freedom of contract, with the reservation that what was contracted could not be contrary to the law or 'the principles of social coexistence' (*infra* 2.2.6.). A clear borderline was drawn between civil law transactions of a unilateral (consumer) and bilateral (professional) character. The first were treated more rigorously against the professional and in favour of the consumer.[44] A separate consumer law emerged, even though it was limited to some particular rules concerning payment, exclusion clauses, prescription periods, modification of the amount under inflationary conditions, and *clausula rebus sic stantibus.* Here, the Council of Ministers could intervene in order, in the interests of consumers, to restore the contractual equality of the parties—a power used in practice under the Regulation of 30 May 1995, even though it was too reminiscent of the old system of contract regulation.[45]

Later changes in consumer law, in particular those imposed by EU directives, were included in the Civil Code. Directive 99/44 was, however, transposed into separate legislation (*infra* 3.2.5.). Poland can therefore be said to have maintained a *mixed system* of contract law. There has been a debate on drafting a new codification, but no concrete proposals have been published to my knowledge.

Letowska,[46] the leading Polish consumer law expert, criticises the attitude of the Polish courts after the change-over. They took an extremely liberal, free

---

42. See Pazdan, 'Zur Änderung des polnischen Zivilrechts', 37 *Osteuroparecht* (1991) 13.

43. See Gralla, *supra* note 41, at 182: a critique of the lack of genuine consumer protection in Poland in the transition phase to market economy has been voiced by Letowska, 'The Constitutional Aspects of Consumer Protection in Poland, in: Thévenoz/Reich, *Droit de la consommation—Liber amicorum Bernd Stauder*, 2006, 237.

44. *Ibid.*, at 192.

45. See Jara, 'Polen—Verbraucherkauf', [1996] *WIRO* 258; St. Heidenhain, *Das Verbraucherschutzrecht in Polen und in der EU (2001)* at 70.

46. Letowska, supra note 43.

market approach to contract law, thus rejecting concept of protecting the weak, especially consumers, despite its role in Art. 76 of the Polish Constitution.

## *1.4. The Importance of the Europe Agreements*

When it became clear that the abovementioned former socialist governments and (Soviet) republics were to become members of the EU, they concluded association agreements (the Europe Agreements) to prepare them for membership and to guarantee the adoption of the so-called '*acquis communautaire*'. The Europe Agreements with Poland and Hungary were concluded in 1993–1994,[47] and with the Baltic states in 1997–1998.[48] They contain provisions on taking over the '*acquis*', for example, in the area of financial services, consumer protection, product liability, and labour law. Obviously, these provisions were so vaguely drafted that they do not have direct effect, in contrast to the non-discrimination rules of the EA,[49] but put an '*obligation de moyen*' on the future Member States which was supported by the so-called PHARE programmes and monitored by the Commission in its accession progress reports. Most countries under scrutiny indeed tried to make their legislation conform as much as possible with EU law.[50] This process terminated with accession on 1 May 2004.

The following analysis will pay special attention to the integration of consumer contract law into the existing civil legislation of the countries under scrutiny. It will be placed into he general concepts of contract law which have been described as autonomy, regulation, and information. Particular attention will be paid to legal-systematic questions which, even though striving to attain the same objectives, have used surprisingly different legal techniques and means of implementation. We will classify them as:

- the monist approach (Estonia);
- the dualist approach (Latvia);
- the parallel approach (Lithuania);

---

47. For Poland see OJ 1993 L 348/1; for Hungary see OJ 1993 L 347/1.

48. For Latvia see OJ 1998 L 26/1; for Lithuania see OJ 1998 L 51/1; for Estonia see OJ 1998 L 68/1.

49. See Reich, 'The Constitutional Relevance of Citizenship and Free Movement in an Enlarged Union', 11 *European Law Journal* (2005) 675.

50. See J. Bober and N. von Redeker, 'Polens Gesetzgebung im Zuge der EG-Rechtsangleichung—Zur polnischen Debatte über Gesetzesfehler und das Gesetzgebungsverfahren', 48 *Osteuroparecht* (2002) 83 with regard to Poland; Vékás and Paschke, *supra* note 13, with regard to Hungary.

- the modified monist approach (Hungary);
- the mixed approach (Poland).

# 2. Autonomy

## *2.1. Recognition of Autonomy in Civil Legislation of New Member States*

Primary Community law presupposes the autonomy of economic actors, but does not in itself guarantee it expressly.[51] We will not go into details.

All Civil Codes or Laws of Obligations of the countries investigated contain a guarantee of freedom of contract, the classical one being written into Article 1415 of the Latvian Civil Code of 1937:

> An impermissible or indecent action, the purpose of which is contrary to religion, laws of moral principles, or which is intended to circumvent the law, may not be the subject matter of a lawful transaction; such transaction is void.

This is a somewhat 'old-fashioned' recognition of the principle of autonomy. The main problem is of course to define the limits of the law which restricts such freedom; here the fundamental freedoms of EC law have to be taken into account but will not be discussed in this context.[52]

A more 'modern definition' can be found in section 5 of the Estonian Code on Obligations and in Article 6.158 of the Lithuanian Civil Code:

- Section 5 of the Estonian Code states: '[u]pon agreement between the parties to an obligation or contract, the parties may derogate from the provisions of this Act unless the Act expressly provides or the nature of the provision indicates that the derogation from this Act is not permitted, or unless the derogation is contrary to public order or good morals or violates the fundamental rights of a person'.
- Article 6.158(1) of the Lithuanian Civil Code states: '[t]he parties to a contract are entitled to conclude contracts freely and to engage on their own will into mutual rights and obligations, and to conclude contracts which are not foreseen by this law, provided it does not violate the law ...'.

---

51. See Müller-Graff, 'Basic Freedoms—Extending Party Autonomy across Borders', in: Grundmann *et al (2001) supra* note 6 at 135–150.

52. See Reich, *supra* note 3, at 269–274; O. Remien, *Zwingendes Vertragsrecht und Grundfreiheiten des EG-Vertrages* (2003) at 178.

The Estonian formula is particularly interesting and innovative, as it limits the 'fundamental freedom of contract' to the equally 'fundamental rights of a person'.

The Hungarian Civil Code recognises private autonomy, but allows a restriction in the sense of a duty to contract (Kontrahierungszwang) in cases where the rejection to conclude a contract is not justified due to the economic situation of the parties, eg if one of the parties is enjoying a monopoly position. If the parties cannot agree on a contract, this will be substituted by court order.[53]

## *2.2. Good Faith and Pre-Formulated Terms in (Consumer) Contracts*

This section will be concerned with defining inherent limitations in the broad autonomy principles. Under continental legal tradition, they have been spelled out by the good faith principle. This has played a role in the control of so-called standard-form and other unilaterally drafted contracts. Article 3(1) of EC Directive 93/13 on unfair contract terms has for the first time recognized this principle in Community law which has thus become part of the *acquis*. It is, however, subject to a number of limitations, the most important being its personal application to a consumer as 'a natural person acting outside his trade, business or profession'. It is also not applicable to individually negotiated clauses and to clauses relating to the subject-matter and the price of the transaction, 'in so far a these terms are in plain intelligible language', Art. 4(2). We will examine whether a more general approach has emerged in the Codes under investigation, which EU law would allow under the minimum harmonization principle.

### 2.2.1. Estonia

Sections 6 and 7 of the *Estonian Act* on obligations recognize the principles of 'good faith' and 'reasonableness'.

Good faith, supplemented by the new principle of reasonableness (probably borrowed from common law), is regarded as a guiding principle of the law of obligations, including the interpretation of contracts: see section 29(5) No. 4. The relationship between the two principles is, however, not clear and has to be shaped by judicial interpretation; no precedents seem to exist.

Standard terms are regulated by sections 35–44 of the Act. Their prominent position makes it clear that they are an inherent limitation of autonomy.

---

53. Udvaros/Tildi, in: Handbuch Wirtschaft und Recht in Osteuopa (WIRO), UNG D.II Rdnr. 8, 35.

The Estonian legislator thereby implemented Directive 93/13, but at the same time extended its sphere of application, thus shaping a general law of standard terms, including such traditional rules on the irrelevance of surprising terms for the contents of the contract (section 37(3)), the priority of individual agreements over standard terms (section 38), the 'battle of forms (section 40), and the '*contra proferentem*' rule of interpretation (section 39(1)).

Specific consumer protection provisions are included in the so-called black list in section 42(3), which widened the material sphere of the 'indicative list' of Article 3(3) of Directive 93/13; a total of 37 terms have been blacklisted. Section 44 provides for a presumption of unfairness of blacklisted clauses which have been inserted 'into a contract for the purposes of economic or professional activities of the person'. This is to some extent surprising, as the function of the black and grey lists is completely different in consumer and in business transactions.[54] Section 36(2) and (3) relates to the international application of the rules on standard terms which is not limited to consumers residing in Estonia. With regard to business entities having '... their economic or professional activities and their places of business related to the contract or the performance thereof ... in Estonia', the rules of the Act on standard terms apply even if another law is applicable to the contract. Such broad application of Estonian law is contrary to the freedom of choice rules of Article 3 and the consumer protection rules of Article 5 of the Rome Convention of 1980.[55] It also goes beyond Directive 93/13 because it is not limited to the law of a non-member country.

An order of the Tartu Court of Appeal of 15.3.2005[56] held that, following the *Océano*-judgment of the ECJ,[57] a jurisdiction clause in a pre-formulated consumer credit agreement cannot be enforced to the detriment of the consumer, and that the court must on its own motion set aside the clause. The court also referred to the Estonian Constitution whereby nobody can be deprived of his competent court.

### 2.2.2. Latvia

Latvian law has enshrined the good faith principle in Article 1 of the Civil Code of 1937, which reads laconically '[r]ights shall be exercised and duties performed in good faith.'

---

54. Vékás, *supra* note 13, at 38; Reich, *supra* note 1.

55. Reich, *supra* note 3, at 270.

56. Order No. 2-2-146/05.

57. Cases C-240-244/98 *Océano Grupo Editorial v Rocio Murciano Quintero* [2000] ECR I-4491.

The place of this norm in the overall structure of the Civil Code is said to be an acknowledgement of its fundamental importance in the implementation of civil law. In court practice, however, a narrow, subjective approach is preferred. The typical cases concern '*abus de droit*': Thus, Article 1 of the Civil Code is considered to be a legal tool that can be used, *inter alia*, to prevent the exercise of rights in conditions when the entitled person has no protected interests, for instance, when the rights are used to achieve unfair aims.[58]

The Latvian Civil Code recognizes the ability of the parties to a contract to use standard-form contracts. This follows from the general civil law provisions allowing the parties to choose freely the form in which to draw up a contract, and not binding them (except for cases when mandatory norms apply[59]) to obey any formalities or models.[60]

In the dualist Latvian system of civil law, the Consumer Rights Protection Act of 1999 (CRP) has implemented Directive 93/13, but has also introduced a number of particularities which may be seen as the emergence of new principles of contract law. Article 5 established the (normative) principle of legal equality between business and consumer, while Article 6(1) prohibits the use of such terms 'as are in contradiction with the principle of legal equality of the contracting parties, this law or other regulatory enactments'. This broad principle is not limited to standard or pre-formulated terms.[61] Only Article 6(3) takes up the wording of Article 3(1) of Directive 93/13 and at the same time blacklists 12 clauses from the 'indicatory list' of the Annex. The most important has been the extension of the concept of consumer to business entities acting outside their market activities:

> Consumer—a natural or legal person who expresses a wish to purchase, purchase or might purchase goods or utilises a service for a purpose which is not directly related to his or her entrepreneurial activity.

This has led to Latvian courts applying the consumer protection legislation to the purchase of cleaning material by a business company because this was outside its normal activity, quite contrary to the relevant case law of the ECJ in

58. See K. Balodis, *The Principle of Good Faith in Latvian Civil Law. Likums und Tiesibas—Law and Justice* (2003), at 2–9, esp. at 7.

59. E.g., Arts. 1475, 1477, 1483, 1484, and 493 Civil Code.

60. Art. 1492 Civil Code.

61. See the critique of similar formulations in the Hungarian law by Vékás, *supra* note 13.

*Idealservice.*[62] This leads to particular problems in the field of consumer credit where section 8(3) of the CRP Act allows the 'consumer' to perform the obligation of repayment before the period specified in the contract, without compensating the bank for lost profits even in the case of mortgage loans. It is not known whether this extension of consumer law to business activities has happened merely by accident or as a result of a misunderstanding of the relevant EC Directive, or whether it can been be seen as the opinion of the Latvian CRP Act.

By Act of 27.10.2005, in force from 25.11.2005 on, legal persons will not be considered consumers anymore. Notwithstanding, a new provision has been introduced providing that several sections of the CRP Act will apply to legal relations existing between producers, sellers, or service providers and a person who expresses the wish to acquire, acquires, or could acquire a good—or use a service—for a purpose that is not connected to the economic or professional activity of that person.

In clear violation of EC law, the Act DID not provide for automatic nullity of unfair terms against the consumer, but allowed only that the term 'shall be declared, upon request of the consumer, null and void, but the contract shall remain effective if it may continue functioning also after exclusion of the unfair provision'. This seems to rule out an *ex officio* disregard of the term by a court of law, as in the *Océano* judgment of the ECJ.[63]

### 2.2.3. Lithuania

Article 1.5 of the Civil Code entrenches general principles of good faith, reasonableness, and justice. Courts must follow these principles in interpreting and applying legal norms. The same rules apply to the situation in which courts have discretion. Article 6.380 provides that obligations must be exercised in good faith; Article 6.158 acknowledges that each party must act in accordance with good faith, and the parties may not exclude or limit this duty. Lithuanian courts have on repeated occasions confirmed these principles.

Article 6.185(1) of the Lithuanian Civil Code provides a definition of standard terms—those contract provisions which are prepared in advance for general and repeated use by one party and which are actually used without negotiation with the other party. This provision basically reiterates Article 2.19

62. Decision of the Riga regional court, No. C 33168300/504/02 against ECJ, Case C-541/99 *Cape snc v Idealservice* [2001] ECR I-9049.

63. Supra note 56.

of the UNIDROIT principles.[64] Article 6.185(2) provides that standard terms of a contract proposed by one party bind the other only if the latter had due opportunity to become acquainted with these standard terms. Accordingly, standard terms cannot be used against a party if he did not have a proper chance to familiarize himself with the standard terms.

Article 6.186 introduces the definition of 'surprising terms.' No term contained in standard terms which is of such a character that the other party could not reasonably have expected it is effective. A term is not surprising if it was expressly accepted by that party, when it was duly disclosed. In determining whether a term is of such a character regard should be had to its content, language, and presentation. Again, the provision in question reiterates UNIDROIT principles.[65] Article 6.186(3) also provides that, when a contract was concluded on the basis of standard terms, the other party has the right to demand the termination or amendment of the contract where standard terms, even if they are not against the law, exclude or limit the legal liability of the party which prepared them, or violate principles of equality of the parties and the balance of their interests, or conflict with the principles of reasonableness, good faith, and fairness.

The currently effective Law on Consumer Protection and the Civil Code centralized regulation of the consumer protection issues. Those laws have been harmonized with the main EU consumer protection legislation,[66] including Directive 93/13. As regards their wording with respect to consumer protection, the Law on Consumer Protection and the Civil Code are almost identical. At present courts applies both in parallel.

Article 6.188 of the Civil Code gives a consumer the right to ask a court to avoid the unfair terms. On the other hand, the court can declare contractual terms void *ex officio* when such terms are contrary to mandatory rules. The Civil Code does not expressly state whether the consumer protection rules entrenched in Article 6.188 are mandatory. It is not clear whether the court is able to set aside the application of the relevant term even where the consumer has not raised the fact that it is unfair; this must be decided now by reference to EC law.

---

64. For the importance of the Unidroit principles see Mikelenas, *supra* note 28, at 252–254.

65. Art 2.20 Civil Code.

66. *Doing business in Lithuania*, available at www.infolex.lt/portal/ml/start.asp?act=dobiz; an overview of the practice of the Lithuanian Consumer Council is given by G. Jakubonyte, 'The Protection of Lithuanian Consumers against Unfair Contract Terms', Journal of Consumer Policy 2006, 79.

The Article also contains a non-exhaustive list of the terms which are regarded as unfair.[67] This list is a verbatim translation of the Annex to the Unfair Terms Directive, but transposed into a blacklist. However, the unfairness of a contractual term is determined by the court, taking into account the nature of the goods or services for which the contract was concluded and taking into account all the circumstances surrounding the conclusion of the contract, and the provision is merely a word-for-word implementation of directive in question.

It is important that this list is not exhaustive—other contractual terms may be regarded as unfair, provided that they are contrary to the requirements of good faith and cause an imbalance in the mutually enjoyable rights and obligations between the seller, service provider, and consumer.[68]

It should be pointed out that the *contra proferentem* rule applies not only in litigation where one party is a consumer; where there is doubt about the meaning or relying on it and in favour of the party which accepted it.[69]

In a judgment of 12.5.2003, the Lithuanian Supreme Court[70] applied the standard form legislation also to a case where the manager of privately owned apartments in a multi-story building had concluded a contract with public utilities. The contract was said to be concluded with the owners as consumers (of water and energy), not with the manager in his professional capacity. Therefore, the consumer protection provisions of the Code were applicable.

### 2.2.4. Hungary

As mentioned above, Act CXIXL of 1997 amended the Civil Code to regulate general contract terms. These broad provisions are not limited to consumer contracts and therefore have a wider application than Directive 93/13, while others, particularly about blacklisted clauses, are limited to consumer contracts. The Hungarian legislator did not go as far as the Estonian.

Section 209/C contains a definition of standard terms which insists that the user (which, against former law, can also be a private party) determines the contract conditions in advance, unilaterally, and for the purpose of repeated contract conclusion without the other party being able to participate. It does not, however, require the clause not to have been individually negotiated.[71] The burden of proof concerning (non-)participation in the drafting of the

---

67. Art. 6.188(2) Civil Code.
68. Art. 6.188(3) Civil Code.
69. Art. 6.193(4) Civil Code.
70. Case 3K-3-579/2003.
71. For a critique see Vékás, *supra* note 13, at 26 f., 32–33. This is probably due that the original draft version of Dir. 93/13 was taken over.

contract is imposed on the user, a rule restricted to consumer contracts.[72] The insistence on 'participation' and not on 'negotiation' may be due to a misunderstanding of the relevant EC law provisions which at that time had not been officially translated.

The concept of unfairness was defined in section 209/B(1) by reference to the concept of 'good faith' under Directive 93/13, well known in Hungarian law. In specifying the Directive, it tries to give two examples of a one-sided and unjustified imposition of rights and duties (section 209/B(2)), namely:

- if the clause deviates substantially from central provisions of contract law,
- if it is incompatible with the subject matter or provisions of the contract.

Vékás observes that this way the non-mandatory provisions of the Civil Code become mandatory.[73]

The main criticism of the Hungarian regulation is concerned with the widening of the ambit of Directive 93/13 (respectively its Hungarian implementation) also to business-to-business (B2B) contracts.[74] If, on the other hand, one starts from the assumption—which is the basis of this chapter—that the good faith principle is also rooted in B2B contracts, even though in a somewhat less intensive way, these contracts should not be excluded from the unfairness control of pre-formulated clauses. The yardstick may be a different and less intrusive one, and the confusion of the Hungarian legislator between 'normal' and 'consumer' contracts may not be a very promising and successful approach.

In a reference of the Hungarian Szombathely City Court[75] the ECJ was asked about the effects of an unfair term on a contract, in particular whether this depended on an express declaration of the consumer. It seems that this case is similar to the *Océano*-judgment of the ECJ; the ECJ however denied jurisdiction.[76]

### 2.2.5. Poland

As mentioned above, the re-establishment of a market economy in Poland and the abolition of special relationships between socialist enterprises led to the recognition of the equality of all civil law subjects and of contractual freedom, and thus the rejection of the privileged position of socialist enterprises.[77]

---

72. *Ibid.*, at 30.
73. *Ibid.*, at. 28, 34.
74. *Ibid.*, at 34–40.
75. Case C-302/04 Ynos kft v Janos Varga [2006] ECRI-371.
76. Case C-302/04 Ynos kft v Janos Varga [2006] 1–371.
77. See Poczobut, 'Zur Reform des polnisches Zivilrechts (mit einigen rechtsvergleichenden Bemerkungen)', 7 *ZEuP* 75, at 82.

According to Article 353.1 of the Civil Code of 1964 as amended in 1990, 'the parties are free to determine their legal relationship according to their free will, provided that its contents and objectives do not contradict the nature of the legal relation, the law and the principles of social coexistence.' The good faith principle is indirectly recognized in Article 7 of the Civil Code: 'if the law determines certain legal consequences by referring to good or bad faith, there is a presumption of good faith.' Art. 354 concerning performance of obligations by the debtor does not mention good faith, but refers to the "content of the obligation, to its socio-economic objective and to the principles of social coexistence;" the creditor has a duty to co-operation.

By Act of 2 March 2000, in force since 1 July 2000, Article 384 *et seq.* of the Civil Code of 1964 were amended to modernize the existing law on standard contract clauses and to introduce specific rules of consumer protection under the impact of EC Directive 93/13 and the Europe Agreement with Poland.[78]

Article 385.3 contains a 'grey list' of 23 clauses which, in cases of doubt, are regarded as 'wrongful provisions.' The provisions of the Code mention the transparency principle of Article 4(2) of the Directive in Art. 385.1(2) first sentence, in conformity with ECJ case law.[79]

The actual practice with regard to the new provisions is not known to me. The structure of the new law is somewhat complicated because general questions of the law of standard contract terms are mixed with specific rules on consumer protection, taking different concepts as starting points. There do not seem to exist rules concerning 'surprising clauses.' The *contra preferentem* rule is only applied to consumer contracts, not as a general principle of the interpretation of standard forms, Art. 385.1(2) second sentence.

# 3. Regulation

## *3.1. Generalities: The Importance of Directive 99/44 for General Contract Law*

The following section will be devoted to analysing the importance of Directive 99/44 for the contract law of the countries studied here. It is meant to

78. Surdek/Binieda, 'Protection of Competition and Consumers', in: Z. Brodecki (ed), *Polish Business Law* (2003) at 470–473; Heidenhain, *supra* note 45 at 222 with detailed references to the Polish legislative procedure.

79. Case C-144/99 *Commission v Netherlands* [2001] ECR I-3541; Heidenhain, *supra* note 45 at 250; Reich, *supra* note 3, at 280; Vékás, *supra* note 13, at 33 with regard to Hungarian law.

be a consumer protection Directive, as clearly stated in paragraph 1 of its 'recitals'. It is therefore limited to consumer sales in a personal and substantive sense:

- personal, in so far as only consumers as 'natural persons acting for purposes which are not related to trade, business or profession' come within its ambit of protection;
- substantive, in so far as only consumer goods as 'tangible movable goods' are covered with some exceptions, and not immovable property, rights, and obligations.

With this limitation, the provisions of the Directive and Member State law implementing it are mandatory and cannot be waived (Article 7(1)).

The importance of the Directive goes far beyond this narrow regulatory approach with respect to consumer protection:

- First, it extends regulation beyond mere consumer protection, because in Article 4 it provides for a right of redress of the last seller against his seller, or the manufacturer, or importer of the product in the chain of distribution. It is not clear how far this right can be contracted out; there is no provision similar to Article 7(1) of the Directive, and paragraph 9 of the 'recitals' is rather ambiguous on this point: on the one hand, it gives the last seller a right to 'pursue remedies against the producer, the previous seller in the same chain of contracts or any other intermediary, unless he has renounced that entitlement.' At the same time, the 'principle of freedom of contract' is said to be safeguarded, and it is left to national law to determine 'against whom and how the seller may pursue such remedies', thereby implicitly stating that the seller must be able as such to pursue these remedies, and that they cannot be completely contracted out of. This ambiguity must, however, be resolved by national law. This chapter will not go into the discussion of such a highly controversial point,[80] but will simply look at the solutions adopted by the Member States under scrutiny.
- Secondly, the concepts used in the Directive itself, especially on conformity stemming from the United Nations Sales Convention, have a much broader sphere of application than consumer sales; they may imply a general paradigm change in sales, and even more in contract, law. It is suggested that dualist systems of contract law will have more problems

80. See N. Reich and H.-W. Micklitz, *Europäisches Verbraucherrecht* (2003), at paras 17.19–17.22.

with implementing the Directive than monist ones, and that countries which decide upon a new codification of contract law will be better off than those that have to merge the imperatives of the Directive into their pre-existing contract law.

- Thirdly, the question of remedies has been intensely debated and resolved in a rather detailed, though not complete, way. This responds to the general Community law principle of '*ubi res ibi remedium*.'[81] It does not, however, refer to compensation, but leaves this to the Member States under the minimum harmonization principle.

## *3.2. The Importance of Directive 99/44 on Contract Law within the Enlargement Process*

### 3.2.1. Estonia

The Estonian Code of Obligations regulates sales law in its sections 208–237. It uses Directive 99/44 to modernize sales law in general, while section 237(1) provides that in consumer sales the legal remedies provided cannot be contracted out of. If 'a contract is entered into as a result of a public tender, advertising or other similar economic activities taking place in Estonia the provisions of this Division apply to contracts of consumer sale entered into with a purchaser residing in Estonia or in a Member State of the European Union regardless of the country whose law is applied to the contract'.

The buyer's remedies are set out in sections 220–225 and are nearly identical for B2B and business-to-consumer (B2C) contracts. Section 228 contains a provision on redress for a seller in consumer sales, but only in cases of 'a statement by the producer, previous seller or other retailer with respect to particular characteristics of the thing.' This is somewhat narrower than Article 4, because there redress can be sought 'because of a lack of conformity resulting from an act or omission by the producer.... 'These rules are not mandatory, but may be caught by the principles of unfair term legislation (*supra* 2.2.1.).

Section 230(1) contains detailed rules on warranties:

> 'A warranty against defects is a promise made by a seller, previous seller or producer (warrantor) to replace or repair a sold thing without charge or for a charge and under the conditions prescribed in the warranty, or to ensure in other ways the compliance of the thing with

81. See Van Gerven, 'Of Rights, Remedies and Procedures', 38 *CMLRev* (2001) 501; Reich, *supra* note 3, at 239.

the conditions prescribed in the warranty whereby the purchaser is given a broader warranty than that provided by law.'

The transparency requirements of the Directive are correctly implemented. In addition to Art. 5 of the Directive, there are certain presumptions concerning the content of the warranty. It is not clear in how far the concept of "warranty against defect" is identical with the broader concept of "conformity" used by the directive. This must eventually be settled according to the rules on "consistent interpretation" of member state law.

### 3.2.2. Latvia

In the dualist system of Latvia, the Civil Code of 1937 does not regulate the remedies for non-conformity in sales contracts as such, but establishes general rules on liability in so-called 'alienation contracts for consideration' (*entgeltlicher Veräußerungsvertrag*), for example, sales, barter, and pledge. The alienator has to guarantee that the 'property has no hidden defects and possesses all the good qualities which are warranted or presumed' (Article 1593). Article 1612 *et seq.* regulate in detail the duties of the alienator and the remedies of the acquirer which are, as in traditional Roman systems, limited to rescission and reduction of the price; the limitation period for the first is six months, and for the second one year (Articles 1633, 1634).

Under the existing Latvian law, Directive 99/44 could not simply be enacted into the Civil Code because it starts from a completely different concept. Therefore, an amendment of the Consumer Rights Protection Act of 1999 (CRP Act) was made on 22 November 2001. This reinforced the dualist system of Latvia law.

The CRP Act lists all the criteria indicating that goods do not conform to the contract by reiterating in the negative form the criteria for goods presumed to be in conformity with the contract listed in the Sales Directive,[82] adding several other grounds, such as counterfeit goods, inappropriate packaging, etc.

The CPR Act restates the four means of redress available to the consumer precisely as defined in the Sales Directive.[83] The peculiarity of Latvian implementation is that when non-conformity is claimed within a period of six month after delivery, the consumer has the free choice of the four remedies provided for by the Sales Directive—a questionable implementation not taking into account the detailed two-step procedure of enforcing claims which the Directive introduced after long debates in the Parliament and the Coun-

82. Art. 14(1) of the CRP Act, transposing Art. 2(2) of the Sales Directive.

83. Art. 28 of the CRP Act, transposing Recital 10 to the Sales Directive, *supra* note 75.

cil, suggesting a complete harmonization of the hierarchy of remedies (with the exception of compensation).[84]

Six months after delivery, priority is given to repair or replacement. If these means are not available or cause considerable inconvenience to the consumer, the contract can be rescinded, but the payment made to the consumer should take natural depreciation of goods into consideration. There are no such provisions in the Sales Directive. It is therefore not clear whether Latvian law conforms to the directive.

Another interesting point is that under Latvian law a guarantee is an undertaking by a seller going beyond (that is, granting more than) the protection of the CRP Act.[85] If the guarantee does not specify something more, it cannot be called a 'guarantee.' Latvian law thus gives more protection to consumers in this respect.

According to section 33 of the CRP Act, the seller is entitled to pursue remedies against the person liable in the contractual chain. It seems that no private arrangement can avoid the liability of the final seller. This right of subrogation has been included in the CPR Act to make enforcement of consumer claims effective, and it therefore cannot be contracted out. The Latvian legislator has not changed the provisions of the Civil Code even though they may be based on a different theory of liability and have shorter prescription periods than foreseen by the Directive.

Latvian implementation, though not formally integrated into the old Civil Code of 1937, will amend general civil law beyond the realm of consumer protection in two directions:

- Questions of redress for the seller from his suppliers will be solved by subrogation, for example, by applying the norms of the CPA Act without allowing the defences under general civil law to be raised.
- Most surprisingly, the rules on conformity have also been extended to cover services, within section 29 of the CPR Act.

The CPR Act may therefore be the starting point for a substantial change in the existing Latvian contract law as such. It is not known how the emergence of a new contract law will be handled by the Latvian legislator and Latvian courts.

---

84. See Rott, 'Minimum Harmonisation for the Completion of the Internal Market? The Example of Consumer Sales Law', 40*CMLRev* (2003) 1107, at 129; Reich, 'Stichtag 1. Mai 2004: Eine erweiterte Union—auch ein erweitertes europäisches Zivilrecht? Zur Rolle der baltischen Privatrechtssysteme in der EU' [2004] *ZEuP* 449.

85. Art. 16 of the CRP Act.

### 3.2.3. Lithuania

All questions of contract law are dealt in the sixth book of the Civil Code of 2000 which first deals with the law of obligations. Then there is a chapter on the law of contracts, followed by one dealing with obligations arising on other grounds, and then the Code contains provisions concerning particular contracts. Sales contracts are dealt with and also regulated by the Law on Consumer Protection[86] (CPL), which is applicable only in the cases mentioned above.

The 23rd section of the fourth part of the sixth book of the Code contains provisions on sales contracts. Its paragraph (4) contains special norms on consumer sales contracts.

The rights of the consumer when he acquires goods that do not conform with the contract in Article 3 of the Sales Directive are transposed in Article 6.363(4) of the Code. These are the right to have the goods brought into conformity by replacement (Article 6.363(4)(1) of the Code) or repair (Article 6.363(4)(3) of the Code) free of charge, the right to have an appropriate reduction in the price (Article 6.363(4)(2) of the Code), and the right to rescind the contract (Article 6.363(8) of the Code). What is different from the Directive is the manner of application of those rights—the Directive provides in Article 3(5) that the consumer is entitled to a reduction in the price or to have the contract rescinded, if he is not entitled to other rights, mentioned above, or under other conditions as specified in the Sales Directive. The Code, however, provides in Article 6.363(4) that the consumer has a discretion to choose one of those rights—a provision similar to the one under Latvian law (*supra* 3.2.2.).

Article 4 of Directive 99/44 provides for a right of redress. This right is indirectly enshrined in Article 6.280 of the Code. This part of the Code deals with questions of the law of torts, which is part of the chapter on obligations arising on grounds other than contract. According to Article 6.280(1), the person who has reimbursed the injury caused to another person has a right of redress equal to that reimbursement, if the law does not provide for a different amount. The Lithuanian rules on subrogation seem to be similar to those of Latvian law (*supra* 3.2.2.) and make redress mandatory.

Article 6 of the Sales Directive lists some important requirements for the content of the guarantee. Special provisions of the Code on consumer sales

86. The Law on Consumer Protection of the Republic of Lithuania, new wording of 2000.10.11, Official gazette No. 85-2581, 2000.10.11, available at http://www3.lrs.lt/c-bin/eng/preps2?Condition1=114309&Condition2.

contracts, namely Article 6.353(1), establish the seller's obligation to provide the necessary information about goods to the consumer, including terms of the guarantee. The Code regulates the term of the guarantee in Article 6.335—it states that the term of the guarantee begins to run from the moment of handover of the goods, unless the parties agree otherwise. It also covers other matters, none of which relate to the contents of the guarantee itself.

### 3.2.4. Hungary

If we follow Vékás'[87] detailed account of the implementation of Directive 99/44 into Hungarian private law, there was agreement to amend the respective provisions of the Civil Code of 1959, and not to create a special law on consumer sales, as in Latvia and Poland. One of the reasons was the modern concept of liability of the seller based on the agreement; the concept used was 'defective performance,' which is identical to 'lack of conformity' in the sense of Article 2 of the Directive. Some provisions of the implementing legislation became less 'consumer-friendly.' In the old Hungarian Civil Code, only positive knowledge of non-conformity excluded the seller's liability, while the Directive, in Article 2(3), extends it to the case where the 'consumer could not reasonably be unaware of the lack of conformity,' which was adopted by section 305/A(2) of the Civil Code.

The remedies of Article 3 of the Directive were transposed into Hungarian law and extended by making use of the former case law of the Hungarian Supreme Court, for example on giving the consumer a right to retain the purchase price in case of non-conformity. There is also a right to self-repair and to the reimbursement of such costs, if the seller does not complete the repair within an adequate time (section 306(3)).[88] As in the earlier law, the consumer must inform the seller of lack of conformity within two months, in accordance with Article 5(2) of Directive 99/44. This period may be extended. Lack of information leads not to a loss of remedies, but only to an obligation to pay the seller the additional costs caused by the delay (section 307 Civil Code). The general time limit for actions against a seller has been extended to two years, but only for consumer sales.

The seller has a right of redress against his prior seller for the costs of fulfilling the consumer's claims, provided that the latter had informed the seller about the lack of conformity. The time limit for redress is 60 days after fulfilling the consumer's claims, and not more than five years in all. This right

87. Vékás, *supra* note 13, at 41–68.
88. Vékás, *supra* note 13, at 65.

of redress can be waived in part or completely[89]—a somewhat problematic solution with regard to Art. 4 to Dir. 99/44.

The Hungarian legislator also made clear that the contractual guarantee does not alter the consumer's rights in law (section 248 Civil Code). The guarantee is not a mandatory instrument. The rights under the guarantee have to be exercised similarly to the remedies for non-conformity. The transparency and form requirements of the guarantee have been transposed into law, but their lack does not avoid the claim.

Vékás[90] summarizes the Hungarian transposition of Directive 99/44 as follows:

> The transposition must be said to be a success. It is practically in full conformity with the directive, except for some minor errors. It must be particularly welcomed that the new rules have been organically integrated into the existing provisions of the Civil Code even where they go beyond the directive, and that the few special rules on consumer sales have been separated. In my opinion, the maintenance of non-mandatory rules including the right of redress must be clearly supported.

### 3.2.5. Poland

Poland has implemented Directive 99/44 not by amending its Civil Code of 1964, but by special Act of 27 July 2002, effective from 1 January 2003. At the same time it tried to create comprehensive consumer sales legislation, going further than Directive 99/44. The information requirements of the Act are dealt with *infra at* 4.2.5.

Section 1 defines its sphere of application similarly to the Directive. Articles 4–7 contain the transposition of Article 2 of the Directive. The provision in Article 2(4) on the cases where a seller is not bound by statements of the producer or his representative has been adopted by Polish law, with the exception of the alternative that 'at the time of conclusion of the contract the statement had been corrected.'

Section 8 of the Polish Act transposes Article 3 of Directive 99/44 on the rights of the consumer. The definition of 'free of charge' in Article 3(4) is extended to cover costs borne by the buyer, 'particularly costs of disassembly, delivery, labour, materials, as well as costs of another installation by other

89. Defended by Vékás *supra* note 13 at 67 referring to the freedom of contract principles which, however, are applicable here only to a limited extent.

90. *Ibid.*, at 68.

means.' The Act therefore confirmed the existence of a far-reaching right of the consumer to self-help, like Hungarian law. The limits of such self-help are not defined. The seller must react to a demand to repair or replace within 14 days. If he does not do so, the demand 'shall be deemed justified.'

Section 10 is concerned with time limits and prescription within the limits allowed by the Directive. Section 9 imposes a two-months notification period. Section 11 makes the rights of the consumer mandatory and tries to avoid their circumvention by a buyer's statement 'that he had the knowledge of the non-conformity of the consumer good with the agreement, or by opting to apply a foreign law.'

Section 13 contains detailed rules on warranties, as regards their contents, transparency, and the giving of the address of the warrantor 'or his representative in Poland'. It must be formulated in Polish.[91] Violation of these requirements does not affect the validity of the warranty, as provided for in Article 6(5) of the Directive.

Art. 12 of the Act contains a general rule on the right of redress. It refers to the general provisions of the Polish Civil Code, which mean that they can be contracted out of in accordance with the general rules of civil law.[92] It is not certain to what extent protection under standard term legislation (*supra* 2.2.5) is available in this context.

# 4. Information

## *4.1. Generalities: EC Law as the Starting Point*

Autonomy requires actors who are informed about their rights and duties. In traditional legal concepts, it is usually left to the actors themselves to acquire the necessary information that makes their freedom of action possible and effective. *Caveat emptor* as the general rule of autonomous transactions in contract law includes the responsibility to keep oneself informed. Autonomy is thus reduced to a formal concept based on the fiction that actors either have or can get the information needed to make decisions. Eventually they will have to 'buy' and pay for it if they do not want to rely on information conveyed through advertising.

Community law as a basically liberal order also started from this principle. However, it has increasingly recognized that autonomy in a substantive sense

91. Cierpial, in: WIRO PL D II para 88.
92. Pasiek, in: WIRO PL D VI para 45.

must be supplemented by the provision of adequate information. In the meantime, information requirements as regards citizens have become part of primary Community law itself, as seen especially in Article 153(1) EC. This contains the consumer's right to information, which of course also includes (pre-)contractual information, even though it has to be implemented by specific directives. The objective of Community law, as a study by Rösler has stated, is the timely, specific, and complete disclosure of relevant information to the consumer as the structurally weaker party to a contract.[93] We will not go into details of the information paradigm in Community law, which can be found on three levels:

- The interdiction of deceptive and misleading information—a rule particularly applicable to marketing practices;
- The transparency principle in pre-contractual negotiations;[94]
- Specific information obligations in consumer directives.[95]

## *4.2. Information Requirements in Contract Legislation of New Member States*

### 4.2.1. Estonia

The Estonian Code of Obligations contains a general information rule concerning pre-contractual negotiations. Section 14(2) reads:

> Persons who engage in pre-contractual negotiations or other preparations for entering into a contract shall inform the other party of all circumstances with regard to which the other party has, based on the purpose of the contract, an identifiable essential interest. There is no obligation to inform the other party of such circumstances of which the other party could not reasonably be expected to be informed.

Obviously, this broad obligation must be filled out by case law which, to our knowledge, does not yet exist. It is worth mentioning that the information obligation is not limited to consumer contracts, even though it will have its main ambit there.

93. See Rösler, *supra* note 15, at 148, 168.

94. For its importance in the implementation of Community law see Case C-144/99 *Commission v Netherlands* [2001] ECR I-3541.

95. For details see Reich, *supra* note 3, at 299–2302.

### 4.2.2. Latvia

The limited application of a general duty to act in good faith also underpins the legal regulation of pre-contractual duties on information in Latvian civil legislation. The Civil Code of 1937 regulates pre-contractual duties only in general terms. Thus, the scope of the *culpa in contrahendo* provision as a basis for pre-contractual information in the Latvian Civil Code is quite narrow, generally covering only intentional misconduct, and not negligence. In the light of this, it has been suggested in Latvian legal literature that amendments need to be made to the law, requiring the pre-contractual negotiations to be conducted in good faith, with the intention of entering into contractual relations.[96]

The principle requiring transparency of pre-formulated terms on price or the subject matter of a contract (Article 4(2) of Directive 93/13) seems to be omitted and not transposed into the CRP Act at all. On the hand, the rules on the transparency of a guarantee in sales contracts have been introduced into the Latvian CPR Act (*supra* 3.2.2.).

Latvia has specific legislation concerning the use of the Latvian language as the official state language (rather than Russian, which was the second or even first language in Soviet times). It is mostly concerned with state activities, but some effects spill over into private law relations which are justified, according to section 2, by concerns of public security, public health, consumer protection, and the like. Thus, section 9 reads:

> Contracts of natural and legal persons regarding provision of medical treatment, health care, public safety and other public services in the territory of Latvia shall be entered into the official language. If a contract is in a foreign language, a translation into the official language shall be attached thereto.

It is somewhat surprising that this strict rule is justified by concerns of consumer protection, because the consumer to be protected may not know Latvian at all. Latvian law also contains a general exception to rules on the use of language in private international law which normally would be either the language of the law applicable to the contract or the language in which the parties negotiated. It is also not clear what the consequences of disregarding this provision are: will the entire contract be avoided if it is drafted in a foreign

96. See Balodis, *supra* note 58.

language without a translation attached to it, or does it only entail an obligation to provide a translation?

### 4.2.3. Lithuania

The Lithuanian Civil Code expressly obliges parties to reveal to each other information essential for the conclusion of a contract.[97] Furthermore, where confidential information is given by one party in the course of negotiations, the other party is under a duty not to disclose that information or to use it improperly for its own purposes, whether or not a contract is subsequently concluded.[98] A party which breaches this obligation is liable for the losses caused to the other party.[99] Article 6.164(2) provides that minimum losses in such situations are equal to the benefit received by the other party.

Under both the Law on Consumer Protection and the Civil Code, consumers are entitled to receive in the Lithuanian language (except when the use of the goods and services is known by custom) correct, complete, and transparent information concerning the terms under which goods and services are purchased, their quality, directions for use, a description of warranties and exchange period, procedures for termination of contracts for goods or services, and other relevant information which is significant to consumers.[100]

If the consumer was not provided with relevant information he has the right to claim damages, or unilaterally to terminate the contract, reclaim sums paid by him, and claim other damages if the contract was concluded.[101] Moreover, if the seller fails to provide the necessary information, he is responsible for defects in the goods which occurred after the goods were delivered to the consumer, when the consumer proves that the defect occurred because of the lack of information.[102]

### 4.2.4. Hungary

The Hungarian Civil Code contains a general information obligation in section 205(4) which reads:

> The parties have to cooperate when concluding a contract and take care of the justified interests of the other side. Before concluding the

97. Art. 6.163(4) Civil Code.
98. Art. 6.164(1) Civil Code.
99. *Ibid.*
100. Art. 6.353 Civil Code and Art. 5 Law on Consumer Protection.
101. Art. 6.353(9) Civil Code.
102. Art. 6.353(10) Civil Code.

> contract they have to inform each other about the relevant essential circumstances concerning the contract to be concluded.

This rule has been extensively used by the Hungarian courts to impose information requirements, particularly in relations in which the parties are not equally informed. It is supplemented by specific information obligations which are derived from transposing EC directives, namely on unfair contract terms and on consumer sales.

The Consumer Protection Act of 1997 gives the consumer two important rights to information:

- Information with regard to the product or service purchased; and
- Information about remedies—certainly an innovative provision.

### 4.2.5. Poland

Specific information requirements are included in the new Act of 27 July 2002 on consumer sales (*supra* 3.2.5.). Section 2 contains a requirement for general information on price, unit price, and the conditions of a hire purchase or similar agreement. At the buyer's request the seller must 'issue a written[103] confirmation of the conclusion of the agreement, including the seller's mark bearing his address, date of sale and specification of the consumer good together with its amount and price.' Section 3 contains a requirement for sales in Poland 'to provide clear, understandable, not misleading information in Polish, necessary for proper and full use of the consumer good.' There are detailed rules with regard to the placement of the information, instructions for use, maintenance manuals, all in Polish. 'At the buyer's request the seller shall explain the meaning of each provision of the agreement.' The Polish language requirement, written into the Act on language which contains this requirement for 'legal transactions performed within the territory of Poland,'[104] is, however, not without problems in the context of party autonomy and free movement of products and services. It is also no sure whether this is a requirement for the validity of a contract which requires written form.[105]

---

103. It is not clear whether this confirmation can also be in an electronic form, which seems to be required by Art. 9 of Dir. 2000/31/EC of 8 June 2000 of the EP and the Council on Electronic Commerce, OJ [2000] L 178/1.

104. See Klapsa, 'Die Auswirkungen des Gesetzes über die polnische Sprache auf die Vertragpraxis' *WIRO* [2000] 233; Surdeck/Binieda, *supra* note 71 at 479

105. Cierpial, WIRO PL D II para 53

# 5. Contract Law 'in the Books' and 'in Action': 'New' Rules for 'Old' Mechanisms of Civil Justice?

## *5.2. A Summary of the 'New' Contract Law of 'New' Member States*

The investigation made above has shown that the principles of autonomy, regulation, and information as basic requirements of a market-conforming contract law, integrating consumer protection requirements, have been adopted by all former socialist countries now members of the EU, but that the methods and instruments chosen for doing so differ widely. We have distinguished between a 'monist approach' (Estonia), a 'dualist approach' (Latvia), a 'parallel approach' (Lithuanian), a 'modified uniform approach' (Hungary), and a 'mixed approach' (Poland). This shows the richness of European legal cultures after the enlargement process which will certainly give impetus to the emergence of a 'modern' European contract law. European contract law is truly an experimental field and maybe even be used for trying out for a 'competition of better rules', for example on how to implement general information requirements written into some modern contract legislation (Estonia, Lithuania, to some extent also Hungary and Poland), on redress of the final seller in consumer sales contracts (Latvia, Lithuania), on transparency of guarantees (Estonia, Latvia, Hungary, to some extent also Poland), in improving remedies under EU law (Lithuania, Hungary), in prescribing spill-over effects to general contract law which has not yet been reformed (Latvia). At the same time, it warns against too much uniformity, and may discourage those who are optimistically promoting a 'European Civil Code.'

European law, in both its general principles and its specific directives, has had an enormous impact on the contract law of the new Member States under scrutiny here. It is even more remarkable that this process has been accomplished before, and not after, membership. There may be certain deficiencies with regard to the implementation of directives, for example on the hierarchy of consumer remedies in sales contracts (Latvia, Lithuania), but they cannot be said to be such as to endanger the European legal integration model—quite the contrary. They have strongly reinforced general contract law principles like good faith and control over standard contract terms. They have allowed specific contract law, most notably on consumer protection, to 'spill over' into general contract law. They have encouraged integrationist models of contract law which have clearly shown the deficits of a dualist model, as in Latvia. *EU law has therefore been an instrument of transformation and modernization of contract law*—similar to the situation in 'old' Member States like Germany.

This chapter is not concerned with the implementation of EC law as such by the new Member States. Two seemingly contradictory trends should however be mentioned:

- All the new Member States analysed here have made great efforts to bring their contract law in line with basic EC directives before membership, even though via different methods as they are entitled to do under Article 249(3) EC.
- On the other hand, there is a certain tendency to extend consumer protection provisions into areas which are not covered by consumer law, for example rules on the territorial application of consumer law (Estonia, Poland), the widening of the concept of consumer to certain B2B transactions (formerly Latvia), applying the rules on pre-formulated contracts also to individually negotiated clauses (Hungary), mandatory language rules beyond the accepted limits of party autonomy and free movement (Lithuania, Poland, and to some extent also Latvia).
- Finally, ambiguities in EU Directives themselves create transposition problems particularly in new Member States, for example the concept of unfair terms (Latvia, Hungary), redress of the seller (different solutions in Latvia/Lithuania on the one hand, Hungary on the other, and a limited solution in Poland, which creates problems with cross-border transactions), and remedies for disrespect of consumer law obligations.

## 5.2. 'Law in Action': Deficits in Civil Justice?

What much less is known about is the working of the 'reconstruction of contract law' in the countries under scrutiny. This is to some extent due to the relative 'youth' of the legislation under examination. Some case law has emerged, little of which is known to the foreign observer. We simply do not know yet how the new 'law in the books' really works, and where the fault lines within the legal systems of new Member countries arise.

This leads to a more fundamental problem: the weakness of the institutions of civil justice after the fall of socialism. Harmathy has said with regard to Hungary that 'the element of insecurity in contractual relationships may also be found in the form that the party crediting his contractual counterpart is unable to know whether the debtor will fulfil his obligations in accordance with the contract.'[106] The quality of judicial decisions in Hungary has been re-

106. See Harmathy, 'Hungarian Civil Law since 1990', 43 *Acta Juridica Hungarica* (2002) 1, at 17.

peatedly criticized;[107] a theory of judicial precedent is only just emerging.[108] With regard to Poland, Letowska[109] criticized the lack of focus on the implementation of new laws; this is 'left to its own resources' (which are scarce). Torgans, the leading Latvian scholar of civil law, criticizes the 'excessive dogmatism or formalism' of Latvian court practice,[110] which makes a flexible adaptation to modern market conditions difficult. The Open Society Institute,[111] in a study done for the EC Commission before accession, voiced concerns over judicial independence in some of the countries under scrutiny. Unfortunately, there is no up-to-date information on this.

A more general and highly critical discussion could be found in a paper done before membership by Emmert.[112] Talking from own experience, he saw problems in applying the law in the new Member States, not so much in the legislative framework but in the missing 'suitable structure ... to ensure the application and enforcement of the new legal rules in practice.'[113] Emmert also identified methodological weaknesses which, in his opinion, are part of the communist heritage. Judges were trained to apply written law only in a rather formal manner. 'They have no training to overcome lacunae in the law, for example by recourse to general principles of law ... The judges have no experience with the concept of justice in contrast to the concept of law.'[114] There was no professional legal argument, nor a thorough discussion of existing case law. Citizens have no confidence in the working of civil justice.[115] 'Legal education has to be reformed more rapidly to reflect not only the changes in leg-

107. See Küper, 'Zivilrechtsprechung in Ungarn: die Metro-Urteile und die ungarische Vertragsrechtsdogmatik' [1999] *WIRO* 366.

108. See Pokol, 'Statutory Interpretation and Precedent in Hungary', 46 *Osteuroparecht* (2000) 262, at 274–288.

109. See Letowska, 'Between Knowledge and Skill: Obstacles to Efficient Implementation of the Community Consumer Law in Poland', in M. Kepinski (ed.), *The Evaluation of the New Polish Legislation in the Matter of Consumer Protection from the European Perspective* (2001), Conference proceedings, Zakrzewo, 21–23 June 2001, at 19–32.

110. See Torgans, 'Contract Law: Latvia an the EU', in University of Latvia, *supra* note 25, at 24, 31.

111. See Open Society Institute (ed.), *Judicial Independence—Monitoring the EU Accession Process* (2001), at 16–69, with detailed recommendations for improvement which will not be taken up here.

112. See Emmert, 'Administrative and Court Reform in Central and Eastern Europe', 9 *ELJ* 288 (2003).

113. *Ibid.*, at 289.

114. *Ibid.*, at 295.

115. See Holmes, 'Citizen and Law after Communism', 7 *East European Con Rev* (1998) 1.

islation but also the (necessary) changes in legal culture.'[116] Critical academic discussion of case law and regulatory action should be encouraged. The system of hierarchical court administration should be changed to allow for more self-administration.

Emmert pointed to structural problems of civil justice which had been more or less present in all countries studied here. On the other hand, with the improved quality of legislation, especially the adoption of new civil codes, as in Estonia and in Lithuania, the administration of justice has also improved. Complicated problems of multi-level application of legislation from completely different traditions, as in Latvia and to some extent Poland, should be avoided in the interest of a more transparent and responsible administration of civil justice.

Some of the arguments of Emmert's study seem anecdotal and exaggerated today. They need to be tested against the development of the countries studied here under the impact of full membership. To conclude, the enormous changes in substantive and procedural law, the role of the judiciary, training of legal personnel, and finally the adoption of the excessively complex *acquis* may necessitate a rethinking of these hypotheses. The Latvian judge at the ECJ, Egils Levits, is probably right in observing:

> [Mastering interpretation methods regarding general clauses] has been a serious problem in Eastern European countries where these ... methods were neither recognised nor used in the inherited socialist traditions of law. In the course of time the situation improved when the content of legal education slowly approached European (continental) education. In recent years, too, in Latvia it can be observed that civil servants' and judges' knowledge of interpretation methods is becoming better.[117]

A similar view was taken by a Polish lawyer, Rafal Manko[118] writing as a result of the necessary reorientation of private law provoked by the enlargement process, while criticising the still prevailing dogmatic method in legal reasoning in Poland:

> "... the paper emphasise(s) the originality and particularity of Polish legal culture, despite the fact that many Western and eastern influ-

116. See Emmert, *supra* note 102, at 302.

117. See Levits, 'General Clauses and Discretionary Power of Administrative Institutions and Courts' [2004] *Law and Justice* 2, at 9, para. 37.

118. Central European Private Law after Enlargement, [2005] ELJ 527 at 548.

ences.... have been moulded together in formation. The particularity of Central Europe should be taken into account by Western academic lawyers, especially in comparative legal research.... One of the ways of facilitating the necessary dialogue seems to be the concentration of discourse on substantive, rather than formal aspects of legal rules and institutions. The formal and dogmatic approach to the law, inherited from Pandectism and fossiled by socialism, should therefore give way to a more transparent, substantive and, to an appropriate extent, also pragmatic and functional approach to legal problems and proposed solutions ..."

# 8

# European Consumer Law

Thomas Wilhelmsson, Geraint Howells & Hans-W. Micklitz

## Summary



## 1. Introduction

Private law in Europe traditionally did not recognise the concept of the 'consumer.' The idea of a particular field of law called 'consumer law' was alien to private law thinking in Europe. Only since the 1970s has consumer protection and the understanding that particular rules for consumer relationships might need to be introduced in private law been on the agenda in at least some European countries. This has been reinforced by the broad intervention of the EC/EU in this area. As will be shown, consumer law is the part of private law on which the European influence has been the strongest to-date.

The emergence of consumer protection and particular rules for consumer relationships has not, however, removed the issue of the relationship between consumer protection rules and general private law from the academic agenda. In particular the discussion on the relationship between contract law in general, or commercial contract law, and consumer contract law is a modern classic in many countries.

The academic debate concerning the possible separation of consumer law from the general body of private law has focused attention on various kinds of arguments.[1] Some refer to the pedagogical argument that consumer rules are more comprehensible, if one does not have continuously to read them in conjunction with general private law rules. Others, however, interpret pedagogics the other way: private law is easier to learn if all its rules, including those regarding consumer protection, are gathered in one comprehensive code. Some underline the legal-technical difficulties arising, if there are different sets of rules for different relationships. Admittedly, certain problems relating to the borderline do arise, as shown below in the section on the definition of the consumer. However, as these are very few in comparison with the quantity of cases dealt with in the area, the legal-technical argument does not seem highly important in this context. Rather one should look at the substantive issue. Is there a different morality or rationality behind the provisions of consumer law that would warrant its separation from general private law? Some would certainly give an affirmative answer to this question. Others, however, would understand the differences as matters of degree rather than of principle. Also, general private law and contract law do contain a 'social' element that can be strengthened by the interaction with consumer law principles. The decisive issue for many seems to be the wished-for interaction between consumer law and general private law. Does one want to infuse more welfarist thinking in general private law by integrating consumer law into it, or is one rather inclined to keep private law 'pure' from such influences? This works the other way around as well: does one fear the weakening of the consumer protection agenda if integrated into a more general private law framework, or does one perhaps even wish for such a development?

As can be seen, all arguments in the integration/separation debate can be met by reasonable counterarguments. Therefore, it is quite natural that in Europe one finds many solutions,[2] from very integrated systems in many coun-

1. See, e.g., T. Wilhelmsson, *International lex mercatoria and local consumer law: an impossible combination, Uniform Law Review* 8 (2003), 141–153.

2. See more closely e.g. C. Joustra, *Consumer Law*, in A. Hartkamp et al. (eds.), *Towards a European Civil Code*, 2nd Edition (The Hague 1998), 134–139. For some reason

tries (like Germany today[3]) to a relatively autonomous consumer contract law in other countries, either with specific consumer codes (like in France and Belgium, as well as Finland) or a largely independent consumer contract legislation (like in Sweden). This makes it difficult to predict where in any given system one may find the provisions on a certain topic.[4]

Consumer law provisions are practically important as they regulate mass transactions and they are also legally interesting, as consumer law often has been the channel for introducing new ideas into European private law. Therefore the approach of the Principles of European Contract Law (PECL) to the consumer law issue is problematic. PECL formally includes consumer relations, but in fact allows arguments related to such relations little influence on the content of the principles. The "general" solutions offered by PECL are not always very suitable for consumer relations.[5] Despite the general scope of PECL, the collection of principles does not "make special provision for consumer contracts."[6] Consumer law is treated as *lex specialis*, general contract law is understood as commercial contract law. Such an approach marginalises consumer law more than is warranted by its societal importance. The recently published draft Common Frame of Reference[7] gives a more central role to consumer law as it in part was inspired by the existing *acquis* that is largely comprised of consumer law.

Consumer law does not only have a relationship to private law. Consumer law has always been multidisciplinary In addition to provisions relating to contract law and other areas of typical private law, various measures of administrative character have been used to protect the consumer as well. Some Member States, like France and the United Kingdom, have also used criminal law measures quite extensively in order to protect the consumer. As the European consumer law directives often leave the enforcement issues to the national im-

---

the particular chapter on consumer law has been omitted from the Third Edition (The Hague 2004) of the book.

3. Most of the consumer contract law rules of European origin were put into the BGB in the well-known *Schuldrechtsreform* at the turn of the century.

4. Joustra, *Consumer Law*, 137.

5. Examples are given e.g. by Joustra, *Consumer law*, 147 and S. C. Lapuente, *The Hypothetical 'European Civil Code': Why, How, When?, ERA-Forum* (2002), 96–97; H-W. Micklitz, The Principles of European Contract Law and the Protection of the Weaker Party, JCP 2004, 339–356.

6. O. Lando and H. Beale (eds.), *Principles of European Contract Law, Parts I and II* (The Hague 2000).

7. C von Bar and H. Schulte-Nölke, *Principles, Definitions and Model Rules of European Private Law*, (Munich, 2008).

plementation, they have not affected to any considerable extent the relatively large variety of different models of consumer protection to be found in Europe with regard to the legal and administrative means used.

Because of the scope of the present handbook, in this chapter we focus mainly on private law. However, in order to understand the place and role of private law consumer protection, in the more general sections at the beginning the variations in European measures and national models have to be described more comprehensively. The narrower focus is then adopted in the analysis of some of the general principles of European consumer law. Here we look mainly at principles embodied in European consumer contract law, in European product liability law and, to some extent, European unfair commercial practices law.

## 2. National and European Consumer Law

Driven by the European Commission, the Community has implemented the crucial statements of the two consumer policy programmes of 1975 and 1981.[8] The five fundamental rights—the right to protection for health and safety, the right to protection for economic interests, the right to claim damages, the right to education as well as the right to legal representation (the right to be heard in a courtroom), have become reality to a large extent. The right of protection of health and safety has not only obtained quasi-constitutional status within the European legal system, but has also assumed well developed contours in the Product Safety Directive.[9] The right of protection of economic interests of the consumer is reflected in several Directives which fall into two categories; on the one hand the protection against unfair and misleading advertising practices and on the other hand the establishment of a genuine European consumer contract law. The right to claim damages constitutes the foundation for the adoption of the Product Liability Directive.[10] The right of education, updated to encompass the right of information, has been moved up the legal agenda and given a constitutionally recognised status upon the adoption of the Treaty

8. Overview over the European consumer policy since the first programme: H. Rösler, *30 Jahre Verbraucherpolitik in Europa, Zeitschrift für Rechtsvergleichung, Internationales Privatrecht und Europarecht* 21 (2005), 134. For its latest agenda see EU Consumer Policy strategy 2007–2013, COM(2007) 99 final.

9. Directive 2001/95 on general product safety, OJ L 11/4.

10. Directive 85/374 on the approximation of the laws, regulations and administrative provisions of the Member States concerning liability for defective products, OJ L 210, 29, amended by Directive 99/34 OJ L 414/20.

of Amsterdam.[11] Its manifold reflection can be found in a broad canon of duties to inform. However, the education of consumers has only partially become an issue within Community law. The right to legal representation (the right to be heard in a courtroom) has been a main theme of numerous activities of the European Commission. Not expressly stated, but closely related to the right of legal representation, is the gradual development by the ECJ of the principle of granting an appropriate and effective legal protection.[12]

European consumer law brought a substantial innovative push in many Member States' legal systems.[13] At present, efforts to divest consumer law of its special characteristics and to reinstate the regulations of traditional civil and public law play a predominant role.[14] The right of protection of health and safety is politically programmatically reduced to the right to purchase safe products.[15] The technical law on the safety of products loses importance.[16] Similar developments can be observed in consumer civil law. Efforts within the European Community to establish a European civil law proceed from the assumption that consumer law is meant to be an integral part of the future European civil law,[17] although it seems as if EC consumer law will remain separate from European civil law. As mentioned in the introduction, the integration of consumer law into civil law carries the prospect of transplanting consumer-welfarist ideas to the general private law, but also the fear of watering down the content of the consumer protection provisions. The Product Liability Directive serves the European Commission as a base point for the es-

---

11. N. Reich, *Verbraucherpolitik und Verbraucherschutz im Vertrag von Amsterdam, Verbraucher und Recht* 14 (1999), 3.

12. N. Reich and H-W.Micklitz, *Europäisches Verbraucherrecht*, 4th edition (Baden-Baden 2003), §§28–30; H-W. Micklitz, Peter Rott and N. Reich, Understanding EU Consumer Law (Antwerpen, Oxford 2009 forthcoming), chapter 8.

13. K. Tonner, *Die Rolle des Verbraucherrechts bei der Entwicklung eines europäischen Zivilrechts, Juristenzeitung* 51 (1996), 533.

14. The notification of the European Commission and the European Parliament on the European contract law COM(2001) 398 final has raised a debate on a large scale on the future of European private law; from a consumer law perspective see S. Weatherill, *The European Commission's Green Paper on European Contract Law: Context, Content and Constitutionality, Journal of Consumer Policy* 24 (2001), 339–399.

15. H-W. Micklitz, *Internationales Produktsicherheitsrecht* (Baden-Baden 1996).

16. C. Schieble, *Deutsches und Europäisches Produktsicherheitsrecht*, (Baden-Baden 2003).

17. H. Schulte-Noelke and R. Schulze in association with L. Bernardeau (ed.), *Europäisches Vertragsrecht im Gemeinschaftsrecht* (Köln 2002); contrary to Lando and Beale (eds.), *Principles of European Contract Law, Part I and II*, prepared by the Commission on European Contract Law; which rather leaves consumer in the hands of nation states. See now the draft Common Frame of Reference.

tablishment of a uniform European liability law.[18] The specific system of legal redress with regards to the consumer is absorbed by reflections to establish and to extend a European judicial system.[19]

Upon the adoption of the first consumer protection programme in the year 1975, the initial position between the Member States and the European Commission changed drastically. Within a few years the Commission took the political initiative and bundled the different national approaches into a common European approach, which led to an increase in consumer protection in the majority of the Member States. At least some Member States appeared politically relieved to be able to hand over the nationally complex, and heterogonous field of consumer politics to the European Commission.

EC law underwent different phases.[20] The first development phase, which lasted until the adoption of the Single European Act, was characterised by social-state considerations, reflecting the Commission's efforts to take the idea of protection into account. This is shown by the development of the Doorstep Selling Directive[21] which sought to protect the consumer in respect of contracts negotiated away from business premises. The change from the EC's concern with consumer *protection* law to simply consumer law, with less emphasis on protection and more on harmonisation, commenced upon the adoption of Single European Act. The extremely influential Sutherland-Report[22] provided the legitimation for the Commission's new approach. Ever since then, consumer protection and consumer law are seen as an integral part of the project to complete the Single European Market. Within a short period of time the Package Tour Directive,[23] the Unfair Contract Terms Directive,[24] the Time-

18. The harmless sounding invitation to tender, A call for tender Markt/2002/11/D—Comparison of the national laws implementing Directive 85/374 on liability for defective products with other existing liability systems, contains in its main feature an important instrument of legal policy which the ECJ has raised in its rulings regarding Art. 13 of the Product Liability Directive.

19. Green book on alternative dispute resolution regarding civil and commercial law COM(2002) 196 final; Green paper on consumer collective redress COM (2008) 794 final.

20. H-W. Micklitz, *Introductory remarks §§13, 14 BGB, 28, 29* in *Münchener Kommentar zum Bürgerlichen Gesetzbuch*, Band 1, 4th edition (München 2001).

21. Directive 85/577 to protect the consumer in respect of contracts negotiated away from business premises, OJ L 372/31.

22. P. Sutherland, *The Internal Market After 1992: Meeting the Challenge. Report presented to the Commission by the High Level Group on the functioning of the Internal Market* (1992), 2277. This paper was meant to define the role and function of the consumer in the Internal Market.

23. Directive 90/314 on package travel, package holidays and package tours, OJ L 158/59.

24. Directive 93/13 on unfair terms in consumer contracts, OJ L 95/29.

share Directive,[25] the Distance Contracts Directive,[26] the Injunctions Directive,[27] the Consumer Sales Directive[28] and the Financial Services Distance Marketing Directive[29] had been adopted.

For a long time it appeared as if the European Community merely pursued a piece-meal approach, limiting its efforts to the selective enactment of provisions. Only towards the end of the nineties did it become evident that the Commission was working towards the development of an all embracing European consumer law. This is particularly striking in the development of consumer civil law. The Directives which govern the modalities of the conclusion of contracts lie at its heart.[30] These include the Doorstep Selling Directive, the Distance Contracts Directive and the Financial Services Distance Marketing Directive. The Unfair Contract Terms Directive opens the possibility to legally scrutinise horizontal standard business conditions. Specific consumer law, as regulated in the above-mentioned directives, governs almost all relevant types of contracts and product liability law; consumer sales, package tours, timesharing, consumer credit and product liability. The development of European consumer private law—with the Consumer Sales and Product Liability Directives as its spearhead—has contributed to the increased discussion about a future European civil law following the publication of the Commission's communication on European contract law.[31]

25. Directive 94/47 on the protection of purchasers in respect of certain aspects of contracts relating to the purchase of the right to use immovable properties on a timeshare basis, OJ L 280/83. See proposal to amend at COM(2007) 303 final.

26. Directive 97/7 on the protection of consumers in respect of distance contracts, OJ L 144,/19.

27. Directive 98/27 on injunctions for the protection of consumers' interests, OJ L 166/51.

28. Directive 99/44 on certain aspects of the sale of consumer goods and associated guarantees, OJ L 171/12.

29. Directive 2002/65 concerning the distance marketing of consumer financial services, OJ L 271/16.

30. H-W. Micklitz, *Vertragschlussmodalitäten*, in H-W. Micklitz, T. Pfeiffer, K. Tonner, A. Willingmann (eds.), *Schuldrechtsreform und Verbraucherschutz*, series of publications VIEW, Volume IX, (Baden-Baden 2001), 191.

31. Cf. Notification of the European Commission and the European Parliament on the European contract law, COM (2001) 398 final, thereto the entire spectrum of all contributions in Schulte-Noelke and Schulze, *Europäisches vertragsrecht in Gesellschaftsrecht*, as well as the two follow-up communications, A more coherent European Contract Law—An action plan, COM (2003) 68 final and European Contract Law and the revision of the acquis: the way forward, COM (2004) 651 final.

Within the past 20 years, the Commission has refined the regulatory techniques. A comparison of the Doorstep Selling Directive and Distance Contracts Directive, which address similar issues provide us with a significant example of this shift. In the Distance Contracts Directive, the Commission generated an approach which it had already outlined in its first draft of the Doorstep Selling Directive at the beginning of the seventies.[32] The regulatory freedom that remains with the member states shrinks. Until the beginning of the 2000s most of the Directives have been based on the principle of minimum harmonisation that left the Member States free to introduce more protective measures than the directive prescribes. For some issues, the Commission in fact has set standards that approached a reasonable maximum harmonisation. Indeed more protective rules could potentially be challenged under free movement rules. In other areas the Directives reflected the minimum on which consensus could be reached and many states with more protective rules were allowed to maintain them in place. Indeed for a time the Commission even encouraged member states to use the minimal harmonization clause to experiment with new stricter consumer protection rules that might serve as a model for the future development of more progressive European minimum standards.

The minimum harmonisation approach was regularly used with respect to the protection of the consumers' economic interests, and their rights of education and legal representation. The protection of health and safety was treated differently. The right to claim compensation for damages is an example. The Product Liability Directive aimed at full harmonisation and only gave limited freedom to the Member States.[33]

From the viewpoint of legal politics, the character of the formula of minimum harmonisation is determined by compromises. Along with the Single European Act, the Commission had acquired competences in the scope of consumer law which were strengthened in the Treaties on the European Community signed in Maastricht and Amsterdam. The Member States defended their national legal cultures and traditions by referring to the requirement for minimum harmonisation. From a legal-theoretical point of view, minimum harmonisation played an increasing role in the discussion on the future of the European private law.[34] With the help of this principle, national tra-

32. Proposal for a Council directive to protect the consumer in respect of contracts which have been negotiated away from business premises, COM(76) 544 final.

33. Case C-183/00, *González Sánchez v Medicina Asturia* (2002) ECR I-3901.

34. J. Stuyck, *Patterns of Justice in the Constitutional Charter: minimum harmonization in the field of consumer law, Liber Amicorum N. Reich, Law and diffuse Interests in the Eu-*

ditions and cultures could be retained and secured against the advance of Community law.[35]

However, the tide has turned. An independent European legal tradition is in the process of being established. This is unlikely to be compatible with the regulatory traditions of the Member States. The Commission has established full harmonisation as the new objective of its politics.[36] Obviously, the Commission intends to stop the Member States minding their "consumer-gardens." The more the Community is going to regulate the Single Market, the less it can tolerate solo efforts. The Commission took a first step in this direction with the EC Directive concerning distance marketing of consumer financial services. It was largely successful in its efforts, although Member States retained some control of matters such as what information should be provided. A decisive breakthrough came with the Unfair Commercial Practices Directive which prohibits unfair commercial practices in B2C relations.[37] The Commission is keen to follow this approach also in the contract law areas. It was central to its philosophy when reforming the Consumer Credit Directive, even if in the end it had to accept many aspects remaining the subject of national law.[38] The Commission has reviewed eight consumer law directives under this perspective. It seems to have be come pragmatic talking of "targeted" maximal harmonization, but the draft Directive seems to have targeted a very broad range of topics for the maximal harmonization treatment.[39] Now the minimum maximum discussion is well and truly on the agenda. It represents a clash between two ideologies—one that believes in consumer protection the other in the internal market and often the unity of civil law.

---

*ropean Legal Order* (Baden-Baden 1997), 279; T. Wilhelmsson, *Is There a European Consumer Law—and Should There Be One?* (Rome 2000).

35. P. Legrand, *European Legal Systems are not converging, International and Comparative Law Quarterly* 45 (1996), 52; same author, *Against a European Civil Code, Modern Law Review* 60 (1997), 44.

36. Communication from the Commission to the European Parliament, the Council, the Economic and Social Committee and the Committee of the Regions—Consumer Policy Strategy 2002–2006, OJ C 137, 8.6.2002, 2.

37. Directive 2005/29 concerning unfair business-to-consumer commercial practices in the internal market and amending Council Directive 84/450/EEC, Directives 97/7/EC, 98/27/EC and 2002/65/EC of the European Parliament and of the Council and Regulation (EC) No 2006/2004 of the European Parliament and of the Council ('Unfair Commercial Practices Directive'), OJ L 149/22.

38. Directive 2008/48/EC of the European Parliament and of the Council of 23 April 2008 on credit agreements for consumers and repealing Council Directive 87/102/EEC: OJ 2008 L 133/66.

39. Draft Directive on Consumer Rights: COM(2008) 614 final.

## 3. Western Models of Consumer Protection

Yet European consumer law is based on different cultures and traditions. It cannot live and it cannot survive without national consumer law. The Member States took the initiative in the sixties and seventies in response to the emerging consumer society. Consumer policy, consumer protection and consumer law have their roots within the nation states. European consumer law as it stands today is largely determined by the fifteen Member States which set the tone in the nineties, when most of the directives were adopted. It might be fair to conclude that these countries represent four '*Rechtskreise*',[40] the common law area, the Romance area as well as the Germanic and Scandinavian areas. Each of the systems has made particular contributions to European law and each has encountered particular difficulties in integrating the European approach.[41]

The *common law countries* tend to react to questions concerning consumer law in a pragmatic way. They rely on precise regulations that limit the way in which traders should behave. Beyond that they rely on self-regulation.[42] Law enforcement is within the responsibility of the state authority. Cooperative structures involving non-governmental bodies are only developed to a limited extent. Therefore, consumers'associations only played a secondary role. The original input of the common law countries to EC consumer law has been mainly confined to the field of product safety in which consumer protection had been realised.[43] They tend to implement the directives into national law correctly and on time. The rules set by Community law gain practical relevance mostly in fields where the common law countries expect them to be beneficial for their own legal order. The linking—inherited within Community law—of rights and legal means is well-established in the common law system. For many continental lawyers it is striking to see how much emphasis the common law system puts on remedies. At the same time, collective remedies granted to consumer organizations are in the common law countries merely supportive to established governmental supervisory authorities.

---

40. Critical view H. Kötz, *Abschied von der Rechtskreislehre, Zeitschrift für Europäisches Privatrecht* 6 (1998), 493.

41. See also on the legal frameworks in the various Member States H-W. Micklitz and J. Kessler (eds.), *Marketing Practices Regulation and Consumer Protection in the EC Member States and the US* (Baden-Baden 2002).

42. Helpful is G. Teubner, *Legal Irritants: Good Faith in British Law or How Unifying Law Ends up in New Divergences, Modern Law Review* 61 (1998), 11.

43. M. H. Whincup, *Consumer legislation in the United Kingdom and the Republic of Ireland* (New York 1980).

The *Romance countries* waiver between *laissez-faire* and interventionism linked with pecuniary sanctions.[44] Consumer policy is exposed to strong political influence and is closely related to social trends. Law enforcement is centrally and bureaucratically organized. Semi-state consumer associations hold a legitimating supportive function. From the beginning these countries took a leading role in the field of consumer information and consumer contract law, not least resulting from the significant measures taken by the French government in the seventies.[45] The Romance countries tend to establish self-contained and coherent national consumer provisions which are fairly congruent with Community law as the national provisions often preceded the EC directives on consumer protection. Community law has improved the existing collective legal competences. Yet, it failed to take up the penal sanction mechanisms which are predominant in the Romance countries. It is a well-established policy in Romance countries to fine those who violate the law even in areas where the Germanic legal system would provide for injunctions only. Thus, from a Romance country point of view, Community law remains deficient.[46]

Countries of *German legal tradition* bank on long-term commitment to policy fields.[47] Legal interventionism with consumer protection tends to be systematic and coherent within the legal system. Law enforcement focuses on safeguarding consumers through court procedures. Cooperative structures in which consumer associations play a significant role are predominant. German consumer policy traditionally focused on an adequate control of standard business conditions, a late heritage of the *Weimarer Republik*.[48] All countries of German legal tradition experience difficulties in integrating consumer directives into their civil legal systems. They require a long time to implement the directives in order to accomplish the degree of perfection strived for in matching Community law and national law. The carefully conducted implementation increases the possibilities of the directive's practical applicability and use. Community law has strengthened collective legal protection. Consolidated administrative executive organs—beyond health protection—are relatively unknown within the countries of German legal roots.[49]

---

44. F. Osman (ed.), *Vers un Code europeen de la Consommation* (Brüssel 1998).
45. J. Calais-Auloy, *Le Droit de la Consommation en France* (New York 1981).
46. Osman (ed.), *Vers un Code europeen de la Consommation.*
47. Micklitz, *Introductory remarks §§ 13, 14 BGB.*
48. N. Reich, K. Tonner, H. Wegener, *Verbraucher und Recht* (Göttingen 1976).
49. Micklitz, Pfeiffer, Tonner, Willingmann (eds.), *Schuldrechtsreform und Verbraucherschutz.*

*Nordic (Scandinavian) countries* regard consumer law as relatively autonomous market behaviour law,[50] with considerable regulatory intervention, often based on broad general clauses. With regard to law enforcement, centrally organized state authorities are predominant solving problems mainly by cooperation. Relatively weak consumer associations rely on the state to provide a developed consumer law. The comparably sophisticated system of legal provisions under the control of a Consumer Ombudsman led to a high standard of provision of legal protection; not only in the field of product safety, but also in relation to the protection of economic interests. A close network of extrajudicial settlement mechanisms provides for efficient legal protection.[51] The Nordic countries appear to be on the losing side with regard to the EC approximation of laws. Its established consumer law system is endangered by Community law based on a market control orientated approach. By contrast in the Nordic countries centralised control organs are predominant. These statutory entities rely mostly on soft forms of law enforcement.[52]

## 4. The Creation of Consumer Law in Eastern Europe

Although most of EC consumer law has been adopted in the nineties, i.e. after the accession contracts between the Middle and Eastern European countries and the European Community had already been concluded, the ten new Member States had practically no chance to influence the content of the directives. The accession contracts obliged them to take over the respective body of consumer law in a three stage mechanism. Some of these countries had already adopted pieces of consumer law, be it before 1990 or after 1990, in order to show their readiness to adapt their legal systems to the requirements of EC law. The majority of their consumer law resulted from EC law. In theory such a starting position should have made it easier for European consumer law to be implanted into their relatively barren national orders. The implementation of European consumer law went hand in hand with a thorough restructuring of the private law systems of these countries.[53]

---

50. B. Dahl, T. Melchior, D. Tamm (eds.), *Danish law in a European Perspective*, 2nd edition (Copenhagen 2002), 413–441.

51. J. M. Scherpe, *Außergerichtliche Streitbeilegung in Verbrauchersachen* (Tübingen 2002).

52. Dahl, Melchior, Tamm (eds.), *Danish law in a European Perspective.*

53. A useful overview and analysis is given by Norbert Reich, *Transformation of Contract law and civil justice in the new EU member countries*, RSGL working papers no. 21 (Riga 2004).

Consumer law had and still has a different role to play in these countries. The reason is that the economic, social and legal environment differs from the old Member States. The establishment of consumer law in the new Member States was and is inherently bound to society, constitution/democracy and market building. Society building refers to the challenge the Eastern European countries had to face as the state and the society had to be separated. This can best be demonstrated by the role consumer organisations—instead of statutory authorities—were expected to play in the new market orientated society. Constitution building was indispensable in order to establish a new democratic order. Consumer policy, consumer law, or even more ambitious, the consumer movement therefore must be seen as an integral part of democracy building. Similar processes might be reported from Greece, Spain and Portugal, 10 to 20 years earlier.[54] Last but not least consumer law was urgently needed to establish a market which did not exist before 1990. Therefore all in all, consumer law is certainly much more 'political' in the new Member States, than it is in the old ones.

The challenge for the new states is to implement a Western legal system without necessary the infrastructure to support it.[55] The reliance placed on consumer organisations has already been mentioned, but the state is unable to subsidise them as in the German model and the consumers are not affluent enough to purchase their magazines in sufficient numbers as under the British model. There has been a shift from state organs controlling the market, to reliance on legal norms enforceable through the court. A consumer who previously would have complained to the state authorities because his purchase did not work properly now has to turn to the judicial system, but with very little, if any, legal assistance; court structures which are not particularly flexible for small claims; and, the prospect of a long wait before the case is ever heard. The new Member States are caught in a trap: having to modernise to become competitive, but not quite able to match the sophistication of the legal regimes for consumer protection in many of the older Western European states.

54. H-W. Micklitz,, *Verbraucherschutz West versus Ost-Kompatibilisierungsmöglichkeiten in der Europäischen Gemeinschaft—Einige Vorüberlegungen,* in H. Heiss (ed.), *Brückenschlag zwischen den Rechtskulturen des Ostseeraums* (Tübingen 2001), 137–182.

55. See A. Barkadjivea-Engelbrekt, The impact of EU enlargement on private law governance in Central and Eastern Europe: the case of consumer protection, in F. Cafaggi/H. Muir Watt (eds.), Making European Private Law, Governance Design (Cheltenham, 2008), 98.

# 5. The Concept and Image of the Consumer

## *5.1. The Scope of European Consumer Law*

The scope of the consumer law provisions is usually delimited with the help of the concept of consumer. The rules of consumer law apply to relationships between consumers and businesses. In national laws the definitions of the consumer concept, as well as the ways in which the scope of consumer protection rules is determined, have varied. However, with regard to many practically important issues the concept of consumer has been largely harmonised in Europe through a number of directives. Therefore the following analysis is mainly restricted to EU law.

EU law has developed its own consumer concept, which has been interpreted independently, without reference to national legal systems. The ECJ when interpreting the concept has expressly referred to the objective of the rules, namely the protection of the economically weaker and legally less experienced party to the contract.[56]

Most consumer protection directives define the consumer in a fairly formal way. The definition is a negative definition, excluding business and professional activities. The definitions are not, however, completely identical on this point. Whilst the first directives, like the Doorstep Selling Directive and the first Consumer Credit Directive used the phrase 'trade or profession' when enumerating activities that were outside the scope of protection, in the Unfair Contract Terms Directive it was enlarged to cover 'trade, business or profession'. In the Unfair Commercial Practices Directive yet another word was added to the list, namely 'craft.' Just as the first enlargement was not understood to reflect any difference in content,[57] the same can be said concerning the addition of 'craft.' It just spells out what was implicit in the definition anyway. The basic message is the same: when a person acts in a professional capacity for an economic purpose that person is not covered by the consumer protection rules.

There has been much discussion on the extent to which consumer protection directives are applicable when a person acquires products both for individual and professional use. At least in situations where the person is acting 'primarily outside his trade or profession' application of EU consumer pro-

---

56. See e.g., *Shearson Lehman Hutton Inc. v TVB Treuhandgesellschaft für Vermögensverwaltung und Beteiligungen MbH*, Case C-89/91 [1993] ECR I-139.

57. G. Howells and T. Wilhelmsson, *EC Consumer Law* (Aldershot 1997), 3.

tection law has been recommended.[58] A somewhat more restrictive approach towards the application of the consumer provisions, at least with regard to European provisions on international jurisdiction, has, however, recently been adopted by the European Court of Justice in a case concerning purchase of materials for a building partially in business use by a farmer.[59] The Acquis Principles and the DCFR propose in reaction to the ECJ a slight modification of the concept of the consumer.[60]

The definition, like the corresponding definitions in several national legislations, is relatively abstract in two respects. On the one hand, it protects all consumers, irrespective of their concrete strength or weakness. It is not relevant to ask whether the consumer, in fact, is the stronger party in an individual case. Neither does the definition pay any special attention to particularly weak consumers or groups of consumers. Moreover, the protection does not cover situations in which the position of a concrete actor may actually be very weak. If he does not meet the requirements of the definition he cannot benefit from consumer protection rules. The definition of the consumer has been criticised for not covering some consumer situations, for example when consumers act in the form of an association or other corresponding group. This is because a legal person falls outside the definition of consumer.[61] Equally the definition does not cover a situation in which a worker buys tools. As most consumer directives are minimum directives, nothing of course prevents the Member States from using broader consumer concepts in those areas.

In some cases a broader definition of consumer has been adopted within EU law. In the Package Tour Directive, a consumer means a person who takes or agrees to take the package or any person on whose behalf the purchase of the package is made or to whom the package is transferred (Article 2(4)). There is no restriction with regard to contracts relating to the trade or profession of the buyer of a package tour. This means that the definition of consumer in the Package Tour Directive is broader and covers, for example, a businessman buying a business trip.

Also in the area of product liability, consumer protection has a larger scope. All personal injuries caused by defective products are within the scope of the directive, regardless of whether the injured person used the product in the ca-

58. See e.g., Howells and Wilhelmsson, *EC Consumer Law*, 3.

59. *Gruber v BayWA AG*, Case C-464/01 [2005] ECR I-439.

60. Article 1:201 of the Acquis Principles and Annex I Definitions of the DCFR.

61. However, the definitions of natural and legal persons may vary. For example, whilst in the United Kingdom a partnership would be seen as a natural person, it would on the Continent rather be classified as a legal person.

pacity of a consumer, businessman or employee. For damage to property the scope of the Product Liability Directive is more limited, however; only damages to property that is of a type ordinarily intended for private use or consumption and was used by the injured person mainly for his own private use or consumption are covered.

There has been much discussion about whether the consumer protection provisions should be extended to cover small enterprises as well. In a case that has aroused a lot of interest, the European Court of Justice deemed that the protection afforded by the Doorstep Selling Directive did not extend outside 'consumers' proper.[62] In this case the Advocate-General of the Court specifically considered that the consumer concept should not be defined abstractly, but in a concrete way connected to the activity in question. The case involved a businessman who sold his undertaking. The Advocate-General considered that he could be compared to a consumer, because the transaction in question was not common to him and thus was outside his trade or profession.[63] The Court, however, did not accept the view of the Advocate-General, but chose the more abstract reading of the Directive. In conformity with this solution the Court has later ruled that a person who concludes a contract with a view to pursuing a trade or profession in the future is not deemed to be a consumer.[64] Businesses acquiring goods for the use of their staff only are also not regarded as consumers.[65]

## *5.2. The Image of the European Consumer*

Even though the legal definition of the consumer is harmonised there has remained obvious variations in the basic consumer images, on which the consumer law in various Member States and in the EU are built. The consumer images are abstractions based on certain perceptions of reality. At the same time, they have a normative quality as they function as starting points *(Leitbilder)* for the regulation of the consumer area.

62. *Patrice di Pinto*, Case C-361/89 [1991] ECR-I 1189.

63. This seems to be in line with the English view, see e.g. Department of Trade and Industry, Implementation of the EC Directive on unfair terms in consumer contracts (93/13/EEC), A Consultation Document, October 1993, at Article 2 and H. Collins, *Good Faith in European Contract Law, Oxford Journal of Legal Studies* 14 (1994), 240.

64. *Francesco Benincasa v Dentalkit*, Case C-295/95 [1997] ECR I-3767.

65. See on automatic drink dispensers *Cape Snc v Idealservice Srl and Idealservice MN RE Sas v OMAI Srl*, Joined Cases C-541/99 and C-542/99 [2001] ECR I-9049.

The active and critical information-seeker is an image used in the practice of building EU consumer policy. Information (transparency) is a central device of this policy.[66] The European consumer image has always, since the beginning of European consumer policy, been that of a well-informed and well-to-be-informed consumer—the active internal-market consumer[67]—who can and shall decide on her or his own affairs at her or his own risk.[68] The stress on the active and critical approach of the consumer is clear from several decisions of the European Court of Justice relating to information requirements in various contexts. The Court's image of the consumer does not seem to be the hasty and relatively uncritical consumer who just throws a quick glance at advertisements and other written materials, but rather a critical and attentive consumer who makes use of all the information offered to him.[69] In particular, the emphasis on labeling and information in many of the cases outlawing substantive regulation presupposes a consumer who really makes an effort to read the information on labels and makes use of information offered otherwise.[70] The Court in several cases has defined the consumer to be used as a measure for assessment as someone 'who is reasonably well informed and reasonably observant and circumspect.'[71] The decision of the Court in the *Nissan*

66. See generally on the central role of information in EU legislative policy, e.g. S. Grundmann, W. Kerber, S. Weatherill (eds.), *Party Autonomy and the Role of Information in the Internal Market* (Berlin 2001) and G. Howells, A. Janssen, R. Schulze, *Information Rights and Obligations* (Aldershot 2005). See more closely below, section 7.

67. C. Joerges and G. Brüggemeier, *Europäisierung des Vertragsrechts und Haftungsrechts*, in P-C. Müller-Graff (ed.), *Gemeinsames Privatrecht in der Europäischen Gesellschaft* (Baden-Baden 1993), 260.

68. P. Hommelhoff, *Zivilrecht unter dem Einfluss europäischer Rechtsangleichung, Archiv für die civilistische Praxis* 192 (1992),93.

69. A. Meyer, *Das Verbraucherleitbild des Europäischen Gerichtshofs—Abkehr vom "flüchtigen Verbraucher", Wettbewerb in Recht und Praxis* (1993), 224.

70. See already the famous Cassis de Dijon-case, *Rewe-Zentral AG v. Bundesmonopol-Verwaltung für Branntwein*, Case 120/78 [1979] ECR 649.

71. See e.g., *Verein gegen Unwesen in Handel und Gewerbe Köln e.V. v Mars GmbH*, Case C-470/93 [1995] ECR I-1923, at 24,, *Gut Springenheide GmbH and Rudolf Tusky v Oberkreisdirektor des Kreises Steinfurt—Amt für Lebensmittelüberwachung*, Case C-210/96 [1998] ECR I-4657, at 31, 37, *Verbraucherschutzverein e V v Sektkellerei G.C. Kessler GmbH und Co.*, Case C-303/97 [1999] ECR I-513, at 36, *Estée Lauder Cosmetics GmbH & Co. OHG v Lancaster Group GmbH*, Case C-220/98 [2000] ECR I-117, at 27, *Verein gegen Unwesen in Handel und Gewerbe Köln e V v Adolf Darbo AG*, Case C-465/98 [2000] ECR I-2297, at 20, *Toshiba Europe GmbH v Katun Germany GmbH*, Case C-112/99 [2001] ECR I-7945, at 52 and *Pippig Augenoptik GmbH & Co. KG v Hartlauer Handelsgesellschaft*, Case 44/01 [2003] ECR I-3095, at 55.

case,[72] where an advertisement was held to be misleading only if it could be demonstrated that a significant number of consumers to which the advertisement was addressed were misled by it, also shows that the EC consumer protection is not necessarily intended to cover the most vulnerable consumer groups.[73]

On the other hand, the passive glancer is one of the images that has been said to dominate, for instance, Nordic consumer protection. So, Nordic marketing regulation is based on the assumption that consumers do not read commercial messages thoroughly, but make their decisions on the basis of the overall impression they get by a short glance at the advertisement. Misleading headings or pictures cannot therefore be validly corrected by accurate information in the text of the commercial. The German approach was similar: one could, on the basis of court practice concerning unfair competition, speak about the so-called "*flüchtige Verbraucher*" who uncritically receives advertising messages.[74] This approach was not necessarily, however, adopted because of consumer policy considerations, as it seems to have been misused to close markets from competition. So, in the light of the European Court of Justice case-law, the German Supreme Court has revised its approach. Since 1999 it uses the formula of the situation-adequate-circumspect consumer (*situationsadäquat aufmerksamer Verbraucher*).[75]

The divergences have recently again been addressed during the preparation of the Unfair Commercial Practices Directive. In the first proposals the benchmark consumer was defined, based on the practice of the European Court of Justice as a consumer 'who is reasonably well informed and reasonably observant and circumspect.'[76] This was later dropped, to reach a compromise with

72. Case C-373/90 [1993] ECR I-131.

73. However, even in EC law, mainly believing in the information-seeker, elements of other kinds may be seen: One may point to decisions of the European Court of Justice such as *Oosthoek's Uitgeversmattschappij* (Case 286/81 [1982] ECR 4575) concerning some rules on the offer of free gifts as marketing devices which "reveals an acceptance on the part of the Court that the consumer may be unable properly to process information", S. Weatherill, *The role of the informed consumer in European Community law and policy, Consumer Law Journal* 2 (1994), 53.

74. Meyer, *Das Verbraucherleitbild des Europäischen Gerichtshofs*, 224.

75. *BGH* GRUR 2000, 619, 621 = WRP 2000, 517—*Orient-Teppichmuster*; stable court practice; see references in T. Wuttke, *Die Konvergenz des nationalen und des europäischen Irreführungsbegriffs, Wettbewerb in Recht und Praxis* (2004), 820, 821; T. Lettl, *Gemeinschaftsrecht und neues UWG, Wettbewerb in Recht und Praxis* (2004), 1079, 1093; R. Sack, *Die relevante Irreführung im Wettbewerbsrecht, Wettbewerb in Recht und Praxis* (2004), 521, 524.

76. Proposal for a Directive of the European Parliament and of the Council concerning unfair business-to-consumer commercial practices in the Internal Market and amend-

Member States not prepared to demand so much of their consumers. Despite this solution, however, the average consumer approach adopted in the Directive seems to give traders more leeway than they have had in those countries in which the credulous consumer was used as benchmark.[77] In fact, despite the revision of the actual sections of the Directive, the formula of the Court is meant to continue to have some relevance in this context, and it is therefore still expressly mentioned in the Preamble of the Directive.[78] The deletion of the vague and not very consistently applied formula[79] from the definitions of the Directive may have the advantage, though, in that it leaves more room for national courts to make a realistic overall assessment of the commercial practice, taking into account the fact that most consumers do not read advertisements and other commercial communications carefully, in an observant and circumspect way, but rather hastily look at the headings and pictures. The 'average consumer' might in some situations act rather as a 'casual observer' and one may therefore very well include elements of hasty observation in the average consumer concept.[80] In fact, the Directive acknowledges this, when noting the importance of the 'overall presentation' when assessing an advertising measure.

One should also note that the general clause in Art. 5 of the Unfair Commercial Practices Directive not only mentions the 'average consumer' as the yardstick to be used in assessing unfairness, but also, as an alternative notes 'the average member of the group when a commercial practice is directed to a particular group of consumers.' In addition, there is a specific provision on

---

ing directives 84/450/EEC, 97/7/EC and 98/27/EC, COM(2003) 356 final, proposed directive Art. 2(b).

77. A. Bakardjieva Engelbrekt, *Fair Trading Law in Flux? National Legacies, Institutional Choice and the Process of Europeanisation* (diss. Stockholm, 2003), 623, sees the Directive as directly targeting the relatively strict German requirements based on the UWG, in this and other respects. The Directive 'may be seen as one collective attempt to shake the UWG at its foundations.'

78. Recital 18.

79. On the incoherence of the decisions of the European Court of Justice in this respect, see, e.g., A. Beater, *Verbraucherschutz und Schutzzweckdenken im Wettbewerbsrecht* (Tübingen 2000), 95.

80. See the interesting analysis of various consumer images (*Verbraucherleitbilder*) in the Member States by T. Lettl, *Der lauterkeitsrechtliche Schutz vor irreführender Werbung in Europa* (München 2004), 306, who distinguishes five such images and thereby uses the focus on 'average' and on 'hasty observation' as different parameters. In his analysis the consumer image of some Member States (Denmark, Finland, the Netherlands and Greece) is then based on *both* the conception of an 'average consumer' and the idea of hasty observation.

the protection of vulnerable consumers, allowing for assessing even such practices that reach the generality of consumers from the perspective of the average member of the vulnerable group. In the Preamble to the Directive it is underlined that a commercial practice that is 'specifically aimed at a particular group of consumers, such as children,' should be 'assessed from the perspective of the average member of that group.'[81]

The 'average consumer' does not necessarily have to be understood as the 'average EU consumer.' One might even seriously doubt the possibility of constructing such an average that would not be purely fictitional—but at least in some cases it might be interpreted as the average consumer on a certain national or local market as well. The average consumer test provides 'a means to take into account relevant social, cultural or linguistic characteristics of targeted groups.'[82] When there is a need for different assessment the courts should, as the European Court of Justice has stated, make use of their understanding of the relevant national 'social, cultural or linguistic factors'[83] in their own environment. This practice of the Court is endorsed in the Unfair Commercial Practices Directive.[84]

## 6. Basic Principles of EU Consumer Contract Law

European consumer contract law, both in Member States in which consumer law is treated as a separate branch of the law and in countries where such a systematisation is less common, is an offspring of general contract law. Therefore, as to its content, on many points it has very similar or even identical rules to those used when assessing business contracts or contracts between private persons. What has been said in other chapters of this handbook on European contract law to a large extent applies to consumer contracts as well.

### *6.1. Mandatory Law*

The most important difference between consumer contract law and general or business contract law is its mandatory character. Unlike contract law

81. Recital 18.

82. COM(2003) 356 final, 8.

83. *Estée Lauder Cosmetics v Lancaster Group ('Lifting')*, Case C-220/98 [2000] ECR I-117, 29. See also *Fratelli Graffione SNC v Ditta Fransa*, Case C-313/94 [1996] ECR I-6039, 22.

84. See Recital 18.

in general, most particular provisions on consumer contracts, both in national as well as in European law, are mandatory. Their basic mandatory character is often one-sided with the obligations being imposed on the trader. As the purpose of consumer law is the protection of consumers, the law does not allow the parties to use the contract to reduce the level of protection guaranteed by the law. On the other hand, there is usually nothing to prevent the trader from contractually placing the consumer in a better position than that required by the law.

Like national consumer provisions, EU legislation in this area is mainly mandatory. However, this should not be seen as an indication that EU consumer law would be in any deep conflict with traditional notions of freedom of contract. As will be shown below, information rules are one of the main means of protection, and such rules are basically in conformity with market-rational ideas of freedom of contract, if these are taken seriously.

One of the most illustrative examples of the strong market-rationality of European consumer law is offered by the discussion on the scope of application of the Unfair Contract Terms Directive during its preparatory stages. Although the grounds for the drafting of the Unfair Contract Terms Directive were largely related to problems appearing in connection with standard form contracts, the starting point of the 1990 proposal for the Directive was that it would be applied to all types of consumer contracts, both to standard form contracts and to individually negotiated contracts.[85] This was criticised in particular in German legal literature, because the fairness control of individually negotiated contracts was said to be in conflict with private autonomy and the functioning of the market economy.[86] The critique emphasised that the German legislation on standard form contracts was not primarily based on the principle of protecting the weaker party, but was directed against the misuse of freedom of contract by users of standard form contracts. Also European legislation on unfair contract terms, according to these views, should be built on such market-rational ideas.

This criticism eventually produced results. The respect for private autonomy led to a solution according to which the Directive only applies to a term 'which has not been individually negotiated' (Article 3). As rational consumers ideally are able themselves to affect the contents of individually negotiated con-

85. Proposal for a Council Directive on unfair terms in consumer contracts, COM(90) 322 final,3; recitals 9 and 10.

86. H. E. Brandner and P. Ulmer, *The Community directive on unfair terms in consumer contracts: some critical remarks on the proposal submitted by the EC Commission, Common Market Law Review* 28 (1991), 652.

tract, they do not need the substantive protection afforded by the Directive. The limitation of the scope of the Directive 'represents a victory for the consumer choice perspective.'[87] The solution was a compromise to make the adoption of the Directive possible. In national laws there are still considerable variations on this point. For example, in the Nordic countries the courts may adjust all parts of the contract, both standardised terms and individually agreed terms, even including the price.

### 6.2. The Principle of Legitimate Expectations

The mandatory rules of EU consumer law, as well as of national laws, that to a considerable extent steer the content of consumer contracts, often relate to specific problems encountered in the respective consumer markets. However, some more general substantive principles seem to be emerging in the area as well.

As to the substantive content of the mandatory provisions of EU law, one important conceptual starting point is the principle of legitimate expectations of consumers.[88] This principle, first elaborated for private law purposes by Hans-W. Micklitz,[89] is on its way to become a leading principle in European consumer law discourse. According to this principle consumer law should protect the legitimate expectations of consumers concerning the products, services and behaviour of businesses.

The principle of legitimate expectations is derived from specific private law materials such as the Product Liability Directive and the Consumer Sales Directive. The general provision in the Product Liability Directive, Art. 6, which considers a product to be defective, 'when it does not provide the safety which a person is entitled to expect' has been read as an expression of the principle of legitimate expectations. The same goes for the provision on conformity in Art. 2 of the Consumer Sales Directive. That contains, among other rules, a general statement that consumer goods should 'show the quality and per-

---

87. H. Collins, *Good Faith in European Contract Law, Oxford Journal of Legal Studies* 14 (1994), 239.

88. See Howells and Wilhelmsson, *EC Consumer Law*, 320–323.

89. See e.g., H-W. Micklitz, *Principles of Justice in Private Law within the European Union*, in E. Paasivirta & K. Rissanen (eds.), *Principles of Justice and the Law of the European Union*, European Commission (DG XIII, Cost A7), (Brussels 1995), 284, as well as H-W. Micklitz, *Legitime Erwartungen als Gerechtigkeitsprinzip des Europäischen Privatrechts*, in L. Krämer, H-W. Micklitz, K. Tonner (eds.), *Law and Diffuse Interests in the European Legal Order* (Baden-Baden 1997), 245–277; H-W. Micklitz, *Social Justice in European Private Law, Yearbook of European Law 19* (1999/2000), 167–204.

formance which are normal in the goods of the same type and which the consumer can reasonably expect'.

However, the principle of legitimate expectations is not limited to private law materials. It has a larger background in EU law, having regard also to the relationship between the Union and its citizens.[90] It can help build a bridge between private law and other branches of EU law.

The principle of legitimate expectations contains two elements. The subjective element—'expectations'—refers directly to the views prevailing among consumers. The objective element—'legitimate'—gives the courts the possibility to screen these expectations by taking into account what enterprises should reasonably be forced to take account of. The principle in other words combines an empirical and a normative approach. The expectations are created on the basis of both prevailing practices and normative values that are deemed acceptable in a certain environment. The concept is particularly useful because it relates to the specific environment of practice and values. It means that the principle of legitimate expectations can have different contents in different settings. What is expected in one type of market and within one legal system might not be expected in another. The principle in other words leaves room for taking into account of the relevant national 'social, cultural or linguistic factors', as has been done by the European Court of Justice.[91]

Such variations can, for example, be based on differences in national commercial practices. The Nordic and German economies, built to a larger extent on relations of co-operation and trust between the actors in the market, may give rise to another interpretation of legitimate expectations than that prevailing in the commercial culture of the United Kingdom, which obviously is founded more directly on the play of market forces.[92]

## 6.3. *Transgressing the Boundaries of Contract*

The principle of legitimate expectations may even lead consumer law to transgress traditional boundaries of contract, as they have been drawn in many national laws. The expectations of consumers do not necessarily relate to the behaviour of the businesses with whom they have established the contractual

90. N. Reich, *Understanding EU law*, 2nd edition (Antwerp 2005).

91. See above section 5.2.

92. See the interesting comparison between Germany and England in this respect in Teubner, *Legal Irritants: Good Faith in British Law And How Unifying Law Ends Up in New Divergences*, 11.

relationship in the traditional sense. For a consumer, the distribution chains and networks may appear not as bundles of independent businesses, but as entities within which the businesses should have combined liabilities.

A small but telling example can be found in the consumer sales law provisions that connect remedies against non-conformity of goods to misleading marketing information. Such provisions already existed in some EU jurisdictions and have now been introduced in the rest. They correspond with what the consumer may legitimately expect.

Already for a long time Nordic sales law, first for consumer sales and nowadays also for commercial sales, has made the seller liable for non-conformity, if the goods do not conform to information given in marketing. The product is deemed to be defective if it does not correspond with particulars given during its marketing or otherwise before purchase and that may be assumed to have influenced the purchase.[93] Also according to the Dutch civil code the seller is bound by public statements, with very narrow exceptions.[94] The Consumer Sales Directive has required a kind of marketing liability to be included in the national legislation. It is implied in the normal quality rule in Art. 2(2)(d), according to which consumer goods are presumed to be in conformity with the contract if they show the quality and performance which are normal in goods of the same type and which the consumer can reasonably expect, given the nature of the goods and taking into account any public statements on the specific characteristics of the goods made about them by the seller, the producer or his representative, particularly in advertising or on labeling. For several Member States this has meant an extension of existing seller's liability. A marketing liability rule of the kind prescribed in the Directive has improved the protection of consumers, in comparison with the previous law, in many Member States.[95]

---

93. See Sec. 18 of the new Nordic Sale of Goods Acts, Sec. 19 of the Swedish Consumer Sales Act and Chap. 5 Sec. 13 of the Finnish Consumer Protection Act.

94. BW 7:18. E. Hondius and H. Schelhaas, *In conformity with the Consumer Sales Directive? Some remarks on transposition into Dutch law, European Review of Private Law* 9 (2001), 331, note that the Dutch rule is more consumer-friendly than the provision of the Consumer Sales Directive.

95. For example, in the United Kingdom, see G. Howells, *Implementation of the EC Consumer Sales Directive in the United Kingdom*, in: S. Grundmann, D. Medicus & Rolland (eds.), *Europäisches Kaufgewährleistungsrecht* (Köln, 2000) 177, as well as S. Watterson, *Consumer Sales Directive 1999/44/EC—The impact on English law, European Review of Private Law* 9 (2001), 208; in Ireland, see T. C. Bird, *Directive 99/44/EC on certain aspects of the sale of consumer goods and associated guarantees: its impact on existing Irish sale of goods law, European Review of Private Law* (2001), 287–288; in Germany, see T. Zerres,

In this context it is of special importance that the provision in Art. 2(2)(d) not only covers marketing information given by the seller, which relatively easily could be interpreted as a part of the contract even with the help of traditional contract principles, but also marketing by persons who do not enter into a contractual relationship with the consumer. The Directive expressly mentions the producer or his representative. By such a broad liability rule it acknowledges that marketing today often is made by other parties than the seller and this should be recognised in contract law. A small concession towards traditional contract thinking is made, however, in the rule that the seller is not bound by public statements made by others, if he shows that he was not, and could not reasonably have been, aware of the statement in question.

In other respects EU law could have gone further in recognising the legitimate expectations of consumers in relation to distributions chains and networks. In fact, in the course of drafting the Consumer Sales Directive the proposal was put forward that the manufacturer of the goods should be jointly liable with the seller in case of non-conformity of the goods. As the Commission noted, '[i]n modern consumer societies, based on systems of mass production and distribution, consumer confidence concerns the product as such, and is bound up more with the consumers' faith in the manufacturers than in the sellers.'[96] Despite this argument; despite the fact that many Member States already give the consumer a direct action against the manufacturer;[97] and despite the practice of many manufacturers being to assume liability by issuing commercial guarantees, manufacturer liability was not included in the adopted version of the Directive. As it is difficult to see the convincing rea-

---

*Das neue Sachmängelrecht beim Kauf, Verbraucher und Recht* 17 (2002), 6 (compare, however, G. Rieger, *Die Richtlinie zu bestimmten Aspekten des Verbrauchsgüterkaufs und der Garantien für Verbrauchsgüter vor dem Hintergrund des geltenden Rechts, Verbraucher und Recht* 14 (1999), 289, who claims that the rule more or less corresponds to prevailing court practice in Germany, and S. Grundmann, *Verbraucherrecht, Unternehmensrecht, Privatrecht—warum sind sich UN-Kaufrecht und EU-Kaufrechtsrichtlinie so ähnlich? Archiv für die civilistische Praxis* 202 (2002), 47, who notes that the really new thing is the liability of the seller for information given by others); in Austria, see C. Jeloschek, *The Transposition of Directive 99/44/EC into Austrian Law, European Review of Private Law* 9 (2001), 169; and in Greece, see G. I. Arnokouros, *The transposition of the Consumer Sales Directive into the Greek legal system, European Review of Private Law* 9 (2001), 269.

96. Green Paper on guarantees for consumer goods and after-sales services, COM(93) 509 final, p. 86.

97. In COM(93) 509 final, p.87, France, Belgium and Luxembourg are expressly named. Finland and Norway (within the EEA) could also be mentioned in this context; Sweden offers direct action only for a limited range of situations. See on the different Nordic solutions e.g. J. Herre, *Konsumentköplagen* (Stockholm 1999), 52–54.

sons for this move, it seems that the lack of success of the proposal followed from formalistic juridical views in some countries emphasising the lack of 'legal basis' for a contractual claim against a manufacturer who was not in a contractual relationship with the consumer. The same problem also led to rejection of the idea of a kind of network liability within selective distribution systems that was also presented in the Green Paper.[98] However, the topic of producer liability is to be considered when the Directive is reviewed.

## 7. Information Rules and Substantive Protection

EU consumer law has produced some substantive liability rules. Liability for defective goods under the Product Liability Directive and for non-conformity under the Consumer Sales Directive come to mind. It also has certain minimum expectations: that products are safe and that contract terms and commercial practices are fair. These standards are mandatory. However, they are not characteristic of EU consumer law. Even within the context of the substantive rules traders are often able to stay within the law so long as they inform consumers about any defects or possible traps in their contracts or offers. Information is the key element of European consumer law. It has been stressed in many consumer policy documents and is expressed in the Treaty by Art.153(1) which talks about promoting the right of consumers to information and education.

The European Court of Justice has set the tone. It has opposed national rules that restrict the flow of information to consumers.[99] In similar vein the Comparative Advertising Directive[100] was also intended to open up Member States to the need to allow comparative advertising and has been interpreted in that manner by the Court.[101] The Court also, in the context of free movement, sees information as an effective mechanism of protection, removing the need for more restrictive regulation.[102] It has used the model of the 'reason-

98. See COM(93) 509 final, p. 97.

99. *GB-Inno-BM v Confederation du commerce luxemburgeois*, Case C-362/88 [1990] ECR I-667, Weatherill, *The Role of the Informed Consumer in European Community Law and Policy*, 49.

100. Directive 97/55 amending Directive 84/450 concerning misleading advertising so as to include comparative advertising, OJ L 290/18.

101. *Toshiba Europe GmbH v Katun Germany GmbH*, Case C-112/99 [2001] ECR I-7945 and *Pippig Augenoptik GmbH v Hartlauer Handelsgesellschaft GmbH*, Case C-44/01 [2003] ECR I-3095.

102. See e.g. J.A. Usher, *Disclosure Rules (Information) as a Primary Tool in the Doctrine on Measures Having an Equivalent Effect*, in S. Grundmann, W. Kerber and S. Weath-

ably observant and circumspect' consumer to justify removing national restrictions on advertising and assumes consumers can process information with a fairly high degree of sophistication.[103]

The legislative preference for information controls is found most clearly in those directives that require the consumer to be provided with a list, often a very long list, of information. The Distance Contracts Directive, Financial Services Distance Marketing Directive, Consumer Credit Directive, E-commerce Directive,[104] the Package Tour Directive and the Timeshare Directive immediately spring to mind. It is underlined in the Unfair Commercial Practices Directive where the exclusion of material information is classed as being misleading (Article 7). Many of these directives list quite considerable numbers of pieces of information that have to be provided to the consumer. The length of the lists sometimes seems to resemble a compilation of information requirements from national law, rather than being geared to the actual needs of consumers. They concern both pre-contractual information and information that has to be provided as part of the contractual documentation. Recently calls have started to be heard for more thought to be given to the amount of information that should be given and which information is actually important to consumers at which particular stage of the contractual process.[105] In essence the suggestion is that in contract formation consumers would benefit from less information that is better targeted. However, information also serves another useful function as a 'contract synopsis' and reference point for post contractual disputes. For that purposes it may be entirely appropriate to provide detailed information as part of the eventual contractual documentation. This may now be realized in a general form under the proposed Directive on Consumer Rights.[106]

---

erill, *Party Autonomy and the Role of Information in the Internal Market* (Berlin 2001), 151–161.

103. See above, Section 5.2.

104. Directive 2000/31 on certain legal aspects of information society services, in particular electronic commerce, in the Internal Market, OJ L 178/1.

105. See, A. Nordhausen, *Information Requirements in the E-Commerce Directive and the Proposed Directive on Unfair Commercial Practices* and B. Wendlandt, *EC Directives on Time-Sharing and for self-employed commercial agents—Apples, Oranges and the Core of the Information Overload Problem* in G. Howells, A. Janssen and R. Schulze (eds.), *Information Rights and Obligations—A Challenge for Party Autonomy and Transactional Fairness* (Aldershot 2004), 93–114 and 67–92. For a policy document in similar vein *see Warning: too much information can harm. A final report by the Better Regulation Executive and National Consumer Council on maximising the positive impact of regulated information for consumers and markets.*

106. Article 5 COM (2008) 614.

The information model is based on overcoming the information asymmetries between trader and consumer. It assumes there is some information the trader might not have sufficient incentives to disclose voluntarily and forces the trader to divulge that information. In theory this means the consumer can compare offers and the information should help assist him in selecting an offer that best suits his preferences. However, there are several reasons why this model will not always produce the desired results. Traders are skilled in manipulating the presentation of information.[107] Even more importantly consumers have problems in processing information. Sometimes this will result from their inability to handle the amount of information given to them; at other times it will be because of problems in processing the information accurately. For instance, they will tend to read information to justify their initial preferences.[108]

Nevertheless, information is a popular information strategy with regulators and this is nowhere more evident than in European regulation. This information policy does impose some restraints on the autonomy of traders, because they are forced to provide some information they might otherwise have chosen not to, either because it reflects poorly on their products or services or because of the costs involved. This restriction on traders is counter-balanced by the growth in autonomy of consumers who can in theory make better informed decisions.[109] It also means that regulation interferes less with the decision-making process of traders. They are allowed greater freedom to design products as they wish and offer them on their preferred terms so long as this information is communicated to the consumer.

Another aspect of European information law that underpins the goal of transparency is the rules on the accuracy of information. Obviously misleading information is not allowed.[110] Moreover the rules not only specify which information should be given, but sometimes provide common rules, for example on the calculation of interest rates,[111] that help ensure meaningful com-

---

107. J. Hanson and D. Kysar, *Taking Behaviouralism Seriously: The Problem of Market Manipulation, NYULR* 74 (1999), 630 and *Taking Behaviouralism Seriously: Some Evidence of Market Manipulation, Harward Law Review* 112 (1999) 1420.

108. This is expanded upon in G. Howells, The *Potential and Limits of Consumer Empowerment by Information, Journal of Law and Society* 32 (2005) 349.

109. C. Willett, *Autonomy and Fairness: The Case of Public Statements* in Howells, Janssen and Schulze (eds.), *Information Rights and Obligations*, 1–15.

110. Directive 84/450 relating to the approximation of the laws, regulations and administrative provisions of the Member States concerning misleading advertising, OJ L 250/17. and the Unfair Commercial Practices Directive.

111. Directive 2008/48/EC: OJ 2008 L 133/66, art 19.

parisons across the Community are possible. The directives also demand that the information is provided in contracts in 'plain, intelligible language'[112] and on labeling in a manner that is 'visible, clearly legible and indelible' and in a language easily understood by the consumer.[113] At times the requirement to provide the information in a language easily understood by the consumer conflicts with the aim of free circulation if goods have to be repackaged to comply with national language requirements and the European Court of Justice has been flexible in encouraging alternative means of providing the information to consumers, such as by the use of symbols.[114]

There is no European right of consumers to be informed in their own language.[115] Of course there are consumer protection issues if this is stretched too far. The Court once again assumes a model of relatively alert and well-informed consumer. However, at least in labeling secondary community law seems to recognise the Member States right to set mandatory standards for using the language of the country.[116]

## 8. Withdrawal Rights as a Specific Feature

European consumer contract law, as expressed in many of the directives in the area, has another particular feature that is closely linked with the focus on information. This feature is the relatively wide use of the right of withdrawal (in some directives also termed cancellation right) by the consumer as a means of consumer protection. In the same vein as information rights the remedy of withdrawal has the purpose of safeguarding the rational decision-making process of the consumer.

It is symptomatic that the remedy of withdrawal is the remedy used already in the first consumer protection directive dealing specifically with contract law, namely the Doorstep Selling Directive. The Directive concerns contracts between traders and consumers for the supply of goods or services

112. Art. 5 of the Unfair Contract Terms Directive.

113. Directive 2000/13 on the approximation of the laws of the Member States relating to the labelling, presentation and advertising of foodstuffs, OJ L 109/29, see art 13(2) and 16.

114. *Piageme v BVBA Peeters*, Case C-85/94 [1995] ECR I-2955.

115. The Timeshare Directive does of course give states the right to require purchasers resident in its state to be giuven a contract in its national language: art. 4.

116. H-W. Micklitz, *Zum Recht des Verbrauchers auf die eigene Sprache, Besprechungsaufsatz zur Entscheidung der Cour de Cassation vom 14. November 2000, Zeitschrift für Europäisches Privatrecht* 11 (2003), 635–655.

which are concluded during an excursion organised by the trader away from his business premises or during a visit to the consumer's home or to the home of another consumer or the consumer's place of work (Art. 1). Although the scope of application of the Directive is narrow, its introduction was theoretically interesting, because of its effects on the basic provisions of contract formation. In the cases which belong to its sphere of application, the Directive prescribes that the consumer shall have the right to renounce the effects of his undertaking within a period of not less than seven days (Art. 5).[117] The period begins when the trader gives the consumer a written notice that informs him of the right of cancellation and contains certain other information as well (Art. 4).

In the Third Life Assurance Directive of 1992 a provision on the right of the policyholder to withdraw from the contract within 14–30 days was adopted.[118] The next step in this development is then represented by the Timeshare Directive that gives the purchaser the right to withdraw without giving any reason within 10 calendar days of both parties' signing the contract (Art. 5). In the Distance Contracts Directive (Art. 6), the European legislator returned to the seven days withdrawal period of the Doorstep Selling Directive, which is not surprising as the policy arguments behind these Directives are at least partially similar. In the Financial Services Distance Marketing Directive (Art. 6), the withdrawal period is extended to 14 days as it is in the Consumer Credit Directive (art. 14). In view of the variations in the length of the withdrawal periods, and in other details as well, the withdrawal directives have offered good examples for those criticising the lack of coherence of EU consumer law and the proposed Consumer Rights Directive seeks a common 14 day period for "distance and off premises" sales.(art.12)

The close connection between the right of withdrawal and information is underlined in these directives by a legal linkage between the withdrawal rights

117. As the Directive is a minimum directive a Member State may, according to the preamble of the Directive, maintain a total or partial prohibition on doorstep selling. However, as such a prohibition may infringe Article 30 as a barrier to trade, there should obviously be specific reasons if such a measure is maintained or introduced. As an example may be mentioned the case *Roger Buet v. Ministere Public,* Case C-382/87 [1989] ECR 1235, where a French prohibition on doorstep selling of educational material was accepted because of the greater risk of ill-considered purchases in this area.

118. Directive 92/96 on the coordination of laws, regulations and administrative provisions relating to direct life assurance and amending Directives 79/267/EEC and 90/619/EEC (third life assurance Directive), OJ L 360/1, Art. 30. Already the Second Life Assurance Directive of 1990 contained, in Art. 15, a right to withdraw from cross-border commitments.

and the information duties of the business.[119] Already according to the Doorstep Selling Directive, the period of cancellation does not commence before the time when the consumer received the required information concerning the right of cancellation and its exercise. If the information is not provided then the cancellation period would seem to be available until such information is supplied however many years later that might be.[120] According to the Timeshare Directive the purchaser may withdraw from the contract within a longer period (three months and ten days) than the ordinary ten days, if certain required information is not provided. The same idea is reproduced in the Distance Contracts Directive, where the beginning of the period of withdrawal is tied to the provision of most of the information required to be given by the articles of the Directive. However, once again there is a maximum period of withdrawal (three months) in case the information is not given. As the Timeshare Directive and the Distance Contracts Directive put much more emphasis on information than the Doorstep Selling Directive the prolongation of the period of withdrawal in these Directives provides a sanction for the information duties concerning many important items. The Financial Services Distance Marketing Directive carries the use of this sanction still further. As it does not mention any maximum period of prolongation it seems to leave the contract open to withdrawal "indefinitely" as long as the information requirements are not fulfilled.[121] In this context one should also mention that this Directive, in Art. 11, offers a general option, not only connected with information, for the Member States to provide that the consumer may be given the right to withdraw from the contract at any time, if the supplier does not comply with the national provisions adopted pursuant to the Directive. Art 13 of the proposed Consumer Rights Directive provides that if the consumer has not been advised of his right of withdrawal then the withdrawal period expires three months after the trader has fully performed his other contractual obligations.[122]

---

119. On a possible generalisation of this connection, see T. Wilhelmsson, *Private Law Remedies against the Breach of Information Requirements of EC Law*, in R. Schulze, M. Ebers and H.C. Grigoleit (eds.), *Informationspflichten und Vertragsschluss im Acquis communautaire* (Tübingen 2003), 245.

120. *Heininger v Bayerische Hypo-und Vereinsbank AG*, Case C-481/99 [2001] 1 ECR I-9945.

121. G. Howells, *The right of withdrawal in European consumer law*, in H. Schulte-Nölke and R. Schulze (eds.), *Europäisches Vertragsrecht im Gemeinschaftsrecht* (Köln 2002), 235.

122. Breach of other information duties is for the most part left to national law: art. 6(2).

The frequent use of withdrawal rights in EU law can be understood as an attempt to increase autonomous rational decision-making of consumers when entering into contracts as individual parties. It is, however, difficult to assess how efficient this tool is in this respect. On the one hand one may claim that the remedy only constitutes a slightly more refined way of giving effect to the traditional market-rational right to self-determination. It might be queried how often the right to withdraw is invoked given the psychological commitment most consumers have to contracts they sign and the fairly short period for withdrawal.[123] On the other hand it at least formally breaks the traditional principle of the binding force of contracts in a fairly radical way.

## 9. General Clauses as an Important Method of Protection[124]

The legitimate expectation principle discussed above is to a large extent derived from the use of general clauses in EC consumer law. General clauses are common in many areas of EC consumer law. We will focus on the unfairness test in the contract and commercial practices directives, but one can also think of the general product safety requirement and even principles like defectiveness in product liability and non-conformity in sale of goods law as general clauses.

General clauses are typically used in situations where the legislator cannot specify or chooses not to specify what conduct is allowed or not allowed; instead the general clause provides the ground rules to steer the parties, regulators and courts towards a decision that correctly balances the interests at stake. In other words it provides the structure for determining how legitimate expectations should be assessed. It is well suited to situations where values are fluid and mixed questions of law and fact pre-dominate so that decisions require individual assessments. Decision-makers can use the general clause to fashion a solution that suits the context.

The openness of general clauses makes them appealing to the European legislator. They can hide compromises and provide a safety valve for tensions caused by increased European influence, as the task of applying the principles

123. Rekaiti and van den Bergh, *Cooling-Off Periods in the Consumer Laws of the EC Member States. A Comparative Law and Econooics Approach, Journal of Consumer Policy*, 33 (2000) 371.

124. In more detail see G. Howells, *General Clauses in European Consumer Law*, in H-W. Micklitz (2005), 397–420.

rest with national institutions that can take account of local conditions and sensitivities. Herein lies a paradox. The flexible features of the general clause that make it so useful as a mechanism for achieving agreement on harmonization at the European level can conflict with the objective of true harmonisation in practice and the need to develop common autonomous legal concepts. The national application of the clauses can permit national traditions and values to re-emerge. There is a danger that the differences between states are simply hidden by practice rather than being transparent on the face of the legislation. Of course, this acceptance of diversity could be celebrated, but officially at least the goal is for consistency of application. There are several reasons, however, why it might not be possible.

Sometimes local conditions simply mean that the way a general clause is applied has to be understood in the local context. In *First National Bank v Director General of Fair Trading*[125] a term relating to interest had to be assessed in the light of national rules on interest chargeable on judgment debts. The local context can determine whether a practice is considered to be fair or not: for example, the Germans have a tradition of trade associations drawing up standard contracts, whereas this is viewed with suspicion in the United Kingdom.[126] In other cases the issues are appreciated in different ways by different societies. For instance, attitudes to risk in the context of product liability and safety laws or the acceptability of marketing practices under the Unfair Commercial Practices Directive. These value differences vary greatly from one area of consumer law to another. For instance, one may suspect that in relation to safety there is a high degree of consensus on appropriate safety levels; by contrast, in the area of marketing the values still seem to differ markedly across the Union. A general clause will therefore seem more likely to provide greater uniformity in the safety than marketing context. However, the general clause is also part of that context. It can help steer European values towards convergence, where this is deemed to be appropriate. This makes general clauses a contribution to the gradual convergence of European law and practice when used as part of a minimal harmonization process; but where, as in relation to unfair commercial practices, maximal harmonization is demanded either national decision-makers will have to step outside the local context and apply the standards according to some yet to be fashioned European values or else, more likely, they will apply the common standard with a local flavour producing a sham full harmonization.

---

125. [2002] 1 AC 481.

126. Teubner, *Legal Irritants: Good Faith in British Law And How Unifying Law Ends Up in New Divergences*, 11.

In moving Europe towards a common application of the general clause the guidance surrounding the application of the clause is very important. The more detailed the guidance the more likely systems are likely to converge in practice. Guidance comes both from the legislation and from court jurisprudence. In the following the chapter will discuss how the legislative guidance is structured for unfair terms and unfair commercial practices law. The role of the European Court of Justice shall also be considered. It will be noted that the Court seems unwilling to become too involved in monitoring the application of general standards.

Finally, before looking at the two case studies on unfair terms and unfair commercial practices it is worth noting that there were very different traditions towards general clauses within Europe. Of course all legal systems have made use of open-textured norms, but civil law countries were far more accustomed to these norms being the foundation principles of their legal systemization. Broad principles are seen by continental lawyers as attractive ways of underpinning core values. By contrast the common law countries preferred specific rules and viewed open textured norms as a necessary evil when it was impossible to be more precise. Common lawyers feel general principles simply hide the real debates that can best be addressed through concrete legal rules.[127] The European preference for general clauses covering broad areas has therefore brought greater disruption to the common than civil law systems. Common lawyers have had to learn new habits.[128] But sometimes a clean break can be the easiest and for continental systems there is perhaps a greater danger that they continue to view the new laws as old wine in new bottles, whereas the rules are in many cases of a different vintage. Civil law systems may be tempted to continue with national rules and practices rather than fully embrace new European concepts. Indeed these national practices provide a certain predictability to the application of general clauses, which may be less easy to discern given the relatively underdeveloped European culture.

The Unfair Contract Terms Directive includes perhaps the paradigm general clause referring to good faith as part of the test of contractual unfairness. Good faith was originally included as an independent criteria for assessing unfairness, but in the final version lack of good faith is a pre-condition before a

---

127. See views of Lord Hoffmann on the right to privacy in *Campbell v MGN Ltd.* Of course not all common law judges are as sceptical: see views of Lord Steyn, *Contract Law Fulfilling the Reasonable Expectations of Honest Men, Law Quarterly Review* 113 (1997), 433.

128. Teubner, *Legal Irritants* and H. Collins, *Good Faith in European Contract Law, Oxford Journal of Legal Studies* 14 (1994), 229.

term can be held to be unfair merely because of an imbalance between the parties. Recital 16 provides some assistance in determining the concept of unfairness. However, the continental understanding of good faith as a substantive control must be borne in mind to appreciate that good faith is not merely concerned with procedural fairness. An imbalance between the parties' rights and obligations can in itself be the basis for a breach of good faith. However, although many lawyers place a lot of trust in good faith as a guiding principle, there is still a sense in which it can be interpreted according to the desires of the decision-maker. Perhaps a firmer steer towards a harmonized European practice has been given by the grey list of indicatively unfair terms found in annex 1. The CLAB database was also a useful experiment in providing a resource to compare approaches to terms across Europe. However, it has been abandoned with the Commission questioning its value for money without ever having promoted its use and without having it made accessible to the broader public.[129] The role of the European Court of Justice in providing guidance is instructive. In *Oceano Grupo Editorial v Murciano Quinto*,[130] it was willing, in a case involving two Spanish parties, to condemn as unfair a clause giving jurisdiction to the traders' local courts. In *Freiburger Kommunalbauten v Hofstetter*[131] the Court said it was the responsibility of the national courts to apply the test set out in the Directive and explained *Oceano* on the basis that the term in that context was always unfair to the consumer. It most cases there will be a need to balance the indirect benefits consumers might gain from agreeing to what might at first glance appear to be a harsh term. This clearly places the emphasis on national courts to make that assessment. Some national courts may be able to spend a lot of time undertaking comparative and European law research,[132] but many may not, giving rise to the risk of divergent national practices. However, the European Court of Justice risks being overwhelmed by requests for interpretation; equally it has developed as a constitutional court and at times seems uneasy with addressing private law questions.

A recent bold use of the general clause at the European level has been the introduction of a general prohibition on unfair commercial practices, formulated as a general clause in Article 5 of the Unfair Commercial Practices Directive. Unfairness is defined in a fairly open way as practices contrary to the

---

129. See H-W. Micklitz and M. Radeideh, *CLAB-Europa—The European database on unfair terms in consumer contracts*, *Journal of Consumer Policy* 28 (2005), 325–360.

130. Case C-240/98 [2000] ECR I-4941.

131. Case C-237/02 [2004] 2 CMLR 13.

132. See judgment of Mr Justice Burton in *A v National Blood Authority* [2001] 3 All ER 289.

requirements of professional diligence that materially distort or are likely materially to distort the economic behaviour of consumers. It includes the concepts of misleading and aggressive practices which are themselves defined in a fairly general manner. The difficulty of predicting which practices will actually be caught led attention during the implementation process to focus on the black list of practices in Annex 1 which will be considered unfair in all circumstances. If the experience of unfair terms legislation is a useful guide it seems unlikely that the European Court of Justice will want to get involved too much in providing guidance on the concept of unfairness. This will be for the national decision-makers. If anything the risk of differential application is greater here than in contract law, for in many states marketing practices law is applied by regulators as well as the courts.[133] However, if this leads to different practices this will undermine the central pillar of the Directive which is the internal market clause that seeks to prevent Member States having more restrictive national rules. The problem with the general clause in the Unfair Commercial Practices Directive is that it does not merely provide the means for national laws and values to converge; rather it demands convergence, but does not provide the direction necessary to achieve that outcome. It will be interesting to see whether any institution emerges with the energy and resources to ensure that the unfair commercial practices are handled uniformly across Europe.

## 10. Judicial Protection of Consumer Rights

The European Community relies on the Member States to provide for appropriate legal means to permit consumer rights to be enforced. Along with the establishment of the Single Market programme, individual and collective consumer rights have gained an ever growing importance as a means for contributing to the completion of the Internal Market. The European Court of Justice even upgraded the legal status of rights and remedies from a human rights point of view, not only to secure the application of Community law, but also to enhance legal protection.[134] While the European Court of Justice focuses on consumer civil law, it appears as if the Commission banks on an

---

133. Regulators might more easily be able to continue national traditions as their decisions will often be less transparent than the courts.

134. F. Snyder, *The Effectiveness of European Community Laws: Institutions, Processes, Tools, Techniques, Modern Law Review* 56 (1993), 19.

improved cooperation of the executive organs of the Member States under the Commission's guidance, as laid down in the Consumer Protection Cooperation Regulation.[135]

As to the judicial protection of consumer rights against the failure of national legislators to fulfil their obligations to implement EU consumer law directives, it is an important question whether the individual consumer can claim compensation if the Member State has failed to enact legislative measures necessary to develop a legal system satisfying Community requirements. This requires that concrete minimum requirements can be ascertained and in many cases this will only be possible with the help of secondary Community law. It concerns possible liability for legislative wrongs in line with *Francovich*. Liability of the Member States for compensation of the damage, which has been incurred from the failure or partial failure to implement a Directive and constitutes a subjective right in favour of the consumer, is relatively unproblematic as it is legally secured as part of the *acquis communautaire*. The most important case so far which had been decided by the European Court of Justice concerned the Package Tour Directive. In *Dillenkofer*,[136] the Court easily found in favour of the individual, who had a subjective legal right and could thus impose state liability on the Federal Republic of Germany for failing to make arrangements for the possible insolvency of the organiser. The imminent risk of liability for the state in Germany as a result of the quadrupling of the duration of warranty obligation (from six months to two years) as a result of the Consumer Sales Directives explains the prompt modernising of the German law of obligations.

The existence of subjective rights in relation to the Member State is more problematic if the relevant Directives primarily constitute supervisory obligations of the Member States. Compliance with these protects the consumer without clearly illustrating whether the consumer is equipped with a separate legal right. As the Community also fails to pursue a uniform policy in secondary law the existence of a subjective right depends on the drafting of the Directive. The Directive on investment services in the securities field[137] purports neither to constitute concrete and determinable supervisory obligations to act nor individual rights of investors.[138] The same applies to the Directive

135. Regulation 2006/2004 on cooperation between national authorities responsible for the enforcement of consumer protection laws (the Regulation on consumer protection cooperation), OJ L 364/1.

136. Case C-178/94 et al. [1996] ECR I-4845.

137. Directive 93/22 on investment services in the securities field, OJ L 197/58.

138. District court Bonn, 6.9.1999, ZIP 1999, 1592.

on the capital adequacy of investments firms and credit institutions[139] and the Directive on the coordination of the laws, regulations and administrative provisions relating to the taking up and pursuit of the business of credit institutions.[140] This is not true for the Directive on deposit-guarantee schemes[141] where a legal right of the consumer can be established.

Turning then to the protection of consumer rights against violations by traders, there are quite a number of directives providing for an injunction in order to set an end to all sorts of marketing practices, such as the Misleading Advertising Directive, the Unfair Contract Terms Directive, the Distance Contracts Directive, the Comparative Advertising Directive, the Unfair Commercial Practices Directive and the Injunctions Directive, which includes particular rules on transborder litigation. There has been much debate in legal doctrine whether the Member States are entirely free to put the control powers into the hands of public authorities or whether the right must be extended to trade/consumer organisations. Although the answer may depend on the precise wording of the directives, nevertheless, relying on Article 153, one might deduce from Community law a legal obligation imposed on the Member States to grant at least consumer organisations the right to file an injunction in the competent national court.[142] The Member States are free to decide, however, whether they intend to grant the same powers equally to competent authorities.

The Injunctions Directive covers national and transborder litigation as well. It has been established in the aftermath of *Direct Shopping*,[143] which demonstrated the inefficiency of the French and German legal order to cope with misleading transborder advertising practices. The directive provided for the establishment of a register run by the Commission and published in the Of-

---

139. Directive 93/6 on the capital adequacy of investments firms and credit institutions, OJ L 141/1; District court Bonn, 6.9.1999, ZIP 1999, 1595.

140. Directive 77/780 on the coordination of the laws, regulations and administrative provisions relating to the taking up and pursuit of the business of credit institutions, OJ L 322/30; Court of Appeal, 4.12.1998, *Three Rivers District Council and Others/Bank of England* (1999) European Law Reports 210, as confirmed by the ECJ, 12.10.2004, *Peter Paul,* Case 220/02 (nyr).

141. Directive 94/19 on deposit-guarantee schemes, OJ L 135/5.

142. See H-W. Micklitz, in Reich and, Micklitz, *Europäisches Verbraucherrecht*, § 30.15 with references.

143. French and German consumer associations had been concerned about the conduct of advertising by firms in the mailorder business with a seat in Germany who, from Germany, approached French consumers using doubtful sales methods (sweepstakes), see judgment, 2.10.1991, 31 Chambre Correctionelle du Tribunal de Grande Instance de Paris, Affaire No P 88 314 2003 6.

ficial Journal[144] under which all consumer organisations and public entities are listed which have the right to sue under national law (*qualité d'agir*). Whether or not the right to sue exists in the particular case at issue has to be investigated by the competent national court (*intéret d'agir*). The scope of application *sedes materiae* is defined in the Annex. Here the relevant directives are enumerated, except those dealing with consumer safety issues. Since its adoption, the Directive has been applied only once in a Belgian/English case.[145]

The Consumer Protection Cooperation Regulation aims at improving the co-operation between public authorities responsible for enforcement of the laws that protect consumers' interests in dealing with intra community infringements, thereby contributing to the smooth functioning of the internal market. The Regulation deals with transborder enforcement in the field of economic consumer protection only. Whilst it was the intention of the Commission to involve public authorities, Germany and Austria insisted on the possibility of delegating the responsibility to consumer and/or trade organisations which are in charge of enforcing unfair terms and unfair marketing practices legislation.

The Regulation distinguishes between information exchange with or without request and requests for enforcement measures. Whilst the mechanisms of co-operation are set out in detail, it must be recognised that the requested authority can not be obliged by the applicant authority to take action, not even to exchange information. That is why the Regulation does not foresee any enforcement mechanism in case the requested authority does not take the required action. The applicant authority may request the Commission to the set the comitology procedure into motion; however, it is not obliged to do so.

These measures relate to the collective enforcement of consumer rights by competent authorities and organisations. Then have not gone so far as to provide means for collective redress of compensation, but this is currently a major priority for the Commission,[146] We do not dwell on this potentially exciting development as the Commissions ambitions are still too uncertain. In addi-

---

144. Commission communication concerning Article 4(3) of Directive 98/27/EC of the European Parliament and of the Council on injunctions for the protection of consumers' interests, concerning the entities qualified to bring an action under Article 2 of this Directive, OJ C 30, 2.2.2002, 2.

145. http://www.oft.gov.uk/news/press+release/2004/208-04.htm, see H-W. Micklitz, Transborder Law Enforcement—Does it exist? in Ulf Bernitz/Stephen Weatherill (eds.), The Regulation of Unfair Commercial Practices under EC Directive, New Rules and New Techniques (Hart Publishing 2006) 235.

146. See EU Consumer Policy strategy 2007–2013, COM(2007) 99 final at 11; now Green Paper on consumer collective redress COM (2008) 794 final, indicating a long lasting consultation process.

tion, some European measures have been adopted concerning individual disputes as well.

The European Commission is strongly advocating for the establishment of alternative dispute resolution systems for the benefit of consumers. Two recommendations[147] set minimum standards on the independency of the members, the transparency of the procedure, the right of the consumer to be heard, efficiency of the procedure, respect of the rule of law, the voluntary character of alternative dispute resolution (ADR) and the right of the consumer to be represented by a lawyer. Currently the Commission is working on a directive on mediation and a regulation on small claims. However, both instruments are only meant to deal with transborder litigation. It has to be recalled that Member States' culture and tradition differ widely in the degree to which ADR systems are regarded as an appropriate means effectively to protect consumers' rights.

Three more recent initiatives seem to indicate a certain shift to using binding directives in order to guarantee access to justice in individual litigations. The Legal Aid Directive establishes a right to legal aid to persons who are partly or totally unable to meet the costs of pre-litigation advice and legal assistance and representation in court in cross border disputes relating to civil and commercial matters.[148] Two further pieces of legislation follow the Legal Aid Directive insofar as they apply to general civil and commercial matters (i.e. not consumers alone). However, unlike the Legal Aid Directive they focus exclusively on transborder litigation. The first concerns a directive on mediation,[149] the second concerns small claim procedures.[150]

Even though EU law has intervened in the area of remedies and enforcement in the above ways, the predominant part of these issues are still regulated by the Member States. The various models of consumer protection, analysed above,[151] are therefore still clearly discernible. Looked at from this

---

147. Recommendations 98/257 on the principles applicable to the bodies responsible for out-of-court settlement of consumer disputes, OJ L 115/31 and 2001/310 on the principles for out-of-court bodies involved in the consensual resolution of consumer disputes, OJ L 109/56.

148. Directive 2003/8/EC to improve access to justice in cross-border disputes by establishing minimum common rules relating to legal aid and other financial aspects of civil proceedings, OJ L 26/41.

149. Directive 2008/52/EC on ceretain aspects of mediation in civil and commercial matters: OJ 2008 L136/3.

150. Regulation (EC) No 861/2007 establishing a European Small Claims Procedure: OJ2007 L 199/1.

151. See section 3 of the chapter.

perspective consumer law in Europe is still in an important respect national law. European remedies are largely non-existent.

## References

Arnokouros G. I., *The transposition of the Consumer Sales Directive into the Greek legal system, European Review of Private Law* 9 (2001), 259–277.

Bakardjieva Engelbrekt A., *Fair Trading Law in Flux? National Legacies, Institutional Choice and the Process of Europeanisation* (diss. Stockholm, 2003).

Beater A., *Verbraucherschutz und Schutzzweckdenken im Wettbewerbsrecht* (Tübingen 2000).

Bianca M.C. and Grundmann, S. (eds.), *EU Sales Directive, Commentary* (Antwerp 2002).

Bird T. C., *Directive 99/44/EC on certain aspects of the sale of consumer goods and associated guarantees: its impact on existing Irish sale of goods law, European Review of Private Law* 9 (2001), 279–295.

Brandner H. E. and Ulmer P., *The Community directive on unfair terms in consumer contracts: some critical remarks on the proposal submitted by the EC Commission, Common Market Law Review* 28 (1991), 647–662.

Calais-Auloy J., *Le Droit de la Consommation en France* (New York 1981).

Collins H., *Good Faith in European Contract Law, Oxford Journal of Legal Studies* 14 (1994), 229–254.

Dahl B., Melchior T., Tamm D. (eds.), *Danish law in a European Perspective*, 2nd edition (Kopenhagen 2002).

Grundmann S., Kerber W., Weatherill S. (eds.), *Party Autonomy and the Role of Information in the Internal Market* (Berlin 2001).

Grundmann S., *Verbraucherrecht, Unternehmensrecht, Privatrecht—warum sind sich UN-Kaufrecht und EU-Kaufrechtsrichtlinie so ähnlich? Archiv für die civilistische Praxis* 202 (2002), 40–71.

Hanson J. and Kysar D., *Taking Behaviouralism Seriously: The Problem of Market Manipulation, New York University Law Review* 74 (1999), 630–749.

Hanson J. and Kysar D., *Taking Behaviouralism Seriously: Some Evidence of Market Manipulation, Harward Law Review* 112 (1999), 1420–1572.

Herre J., *Konsumentköplagen* (Stockholm 1999).

Hommelhoff P., *Zivilrecht unter dem Einfluss europäischer Rechtsangleichung, Archiv für die civilistische Praxis* (1992), 71–107.

Hondius E. and Schelhaas H., *In conformity with the Consumer Sales Directive? Some remarks on transposition into Dutch law, European Review of Private Law* 9 (2001), 327–336.

Howells G., *Implementation of the EC Consumer Sales Directive in the United Kingdom*, in: Grundmann, S., Medicus, D. and Rolland (eds.), *Europäisches Kaufgewährleistungsrecht* (Köln, 2000), 40–71.

Howells G., *The Potential and Limits of Consumer Empowerment by Information, Journal of Law and Society* 32 (2005), 349–370.

Howells G., *The right of withdrawal in European Consumer Law*, in Schulte-Nölke H. and Schulze R. (eds.), *Europäisches Vertragsrecht im Gemeinschaftsrecht*, (Köln 2002), 229–238.

Howells G., *General Clauses in European Consumer Law*, in Micklitz H-W., Stand und Perspektiven des Verbraucherrechts in Deutschland, (Baden-Baden, to be published 2005), 397–420.

Howells G., Janssen A. and Schulze R. (eds.), *Information Rights and Obligations—A Challenge for Party Autonomy and Transactional Fairness* (Aldershot 2005).

Howells G., Micklitz, H-W. and Wilhelmsson, T., *European Fair Trading Law—The Unfair Commercial Practices Directive* (Aldershot 2006).

Howells G. and Wilhelmsson T., *EC Consumer Law* (Aldershot 1997).

Jeloschek C., *The Transposition of Directive 99/44/EC into Austrian Law, European Review of Private Law* 9 (2001), 163–175.

Joerges C. and Brüggemeier G., *Europäisierung des Vertrags-und Haftungsrechts*, in Müller-Graff P-C. (ed.), *Gemeinsames Privatrecht in der Europäischen Gesellschaft* (Baden-Baden 1993), 233–286.

Joustra C., *Consumer Law*, in Hartkamp A. et al. (eds.), *Towards a European Civil Code*, 2nd Edition (The Hague 1998), 133–148.

Kötz H., *Abschied von der Rechtskreislehre, Zeitschrift für Europäisches Privatrecht* 6 (1998), 495–505.

Lando O. and Beale H. (eds.), *Principles of European Contract Law, Parts I and II* (The Hague 2000).

Lapuente S.C., *The Hypothetical 'European Civil Code':Why, How, When?, ERA-Forum* (2002), 89–99.

Legrand P., *European Legal Systems are not converging, International and Comparative Law Quarterly* 45 (1996), 52–81.

Legrand P., *Against a European Civil Code, Modern Law Review* 60 (1997), 44–63.

Lettl T., *Gemeinschaftsrecht und neues UWG, Wettbewerb in Recht und Praxis* (2004), 1079–1132.

Lettl T., *Der lauterkeitsrechtliche Schutz vor irreführender Werbung in Europa* (München 2004).

Meyer A., *Das Verbraucherleitbild des Europäischen Gerichtshofs—Abkehr vom "flüchtigen Verbraucher", Wettbewerb in Recht und Praxis* 39 (1993), 215–224.

Micklitz H-W., *Principles of Justice in Private Law within the European Union*, in Paasivirta E. and Rissanen K. (eds.), *Principles of Justice and the Law of the European Union*, European Commission (DG XIII, Cost A7) (Brussels 1995), 259–298.

Micklitz H-W., *Internationales Produktsicherheitsrecht* (Baden-Baden 1996).

Micklitz H-W., *Legitime Erwartungen als Gerechtigkeitsprinzip des Europäischen Privatrechts*, in Krämer L., Micklitz H-W., Tonner K. (eds.), *Law and Diffuse Interests in the European Legal Order* (Baden-Baden 1997), 245–277.

Micklitz H-W., *Social Justice in European Private Law, Yearbook of European Law* 19 (1999/2000), 167–204.

Micklitz H-W., *Vertragschlussmodalitäten*, in Micklitz H-W., Pfeiffer T., Tonner K., Willingmann A. (eds.), *Schuldrechtsreform und Verbraucherschutz* (Baden-Baden 2001), 191–248.

Micklitz H-W., *Verbraucherschutz West versus Ost—Kompatibilisierungsmöglichkeiten in der Europäischen Gemeinschaft—Einige Vorüberlegungen*, in Heiss H. (ed.), *Brückenschlag zwischen den Rechtskulturen des Ostseeraums* (Tübingen 2001), 137–182.

Micklitz, H-W., *Introductory remarks §§13, 14 BGB, Münchener Kommentar zum Bürgerlichen Gesetzbuch, Band 1,* 5th edition (München 2008).

Micklitz, H-W., *Zum Recht des Verbrauchers auf die eigene Sprache, Besprechungsaufsatz zur Entscheidung der Cour de Cassation vom 14. November 2000, Zeitschrift für Europäisches Privatrecht* 11 (2003), 635–655.

Micklitz H-W. and Kessler J. (eds.), *Marketing Practices Regulation and Consumer Protection in the EC Member States and the US* (Baden-Baden 2002).

Micklitz H-W. and Radeideh M., *CLAB-Europa—The European database on unfair terms in consumer contracts, Journal of Consumer Policy* 28 (2005), 325–360.

Micklitz H-W., The Principles of European Contract Law and the Protection of the Weaker Party, JCP 2004, 339–356.

Micklitz H-W., Transborder Law Enforcement—Does it exist? in Ulf Bernitz/Stephen Weatherill (eds.), The Regulation of Unfair Commercial Practices under EC Directive, New Rules and New Techniques (Hart Publishing 2006) 235

Micklitz H-W., Peter Rott and N. Reich, Understanding EU Consumer Law (Antwerpen, Oxford 2009 forthcoming)

Nordhausen A., *Information Requirements in the E-Commerce Directive and the Proposed Directive on Unfair Commercial Practices,* in Howells G., Janssen A. and Schulze R. (eds.), *Information Rights and Obligations—A Challenge for Party Autonomy and Transactional Fairness* (Aldershot 2005), 93–114.

Osman F. (ed.), *Vers un Code europeen de la Consommation* (Brüssel 1998).
Radeideh M., *Fair Trading in EC Law* (Groningen 2005).
Reich N., *Understanding EU law*, 2nd edition, (Antwerp 2005).
Reich N., Tonner K., Wegener H, *Verbraucher und Recht* (Göttingen 1976).
Reich N., *Transformation of Contract law and civil justice in the new EU member countries*, RSGL working papers no. 21 (Riga 2004).
Reich N., *Verbraucherpolitik und Verbraucherschutz in Vertrag von Amsterdam, Verbraucher und Recht* 14 (1999), 3–10.
Reich N. and Micklitz H-W., *Europäisches Verbraucherrecht*, 4th edition (Baden-Baden 2003).
Rieger G., *Die Richtlinie zu bestimmten Aspekten des Verbrauchsgüterkaufs und der Garantien für Verbrauchsgüter vor dem Hintergrund des geltenden Rechts, Verbraucher und Recht* 14 (1999), 287–293.
Rösler H., *Europäisches Konsumentenvertragsrecht* (München 2004).
Rösler H., *30 Jahre Verbraucherpolitik in Europa, Zeitschrift für Rechtvergleichung* 21 (2005), 134–147.
Sack, R., *Die relevante Irreführung im Wettbewerbsrecht, Wettbewerb in Recht und Praxis* 50 (2004), 521–529.
Scherpe J. M., *Außergerichtliche Streitbeilegung in Verbrauchersachen* (Tübingen 2002).
Schieble C., *Deutsches und Europäisches Produktsicherheitsrecht* (Baden-Baden 2003).
Schulte-Noelke H. and Schulze R. in association with Bernardeau L. (ed.), *Europäisches Vertragsrecht im Gemeinschaftsrecht* (Köln 2002).
Snyder F., *The Effectiveness of European Community Law: Institutions, Processes, Tools and Techniques, Modern Law Review* 56 (1993), 19–53.
Lord Steyn, *Contract Law: Fulfilling the Reasonable Expectations of Honest Men, Law Quarterly Review* 113 (1997), 433–442.
Stuyck J., *Patterns of Justice in the Constitutional Charter: minimum harmonization in the field of consumer law*, Liber Amicorum N. Reich, *Law and diffuse Interests in the European Legal Order* (Baden-Baden 1997), 279–289.
Teubner G., *Legal Irritants: Good Faith in British Law or How Unifying Law Ends up in New Divergences, Modern Law Review* 61 (1998), 11–32.
Tonner K., *Die Rolle des Verbraucherrechts bei der Entwicklung eines europäischen Zivilrechts, Juristenzeitung* 51 (1996), 533–541.
Usher J.A., *Disclosure Rules (Information) as a Primary Tool in the Doctrine on Measures Having an Equivalent Effect*, in S. Grundmann, W. Kerber and S. Weatherill, *Party Autonomy and the Role of Information in the Internal Market* (Berlin 2001), 151–161.

Watterson S., *Consumer Sales Directive 1999/44/EC—The impact on English law, European Review of Private Law* 9 (2001), 197–221.

Weatherill S., *The European Commission's Green Paper on European Contract Law: Context, Content and Constitutionality, Journal of Consumer Policy* 24 (2001), 339–399.

Weatherill S., *The role of the informed consumer in European Community law and policy, Consumer Law Journal* 2 (1994), 49–69.

Weatherill, S., *EU Consumer Law and Policy* (Cheltenham 2005).

Wendlandt B., *EC Directives on Time-Sharing and for self-employed commercial agents—Apples, Oranges and the Core of the Information Overload Problem* in Howells G., Janssen A., Schulze R. (eds.), *Information Rights and Obligations—A Challenge for Party Autonomy and Transactional Fairness* (Aldershot 2004), 67–92.

Whincup M. H., *Consumer legislation in the United Kingdom and the Republic of Ireland* (New York 1980).

Wilhelmsson T., *Social Contract Law and European Integration* (Aldershot 1995).

Wilhelmsson T., *International lex mercatoria and local consumer law: an impossible combination, Uniform Law Review* 8 (2003), 141–153.

Wilhelmsson T, *Is There a European Consumer Law—and Should There be one* (Rome 2000).

Wilhelmsson T., *Private Law Remedies against the Breach of Information Requirements of EC Law*, in Schulze R., Ebers M. and Grigoleit H. C. (eds.), *Informationspflichten und Vertragsschluss im Acquis communautaire* (Tübingen 2003), 245–265.

Wilhelmsson T., Tuominen S. and Tuomola H. (eds.), *Consumer Law in the Information Society* (The Hague 2001).

Willett C., *Autonomy and Fairness: The Case of Public Statements* in Howells G., Janssen A., Schulze R. (eds.), *Information Rights and Obligations—A Challenge for Party Autonomy and Transactional Fairness* (Aldershot 2004), 1–15.

Wuttke, T, *Die Konvergenz des nationalen und des europäischen Irreführungsbegriffs, Wettbewerb in Recht und Praxis* 50 (2004), 820–828.

Zerres T., *Das neue Sachmängelrecht beim Kauf, Verbraucher und Recht* 17 (2002), 3–15.

## Legislation

Directive 77/780 on the coordination of the laws, regulations and administrative provisions relating to the taking up and pursuit of the business of credit institutions.

Directive 84/450 relating to the approximation of the laws, regulations and administrative provisions of the Member States concerning misleading advertising.

Directive 85/374 on the approximation of the laws, regulations and administrative provisions of the Member States concerning liability for defective products, amended by Directive 99/34.

Directive 85/577 to protect the consumer in respect of contracts negotiated away from business premises.

Directive 87/102 concerning consumer credit agreements, amended by Directive 98/7.

Directive 90/314 on package travel, package holidays and package tours.

Directive 92/96 on the coordination of laws, regulations and administrative provisions relating to direct life assurance and amending Directives 79/267/EEC and 90/619/EEC (third life assurance Directive).

Directive 93/6 on the capital adequacy of investments firms and credit institutions.

Directive 93/13 on unfair terms in consumer contracts.

Directive 93/22 on investment services in the securities field.

Directive 94/19 on deposit-guarantee schemes.

Directive 94/47 on the protection of purchasers in respect of certain aspects of contracts relating to the purchase of the right to use immovable properties on a timeshare basis.

Directive 97/7 on the protection of consumers in respect of distance contracts.

Directive 97/55 amending Directive 84/450 concerning misleading advertising so as to include comparative advertising.

Directive 98/27 on injunctions for the protection of consumers' interests.

Directive 99/44 on certain aspects of the sale of consumer goods and associated guarantees.

Directive 2000/13 on the approximation of the laws of the Member States relating to the labelling, presentation and advertising of foodstuffs.

Directive 2000/31 on certain legal aspects of information society services, in particular electronic commerce, in the Internal Market.

Directive 2001/95 on general product safety.

Directive 2002/65 concerning the distance marketing of consumer financial services.

Directive 2003/8/EC to improve access to justice in cross-border disputes by establishing minimum common rules relating to legal aid and other financial aspects of civil proceedings.

Directive 2005/29 concerning unfair business-to-consumer commercial practices in the internal market and amending Council Directive 84/450/EEC,

Directives 97/7/EC, 98/27/EC and 2002/65/EC of the European Parliament and of the Council and Regulation (EC) No 2006/2004 of the European Parliament and of the Council ('Unfair Commercial Practices Directive').

Regulation 2006/2004 on cooperation between national authorities responsible for the enforcement of consumer protection laws.

# 9

# Western Tort Law: A Jurisprudence of Injury[1]

Gert Brüggemeier

## Summary



## 1. Introduction

Today, at the dawn of the 21st century and after a long history of western private law and its diversity, some rough consensus might be attainable that the branch of private law called *delict* or *tors* is at best characterised as the *law of injuries*. The essence of tort law is to "make whole" the injuries incurred, mostly by payment of damages to the victim, and to prevent injuries to occur

1. The subtitle is "borrowed" from M.S. Shapo, *Towards a Jurisprudence of Injury*, Chicago 1984.

by adequate tort remedies. The basic morality of tort law through the centuries was "Do not injure your neighbour"/"*neminem laede!*" The fundamental principle of non-contractual liability can therefore today still be stated as follows: *One who in a legally attributable way*[2] *injures the protected interest of others is bound to compensation: for the economic or non-economic loss resulting therefrom and for the injury as such.* A person who, for example, takes a property away from its owner or possessor has to restitute it.[3] A person who injures the bodily integrity or who damages the property of another person, has to pay the money needed to redress the damage (*damna sunt praestanda*). One who violates the dignity, autonomy or privacy of a persona, is bound to an equitable indemnification.

This principle forms the basis of most, if not all, national and transnational liability rules, notwithstanding how different and diffuse these rules at various times in history may have been formulated: from the Aristotelian principle of corrective/commutative justice (4th century B.C.) to the action of *damnum iniuria datum*[4] of the Roman *Lex Aquilia* (3rd century B.C.); from the general heads of liability in Articles 1382 and 1383 of the French *Code civil* of 1804[5] to the three "small general clauses" in Sections 823 (1), 823 (2), and 826 of the German *Bürgerliches Gesetzbuch* (*BGB*) of 1896/1900; from the English Common Law with its pigeonhole system of enumerated torts[6] and its

---

2. The English juristic language lacks a familiar term for *Zurechnung/Toerekening*. *Wrongfulness* is more or less synonymous with fault/negligence. The (Vienna) European Group on Tort Law uses both terms, *attribution* (Art. 1:101 (1)) and *imputation*; the Study Group on a European Civil Code (SGECC) speaks of *accountability* (DCFR Art. VI-1:101 (1)). More to this below in fn. 8 and in the text.

3. The Canonist doctrine of "restitution" influenced strongly the modern development of tort law, esp. the Austrian and German law of damages. See K. Weinzierl, *Die Restitutionslehre der Frühscholastik*, München 1936; id., *Die Restitutionslehre der Hochscholastik*, München 1939.

4. "Wrongfully inflicted damage (to property)/economic loss". See U. von Lübtow, *Untersuchung zur lex Aquilia de damno iniuria dato*, Berlin 1971 ; B. Winiger, *La responsabilité aquilienne romaine—Damnum iniuria datum*, Bâle 1997.

5. This seems to hold true also for the French law: "Le demandeur d'une indemnité délictuelle ... doit justifier non d'un dommage quelconque, mais da la lésion certaine d'un intérêt légitime, juridiquement protegé. » Cass. civ., 27.7.1937, Gaz. Pal. 1937.2.376; see also G. Viney and P. Jourdain, *Les conditions de la responsabilté*, 2d edn. Paris 1998, pp. 9 («intérêt protégé»). The French «Avant-Projet de réforme du droit des obligations et de la prescription» of September 22, 2005, intends to introduce beneath the broad category of «dommage» the terms *atteinte* à la personne ou aux biens and *préjudice réparable*. For Swiss law see F. Werro, *La responsabilité civile*, Bern 2005, pp. 21.

6. For a list up see B. Rudden, Torticles, 6/7 Tul. Civil L.F. 105 (1991/92).

general tort of negligence[7] to the "basic norms" in the recent proposals for a harmonised European law of delict/tort.[8,9] Finally it can be found in the first contours of a European Community liability law.[10]

This tort principle is less Germanic than it may appear at first glance. It does *not* list enumerated interests, instead it pursues two aims: (1) It tries to pave a way *between* the too broad French and the too narrow German law of delict by referring generally on "legally protected interests."[11] (2) It insists on the fundamental distinction between *conditions* (injury/*lésion*) and *effects* (recoverable damage/*préjudice réparable*) of liability! Both ends have as early as 1898 already been attained in the Far East by the Japanese Civil Code.[12] However, the two central elements of this tort concept—*which* are the legally protected interests and *when* is an injury legally attributable—today have become to a large extent a matter of public policy.

---

7. It means "general liability for wrongfully inflicted damage". This common law tort of negligence seems, indeed, to fit the less under the umbrella of the above mentioned basic principle; but the opposite is true. See in general Shapo, *Towards a Jurisprudence of Injury*, 1984.

8. European Group on Tort Law (ed.), *Principles of European Tort Law* (PETL), Vienna/New York 2005, Art. 1:101 (1): "A person to whom damage to another is legally attributed is liable to compensate that damage." And damage is "harm to a legally protected interest" (Art. 2:101)!

9. C. von Bar, E. Clive and H. Schulte-Nölke (eds), *Principles, Definitions and Model Rules of European Private Law. Draft Common Frame of Reference (DCFR)*, Munich 2008. The "basic rule" (Art. VI-1:101 (1)) of the provisions on non-contractual liability speaks of "legally relevant damage". Legally relevant damage is "loss or injury to a right or legally protected interest" (Art. VI-2:101 (1))!

10. There are three paths of EC liability law: (1) liability of EC institutions according to Art. 288 (2) EC; (2) member states' liability for breach of EC law ("Francovich doctrine"). This requires (i) the conferment of a right to a private party by EC law; (ii) sufficiently serious breach, (iii) loss and (iv) causation between breach and loss of the private party: ECJ, 19.11.1991, cases C-6/90 and 9/90, *Francovich* v. *Italy* [1991] ECR I-5357; 5.3.1996, cases C-46/93 and 48/93, *Brasserie du Pêcheur* v. *Germany* [1996] ECR I-1029; (3) breach of directly applicable EC law (e.g. Art. 81 EC). This is by Member States' domestic law treated as breach of statutory duty in tort. See in greater detail W. van Gerven, Bridging the Unbridgeable (1996) 45 ICLQ 507; W. van Gerven et al., *Tort Law*, Oxford 2000, chap 9.1 (respective case law of the European Court of Justice); C. van Dam, *European Tort Law*, Oxford 2006, pp. 15–40; pp. 247–254; U. Haltern, *Europarecht*, 2nd edn. Tübingen 2007, pp. 388.

11. This is considered by „neutral" observers to be the current "mission" of modern law of delict; see e.g. V. Roberto, Schweizerisches Haftpflichtrecht, Zürich 2002, p. 13.

12. See esp. Sects. 709, 710. The Japanese Civil Code is available in English on the homepage of the Japanese government: http://www.cas.gojp/jp/seisaku/hourei/data2.html); but see also Art. 483 (1) of the Portuguese Civil Code of 1966.

The continental European liability rules originate from two sources, one is Roman Law, the other is the context of Christian ethic, Canon and Natural law.[13] Traces of both remain evident in modern European civil laws.

The whole concept of western private law, its form and substance, its categories and types of torts, as well as its systematic approach are deeply rooted in *Roman Law*. Another legacy of Roman (and Germanic) law is the close relationship between tort law and criminal law. Penal claims with their punishment of committer-function and civil claims with their compensation of loss-function did not break away from each other in a material and procedural sense until a relatively late stage. For a long time, three legal remedies have been applied simultaneously: damages, criminal punishment and civil fine (punitive damages). This is still true for the common law in the US; in English law exemplary damages are basically restricted to criminal-like defamations. In continental civil law the equitable compensation of infringements of the personality is still related to this tradition of interwoveness.

The primary legacy of *Canon* and *Natural Law*[14] is the strengthening of the *personalist* orientation of modern tort law. The focus is on the individual and his/her free will and reason. This perspective backed up the prominence of legal categories like human conduct and guilt/fault.[15] Another Natural law legacy is the *formality* of law. In association with the birth of the nation states and the emerging market economies, this led in Continental Europe to the grand codifications of the 19th century building upon liberal principles like property, freedom of contract and fault.

Although officially a Roman colony, the impact of Roman law was negligible in *England*. After the conquest of the Normans in 1066, modern English law developed indigenously from the practice of the centralised jurisdiction of the crown, building on Saxon and Norman legal traditions. Continental Canon and Natural law had only an indirect effect. It was not until the 19th century, with the development of fault liability (negligence), that the English common law was definitively influenced by the dominant European legal theories.

---

13. See F. Wieacker, *Privatrechtsgeschichte der Neuzeit*, 2d edn. Göttingen 1967, chap. 4 (pp. 249–347; in English id., *A History of Private Law in Europe*, Oxford 1995, transl. T. Weir) with further references.

14. Cf. especially N. Jansen, *Die Struktur des Haftungsrechts*, Tübingen 2003, pp. 313–360.

15. See S. Kuttner, *Kanonistische Schuldlehre von Gratian bis auf die Dekretalen Gregors IX*, Vatikan 1935.

However, before the end of the 19th century, the societal requisites of both the idea of the autonomous individual and the corresponding "social model"[16] were called into question. The Industrial Revolution of the 19th century changed the forms in which people lived and moved about radically. It was also an organisational and legal revolution.[17] It brought about an overthrow of social institutions *and* a reassessment of juristic values. In liability law new anti-personalist paradigms came to the fore. These were *technical risks*, *enterprises*, and *insurance*. The actual status of liability laws in Western Europe (and North America) is characterised by an unresolved conflict between these two dominant influences: natural law and economic liberalism (modernity)—and risk society (post-modernity),[18] i.e.: individual responsibility for damages caused by impersonal production processes and covered by liability insurers.

In the next section I briefly sketch the problems which characterise the Western tort laws as they stand now. In the sections which follow I discuss these problems in more detail.

## 2. Stock Taking of Problems

### *2.1. Fault Principle*

Under the basic principle of liability, above introduced, three main categories of accountability can be distinguished: intentional unlawful injuring, negligent wrongdoing, and strict liability.[19] The notion of fault comprises unlawful intent and negligence, although the two are clearly different subjects.[20] The fault principle dominated 19th century's private law of delict and tort in

16. See especially F. Wieacker, *Das Sozialmodell der klassischen Privatrechtsgesetzbücher*, Heidelberg 1953; id., Pandektenwissenschaft und industrielle Revolution, 9 Juristen-Jahrbuch 1 (1968/69).

17. See as locus classicus M. Weber, *Wirtschaft und Gesellschaft*, Tübingen 1925 (in English id., *On Law in Economy and Society*, Cambridge (Mass.) 1954, transl. Rheinstein).

18. See U. Beck, *Risikogesellschaft. Auf dem Weg in eine andere Moderne*, Frankfurt 1986 (in English id., *Risk Society. Towards Another Modernity*, London 1992).

19. See J. Gordley and A.T. von Mehren, *An Introduction to the Comparative Study of Private Law*, Cambridge 2006, pp. 335–412; see also G. Brüggemeier, *Haftungsrecht. Struktur, Prinzipien, Schutzbereich*, Heidelberg 2006, pp. 20–116. This triad fits the less to the English law as it is.

20. Intent and negligence are accurately separated in the DCFR proposals (Arts. VI-3:101 and 3:102); they are confusingly mixed up in the Vienna Group's PETL, see Art. 4:101: "*intentional and negligent violation of the required standard of conduct*".

the whole Western world. However, it proved itself unsuited to the "new torts" occurring en masse in the upcoming arenas of the industrialising society (*accidents at work, road traffic accidents*). The resulting non-responsibility of principals and enterprises for these risk-related accidents was considered as a part and parcel of industrialisation. It was internationally tolerated.[21] Soon this gap was filled by (i) *loss spreading* through insurance, (ii) liability without fault (*strict liability*),[22] and (iii) an overstressing of the fault concept by the courts when applying duty of care.[23]

By the end of the 19th century, French courts began to develop a clear no-fault liability *contra legem* within the framework of the Civil Code's general law of delict, particularly by re-designing and placing the previously marginal Art. 1384 (1) C. civ. at the head of this new liability regime.[24] In most of the other civil law regimes on the continent, strict liability for "dangerous" technical risks has been introduced outside the Code by special legislation.[25] In some social areas like accidents at workplace, social security schemes have gradually replaced liability law;[26] in other fields like road accidents, a strict liability regime together with a—concurring (e.g. Germany) or exclusive (e.g.

---

21. On subsidisation of industrial growth through negligence liability, see the controversial American discussion: M.J. Horwitz, *The Transformation of American Law, 1780–1860*, Cambridge (Mass.) 1977, pp. 63; M. Friedman, Civil Wrongs: Personal Injury Law in the Late 19th Century, 1987 Am. B. Found. Res. J. 351; G.T. Schwartz, Tort Law and the Economy in 19th Century America: A Reinterpretation, 90 Yale L.J. 1717 (1981).

22. For a comparative account, see F. Werro and V.V. Palmer (eds.), *The Boundaries of Strict Liability in European Tort Law*, Bern 2004.

23. See the well known example of the Superior Appeal Court of Munich which held in 1861 that "operating a railway with locomotives (by a corporation) *constitutes necessarily and inevitably a culpable behaviour*". [1861] 14 Seuffert's Archiv no. 208, p. 354 et seq.; in greater detail see J. Esser, *Grundlagen und Entwicklung der Gefährdungshaftung*, Berlin 1941 (Munich 2nd edn. 1969).—In England the negligence liability for road accidents can hold as an example.

24. From Cass. civ., 16.6.1896 (Teffaine), S. 1897.1.17, note Esmein; D.P. 1897.1.433, concl. Sarrut—Cass. Réun., 13.2.1930 (Jand'heur II), S. 1930.1.121, note Esmein—up to Cass. civ., 19.2.1997 (Bertrand), D. 1997, 265, note Jourdain; as leading monograph see G. Viney, *Le déclin de la responsabilité individuelle*, Paris 1965.

25. An introduction of a general clause of strict liability for "abnormally dangerous activities" has been discussed in Austria, Germany and Switzerland. See now, in this respect also influenced by American law (Restatement (Second) Torts, vol. 3, 1977, §§519, 520), PETL, Art. 5:101 with comments pp. 101; cf. also J. Gordley, *Foundations of Private Law*, Oxford 2006, chap. 11, pp. 204.

26. For a comparative account, see U. Magnus (ed.), *The Impact of Social Security on Tort Law*, Vienna/New York 2003.

Sweden)—direct claim against liability insurers ("*action directe*") has rolled back the influence of tort law.[27]

In the last two centuries, the grand old Civil Codes have been supplemented by two important elements: *special legislation* and *judge-made law*. Thus, the Civil Laws of delict in continental Europe today can be described as thoroughly decodified and pluralised legal systems. In addition, liability law is further supplemented "from above", e.g. by the increasing influence of European (ECHR) or national *human rights* and of *public safety law*,[28] and "from below" by *self-regulatory instruments* developed by private parties ("soft law"), e.g. general contract terms, *lex mercatoria*, technical standards by non governmental standardisation agencies like *Comité Européen de Normalisation (CEN)*, *Deutsches Institut für Normung (DIN)*, *Association Francaise de Normalisation (AFNOR)*, British Standards Institute (BSI), etc.

The English Common Law did not follow this path of Continental liability law. Apart from a single House of Lords' judgment of 1868 (*Rylands v Fletcher*[29]) the English law, unlike the American, was reluctant to depart from negligence and to develop a no-fault liability in tort.[30] Some exceptions only have to be made for the field of breach of statutory duty.[31]

## 2.2. Enterprises

The "modern" fault liability faced pressure to cope with the new incorporated entities ("organisational revolution"[32]) and the new social mechanisms of loss spreading (insurance).[33] Reduced in the personalist context to the notion of "liability for others," the category of *enterprise liability* gained central

---

27. G. Wagner (ed.), *Tort Law and Liability Insurance*, Vienna/New York 2005.

28. See e.g. the amended Council Directive on General Product Saftey 2001/95/EC, 2002 OJ L 11, pp. 4.

29. [1868] LR 3 HL 330; see Clerk & Lindsell (Buckley), *On Torts*, 19th edn. London 2006, chap. 21.

30. To the recent development, see E. Reid, Liability for Dangerous Substances (1999) 48 ICLQ 731.

31. See K.M. Stanton, *Statutory Torts*, London 2003, C. van Dam, *European Tort Law*, 2006, pp. 238.

32. K.E. Boulding, *The Organizational Revolution*, New York 1953.

33. As comparative accounts see Magnus, *The Impact of Social Security*, 2003; Wagner, *Tort Law and Liability Insurance*, Vienna/New York 2005.

significance in industrial society.[34] Beyond the narrow fields of coverage by social security and availability of strict liability for technical risks, a broader model of enterprise liability for insurable losses was to be formulated.[35] The industrial society was in search for it. In many continental civil law systems, this occurred when the judiciary created a quasi-strict liability of organisations, whatever their legal form, for presumed organisational fault (*Organisationspflichtansatz*). The scope of this concept still varies in the individual States. A subsequent problem was then the liability of agents for breaches of duty, from low-ranked workers to high-ranked executives. The 19th century model of the "autonomous private person" was incompatible with dependent individuals acting on behalf of the economic interests of others, employers or shareholders, in an organisational setting.[36]

## *2.3. Protected Interests*

A fundamental change has taken place during the past 100 years in the area of protected interests. This concerned, in the first instance, the physical person and the non-physical personality interests. While bodily integrity and property were the classical objects of protection of liability law, under Natural Law influence claims for compensation brought by dependants in wrongful death cases were recognised relatively early on the continent. In England and the US, the blood let of fatal workplace accidents during industrialisation led to corresponding special legislative initiatives (Lord Campbell's Act/Wrongful Death

---

34. This category still passes through the nets of mainstream comparative jurisprudence; cf. the world-wide International Encyclopedia of Comparative Law: Enterprise liability neither pops up in the Tort volume (XI), nor in the volume on Business and Private Organizations (XIII); the same holds true for J. Gordley and A.T. von Mehren, *Comparative Study of Private Law*, 2006; but see M. Faure and T. Hartlief, Towards an Expanding Enterprise Liability in Europe?, (1996) MJ 235; G. Brüggemeier, Unternehmenshaftung—Enterprise Liability. Eine europäische Perspektive?, HAVE/REAS 2004, 162; K. Wantzen, *Unternehmenshaftung und Enterprise Liability*, Tübingen 2007 with further references.

35. In the US this was the working programme of the eminent tort scholar Fleming James of Yale (cf. F.V. Harper, F. James and O.S. Gray, *The Law of Torts*, 5 vols. Boston 1986); in England that of Patrick Atiyah of Oxford (cf. id., *Accidents, Compensation and the Law*, London 1970). See also A. Ehrenzweig, *Negligence Without Fault: Towards an Enterprise Liability for Insurable Loss*, 1951.

36. It is just the reverse side of the non-attention of enterprise liability. The PETL mention the liability of employees, but let its regulation up to the national legislator (Art. 9:101 (1) (c)); the DCFR explicitly excludes this highly controversial topic from harmonisation (Art. VI-7:104 (a))!

Statutes[37]). Until today, a civil law remedy for wrongful death itself (*pretium mortis*; "bereavement damages"), as distinct from liability to the dead person and the dependants, remains controversial.[38]

Even more controversial is the legal protection of certain *intangible personality interests*: privacy; the right to image, name and likeness; bodily, sexual, and informational self-determination, etc. It developed relatively uninterrupted in France from the middle of the 19th century[39] and in the US from the beginning of the 20th century.[40] In Germany, the historical school of jurisprudence (*F.C. v. Savigny*) in the 19th century broke away from the tradition of the Roman law *actio iniuriarum*. The new focus was on economic rights (property rights and obligations) and compensation for economic loss. Personality rights were alien to the *BGB* of 1896/1900.[41] Honour and reputation were only protected by provisions of penal law. This legal situation did not change until after the Second World War on the basis of the Constitution of 1949.[42]

In England and Scotland, the incorporation of the European Convention of Human Rights into domestic law through the Human Rights Act of 1998 helped to put a more extensive personality protection in motion which goes beyond

37. See Malone, American Fatal Accident Statutes, 4 Duke L.J. 673 (1965).

38. In the majority of western European countries accordant rules exist today or they are in preparation. DCFR and PETL also support concurringly bereavement damages/Angehörigenschmerzensgeld (Art. VI-2:202 (1); PETL, Art. 10:301 (1) (ii)). For a detailed comparative account see A. Janczuk and M.M. Veloso, Claims for Non-Pecuniary Losses by 'Third Persons' upon Death and Injury, in G. Brüggemeier, A.C. Ciacchi and G. Comandé (eds.), *Fundamental Rights and Private Law in the European Union*, vol. 2, Cambridge 2008 (forthcoming); for a German monograph see N. Stahmer, *Entschädigung von Nichtvermögensschäden bei Tötung*, Hamburg 2004.

39. Trib. civ. Seine, 16.6.1858 (Rachel), D. 1858,3,62; see E.H. Perreau, Des droits de la personnalité, RTD civ. 1909, 501.

40. S.D. Warren and L.D. Brandeis, The Right to Privacy, 4 Harv. L. Rev. 193 (1890). Initially, nothing followed this article. With the decision of the Georgia Supreme Court, *Pavesich* v. *New England Life Insurance Co.*, 50 S.E. 68 (1905) a Common Law „tort of invasion of privacy" started to become recognised in the US; cf. W. Prosser, Privacy, 48 Cal. L. Rev. 383 (1960). For an American-European comparison, see J. Whitman, The Two Cultures of Privacy: Dignity Versus Liberty, 113 Yale L.J. 1151 (2004).

41. RG, 7.11.1908, RGZ 69, 401 (Nietzsche letters). The only exception is the "right to one's name" (§ 12 BGB).

42. The landmark decision is BGH, 25.5.1954, BGHZ 13, 334; NJW 1954, 1404; JZ 1954, 698, note Coing (Schacht-Leserbrief) [Many of the German judgments are in English available on the website of UCL Law School, Institute for Global Law: http://www.ucl.ac.uk/laws/global_law/german-cases].

long existing defamation law. Highly disputed judgments at the national[43] and European levels[44] brought this area of law to the centre of juristic interest.

Liability law also broke new ground in the 20th century with the gradual transition to non-contractual compensation for *pure economic loss.*[45] In the 19th century, outside France, Belgium and Luxembourg, it was widely accepted that pure economic loss was not to be compensated through negligence liability in tort. Remedying pure economic loss generally required a showing of intentional unlawful causation of loss.[46] In Austrian and German law, it depended in addition upon intentional unconscionable infringement of economic interests (§§ 1295 (2) *ABGB*, 826 *BGB*). Internationally (except in France, Belgium and Luxembourg), the so-called exclusionary rule was to the fore but did not last through the 20th century. The contentious cable cases (regarding compensation of production costs) and liability for disclosure of wrongful information without a contract are just two examples of the advancement of negligence liability for pure economic loss. The judgment of the House of Lords in *Hedley Byrne & Co Ltd* v *Heller & Partners* (1963)[47] became the Common Law basis for negligence liability for misstatements. By contrast, in Germany, because of the narrow requisites of § 826 *BGB*, the departure from tort to contract law began early in the form of fictional contracts to supply information (*Auskunftsverträge*).[48]

## *2.4. Differentiation of Tort Law*

Tort law and its principle of liability (attributable injury of a protected interest)[49] is made more complex, in that—internationally—special rules for certain professionals' and business sectors have been developed, partly with a reversal of burden of proof, partly without. In addition, a multitude of causes of actions have been made available. For example, for harm caused

43. In England see *Campbell* v *MGN Ltd* [2004] 2 AC 457, 2 WLR 1232, and *Douglas* v *Hello! Ltd* [2006] QB 125; [2007] UKHL 21.

44. Cf. especially ECtHR, 24.6.2004, *C. von Hannover* v. *Germany*, (2004) 40 EHRR 1; [2004] EMLR 21; NJW 2004, 2647; JZ 2004, 1015, note Stürner.

45. For a comparative account see M. Bussani and V.V. Palmer (eds.), *Pure Economic Loss in Europe*, Cambridge 2003.

46. Basic judgment in England is: *Allen* v *Flood* [1898] AC 1; cf. T. Weir, *Economic Torts*, Oxford 1997.

47. [1964] AC 465, [1963] 2 All ER 575.

48. Since RG, 27.10.1902, RGZ 52, 365.

49. Cf. above p.1. The European Group on Tort Law lists three main sources of imputability (PETL: Art. 1:101 (2)): fault, abnormally dangerous activity, and respondeat superior.

by defective products[50] and for environmental harm, a regime of both enterprise liability (presumption of organisational fault) and strict liability has emerged today in Europe and in the US. There is also an influential additional area of the law: public product safety regulations.[51] These can serve as protective statutes thus providing for a third branch of product liability law: statutory torts.

Medical cases are unique in that they are not concerned with "accidents," but with medical treatments occurring within the privity of a contractual relationship between the patient and her doctor or hospital. Contractual liability provides the appropriate framework to remedy medical related pecuniary losses and non-pecuniary harm. Only particularities of the national laws lead to the application of tort liability. This was the case in Germany until 2002 where compensation for pain and suffering, which in medical cases plays a central role alongside the treatment costs, could only be settled on a tortious basis (ex § 847 (1) *BGB*).[52] In England, the coverage of medical expenses by the National Health Service precludes the application of English contract law. French law differentiates between the private and public medical sectors: contract law is applicable in the former, non-contractual liability law in the latter. No-fault compensation schemes are also gaining importance in the medical sector. Sweden took the lead as a model for replacing medical liability through insurance coverage. Belgium followed suit in 2006. France introduced a modified system in 2002 (only where losses are unrecoverable via contract/tort law).[53]

## 2.5. Damages

The law of damages is an independent branch of delict/tort.[54] Some legal systems, such as that of Germany, the Netherlands, Portugal and Japan, establish a clear separation between the foundation of liability (*Haftungsgrund*)

---

50. Cf. in more detail F. Werro, Products Liability (in volume II).

51. Cf. especially on the European level the amended Council Directive on General Product Safety 2001/178/EC, 2002 OJ L 11, p. 4.

52. The Second Damages Law (Amendment) Act (Zweites Schadensersatzrechtsänderungsgesetz) came into force on August 1, 2002. Cf. G. Wagner, *Das neue Schadensersatzrecht*, Baden-Baden 2002; A. Cahn, *Einführung in das neue Schadensersatzrecht*, München 2003.

53. To Sweden and France see in more detail J.C.J. Dute, M.G. Faure & H. Koziol (eds.), *No-Fault Compensation in the Health Care Sector*, Vienna/New York 2004, pp. 210/367.

54. Cf. H. Lange and G. Schiemann, *Schadensersatz*, 3d edn. Tübingen 2003; McGregor, *On Damages*, 17th edn. London 2003; G. Viney and P. Jourdain, *Les effets de la responsabilité*, 2d edn. Paris 2001; for a transnational perspective see U. Magnus (ed.), *Uni-*

and the extent of liability (*Haftungsausfüllung*). That distinction is not evident in the private law regimes with a general clause like e.g. the French law of delict (Art. 1382 C. civ.), but it is still familiar to the doctrine in these countries.[55]

The distinction between pecuniary and non-pecuniary loss is broadly accepted.[56] There are also nominal or symbolic damages. Only in the US do exemplary or punitive damages still play a considerable role.[57] In continental Europe, US punitive damages awards are generally not enforceable. They are regarded as a violation of the *ordre public*.

As mentioned above, the following text discusses some highly disputed subjects of modern tort law such as negligence liability, forms of enterprise liability, protection of personality interests and compensation for non-pecuniary damage.[58]

---

*fication of Tort Law: Damages*, Vienna/New York 2001; N. Jansen, Konturen eines europäischen Schadensrechts, JZ 2005, 160.

55. The leading tort textbook in France by G. Viney and P. Jourdain sticks to this distinction. Besides the introductory volume the two main volumes are dedicated to "*Les conditions de la responsabilité*" and to "*Les effets de la responsabilité* ». For the distinction between *dommage* (atteinte à la personne ou aux biens) and *préjudice réparable* see Avant-Projet (fn. 5).—For the „general clause country" Switzerland see Roberto, *Schweizerisches Haftpflichtrecht*, 2002 ("Haftungstatbestand"; "Haftungsfolgen"); Werro, *La responsabilité civile*, 2005.

56. As to the differences arising from a comparative perspective in compensation for non-pecuniary loss, see e.g., for Europe (and Israel), W.V.H. Rogers (ed.), *Damages for Non-Pecuniary Loss in a Comparative Perspective*, Vienna/New York 2001.

57. See recently G. Calabresi, The Complexity of Torts—The Case of Punitive Damages, in M.S. Madden (ed.), *Exploring Tort Law*, Cambridge 2005, pp. 333; for an English perspective see the Law Commission Report, *Aggravated, Exemplary and Restitutionary Damages*, Law Com no. 247, 16 Dec. 1997.—However, the French "Avant-Projet du droit des obligations", 2005, now plans to introduce punitive damages; clarifying that they shall not be insurable.

58. For stock takings of Europe's laws of delict/tort see C. von Bar, *Gemeineuropäisches Deliktsrecht*, vol. 2, Munich 1999 (in English id., *The Common European Tort Law*, vol. 2, Oxford 2000); W. van Gerven et al., *Tort Law*, Oxford 2000; C. van Dam, *European Tort Law*, OUP 2006; but see also G. Brüggemeier, *Haftungsrecht. Struktur, Prinzipien, Schutzbereich*, Heidelberg 2006 and G. Wagner, in R. Zimmermann (ed.), *Grundstrukturen des Europäischen Deliktsrechts*, Baden-Baden 2003, pp. 189–340.

# 3. Negligence Liability

Negligence liability is the law of non-intentional wrongdoing, in other words, the *law of accidents*.[59] Quite simply, negligence liability is *the* modern tort law.[60] The breaks between the modern and the post-modern approach are most evident in the area of negligence as is clearly demonstrated in the Common Law. In continental private laws, negligence liability had to first reluctantly detach itself from its supposed similarity to liability for intentional infliction of harm. To this day unresolved problems with the notion of unlawfulness and/or wrongfulness,[61] the distinction between "inner" and "outer" care,[62] and the subjective requisites for fault persist,[63] particularly in Austria, Switzerland, Germany, Greece, and the Netherlands, but also in Italy. The development of the French and English negligence liability laws, as different as they are, seem to be free from these doctrinal side effects. Here the example of the Common Law is chosen because its structure is more elaborated and less clandestine, in addition demonstrating other interesting shortcomings.[64]

## *3.1. General Conditions*

The Common Law tort of negligence is a product of the 19th century, even if its roots go back further.[65] It developed independently in England and in the US though at the same time. In England, this new tort originated from three

---

59. The law of accidents has been treated nearly simultaneously in the last century by three great monographs: G. Calabresi, *The Costs of Accidents*, New Haven 1970; P.S. Atiyah, *Accidents, Compensation and the Law*, 1st edn. London 1970; H.L. Weyers, *Unfallschäden*, Frankfurt/M. 1971; in addition see D. Dewees, D. Duff and M. Treblicock, *Exploring the Domain of Accident Law*, Oxford 1996.

60. On this in more detail see Brüggemeier, *Haftungsrecht*, 2006, pp. 42–103; and as an earlier treatise, Brüggemeier, *Prinzipien des Haftungsrechts*, Baden-Baden 1999 (in English id., *Common Principles of Tort Law*, London 2004/2006).

61. For a comparative account see H. Koziol (ed.), *Unification of Tort Law: Wrongfulness*, Vienna/New York 1998.

62. For this German "invention" see E. Deutsch, *Allgemeines Haftungsrecht*, 2nd. edn. Cologne etc. 1996, pp. 248 and in English: C. von Bar, *Common European Tort Law*, vol. 2, 2000, p. 255 et seq.; C. van Dam, *European Tort Law*, 2006, p. 191.

63. Cf. P. Widmer (ed.), *Unification of Tort Law: Fault*, Vienna/New York 2005.

64. See esp. B.A. Hepple, Negligence: The Search for Coherence (1997) 50 CLP 69, P. Birks and D.J. Ibbetson, in Schrage (ed.), *Negligence. The Comparative Legal History of the Law of Torts*, Berlin 2001, pp. 173/229.

65. See esp. E.J.H. Schrage (ed.), *Negligence. The Comparative Legal History of the Law of Torts*, Berlin 2001; Gordley, *Foundations of Private Law*, 2006, pp. 196.

sources: 1) the writ of trespass on the case for indirect injuries, 2) the concept of duty in Natural Law ("*Every Man ought to take reasonable Care that he does not injure his Neighbour.*"[66]), and 3) the dominant influence of the continental categories of fault in the 19th century ("*Nicht der Schaden verpflichtet zum Schadensersatz, sondern die Schuld.*"[67]). The result was an unstructured *actio culpae*, making liable for every kind of damage. It appeared alongside the well established pigeonhole torts such as trespass, battery, libel, slander, conversion etc. Five requisites were ultimately formulated as the complete rubric of negligence: duty of care, breach, damage, causation, and proximity.

## *3.2. Duty of Care*

Fault, damage (to property), conduct, and causation[68] were the elements of the Aquilian delict *damnum iniuria datum*.[69] The duty category is new and somewhat perplexing. It seems to be Natural Law-related.[70] Today a distinction is made between a notional and a threshold function.[71] The *notional* function specifies an area of protection: what interests of which persons are legally

66. F. Buller, *An Introduction to the Law relative to Trials at Nisi Prius*, 1781, p. 25 (cited from Birks, Negligence in the Eighteenth Century Common Law, in Schrage, *Negligence*, 2001, pp.173, at 192).

67. "Not the causation of damage binds to liability, but fault." R. von Jhering, *Das Schuldmoment im Römischen Privatrecht*, Gießen 1847, p. 40. The same holds true for the 19th century France, see S. Galand-Carvan, France, in Widmer, *Fault*, 2005, p. 89: "Fault was more than a ground for tortious liability: it constituted its very foundation."

68. *Factual causation* is not further expanded on in this contribution, see now B. Winiger et al. (eds.), *Digest of European Tort Law*, vol. 1: *Essential Cases on Natural Causation*, Vienna/New York 2007. The proof of causation raises a lot of problems in cases of toxic torts and in situations of a multitude of tortfeasors. To the problem of "indeterminate defendants" and the shifting from solidary to proportionate liability in the English law see e.g. the two contradictory judgments of the House of Lords: *Fairchild* v *Glenhaven Funeral Services Ltd* [2002] UKHL 22, [2002] 3 WLR 89, and *Barker* v *Corus UK Ltd* [2006] UKHL 20, [2006] 2 AC 572.

69. See in more detail B. Winiger, *La responsabilité aquilienne romaine—Damnum iniuria datum*, Bâle 1997.

70. See fn. 66. In French law, the idea of a duty of care ("obligation préexistante") has been introduced by Planiol. Cf. M. Planiol, *Traité élémentaire de droit civil*, vol. 2, 4th edn. Paris 1952, no. 445.

71. Cf. e.g. Norrie, in *The Laws of Scotland, Stair Memorial Encyclopaedia*, vol. 15: *Obligations*, 1995, para. 265.—A third function is the „affirmative duty" which constitutes liability for omissions and for malfeasance in cases of indirect injuries. See also below in the text.

protected against negligent injury. This function is redundant or just purely formal in the traditional situations of accidents causing direct injuries. For it is self evident, that persons are not allowed to injure other persons or damage other persons' property, if it can be avoided. The law of delict/tort prohibits wrongful injuries (*neminem laedere*)! In such cases, a legal duty of care is a "non-issue," as the late *G.T. Schwartz* put it;[72] it "adds nothing to ... the tort of negligence itself," as *P.S. Atiyah* aptly formulated.[73]

With regard to *indirect injuries*, which are caused by negligent conduct, the search for liability takes on the material question of imputation/*Zurechnung*: whether a caused remote injury is attributable to the given negligence of the defendant (remoteness issue/"neighbour principle"/*threshold function*).[74] A classic example is the *Palsgraf* case of the New York Court of Appeals from 1928.[75] In trying to catch a moving train, a passenger dropped a package with fireworks when a guard helped him to enter the train and inattentively touched the package. The fireworks subsequently exploded. The pressure of the explosion threw down a weighing scale at the other end of the platform and injured a waiting passenger (Ms. *H. Palsgraf*). *B. Cardozo*, C.J., writing for the close majority of the court, made it clear that it is not a case of causation[76] or negligence, but of imputation/duty of care. There is not a duty of care against the world at large ("negligence in the abstract"). Negligence liability is a relational problem in cases of indirect injury: the respective injured party must be owed a duty of care (*relational tort*). In *Palsgraf*, the majority denied a duty of care by the guard towards Mrs. Palsgraf, on the part of the railway guard who helped the passenger with his fireworks onto the train.

While a duty of care is purely notional for a finding of liability in accidents, it is identical to the proximity requirement in the indirect (relational) cases of injury. Often described as legal cause, proximity is often confused with causation (cause in fact). The most well-known examples are the two *Wagon Mound* judgments of the House of Lords acting as Privy Council.[77] This Aus-

72. *Restatement (Third) Torts: General Principles (Draft)*, 1999, §6 (p. 83).

73. P.S. Atiyah, *Accidents, Compensation and the Law*, 3rd edn. 1980, p. 66; see also at pp. 70/71 (road accidents).

74. From an Aristotelian corrective/commutative justice-point of view see E. Weinrib, The Disintegration of Duty, in Madden, *Exploring Tort Law*, 2005, pp. 143.

75. *Palsgraf* v. *Long Island R. Co.*, 162 N.E. 99 (1928).

76. "The law of causation,..., is thus foreign to the case before us." 162 N.E. 99, at 105.

77. *Overseas Tankship (U.K.) Ltd* v *Marts Dock & Engineering Co Ltd (The Wagon Mound No 1)* [1961] AC 388; *Overseas Tankship (U.K.) Ltd* v *The Miller Steamship Co Pty Ltd (The Wagon Mound No 2)* [1967] 1 AC 617.

tralian case concerned the ignition of furnace oil on the water surface through sparks in Sydney Harbour. Two ships and a wharf were destructed by the fire. In fuelling the ship, the crew of the *Wagon Mound* by its inattendance let the fuel overflow. As in *Palsgraf*, negligence, causation and damage were given. In contrast to *Palsgraf*, the condition for liability was not treated as a duty of care problem, but as a problem of foreseeability of the damage. The Australian courts affirmed the foreseeability in one trial (owners of the wharf), and denied it in the other one (owners of the ships). The House of Lords considered itself tied to these supposed statements of facts. The less than satisfactory outcome is one of two contrary judgments on the same issue. However, if the Law Lords had recognized the central question as a *question of law* (duty of care/threshold function), which is within the jurisdiction of the High Court, contrary judgments would then not have been the outcome in the *Wagon Mound* cases.

To avoid incoherence in cases of negligence liability in Common Law *and* in Civil Law, it is helpful to keep in mind the elements of the Aquilian delict *damnum iniuria datum*: damage/injury (to a protected interest), conduct/fault (negligence) and causation. These are the necessary and sufficient conditions of negligence liability for accidents or direct injuries. With regard to relational torts or indirect injuries, there is only the additional normative question of imputation/*Zurechnung* (remoteness issue/proximity/threshold duty) as a matter of public policy to be answered. Whether appropriate or not, the *duty of care/Verkehrspflicht* has internationally become the term to deal with this problem of fair, just and reasonable imputation.[78]

### 3.3. Fault

Fault remained the central condition for liability in tort (*Fahrlässigkeit*/breach of duty of care/*négligence*). In Continental Europe negligence is overloaded with the fault concept of intentional wrongdoing (e.g. in Germany with the prerequisite of unlawfulness and the difference between "outer and inner care" (*äußere/innere Sorgfalt*)[79]) or of criminal law (e.g. in Austria and Switzerland which still tend to hold on to subjective blameworthiness

78. "This talk of 'duty' or 'no duty' is simply a way of limiting the range of liability for negligence." *Dorset Yacht Co Ltd* v *Home Office*, [1969] 2 QB 412, at 426 (Lord Denning); [1970] AC 1004, at 1058 (HL, Lord Diplock).

79. See fn 62.

(*Schuldvorwurf*)).[80] In the Common Law as well as in the French and Dutch law the structure of negligence as fault has been articulated with absolute clarity. In this sense, negligence has three elements: (i) the establishment of the concrete conduct causing injury (question of fact); (ii) the judicial definition of the standard of required conduct or due care (question of law)—and (iii) the decision whether or not the concrete conduct fulfils the standard. *Substandard conduct is negligence.* In this respect §276 (2) *BGB* defines correctly: "A person acts negligently if she disregards the objectively required care."

The most difficult task is to define the required conduct under a given set of facts—the normative concrete standard of care. In contrast to criminal law, the standard of care in civil law is objective.[81] The starting point is the *bonus paterfamilias/the reasonable man of ordinary prudence/l'homme prudent et avisé.* The conduct of this ideal person must however be assigned to the concrete situation of the individual case. There is no "negligence in the abstract"/"Fahrlässigkeit an sich." The standard of conduct is always to be defined in a *concrete way,* related to roles and to the situation—but irrespective of the subjective attributes of the individual actor. Complex societies, *Luhmann* formulated, "guarantee the trustworthiness of expectations of conduct more through roles than through persons."[82] In this sense, the civil law notion of objective negligence (as a kind of fault) imposes upon members of society a type of strict liability to fulfil the general standards of the reasonableness test.

The rule rewards the individual who takes extra precautions against damage to others so as not to have to compensate them. The participant in societal interaction will be protected in his expectation that others will conduct themselves reasonably. The person who undertakes a role, the standards of which he is not able to fulfil, will be liable (*Übernahmeverschulden*). Where this concept of negligence, in all its variable contents, goes on to cause social hardship (e.g. protection of children[83] and disabled persons, of the old and

80. A comparative account is given by Widmer, *Unification of Tort Law: Fault*, 2005. For a critique of this approach, see F. Werro, Die Sorgfaltspflichtverletzung als Haftungsgrund, ZSR 1997, pp. 343.

81. This holds true esp. for the Dutch, French and German Civil Law, and for the Common Law tort of negligence. See the summarising discussion in *Principles of European Tort Law*, 2005, p. 64 et seq.

82. N. Luhmann, in J. Habermas & N. Luhmann, *Theorie der Gesellschaft oder Sozialtechnologie*, Frankfurt 1971, p. 23.

83. With respect to *liability of minors* the new Dutch Burgerlijk Wetboek provides exemplary provisions (Art. 6:169 BW): no liability till the completion of 14 years; discerne-

the weak), the legislature is called upon to carry out corrections of which the French *Loi Badinter* (1985) is an example: Youth under the age of sixteen years and seniors older than seventy years are given some privilege in the assignment of liability in automobile accidents.

Put another way, negligence is not a simple "fact" which can be proven.[84] Rather, it is the result of the *evaluation of empirical conduct with a normative benchmark.* It involves mixed questions of law and fact. On the European continent, in the Nordic countries, and in England, Scotland and Ireland, the determination of negligence is the business of the competent career judge, if necessary counselled by experts. In the individual State jurisdictions of the US, this decision is left in the hands of the lay judges of the civil juries.[85]

## 3.4. Learned Hand-Formula

Since the mid-20th century, American courts have employed a balancing test when weighing costs and benefits—the so-called Learned Hand formula. The goal of this approach is to reduce the ambiguity in determining the standard of care ("negligence lottery"). Under this approach, an activity is always negligent, if the costs of adequate precaution are lower than the expected losses (N = B < P x L[86]). Conversely, there is no negligence, if the precautionary costs are higher than the avoidable losses. Here only a strict liability regime would trigger an obligation to compensate the caused losses. Accurate information about the losses attributable to the tortious activity and about the costs of the precautionary measures is presumed in this test. Access to such information may solely exist, if at all, in the hands of enterprises and their accounting departments.

The Learned Hand test is not suited to simple human mistakes. Just as the Natural Law idealistic concept of fault subsumed enterprises and individuals indiscriminately under the ideal autonomous person, similarly the rationality assumption of economic theory generalizes corporate decisions indiscriminately in respect of all participants in market transactions, whether a private

---

ment and fault als conditions of liability for minors of 14–16 years; regular liability for minors who are older than 16 years.

84. Likewise Atiyah, *Accidents, Compensation and the Law*, pp. 38.

85. Cf. R.E. Litan (ed.), *Verdict: Assessing the Civil Jury System*, Washinton 1993.

86. *United States* v. *Carroll Towing Co., Inc.*, 159 F.2d 169 (1947); cf. R. Posner, A Theory of Negligence, 1 J. Legal Stud. 29 (1972); id., *Economic Analysis of Law*, 5th edn. New York 1998.

individual, employee, or commercial enterprise, *and* on human behaviour beyond market transactions.[87]

# 4. Liability of Principals and Agents

The business orientated Learned Hand Formula has highlighted an important shortcoming of 19th century tort law. The emphatic negligence concept of the personalist tort law (in Civil *and* in Common Law) stems from the assumption of individual human wrongful conduct. Complex entities such as industrial corporations do not conduct themselves like people nor are they guided by a free will like individuals. Organised processes come into existence; system rationality replaces human behaviour logic. People are, as employees and managers, only the holders of a function in this process. Mistakes occur as system defects or quality deficiencies independent of clear-cut wrongful conduct on the part of any individual. Industrialisation brought with it the biggest challenge for the personalist law of torts of the 19th century. It expanded the reasonable person concept to its logical ends and to its partial abdication—i.e., its replacement through functional equivalents like social insurance or strict liability for insurable losses.

## *4.1. Alternatives to Negligence Liability*

Workplace and traffic accidents (first railway, then automobiles) mark the point at which the fault principle and industrial society intersected from the mid-19th century onwards. Most western industrial states reacted to the inadequacy of the fault principle in such cases with special legislation, even if with somewhat of a delay. After German unification in 1871, an attempt to introduce an industry-wide strict liability based on the model of §25 of the Prussian Railway Act of 1838 failed in the face of opposition from heavy industry. Fifteen years later, a completely new path was decided upon: the *substitution of tort law through insurance protection.* Through the statutory workmen's accident insurance (*Arbeiterunfallversicherung*) of 1884 the primary care of workers involved in accidents at the workplace was secured, independent of liability claims and their implementation and enforceability. Since 1926 the coverage also comprised occupational diseases. In France, scholarship developed a "*théorie du risque*," which

87. To the REMM hypothese (resourceful, evaluating, maximizing man) see H.B. Schäfer and C. Ott, *Lehrbuch der ökonomischen Analyse des Zivilrechts*, 4th edn. Heidelberg 2005, pp. 58 (in English id., *The Economic Analysis of Civil Law*, Cheltenham 2004).

forced a further development of tort law to cover work-related accidents. The *Cour de Cassation* drew back at the end of the 19th century and developed Art. 1384 (1) C. civ. (liability for things), an unimportant provision up until then, into an employer's liability independent of fault.[88] Soon after, the legislature reacted with social insurance based legal regulations for the area of work-related accidents. In continental Europe, this led to the rise of the "état providence."[89]

In the US in the second half of the 19th century, the "unholy alliance" of three Common Law rules—the requirement of fault on the part of the employer, the assumption of risk on the part of the employee, and the fellow servant rule—led to a non-compensation system in the area of industrial workplace accidents.[90] Relatively late, at the beginning of the 20th century, these common law rules were replaced by the Federal and State special legislation of the Workmen's Compensation Statutes.[91] Developments in England followed a similar path.[92]

At the same time, in continental Europe special legal regimes of strict liability for risky activities, mostly performed by enterprises, were developed. In the area of road accidents, a workable system of combining strict liability of the keepers of automobiles and obligatory liability insurance was put in place. Both, keeper of the automobile and the insurer, can be sued directly. In Sweden, the liability insurer is the only party to be addressed by the accident victim.

## *4.2. Enterprise Liability*

### 4.2.1. Respondeat Superior

Beyond workplace and traffic accidents and beyond special rules of strict liability, the problem of a general enterprise liability in tort for injury to life, limb, and property remained unresolved. The traditional answer, offered by personalist tort law, was *respondeat superior*. The master/employer was generally responsible for the torts of employees acting within the scope of their

88. Cass. civ., 16.6.1896 (Teffaine), S. 1897.1.17, note Esmein; D.P. 1897.1.433, concl. Sarrut; cf. Saleilles, *Les accidents du travail et la responsabilité civile*, 1897.

89. The locus classicus is F. Ewald, *L'état providence*, Paris 1986.

90. Cf. especially M. Friedman, Civil Wrongs: Personal Injury Law in the Late 19th Century, 1987 Am. B. Found. Res. J. 351.

91. As a partisan of a further replacement of tort law through social insurance compensation schemes, see S. Sugarman, *Doing Away with Personal Injury Law*, New York 1989. But this would have as a precondition that also damage to property and compensation for pain and suffering are covered by the social insurance schemes; this is e.g. not the case in the German system.

92. See Atiyah, *Accidents, Compensation and the Law*, 1980, chap. 14 ("The common law and the welfare state").

employment (vicarious liability); the corporation was responsible for the personally committed torts of its executive officers. As far as vicarious liability is concerned, the Germanic legal family has evolved the least since the 19th century: in principle, for liability of the employer to be established the employer's *own* fault has to supervene. Admittedly this is presumed, on the existence of an employee's tort (§831 (1) *BGB*; Art. 55 (1) Swiss *OR*).[93] The exculpatory proof remains open to the employer.

A special case in this respect is *governmental liability*. In continental Europe, the state is (exclusively) responsible for the damages caused by the fault of its public servants.[94] It is in this marginal field of tort law that the European Community law exercised a strong influence on the national laws. Through the rulings of the ECJ in *Francovich*[95] and *Brasserie du Pêcheur/Factortame*[96] it became imperative to have a common liability regime for violations of Community law, be they committed by European institutions, Member States' authorities or even by private parties. Given the direct applicability of the respective EC law, and the infringement of the right of a private party through a "sufficiently serious breach" of Community law, the damage thereof has to be compensated. The criteria are listed in the *Brasserie* judgment. According to the case law of the ECJ breaches of Community Law and similar breaches of national law must be treated equally.[97]

### 4.2.2. The Organisational Duty Approach

*Respondeat superior* is the conventional pillar of tortious enterprise liability ("liability for acts of others"). It is still indispensable in cases of direct torts of individual employees, e.g. the malpractice of the doctor of a hospital; the carelessness of a bus driver. It is of no help where there are losses to third parties through industrial processes, without existing concrete injurious conduct through an individual employee.[98] Examples are products lia-

---

93. For Austria see H. Koziol, *Österreichisches Haftpflichtrecht*, vol. 1, 3d edn. Vienna 1997, pp. 400.

94. For a recent European comparative account see D. Fairgrieve, M. Andenas and J. Bell (eds.), *Tort Liability of Public Authorities in Comparative Perspective*, London 2002; for the US see P.H. Schuck, *Suing Government. Citizen Remedies for Official Wrongs*, New Haven 1983.

95. ECJ, 19.11.1991, cases C-6/90 and 9/90, *Francovich* v. *Italy* [1991] ECR I-5357.

96. ECJ, 5.3.1996, cases C-46/93 and 48/93, *Brasserie de Pêcheur* v. *Germany* [1996] ECR I-1029.

97. See esp. W. van Gerven, Bridging the Unbridgeable, (1996) 45 ICLQ 507.

98. See ALI (ed.), *Reporters' Study—Enterprise Responsibility for Personal Injury*, 2 vols 1991.

bility, environmental liability and—in wide areas—hospitals' liability. Here, in the western industrial nations, a new type of *direct* enterprise liability (i.e. without an antecedent tort on the part of the agent) has developed as a second pillar: the organisational duty liability (*Organisationspflichthaftung*). This type of enterprise liability has now been incorporated into the Principles of European Tort Law[99] and in the French *Avant-Projet de Réforme du Droit des Obligations.*[100]

The enterprise or the enterprise operator, whatever its legal form, does not produce itself. It initiates and organises the production through the combination of know-how, capital, labour and resources. In order to establish a direct liability of enterprises for "production-related losses," a legal duty is placed on the addressees—the enterprises—to organise the production process in a clinical and functional way (also with reference to human resources and finances), so that losses to third parties can be avoided.[101] The executive officers are in charge of fulfilling this organisational duty such that any defect in its appropriate fulfilment is attributable to the enterprise. *Damage to third parties through production-related activity* and *organisational fault of management constitutes the tort of the enterprise.* The same principles apply *mutatis mutandis* in the service sector.[102]

Three landmark decisions of the 20th century form the bedrock of this type of enterprise liability: *MacPherson* v. *Buick Motor Co.* (1916) in the US,[103] *Donoghue* v *Stevenson* (1932) in England and Scotland,[104] and the *Hühnerpest* case of the *Bundesgerichtshof* (*BGH*) in Germany (1968).[105] The per-

99. PETL Art. 4:202; see the comments on p. 93 et seq. This Article follows the model of Art. 49a of the Swiss project on the reform of federal liability law (Draft 2000; see the reprint in Werro, *La responsabilité civile*, 2005, pp. 415). For comments on this project see B. Foëx and F. Werro (eds.), *La réforme du droit de la responsabilité civile*, Zürich 2004.

100. Art.1353: "La faute de la personne morale s'entend non seulement de celle qui est commise par un représentant, mais aussi de celle qui résulte d'un défaut d'organisation ou de fonctionnement."

101. At this point the *duty of care* appears in a third function next to the notional and threshold function: as affirmative duty. Affirmative duties are needed for the liability for non-feasance (Unterlassenshaftung). The borderline between liability for non-feasance and negligence liability for mal-feasance cannot be expanded on here.

102. Cf. the withdrawn Proposal of a Council Directive on the Liability of Suppliers of Services, 1991 OJ C 12, p. 8; see e.g. J. Haas, *La responsabilité de l'entreprise en Europe: Un droit unique pour le Marché unique?*, Bern 2004, pp. 144.

103. 217 N.Y. 383, 111 N.E. 1050 (1916).

104. [1932] AC 580, [1932] All ER 1, 1932 SLT 317.

105. BGH, 26.11.1968, BGHZ 51, 91; NJW 1969, 269, note Diederichsen; JZ 1969, 387, note Deutsch.

sonalist accountability of individual wrongful conduct fell into the background. Already in *MacPherson* the employees disappeared completely behind the veil of the manufacturing company. The case concerned organisational and system defects. Such American developments ushered in the trend of imposing liability independent of fault from 1963 onwards (strict products liability).[106] The German *Hühnerpest* judgment created a presumption of (organisational) fault in cases of third party loss caused by business activities of the enterprise. An exception is only made for product monitoring and the post-market duty to warn.[107] These principles of corporate liability for presumed organisational fault have been adopted by areas of law such as environmental and hospital liability as well as liability of owners of commercial premises.

Only England, after having admitted liability in tort (negligence) in defect product cases with *Donoghue* in 1932, has not followed suit though there has been an alleviation of the burden of proof in isolated cases. This is, however, not a general rule. In France products liability to a large extent has traditionally been governed by contract law ("*action directe*"); this provided for a liability without fault ("*obligation de résultat*").

## *4.3. Agent Liability*

A downside of increasing channelling of liability towards enterprises, through the construction of no-fault liability and mechanisms of quasi-strict liability for organisational fault, is the problem of personal tortious liability of agents. Western liability laws have responded to that problem in various and even incoherent ways. We only scratch the surface herein.

Regarding governmental liability, personal tort liability of public servants is almost entirely lacking, even when the challenged conduct was intentional. Only the government, not the individual agent, faces liability in respect of third parties in most of the EU member-states. The state may then have recourse against its tortious agent.

In private industry, the agent, whether employee or executive, is always liable under German law. This is true for both the classic personal tort (e.g. a bus driver hitting a pedestrian) and for relational torts (e.g. an organisational

---

106. *Greenman v. Yuba Power Products, Inc.*, 377 P.2d 897 (1963). On the American products liability law see: Restatement (Third) Torts: Products Liability, 1998; D. Owen, *Products Liability Law*, St. Paul 2005; but see also ALI, *Reporters' Study—Enterprise Responsibility for Personal Injury*, 1991.

107. The leading case is BGH, 17.3.1981, BGHZ 80, 186; NJW 1981, 1603 (Apfelschorf).

mistake on the part of the manager[108]). The employee has a right of recourse against his employer which is dependent upon the degree of his/her fault. However, there is no help for the agent of an insolvent principal lacking liability insurance. In France, by contrast, case-law treats public and private sector employees equally.[109] One who acts within the scope of his employment when negligently causing loss to a third party is not personally liable. He is only liable if he overstepped the "*limites de la mission*", e.g. in cases of intentional infliction of harm. The same is true in French law for corporate directors and officers.—The same rules determine the law in Sweden. The non-liability of employees is explicitely provided for in the Tort Liability Act (Art. 3:1 (1)). The employer is bound to purchase liability insurance.

The extreme incoherence in this field of liability law reveals a need for European harmonisation.[110]

## 5. Personality Interests

In the second half of the twentieth century, non-economic personality interests, sometimes called personality rights, entered the debate alongside the classically protected interests of tort law such as bodily integrity and property. Personality interests include: dignity, privacy, right to one's image, name and likeness, and rights of self-determination. In the industrial states of the west, the law regarding the protection of personality interests is extremely disparate. Developments in France and in Switzerland have diverged from those in Germany (followed by Austria and Italy to a certain extent). The American and English Common Law have taken their own paths in the protection of personality interests.[111] The Nordic countries, on the contrary, still do not ac-

---

108. The leading case is BGH, 5.12.1989, BGHZ 109, 297; NJW 1990, 976; JZ 1990, 486, note Mertens/Mertens.

109. Cass. Ass. plén., 25.2.2000, Costedoat, JCP 2000 II 10295, rapport Kessous, note Biliau; D. 2000, 673, note Brun.

110. Interestingly though is that the DCFR excluded precisely this subject from its proposals (Art. 7:101 (a)), and the Vienna Group leaves it to the national legislator (PETL Art. 9:101 (1) (c)).

111. Cf. the two collections of basic articles: R. Wacks (ed.), *Privacy*, 2 vols, Aldershot/New York 1993, and E. Barendt (ed.), *Privacy*, Aldershot 2001; for a European comparative account see the Common Core of Private Law-Project: G. Brüggemeier, A.C. Ciacchi and P. O'Callaghan (eds.), *Personality Rights in European Tort Law*, Cambridge 2008 (forthcoming); for a perspective "from down under" see A.T. Kenyon and M. Richardson (eds.), *New Dimensions in Privacy Law*, Cambridge 2006.

knowledge any civil personality right or any by tort law protected personality interest. Civil remedies in tort law are only available if the conditions of a criminal act under Penal law are fulfilled.

Again, the starting point on the Continent is with both Roman law and Natural law, building on Christian ethic and Canon law.[112] The *actio iniuriarum* originally protected two aspects of the persona: bodily integrity *and* honour and dignity (*fama et dignitas*) of Roman citizens.[113] Injuries were sanctioned with an equitable monetary fine (*poena*). Natural Law stressed the basic right of a human being to be respected in her dignity and freedom. It acknowledged a far reaching general duty not to injure another person (*neminem laedere*).

In *France*, at least three phenomena are worth noting: (i) the impact of the *actio iniuriarum* in the late *Ius Commune*, (ii) the influence of Natural law with its general clause of tort law, and (iii) the Declaration of Rights of 1789.[114] The equal treatment of economic loss (*dommage patrimonial*) and non-economic loss (*dommage moral*) by the general clauses of the *Code Civil* (Arts. 1382, 1383) allowed for the provision of monetary compensation for infringements on non-economic personality interests. One famous early example of this is the *Rachel* case of 1858,[115] where photos were taken of the drawing of a famous actress on her death bed and were used commercially without consent. The notorious conflict between freedom of press and the protection of one's honour was addressed in a very progressive way through the Press Act of 1881: *in dubio pro libertate*. The legal nature of new personality rights and their modified application to the commercial personality rights of artists, authors, and inventors remained controversial: the latter being transferable, inheritable, and of economic value, while the former remained non-transferable, uninheritable, and without economic value.[116] The right of privacy also became the subject of legislation in France. After a series of spectacular cases dealing with personality interests of celebrities in the 1950s and 1960s, the protection of privacy was inserted into the *Code civil*. The new Article 9 (1) C. civ. reads: «*Chacun a droit*

112. For the Aristotelian and scholastic roots see Gordley, *Foundations of Private Law*, 2006, chap. 11 ("Liability in Tort for Harm to Reputation, Dignity, Privacy, and 'Personality'").

113. In the late Ius Commune the actio iniuriarum has been reduced to the protection of honour and reputation. For its impact on modern law, see R. Zimmermann, *The Law of Obligations. Roman Foundations of the Civilian Tradition*, Cape Town 1990, chap. 31.

114. Déclaration des droits de l'homme et du citoyen of August 26, 1789.

115. Trib. civ. Seine, 16.6.1858 (Rachel), D. 1858,3,62.

116. See as an early contribution E.H. Perreau, Des droits de la personnalité, RTD civ. 1909, 501; as a Franco-German comparison see A. Lucas-Schloetter, *Droit moral et droits de la personnalité*, Aix/Marseille 2002.

*au respect de sa vie privée.*» Thereafter, infringements of one's right of privacy allowed for compensation independent of fault. Art. 9 C. civ. thus represented yet another step in the broad trend within French private law whereby fault liability was changing into strict liability.[117]

As stated above, developments in 19th century *Germany* were completely different. The historical school of jurisprudence (*F.C. v. Savigny*) pursued an emphatic re-orientation towards genuine Roman law, not alienated through Canon and Natural law. German scholars sought to completely separate the penal and civil elements entirely removing the former from civil tort law. The historical school, and the Pandectists as its successors, tried to build a system of subjective economic rights. In the tradition of the *Lex Aquilia*, compensation was limited to concrete pecuniary loss. The *actio iniuriarum* with its punitive elements and its equitable monetary fine did not suit this. It was formally set out of force in 1879. Monetary compensation of non-economic loss was only exceptionally allowed for remedying pain and suffering in cases of bodily injuries.[118] In contrast to Roman law and Common law, damages for infringements of honour and reputation no longer existed! The protection of honour was taken over by criminal law. The *Reichsgericht* clearly stated in 1908, "A general subjective personality right is alien to the effective (German) civil law."[119]

It was not until after the Second World War that there was a fundamental change. Its normative basis was the new West German constitution, the "*Grundgesetz*" of 1949; its empirical basis was the history of the totalitarian national socialist State. In a virtually revolutionary judgment in 1954, the (new) highest civil court, the *Bundesgerichtshof* (*BGH*), abruptly ended a more than 100 year old tradition of suppressing the *actio iniuriarum* out of private law. With reference to the fundamental values of the new constitution (Art. 1 (1): dignity of human beings, and Art. 2 (1) *GG*: free development of personality), the Court recognized a *private law* personality right.[120] The task of integrating non-economic personality interests into the system of *BGB* law of delict proved extremely difficult. The landmark *Herrenreiter* case represents that effort.[121] The Federal Court of Justice found a non-economic loss result-

---

117. To this process see G.Viney, *Le déclin de la responsabilité individuelle*, 1965.

118. After one decided to conceive Schmerzensgeld no longer as a private law fine (poena)—but as compensation of immaterial harm. B. Windscheid, *Lehrbuch des Pandektenrechts*, 4th edn. Frankfurt/Main 1875, §455 A 31.

119. RGZ 69, 401, at 403 (Nietzsche letters).

120. BGH, 25.5.1954, BGHZ 13, 334; NJW 1954, 1404; JZ 1954, 698, note Coing.

121. BGH, 14.2.1954, BGHZ 26, 349; NJW 1958, 827; JZ 1958, 571.

ing from the commercial use of a private individual's picture which had damaged his reputation. Contradicting the clear wording of the Code (ex § 847 (1) *BGB*) the court also awarded equitable monetary compensation. Despite decades-long opposition in the neo-pandectist literature, this judge-made law was upheld.[122] The protection of a civilian "general" personality right was further expanded through the combined efforts of the Federal Court of Justice and the Federal Constitutional Court leading to the right to protection of the private sphere, the right to name, image, word, etc.[123] Yet, to this day, a legislative regulation has not been created.

With regard to German legal developments, there are three points to remember:

- The equitable monetary compensation of personality infringements today is completely removed from traditional pain & suffering awards. It is qualified as a *remedy sui generis*, which goes directly back to the protective duties of the Constitution (Arts. 1 (1), 2 (1) *GG*).
- In contrast to other legally protected interests, compensation will be awarded only (i) in cases of *serious impairment* of the personality and (ii) if no other cure is at hand.[124]
- In the mean time, German law has also recognised commercial personality rights (*publicity rights*), which are treated like intellectual property rights.[125]

In the *Common Law*, protection from defamation has had a long tort law tradition. Libel (defamation in the written form) and slander (in the oral form) emerged from different historical sources. Libel guarantees a particularly wide reaching protection. It is actionable per se. For compensation, the plaintiff need not show fault or injury. The defendant has however an array of avail-

---

122. Constitutionally becked through BVerfG, 14.2.1973, BVerfGE 34, 269; NJW 1973, 1221—Soraya.

123. Cf. in more detail Brüggemeier, *Haftungsrecht. Struktur, Prinzipien, Schutzbereich*, 2006 (§ 5 B); Baston-Vogt, Der sachliche Schutzbereich des zivilrechtlichen allgemeinen Persönlichkeitsrechts, 1997.

124. This seems to be a Germanic „Sonderweg". See Art. 49 (1) Swiss OR; BGH, 19.9.1961, BGHZ 35, 363 (Ginseng); Koziol, *Österreichisches Haftpflichtrecht*, vol. 1, 1997, p. 352.

125. BGH, 1.12.1999, BGHZ 143, 214; NJW 2000, 2195; JZ 2000, 1056, note Schack; leading German monographs are H.P. Götting, *Persönlichkeitsrechte als Vermögensrechte*, Tübingen 1995; T. Dreier, *Kompensation und Prävention*, Tübingen 2002; as comparative analysis see H. Berverly-Smith, A. Ohly and A. Lucas-Schloetter, *Privacy, Property and Personality. Civil Law Perspectives on Commercial Appropriation*, Cambridge 2005.

able defences. Due to the historical interwoveness of libel and slander with criminal acts, in this field of English common law exceptionally civil juries at trial and exemplary damages are still acknowledged.

The *US* Common Law took a completely different path. Anti-defamation law is framed by the First Amendment to the US constitution as well as by landmark US Supreme Court decisions such as *New York Times* v. *Sullivan* (1964).[126] English defamation judgments, therefore, are sometimes declared unenforceable in the US for constitutional reasons.[127]

In the US, a second branch of personality protection developed independently of defamation law. As far back as 1890 Warren and Brandeis famously took an important step forward in the protection of privacy rights.[128] They appeared to be inspired by French legal developments. In 1902, the New York Court of Appeals, was still divided over the question of recognition of the tort of invasion of privacy.[129] It was not until 1905 that the tort law protection of non-economic personality interests entered the American Common Law through a decision handed down by the Supreme Court of Georgia.[130]

In many states where the courts had not yet defined a clear-cut right of privacy, state legislatures eventually set about creating statutes with similar effects. The state of New York, for example, sought to prohibit the misuse of photographs of individuals for advertising purposes. All the while, the protection of other personality interests was expanding in the American common law alongside the traditional anti-defamation law. The first Restatement of Torts in 1939 included a loose formulation of this new tort.[131] At the beginning of the 1960s W. Prosser distinguished four aspects of personality protection:[132] the commercial appropriation of another's image, name, and likeness; the intrusion

126. 376 U.S. 254 (1964); cf. A. Lewis, *Make No Law: The Sullivan Case and the First Amendment*, 1992.

127. Cf. *Telnikoff* v. *Matusevich*, 702 A.2d 230 (Md. 1997).

128. Warren and Brandeis, The Right to Privacy, 4 Harv. L. Rev. 193 (1890).

129. *Roberson* v. *Rochester Folding Box Co.*, 64 N.E. 442 (1902): The photo of a young woman was used for the promotion of flour.

130. *Pavesich* v. *New England Life Insurance Co.*, 50 S.E. 68 (1905): "A right of privacy in matters purely private is therefore derived from natural law."

131. 4 Restatement of Torts, 1939, §867: "A person who unreasonably and seriously interferes with another's interest in not having his affairs known to others or his likeness exhibited to the public is liable to the other."

132. Prosser, Privacy, 48 Cal. L. Rev. 383 (1960); but see also E.J. Bloustein, Privacy as an Aspect of Human Dignity, 39 N.Y.U.L. Rev. 962 (1964). For two collections of basic articles see Wacks (ed.), *Privacy*, 2 vols. Aldershot 1993, and Barendt (ed.), *Privacy*, Aldershot 2001.

into another person's private sphere; the publication of private facts; placing someone publicly in a false light.[133] They subsequently gained entry into the Restatement (Second) of Torts, to which Prosser was the reporter.

The right of privacy is subject to the same rule as is the right of anti-defamation: the media enjoys a fundamental freedom of speech (First Amendment).[134] Since the 1950s, an independent *right to publicity* has developed as relates to the use of pictures and names of famous individuals. That right was upheld, if not created, in *Haelan Laboratories, Inc.* v. *Topps Chewing Gum, Inc*,[135] and was treated like a property right. The contours of that right remain somewhat imprecise—partly recognized by the courts, partly introduced by lawmakers such as those of California.[136]

In contrast to American jurisprudence, the *English* courts to this day at least formally refuse to recognise a right to privacy. The discussion has intensified due to the Human Rights Act 1998. Art. 8 (1) ECHR obliges the Contracting States to protect private life of their citizens. The courts look to Parliament which has shown no readiness to act in this area. As a substitute, courts employ the equitable doctrine of breach of confidence which no longer requires the existence of a confidential relationship.[137] Where the situation does not involve informational privacy (press reports, publication of pictures), the gaps in personality protection remain problematic.[138] As for Scotland, it remains to be seen whether it will revitalise its Roman law legacy and return to the *actio iniuriarum*.

## 6. Damages and Non-Economic Loss

The injury of a protected interest usually leads to a pecuniary loss. The reparation of the damaged thing costs money; as is the case of the medical treatment of bodily injury. Additional consequential losses can also flow from injury including loss of profit or income due to a reduced capacity to work. In that respect, complicated questions of legal imputation can arise. We will

---

133. 3 *Restatement (Second) Torts*, 1977, §652.

134. The leading case is *Time, Inc.* v. *Hill*, 385 U.S. 374 (1967).

135. 202 F.2d 866 (2d Cir. 1953). The Court decided on the basis of the law of the State of New York, without such a law being recognised there.

136. Cf. McCarthy, The Rights to Publicity and Privacy, 2 vols. 2d edn. 2002.

137. Cf. especially *Campbell* v *MGN Ltd* [2004] 2 WLR 1232 and *Douglas et al* v *Hello! Ltd* [2006] QB 125; [2007] UKHL 21.

138. E.g. *Wainwright* v *Home Office* [2003] 4 All ER 969 (Body Strip).

not consider those questions here. Instead the focus will be on two dimensions of the increasingly important category of non-economic loss: pain and suffering (*Schmerzensgeld/Smartengeld/pretium doloris*), and damage per se/injury itself.

## *6.1. Pain and Suffering*

Pain and suffering awards in personal injury cases were alien to the Roman law. But it was broadly accepted in the Germanic laws. So even the restrictive, Roman law and economic loss oriented German *BGB* recognised an equitable compensation for pain and suffering (*Schmerzensgeld*) in cases of bodily injury or injury to health (ex §847 *BGB*). The legal nature of *Schmerzengeld* and the criteria for its assessment, however, remained controversial. In the tradition of the *actio iniuriarum* it was in the form of an equitable fine (*Privatstrafe/peine privée/poena*). In 1875, *Windscheid* adopted *Waechter's* interpretation of *Schmerzensgeld* as a category of private law damage—non-economic loss.[139] *Schmerzensgeld* was thus treated much like an economic loss; the negative emotions associated with bodily injury were compensated with the positive emotions associated with the receipt of a money payment ("emotional difference hypothesis"). A widespread opinion was that *Schmerzensgeld* served not only the compensation of pain and suffering but also the satisfaction ("*Genugtuung*"[140]) of the injured.

Internationally, this concept of compensation for pain and suffering led to a problem. What is to be said of those compensation payees who are incapable of sensation and can gain no satisfaction from money payment? In those cases, the German courts were content to award a symbolic *Schmerzensgeld*. The Federal Court of Justice (*BGH*) parted with that reasoning in a seminal 1993 judgment.[141] The case involved medical malpractice in the birth of a severely disabled child incapable of sensation. In addition to an award for the compensation of the costs of medical treatment, the Court saw in the irreparable "destruction of personality" sufficient ground for awarding extensive equitable compensation for "pain and suffering." Clearly, here the boundaries of *damage per se* have been crossed. However, with some hesitation, many national courts

---

139. Windscheid, *Lehrbuch des Pandektenrechts*, 4. edn. 1875, §455 A 31, giving up his earlier opposite opinion.

140. In the Swiss law of obligations every compensation of non-economic loss serves the "Genugtuung" of the injured (Arts. 47, 49 OR).

141. BGH, 13.10.1992, BGHZ 120, 1; NJW 1993, 781, note Deutsch; JZ 1993, 516, note Giesen.

proceed in this fashion today.[142] In Britain the House of Lords denies pain and suffering payments to unconscious patients but awards compensation for loss of amenities.[143]

Compensation for pain and suffering is traditionally awarded to remedy emotional harms connected with bodily injury or injury to health. This the broadly accepted stand of the law of damages. Can the causation of pain and suffering without preceding bodily injury also lead to a claim for compensation? Take the example of the hostage taken by terrorists,[144] the fear of death in a burning shuttle (e.g. the *Kaprun* accident of ski tourists in Austria, Nov. 2000), and the daily contact with a severely disabled child. Many private law regimes, particularly the Dutch, English and German, do not go so far. In nervous shock cases, the evidence of a medically diagnosed illness has to be shown and the additional requirements of a fatal accident or severe personal injury and of a close relationship must be met.[145] Certain Romanist legal systems and the EC courts are somewhat more willing to redress these pains.[146] English and American Common Law recognise the tort of intentional infliction of mental distress.[147] In addition to intent and the extreme misconduct on the part of the acting party, the injured party must have suffered serious injuries to her feelings.

A notorious problem with compensation of pain and suffering is the equal treatment of comparable cases. To achieve some sort of standardisation, courts and lawyers in a couple of EU-Member States make recourse to pain and suffering tables when assessing these general damages (*Schmerzensgeldtabellen*/*Smartengeldbundel*/Guidelines for the Assessment of General Damages). Eventually such tables may be made available for the whole area of the EC or EEA. Yet, the unique aspects of individual cases will remain of primary importance.

---

142. Cf. W.V.H. Rogers (ed.), *Damages for Non-Pecuniary Loss in a Comparative Perspective*, 2001, p. 257 (para. 23).

143. *West & Son Ltd* v *Shepard* [1964] AC 326.

144. This case would cause no legal problems in legal regimes like e.g. Germany, where the impairment of freedom to move also entitles the impaired party to Schmerzensgeld (ex §847 (1) BGB; §253 (2) BGB 2002). Cf. BGH, 29.11.1994, BGHZ 128, 117 (hostage taking).

145. Cf. the judgment of the Dutch Hoge Raad, 22.2.2002, NJ 2002, no. 240; 2003 ERPL 412–476 (with comparative comments).

146. Cf. Rogers, *Damages for Non-Pecuniary Loss in a Comparative Perspective*, 2001, pp. 260; W. Wurmnest, *Grundzüge eines europäischen Haftungsrechts*, Tübingen 2003, pp. 292–294 (references to actions of civil servants).

147. See *Wilkinson* v *Downton* [1897] 2 QB 57; W. Prosser, Intentional Infliction of Mental Suffering: A New Tort, 37 Mich. L. Rev. 874 (1939); 1 *Restatement (Second) Torts*, 1965, §46.

## *6.2. Damage per se/Injury as Such*

Next to the classical harm to feelings (pain & suffering), mostly in connection with bodily injury, another variant of non-economic loss has recently stepped into the foreground—*damage per se.* It is now prominently advocated for by the Study Group on a European Civil Code in its proposals on liability law.[148] *Damage per se means injury without loss.* The "injury itself" of a protected interest is sanctioned with an equitable monetary compensation, independent of whether pecuniary loss results therefrom. *Ubi ius, ibi remedium!*[149] There are two big groups of cases: lasting bodily impairment and the infringement on personality rights. Between these two cases can be located the Italian "revolution of damages law" which became known as *danno biologico* or *danno alla salute*

### 6.2.1. Lasting Bodily Impairment

A lasting irreparable injury to bodily integrity demands equitable compensation. This is widely accepted. Regarding the curable injury to body or health, the treatment costs are viewed as pecuniary loss, including economic consequential damage like loss of earnings due to a reduced capacity to work, etc. However, the irreparable loss of a body part (finger, arm, foot, or frozen sperm[150]) or of a bodily capacity (blindness, deafness, sterility, or infertility) as such is expressed as damage *per se.* This kind of injury has been extensively recognised. Yet until now it has been subsumed by the traditional compensation for pain and suffering, although here the compensation is granted regardless of actual pain.[151] In England the bodily "injury itself" seems to be recognised when the courts award money for the loss of faculty and the loss of amenities of life.[152]

Damage per se has attained a new independent dimension in cases of so called destruction of personality. The irreparable severe disability of a child through medical malpractice during the delivery is compensated as such, independent of the economic consequential losses (on-going medical treatment and care costs) of this injury to bodily integrity.

---

148. See esp. DCFR, Book VI: "Non-Contractual Liability arising out of Damage caused to another", Art. 6:204: "Injury as such is to be compensated independent of compensation for economic or non-economic loss."

149. For the reversing of "ubi remedium, ibi ius" in the Common Law see P. O'-Callaghan, (2007) ERPL 659–683.

150. See BGH, 9.11.1993, BGHZ 124, 52 (Sperma).

151. Cf. to this the above mentioned internationally prepared "pain and suffering tables"/"guidelines" etc.

152. *West & Son Ltd* v *Shepard* [1964] AC 326.

A third and most important aspect of this bodily damage per se is the *wrongful death of a human being*. This non-restorable injury to the highest legal interest, which western constitutions recognise—human life (born and unborn), demonstrates the most important damage per se. Primarily in order to avoid contradictions of values and secondly from preventive grounds,[153] the mere act of wrongful killing of a human being has to be sanctioned by private law.[154] This compensation claim is entirely separate from those of other individuals whose livelihoods are dependent upon the injured. Germany, Finland and Poland are among the few states which refuse such a compensation.[155] The economic loss orientation of 19th century still dominates here. In one form or another, most legal systems have recognised the damages claims of relatives in wrongful death cases. In Portugal, it is regulated in the Civil Code; in England, bereavement damages have been introduced by legislation (Amendment to the Fatal Accident Act).[156] Also in the US, the various states have enacted special legislative rules to that effect.[157]

### 6.2.2. Personality Rights/Privacy Rights

The second category of damage per se is composed of injuries to so-called personality rights.[158] Again, here the infringement itself is the damage;[159] rarely is economic loss to be found. Where there is no economic loss, law by definition is less concerned with loss compensation than with the sanctioning of unlawful infringements which is carried out through the award of an equitable sum of money as an independent remedy differentiated from the classical

---

153. Although the amount of money paid e. g. under the English Fatal Accident Act (£10.000), payable to spouses and parents only, is not a powerful incentive to avoid wrongful deaths.

154. See also the case law of the ECtHR, 8.7.2004, appl. no. 53924/00, *Vo* v. *France*, [2004] 40 EHRR 12; ECtHR, 17.3.2005, appl. no. 50196/99, *Bubbins* v. *United Kingdom*, [2005] EHRR 458.

155. In the Netherlands a corresponding Bill on "affectieschade" has been introduced in Parliament.

156. See the detailed comparative account by A. Janczuk and M.M. Veloso, Claims for non-pecuniary losses by 'third persons' upon death and injury, in Brüggemeier, Ciacchi and Comandé (eds.), *Fundamental Rights and Private Law in the European Union*, vol. 2, Cambridge 2008 (forthcoming); as a German monograph see Stahmer, *Entschädigungsansprüche in Tötungsfällen für Angehörige*, 2004.

157. Cf. D.B. Dobbs, *The Law of Torts*, St. Paul 2000, § 297.

158. See above in the text.

159. W. van Gerven, Remedies for Infringements of Fundamental Rights (2004) 10 Eur. Public L. 261, 276 et seq.

*Schmerzensgeld.*[160] In determining the amount of the award, all relevant circumstances are to be taken into account. Goals of deterrence should not be confused with punitive purposes though the distinction is easily blurred. In the US, as far as they are recognised in the individual states, and to a restricted extent in England, punitive damages complement as an additional independent remedy the equitable compensation for the infringement on personality interests.

In Europe some punitive elements are existent when the amount of the equitable compensation is raised with regard to the degree of fault: less in cases of negligence—more in cases of intentional and reckless violations. Insofar one may speak of aggravated damages.[161]

### 6.2.3. Danno Biologico/Danno alla Salute

Somewhat linked to the debate on damage is the revolution in the Italian law of damages which became known under the title "*danno biologico.*" Between the end of the 1970s and the end of the 1980s, a major turnabout in Italian private law was achieved via constitutionalisation of tort liability. With reference to Art. 32 of the Italian Constitution of 1948 ("right to health") the strict boundaries of compensation for non-economic loss in personal injury cases (Art. 2059 C. civ.) were abolished by the judiciary. In a first step, the concept of *danno biologico* was developed. As a result, three categories of damage in cases of bodily injury and harm to health can be distinguished: (i) the economic loss of medical treatment costs (*danno patrimoniale*), (ii) non-pecuniary loss of pain and suffering (*danno morale soggettivo*), and (iii) the bodily or health *injury as such* to be remedied by an equitable compensation (*danno alla persona*), which will be assessed in proportion to the injury's gravity, and is justified by the high constitutional rank of the violated personal right.[162] This third category of damage was directly placed under the umbrella of the general clause of tort liability (Art. 2043 C. civ.).

Finally, in 2003 the principle was established that an award for non economic loss must always be available in case of the violation of any constitutionally protected right of the person.[163] This led in substance to an *interpretatio contra*

---

160. Finally recognised in Germany by BGH, 15.11.1994, BGHZ 128, 1, at 17.

161. See again the seminal case BGHZ 128, 1, at 17 (Caroline of Monaco). To the aggravated damages in English law see Law Commission, *Aggravated, Exemplary and Restitutionary Damages*, Law Com no 247, 16 Dec 1997.

162. Cf. F. Busnelli, *Il danno biologico*, 2001; G. Alpa, *Il danno biologico*, 1993.

163. Cass., 311.5.2003, n. 8828, [2003] Foro it., I, 2272 and Cass., 31.5.2003, n.8827, [2003] Foro it., I, 2273; Corte const., 11.7.2003 Foro it., I, 2201. To this Italian development see in English the comparative account by S. Wünsch and F. Panetti, Non-Pecuniary

*codicem* justified by a constitution-based reasoning. As Art. 2059 C. civ. has been definitively deemed applicable by the judiciary in all subject matters concerning "the person," nowadays Italian scholars and courts no longer need to create special categories of damages such as *danno biologico* or *danno esistenziale* to justify exceptions to the principle of non-recoverability of non-economic losses.

## 7. Conclusion

Can there be an approximisation of liability rules in Europe and North America? Firstly one should remember the accurate observation of *R. Zimmermann*: "English law is European, America is different."[164] From the European perspective, the American law of torts is characterized by many court and procedural particularities (including civil juries, punitive damages, pretrial discovery, and contingent fees), which have no equivalent in Europe. US pain and suffering awards, to give another well known example, are far beyond any payments conceivable in Europe. So, it would appear that any approximisation will concentrate primarily on the twenty-eight legal systems of the EC[165] or the thirty-one that comprise the European Economic Area (EEA).[166] However, this does not mean that substantive American liability law is of no comparative value.

Unification or approximization in Europe? The complexities of society, the cultural diversities of member states (Art. 151 EC), the great variety of legal problems, the disparity and (functional) plurality of private law, and the dynamics of social developments all count against transnational unification through general legal provisions. However, in light of the foregoing survey of the diversity and plurality of European liability laws, an approximisation on the ground of the national legal systems, if at all possible, seems a more realistic legal policy. The dream of the Enlightenment—the plain, simple and eternal Civil Code—has ended. Unification does not hurt, but neither does it really help. The phenomenon of decodification cannot simply be ignored. The

Damages: How Fundamental Rights Shake Traditional Barriers, in Brüggemeier, Ciacchi and Comandé, *Fundamental Rights and Private Law*, vol. 2, Cambridge 2008 (forthcoming).

164. R. Zimmermann, „Common law" und „civil law", in R. Zimmermann (ed.), *Amerikanische Rechtskultur und europäisches Privatrecht*, Tübingen 1995, 1, at 9.

165. 25 member states (plus Scotland) and since Jan. 1st 2007 Bulgaria and Romania.

166. 27 EC member states (with 28 legal systems) plus Iceland, Liechtenstein and Norway.

"*Common Frame of Reference* process," initiated by the European Commission's Action Plan 2003[167] and executed by the *Joint Network on Europea Private Law,*[168] will finally produce another (optional) private law regime for the EEA—but no effective European Civil Code.[169] In particular, in respect of damages claims in tort, the possibility to opt into the CFR rules will hardly have any substantial effects. At the best the CFR rules may—like other academic proposals—serve as a source of inspiration for the law reforms by the national legislators.

The living tort laws in continental Europe today are to be found much more in case law and statutes—a body of sources that lacks inner structure—than in the Civil Codes. The Code itself is an anathema to the Common law countries. Common ground, however, can be found in transnational cooperation: The legal material in its plurality is to be structured; old or new principles and rules are to be carved out, there is still a lot of doctrinal strife; conflicting judgments are, as far as possible, to be reconciled or eliminated. Such a comparative orientation of scholarly work and of judiciaries' case adjudicating may lead to a convergence of the national laws.

# References

Alpa, G., Il danno biologico, Padova (Cedam) 1993.

American Law Institute (ed.), Restatement of Laws: Torts, 4 vols, 1934–39.

American Law Institute (ed.), Restatement (Second) of Torts, 4 vols, St. Paul 1965–79.

American Law Institute (ed.), Reporters' Study—Enterprise Responsibility for Personal Injury, 2 vols, Philadelphia 1991.

American Law Institute (ed.), Restatement (Third) of Torts: Products Liability, St. Paul 1998.

---

167. See the European Commission's Communication 'European Contract Law: An Action Plan', COM (2003) 68 final; on the process see M.W. Hesselink (ed.), *The Politics of a European Civil Code*, The Hague 2006.

168. Cf. C. von Bar, E. Clive and H. Schulte-Nölke (eds), *Principles, Definitions and Model Rules of European Private Law. Draft Common Frame of Reference (DCFR)*, Munich 2008; on this see M.W. Hesselink, *CFR & Social Justice*, Munich 2008 and A. Somma (ed).), *The Politics of the Draft Common Frame of Reference*, The Hague 2009 (forthcoming).

169. Cf. A. Hartcamp et al. (eds), *Towards a European Civil Code*, 3rd edn. Nijmegen 2004; see also the chairman of the SGECC, C. von Bar, From Principles to Codification: Prospects for European Private Law, 8 Colum. J. Eur. L. 379 (2002) and his most pronounced opponent P. Legrand, European Legal Systems are not Converging, (1996) 55 ICLQ 52, id., Antivonbar, (2006) 1 JCL 13.

American Law Institute (ed.), Restatement (Third) of Torts: General Principles, Draft 1999.

Atiyah, P.S., Accidents, Compensation and the Law, 3rd edn. London (Weidenfeld and Nicolson) 1980.

Avant-Projet de réforme du droit des obligations et du droit de la prescription—Rapport à M. Pascal Clément Garde de Sceaux, Ministre de la Justice, 22 Septembre 2005.

Bar, C. v., Gemeineuropäisches Deliktsrecht, vol. II, München (Beck) 1999 (in English id., The Common European Law of Torts, vol. 2, Oxford (OUP) 2000).

Bar, C. v., From Principles to Codification: Prospects for European Private Law, 8 Colum. J. Eur. L. 379 (2002).

Bar, C. von, Clive, E. and Schulte-Nölke, H. (eds), Principles, Definitions and Model Rules of European Private Law. Draft Common Frame of Reference (DCFR), Munich (Sellier) 2008.

Barendt, E. (ed.), Privacy. The International Library of Essays in Law and Legal Theory, Aldershot (Dartmouth)/New York (NYUP) 2001.

Baston-Vogt, M., Der sachliche Schutzbereich des zivilrechtlichen allgemeinen Persönlichkeitsrechts, Tübingen (Mohr Siebeck) 1997.

Beck, U., Risikogesellschaft. Auf dem Weg in eine andere Moderne, Frankfurt/Main (Suhrkamp) 1986 (in English id., Risk Society. Towards Another Modernity, London 1992).

Beverly-Smith, H., Ohly, A. and Lucas-Schloetter, A., Privacy, Property and Personality. Civil Law Perspectives on Commercial Appropriation, Cambridge (CUP) 2005.

Birks, P., Negligence in the Eighteenth Century Common Law, in Schrage, E.J.H. (ed.), Negligence, Berlin (Duncker & Humblot) 2001, pp. 173.

Bloustein, E.J., Privacy as an Aspect of Human Dignity, 39 N.Y.U.L. Rev 962 (1964).

Boulding, K.E., The Organizational Revolution, New York (Harper) 1953.

Brüggemeier, G., Prinzipien des Haftungsrechts, Baden-Baden (Nomos) 1999. (in English id., Common Principles of Tort Law. A Prestatement of Law, London (BIICL) 2004; reprinted 2006).

Brüggemeier, G., Unternehmenshaftung—Enterprise Liability. Eine europäische Perspektive?, HAVE/REAS 2004, 162.

Brüggemeier, G., Haftungsrecht. Struktur, Prinzipien, Schutzbereich—Ein Beitrag zur Europäisierung des Privatrechts, Heidelberg (Springer) 2006.

Brüggemeier, G., Ciacchi, A.C. and Comandé, G. (eds.), Fundamental Rights and Private Law in the European Union, vol. 2: Comparative Analyses of Selected Case Patterns, Cambridge (CUP) 2008 (forthcoming).

Brüggemeier, G., Ciacchi, A.C. and O'Callaghan, P. (eds.), Personality Rights in European Tort Law, Cambridge (CUP) 2008 (forthcoming).
Busnelli, F.D., Il danno biologico. Dal "diritto vivente" al "diritto vigente", Torino (Giappichelli) 2001.
Bussani, M., Palmer, V.V. (eds.), Pure Economic Loss in Europe, Cambridge (CUP) 2003.
Cahn, A., Das neue Schadensersatzrecht, München (Beck) 2002.
Calabresi, G., The Costs of Accidents. A Legal and Economic Analysis, New Haven/London (Yale UP) 1970.
Calabresi, G., The Complexity of Torts—The Case of Punitive Damages, in Madden (ed.), Exploring Tort Law, New York (CUP) 2005, pp. 333.
Clerk, J.F. and Lindsell, W.H.B., On Torts. The Common Law Library, 19th edn. London (Sweet & Maxwell) 2006.
Dam, C. van, European Tort Law, Oxford (OUP) 2006.
Dewees, D, Duff, D. and Trebilcock, M.J., Exploring the Domain of Accident Law. Taking the Facts Seriously, Oxford (OUP) 1996.
Deutsch, E., Allgemeines Haftungsrecht, 2d edn. Cologne etc. (Heymanns) 1996.
Dobbs, D.B., The Law of Torts, St. Paul (West) 2000.
Dreier, T., Kompensation und Prävention. Rechtsfolgen unerlaubter Handlung im Bürgerlichen, Immaterialgüter-und Wettbewerbsrecht, Tübingen (Mohr Siebeck) 2002.
Dute, J., Faure, M.G. & Koziol, H. (eds.), No-Fault Compensation in the Health Care Sector, Vienna/New York 2004.
Ehrenzweig, A. A., Negligence without Fault. Trends toward an Enterprise Liability for Insurable Loss, Berkeley (Univ. Cal. Press) 1951.
Esser, J., Grundlagen und Entwicklung der Gefährdungshaftung, Berlin (Beck) 1941.
European Group on Tort Law (ed.), European Principles of Tort Law. Text and Commentary, Vienna/New York (Springer) 2005.
Ewald, F., L'état providence, Paris (Grasset) 1986.
Fairgrieve, D., Andenas, M. and Bell, J. (eds.),Tort Liability of Public Authorities in Comparative Perspective, London (BIICL) 2002.
Faure, M. and Hartlief, T., Towards an Expanding Enterprise Liability in Europe?, (1996) MJ 235.
Friedman, M., Civil Wrongs: Personal Injury Law in the Late 19th Century, 1987 Am. B. Found. Res. J. 351.
Foëx, B. and Werro, F. (eds.), La réforme du droit de la responsabilité civile, Zürich (Schulthess) 2004.
Gerven, W. van, Bridging the Unbridgeable: Community and National Tort Law After Francovich and Brasserie, (1996) 45 ICLQ 507.

Gerven, W. van, Lever, J. and Larouche, P., Cases, Materials and Text on National, Supranational and International Tort Law, Oxford (Hart) 2000.

Gerven, W. van, Remedies for Infringements of Fundamental Rights (2004) 10 EurPublicL 261.

Gordley, J. and Mehren, A.T. von, An Introduction to the Comparative Study of Private Law. Readings, Cases, Materials, Cambridge (CUP) 2006.

Gordley, J., Foundations of Private Law—Property, Tort, Contract, Unjust Enrichment, Oxford (OUP) 2006.

Götting, H.P., Persönlichkeitsrechte als Vermögensrechte, Tübingen (Mohr Siebeck) 1995.

Haas, J., La responsabilité de l'entreprise en Europe: Un droit unique pour le Marché unique?, Bern (Stämpfli) 2004.

Haltern, U., Europarecht. Dogmatik im Kontext, 2nd edn. Tübingen (Mohr Siebeck) 2007.

Harper, F.V., James, F. and Gray, O.S., The Law of Torts, 5 vols., Boston etc. (Little, Brown & Co.) 1986.

Hartcamp, A., Hesselink, M. and Hondius, E. (eds.), Towards a European Civil Code, 3rd edn. Nijmegen (Ars Aequi Libri) 2004.

Hepple, B.A., Negligence: The Search for Coherence (1997) 50 CLP 69.

Hesselink, M.W. (ed), The Politics of a European Civil Code, The Hague (Kluwer) 2006.

Hesselink, M.W., CFR & Social Justice, Munich (Sellier) 2008.

Horwitz, M.J., The Transformation of American Law, 1780–1860, Cambridge Mass. (Harvard UP) 1977.

Ibbetson, D.J., The Tort of Negligence in the Common Law in the Nineteenth and Twentieth Centuries, in Schrage, E.J.H. (ed.), Negligence, Berlin (Duncker & Humblot) 2001, pp. 229.

Jansen, N., Die Struktur des Haftungsrechts. Geschichte, Theorie und Dogmatik außervertraglicher Ansprüche, Tübingen (Mohr Siebeck) 2003.

Jansen, N., Konturen eines europäischen Schadensrechts, JZ 2005, 157.

Jhering, R. von, Das Schuldmoment im Römischen Privatrecht, Gießen (Roth) 1867.

Kenyon, A.T. and Richardson, M., New Dimensions in Privacy Law. International and Comparative Perspectives, Cambridge (CUP) 2006.

Koziol, H., Österreichisches Haftpflichtrecht, vol. 1, 3d edn. Wien (Manz) 1997.

Koziol, H. (ed.), Unification of Tort Law: Wrongfulness, Vienna/New York (Springer) 1998.

Lange, H. and Schiemann, G., Schadensersatz, 3rd edn. Tübingen (Mohr Siebeck) 2003.

Law Commission, Aggravated, Exemplary and Restitutionary Damages, Law Com no 247, 16 Dec 1997.

Legrand, P., European Legal Systems are not converging, (1996) 55 ICLQ 52.

Legrand, P., Antivonbar, (2006) 1 JCL 13.

Litan, R.E., Verdict : Assessing the Civil Jury System, Washington (Brookings Institution Press) 1993.

Lucas-Schloetter, A., Droit moral et droits de la personnalité, Aix en Provence/Marseille (Presse Univ.) 2002.

Luhmann, N., Moderne Systemtheorien als Form gesamtgesellschaftlicher Analyse, in Habermas, J. and Luhmann, N., Theorie der Gesellschaft oder Sozialtechnologie, Frankfurt/Main (Suhrkamp) 1971, pp. 7.

Madden, M.S. (ed.), Exploring Tort Law, New York (CUP) 2005.

Magnus, U. (ed), Unification of Tort Law: Damages, Vienna/New (Springer) 2001.

Magnus, U. (ed.), The Impact of Social Security on Tort Law, Vienna/New York (Springer) 2003.

McCarthy, J.T., The Rights of Publicity and Privacy, 2d edn. New York (Boardman) 2004.

McGregor, C.T., On Damages, 17th edn London (Sweet & Maxwell) 2003.

Norrie, K. McK, Stair Memorial Encyclopeadia: Laws of Scotland, vol. 15: Obligations, 1995.

Owen, D., Products Liability Law, St. Paul (West) 2005.

Perreau, E.H., Des droits de la personnalité, RTD civ. 1909, 501.

Planiol, M., Traité élémentaire de droit civil, vol. 2, 4th edn. Paris (L.G.P.J) 1952.

Posner, R., A Theory of Negligence, 1 J. Legal Stud. 29 (1972).

Posner, R., Economic Analysis of Law, 5th edn New York (Aspen) 1998.

Prosser, W., Intentional Infliction of Mental Suffering: A New Tort, 37 Mich. L. Rev. 874 (1939).

Prosser, W., Privacy, 48 Cal. L. Rev. 383 (1960).

Roberto, V., Schweizerisches Haftpflichtrecht, Zürich (Schulthess) 2002.

Rogers, W.V.H. (ed.), Damages for Non-Pecuniary Loss in a Comparative Perspective, Vienna/New York (Springer) 2001.

Rudden, B., Torticles, 6/7 Tul. Civ. L.F. 105 (1991/92).

Saleilles, R., Les accidents du travail et la responsabilité civile, Paris (Rousseau) 1897.

Schäfer, H.-B. and Ott, C., Lehrbuch der ökonomischen Analyse des Zivilrechts, 4th edn. Heidelberg (Springer) 2005 (in English id., The Economic Analysis of Civil Law, Cheltenham (Elgar) 2004).

Schrage, E.J.H. (ed.), Negligence. The Comparative Legal History of the Law of Torts, Berlin (Duncker & Humblot) 2001.

Schuck, P.H., Suing Government. Citizen Remedies for Official Wrongs, New Haven (Yale UP) 1983.

Shapo, M.S., Towards a Jurisprudence of Injury: The Continuing Creation of a System of Substantive Justice in American Tort Law, Chicago (American Bar Association) 1984.

Somma, A. (ed).), The Politics of the Draft Common Frame of Reference, The Hague (Kluwer International) 2009 (forthcoming).

Stahmer, N., Entschädigung von Nichtvermögensschäden bei Tötung, Hamburg (Kovac) 2004.

Stanton, K.M., Statutory Torts, London (Thomson) 2003.

Sugarman, S.D., Doing Away with Personal Injury Law: New Compensation Mechanisms for Victims, Consumers, and Business, New York (Quorum Books) 1989.

Viney, G., Le déclin de la responsabilité individuelle, Paris (L.G.D.J) 1965.

Viney, G. and Jourdain, P., Traité de Droit Civil: Les conditions de la responsabilité, 2nd edn. Paris (L.G.D.J) 1998.

Viney, G. and Jourdain, P., Traité de Droit Civil: Les effets de la responsabilité, 2d edn. Paris (L.G.D.J) 2001.

Wacks, R. (ed.), Privacy, 2 vols, The International Library of Essays in Law and Legal Theory, Aldershot (Dartmouth) 1993.

Wagner, G., Das neue Schadensersatzrecht, Baden-Baden (Nomos) 2002.

Wagner, G., Grundstrukturen des Europäischen Deliktsrechts, in R. Zimmermann (ed.), Grundstrukturen des Europäischen Deliktsrechts, Baden-Baden (Nomos) 2003, pp. 189–340.

Wagner, G. (ed.), Liability in Tort and Liability Insurance, Vienna/New York (Springer) 2005.

Wantzen, K., Unternehmenshaftung und Enterprise Liability, Tübingen (Mohr Siebeck) 2007.

Warren, S.D. & Brandeis, L.D., The Right to Privacy, 4 Harv. L. Rev. 193 (1890).

Weber, M., Wirtschaft und Gesellschaft, Tübingen (Mohr Siebeck) 1925 (in English id., On Law in Economy and Society, Cambridge (Mass.) 1954, transl. Rheinstein).

Weinrib, E.J., The Disintegration of Duty, in Madden (ed.), Exploring Tort Law, New York (CUP) 2005, pp. 143.

Weir, T., Economic Torts, Oxford (Clarendon Press) 1997.

Werro, F. and Palmer, V.V. (eds.), The Boundaries of Strict Liability in European Tort Law, Bern (Stämpfli) 2004.

Werro, F., La responsabilité civile, Bern (Stämpfli) 2005.

Weyers, H.L., Unfallschäden, Frankfurt/Main (Athenäum) 1971.

Whitman, J.Q., The Two Cultures of Privacy: Dignity Versus Liberty, 113 Yale L.J. 1151 (2004).

Widmer, P. (ed.), Unification of Tort Law: Fault, Vienna/New York (Springer) 2005.

Wieacker, F., Das Sozialmodell der klassischen Privatrechtsgesetzbücher und der Entwurf der modernen Gesellschaft, Heidelberg (C.F. Müller) 1953.

Wieacker, F., Pandektenwissenschaft und industrielle Revolution, 9 Juristen-Jahrbuch 1 (1968/69).

Wieacker, F., Privatrechtsgeschichte der Neuzeit, 2d edn. Göttingen (Vandenhoeck & Ruprecht) 1967 (in English id., A History of Private Law in Europe, Oxford (Clarendon Press) 1995, transl. T. Weir).

Windscheid, B., Lehrbuch des Pandektenrechts, 4th edn Frankfurt on Main (Rütten & Loenig) 1875.

Winiger, B., La responsabilité aquilienne romaine—Damnum iniuria datum, Bâle etc. (Helbing & Lichtenhahn) 1997.

Zimmermann, R., The Law of Obligations. Roman Foundations of the Civilian Tradition, Cape Town (Juta) 1990.

Zimmermann, R., "Common law" und "civil law", Amerika und Europa, in Zimmermann, R. (ed.), Amerikanische Rechtskultur und europäisches Privatrecht, Tübingen (Mohr Siebeck) 1995, pp. 1.

Zimmerman. R. (ed.), Grundstrukturen des Europäischen Deliktsrechts, Baden-Baden (Nomos) 2003.

# 10

# Eastern Tort Law

Attila Menyhárd

## Summary



## 1. Introduction

Tort law of the East European legal systems is far from being an easy subject to analyze. The first obstacle is that tort law in all of the European legal systems is a law in action: the law can be found rather in court practice than in books and discussion of the regulation itself may lead us to shallow and incorrect conclusions. The second obstacle is the transitional status of these legal systems today. The transition into the market economy is not to be seen as a moment in time but as a longer and continuous social development. The third problem is that a comprehensive analysis would take more volumes instead of a few pages. From all of this follows that the analysis below could be only a selection of trends, developments and a presentation which is necessarily a subjective one but may give an aerial perspective attempting to make the most important features and developments of these legal systems' tort law recognizable. This overview cannot be by any means complete. The analysis provided here focuses on the basis of liability and some features giving the main characteristics of a tort law system.

Tort law as it stands today in the Eastern European legal systems can be understood as a result of different impacts and developments. The transformation of social and economic system, the transition to market economy in these countries, and the consequences of enlargement of the European Union confronted not only the regulation and court practice but tort law theory as well with new challenges. The picture we see now is a moment of changes in the progress of development and these changes are quick and drastic. Looking back, the observer may see the disappearing contours of the remnants of the socialist civil law while looking ahead the outlines of a new regulation, a new philosophy and changing court practice are growing very rapidly stronger.

In spite of the common background presented by the socialist legal theory and legal policy, the civil law of socialist countries had not been the result of coherent development—neither in general nor at the national level. Each Eastern European country had its own legal traditions before World War II, which was a mixture of influence of the German, Austrian and French private and commercial law and of an internal development in different proportions. This has been reflected in tort law as well in regulation as in practice.

The socialist civil codes in the Eastern European countries have been built upon these traditions. In the former socialist Czechoslovakia, the civil law was codified in 1950 and again in 1964. In the Czech Republic and Slovakia the basis of tort law regulation today is the Civil Code of 1964 along with the Commercial Code. There are, however, strong efforts in both of these countries to re-codify the civil law, which sometimes seem to be very close to success.[1] The basis of tort law regulation in Poland is the Civil Code of 1964,[2] although the Commission for the Civil Law Codification has decided—besides working on the reform of existing law—to consider the drafting of principles and propos-

1. After an unsuccesful effort the Slovak Government resolved in 2002 again to have a final draft in the summer of 2005. J. Lazar, *Die Aufgaben der Neukodifikation des slowakischen Privatrechts im Kontext seiner Europäisierung*, in P. Blaho and J. Śvidroň (eds.), *Kodifikácia, europeizácia a harmonizácia súkromného práva/Kodifikation, Europaisierung und Harmonisierung des Privatrechts* (Bratislava, 2005), 132. The recodification of the civil law in the Czech republic is in progress as well, although with uneven intensity. J. Dvořák, *Kodifikace občanského práva v České Republice (včera, dnes a zítra)* with a summary in German, Blaho and Śvidroň (eds.) *Kodifikácia*, 250.

2. Dz. U. 1964 Nr.16, Pos 93 [KC]. See also J. Poczobut, *Deliktsrecht in Europa, Landesbericht Polen*, Köln/Berlin/Bonn/München, 1996, 11.

als for a new Polish Civil Code.[3] In Hungary, the Civil Code of 1959 is the basic regulation of the civil law relationships including tort law. The re-codification of the civil law in Hungary is in progress as well.[4] The Principles and Proposals for a new Hungarian Civil Code were published in 2004 and the Government of the Hungarian Republic has submitted in June 2008 the bill of the New Hungarian Civil Code in the Parliament. The general discussion of the Bill is ongoing. The tort law regulation of the Bill for the New Hungarian Civil Code would not bring any great substantial or revolutionary changes into Hungarian tort law. The main attempt of the legislator (at least as it has been presented) seems to be revising the existing law and, as a result of this revision, keeping the structure of current regulation, incorporating settled court practice and making slight corrections where it seems to be necessary.

The re-codification of the civil law was quicker and is generally in a more advanced stage in those Eastern European countries that became independent countries as a result of disintegration of a federal state (i.e. the successor states of the former Soviet Union or Yugoslavia).[5] In these countries, the pressure for having a new, independent, and self-developed legislation reflecting their identity too might have been stronger than in other countries. In 2003, the Slovenian Code of Obligations came into force.[6] In Croatia, the basis of tort law regulation remained the former Yugoslavian Law of Obligations 1978, which was amended with special regulation. The main focus of civil law reform in Croatia is the correction of existing laws instead of codification—however, they did enact new laws, too.[7] As for the Baltic States, in Estonia,[8] the new Law of Obligations came into force in 2002, which included the gen-

3. Z. Radwański, *Kodifikationsprobleme des Zivilrechts in Polen*, Blaho and Švidroň (eds.) *Kodifikácia*, 174.

4. For more on the process and background of recodification of the new Hungarian Civil Code see e.g. L. Vékás, *Über die Grundzüge der ungarischen Privatrechtsreform*, Blaho and Švidroň (eds.) *Kodifikácia*, 149 ff.

5. Even if in Slovenia, in Croatia and in Estonia the process of revision and reform does not necessarily aim at the elaboration of a new civil code.

6. For the recodification of civil law in Slovenia see A. Polajnar-Pavčnik, *Neukodifikation des Privatrechts in Slowenien*, Blaho and Švidroň (eds.) *Kodifikácia*, 202 ff. Esp. for the tort law regulation I. Strnad and R. Lampe, *Country Report for the Republic of Slovenia* in H. Koziol and B. C. Steininger, *European Tort Law 2002—Tort and Insurance Law Yearbook* (ECTIL, Wien, 2003) 364 ff.

7. T. Josipovič, *Rekodifizerung des Privatrechts in Kroatien*, Blaho and Švidroň (eds.) Kodifikácia, 222 ff.

8. I. Kull, *Country Report for Estonia* in H. Koziol and B. C. Steininger, *European Tort Law 2004—Tort and Insurance Law Yearbook* (ECTIL, Wien, 2005) 248 ff.

eral tort law regulation.[9] In Lithuania, a new Civil Code was adopted in 2001, which replaced the former Soviet code from 1964.[10]

The overall picture shows that the main source of tort law regulation in the Czech Republic, Slovakia, Hungary, and Poland is still the former socialist civil code, although there is ongoing reform in these countries. In Slovenia, Croatia, Estonia, and Lithuania, a new regulation already came into force. The civil code or the law of obligations in these countries provide only the basic regulation, there are in all of these legal systems special acts and special regulation covering certain areas of tort law.

The social and economic circumstances of the former socialist codification were completely different from those of the market economy. The social and economic environment of civil law regulation and practice has significantly changed with the transition to market economy in the Eastern European countries. The socialist economy was based on central state control; the role of the private economy was negligible. The central control did not postulate free action—neither in economy nor in society. Insurance played almost no role at all; the main source of covering and spreading risks was the state budget. Insurance also had been used as a channel of state aid since insurance for socially sensible risks was subsidized from the state budget paid to the insurer. In Hungary e.g. in the socialist economy, there was only one insurance company. This company was owned by the state and one form of subsidization in the agricultural sector was providing cheap insurance to the producers for high risk events such as ice or storm damage in the plants. These insurance policies were underpriced and the "loss" of the insurance company was covered from the state budget. As another important insurance aspect, in the sixties there were relatively few cars and relatively few accidents. In general, private property was insignificant and—even if certain benefits existed for some people—there weren't great differences between the financial standing of members of the society, which are normally induced in market economy. World

9. The text of the Estonian Law of Obligations (Võlaõigusseadus) has been translated and published in English at www.legaltext.ee by the Estonian Legal Language Centre. The direct references to the relevant provisions of the Estonian Law of Obligations are according to this translation.

10. In the course of the recodification of civil law the new Dutch Civil Code of 1992 and the Civil Code of Quebec of 1991 were especially taken into consideration. See H. Gabartas and M. Laučienė, *Country Report for Lithuania* in H. Koziol and B. C. Steininger, *European Tort Law 2004—Tort and Insurance Law Yearbook* (ECTIL, Wien, 2005) 405 ff. The text of the Civil Code of the Republic of Lithuania has been translated and published in English at www.lrs.lt. The direct references to the relevant provisions of the Civil Code of the Republic of Lithuania are according to this translation.

War II and the post-war changes to society had a serious impact on moral values. As a consequence, we can speak about the crisis of moral values without exaggeration. Christian values had been pushed into the background and appreciation of human life and wealth had been changed fundamentally compared to before World War II. These were not necessarily reflected in the regulation itself but constituted the social milieu for it and influenced court practice, too.

The change of social and economical circumstances was not a quick development but began relatively early. In the sixties and seventies, the general standard of living and—together with that—the financial differences within the society started to increase (mostly as a result of foreign loans which were allotted simply to this aim out of political considerations). The systems became open for some forms of small scale private entrepreneurship. The importance of state activity in the economy slowly started to decrease. The role of insurance also increased and mandatory motor vehicle liability insurance schemes were introduced.

As a significant development—and the consequences of this are yet to be seen in its entirety—the central (budgetary) financed social security system became unsustainable and building a new, privately financed system was unavoidable. The age limit for pension was increased, which influenced the amount of damages awarded, as in the course of assessing damages for personal injuries resulting in disability to work the courts had to assess the relevant period the victim could have spent in work and calculated the compensation (allowance) for lost salary accordingly The boundaries and the scope of free economic activity have been significantly broadened and it became questionable whether cases of professional liability (liability of doctors, lawyers, building designers etc.) could be assessed according to the same standards as before. The demographic changes—the decreasing number of birth since the sixties, which is leading to a general ageing of society—will also have consequences. This progression is tightly connected to changes in social policy.

A common feature of tort law regulation in the Eastern (as well as in Western) European Countries is that one has to take them as systems built upon open rules, which leave a wide power to the courts and allow them to establish and use their proper guidelines in adjudicating tort cases and to adapt the practice to changing social circumstances. Tort law as a law in action is a flexible system[11] where the courts apply complex criteria in the course of decid-

11. As it has been described by Walter Wilburg. See W. Wilburg, *Entwicklung eines beweglichen Systems im Bürgerlichen Recht* (Rede gehalten bei der Inauguration als Rector

ing tort cases and drawing the boundaries of liability. As a result of this flexible system, the fundamental changes in society and economy that brought forth the changes of moral values did not call for the necessity of changes to the basic tort law regulation of the civil codes.

In general, the main aim of legislation is modernizing the existing law, the harmonization of it with the requirements of the European Union community law and the reaction to the challenges created by the new social and economic system as well as by the technical and industrial development. These challenges are the same as those that other modern legal systems have to face. As economy and society are built upon similar legal and moral values in European countries, the problems and possible answers are similar too. However, different traditions and differences in the legal way of thinking mark out different tracks for solutions.

## 2. The Basis of Liability

### *2.1. Functions of Liability*

According to socialist legal theory, liability is the sanction of an unlawful conduct in civil law, which aims at reducing the number of illegal conducts in society by means of persuasion and holding out the prospect of exercising the power of the state in case of illegal actions. From this follows that the main aim of liability—at least as Ioffe and other socialist legal theorists formulated it—was the education of people by sanctioning their wrongful behavior.[12] One must not take this philosophical—or rather ideological—background too seriously, because neither the legislator nor socialist legal theory has drawn far-reaching inferences from this starting point. This approach has led only to emphasizing prevention as the primary goal of tort law and accepting the reparatory (or compensatory) function as the main pillar of the system. It also has been fixed that since the purpose of liability is protecting the existing order of society, socialist and capitalist tort law cannot be the same because of the fundamental differences in the order of society.[13] This approach strongly in-

magnificus der Karl-Franzes Universität in Graz am 22 November 1950, Graz, um 1950.) and *Zusammenspiel der Kräfte im Aufbau des Schuldrechts*, 163 AcP (1964) 364 ff. B. A. Koch, *Wilburg's Flexible System in a Nutshell* in H. Koziol and B. C. Steininger, *European Tort Law 2001—Tort and Insurance Law Yearbook* (ECTIL, Wien, 2002) 545 ff.

12. G. Marton, *A polgári jogi felelősség* (Budapest, 1993) 245 ff.

13. F. Mádl, *A deliktuális felelősség a társadalom és a jog fejlődésének történetében* (Budapest, 1964) 454 ff.

fluenced both theory and practice where these differences presented themselves but—as a result of the flexible system, which did not make such changes necessary—not so obviously the regulation itself.

Generally, socialist legal theory attributed the same main functions to tort law as traditional legal theories do, i.e. providing corrective justice by rendering compensation and prevention. Loss shifting (and loss spreading) and avoiding economically inefficient behavior[14] however, did not appear as functions of tort law, even if it has been widely accepted that tort law has different functions which are to be seen in their complexity. The fundamental changes in social and economic order and also in moral values brought by the switchover to a market economy necessarily influenced theories of tort law too. This tendency seems to be obvious but the theoretical frameworks in the literature have not yet been redrawn.

Along with the approach prevailing in general in continental legal systems, attributing a compensatory role to tort law punitive damages are not accepted in Eastern European legal systems,[15] although there exist specific sanctions of punitive character supporting the general policy of prevention underlying private law regulation too. One of the most significant punitive elements of Eastern European private laws is the public penalty provided as a special punitive sanction of wrongful interference with personality rights or intellectual property rights. Such punitive sanctions are known e.g. to Slovenian, Lithuanian[16] or Hungarian tort law. In Hungary, §84 subpar. (2) of the Hungarian Civil Code provides that if the defendant interfered wrongfully with the plaintiff's personal (or inherent) rights and the sum to be awarded as damages would not be proportionate to the gravity of the wrongfulness of the tortfeasor's conduct, the court may impose a fine on the defendant to be turned to public

14. Gy. Eörsi, *Összehasonlító polgári jog* (Budapest, 1975) 327.

15. E.g. in context of Estonian tort Law K. Sein argues that punitive damages would not only be incompatible with Estonian Constitution but neither is a need for them as wrongful interference with personalty rights may properly be sanctioned with other means of private law (Juridica International 2007, 46 ff.). J. Lahe/I. Kull, *Country Report for Estonia* in H. Koziol and B. C. Steininger, *European Tort Law 2007—Tort and Insurance Law Yearbook* (ECTIL, Wien, 2008) 267 ff.

16. R. Lampe, *The Protection of Personality Rights against Invasions by Mass Media in Slovenia* in H. Koziol and A. Warzilek, *Persönlichkeitsshutz gegenüber Massenmedien/The Protecion of Personality Rights against Invasions by Mass Media* (ECTIL, Wien, 2005) 258. f. There is a special compensation system allowing compensation above the suffered loss also in Lithuania. H. Gabartas and M. Laučienė, *Country Report for Lithuania* in H. Koziol and B. C. Steininger, *European Tort Law 2006—Tort and Insurance Law Yearbook* (ECTIL, Wien, 2007) 328 f.

purpose. The prerequisites of imposing such a public fine on the defendant are wrongful interference with the plaintiff's personal (inherent) rights; according to the general rules of liability (§339 ff. of Hungarian Civil Code), the defendant shall be liable for damages for wrongful interference with the plaintiff's personal rights; and the awarded damages would not be proportionate to the gravity of the wrongfulness of the defendant's conduct. The sum of this public fine shall not be paid to the plaintiff but to the state, and is to be imposed *ex officio*, even in absence of claim for it,[17] and even in absence of claim for damages, too. In a relatively recent decision, the Hungarian Supreme Court established that if the aggrieved party in the court procedure does not make a claim for damages, but the court recognizes that the interference with the plaintiff's personal rights was wrongful and the wrongful interference was unreasonably gross and it cannot be excluded that damages had been awarded in case of submitting a claim for that, the prerequisites of imposing a public fine shall be established as if actually awarded damages had been disproportionate to the gravity of wrongfulness.[18] In the course of preparation of the New Hungarian Civil Code, it has been established—already at the outset—that the public penalty provided in §84 subpar. (2) of the Hungarian Civil Code shall be abolished.[19] The Bill of the New Hungarian Civil Code abandoned the public penalty accordingly, leaving the functions of it to the new indemnity compensation provided as a special sanction of wrongful interference with the other party's personal rights. Moreover, the Bill also suggests that the sanctions of unlawful interference with personal rights shall be amended with a new restitutionary sanction (as a special form of unjust enrichment), allowing the courts to deprive the defendant of the benefit she gained at the "price" of the wrongful interference with the plaintiff's personality rights. According to §2:88 of the Bill of the New Hungarian Civil Code, in case of unlawful interference with the plaintiff's personality rights, the plaintiff shall be entitled to claim to assign to herself the benefit the defendant has gained as a result of the unlawful interference. This restitutionary sanction—modelled after similar solutions for sanctioning unlawful interference with intellectual property rights—shall be applied as an objective (or strict) one, i.e. the plaintiff shall have a claim for restitution even if the defendant was not at fault in the unlawful interference.

---

17. Supreme Court, Legf. Bír. Pfv. IV. 20555/1994. sz.—BH 1995. 395. sz. [BH = Reports of the Hungarian Supreme Court Decisions].

18. Supreme Court, Legf. Bír. Pfv. IV. 20.822/2001. sz.—BH 2003. 150. sz.

19. Principles and Proposals for a New Hungarian Civil Code Part 6, 2.4. (Published as an appendix to the Official Journal of the Hungarian Republic 2002. 15/II).

## *2.2. Liability for Torts and Breach of Contract*

Tort law is, by definition, about liability for violation of duties imposed on persons by law and not by contract. If an obligation is a contractual one, the sanction of violating it is a liability for breach of contract and not a liability in tort. There is a strict and consequent division between delictual (in tort) and contractual liability in theory and structure of civil law. This, however, does not necessarily mean that such a distinction is reflected on the level of regulation too. Moreover, if one explains liability as a civil law sanction of violating a civil law obligation, it seems to be a palpable approach keeping them together and providing a common regulation for them. The question is however, whether the difference arising from the contractual or non-contractual nature of the infringed obligation, i.e. whether the basis of liability is a violation of a voluntary promise or a legal norm (a general obligation to prevent harm or a general prohibition of causing harm to others in the society), and whether the inevitable differences in the underlying policies justify and call for different regulation or not. The legal systems in Eastern Europe are giving different answers to this question.

The Civil Code of Poland does not make a sharp distinction between delictual and contractual liability. There are common provisions for contractual and non-contractual liability, which relate to the compensation as an obligation[20] and also provide special regulation for the concurrent liabilities. Art. 443 of the Polish Civil Code leaves open the application of tort law regulation also to cases of breach of contract. According to this provision, the fact that the tortfeasor's conduct constitutes a breach of contract, does not preclude claims under delictual (tort) liability, unless from the content of the infringed obligation otherwise follows.[21] Although in situations of concurrence of liabilities, the plaintiff has a choice to bring his action either on tort or as a remedy for breach of contract, there is a strong view in Poland that the court may not apply contractual and tortuous regime in a mixed way but the court shall apply the contractual or the tortius system of liability as whole.[22]

Neither in Czech nor Slovakian tort law (where the Civil Code of 1964 is still in force) can be found a sharply marked off division of delictual and contractual liability. These two types of liabilities are distinguished, but the start-

20. Art. 361 (2) and 363 of the KC. Poczobut, *Deliktsrecht Polen*, 11.

21. For translation of the relevant text see Poczobut, *Deliktsrecht Polen*, 60.

22. E. Bagińska, *Country Report for Poland* in H. Koziol and B. C. Steininger, *European Tort Law 2006—Tort and Insurance Law Yearbook* (ECTIL, Wien, 2007) 383.

ing point of the theory is that a sanctionable wrongful conduct comprises illegality, where illegality is violation of a legal obligation, be the obligation established by legal norm or by contract.[23] On the level of the Civil Code there aren't two separate distinguished regimes for delictual and contractual liability: §420 subpar. 1 of the Civil Code 1964 makes the tortfeasor liable for the damage that has been caused with the violation of his legal obligation. However, *some differences between the liability for tort and breach of contract present themselves according to the nature* of the legal relationship. For contracts coming under the application of the Commercial Code, special liability rules are to be applied, as in commercial relationships liability cannot be reduced. *In the Czech Republic there is an attempt to make—in a possible civil law reform—a distinction between contractual and non-contractual liability by shifting the exculpation to the level of strict liability in case of breach of contract.*[24]

In Hungary, the policy underlying tort law regulation of the Civil Code 1959 was to provide a unified system of liability. This idea included the unitary regulation of liability for torts and breach of contract. According to §318 subpar. (1) of the Hungarian Civil Code the rules of delictual (tort) liability are to apply to liability for breach of contract as well, except it is otherwise provided by the law. This solution reinforces the idea of common moral basis of liability—as it is always a breach of an obligation, having the obligation rested on a contractual promise or followed from the law itself—and makes the system a simple one through avoiding borderline problems and the constant necessity of classifications. The difference the Hungarian Civil Code declares [§318 subpar. (1)] is that liability for breach of contract cannot be reduced on equitable ground (which is allowed in case of delictual liability according to §339 subpar. (2)), and there are differences in the preconditions of the validity of exclusion clauses and the liability for third persons as well. The system of the Law of Obligations of the Hungarian Civil Code would allow the concurrence of contractual and non-contractual (tort) liabilities and the court practice also seems to accept this concurrence as the plaintiff is not sealed off from suing in tort even if the defendant's conduct causing harm constitutes a breach of contract. Moreover, since in Hungarian case-law the courts shall not be bound to the title represented by the plaintiff as a ground of his claim, the court would consider—even without request of the parties—the preconditions of tort liability *as well even if the plaintiff has relied only on the*

23. L. Tichý, *Development of Czech Law of Tort*, in H. Koziol and B. C. Steininger, *European Tort Law 2001—Tort and Insurance Law Yearbook* (ECTIL, Wien, 2002) 115.

24. L. Tichý, *Development of Czech Law of Tort*, 119.

*defendant's breach of contract.*[25] The earlier court practice in Hungary was somewhat confusing, since decisions were often based on the basic rule of liability [§339 Hungarian Civil Code] instead of referring to the special rule for contractual liabilities [§318 Hungarian Civil Code] in cases of remedies for breach of contract too. Already at the beginning of the seventies, a tendency towards preferring the contractual basis could be detected[26] and this tendency has developed to a clear standpoint for today. If there is a concurrence of contractual and non-contractual (tort) liability, courts refer to the special rule of liability for breach of contract provided in §318 of the Hungarian Civil Code and decide the case on the basis of contractual liability.[27] One obvious and significant difference has, however, been clearly developed in the court practice and this is the *different measure for exculpation*: in contractual cases courts apply stricter tests in assessing whether the tortfeasor has *acted as it was in the given situation generally expected and allow exculpation* only if the defendant can prove that the harm in the given circumstances was unavoidable. Thus, the level of required standard of conduct in contractual liability is higher than in tort cases.[28] This tendency and the obvious difference between the relationship of the parties in contractual and non-contractual cases involving the need for different *limitation measures* too (such as the foreseeability doctrine for liability for breach of contract) led the Hungarian legislator to *the conviction that the unified system shall be replaced by division of contractual and non-contractual liability, even if they would basically remain congruent with respect to the measure of damages. Regulation on calculation of damages and the way of compensation itself—except the foreseability limit for damages for breach of contract*[29]*—will be the same for liability for torts and for breach of contract in the New Hungarian Civil Code, too.*[30] A remarkable recent development in Hungarian tort law theory is the emergence of the doctrine of protective purpose of the norm in the *professional discussions* on contractual and non-contractual liability. The protective purpose of the norm has not yet been formulated in the Hungarian court practice or legal theory *in the form as it is present in Ger-*

25. A Menyhárd, *A kártérítési jog egyes kérdései* (Polgári Jogi Kodifikáció 2004/1-2.) 47 ff.

26. A. Harmathy, *Felelősség a közreműködőért* (Budapest, 1974) 202.

27. J. Gyevi-Tóth, *A szerződéses és a deliktuális felelősség egymáshoz való viszonya*, in: Jogi Tanulmányok (Budapest, 1997) 178.

28. I. Kemenes, *A gazdasági szerződések követelményei és az új Hungarian Civil Code* (Polgári Jogi Kodifikáció 1/2001) 9 ff.

29. Bill of the New Hungarian Civil Code §5:118.

30. Bill of the New Hungarian Civil Code §5:121 and §5:447 ff.

*man and Austrian legal doctrine.*[31] Professional debates on indirect causation so far have been focusing on the problem of whether the damage suffered by the company can be a ground of a tort claim for the shareholder (member) of the company too, referring to the shareholder's suffered loss in value of the share. Neither these debates nor the court practice reached to the conclusion that the tortfeasor's—mostly contractual—obligations are limited in their scope to protecting the company's interests and should not cover the protection of its shareholders' interests. *An approach is, however, taking shape that if the plaintiff based his tort claim on a conduct constituting a breach of a contractual obligation vis-à-vis him or third persons, the tort claim shall not be decided without deciding the contractual claim. Deciding the claim for damages for breach of contract—i.e. establishing liability for breach of contract—is a necessary preliminary question of the tort claim in such cases and the court has to take into account that the contracting parties are as a main rule privy, that is, a contract creates obligations vis-à-vis the other party but not vis-à-vis anyone.*[32]

Chapter 53 of the Estonian Law of Obligations on liability for unlawfully caused damage establishes a distinction between contractual and non-contractual liability. § 1044 subpar. (2) of the Estonian Law of Obligations explicitly provides that compensation for damage arising from the violation of contractual obligations shall not be claimed on tort bases, unless otherwise provided by law. The main principle behind this distinction seems to be the protective purpose of the norm, as § 1044 subpar. (2) also provides that compensation for damage arising from the violation of contractual obligations may be claimed on tort bases if the objective of the violated contractual obligation was other than to prevent the damage for which compensation is claimed. Art. 6.245 of the Civil Code of Lithuania follows a similar approach in distinguishing contractual and delictual liability as it defines non-contractual (delictual) liability as a pecuniary obligation which is not related with contractual relations, except in cases where it is established by the law that delictual liability shall also result from damage related with contractual relations.

---

31. H. Koziol, *Österreichisches Haftpflichtrecht I* (Wien, 1997) 246 ff.

32. This opinion has been formulated on *professional* discussions and seems to be supported by some unreported decisions of the Hungarian Supreme Court. Á. Fuglinszky and A. Menyhárd, *Felelősség "közvetett" károkozásért*, *Magyar Jog* 5 (2003) 283 ff. In a recent judgement the Supreme Court established that the lawful termination of a contract for loan with the company does not establish the claim of the shareholder for damages *vis-à-vis* the bank terminating the contract for loan. The Supreme Court, however, did not go as far as establishing that shareholders' claims for—indirect—damages on the basis of the damage suffered by the company (e.g. as compensation for loss in value of the shares) are to be excluded *per se*. Supreme Court, Legf. Bír. Gfv. IX. 30.252/2005. sz.—BH 2006. 117. sz.

## *2.3. Structure of Regulation: Basic Norm and Special Forms of Liability*

The structure of tort law regulation in the Eastern European countries presents remarkable similarities even if this structure is the result of traditional method of tort law codification.[33] There is a basic norm of liability as a general rule and there are special forms of liability for different situations, which make the divergence from the general rule necessary or where establishing liability is necessary but would not follow from the general norm.[34] There are, however, differences in shaping the special forms of liability which also may present different trends in the codification and indicate divergences in the way of thinking or in the legal traditions. After discussing the basic rules of liability we will highlight two groups of special forms of liability here: strict liability on the one hand and employers' vicarious liability (as one of the most important forms of liability for damage caused by other persons) on the other hand.

## *2.4. Basic Norm and Preconditions of Liability*

At the heart of tort law in a codified legal system typically lies a basic norm of liability, which determines the general prerequisites to liability and the whole structure of tort law. The basic norm and preconditions of liability provide the most significant characteristics of tort law in codified legal systems. All of the systems in Eastern Europe are fault based regimes and are built on the doctrine of objective fault. This means that according to the basic or general rule of liability the tortfeasor shall be liable if he was at fault in causing the damage. Fault is a concept which transmits objective and general social requirements on the abstract level of a general clause to be standardized and concretized in court practice. Preconditions of liability in general are wrongfully caused damage, fault, and the causation link between the damage and the tortfeasor's conduct. The tortfeasor shall be liable in tort only if the damage has been caused unlawfully. *Limitation of liability, however,* is as much inherent in a tort law system as liability itself. The conclusion that "tort-law is as much about non-liability as it is about liability"[35] holds true also for Eastern European tort laws. The three main aspects of liability providing the general *limi-*

33. The Principles of European Tort Law present the generality of this solution: see European Group on Tort Law: *Principles of European Tort Law—Text and Commentary* (Wien/NewYork, 2005).

34. H. Küpper, *Deliktsrecht in Osteuropa*, OER 2003, 495–541, 500.

35. See e.g. C. von Bar, *Gemeineuropäisches Deliktsrecht* (München, 1999) II. s.2. Fn.1.

*tation measures too* are the concept of fault (accountability), causation, and unlawfulness of damage. From the flexible structure of the tort law regulation follows that the legislator in the most important aspects of liability—i.e. accountability and causation—makes way to the greatest extent to the court practice leaving the consideration of the case in the hand of the judges. That may be true for the unlawfulness requirement as well: the doctrine of protective purpose of the norm, *either in normative form or in theory and practice as well as defining or listing illegal causation of damage serve the purpose of limitation. This possibility seems to be lost in those legal systems which are insisting on the starting point that every damage is unlawful except otherwise provided by the law and aren't open for the doctrine of protective purpose of the norm. From the flexible system also follows that if one tries to seek the limits of liability they also shall be found in the court practice.*

Basic norm of liability in Polish tort law is provided by Art. 415 of Polish Civil Code. According to this basic rule if someone causes harm at fault, he shall be obliged to pay damages. The concept of fault—since it is not defined in the Code—has been elaborated in legal theory and court practice. Fault comprises objective and subjective elements. The objective element of fault is unlawfulness, which may consist of the infringement of a legal norm, the general precautionary principle of refraining from causing damage to others, or norms of social coexistence. Subjective element of fault is deliberateness or negligence of the tortfeasor. Measure is the due care which is an objectivized and abstract requirement, independent from the personal qualities of the tortfeasor.[36] The burden of proof regarding all of the preconditions of liability rests on the victim.[37]

According to §420. subpar (1) of the Civil Code of the Republic of Slovakia, and the same provision in the Czech Republic, the tortfeasor is obliged to compensate damage that has been caused by him through the infringement of a legal duty. The basic legal duty is a duty not to cause harm to others, which is a normative general prevention principle, a requirement provided by §415 of the Civil Code. The tortfeasor may *exculpate himself* from liability by proving that he was not at fault in causing harm to the victim [§420 subpar. (3) both in the Slovakian and Czech Civil Codes]. Negligence of the tortfeasor is presumed with the limit that presumption of fault does not extend to deliberateness.

At the heart of Hungarian tort law regulation there is the basic rule of liability: according to §339 subpar. (1) of Hungarian Civil Code, if someone

36. Poczobut, *Deliktsrecht Polen*, 18.
37. Poczobut, *Deliktsrecht Polen*, 17.

causes harm unlawfully to another person, the tortfeasor shall be obliged to pay damages, unless he proves that he acted *as it was generally expected under the given circumstances of the case. With the special standard of "under the given circumstances generally expected behavior" the Hungarian Civil Code has been enacted under the influence of the theory of fault-based liability with a special objectivized standard putting the basis of accountability somewhere between subjective and objective liability.* The burden of proof regarding damage and causation link between the tortfeasor's conduct and damage as preconditions of liability is allocated to the plaintiff. The burden of proof of being compliant with the generally required standard of conduct (*"under the given circumstances, generally expected behavior"*) i.e. the absence of fault is allocated to the tortfeasor. Unlawfulness of the damage is presumed and the tortfeasor has to prove that in the given situation, causing damage was permitted by the law in order to exempt himself from liability. The Hungarian Civil Code rests on the—implied—theoretical basis that causing harm to others is always unlawful, unless it is otherwise provided by the law. As a general principle, the conduct resulting in damage to others is unlawful and from this follows that causing harm is always unlawful. If the tortfeasor can prove that causing harm in that specific case explicitly and exceptionally was permitted by the law, he shall not be liable.[38] It means that if the victim (the plaintiff) proves that he suffered damage and this was the result of the tortfeasor's (the defendant) conduct, the defendant shall be liable, except if he proves that he acted according to the generally required standard of conduct or if he proves that causing harm in the given situation was lawful.

The basic norm in the Slovenian tort law is fault-based liability with shifted burden of proof, *where under fault intention or negligence shall be understood.* The plaintiff has to prove the unlawful act, the damage, and the causal link between the tortfeasor's conduct and the occurrence of damage. The tortfeasor has to prove that he was not at fault. There is a rebuttable presumption of fault, but the presumption covers only minor negligence (culpa levis), that is, if the *plaintiff's interest is proving the intention or gross negligence of the tortfeasor, it must be proven by the plaintiff.*[39]

Tort law system of the Estonian Law of Obligations is a fault-based liability with rebuttable presumption of fault.[40] A significant difference between the Es-

---

38. Gy. Eörsi, *A polgári jogi kártérítési felelősség kézikönyve* (Budapest, 1966) 221. The defences are such as the consent of the aggrieved person, necessity, the authorized exercise of rights etc.

39. I. Strnad and R. Lampe, *Country Report for Republic of Slovenia 2002*, 367.

40. I. Kull, *Country Report for Estonia 2004*, 250.

tonian legal system and the Polish, Czech, Slovakian, Slovenian, and Hungarian ones is that the Estonian Law of Obligations defines unlawfulness with determining—even if the list is not an exhaustive one—in its § 1045 the protected interests. This is also the basis for providing a special normative interpretation of *unlawfulness in the context of wrongful interference with personality rights, disclosure of incorrect information, giving incorrect expert opinion and halting of economic or professional activities* [§§ 1045 ff.]. According to § 1043 of the Estonian Law of Obligations, the tortfeasor who causes damage unlawfully to another person shall compensate the victim for the damage if the tortfeasor was at fault in causing the damage or otherwise shall be deemed liable for the damage by the law. Unless otherwise provided by law, a tortfeasor shall not liable for the damage if he proves that he was not at fault in causing the damage [§ 1050 subpar. (1)]. The tortfeasor is at fault if he caused the damage with intention or negligence. In this system, the concept of negligence follows —similarly to § 276 of the German BGB—an objective doctrine. The concept of negligence in the Estonian Law of Obligations "stresses an objective standard of care,"[41] even if according to § 1050 subpar. (2) the "situation, age, education, knowledge, abilities and other personal characteristics" of a person as subjective criteria shall be taken into consideration upon assessment of fault.

The Lithuanian Civil Code—just like the Czech and Slovakian ones—establishes a general duty of prevention providing that "every person shall have the duty to abide by the rules of conduct so as not to cause damage to another by his actions or omissions" [Art.6.263. subpar. (1)]. According to Art. 6.248 subpar. (1) of Lithuanian Civil Code, liability shall arise only upon fault, *except if it is otherwise provided by the law or by contract resulting in strict liability.* The tortfeasor's fault shall be presumed, except in cases otherwise provided by the law. Fault is an objective concept also in the Lithuanian tort law. From Art. 6.248 subpar. (3) of Lithuanian Civil Code follows that a person shall be deemed to have committed fault where if he—taking into consideration the essence of the obligation and other circumstances of the case—failed to behave with the care and caution necessary under the given conditions.

# 3. Special Forms of Liability

## *3.1. Strict Liability*

In a continental context the concept of strict liability is far from being clear and this holds in general for Eastern European legal systems as well. There is

41. I. Kull, *Country Report for Estonia 2004*, 250.

not any independent category of torts such *as strict liability* in Eastern European legal systems. If this term is used in relation to these legal systems, the remark, that strict liability is a multifaceted notion, which "may well mean different things to different people in different contexts and in different times"[42] *is really* apt. In the followings one typical form of strict liability, i.e. the liability for especially hazardous activities and one typical form of vicarious liability, i.e. the liability for damages caused by employees shall be dealt with. There are, of course, many other special forms of liability under these headings (liability for people with lack of mental ability, liability for animals, damage caused by buildings or objects thrown out from buildings, liability for nuclear activity, etc.), which are not analyzed here. The reason for this choice is that over and above the basic norm of liability, these two special forms of liability emphasized here may present significant characteristic differences and similarities of legal systems. We address product liability and state liability under separate heading.

Art. 435 of Polish Civil Code provides the basic regulation for strict liability, specifying activities that fall under this heading *as enterprises working with* natural power such as steam, gas, electricity, fluid burn materials, etc., *and allowing exculpation from liability for the holder of the enterprise only in cases of vis maior, or* if the damage has been caused exclusively by the fault of the victim or a third party for whom the defendant shall not be liable. Art. 436 subpar. (1) of Polish Civil Code *extends this strict liability over vehicles powered with natural energy. As vis maior—which is not defined in the* Polish Civil Code *itself—shall be held events which are unavoidable, extraordinary and fall outside the scope of the activity establishing application of strict liability regime.*[43] Legislation has established strict liability for other activities as well, *extending strict liability over cases originally not covered by* Art. 435 and 436. of Polish Civil Code. Such examples are the law of 27 August 1997 on the safety of mass events (sporting events, concerts, etc.) which declares the organizer liable for persons employed by him or the amendment of tort law regulation by the law on the Revision of the Civil Code of 17 June 2004 which established strict liability for unlawful exercise of public authority.[44]

§432 of the Czech Civil Code and the same provision of the Slovakian Civil Code establish strict liability for damage caused by hazardous activity. The hazardous nature of the activity shall be assessed by the courts on the ground of the circumstances of the case. In the course of assessment of the activity all

42. I. Gilead, *On the Justifications of Strict Liability*, in H. Koziol and B. C. Steininger, *European Tort Law 2004—Tort and Insurance Law Yearbook* (ECTIL, Wien, 2005) 29.

43. Poczobut, *Deliktsrecht Polen*, 27.

44. E. Bagińska, *Country Report for Poland* in H. Koziol and B. C. Steininger, *European Tort Law 2004—Tort and Insurance Law Yearbook* (ECTIL, Wien, 2005) 462 ff.

of those circumstances must be taken into account, which make the activity connected with a higher degree of risk of serious damage.[45] In Slovakian legal theory and practice in general activities where technical instruments, things or natural power are used and which cannot be—according to the scientific and technical knowledge and under the given circumstances—fully controlled even by the required due care, shall be deemed hazardous and falling under application of §432 of the Slovakian Civil Code. If the cause of the damage was falling within the scope of *the operation,* the operator carrying out such an activity can exempt himself from liability *only by* proving that the cause of the damage could not have been avoided even with all the expected efforts. There are special provisions for damage caused by motor vehicles (§§432–431 of the Slovakian and the Czech Civil Code). Both in the Czech Republic and in Slovakia there are special forms of statutory strict liabilities—in the Czech Republic the strict liability provided by the State Liability Act of 1998,[46] the liability of the state for damage caused by species of protected animals[47] and both in the Czech and Slovakian Republic §420a of the Civil Code establishing enterprise liability as strict liability for damage caused by the activity of the enterprise. Under this enterprise liability regime, the defendant can exempt itself from liability only by proving that the cause of the damage was falling outside of the scope of the enterprise activity or by proving that the victim himself caused the harm.[48]

In Hungary, §345 of Hungarian Civil Code provides that a person who carries on an activity involving considerable hazards is liable for any damage the activity causes. The operator shall be relieved of liability if he proves that the damage occurred due to an unavoidable cause that fell beyond the scope of the activity involving considerable hazards or resulted from the victim's wrongful conduct. Neither the scope of the considerably hazardous activities nor the carrier or operator of the activity is defined nor are guidelines provided for this in the Hungarian Civil Code. The guidelines for assessment and scope of considerable hazardous nature of the activity and defining the person (the operator) who shall be liable for that activity have been elaborated in court prac-

45. J. Hrádek, *Country Report for the Czech Republic,* in H. Koziol and B. C. Steininger, *European Tort Law 2002—Tort and Insurance Law Yearbook* (ECTIL, Wien, 2003) 130.

46. Act No. 82/1998 Coll. J. Hrádek, *Country Report for the Czech Republic 2002.* 121 ff.

47. J. Hrádek, *Country Report for the Czech Republic,* in H. Koziol and B. C. Steininger, *European Tort Law 2003—Tort and Insurance Law Yearbook* (ECTIL, Wien, 2004) 91.

48. See also the recent Draft of the New Czech Civil Code §. 2425 and §. 2426 (unofficial translation by *J. Hrádek.*)

tice. In the course of qualifying an activity as a considerably hazardous one, the court shall consider all the circumstances of the case. There are activities which under certain circumstances *shall be considered as considerably hazardous one resulting strict liability, while under other circumstances not.* In court practice operation of motor vehicles or industrial machines; chemicals, explosives, acids or other dangerous materials; activities requiring special prevention such as mining, well-digging, etc. are specified as considerably hazardous one triggering the application of strict liability regime. Liability for wild animals and traditional environmental damage are also governed by the regime of strict liability for hazardous activity. Building construction work also can be qualified as extremely hazardous, *while certain activities—such as using household machines, using fire like lighting a cigarette—are regularly not, even if they can really be dangerous. The concept of* extremely hazardous activity establishing the application of this strict liability regime is an open category allowing a wide "playing field" to the courts. Even if there are typical activities belonging to this category, sometimes courts use the openness and abstract nature of this notion simply to allocate the risk as they think fit through establishing strict liability.[49] The person who is the owner, being in the situation to control the activity, or whose direct interest is pursuing the activity (e.g. the landowner who orders chemical vaporization) can be treated as operator of the activity and as such liable under strict liability regime provided in § 345 of Hungarian Civil Code. There is no distinction between holding a dangerous thing and pursuing dangerous activity; holding a dangerous thing can be a dangerous activity falling under application of § 345 of Hungarian Civil Code according to the normal tests. There is not any special form of enterprise liability in Hungarian tort law.

---

49. It is well presented in a recent decision of the Hungarian Supreme Court establishing strict liability of a hospital for an accident that has been caused by flammable material used during surgery. The plaintiff's father underwent a surgery in the defendant's hospital and during surgery the doctors used a special tincture containing alcohol in order to sterilize the skin of the patient. This tincture was flammable. An electrical folding knife had been used for the operation. When the doctors started the operation, this material on the skin of the plaintiff's father caught fire. The plaintiff's father died as a result of the serious injuries he suffered and the plaintiff claimed damages for the death of his father. The Court established that performing the operation in a situation like this using flammable material shall be deemed as an extremely hazardous activity so the liability of the hospital is strict. From this it follows that the hospital, in order to exculpate itself, would have had to prove that the cause of the damage fell outside the scope of the activity and was unavoidable. The proof of required duty of care would not have been sufficient. Supreme Court, Legf. Bír. Pf. III. 25.423/2002. sz.—BH 2005. 251. sz.

*Slovenian tort law provides strict liability for holding a dangerous thing or pursuing a dangerous activity, where the decisive circumstance establishing strict liability is the actual relationship between the thing and possessing it or between the occupier and the activity.* Strict nature of liability means that the possessor of the dangerous thing *or the occupier of the dangerous activity shall be liable* for the damage caused by the thing or activity unless he proves that the cause of the harm was a *vis maior* or the victim's or third person's exclusive act. The defendant shall also not be liable if and in so far as he proves that the cause of the damage was the fault of the victim.[50] Slovenian courts consider all the circumstances of the case in the course of deciding whether the activity or the thing shall be deemed as an especially dangerous one establishing strict liability or not.[51] An important factor of assessment is whether the activity presents a high risk for the life or health of other people.[52]

§§ 1056–1059 of Estonian Law of Obligations provides strict liability for dangerous activities, damage caused by dangerous things and motor vehicles in a more sophisticated and elaborated way then other Eastern European legal systems do. § 1056 provides general rules on liability for damage caused by major source of danger *declaring in its subpar. (1) that if damage has been caused as a result of danger being characteristic to a thing and constituting* a major source of danger or from an extremely dangerous activity, the person who manages the source of danger shall be liable regardless of the person's *culpability.* In § 1056 subpar. (2), of Estonian Law of Obligations the Estonian legislator—going further than other systems do—gives normative guidelines for the courts in assessing the dangerous nature of the thing or activity, providing that a thing or an activity is deemed to be a major source of danger if, due to its nature or to the substances or means used in connection with the thing or activity, major or frequent damage may arise therefrom even if it is handled or performed with due diligence by a specialist. Moreover, if liability for causing damage by means of a source of danger is prescribed by law, any thing or activity similar to such source of danger is also deemed to be a source of danger, regardless of whether the person who manages the source of danger was

50. I. Strnad and R. Lampe, *Country Report for Republic of Slovenia 2002*, 368.

51. E.g. a switchgear could be qualified as especially dangerous depending on the height of it. R. Lampe, *Country Report for the Republic of Slovenia* in H. Koziol and B. C. Steininger, *European Tort Law 2004—Tort and Insurance Law Yearbook* (ECTIL, Wien, 2005) 529 Nr. 26.

52. R. Lampe, *Country Report for the Republic of Slovenia* in H. Koziol and B. C. Steininger, *European Tort Law 2003—Tort and Insurance Law Yearbook* (ECTIL, Wien, 2004) 378 ff.

at fault *or not*. §§ 1057 ff. provide special rules for liability of possessor of motor vehicle and the liability of owner of dangerous structures or things.

In Lithuania, Art. 6.270 of the Civil Code provides for special form of liability arising from the exercise of hazardous activities. Art. 6.270 subpar. 1 provides a special form of strict liability for persons whose activity is connected with potential hazards for other persons (operation of motor vehicles, machinery, electric or atomic energy, use of explosive or poisonous materials, activities in the sphere of construction, etc.). Such a person as operator shall be liable for compensating the damage caused by the operation of the potentially hazardous objects constituting a special danger for surrounding persons, unless he proves that the damage was caused by *superior* force or it occurred due to the aggrieved person's actions exercised either intentionally or by the latter's own gross negligence.

### *3.2. Employers' Vicarious Liability*

Basic forms of vicarious liability are the liability of employer for the employee and the liability for mentally incapable persons. An important feature of this form of liability is that it is a liability for others' conduct where the link between the liable person and the actual tortfeasor is established by the law: the liable person shall not become obligor because of his own conduct but because of the legal norm providing it. In this sense this liability is also a strict one. Here we put the emphasis on the liability of employers because this form of vicarious liability may present significant convergences and divergences of legal systems providing a ground for drawing further conclusions.

The principle of "*respondeat superior*" itself is a very old one and goes back to the ancient idea of criminal and civil law liability that the household and its head, the *pater familias* shall be liable for delicts committed by persons belonging to the household community (such as wife, children and others). The basic principle (as form) has been remained and adapted to the always developing economic and social circumstances with different importance and often with different ideas behind it. Liability of the master for torts committed by his servants (as servants) was always treated as just and socially necessary.[53] The roots of the liability of the employers for the employees may be traced back to this ancient principle, but—as it stands now in modern private law systems—is a result of a relatively new development. The employers' liability for damages caused by their employees in the course of their employment is

53. E. von Caemmerer, *Reformprobleme der Haftung für Hilfspersonen* (in *Gesammelte Schriften III.*, hrsg. von Hans G. Leser, Tübingen, 1983) 286.

the result of the dominance of business entities and the complex and well organized system of producing and providing services which is the result of the division of labour and which is based on using services of other persons for one's own economic interests.[54] The special form of liability of employers for the delicts of employees committed in the course of employment is an inherent principle of modern private law systems but—presumably because of the partly different underlying policies—there are remarkable differences in some aspects of the rule. The regulation is a result of collisions and compromises of different policies. Risk allocation, in general, is one of the main traditional policies for vicarious liability; at the heart of this risk allocation aspect is the understanding that the employer benefits from the servant's work and that is why the law should shift the risk of the employee's activity upon him. The employer or master extends his own activity through employing others, so he has to bear the risk of damage caused by the employees in the course of their activity for the employer. A further argument for employer's vicarious liability is that the employer may and should internalize the risk of the activity of his employees; he can calculate the costs of this risk into his normal costs of business activity and is able to optimalize the risk avoidance costs by insuring against the risk.[55] An important feature of employer's vicarious liability is whether the regulation makes the employer and the employee joint and severally liable or it shifts the liability only to the employer.

The basic problem of codification is how to define normatively the relationship between the actual tortfeasor and the liable person, establishing liability of the latter. At the heart of this special form of vicarious liability lies a qualification problem drawing the doctrinal limits of this form of vicarious liability too, *that is, who shall be deemed as employee.* The very important distinction between employee and independent contractor cannot be assessed in the relevant cases on the basis of a rigid definition. It would necessarily lead to an insensitive practice being unable to reflect the underlying policies of vicarious liability, if distinction between employee and independent contractor was a direct result of qualification of the contract between the employer and the person causing the harm actually.

Codification in Poland followed a way of making difference between liability for self-employed persons acting as agent of the employer and liability for employees acting under labour law relationship for the employer. In the former case (liability for agents) the employer may exempt himself from lia-

---

54. B.S. Markesinis, *The German Law of Obligations Vol II.* (2nd ed.Oxford, 1997,) 677.
55. Von Caemmerer, *Reformprobleme der Haftung für Hilfspersonen* 290.

bility with proving either that in choosing the agent he acted in compliance with the generally required duty of care (i.e. there is not *culpa in eligendo*) or that the chosen agent was an enterprise or an establishment undertaking the agency within the scope of its business activity (Art. 429 of Polish Civil Code). In the latter case (acting under labour law relationship) the employer shall be liable for the employee even in absence of *culpa in eligendo*: liability of the employee is a necessary and sufficient precondition of employer's liability and the employer shall be liable even if in the course of choosing the employee he acted according to the generally required duty of care (Art. 430 of Polish Civil Code). Absence of *culpa in eligendo* does not relieve the employer of liability. The underlying policy of employer's strict liability for the damage caused by the employee wrongfully in case of employment relationship is providing proper risk allocation. The basis of liability is the control over the employee, where the employee is obliged to act according to the instructions of employer due to a hierarchical relationship.[56] The Polish solution makes the employer and the employee as multiple tortfeasors joint and severally liable for the damage caused by the employee according to Art. 441 of Polish Civil Code; the employee is liable on the ground of the general rules, the employer on the ground of Art. 430 of Polish Civil Code.[57] An interesting feature of employer's vicarious liability is that the employer's liability puts liability for medical malpractice into a special context and this has been recognized in Polish court practice too. The hospital as employer is liable for doctors and other personnel who are employees of the hospital under vicarious liability, but not for the independent contractors. In fact, more and more physicians are being employed as independent contractor, working in team with the hospital's employees and making difference between them from the point of view of the vicarious liability of the hospital seems to be very questionable. In Poland, the solution has been suggested that the hospital should be liable for those physicians who are employed by the hospital even if they are not in a labour employment relationship with the hospital if they are financed by the National Health Fund. Physicians, however, providing services for the hospital as independent entrepreneurs should not be regarded as servants and for their wrongdoing the hospital shall not be liable.[58]

The Hungarian Civil Code applies a similar distinction between liability for the agent and liability for the employee. The principal shall be liable joint and

---

56. Poczobut, *Deliktsrecht Polen*, 21.
57. Poczobut, *Deliktsrecht Polen*, 22.
58. E. Bagińska, *Country Report for Poland 2004*, 473 ff.

severally with his agent for any damage caused to a third person by the agent in this capacity. Except strict liability regime for especially dangerous activites the principal shall be relieved of liability by proving that in choosing, instructing, and supervising his agent he acted *in compliance with the standard of generally required duty of care* (i.e. if *culpa in eligendo* shall not be established). In case of permanent agency or if both the principal and the agent are economic organizations, the court may apply the regime of employers' vicarious liability *in the relationship of the victim and the principal* (§ 350 Hungarian Civil Code). According to § 348 of Hungarian Civil Code, if an employee causes damage to a third person in the scope of his employment, the employer shall bear liability *vis-à-vis* the injured person unless it is otherwise provided by law. The underlying policy of this solution in the Hungarian Civil Code has been the idea that the agent and the employee are primarily acting in the interest of the employer. The basis of the difference between the employer—employee and the principal—agent relationship (which is a question of legal qualification of the legal relationship according to its content) is the permanent character of employment relationship and the normally incidental one of agency. That is why the Hungarian Civil Code provides the possibility to apply the rules of employers' liability to the cases where agency has a permanent character. The Motives to the Draft of the Civil Code emphasize that the damage caused by employee shall be treated as if it would have been caused by the enterprise (the employer) itself. According to this reasoning, the acts of the employee shall be attributed to the corporate entity (the employer) itself. In Hungarian court practice, the decisive factor is the qualification of the contractual relationship between the employer and the employee. The qualification is based on the normal tests of drawing the line between contracts for work on goods, agency and employment (labour) contract. *The main bordering factors are the right and degree of control and instructions, the ownership of the means that are necessary to pursue the given activity, the management of work and the way of pricing or remuneration.* As a main rule, employee is only the party to an employment—i.e. labour—contract. If the parties are principal and agent, § 350 of the Hungarian Civil Code is applicable (which means joint and several liability of principal and agent). An independent contractor shall not be treated as employee and there is not any special form of vicarious liability to be applied. There are cases where the courts extended the application of § 348 of the Hungarian Civil Code to contractual relationships that have not been qualified as contract for employment[59] but it seems that in absence

59. Supreme Court, Legf. Bír. Pf. III. 20 854/1990. sz.—BH 1991 314. sz.

of contractual relationship one cannot be held as employer of another person. § 348 of the Hungarian Civil Code requires that the employee shall act within the scope of his employment in order to establish the employer's vicarious liability. This formulation is relatively wide. If, for instance, an employee exceeds his authorization and without the right to act in the name of his employer, as a false procurator, creates false documents, orders goods and this way causes harm to the buyer, the employer shall be vicariously liable *vis-à-vis* the other party with whom the contract could not have been concluded (*but the other party acted as if the contract had been concluded knowing nothing about the false representation*).[60] If a doctor, on the other hand, during his holiday was acting outside the territory of his practice without remuneration, his employer is not vicariously liable because the doctor's activity would not fall within the scope of the employment.[61] The underlying policy of employer's vicarious liability regime in Hungarian tort law was the social risk allocation function of employer's vicarious liability. Under this regime (provided by Hungarian tort law) the injured party may have a claim against the employer only[62] and the employer may seek indemnity according to the rules of labour law which limit very strongly the liability of the employee (the maximum of one and half or three month salary). Only the employer is liable, and he may seek only a very limited recovery from the employee; the regime does not simply *extend the funds for compensating the victim's loss* but provides protection to the employee too by allowing only a limited counter-claim according to labour law liability rules.

According to Art, 147 of the Slovenian Code of Obligations, under employer's vicarious liability regime, the liability of the employee establishes the employer's liability The system of employer's vicarious liability as a main rule provides—like in the Hungarian and unlike in the Polish tort law—protection for the employee but if the employee caused the damage intentionally or with gross negligence, he remains fully liable for damages *vis-à-vis the employer*.[63]

The Estonian Law of Obligations attempts to provide a flexible formulation of employer's vicarious liability. Its § 1054 subpar. (1) provides that if someone engages another on a regular basis within the scope of his economic or professional activity, he shall be liable for any damage unlawfully caused by the employed person if the employed person shall be held liable according to the general rules of liability, and the wrongful conduct of the employed per-

60. Supreme Court, Legf Bír. Gf. I. 31 500/1993. sz. BH 1994–96. sz.
61. Supreme Court, Legf. Bír. Pf. V. 20.063/1995. sz. BH 1996–89. sz.
62. Eörsi, *A kártérítési felelősség kézikönyve* 299.
63. I. Strnad/R. Lampe, *Country Report for Republic of Slovenia 2002*, 367.

son falls within the scope of the economic or professional activity. This definition of the relationship establishing vicarious liability is close to the German one and tries to avoid the bordering problems those legal systems—such as the Hungarian one—have to confront with which make the liability depending on the qualification of the legal relationship between the actual tortfeasor and person held liable for it. The Lithuanian Civil Code attempts to provide a relatively elaborated norm for the employer's liability providing normative guidelines for the assessment of the relationship establishing employer's vicarious liability. According to Art. 6.264 subpar. (1) and (2) the employer shall be liable for the damage caused wrongfully by its employees in the course of performing their service (official) duties, where persons exercising their functions on the ground of a labour or civil law contract and acting under the supervision or in accordance with the orders of the corresponding legal or natural person are considered as being employees. The Lithuanian Civil Code does not provide protection to the employee. Art. 6.264 subpar. (3) provides that the employer and the employee shall be joint and severally liable for damages and the employee shall be liable *vis-à-vis* the employer exclusively in case of intention or negligence.

### *3.3. Product Liability*

Producer's liability for compensating damage caused by defective products as a subject of special regulation is the result of the impact of European Community legislation. Eastern European countries being members of the EU have been obliged to implement the Council Directive 85/374/EEC of 25 July 1985 (Product Liability Directive). Before the implementation, product liability, cases were governed by general tort law regulation and practice. The aim of product liability regime is to give better protection to the victim against the manufacturer. Traditional tort law theory, doctrine, and regulation made claiming damages for persons who were not contracting parties very difficult and fault-based liability provided neither for producers nor for consumers a predictable regime. Product liability makes the victim's position better in two main ways: it allows the claims of victims not being contracting parties and makes the producer's liability strict. Product liability might not introduce revolutionary changes in tort laws being able to provide these two advantages without implementing such a special form of liability. The interpretation of the European Court of Justice for the Product Liability Directive in 2002 in three decisions made it clear that the Directive—in contrast with the character of consumer protection directives providing only minimum requirements—does provide a regime from which the legislator cannot deviate, not even with providing a more advantageous system to the victims.[64] Thus, the Product Liability Directive shall not be held as a minimum but a maximum legislation. The impact of this interpretation cannot yet be seen in the Eastern European countries' tort law regulation and practice.

In Poland, the Product Liability Directive has been implemented with the Act of 2 March 2000 on The Protection of Some Consumer Rights and Products Liability, which amended the Civil Code with the new Artt. 449.1-449.11 under the heading "Damage Caused by Dangerous Products." Until this new regulation came into force on 1 July 2000, product liability cases have been decided under the fault-based liability regime of Art. 415 of Polish Civil Code. The impact of the implementation in Poland is not yet clear but it seems that it did not bring revolutionary changes to Polish tort law and in certain aspects it is not more favorable for the victim than the old regime. As Polish authors stress it, under the new product liability regulation the producer may plea successfully as a defense that the product conformed to the compulsory technical standards set by the appropriate state agency as binding law and the victim may only question the level of the legal standards as obsolete and not meeting the "ordinary consumer expectation test."[65] Concerning a case where the plaintiff sued the car dealer for damages because of a *disfunctionally* exploded airbag, a Polish commentator reckoned that the dealer's liability might have been occasionally stricter than the producer's because he might not make use of defenses available such as the development risk defense.[66]

Product liability regime had been introduced in the Czech tort law as well under the influence of the EC product liability legislation in 1998 with the Product Liability Statute No. 59/1998 Coll. and has been amended in 2000 in order to bring it in line with the EC Product Liability Directive. Product liability is a strict liability in the Czech legal system too. Since product liability regulation is relatively new in the Czech Republic, there aren't any experiences yet which would allow drawing consequences on its impact on Czech tort law theory and practice.[67] In the Slovak Republic, product liability regime has been

64. ECJ 25 April 2002—C-183/00 *Maria Victoria González Sánchez v. Medicina Asturiana SA* [2002] ECR I-3901; ECJ 25 April 2002—C-52/00 *EC Commission v. French Republic* [2002] ECR I-3827; and ECJ 25 April 2002—C-154/00 *EC Commission v. Hellenic Republic* [2002] ECR I-3879. See for more detailed comments Bernhard A. Koch, *Report on European Union* in H. Koziol and B. C. Steininger, *European Tort Law 2002—Tort and Insurance Law Yearbook* (ECTIL, Wien, 2003) 448 ff.

65. E. Bagińska, *Country Report for Poland 2001* 388.

66. E. Bagińska, *Country Report for Poland 2001* 390.

67. B. Klein/K. Knuschke/M. Dolecek, *Country Report for Czech Republic* in Gregory L. Fowler, International Product Liability Law (Aspatore Books 2003)170.

introduced with the Product Liability Act No. 294/1999 Coll. which came into effect on 1 December 1999. The basis of this regulation is also the EC Product Liability Directive; the aim of the legislation was harmonizing the Slovak law with the Directive. Lawyers in Slovakia consider this new regulation as making the position of the victim more favorable, as he may „as an alternative to the general liability rules, choose to sue the tortfeasor in product liability regime on the ground of strict liability.[68] In the light of the interpretation of the Directive given by the European Court of Justice and holding the Directive as providing a maximum protection it is very questionable whether such solutions—i.e. handling product liability as an alternative regime—are compatible with European law.

In Hungary, the Product Liability Directive has been implemented by the Act X of 1993 on Product Liability. The implementation of the Directive does not seem having impact on the Hungarian tort law at all. Although the Product Liability Act *implementing the Directive has been in force for more than ten years now, there has not been developed any practice yet to be analyzed.*There are only two reported decisions of the Hungarian Supreme Court[69] regarding the application of the provisions of the Product Liability Act and they deal only with marginal problems. It seems *as if the Hungarian legal practice would not have found for itself the product liability regulation in tort law.* One reason for that may be that the implementation *did not bring revolutionary changes* either to the Hungarian tort law which has been built on the flexible system of abstract and open rules. Court practice could reach the same result through the application of general tort law regulation. It may be best presented by a Supreme Court decision from 1993 (before enacting the Product Liability Act). A child wanted to buy hydrochloric acid in a shop at the request of her mother. Because of a defect in the bottle, the acid splashed onto her face and made her blind. Thc claimant sucd thc shop and the assumed manufacturer. The Court rejected the claim against the manufacturer because it turned out that the shop had bought hydrochloric acid from two manufacturers and it was impossible to decide which one of the two manufacturers had produced the defective product. The Court found the shop liable on the ground of liability for extremely hazardous activities (§ 345 of Hungarian Civil Code) and established the strict liability of the shop. If the shop as seller could have proved which

68. A. Blaha/P. Erben/P. Jurek/K. Hatapka/T. Kozovsky, *Country Report for Slovak Republic* in Gregory L. Fowler, International Product Liability Law (Aspatore Books 2003) 715 f.

69. Supreme Court, Legf. Bír. Pfv. VI. 23.641/1998. sz.—BH 2000. 350. sz. and Supreme Court, Legf. Bír. V. Pfv. VII. 20.620/2004. sz.—BH 2005 354. sz.

manufacturer produced the product, the manufacturer had been held liable. The Court should reach the same result under the Product Liability Act of 1993.[70]

The Republic of Slovenia implemented the Product Liability Directive as a primarily strict liability regime in 1998 as incorporated into the Consumers Protection Act and this regulation remained unchanged with the enactment of the new Slovenian Code of Obligations.[71] The regulation is in line with the EC product liability legislation and the impact of the regulation on tort law is yet to be seen.

In Estonia, the product liability regulation is incorporated into the Law of Obligations Act [§§ 1061 ff.] with the aim of implementing the Product Liability Directive and providing additional alternative mechanism to the consumers to bring them in a more favorable position. Product liability is strict in Estonia too.[72] Also in Lithuania, the product liability regime incorporated into the Civil Code is the result of implementation of the Product Liability Directive. Artt. 6.292 ff. on the liability of a producer and a supplier of services are covering product liability cases. Liability of the producer is strict, exemptions from liability in Art. 6.298 are designed according to the Directive. The burden of proof has been provided in Art. 6.295, according to which damage shall be compensated if the aggrieved person proves the occurrence of damage, existence of defect in the product (service) and the causal link between the defect and the damage.

### 3.4. Public Liability

Public liability in general, and especially the liability of the state, is perhaps the most sensitive tort law problem in the former socialist countries, both in contract and in tort. The double role of the state in the market economy as a private player in the market and as the possessor of the public power is inevitable and these two roles seem to be incompatible. The questions of whether the state can be liable for harms caused by legislation or whether the state as contracting partner is bound by the contract if the obligations interfere with public law regulation are very hard to answer. The basic problem here seems to be setting the boundaries of state immunity. The former view, that natural and legal persons are simply subjects who are obliged to obey the order of

---

70. Supreme Court, Legf. Bír. Pf. III. 21 046/1992. sz.—BH 1993. 678. sz.

71. I. Strnad/R. Lampe, *Country Report for Republic of Slovenia 2002*, 371.

72. A. Tark/P. Luiga, *Country Report for Estonia* in Gregory L. Fowler, International Product Liability Law (Aspatore Books 2003) 207.

the state, is clearly untenable in a market economy and under the rule of law that requires the state to face the consequences of its act and which makes the state responsible not only *vis-à-vis* the society as a whole, but towards natural and legal persons as individuals, as well. This approach cannot ignore that the state as legislator has the power to provide the objective and subjective law and set its limits. State, on the other hand, has several authorities and institutions which are involved in acquiring and enforcing rights of the persons. In this wide context, a very important task of the legislation—court practice and theory—is to draw the limits of state immunity without depriving the state of its public function. Increasing number of public liability cases is a tendency which may have two parallel phenomena behind it: demand for depriving the state of its privileges in civil law relationships on the one hand, and the claim for more protection[73] and avoidance of self-responsibility on the other hand.[74] One of the most significant developments of the last decade in the Eastern European countries is the recognition of this problem and the attempts to provide legislative and theoretical answers to it. There are significant differences between legal systems about how far the legislator could go in providing such a regulation for state liability being held as still compatible with the requirements of market economy and the rule of law. The tendency is to provide public liability on a strict basis as a special form of liability instead of taking it as a form of vicarious liability: the Polish, Czech, Slovak, Estonian, and Lithuanian legislator has been moving clearly in this direction, while in Hungary, the traditional form of vicarious liability for public liability is still in force and the New Hungarian Civil Code would not bring significant changes to this approach.

Liability of the state in tort seems to be one of the *most current problems* of Hungarian tort law theory and practice. Problems of state liability today in Hungary shall also be assessed from the perspective of liability of the state for failing to enforce human rights and failing to implement EU legislation and these perspectives are new. Discussions on state liability had got new impulses in recent years. It seems that the arguments of the courts as they reject claims against the state for damages from improper legislation will be revisited and a new doctrine of state immunity should be outlined. Hungarian theory seems to accept the possibility of a new form of liability established by the ECJ practice and there is a strong argument for that liability of the state in tort for leg-

73. H. Koziol, *Comparative Remarks* in H. Koziol and B. C. Steininger, *European Tort Law 2001—Tort and Insurance Law Yearbook* (ECTIL, Wien, 2002) 522.

74. B. A. Koch, *Comparative Remarks* in H. Koziol and B. C. Steininger, *European Tort Law 2002—Tort and Insurance Law Yearbook* (ECTIL, Wien, 2003) 525.

islation and state liability for failure of implementing European legislation shall be assessed together and shall be brought under the same theoretical approach. Discussions about the role of the state in private law relationships got also new impulses from an important decision of the Hungarian Supreme Court and the debate following this decision, where the Court declared that the Hungarian State shall not be unconditionally bound to a contract where the performance of the obligation was depending on administrative decisions and legislation. It meant that if the state undertakes a long term obligation for providing financial support to a project, the enforceability of the obligation of the state is always depending on administrative decision of Parliament on passing the yearly budget containing the financial coverage for the contribution of the state. This approach concerning the state as subject of private law relationships surely has important implications and consequences for the state liability in tort but these are yet to be considered. Today the original regulation of Civil Code is in force, which provides regulation for public liability under vicarious liability. *Liability for damage caused within the jurisdiction of government administration shall be established only if common legal remedies cannot abate the damage or the aggrieved person resorts to the ordinary legal remedies in order to avoid damage.* Unless otherwise provided by regulation, these provisions shall also be applied to liability for damage caused by judges and public prosecutors within their official activity [§349 of Hungarian Civil Code]. Neither this approach nor the system seems to be changed in the New Hungarian Civil Code. The §§5:524–5:526 of the Bill specify three cases of liability for exercising public power including liability for improper decision making in the course of exercising executive power, liability for failure of judges and public prosecutors and liability for unfair or unreasonably slow court procedure. This form of liability is a fault-based one and is limited to exercising executive power. Hungarian court practice rejects the claims for damages against legislative bodies and refuses to establish liability for improper legislation.[75]

In the Czech Republic, the Act No. 82/1998 Coll. (State Liability Act) provides regulation of public liability for misadministration and unlawful decision-making. The State Liability Act as *lex specialis* to the Civil Code establishes strict liability for damage caused by administration activities of the state and of local authorities. A decision of the Czech Constitutional Court established that liability of the state for misadministration, wrongful court decisions or wrongful decisions of local authorities *is strict, without the possibility of exoneration.* The State Liability Act limits the representative power

75. Supreme Court, Legf. Bír. Pf. V. 24.375/1998. sz.—BH 2002. 264. sz.

of the state and that of the local authorities.[76] Similar legislation came into force in Slovakia in July 2004 [Act 514/2003]. The Estonian legislation also went relatively far in regulating state liability. The Estonian State Liability Act of May 2001 establishes strict liability for compensating actual damage and costs caused by wrongful decisions of government authorities and failure to comply with a statutory duty to act *(including making a decision)* within the statutory limit.[77] Provisions of the Lithuanian Civil Code cover liability for compensation of damage caused by wrongful acts of institutions of public authority and liability for damage caused by wrongful acts of preliminary investigation officials, prosecutors and judges [Art. 6.271 and Art. 6.272]. Liability is strict, as Art. 6.271 subpar. (1) provides that damage caused by wrongful acts of institutions of public authority must be compensated by the state from the means of the state budget, irrespective of the fault of a concrete public servant or other employee of public authority institutions. Damage caused by wrongful acts of municipal authority institutions must be redressed by the municipality from its own budget, irrespective of its employee's fault.

Liability of the state and municipial authorities for unlawful arrest or imprisonment and for failure in executing court decisions or decisions of public authorities,[78] as well as liability for improper decisions of administrative bodies,[79] seems to be generally accepted.

## 4. Non-Pecuniary Damages

Traditional concept of damage covers actual harm, loss of income and costs of restoring the state as it was before the damage. All of the Eastern European legal systems take as starting point this traditional concept of damage. The development which extended the concept of damage to non-pecuniary loss (immaterial harm or damage) is common as well. In Hungarian legal

---

76. J. Hrádek, *Country Report for the Czech Republic 2002*, 121 sk.

77. I. Kull, *Country Report for Estonia 2004*, 251 ff.

78. J. Hrádek, *Country Report for the Czech Republic*, in H. Koziol and B. C. Steininger, *European Tort Law 2005—Tort and Insurance Law Yearbook* (ECTIL, Wien, 2006), 197 ff, 205 ff., Hungarian Supreme Court, Legf. Bír. Pfv. VI. 22.288/2004. sz.—BH 2005. 430. sz.

79. E.g. E. Bagińska, *Country Report for Poland* in H. Koziol and B. C. Steininger, *European Tort Law 2003—Tort and Insurance Law Yearbook* (ECTIL, Wien, 2004) 7 ff., 30 ff. J. Hrádek, *Country Report for the Czech Republic*, in H. Koziol and B. C. Steininger, *European Tort Law 2007—Tort and Insurance Law Yearbook* (ECTIL, Wien, 2008) 213 ff.

theory, however, there are strong arguments that in context of non-pecuniary damages one cannot speak of damage in the traditional sense of this word. The theoretical starting point of this idea—followed by the courts as well[80]—is that awarding non-pecuniary damages is a special sanction for wrongful interference with others' personality rights. That is why in the context of non-pecuniary damages the damage as a precondition of liability is replaced with the fact of wrongful interference with personality rights of the victim and the aggrieved person shall be entitled for awarding non-pecuniary damages without proving any actual harm, costs or loss in the traditional sense of the word.[81]

There is an obvious extensive tendency toward recognizing immaterial or moral harms as compensable loss and awarding compensation for them,[82] which is also strongly influenced by the growing impact of human rights.[83] Problems the courts have to face with, in general, are the same as in other European legal systems: setting the limits on non-pecuniary damages, cases of wrongful death, wrongful birth, wrongful life, claims of relatives of the dead person, assessment of the damages etc. The Czech and Slovakian legislation[84] and the Hungarian and Slovenian[85] legal theory and court practice explicitly define non-pecuniary damages as a special sanction of wrongful interference with the inherent rights of another person. In Hungary, this approach is so strong that one of the great reforms of the New Hungarian Civil Code in the field of tort law would be the abolition of non-pecuniary damages and replacing it with the *special consequence of payment of indemnity compensation* (Schmerzensgeld). This indemnity would be able to provide the necessary compensation in case of personal injury or other wrongful interference with personality rights relieving the victim from the special preconditions and burden of proof concerning damage that would come from application of liabil-

80. Supreme Court, Legf. Bír. Pf. III. 26.339/2001. sz.—EBH 2003. 941. sz. [EBH = Official Collection of the Decisions of the Supreme Court of the Republic of Hungary. Decisions published in this collection are selected and highlighted decisions of the Hungarian Supreme Court.]

81. T. Lábady, *A nem vagyoni kártérítés újabb bírói gyakorlata* (Budapest, 1992) 31. and F. Petrik, *Kártérítési jog* (Budapest, 2002) 74.

82. See e.g. the amendments to the Latvian Civil Code in 2006. A. Bitāns, *Country Report for Latvia*, in H. Koziol and B. C. Steininger, *European Tort Law 2006—Tort and Insurance Law Yearbook* (ECTIL, Wien, 2007) 311 ff.

83. B. A. Koch, *Comparative Overview* in H. Koziol and B. C. Steininger, *European Tort Law 2005—Tort and Insurance Law Yearbook* (ECTIL, Wien, 2006) 606 ff.

84. § 1 ff. of the Czech and the Slovakian Civil Code.

85. I. Strnad and R. Lampe, *Country Report for Slovenia 2002*, 367.

ity rules. *In introducing this new sanction, preserving non-pecuniary damages as parallel consequence could be disturbing and seems to be superfluous.*[86] The great question is, however, whether the assumption of the legislator (i.e. that courts award non-pecuniary damages in cases of wrongful interference with personality rights only and that this direct compensation could replace non-pecuniary damages) is correct. There is already one important exception from the doctrine that non-pecuniary damages are specific sanctions of wrongful interference with personality rights: in case of breach of travel contracts, the disappointed victim may claim non-pecuniary damages *even in absence of proving* wrongful interference with his personal rights. In a decision from 1998, the Hungarian Supreme Court awarded non-pecuniary damages to the plaintiff on the ground that the defendant travel agency failed to inform the plaintiff about the difficult conditions of approaching the rented resort house lying upon a hill, far from the village. The Court found that, since the plaintiff could not spend his holiday in a quiet place as he contracted for with the travel agency, he lost his possibility for recreation and lost the holiday experiences as well as the entertainment and relaxation of a holiday abroad.[87] This also shows that the Hungarian Court practice is in line with the ECJ's one, as established in the Leitner-case.[88]

As far as the assessment of amount of damages is concerned, the general approach is that the courts have to consider all the circumstances of the case.[89] Courts try to consider the general living conditions in the society[90] *and the ability of the society to bear the costs of awarded non-pecuniary damages as well. This may result in relatively low level of damages which is very problematic not only concerning certain groups of society but also in cases where the victim is a member of a society where the level of damages—as well as the general living conditions—are higher. This may cause tension on European level too.*

---

86. This assumption may prove to be false. A. Menyhárd, *Country Report for Hungary* in H. Koziol and B. C. Steininger, *European Tort Law 2004—Tort and Insurance Law Yearbook* (ECTIL, Wien, 2005) 349 ff. and 356 ff. For the explicit critic of this solution see F. Petrik, *A nem vagyoni kár megtérítése védelmében*, Polgári Jogi Kodifikáció, 2003/2 6 ff.

87. Supreme Court, Legf. Bír. Pfv. VIII. 23.243/1996. sz.—BH 1998. 278. sz.

88. ECJ preliminary ruling 12 March 2002, in case C-168/00 *Simone Leitner* v. *TUI Deutschland GmbH & Co. KG.*

89. M. Nesterowicz and E. Bagińska, *Country Report for Poland* in W.V. Horton Rogers, *Damages for Non-Pecuniary Loss in a Comparative Perspective* (Wien/New York, 2001) 176. A. Dulak, *Country Report for Slovakia* in H. Koziol and B. C. Steininger, *European Tort Law 2004—Tort and Insurance Law Yearbook* (ECTIL, Wien, 2005) 518 f.

90. Eg. M.Nesterowicz and E. Bagińska, *Damages for Non-Pecuniary Loss Country Report for Poland* 177.

The general tendency seems to be that even if courts in Eastern Europe are giving similar answers and seeming to present the same uncertainties regarding the current basic problems emerging in practice just like the *courts in Western Europe do*, there may be great differences in the approach and sometimes one cannot speak of well settled court practice but *only the first decisions are marking some ways of thoughts.* The Polish Supreme Court in a recent decision *in abstracto* accepted the wrongful birth of a healthy child as a possible ground for awarding non-pecuniary damages to the mother as a consequence of wrongful interference with the mother's personality rights.[91] In Hungary, the Supreme Court in a very similar case rejected the plaintiff's claim on *the ground that the plaintiff could not present wrongful interference with her personality rights as the birth of a child could not be such an interference.*[92] It is, however, very hard to decide whether it was the reinforcement of the principle that non-pecuniary damages is the special sanction of infringement of personality rights or the Court only tried to find a reason for its decision based on the maxim that life in itself cannot be deemed as harm.

The most sensible cases in Eastern Europe involve the difficult ethical issues of life and death. The parents' right for compensation in wrongful birth cases is generally acknowledged also in Eastern European jurisdictions.[93] In Poland, in a recent wrongful birth decision of the Supreme Court, the violation of the parents' right to family planning has been established.[94] Damages for wrongful life, i.e. the child's own claim for compensation of being born is—after a very recent statement of the Hungarian Supreme Court—generally rejected. The Hungarian Supreme Court has revisited its practice of acknowledging the claim of the child[95] and reversed its apparently settled practice of awarding damages to the child, too, in wrongful birth cases in 2008. In its authoritative ruling of no 1. of 2008, the Hungarian Supreme Court[96]—considering the European trends as well as constitutional and human rights aspects—explicitly declared that the child shall not have a right to get com-

---

91. E. Bagińska, *Country Report for Poland 2004* 466 ff.

92. Supreme Court, Legf. Bír. Pf. III. 26.339/2001. sz.—EBH 2003. 941. sz.

93. B. A. Koch, *Comparative Overview 2005 (Tort and Insurance Law Yearbook* 2006) 608. See also as an example the decision of the Hungarian Supreme Court, Legf. Bír. Pfv. III. 22.193/2004. sz.—EBH 2005. 1206. sz.

94. E. Bagińska, *Country Report for Poland 2006* 384 f.

95. B. A. Koch, *Comparative Overview 2005 (Tort and Insurance Law Yearbook* 2006) 609., Hungarian Supreme Court, Legf. Bír. Pfv. III. 22.193/2004. sz.—EBH 2005. 1206. sz.

96. Magyar Közlöny [Official Journal of the Hungarian Republic] 2008/50 (III. 26.)

pensation for being born with genetic deficiency towards the hospital or the doctors who failed to recognize it at the adequate stage of pregnancy.

Discrimination as a human rights (or personality rights) problem is a *very current issue* of Eastern European private laws[97] too and it has a great tort law relevance, since one of the possible consequences of infringement of human rights is awarding non-pecuniary damages. Increasing number of discrimination cases is a great challenge to courts, especially in cases *where contracting is at stake*. Freedom of contract is a fundamental principle of contract law. According to its nature, it would leave—except in compulsory contracting—no place for arguments such as discrimination. It is very hard to provide the proper guidelines which are currently generally absent in court practice to allow human rights issues to make their way into private law (as well as contract law) without frustrating the basic paradigms of contract law. This is a great problem still to be solved. In Hungary, for example, there are two opposing views nowadays. On the one side, there are legal practitioners and scholars who say that human rights have superiority over private law principles. According to this opinion human rights overwrite the whole private law regulation including contract law. In other words, human rights are the limits of the private law principles. On the other side, there are scholars and practitioners (mainly private lawyers) who defend the classical principles of private law and argue that enforcing human rights should not overwrite the principle of freedom of contract and cannot be enforced against it otherwise the inner market-oriented integrity of contract law would be ruined. It became clear for today that even if the traditional view of private law rejected the enforcement of prohibition of discrimination in private law relationships and courts dismissed the claims established on discrimination, private law relationships cannot remain untouched by the anti-discrimination principle. Private law theory and practice have to face the problem of enforcing prohibition of discrimination in private law relationships. The idea of anti-discrimination and requirement of equal treatment seems to be completely inconsistent to the principles of private law built on market paradigm. While prohibition of discrimination became overall generally accepted human rights norm and constitutional requirement, for theory and practice of contract law it is very hard to accept that freedom of contract is limited by such an abstract and vague (in its content) principle. Prohibition of discrimina-

97. See e.g. the amendments to Latvian Civil Code of 9 February 2006 (A. Bitāns, *Country Report for Latvia 2006)* 312, A. Dulak, *Country Report for Slovakia*, in H. Koziol and B. C. Steininger, *European Tort Law 2006—Tort and Insurance Law Yearbook* (ECTIL, Wien, 2007) 416.

tion is, however not as far from private law as one could think and as it seems to be so in theory. Cases of common calling in medieval English common law and in German *Gemeines Recht* show, that prohibition of discrimination was always a general requirement in societies burdening people pursuing certain activities. Innkeepers, owners of public houses, common carriers etc. under normal circumstances were obliged to provide services without discrimination to anyone who asked for it and common callings were never seriously questioned in private law theory. Courts in Hungary seem to be very open to accept the discrimination argument and are ready to declare the infringement of the plaintiff's personality rights and to award some non-pecuniary damages[98] and a similar trend seems to be outlined in Latvian court practice too.[99]

The problem is, however, that discrimination is a social problem, and private law built on market paradigm can only be adequate in a limited way to pursue such aims. Prohibition of discrimination should be limited to cases of monopoly and narrowly understood public offers if contracting is at stake. A further reference point in the course of application of anti-discrimination principle could be the prevention of social exclusion. Private law cannot allocate the social costs of anti-discrimination. As a result, costs are to be borne by certain market players or—as an adverse effect—members of the protected groups. In a great bulk of anti-discrimination cases courts try to solve social problems with inadequate means and as a result, even if decisions and aims are morally correct, consequences going beyond the relationship of the parties remain unmanageable.

## 5. Pure Economic Loss

Pure economic loss as an independent category of damage is not known in Eastern European legal systems, even if it is a very important type of loss in tort law. The main conceptual feature of pure economic loss is that it is a loss without antecedent harm to the plaintiff's person or property, which is not a consequential loss in the same patrimony in which property has been damaged *and which is not the loss of the plaintiff, who as person has been injured.*[100]

98. Supreme Court, Legf. Bír. Pfv. IV. 21.269/2001. sz.—EBH 2002. no. 625 (BH 2003 no. 150.)

99. A. Bitāns, *Country Report for Latvia*, in H. Koziol and B. C. Steininger, *European Tort Law 2005—Tort and Insurance Law Yearbook* (ECTIL, Wien, 2006) 392 ff.

100. M. Bussani and V. Palmer (eds.) *Pure Economic Loss in Europe* (Cambridge 2003) 5.

Pure economic loss is an "harm not causally consequent upon an injury to the person (life, body, health, freedom or other rights to personality) or to property (tangible or intangible assets)."[101] Eastern European case law in this area of tort law is poor. One reason for this is that the concept of economic loss itself had been for a long time incompatible with the socialist social and economic approach, which did not respect profit and the chance of gain. A further consideration relates to the fact that courts normally apply the flexible system of tort law without explicitly referring to it. The problem of pure economic loss is the problem of *limitation of liability* and mostly it is a problem of legal causation in the Eastern European case law and legal theory. In Hungarian legal theory Eörsi *exposed summarizing the impact of limitation doctrines in the court practice that the court may* refuse full compensation by dismissing the claim for damages if the harm was unforeseeable to the tortfeasor (foreseeability doctrine); *it was beyond rational probability, was untypical or unique (adequate causality); was beyond the normal consequences and was too unexpected; if the harm as the consequence of the tortfeasor's conduct was too remote; if in the causal link the interference of an unexpected cause altered the normal foreseeable consequences and contributed to the causing of the harm; if the damage is within the normal risk imputed to the aggrieved party; or if it would be disproportionate considering the amount of damages and the degree of fault.*[102]

There are some recent remarkable decisions which show the first contours of the courts' approach. Both the Czech and the Hungarian court practice seem to be open to award compensation for so called ricochet loss. The Hungarian Supreme Court in a case where a sales representative suffered a car accident which was caused negligently by another car driver and the concluding of the contract between the sales representative's employer and another party has failed because the accident prevented the sales representative from coming to the place of contracting held that the unrealized net income, which the employer would have earned from the performance of the contract if contracting had not been frustrated through the accident, is a compensable economic loss of the employer. The driver causing the accident of sales representative has caused this economic loss. On this ground the Court held the driver liable for the economic loss of the employer and ordered the defendant (the insurer of the driver who caused the accident) to pay the lost net income

101. H. Koziol, *Compensation for Pure Economic Loss from a Continental Lawyer's Perspective* in W. H. van Boom/H. Koziol/C. A. Witting (eds.) *Pure Economic Loss* (Wien New York, 2004, ECTIL Tort and Insurance Law Vol. 9.) 141 ff.

102. Gy. Eörsi, *A közvetett károk határai* in *Emlékkönyv Beck Salamon születésének 100. évfordulójára* (Budapest, 1985) 62 ff.

as compensation to the plaintiff.[103] In a very similar case the Czech Supreme Court—albeit also with restrictions—was open to award damages as well and refused to cut the causatal link, reversing a well established court practice dating back to 1979.[104] It is remarkable that the defendant in both of the cases was the tortfeasor's liability insurer and there *seems to be a tendency in court practice that courts are more willing to order compensation* if the risk is shifted to an insurance company.

## 6. Summary

After the transition, the basic problems of liability the Eastern European legal systems are facing are the same as those the Western European countries have to cope. The similar social and economic background produces similar challenges. The most challenging questions, touching upon the strength of the basic moral values of the society (like cases of wrongful birth and wrongful life) or those implying social policy considerations and important risk allocation choices (like employer's vicarious liability) are given different answers, depending on the result of weighing different interests. Courts are seeking the limits of liability and are trying to provide compensation as far as the general capacity of the society for bearing and spreading the burden of losses allows that. The basic inherent structures of tort law are similar across the Eastern European countries but that does not necessarily result in similar regulation and/or court practice and does not prevent differences in the approach or in the decisions. This is partly a result of the flexible system of tort law, partly the differences in the stage of development of transition. *The clear and increasing willingness for respecting* individuals' freedom, dignity and wealth is combined with inclination of giving scope to social policy considerations as anti-discrimination cases present it. The revisiting of the role of the state in the society, the necessity of re-interpreting the state immunity doctrines are obvious as the public liability cases show it. *New problems are, however, enforcing the revision of such basic categories as the meaning and content of unlawfulness as prerequisite for liability. The task is now to give* an answer to the triple challenge of the economic and social transition, the modernization and the requirements of the supra-national legislation.

It also seems to become clear that tort law is only one of the risk allocation and risk spreading systems in society being strongly correlated and interre-

---

103. Supreme Court, Legf. Bír. Pfv. VIII. 20.295/1999. sz.—BH 2001 no. 273.

104. J. Hrádek, *Country Report for the Czech Republic*, in H. Koziol and B. C. Steininger, *European Tort Law 2004—Tort and Insurance Law Yearbook* (ECTIL, Wien, 2005) 206 ff.

lated to other risk spreading systems, like private insurance and the social security system. The growing pressure on governments to reduce budgetary expenses, to ease the burden of employers by reducing their obligatory contribution to social security system, and the general tendency of withdrawal of the state from social welfare may lead to limited availability of compensation from social security systems for victims of personal injury. If this would occur, victims would presumably tend to use tort law in order to get compensation. Tort law—as experiences of deregulation in the eighties in Western European countries already presented it—has the capability of releasing social security system, at least partly, from the burden of providing compensation to victims of accidents. If the burden of compensating victims of accidents would shift from social security system to tort law, this would result in an increasing role for private insurance in risk spreading, which would not only counterbalance this tendency, but also would strengthen the role of private insurance as an alternative of social insurance.

# 11

# The Law of Restitution: A Perspective from Western Europe

Anne-Catherine Hahn*

## Summary



## 1. Introduction

Contract and tort have an established place in Western European private law, and although there are many controversies over details, their basic role and core requirements are rarely contested. Contract and tort law have also long been on the agenda of comparative lawyers, and can to a large extent be

*Dir. iur., LL. M. (Michigan), attorney-at-law, Zurich.

discussed on a European, rather than national level. Although it has in recent years attracted a steadily growing interest from comparative lawyers, no such affirmation can as yet be made for the law of restitution.[1] There is today not a single term that would be able to grasp the different conceptions of the subject existing within Western Europe. In the languages of the civil law, the subject is referred to as "ungerechtfertigte Bereicherung", "enrichissement sans cause", "arrichimento senza causa", "enriquecimiento sin causa," or "ongerechtvaardigte verrijking." All of these labels suggest that a benefit received has to be returned because the resulting enrichment lacks sufficient justification.[2] In contrast, the common law term "law of restitution" focuses on the remedial side rather than on the liability-triggering event without, however, specifying when and why restitutionary remedies should be granted. It is only in recent years that this has begun to change, and that attempts have been made to explain the grounds for restitutionary liability in terms of a single theory similar to the one prevailing in the civilian systems (2.2 below).

Comparative approaches to the subject are further complicated by the fact that it covers a wide array of constellations that raise very different policy issues,[3] and that are addressed through different doctrinal concepts.[4] Situations

---

1. This interest is evidenced by numerous publications that explore specific aspects of the subject, often in a German/English perspective, or that purport to provide a comprehensive overview in a European perspective, such as Peter Schlechtriem in *Restitution und Bereicherungsausgleich in Europa*, vol. I and II, Tubingen 2000 and 2001. The law of restitution is also increasingly being included in research projects on the European harmonization of private law, as the one carried out by the Study Group on a European Civil Code, see on this S. Swann, *The Structure of Liability for Unjustified Enrichment: First Proposals of the Study Group on a European Civil Code*, in: R. Zimmermann (ed.), *Grundstrukturen eines europäischen Bereicherungsrechts*, Tubingen 2005, 265; J.M. Smits, *A European Law on Unjustified Enrichment? A Critical View of the Law of Restitution in the Draft Common Frame of Reference*, in: Antoni Vaquer (ed.), *European Private Law Beyond the Common Frame of Reference*, Groningen 2008, 153. The "Principles of European Unjustified Enrichment Law" are available on the website of the Study Group, <www.sgecc.net/media/download/unjustified_enrichment.pdf>.

2. As becomes clear from the analysis of the different instances in which liability for unjustified enrichments can arise, these theories serve, however, primarily as policy statements and not as directly applicable rules, see P. Schlechtriem, *Introduction*, in: E. von Caemmerer and P. Schlechtriem, *International Encyclopedia of Comparative Law, vol. X: Restitution, Unjust Enrichment and Negotiorum Gestio*, Tubingen, Leiden, Boston 2007, 6.

3. For a challenging discussion of policy issues in different scenarios of restitutionary liability see H. Dagan, *The Law and Ethics of Restitution*, Cambridge 2004.

4. See, generally, P. Schlechtriem, C. Coen and R. Hornung, *Restitution and Unjust Enrichment in Europe*, European Review of Private Law 2001, 377, 379 *seq.*

that may be regarded as instances of liability in unjustified enrichment, or of restitutionary liability, range from intentional transfers of benefits over mistaken improvements to another's assets and encroachments on another's resources to altruistic acts undertaken in view of protecting another's life, limb or property[5] to self-interested investments with incidental benefits for third parties.[6] There are rather different views within Western Europe as to which of these claims are really part of the law of restitution. For example, cases of wrongful interference with another's resources are in French law typically addressed through tort law alone while they can lead to both delictual and restitutionary remedies in German and English law. By the same token, recovery claims resulting from the voluntary management of another's affairs (*negotiorum gestio*) or from improvements made to another's property are in some legal systems regarded as part of the law of restitution, but are treated as distinct matters in others. In addition, the civilian understanding of restitutionary liability is limited to personal claims, whereas the common law conception also includes certain proprietary remedies that afford the claimant a privileged position in the defendant's insolvency (see 3.1.2.1).

Given the breadth and unclear borders of the subject, this introduction to the law of restitution in Western Europe will concentrate on two core scenarios of restitutionary liability, namely liability for intentional transfers and liability for wrongful interference with another's resources. In discussing these core cases, the focus will be placed on German, French, and English law. These three legal systems illustrate three different ways of dealing with the law of restitution, and to a greater or lesser degree, their solutions have been emulated in many other legal systems of Western Europe.[7] While this selective approach does not allow to fully reflect the variety of national solutions that have

---

5. The last category is peculiar in that as claims resulting from the spontaneous management of another's affairs are not truly restitutionary in nature, but primarily aimed at obtaining a remuneration for efforts voluntarily undertaken for another's benefit. This is also reflected in the fact that *negotiorum gestio* claims are in the civilian tradition embedded into a quasi-contractual relationship that creates not only claims, but also obligations for the acting party.

6. This latter category has received growing attention in recent years, see for example D. Friedmann, *Unjust Enrichment, Pursuance of Self-Interest, and the Limits of Free Riding*, Loy. L. A. L. Rev. 36 (2003), 831; Dagan, *Law and Ethics*, 123 *seqq.*; A.-C. Hahn, *Vergütungsansprüche für Dienstleistungen bei fehlender vertraglicher Grundlage*, Berne/Baden-Baden 2004, 61 *seqq.*

7. The approach taken in the European principles on unjustified enrichment, as reflected in the Draft Common Frame of Reference, does not follow any of the established national taxonomies, as it is based in a first step on a general clause while the circumstances

evolved out of or in parallel with these three traditions and the many doctrinal controversies existing within the three large traditions of Western Europe, the additional degree of detail gained from a more comprehensive approach would ultimately probably obfuscate, rather than highlight the understanding of core issues in the law of restitution.

## 2. The General Structure and Role of Restitutionary Liability

### *2.1. The Civilian Approach*

As seen above (1), the civilian systems normally approach the law of unjustified enrichment in terms of liability-triggering events, while the common law focuses on the resulting remedies. These terminological differences are not accidental, but reflect underlying conceptual divergences. In the civilian tradition, the law of unjustified enrichment is regarded as a separate type of obligations ranking next to contract and tort. The specificity of these obligations lies in their origin: while contractual obligations are created through consent, and delictual obligations result from the unlawful infliction of harm, claims in unjustified enrichment originate from the receipt of a benefit that lacks legal justification. Thus, liability in unjustified enrichment in a sense mirrors tort law: while the latter imposes liability for unlawful losses, the former deals with unlawful benefits.[8]

At first glance, this focus on a common causative event appears strikingly simple and elegant. However, a closer look shows that this impression is deceiving. Notwithstanding this broad approach, it comprises different claims that depend on rather different conditions. It would also be wrong to assume that all civil law systems share the same conception of liability in unjustified enrichment. More particularly, two main approaches can be distinguished within Western Europe.[9] The first has its origins primarily in French law, and

---

for qualifying the enrichment as unjustified are specified in a second step, see Smits, *European Law*, 153 *seqq*.

8. See on this idea H. Hagen, *Funktionale und dogmatische Zusammenhänge zwischen Schaden-und Bereicherungsrecht*, in: *Festschrift Larenz*, Munich 1973, 867.

9. The Scandinavian systems have developed a third, distinct tradition. This tradition —which cannot be addressed in the present contribution—is characterized by the fact that the question as to when and why restitution should be ordered is primarily decided on the basis of a case-by-case evaluation, rather than on the basis of abstract legal rules, see Schlechtriem, *Restitution*, vol. I, 49 *seqq*.

has marked the development of Italian, Spanish, Dutch, and—to a certain extent—Scottish law (2.1.1). The second conception was developed in Germany during the 19th century. Its influence is not only notable in Germany and Switzerland, but also in Greece and Portugal as well as in many Eastern European countries (2.1.2).

### 2.1.1. The Romanist Tradition

In the Romanist tradition, three different types of restitutionary claims can be distinguished: claims for the recovery of money or things not owed to the recipient (*répétition de l'indu*[10]), claims for the reimbursement of outlays spontaneously incurred to protect another's interest (*gestion d'affaires d'autrui*), and claims for the return or compensation of an unjustified enrichment (*enrichissement sans cause*).[11] Initially, only the first two of these categories were recognized in the Codes. Both of them were seen as instances of quasi-contractual liability, *i.e.* liability that does not depend on consent, but that entails contract-like consequences.[12] This understanding goes back to Roman law.[13] Thus, both under the *condictio indebiti* of Roman law and under the *répétition de l'indu* of modern French law, the receipt of money or chattels transferred under the influence of a mistake obliges the recipient to return the benefit received like a borrower under a loan agreement. Similarly, liability under the concept of *gestion d'affaires d'autrui* is described as quasi-contractual because the spontaneous intervention made to preserve another's life, limb or

10. Its equivalents in other Romanist systems are the *ripetizione dell'indebito* of Italian law, the *cobro de lo indebido* of Spanish law, the *onverschuldigde betaling* of Dutch law, and the *repetition* of Scottish law.

11. In Scottish law, the claim for the recovery of involuntary transfers is called "repetition", and the claim for reimbursement of improvements is called "recompense", while the general enrichment action is simply referred to as "restitution", see M.A. Hogg, *Lowlands to Low Country: Perspectives on the Scottish and Dutch Law of Unjustified Enrichment*, vol. 5.1 Electronic Journal of Comparative Law (March 2001), <www.ejcl.org/ejcl/51/art51-1.html>, para. 2.2.

12. See Articles 1371, 1372 and 1376 of the French Civil Code; see J. Honorat, *Rôle effectif et rôle concevable des quasi-contrats en droit actuel*, RTD civ. 1969, 653, 676; M. Douchy, *La notion de quasi-contrat en droit positif français*, Paris, 1997, 8.

13. For further details see R. Zimmermann, *The Law of Obligations: Roman Foundations of the Civilian Tradition*, Oxford 1996, 15 *seqq.*; B. Huwiler, *Zur Anspruchsgrundlage der Obligation aus ungerechtfertigter Bereicherung im Schweizerischen Obligationenrecht*, in: *Der Allgemeine Teil und das Ganze, Liber Amicorum für H. Schulin*, Basle 2002, 41, 50; for a brief summary of the Roman and modern civilian understanding of quasi-contractual liability see Hahn, *Vergütungsansprüche*, 74 *seqq.*

property assets results in a legal relationship with mutual rights and obligations resembling a contract for mandate.[14]

The *répétition de l'indu* and its equivalents in other Romanist systems are generally limited to the recovery of money and other fungible assets which have been intentionally transferred on another person.[15] To allow recovery in situations that were not covered by this narrow claim, French courts gradually extended the concept of *gestion d'affaires d'autrui* in the course of the 19th century by relaxing the traditional requirement of intent to act for the benefit of another.[16] This practice attracted widespread criticism from legal writers, who suggested that cases falling outside the scope of the *repetition de l'indu* should be discussed on the basis of a general clause of liability in unjustified enrichment,[17] as had arguably been the case in Roman law,[18] rather than being forced under the *negotiorum gestio* rules.

In the *Boudier*-decision of 1892, the *Cour de Cassation* ultimately followed these suggestions.[19] Invoking a general, equity-based principle in terms that recall the famous maxim of Pomponius,[20] it recognized a gen-

14. See J. Carbonnier, *Droit civil: Les obligations* (vol. IV), 22nd ed., Paris 2000, n. 298 f.; J.P. Dawson, *Negotiorum Gestio: The Altruistic Intermeddler*, Harv. L. Rev. 74 (1961), 817 and 1073, 824.

15. See M. Planiol/G. Ripert/P. Esmein, *Traité pratique de droit civil: Obligations* (vol. VII), 2nd ed., Paris 1954, n. 737. However, the Spanish rules of liability in unjustified enrichment deviate on this point from the Code Civil as they are based on a broader concept of receipt, see Schlechtriem, *Restitution*, vol. I, 15.

16. See, *e.g.*, Civ., 16 July 1890, S. 1894, I, 19.

17. See in particular C. Aubry and C. Rau, *Cours de droit civil français d'après la méthode de Zachariae*, 4th ed., Paris 1869–1876, vol. IV, 578.

18. Apart from the *condictio indebiti*, which was of particular practical importance, the Roman jurists of the classical period had recognized a range of other, more or less narrowly defined claims, namely the *condictio causa data causa non secuta* (Dig. 12.4), the *condictio ob turpem vel iniustam causam* (Dig. 12.5), the *condictio furtiva* (Dig. 13.1, and—as a sort of "catch-all" clause, the *condictio sine causa* (Dig. 12.7), see Zimmermann, *Roman Foundations*, 841. In later years, these claims were taken together under a broad general claim, the *condictio sine causa*, see Zimmermann, *Roman Foundations*, 856 *seq.*; B. Kupisch, *Ungerechtfertigte Bereicherung, Geschichtliche Entwicklungen*, Heidelberg 1987, 24.

19. Req., 15 June 1892, S. 1893, I, 281, 283.

20. The maxim is generally translated to read "by the law of nature it is right that nobody should be unjustly enriched at another's expense, see D. 12, 6, 14 for the original text. While this maxim may have been seen as a general guideline by the late Roman jurists, it was never considered an applicable rule of law, see R. Feenstra, *Grotius' Doctrine of Unjust Enrichment as a Source of Obligations: Its Origin and its Influence in Roman-Dutch Law*, in: E. Schrage (ed.), *Unjust Enrichment, The Comparative Legal History of the Law of Restitution*, 2nd ed., Berlin 1999, 197; D. Johnston and R. Zimmermann, *Unjustified Enrichment:*

eral clause of liability in unjustified enrichment which has since become known as *action de in rem verso*.[21] In the case underlying the decision, a farmer had purchased manure and used it on leased land. When he became insolvent, the seller claimed recovery from the owner of the land, arguing that the latter had been enriched because his land had become more valuable. The *Cour de Cassation* accepted this reasoning, thus jettisoning the principle of contractual privity and allowing the claimant to shift the insolvency risk of his contractual partner to the landlord. While this outcome[22] and the extremely broad ambit of the claim rightly attracted a fair amount of criticism,[23] the *action de in rem verso* was soon considerably narrowed down. Thus, French courts require the defendant's enrichments to be matched by a corresponding loss on the claimant's part, which must not be attributable to the claimant's own fault.[24] In addition, claims in unjustified enrichment can only be brought in circumstances where no other claim or action lies.[25] Nevertheless, it is still true that the *action de in rem verso* and its equivalents in the other Romanist systems[26] are construed more broadly and more flexibly than the general clauses of liability in unjustified enrichment existing in legal systems inspired by German law, among other things because the courts often refrain from requiring strict evidence of the

*Surveying the Landscape*, in: *id.* (eds.), *Unjustified Enrichment—Key Issues in Comparative Perspective*, Cambridge 2002, 3.

21. This name was derived from an action of Roman law that could be brought in specific cases of indirect enrichment, see B. Kupisch, *Die Versionsklage*, Heidelberg 1965.

22. In the Germanic systems, the claim would most likely have been rejected because the seller intended to transfer an asset to the farmer, rather than to the owner of the land, see 3.1.1.

23. See, *e.g.*, A. Rouast, *L'enrichissement sans cause et la jurisprudence civile*, RTD civ. 1922, 35, 44.

24. See Civ., 12 June 1914, S. 1918, I, 41, and 2 March 1915, S. 1920, I, 102; Rouast, *enrichissement*, 47; G. Bonet, *La condition d'absence d'intérêt personnel et de faute chez l'appauvri pour le succès de l'action de in rem verso*, in: Mélanges offerts à P. Hébraud, Toulouse 1981, 59.

25. See P. Drakidis, *La subsidiarité, caractère spécifique et international de l'action d'enrichissement sans cause*, RTD civ. 1961, 38; J. Flour/J.-L. Aubert/E. Savaux, *Les obligations: Le fait juridique* (vol. 2), 10th ed., Paris 2003, n. 53.a).

26. In the other Romanist systems, general clauses for liability in unjustified enrichment were formally introduced in the course of the 20th century, either through case law or through legislation, see C. Wendehorst, *Die Leistungskondiktion und ihre Binnenstruktur in rechtsvergleichender Perspektive*, in: R. Zimmermann (ed.), *Grundstrukturen eines europäischen Bereicherungsrechts*, Tubingen 2005, 47, 61 *seq.*, with further references.

parties' respective loss and enrichment,[27] and because an indirect relation between the two is considered sufficient to trigger liability.[28]

### 2.1.2. The Germanic Tradition

The Germanic model of liability in unjustified enrichment was initially developed by Friedrich Carl von Savigny, the founding father of the 19th century historical school of law. Von Savigny, too, drew heavily on the Roman sources, and placed particular importance on the *condictio indebiti*. However, unlike the French authors who had paved the way for the *Code Civil*, he viewed this claim from the outset as mere application of a wider principle against unjustified enrichment. According to this conception, all claims in unjustified enrichment are based on a common requirement, namely the absence of a legal cause entitling the recipient to keep the benefit in question.[29] This requirement is met if a benefit is transferred or appropriated in the absence of a contractual obligation, unless the other party is as of law authorized to keep the benefit in question. Hence, claims in unjustified enrichment essentially allow people to regain control over assets involuntarily lost to another. In this respect, their function is similar to that of the *rei vindicatio* which can be invoked by an owner who has lost possession of an asset to a third party, but continues to hold title to it.[30] The fundamental difference between the two remedies lies in their enforcement: the *rei vindicatio* is proprietary in nature, and allows the owner to recover his property even if the recipient has meanwhile become bankrupt, or if the asset has been passed on to a third party.[31] In contrast, unjustified enrichment claims only come into play once the claimant has lost title to the asset in question, and are purely personal in nature.

Under the model of German law, an enrichment lacking a sufficient legal cause can result from multiple causes. It may be triggered by a conscious transfer of wealth that does not correspond to the transferor's true will, for exam-

---

27. See for example Civ. 1re, 15 October 1996, D. 1997, Som. 177, with note by R. Libchaber.

28. See Planiol/Ripert/Esmein, *Traité*, n. 755; Bonet, *intérêt personnel*, n. 117; G. Marty and P. Raynaud, *Droit civil, Les obligations*, vol. 2, 2nd ed., Paris 1988, n. 394.

29. See F. C. v. Savigny, *System des heutigen Römischen Rechts*, vol. 5, Berlin 1841, 511 *seqq.*, and Huwiler, *Anspruchsgrundlage*, 41 *seqq.* on von Savigny's influence on the German and Swiss conceptions of unjustified enrichment.

30. See von Savigny, *System*, 512 *seqq.*

31. Recovery from a third party is, however, excluded in cases of bona fide acquisition of title.

ple when money is paid in performance of an invalid contract. An unjustified enrichment can also follow from the payment of another's debts, or from the unlawful appropriation of another's resources. This variety of events susceptible of triggering liability in unjustified enrichment is reflected in §812 (1) BGB, where enrichments as a result of performance ("*durch die Leistung eines anderen*") are explicitly juxtaposed to enrichments caused "in another way" ("*in sonstiger Weise*"). Starting from this distinction, 20th century authors such as Wilburg and von Caemmerer argued that liability in unjustified enrichment covers a variety of claims, ranging from the recovery of failed transfers over reimbursement claims for improvements made to another's property or for the payment of another's debts to claims sanctioning encroachments on another's property.[32] In all of these situations, the necessary nexus between claimant and defendant is primarily established on the basis of the action or event leading to liability, rather on the basis of the more traditional requirement of a disenrichment on the claimant's part. This approach and the underlying typology of claims have proven extremely influential, both in German law and in many of the legal systems influenced by it. This notwithstanding, the questions as to whether liability in unjustified enrichment should be understood in terms of an all-encompassing general clause or in terms of specific claims and what abstract criteria should be used for identifying the persons or entities among which restitution should be ordered continue to fuel heated debates,[33] as is also illustrated at European level by the recent proposals of the Study Group on a European Civil Code.[34]

32. See W. Wilburg, *Die Lehre von der ungerechtfertigten Bereicherung nach österreichischem und deutschem Recht*, Graz 1934, 22 *seqq*; E. v. Caemmerer, *Bereicherung und unerlaubte Handlung*, in: H.G. Leser (ed.), *Gesammelte Schriften: Rechtsvergleichung und Schuldrecht* (vol. 1), Tubingen 1968, 209, 217 *seqq*.

33. See, *e.g.*, B. Kupisch, *Einheitliche Voraussetzungen des Bereicherungsanspruchs—ein Missgriff des Gesetzgebers?*, in: Festgabe für U. v. Lübtow, Berlin 1980, 501, 504; J. Gordley, *The Principle Against Unjustified Enrichment*, in: *Gedächtnisschrift Lüderitz*, Munich 2000, 213, 216 *seqq*. These controversies are in particular illustrated by the sophisticated (not to say sophistic) debates over liability in three-party-situations, see C.-W. Canaris, *Der Bereicherungsausgleich im Dreipersonenverhältnis*, in: *Festschrift Larenz*, Munich 1973, 799. There are also national differences. For example, based on the wording of Art. 62 I Swiss Code of Obligations, Swiss courts and writers have traditionally insisted on the idea of general clause and on the requirement of a loss on the claimant's side, although distinctions are made between liability for transfers and liability for encroachments, with no loss having to be shown in the latter case, see Schlechtriem, *Restitution*, vol. I, 231 *seq*.; Hahn, *Vergütungsansprüche*, 191 *seqq*., with further references.

34. The Study Group proposes the following "basic rule" (Article 1:101) as introduction to its principles of European Unjustified Enrichment Law: "A person who obtains an

## *2.2. The Common Law Approach*

In contrast to the Continental conceptions of unjustified enrichment, the modern English law of restitution is not the result of any comprehensive theory. This is in large part due to the procedural constraints that marked the adjudication of claims in the English courts, and that greatly limited the practical influence that Roman law has had on the development of English law. For centuries, claims were not phrased in terms of substantive arguments, such as the conclusion of a contract, but in terms of specific forms of actions.[35] Nevertheless, several forms of actions aimed at recovering benefits conferred on another gradually came to be recognized, both at common law and in equity. These included in particular remedies for the recovery of money *(action for money paid)* and for the value of things (*action for quantum valebat*) transferred by mistake, for the recovery of money spent on another's debts (*action for money had and received*), or for the remuneration of work done outside a valid contract (*action for quantum meruit*). All of these actions developed out of the action of *assumpsit*, which was essentially a contractual action,[36] and all of them were justified on the basis that the defendant had implicitly promised to return or pay for the benefit received.[37] A second type of restitutionary action evolved out of the *waiver of tort*-doctrine. Under this theory, claimants could, instead of claiming damages, demand that a tortfeasor be ordered to disgorge whatever he had obtained through his tortious conduct, in which case the delictual relationship existing between the parties was supposedly "transformed" into a quasi-contractual relationship.[38] Still other remedies originated from the law of equity—most notably the constructive and the result-

---

unjustified enrichment which is attributable to another's disadvantage is obliged to that other to reverse the enrichment. This rule applies only in accordance with following provisions of this Book". The question when an enrichment qualifies as unjustified is clarified in the subsequent rules, but enrichments resulting from transfers and from encroachments are not systematically distinguished, see also Swann, *First Proposals*, 275 *seq.*

35. See J.H. Baker, *An Introduction to English Legal History*, 4th ed., London 2002, 53.

36. The history of the action of *assumpsit* is complex. It developed out of different, older actions with a much narrower scope of application, including the *action of debt*, which resembled the *condictio indebiti* of Roman law, and the delictual action *trespass on the case*, but it gradually came to be used as a general claim for breach of contract, see A.W.B. Simpson, *A History of the Common Law of Contract. The Rise of the Action of Assumpsit*, Oxford 1975.

37. See A. Burrows, *The Law of Restitution*, 2nd ed., London 2002, 7 *seq.*

38. See Burrows, *Restitution*, 462; *United Australia Ltd. v. Barclays Bank Ltd.* [1941] A.C. 1.

ing trust, which allow the holder of equitable title to recover an asset from its legal owner.[39]

The old forms of action influenced the legal reasoning of courts and lawyers long after they had been formally abolished in the judicial reforms of the 19th century.[40] As a result, the different restitutionary remedies recognized in English law continued for a long time to be seen as mere annexes to contract and tort.[41] In addition, the underlying liability-triggering events were considered far too diverse to be explained in terms of a single uniting principle or policy. This traditional understanding of the English law of restitution has, however, undergone fundamental changes in recent years. In a remarkable renunciation of the common law's traditional skepticism of abstract concepts and general clauses, a growing number of academics,[42] and in their wake also of courts,[43] has begun to reconceptualize the various restitutionary remedies of English law as manifestations of a general "principle against unjust enrichment."[44] According to this view, the law of restitution should be understood as a unified subject that is concerned with reversing unjust enrichments, whether resulting from transfers ("unjust enrichment by subtraction") or from wrongful conduct ("restitution for wrongs").[45]

---

39. See P.J. Millet, *Restitution and Constructive Trusts*, LQR 114 (1998), 399, 400 *seq.*

40. See F.W. Maitland, *The Forms of Action at Common Law, A course of Lectures* (ed. A.H. Chaytor and W.J. Whittaker), Cambridge 1976 (reprint), 6 *seq.*; R.C. van Caenegem, *An Historical Introduction to Private Law*, Cambridge 1992, 163 *seq.*

41. See, *e.g.*, Viscount Haldance LC in *Sinclair v. Brougham* (1914) A.C. 398, 415.

42. An initial effort at a systematic and comprehensive presentation of the subject was made by Robert Goff and Gareth Jones in their book on *The Law of Restitution*, which first came out in 1966. Building on their work, Peter Birks developed a comprehensive theory of the subject in "An Introduction to the Law of Restitution", the last edition which is now simply called "Unjust Enrichment", thus underlining the unity of the subject. See generally on Peter Birk's contribution to the subject R. Grantham and C. Rickett, *Unjust Enrichment—Reason, Place and Content*, in: id., *Structure and Justification in Private Law, Essays for Peter Birks*, Oxford/Portland 2008, 5.

43. See *Lipkin Gorman v. Karpnale (Ltd.)* [1991] 2 A.C. 548 and *Banque Financière de la Cité v. Parc (Battersea) Ltd.* [1998] 2 WLR 475, 479 for explicit endorsements of the new principle.

44. This development is part of a more general tendency to describe and re-organize English law in terms of a rational system, see critically, G. Samuel, *English Private Law: Old and New Thinking in the Taxonomy Debate*, OJLS 2004, 335; S. Waddams, *Dimensions of Private Law: Categories and Concepts in Anglo-American Reasoning*, Cambridge 2003, 2.

45. See on this separation Burrows, *Restitution*, 25 *seqq.*, 455. While recalling the distinction between different types unjustified enrichment claims that is practiced in the Germanic systems, the category of "enrichment by subtraction" is considerably broader than the concept of "Leistungskondiktionen" as it does not require evidence of an intent to make a transfer. Also, unlike in the Germanic systems, the same case may in English law alter-

The different ramifications of this new understanding remain controversial.[46] What seems, however, uncontestable is that the law of restitution has in the course of the past ten years conquered a prominent place on the agenda of English legal writers and, though to a somewhat lesser extent, English courts. Moreover, as the subject is now discussed in terms that are very similar to those used on the Continent, it has become much easier for outsiders to understand the English law of restitution, and to assess the extent to which its solutions differ from those reached in the civilian tradition. As a result there is also a sense that many divergences may be less fundamental than was traditionally thought to be the case.[47]

## 3. Core Cases of Restitutionary Liability

Both the general clauses of unjustified liability of the civilian systems and the newly recognized principle against unjust enrichment of English law have the potential of covering a broad array of situations in which benefits are received by one person to another's detriment. While it is generally accepted that this alone is not sufficient to hold the recipient liable, all Western European systems have struggled with the question as to when an enrichment can be qualified as "unjust" or "unjustified" and should, therefore, be subject to recovery. These efforts have generally resulted in the differentiation of typical cases of restitutionary liability. The most important of these distinctions concerns the one between liability for intentional transfers (3.1), and liability for unlawful encroachments on another's resources (3.2). While the importance

---

natively give rise to claims under either of the two concepts, see Burrows, *Restitution*, 456; Birks, *Unjust Enrichment*, 4 *seqq.*, 83 *seqq.*, who insisted in his later writings that restitution for wrongs is completely unrelated to "unjust enrichment".

46. Among other things, these controversies concern the role of "unjust factors" and the relation between these causative events and restitutionary remedies as response to such, but possibly also to other events, see Birks, *Unjust Enrichment*, 4 *seqq.*; Burrows, *Restitution*, 5 *seq.* On a more fundamental level, it has been objected that the new approach cannot truly explain why liability should be imposed in specific instances and not in others, see, *e.g.*, S. Hedley, *Unjust Enrichment*, CLJ 199, 578.

47. A striking example of such a "rapprochement" is provided by Peter Birks' swing towards the civilian understanding of liability for intentional transfers: While he himself played a substantial role in developing the "unjust-factors" as triggers to liability (3.1.1.2), he later argued that restitutionary liability for transfers is more appropriately explained on account of a general "absence as basis" requirement, see Birks, *Unjust Enrichment*, 113 *seqq.*; see also Zimmermann, *Bereicherungsrecht*, 40. The adequacy of this approach remains controversial, see Grantham/Rickett, *Unjust Enrichment*, 13.

attributed to this distinction varies considerably from country to country,[48] it certainly provides a useful framework for gaining an overview over core cases of restitutionary liability in Western Europe.

## *3.1. Liability for Intentional Transfers*

Claims for the recovery of intentional transfers have historically played an important role in the development of the law of restitution, and continue to be of eminent practical relevance. Although the civil law and common law systems have traditionally relied on different methodologies for deciding when transfers are subject to recovery, the outcomes reached are often similar (3.1.1.) while differences in the types of available remedies are relatively important (3.2.2.).

### 3.1.1. Grounds for Recovery

#### *3.1.1.1. In the Civil Law Systems*

In the civilian systems, benefits consciously conferred on another are in principle subject to recovery whenever the benefit was not owed to the transferee, such that the latter lacks a valid claim to keeping it.[49] The existence of such a claim is determined on the basis of rules that lie outside the law of restitution, in particular on the basis of contract law. Restitution is excluded whenever money or things have been transferred, or when services have been rendered in discharge of a contractual duty.[50] To claim recovery for benefits transferred under a presumptive contract, the claimant has to prove the invalidity or subsequent disappearance of the underlying contract—for example,

48. For example, the Germanic concept of liability enrichments resulting from performance is narrower than the (roughly equivalent) English concept of enrichment by subtraction, which, unlike the former, does not necessarily suppose a conscious transfer by the claimant, as evidenced, for example, by the case *Lipkin Gorman v. Karpnale Ltd.* [1991] 2 A.C. 548.

49. This idea is most clearly expressed in the Romanist systems through the concepts of "indu" or "indebito" that underlie the *répétition de l'indu* claim, see also Birks, *Unjust Enrichment*, 102.

50. Transfers that were made in performance of a time-barred contractual claim are, however, exempt from recovery even though the recipient would not have been able to enforce such a claim, see G. Dannemann, *Unjust Enrichment by Transfer: Some Comparative Remarks*, 79 Texas Law Review (2001), 1837, 1842, with further references. While contractual rules are of particular practical importance for determining whether or not a benefit is subject to restitution, statutory obligations, such as maintenance duties or delictual duties to pay damages, can also preclude such a claim.

because of lack of sufficient agreement, non-compliance with mandatory form requirements, or termination as a result of a breach.[51]

Ordering liability in unjustified enrichment whenever the defendant lacks a valid contractual claim to the benefit received is a way of implementing contractual policies. In other constellations, however, contract law and restitutionary liability are less easily reconciled. Thus, recovery is sometimes also available when benefits have been transferred in anticipation of an expected contract or other event that does not materialize, rather than in performance of a presumptive contract. To allow transferors to recover such benefits in unjustified enrichment—whether under the *condictio causa data causa non secuta* of the Germanic systems,[52] or under the general clause of the Romanist systems,[53] is problematic because expectations as to another party's future conduct are in principle only protected through contract law, while non-contractual transfers are generally made at the transferor's own risk.[54] Similar issues are raised by recovery claims for indirect enrichments. Thus, when a craftsman is hired by a lessee to do work in an apartment, his work is likely to increase the value of the landlord's property. In this situation, the Romanist systems in principle allow the craftsman to seek recovery from the landlord under the general clause of liability in unjustified enrichment if the contractual claim against the lessee turns out to be unenforceable.[55] In contrast, the

---

51. See Wendehorst, *Leistungskondiktion*, 68 *seqq*, for a brief comparative overview of the grounds for recovery.

52. The *condictio causa data causa non secuta* has been taken over from Roman law, where it was used to moderate the of the *numerus clausus* of enforceable contractual claims, see Zimmermann, *Roman* Foundations, 843.

53. See Rouast, *enrichissement*, 76; Schlechtriem, *Restitution*, vol. 1, 195. Restitution is, however, excluded if the claimant is considered to have acted at his own risk and peril, see, for example, Civ. 1re, 19 October 1976, Bull. civ. I, Nr. 300; Civ. 3ème, 26 February 1992, D. 1992, IR 109; Flour/Aubert/Savaux, *Le fait juridique*, n. 50.

54. See von Caemmerer, *Bereicherung*, 222 *seq*.; D. Reuter and M. Martinek, *Handbuch des Schuldrechts in Einzeldarstellungen: Ungerechtfertigte Bereicherung*, vol. 4, Tubingen 1983, 158 *seqq*.; Hahn, *Vergütungsansprüche*, 197 *seqq*.

55. It is in this very type of constellation that the general claim in unjustified enrichment was first recognized by the *Cour de Cassation* in 1892, see n. 19 above. Subsequently, claims of this type were restricted to situations in which the defendant's enrichment finds no justification in his contractual relationship with the direct recipient of the benefit, and where (contractual or other) claims against the contractual partner are barred due to factual or legal reasons, see Req., 12 February 1923, D. 1923, 1, 64; Req., 22 February 1939, Gaz. Pal. 1939, 1, 779; Req., 11 September 1940, S. 1941, I, 121, with note by Paul Esmein. Nevertheless, the general principle remains; see Flour/Aubert/Savaux, *Le fait juridique*, n. 55.

Germanic systems do not allow restitution for this type of indirect enrichments—a position that is arguably more faithful to the idea of contractual privity.[56]

Moreover, while transfers made in the absence of an underlying contractual claim are in principle subject to recovery, restitution may be excluded when both parties have executed the contract over a protracted period of time. Such contracts are often treated as valid for the time of their performance in order to avoid the practical difficulties associated with requiring full restitution of all benefits exchanged. Thus, when a contract is void because form requirements with an exclusively evidentiary function have been disregarded, many legal systems allow this flaw to be cured through voluntary execution of the contract.[57] Conversely, when form requirements are supposed to protect the parties from making rash decisions, or when one of the parties did not have the necessary capacity to enter into the contract, the impulse for ordering restitution is generally much stronger. Still other considerations come into play when the underlying contract has an illegal content—in this case, many legal systems have traditionally taken the position that the contract is not only unenforceable, but that the law should also not assist a party that has voluntarily performed its obligations and that later seeks restitution because the other party fails to do the same.[58]

Finally, even if contractual policies do not oppose the recovery of benefits transferred under an invalid or terminated contract, recovery may still be excluded if the transferor was aware—and sometimes also if he should have been aware—that he was under no obligation to make the transfer. The underlying idea is that, if someone voluntarily confers a benefit on another knowing that he is not required to do so, the other party is to be protected in his reliance on the stability of the receipt, even if he did not have any claim to the benefit.[59] Although this idea is widely acknowledged, its role and implemen-

56. See von Caemmerer, *Bereicherung*, 245 *seqq.*; Reuter/Martinek, *Handbuch*, 18 *seqq.*; E. Schrage, *Contract and Restitution: A Few Comparative Remarks*, in: F.D. Rose (ed.), *Failure of Contracts, Contractual, Restitutionary and Proprietary Consequences*, Oxford 1997, 231, 237. In this scenario, the claimant is in particular not authorized to bring an action for enrichment "other than through transfer", see BGHZ 40, 272, 278.

57. Schlechtriem, *Restitution*, vol. I, 591 *seqq.*

58. Both this justification, and the practical scope of the defense are controversial, see G. Dannemann, *Illegality as Defence Against Unjust Enrichment Claims*, (2000) Oxford U Comparative L Forum 4, <www.ouclf.iuscomp.org>.

59. A mistake in the sense of the law of unjustified enrichment need not be such as to simultaneously invalidate the underlying obligation. Instead, it is sufficient that the transferor erroneously believed to owe an obligation to the transferee, and that this obligation did, for whatever reason, not exist.

tation vary from country to country. In the German tradition, the absence of mistake is a broad defense that can be invoked under all transfer-based recovery claims. In contrast, in the French-inspired systems, the element of mistake only comes into play when the recipient is in fact entitled to receive the benefit in question, but from a different person. In this situation of so-called "indu objectif", the transferor has to show that he was mistaken about his obligation to the recipient—otherwise he is presumed to have voluntarily paid another's debt. In the new Dutch Civil Code, the requirement of mistake has been completely abandoned. Under this approach, unjustified enrichment claims for intentional transfers are only excluded if they would, due to the transferee's contradictory conduct, amount to a violation of the general principle of good faith (Art. 6:203 NBW).[60]

### *3.1.1.2. In English Law*

Unlike the civilian systems, English law has traditionally not relied on a single, all-encompassing criterion, such as the absence of legal cause, to determine the recoverability of benefits intentionally conferred on another. Instead, English courts have over time identified different "unjust-factors" that indicate that the transfer was flawed in one way or the other. Thus, recovery has traditionally been allowed if the transferor acted under the influence of a mistake, especially if he acted under the mistaken belief that he was under an obligation to make a payment.[61] Restitution is also possible if the transferor's will was vitiated due to duress, compulsion or the exercise of undue influence,[62] or if the transfer was made in view of a consideration which failed to materialize.[63] Unlike the grounds that can in the civilian tradition cause a contractual obligation to become invalid or void, thereby removing the presumptive cause of a transfer and opening the way to recovery in unjustified enrichment, the "unjust-factors" of English law are proper to the law of restitution. Therefore, benefits transferred on the basis of a void, invalid or frustrated contract

---

60. See P. Schlechtriem, *Europäisierung des Bereicherungsrechts*, vol. 7.4 Electronic Journal of Comparative Law (November 2003), <www.ejcl.org/74/art74-3.html>, para. 1.3.

61. See Parke B. in *Kelly v. Solari* (1841) [1835–42] All ER Rep. 320, 322 (Court of Exchequer). In contrast, mistakes about the underlying legal premisses were not considered sufficient, see below.

62. See, for example, *Barclays Bank plc. v. O'Brien* [1994] 1 A.C. 180 (H.L).

63. This unjust-factor resembles, and is often associated with the *condictio causa data causa non secuta* of the civilian systems, see G. Virgo, *Failure of Consideration: Myth and Meaning in the English Law of Restitution*, in: R. Zimmermann and D. Johnston (eds.), *Unjustified Enrichment—Key Issues in Comparative Perspective*, Cambridge 2002, 103.

are in principle only recoverable if the claimant can in addition establish a specific unjust-factor.[64] Nevertheless, the results reached are often similar to those reached in the civilian systems.[65] Thus, although restitution is in the latter based on the absence of an underlying obligation, recovery is generally denied when the claimant knew that he was not bound to make the transfer (3.1.1.1). In contrast, in English law, it is the tranferor's mistake that entitles him to restitution. In a second step, the recipient can, however, defend himself by showing that he had an enforceable claim to the benefit received, in which case no action lies against him.[66]

Beyond these similarities in outcomes reached, there are also indications of a gradual rapprochement in the methodologies used. To a large extent, this development is attributable to the so-called swap litigation—a wave of cases on the recovery of payments made under interest swap contracts between financial institutions and local authorities.[67] Such contracts had been made since the 1980s, but in 1992 the House of Lords held that they were *ultra vires* the local authorities and hence void.[68] This decision prompted a number of banks to sue their contractual partners for the return of net payments made under such contracts. The initial response of English courts was to allow restitution on the sole basis that the underlying contracts were void[69]—an approach strikingly similar to the one adopted in the civilian systems. It looked as if English law was about to, or had already abandoned its traditional focus on specific unjust-factors in favor of a broad, general ground for restitution "absence of basis."[70] However, these expectations were at least temporarily frustrated when a related case was brought before the House of Lords. Renouncing the old distinction between mistakes of fact and mistakes of law, the House of Lords al-

---

64. Differences between the contractual and restitutionary concepts exist in particular with regard to the unjust-factors mistake and failure of consideration, see Dannemann, *Transfers*, 1855 *seq.*, with further references.

65. See Schlechtriem, *Restitution*, vol. I, 135; Zimmermann, *Bereicherungsrecht*, 32.

66. See Robert Goff J. in *Barclays Bank v. W. J. Simms Ltd.* [1980] 1 QB 677, 695.

67. See, generally, Birks, *Unjust Enrichment*, 108 *seqq.*

68. *Hazell v. London Borough of Hammersmith and Fulham* [1992] 2 A.C. 1.

69. Hobhouse J. in *Westdeutsche Landesbank v. Islington LBC* [1994] 4 All ER 890, 955; *Guinness Mahon & Co. Ltd. v. Kensington & Chelsea Royal London BC* [1999] QB 215 (CA).

70. This view has in particular been promoted by comparative lawyers such as Zimmermann, *Bereicherungsrecht*, 33 *seq.*, and S. Meier, *Irrtum und Zweckverfehlung*, Tubingen 1999, 371 *seqq.* At least initially, English restitution scholars reacted more skeptically, see for example M. Chen-Wishart, In *Defence of Unjust Factors: a Study of Rescission for Duress, Fraud and Exploitation*, in: R. Zimmermann and D. Johnston (eds.), *Unjustified Enrichment—Key Issues in Comparative Perspective*, Cambridge 2002, 159.

lowed recovery because the claimant had acted under a "settled understanding of the law," and had wrongly believed to be under an obligation to make the payment—a belief that proved wrong when the swap contracts were later declared void.[71] This view led to rather controversial debates about the underlying assumptions about judicial interpretations: by treating the case as one of mistake, the House of Lords suggested in fact that it had, in its 1992 decision on the *ultra vires* character of the swap agreements, only declared the law as it had always been, rather than having changed its content—an argument that met with considerable scepticism as the decision marked a significant departure from established case law.[72] Against this background, the view that restitution was in reality, and should have been, ordered solely because payments had been made in the absence of a valid (contractual) basis has increasingly been gaining ground in recent years.[73] Even though the traditional analysis of specific unjust-factors still dominates in practice, there is, therefore, a considerable likelihood that the broad "absence of basis"-approach that has long marked the civilian conception of unjustified enrichment will in due course also prevail in English law.

### 3.1.2. Remedies

Once it has been decided that a benefit voluntarily conferred on another is subject to recovery, the next question is through what remedies the defendant's liability is implemented, and how strictly it is defined. The most fundamental choice in this context is that between proprietary and purely personal remedies (3.1.2.1). In the latter case, it also needs to be decided if and to what extent recipients should remain liable even though the original receipt cannot be returned in nature, or does not have any value for them (3.1.2.2). Unlike the definition of liability-triggering events, this area presents considerable and profound differences between the civilian and common law traditions.

---

71. See *Kleinwort Benson Ltd v. Lincoln City Council* [1998] 2 All ER 513. This different analysis was triggered by limitation issues, as claims for relief from the consequences of a mistake are subject to a longer limitation period, see Birks, *Unjust Enrichment*, 112, 239.

72. See the vote of the dissenting judge Lord Browne-Wilkinson in *Kleinwort Benson Ltd v. Lincoln City Council* [1998] 4 All ER 513, 522; see also S. Meier and R. Zimmermann, *Judicial Development of the Law, Error Iuris, and the Law of Unjustified Enrichment—a View from Germany*, LQR 15 (1999), 556, 559 *seq.*

73. The most prominent support for this view has come from Peter Birks, who adopted this understanding in the last edition of his textbook, see Birks, *Unjust Enrichment*, 113 *seqq.*, 115: "Absence of basis is now the only unjust factor in English law"; see also Meier/Zimmermann, *Judicial Development*, 556 *seqq.*

### *3.1.2.1. The Choice between Personal and Proprietary Claims*

In the civilian systems, unjustified enrichment claims are always personal in nature. Consequently, they do not afford the claimants any privileged position in the recipient's bankruptcy. Any such privileges exist only as long as title to the assets subject to recovery has not passed to the recipient. In this case, the transferor can reclaim his property by invoking the *rei vindicatio* (2.1.2 above), even if the assets have in the meantime come into the possession of a third party.[74] Thus, the practical importance of unjustified enrichment claims within a given legal system depends on the rules on the acquisition and loss of title.[75] In most civil law systems of Western Europe, the transfer of title requires a valid cause.[76] In these systems, unjustified enrichment claims for transfers only become relevant when title to the benefit subject to recovery has exceptionally passed in spite of the absence of a valid cause, or when the benefit received can, due to its nature, not be returned in nature, as is typically the case with services. In contrast, under the German model of "abstract" transfers of title, unjustified enrichment claims play a much more important role as title passes without regard to the validity of the underlying obligation.[77]

The distinction between the law of property and the law of obligations is fundamental to the civilian conception of patrimonial law in general and, as seen just before, to the role of unjustified enrichment claims in particular. In the tradition of English law, personal and proprietary claims are separated much less clearly.[78] To start with, the range of recognized property rights is

---

74. Recovery from a third party is, however, excluded in case of bona fide acquisition of title by that party. It should also be noted that the distinction between the *in rem* claim (*revendication*) and the purely personal unjustified enrichment claim (*répétition de l'indu*) is not always very clear in the Romanist systems, see Schlechtriem, *Restitution*, vol. I, 290 *seqq*.

75. This is also one of the main difficulties which the Study Group on a European Civil Code has been facing in its efforts to prepare European-wide proposals on liability for unjustified enrichment, see Swann, *First Proposals*, 268 *seq*.

76. This is in particular the case for French law, under which title passes automatically once a valid (unconditional) obligation to this effect has come into existence, see Articles 711, 1138 and 1583 of the French Civil Code. The French model was taken over in the Benelux countries, Italy, Portugal and also in England. In Austrian and Swiss law, transfer of title also requires a valid cause, but depends in addition on the delivery of the thing. See, generally, Schlechtriem, *Restitution*, vol. I, 283 *seqq*.; Wendehorst, *Leistungskondiktion*, 70 *seq*.

77. This is also the solution of Greek law, see Schlechtriem, *Restitution*, vol. I, 288.

78. See, generally, W. Swadling, *Property: General Principles*, in: Peter Birks (ed.), *English Private Law*, vol. 1, Oxford 2000, 203, 210 *seqq*.; more specifically on the differences

far more complex than in the civilian systems, as property rights exist at common law and in equity, and as the same asset can simultaneously be subject to property interests under both sets of rules. In addition, the remedies available for the protection of property interests are far more diverse than in the civilian tradition. There is in particular no proper equivalent to the *rei vindicatio*. Instead, property interests are often protected through delictual claims, while unjust enrichments are sometimes reversed through equity-based proprietary remedies.[79] Thus, the rules of tracing allow asserting property rights in assets that the defendant obtained in exchange for a benefit originally received or taken from the claimant.[80] In other situations, funds that the recipient is considered to hold on trust for another person may be recovered under a constructive or resulting trust without the claimant having to compete with other creditors. Notwithstanding this diversity of remedies, unjust enrichments resulting from intentional transfers (as opposed to encroachments, see 3.1.2.3) are typically corrected through *in personam* claims directed at recovering the value of the benefit received.[81]

### *3.1.2.2. Liability under Unjustified Enrichment Claims*

Apart from the fact that unjustified enrichment claims do not afford privileges in the event of insolvency, they are also subject to relatively generous defenses. This is especially so in legal systems influenced by German law, where liability in unjustified enrichment is subject to a general defense of change of position (§818 sec. 3 BGB, Article 64 Swiss Code of Obligations). This defense used to be interpreted very broadly, as defendants were traditionally al-

---

between civil law and common law G. Gretton, *Proprietary Issues*, in: R. Zimmermann and D. Johnston (eds.), *Unjustified Enrichment—Key Issues in Comparative Perspective*, Cambridge 2002, 571.

79. Birks, *Unjust Enrichment*, 32 *seqq*., who notes that property is in the tradition of English law a response, rather than a causative event for liability. The reasons for this diversity lie in the historical origins of the claims today referred to as law of restitution. The common law remedies that developed out of the old action of *assumpsit*, such as the *action for money had and received* or the *action for quantum meruit*, are purely personal in nature. In contrast, most proprietary remedies developed in the law of equity, see Burrows, *Restitution*, 53.

80. Whether the rules of tracing are a remedy for reversing unjust enrichment, or whether they only vindicate an existing property right is a matter of controversy, see *Foskett v. McKeown* [2001] 1 AC 102; Burrows, *Restitution*, 65 *seqq*.; Birks, *Unjust Enrichment*, 34 *seqq*.

81. Birks, *Unjust Enrichment*, 168 *seq*.

lowed to deduct all losses and expenses incurred in relation with the unjustified receipt, even if they had not been made in reliance on the latter's stability.[82] Quite apart from any subsequent loss of the benefit received, the change of position defense was also thought to imply that there could be no liability if the receipt had not resulted in a subjective enrichment for the defendant.[83] This broad deference to the defendant's idiosyncratic values has long been criticized for failing to adequately protect the interests of transferors, especially as claimants who are able to seek recovery under the *rei vindicatio* are subject to no similar restrictions. Due to this criticism, the scope of the defense has been greatly reduced. The now prevailing view is that the recipient of a benefit transferred without cause is in principle required to return that benefit in nature, even if he has not derived any subjective enrichment from it.[84] If this is impossible, he is in principle required to pay compensation at market values.[85] A defense from change of position can only be invoked if the benefit received was lost, or if additional losses were incurred, because the defendant had in good faith assumed that he would be able to keep it.[86]

The Romanist systems have always taken a more differentiated approach to defining the standard of liability in unjustified enrichment. As seen before, claims for the recovery of intentional transfers are primarily based on the special action of *répétition de l'indu* rather than on the general clause of liability in unjustified enrichment (2.1.1). Under this claim, the recipient is strictly liable for the money or thing received, even if he has not been enriched by it.[87] However, as this claim is based on a narrow concept of "payment," it does not apply to services and use rights. Restitution for these latter types of benefit

---

82. See, *e.g.*, RGZ 118, 185, 187; BGHZ 1, 75,81; 55, 128, 131.

83. See Reuter/Martinek, *Handbuch*, 11 *seqq.*, J. Gordley, *Restitution without enrichment? Change of position and Wegfall der Bereicherung*, in: R. Zimmermann and D. Johnston (eds.), *Unjustified Enrichment—Key Issues in Comparative Perspective*, Cambridge 2002, 227, 229 *seq.*, with further references.

84. See K. Larenz and C.-W. Canaris, *Lehrbuch des Schuldrechts*: Besonderer Teil (vol. II/2), 13th ed., Munich 1994, 254 *seqq.*; von Caemmerer, *Bereicherung*, 226 *seq.*; Wilburg, *Lehre*, 124 *seq.*

85. See, *e.g.*, BGHZ 5, 197, 201; 10, 171, 180; Larenz/Canaris, *Lehrbuch*, 256, 275; Reuter/Martinek, *Handbuch*, 568.

86. The defense is also available if benefits, such as services, cannot be returned in nature: provided the recipient was not aware that he was not entitled to their receipt, he can object that his personal situation has not been improved by them, see Hahn, *Vergütungsansprüche*, 242 *seq.*, with further references.

87. See Com., 10 February 1998, RTD civ. 1999, 102, with note by Jacques Mestre; Planiol/Ripert/Esmein, *Traité*, n. 746.

can only be demanded under the general clause of liability in unjustified enrichment, under which the defendant's liability depends in principle on the presence of a subjective benefit.[88] In practice, the requirements for showing such an enrichment are, however, very low and, unless specific circumstances suggest that the defendant did not wish to receive the service or thing in question, he is generally held liable for its market price.[89]

In comparison with the Continental systems, English law clearly places more importance on protecting defendants from liability for things or services that were received in the absence of a valid contract. People are in principle not to be held liable for benefits for which they did not agree to pay, or which cannot at least be easily exchanged into money. Based on this idea, different criteria are applied depending on the type of benefit received. The receipt of money is considered to be *per se* enriching,[90] and the recipient only escapes liability if he can invoke a defense from change of position.[91] Conversely, where benefits in kind or for services are in issue, the recipient can object that he did not want to receive those benefits, or that he would not have been willing to pay for them at market prices.[92] However, when there are indications that the recipient has been saved a necessary expense or that he has effectively realized the market value of the benefit received—for example by selling a thing that was improved against his will[93]—he is not allowed to "subjectively devalue" the receipt in this way. The same is true if the defendant has, through his prior conduct, manifested a willingness to pay for the benefit received. In all of these cases, he is in principle required to pay the benefit at its market price, as if he had previously agreed to do so.[94]

---

88. Rouast, *enrichissement*, 52 *seq.*; Planiol/Ripert/Esmein, *Traité*, n. 753.

89. See, *e.g.*, Civ. 1re, 9 January and 30 May 1979, D.1981. Jur. 241; Civ. 1re, 26 October 1982, JCP 1983, II, 19992.

90. See Birks, *Unjust Enrichment*, 53; R. Goff and G. Jones, *The Law of Restitution*, 6th ed., London 2002, 16.

91. See *Lipkin Gorman v. Karpnale Ltd* [1991] 2 A.C. 548.

92. See Birks, *Unjust Enrichment*, 54; Goff/Jones, *Restitution*, 18; see also *BP Exploration Co. (Libya) Ltd. v. Hunt (No. 2)* [1979] 1 WLR 783, 799 (QBD.); *Stovin v. Wise* [1996] 3 All ER 801, 819.

93. See Birks, *Unjust Enrichment*, 61. Goff/Jones, *Restitution*, 23, and Burrows, *Restitution*, 19, consider it sufficient that the market value of the benefit received can be realized with reasonable certainty.

94. Again, there are different views as to which circumstances allow concluding to such a willingness to pay, see Birks, *Unjust Enrichment*, 56 *seq.*; Goff/Jones, *Restitution*, 18; Burrows, *Restitution*, 14 *seqq.*

In addition to these general principles, it is important to note that almost all European legal systems have developed special rules and concepts for dealing with situations in which void, invalid or frustrated contracts have been wholly or partly executed by both parties.[95] The purpose of these special rules is generally to minimize the complications associated with unwinding executed contracts (see also 3.1.1.1), and to maintain a nexus between the parties' respective obligations so that none of them can escape liability, for example under the change of position defense, while at the same time claiming full recovery from the other. The dogmatic solutions used for implementing these objectives vary considerably. In some cases, recovery for transfers made in contractual settings is totally excluded from the law of restitution and solely addressed through contractual remedies.[96] In other cases, unjustified enrichment rules continue to be relevant, but are adjusted to reflect the underlying contractual considerations, for example through limitations on the change of position defense. As a result of these differentiations, restitution for executed contracts is clearly more complex, and in comparative perspective also far more diverse than the rules on restitutionary liability for unilateral transfers.

### *3.2. Liability for Encroachments*

Historically, the debate over liability in unjustified enrichment mostly focused on intentional transfers. There is, however, a second, large category of benefit-based remedies, which is today at least as important, and which is concerned with undoing certain monetary consequences of encroachments another's resources. Before discussing the conditions under which such remedies are available in different European jurisdictions (3.2.2), a brief overview will be given over the possible remedies and underlying rationales (3.2.1).

---

95. See P. Hellwege, *Die Rückabwicklung gegenseitiger Verträge als einheitliches Problem*, Tubingen 2004; for a Swiss perspective S. Hartmann, *Die Rückabwicklung von Schuldverträgen: kritischer Vergleich der Rechtslagen bei Entstehungs-und Erfüllungsmängeln*, Zurich 2005.

96. See, *e.g.*, for French law, Y.-L. Sage and A.H. Angelo, *Some Reflections on the Economic Consequences of the Cancellation of a Contract in French Law*, (2000) 31 Victoria University of Wellington Law Review. In English law, rescission is considered a separate remedy that revests the proprietary rights to goods or land transferred under the contract, see, *e.g.*, *Car and Universal Finance Co. Ltd. v. Caldwell* [1965] 1 QB 525; Burrows, *Restitution*, 58 *seq.*

### 3.2.1. Types of Relief and Underlying Rationales

When talking about liability for encroachments, it is useful to distinguish between remedies that aim to restore control over a specific asset or resource as such (3.2.1.1), and remedies that purport to transfer the economic benefits of an unlawful infringement to the person affected thereby (3.2.1.2).

#### *3.2.1.1. Recovery of Assets Withdrawn against the Owner's Will*

Claims for the recovery of assets that have been withdrawn from their owner against his will exist in all legal systems of Western Europe. In the civilian tradition, owners can in this situation normally invoke the proprietary claim of *rei vindicatio*, which is also available in respect of voluntary transfers that do not result in a passing of title (3.1.2.1). The common law position is more complicated, as real property (land and related chattels) and personal property (all other property rights) are protected through a range of different remedies.[97] Thus, the unauthorized retention or disposal of movables can give rise to the actions of conversion, trespass to chattels or detinue.[98] Typically, all of these actions result in a duty to pay damages for the value of the thing appropriated.[99] Similarly, acts of unlawful interference with land are sanctioned through the actions of *ejectment* or *trespass to land*, both of which are tort actions.[100]

#### *3.2.1.2. Recovery of Economic Benefits Realized without the Owner's Consent*

Unlike the *rei vindicatio* of the civilian systems and the various remedies of English law described above, the terms "restitution for wrongs" or "restitutionary remedies" are generally reserved to remedies that do not purport to recover an asset or resource as such, but rather the economic benefits that are

97. See Swadling, *Property*, 219, 221; P. Huber, *Eigentumsschutz durch Deliktsrecht. Vergleichende Betrachtung zum englischen Recht der Wrongful Interference with Goods*, RabelsZ 62 (1998), 59.

98. Trespass to chattels and detinue cannot only be invoked by owners, but also by mere possessors, while conversion requires ownership of the goods. The choice of the remedy also depends on the severity of the damage suffered, see generally S. Deakin, A. Johnston and B. Markesinis, *Markesinis and Deakin's Tort Law*, 5th ed., Oxford 2003, 436 *seqq.*

99. See Deakin/Johnston/Markesinis, *Tort Law*, 442 *seq.*, on the (very limited) possibility to demand the return of the thing appropriated.

100. Deakin/Johnston/Markesinis, *Tort Law*, 444 *seqq.*

associated with it, and that an infringer may have used without the owner's consent. Situations of this type can, for example, arise when land is unlawfully occupied, when products are sold under another's trade name, when unauthorized photographs are commercially exploited, or when a patient's body tissue is used for research without his consent.[101] In all of these situations, the persons affected by such encroachments are—apart from regaining physical control over their resource—generally interested in obtaining some form of remuneration for the unauthorized use that has been made of their rights.[102]

One way to sanction infringements of this type is by awarding compensatory damages. The purpose of such damage awards is to compensate the claimant for the subjective loss sustained as a result of the infringement, whether in the form of a decrease in his existing wealth, or in the from of lost income.[103] Thus, owners whose premises have been used against their will can, if they intended to lease out those premises, demand compensation for the income lost through the unlawful occupation, while the unauthorized use of a trade name may give rise to damage claims for reputational harm suffered due to the interference. Likewise, the unauthorized withdrawal of body tissue from a patient can result in a duty to pay damages for harm inflicted in the course of this process. However, compensatory damages always require evidence of a measurable loss, whether through a deterioration of the claimant's existing situation or through a loss of profits that the claimant could have realized. No such loss can be established in situations when claimants did not intend to commercially exploit their resources, or when they would not have succeeded

---

101. See *Moore v. Regents of University of California*, 793 P.2d 479 (Cal. 1990), where cell lines derived from a patient's body tissues were without his knowledge used to develop and patent anti-cancer therapies. In a highly debated decision, the Supreme Court of the State of California found that the patient was not entitled to participate in the resulting profits because he had no property interest in his body tissues and was, therefore, not entitled to bring an action in conversion, see also Dagan, *Law and Ethics*, 240 *seqq.*

102. See P. Schlechtriem, *Unjust Enrichment by Interference with Property Rights*, in: E. von Caemmerer and P. Schlechtriem, *International Encyclopedia of Comparative Law, vol. X: Restitution, Unjust Enrichment and Negotiorum Gestio*, Tubingen, Leiden, Boston 2007, 1 *et seqq.* for a discussion of the assets thus protected in different jurisdictions.

103. See for example Megarry V-C in *Tito v. Waddell (No 2)* [1977] Ch.D. 106, 332: "[I]t is fundamental to all questions of damages that they are to compensate the plaintiff for his loss or injury by putting him as nearly as possible in the same position as he would have been in had he not suffered the wrong", see also D. Friedmann, *Restitution for Wrongs: The Measure of Recovery*, 79 Tex. L. Rev. 1879, 1882 *seq.*, on the (factual and legal) limits of full subjective compensation.

in doing so.[104] This is where the interest of restitutionary remedies lies: Unlike compensatory damages, they are based on the earning opportunities associated with a specific resource, or on the profits derived from its appropriation, rather than on the losses sustained by the proprietor. By allowing the proprietor to recover all or part of these benefits, they help to reassert his control over the underlying resource, or ensure at least that he does not end up worse off than as if he had previously sold his use right to the infringer under market conditions.[105]

In most legal systems, the extent of restitutionary liability for encroachments varies depending on the gravity of the encroachment. Sometimes, defendants have to disgorge all of the profits obtained through the unauthorized use of another's resources. In other cases, their liability is limited to the market price that they would have had to pay to purchase the right to use that resource. Obviously, the protection afforded by these two types of remedies is not the same: In the first case, the encroachment loses its economic appeal as all benefits derived therefrom are transferred to the claimant. In contrast, if the infringer's liability is limited to the fair market value of the right appropriated by him, the remedy is unlikely to have any deterrent effect as the infringer can keep any additional gains.[106] This notwithstanding, both types of remedies afford greater protection than compensatory damages as they can also be invoked by claimants who would never have exploited their rights in the same way as the infringer. As is illustrated by recent developments in the areas of publicity and privacy, where profit-based remedies are becoming more and more frequent,[107] restitutionary remedies thereby not only help to protect

104. But see R.J. Sharpe and S.M. Waddams, *Damages for lost opportunity to bargain*, OJLS 1982, 290, who argue that compensatory damages can and should be awarded because the claimant has lost the opportunity to sell a use right to the defendant.

105. An alternative form of protecting resources is afforded through injunctions that are granted before, rather than after the act of interference has occurred. Injunctions leave potential infringers no other choice but to enter into negotiations over the right to use the resource they are interested in, thus affording owners maximum control over their resources. Restitutionary remedies that transfer all profits from an infringement to the affected owner produce similar incentives. These issues have received considerable attention in recent years, see *e.g.* H. Dagan, *Unjust Enrichment: A Study of Private Law and Public Values,* Cambridge 1997, 16 *seqq.*, and the article by G. Calabresi and A. D. Melamed on *Property Rules, Liability Rules, and Inalienability: One View of the Cathedral*, Harv. L. Rev. 85 (1972), 1089, 1092, which has inspired the more recent debates.

106. See, generally, Dagan, *Law and Ethics*, 213 *seqq.;* see also J. Edelman, *Gain-based damages: contract, tort, equity and intellectual property*, Oxford 2002, 73 *seqq.*

107. See the "Caroline of Monaco case", in which the German Supreme Court took the view that the gains made by a publisher, who had printed an invented interview with the

long-established property rights, but also contribute to the creation of new, commercially exploitable entitlements that were not traditionally thought of as property interests.[108]

## 3.2.2. Conditions and Extent of Liability

Most legal systems of Western Europe recognize the role that restitutionary remedies can play for sanctioning encroachments on another's rights or resources. This notwithstanding, the practical relevance of such remedies, and the doctrinal mechanisms used for their implementation vary considerably from country to country.

### *3.2.2.1. The Germanic Tradition*

Cases of encroachments did not play an important role under the model of liability in unjustified enrichment that was originally developed by von Savigny (2.1.2). One central element of this model was the requirement of a transfer of wealth from the claimant to the defendant. This was understood to imply that encroachments on use rights or intellectual property could only lead to liability in unjustified enrichment when the defendant's enrichment was matched by a corresponding loss by the claimant, but as described above, it is often difficult to establish such a loss. The growing desire to protect resources regardless of any provable losses yielded different doctrinal solutions. In the area of intellectual property law, German courts began to deviate from traditional tort rules by measuring—supposedly compensatory—damages on the basis of usual license fees, or even on the basis of the profits resulting from the infringement.[109] On a more general level, legal writers suggested to re-consider the understanding of liability in unjustified enrichment and to recognize

---

princess, had to be taken into account for measuring the pain and suffering award made to the claimant, BGHZ 128, 1; see also the English case *Douglas v. Hello! Ltd (No 2)* [2003] EWHC 786 (Ch.), and, for an analysis of these tendencies C.-W. Canaris, *Gewinnabschöpfung bei Verletzung des allgemeinen Persönlichkeitsrechts*, in: *Festschrift Deutsch*, Cologne 1999, 85; P. Schlechtriem, *Privacy, Publicity and Restitution of Wrongful Gains: Another New Economy?*, (2001) Oxford U Comparative L Forum 3 at <www.ouclf.iuscomp.org> and F. Werro, *Faut-il renforcer la protection de la personnalité? La tentation des dommages-intérêts punitifs en droit des médias*, Medialex 2002, 81.

108. See generally Dagan, *Law and Ethics*, 215 *seqq*.; D. Friedmann, *The Protection of Entitlements via the Law of Restitution—Expectancies and Privacy*, LQR 121 (2005), 400, 407 *seqq*.

109. See BGHZ 44, 372; 60, 206; 77, 16; R. Ellger, *Bereicherung durch Eingriff: Das Konzept des Zuweisungsgehalts im Spannungsverhältnis von Ausschließlichkeitsrecht und Wettbewerbsfreiheit*, Tubingen 2002, 597 *seqq*. On the role of intellectual property rights in the

acts of unlawful interference with another's resources as a distinct, liability-triggering event, provided that the resources in question are commercially exploitable.[110] Thus, the unauthorized use of land, movables, patents, trade names and trade secrets can all lead to liability in restitution because the commercial benefits associated with these entitlements are considered to be reserved to their owners. Conversely, the appropriation of resources that are in the public domain, or violations of legal rules that do not confer exclusionary rights on specific persons, such as, for example, acts of unfair competition, do in principle not give rise to restitutionary liability. This conception has gradually been accepted by the overwhelming majority of courts and scholars in Germany as well as in most of the legal systems inspired by German law.[111]

According to the prevailing view, liability in unjustified enrichment for encroachments is always limited to the market value of the right or resource that has been appropriated by the infringer.[112] In cases of patent infringements, the patent holder can, for example, claim the payment of a reasonable license fee, while profits exceeding this amount can be kept by the infringer. Such profits are only subject to recovery if they are the result of an intentional infringement.[113] In this case, the claimant can, in addition to relying on unjustified enrichment principles, demand the disgorgement of profits realized on the theory that the infringer was unlawfully managing the claimant's affairs, and that he is, therefore, accountable in the same way as if he had acted as an agent.[114] Thus, voluntary infringements are sanctioned (and deterred) with

gradual reform of liability in unjustified enrichment see also C. Joerges, *Bereicherungsrecht als Wirtschaftsrecht*, Cologne 1977, 14 *seqq.*

110. See in particular E. v. Caemmerer, *Grundprobleme des Bereicherungsrechts*, in: H.G. Leser (ed.), *Gesammelte Schriften: Rechtsvergleichung und Schuldrecht* (vol. 1), Tubingen 1968, 371, 378.

111. See BGHZ 68, 90; 82, 299; 107, 117; J. Esser and H.-L. Weyers, *Schuldrecht, Besonderer Teil, Gesetzliche Schuldverhältnisse* (vol. II/2), 8th ed., Heidelberg 2000, 75 *seq.*; Reuter/Martinek, *Handbuch*, 257; W.R. Schluep, *Über Eingriffskondiktionen*, in: Mélanges Piotet, Berne 1990, 173, 199, all with further references.

112. See BGHZ 82, 299; von Caemmerer, *Bereicherung*, 232 *seqq.*

113. In Swiss law, negligence is also sufficient, see BGE 119 II 40, 43; 126 III 69, 72; 129 III 422, 425.

114. This results from §687 sec. 2 BGB in combination with §681 BGB and §667 BGB, see R. Wittmann, Commentary to §§652–704 BGB, in: J. v. Staudinger, *Kommentar zum Bürgerlichen Gesetzbuch mit Einführungsgesetz und Nebengesetzen, Zweites Buch: Recht der Schuldverhältnisse*, 13th ed., Berlin 1995, §687 n. 20, for further references. Under the case law on the calculation of damages in cases of intellectual property infringements, the surrender of profits can also be demanded in tort law, see BGHZ 44, 372; 60, 206; 77, 16.

the help of a profit-based remedy whereas other infringements only lead to a duty to compensate the plaintiff for the income that he could have realized by selling his resource to the infringer under market conditions.

### *3.2.2.2. The Common Law Tradition*

English law has traditionally recognized the possibility to sanction specific torts through restitutionary remedies, both at common law and in equity.[115] In contrast, the tendency to describe these situations as instances of "restitution for wrongs," and to emancipate them from the underlying torts is relatively recent.[116] As yet, it is not clear to what extent this new understanding can help to develop a systematic approach for identifying the types of conduct in which restitutionary remedies are appropriate.[117] One suggestion, which is to a certain extent reminiscent of debates in the Germanic systems (3.2.2.1), is to limit restitutionary liability to situations in which the claimant is, or should be, entitled to the earning opportunities associated with the underlying right or resource.[118] This is a useful approach, but it does not explain why in English law, too, recovery is sometimes limited to the use value of the appropriated resource, but other times extends to the profits resulting from the encroachment. The reason for this distinction lies probably in the fact that certain resources are considered more important than others, and that any infringements thereof are from the outset to be deterred through a profit-based remedy.[119]

Although for the time being there is no established methodology in English law for determining the types of conduct that can lead to restitutionary liability, and the extent of such liability, it is possible to identify certain categories of cases in which restitutionary remedies have traditionally been ad-

115. This includes in particular the "waiver of tort" doctrine, see 2.2 above, and the "account of profits" that developed out of the law of equity, see Burrows, *Restitution*, 467.

116. See Birks, *Unjust Enrichment*, 83 *seq*.; T. Krebs, *Eingriffskondiktion und Restitution for Wrongs im englischen Recht*, in: R. Zimmermann and D. Johnston (eds.), *Unjustified Enrichment—Key Issues in Comparative Perspective*, Cambridge 2002, 141.

117. See S. Worthington, *Reconsidering Disgorgement for Wrongs*, MLR 62 (1999), 218. On a very general level, it is often assumed that such liability should be imposed in respect of torts that are not adequately sanctioned through compensatory damages, see for example *Swordheath Properties Ltd. v. Tabet* [1979] 1 WLR 285, 288; Burrows, *Restitution*, 455. This, however, seems to beg, rather than answer, the question as to when exactly monetary relief is appropriate although the claimant has not suffered a measurable loss.

118. See Birks, *Unjust Enrichment*, 82 *seqq*.; Krebs, *Eingriffskondiktion*, 164 *seqq*.

119. See generally Dagan, *Unjust Enrichment*, 16 *seqq*. See also Worthington, *Disgorgement*, 218 *seqq*., who argues that profit-based remedies should be limited to breaches of "good faith or loyalty".

mitted. A first group concerns the unauthorized use of another's premises (*trespass to land*)[120] or movables (*trespass to goods*).[121] In both situations, defendants are required to pay the owner a reasonable use fee for the use of his property.[122] Restitutionary remedies have also long been granted in view of intellectual property right infringements—first under the equitable doctrine of "account of profits," and today primarily on the basis of specific provisions in the relevant statutes.[123] Unlike in cases of proprietary torts, claimants can in this type of scenario demand the disgorgement of all (net) profits resulting from the infringement.[124] A third category deals with breaches of fiduciary duties that arise whenever someone has undertaken to act, or is retrospectively qualified, as trustee of another person.[125] Based on this qualification, he is required to show loyalty to the beneficiary and must refrain from exploiting his position for his own profit.[126] If these duties of loyalty are breached, the trustee can be required to surrender all resulting profits to the beneficiary.[127] When trusts funds have unlawfully been misused and invested into other assets, the beneficiary may also be able to recover these substitute assets with the help of a proprietary remedy.[128] Thus, when a corrupt prosecutor had accepted bribes,

120. See *Penarth Dock Engineering Co. Ltd. v. Pounds* [1963] 1 Lloyd's Law Reports 359 (QBD); *Bracewell v. Appleby* [1975] Ch.D. 408; *Ministry of Defence v. Ashman* (1993) 66 Property Planning and Compensation Reports 195 (C.A.), but see *Phillips v. Homfray* (1883) 24 Ch.D. 439, where a tortfeasor had transported coal over the plaintiff's land without previously seeking the latter's consent and paying for the passage right. Here, restitution was denied on the basis that the saved expenses did not directly result from the plaintiff's property, see Burrows, *Restitution*, 473 *seq.*

121. *Strand Electric & Engineering Co Ltd v. Brisford Entertainments Ltd* [1952] 2 QB 246. Restitution was denied in *Stoke-on-Trent City Council v. W. & J. Wass Ltd.* [1988] 1 WLR 1406, where the defendants had, by operating a market, infringed on the claimant's proprietary market right, thereby committing the tort of nuisance.

122. See *Strand Electric & Engineering Co Ltd v. Brisford Entertainments Ltd* [1952] 2 QB 246, 254; *Ministry of Defence v. Ashman* (1993) 66 Property Planning and Compensation Reports 195.

123. See section 61 (1) Patent Act 1977; section 96 (2) and 229 (2) Copyright, Designs and Patents Act 1988; section 14 (2) Trade Marks Act 1994.

124. See, for example, *Colbeam Palmer Ltd. v. Stock Affiliates Property Ltd.* (1968) 122 CLR 25; *Redwood Music Ltd. v. Chappell & Co. Ltd.* [1982] RPC 109.

125. See Goff/Jones, *Restitution*, 704.

126. See *Bristol and West Building Society v. Mothew* [1996] 4 All ER 698, 711.

127. See for example *Reading v. AG* [1951] A.C. 507; *Boardman v. Phipps* [1967] 2 A.C. 46; Goff/Jones, *Restitution*, 713 *seqq.*

128. Behind this concept stands the idea that the law of equity, from which these proprietary remedies are derived, "regards as done that which ought to have been", see Gretton, *Proprietary Issues*, 572.

the government was considered to hold an equitable interest in the monies received and was allowed to invoke a proprietary interest to the assets in which the illegal funds had been invested.[129] By the same token, when a former spy had revealed state secrets in his memoirs, he was made to surrender the profits realized through his publication to the government on the basis that he had breached his fiduciary duties to his former employer.[130] Subsequently, a similar result was reached in a case where information had been disclosed in breach of a post-contractual confidentiality undertaking without simultaneously violating any equity-based fiduciary duties.[131] It is unclear whether other, less "exceptional" breaches of contract can also lead to liability in restitution, for example when contractual damages present a risk of under-compensation because lost profits cannot be proved. The general feeling is, however, that these issues should primarily be tackled through contractual remedies, such as specific performance awards or liquidated damages.[132]

### 3.2.2.3. The Romanist Tradition

While the adequacy of restitutionary liability for encroachments is still being vividly discussed in common law jurisdiction and in legal systems inspired by German law, this question has to date not received much attention in French law and other Romanist systems.[133] Unlike in German and English law, acts of unlawful interference with another's resources are not seen as a potential source of liability in unjustified enrichment, but are exclusively addressed through tort law. Given that such acts generally qualify as delictual, parallel claim in unjustified enrichment are in fact automatically barred due to the strictly subsidiary nature of unjustified enrichment claims (2.1.1 above). This

---

129. *Attorney-General of Hong-Kong v. Reid* [1994] 1 AC 324 (PC NZ); see also *Boardman v. Phipps* [1967] 2 AC 46, and, generally, on the underlying concept of constructive trust Burrows, *Restitution,* 493 *seqq.*

130. *Attorney General v. Guardian Newspapers Ltd. (No. 2)* [1990] 1 A.C. 109.

131. *Attorney General v. Blake* [2000] 3 WLR 625 (HL).

132. See also *Experience Hendrix LLC v PPX Enterprises Inc.* [2003] EWCA Civ. 323, [2003] 1 All ER and on this A. Burrows, *Remedies for Torts and Breach of Contract,* 3rd ed., Oxford 2004, 405 *seq.*, suggesting that breaches of contract resulting in the unauthorized use of another's resources may result in a duty to pay for the fair market value of the resource regardless of the plaintiff's losses, while a disgorgement remedy should only be available in cases of egregious breach of conduct calculated to make gains; more generally Dagan, *Law and Ethics,* 261 *seqq.*

133. See A. Marx, *Abschöpfung der Bereicherung aus Eingriff in fremde Rechtsgüter im französischen und deutschen Recht,* Frankfurt am Main 1999, 90 *seq.*, with further references.

notwithstanding, profits realized through unlawful infringements are often taken into account for measuring tort damages. Thus, where intellectual property rights have been violated, French courts typically award the claimant a reasonable license fee, which is often increased by a certain amount in order to deter future violations.[134] Profit-based damage awards are also made when someone's personality rights have been commercially exploited without consent—for example, through the reproduction and distribution of unauthorized photographs.[135] However, even within the realm of tort law, these types of awards have something of a "niche" existence, and are generally not seen as expression of a broader principle.

## 4. Conclusion

There is a broad consensus in Western Europe that obligations cannot only arise from voluntary agreement and from the unlawful infliction of harm on another, but also from the receipt of benefits that belong to another person. This survey focused on two particularly important and widely recognized sources of such benefit-based liability: on the one hand, voluntary transfers of benefits made without sufficient cause and, on the other hand, unlawful encroachments on another's resources. Both illustrate that restitutionary remedies are essentially an instrument for re-asserting control over property rights and similar entitlements in situations of involuntary loss or appropriation. In doing so, restitutionary remedies complement and reinforce the law of property and other legal rules that create and define exclusionary entitlements, and occasionally they also contribute to the creation of new entitlements.

Although benefit-liability is, as a matter of principle, widely accepted in Western European legal systems, there are substantial divergences in the practical role that it plays within different jurisdictions, and in the doctrinal rules through which it is implemented. One primary reason for this variation lies in the law of property. As the rules on the transfer of title differ from one country to another, the important question as to whether assets lost can be recovered through *in rem* claims or through merely personal claims is often

---

134. See Paris, 10 July 1986, JCP 1986, II, 20720; generally Marx, *Abschöpfung*, 203 *seqq*.

135. See Trib. gr. inst. Seine, 1 April 1965, JCP 1966, II, 14572; Trib. gr. inst. Paris, 12 December 1984, D. 1985, IR, 323; Paris, 19 September 1985, D. 1986, IR, 189; Trib. gr. inst. Paris, 4 March 1987, JCP 1987, Jur. 20904; Lyon, 27 October 1988, D. 1988, IR 284; see also Werro, *protection de la personnalité*, 83 *seq*.

answered differently. Moreover, while unjustified enrichments are in the civilian systems always reversed through purely personal remedies, this is not the case in the common law, where the distinction between personal and proprietary claims is much less clear than in the civilian tradition. In addition, the delimitation from contractual and delictual claims also varies among jurisdictions. Sometimes, claims in unjustified enrichment are also superseded by concepts that have no proper equivalent in other systems, such as, for example, the unauthorized management of another's affairs of the Germanic systems, or the common law concepts of constructive and resulting trusts.

Apart from these delimitation issues, differences and controversies also exist with regard to the internal organization of the law of restitution. One of the questions that has occupied lawyers in all Western European systems is whether liability in unjustified enrichment should be discussed in terms of a broad general clause or on the basis of narrowly defined types of cases. The idea of a general clause has a long tradition in the civilian systems. It also seems to find additional support in the recent developments of English law and in the proposals of the Study Group on a European Civil Code.[136] Nevertheless, it is widely acknowledged that the analysis required for qualifying an enrichment as "unjustified" varies, depending on how it was brought about. Thus, legal systems influenced by German law today generally approach liability in unjustified liability on the basis of a typology of cases that are only loosely connected to each other, and that are at least in part subject to distinct rules. English law seems to be evolving along similar lines, even though the restitutionary remedies that have traditionally been recognized are now seen as emanations of a general principle against unjust enrichment. Finally, while the Romanist systems do recognize a general clause in unjustified enrichment, its scope is rather limited, as it does not cover the important category of claims for the recovery of failed transfers, and as cases of encroachments are exclusively addressed through tort law.

Once the focus of analysis shifts to specific categories of liability in unjustified enrichment, additional divergences become apparent. Thus, the role of restitutionary remedies in contractual contexts varies considerably, for example with regard to the question whether and through what mechanisms restitution should be ordered in the wake of failed contracts. There are also different views as to whether unjustified enrichment claims can be brought against a person who has indirectly benefited from a contract to which he or she is

136. See Article 1:101 of the Principles of European Unjustified Enrichment Law and 2.1.2 above.

not a party. In the area of liability for encroachments, the main difficulties are to identify the entitlements that are to be protected through restitutionary remedies, and to determine the appropriate measure of recovery.

As this list illustrates, it would be wrong to assume that European legal systems are firmly committed to one specific model of liability in unjustified enrichment, and that divisions only exist between, but not within individual jurisdictions. The French, German and English approaches to liability in unjustified enrichment undoubtedly differ on numerous doctrinal issues, and some of them appear to be the result of historical coincidences, not deliberate choices. However, many of the fundamental controversies, for example with regard to the choice between personal and proprietary remedies, the coordination of unjustified enrichment claims with contract law, or the availability of profit-based remedies, transcend national boundaries and reflect underlying disagreements on policy issues. While it would, therefore, be a mistake to assume that these divergences could easily be eliminated by harmonizing national rules and concepts, the recent re-conceptualization of the English law of restitution, and the gradual rapprochement to civilian concepts associated with it, have certainly made it easier to unveil and discuss these policy issues in a comparative perspective, as I hope to have shown in this survey.

## References

Aubry C. and Rau C., Cours de droit civil français d'après la méthode de Zachariae, 4th ed., Paris 1869–1876, vol. IV.

Baker J.H., An Introduction to English Legal History, 4th ed., London 2002.

Birks Peter, Unjust Enrichment, 2nd ed., Oxford 2005.

Bonet Georges, La condition d'absence d'intérêt personnel et de faute chez l'appauvri pour le succès de l'action de in rem verso, in: Mélanges offerts à Pierre Hébraud, Toulouse 1981.

Burrows Andrew, The Law of Restitution, 2nd ed., London 2002.

Burrows Andrew, Remedies for Torts and Breach of Contract, 3rd ed., Oxford 2004.

Caemmerer Ernst von, Bereicherung und unerlaubte Handlung, in: Hans G. Leser (ed.), Gesammelte Schriften, vol. 1: Rechtsvergleichung und Schuldrecht, Tubingen 1968, 209.

Caemmerer Ernst von, Grundprobleme des Bereicherungsrechts, in: Hans G. Leser (ed.), Gesammelte Schriften, vol. 1, Rechtsvergleichung und Schuldrecht, Tubingen 1968, 371.

Calabresi Guido and Melamed A. Douglas, Property Rules, Liability Rules, and Inalienability: One View of the Cathedral, Harv. L. Rev. 85 (1972), 1089.

Canaris Claus-Wilhelm, Der Bereicherungsausgleich im Dreipersonenverhältnis, in: Festschrift Larenz, Munich 1973, 799.

Canaris Claus-Wilhelm, Gewinnabschöpfung bei Verletzung des allgemeinen Persönlichkeitsrechts, in: Festschrift Deutsch, Cologne 1999, 85.

Carbonnier Jean, Droit civil, vol. IV: Les obligations, 22nd ed., Paris 2000.

Chen-Wishart M., In Defence of Unjust Factors: a Study of Rescission for Duress, Fraud and Exploitation, in: Reinhard Zimmermann and David Johnston (eds.), Unjustified Enrichment—Key Issues in Comparative Perspective, Cambridge 2002, 159.

Dagan Hanoch, The Law and Ethics of Restitution, Cambridge 2004.

Dagan Hanoch, Unjust Enrichment: A Study of Private Law and Public Values, Cambridge 1997.

Dannemann Gerhard, Illegality as Defence Against Unjust Enrichment Claims, (2000) Oxford U Comparative L Forum 4, <www.ouclf.iuscomp.org>.

Dannemann Gerhard, Unjust Enrichment by Transfer: Some Comparative Remarks, 79 Texas Law Review (2001), 1837.

Dawson John P., Negotiorum Gestio: The Altruistic Intermeddler, Harv. L. Rev. 74 (1961), 817 and 1073.

Deakin Simon, Johnston Angus and Markesinis Basil, Markesinis and Deakin's Tort Law, 5th ed., Oxford 2003.

Douchy Mélina, La notion de quasi-contrat en droit positif français, Paris 1997

Drakidis Philippe, La subsidiarité, caractère spécifique et international de l'action d'enrichissement sans cause, RTD civ. 1961, 38.

Edelman James, Gain-based damages: contract, tort, equity and intellectual property, Oxford 2002.

Ellger Reinhard, Bereicherung durch Eingriff: Das Konzept des Zuweisungsgehalts im Spannungsverhältnis von Ausschließlichkeitsrecht und Wettbewerbsfreiheit, Tubingen 2002.

Esser Josef and Weyers Hans-Leo, Schuldrecht, Besonderer Teil, Gesetzliche Schuldverhältnisse (vol. II/2), 8th ed., Heidelberg 2000.

Feenstra Robert, Grotius' Doctrine of Unjust Enrichment as a Source of Obligations: Its Origin and its Influence in Roman-Dutch Law, in: Eltjo Schrage (ed.), Unjust Enrichment, The Comparative Legal History of the Law of Restitution, 2nd ed., Berlin 1999, 197.

Flour Jacques/Aubert Jean-Luc/Savaux Eric, Les obligations, vol. 2: Le fait juridique, 10th ed., Paris 2003.

Friedmann Daniel, Restitution for Wrongs: The Measure of Recovery, 79 Tex. L. Rev. 1879.

Friedmann Daniel, The Protection of Entitlements via the Law of Restitution—Expectancies and Privacy, LQR 121 (2005), 400.

Friedmann Daniel, Unjust Enrichment, Pursuance of Self-Interest, and the Limits of Free Riding, Loy. L. A. L. Rev. 36 (2003), 831.

Goff Robert and Jones Gareth, The Law of Restitution, 6th ed., London 2002.

Gordley James, Restitution without enrichment? Change of position and *Wegfall der Bereicherung*, in: Reinhard Zimmermann and David Johnston (eds.), Unjustified Enrichment—Key Issues in Comparative Perspective, Cambridge 2002, 227.

Gordley James, The Principle Against Unjustified Enrichment, in: Gedächtnisschrift für Alexander Lüderitz, Munich 2000, 213.

Grantham Ross and Rickett Charles, *Unjust Enrichment—Reason, Place and Content*, in: id., *Structure and Justification in Private Law, Essays for Peter Birks*, Oxford/Portland 2008, 5.

Gretton George, Proprietary Issues, in: Reinhard Zimmermann and David Johnston (eds.), Unjustified Enrichment—Key Issues in Comparative Perspective, Cambridge 2002, 571.

Hagen Horst, Funktionale und dogmatische Zusammenhänge zwischen Schaden-und Bereicherungsrecht, in: Festschrift Larenz, Munich 1973, 867.

Hahn Anne-Catherine, Vergütungsansprüche für Dienstleistungen bei fehlender vertraglicher Grundlage, Berne/Baden-Baden 2004.

Hartmann Stephan, Die Rückabwicklung von Schuldverträgen: kritischer Vergleich der Rechtslagen bei Entstehungs-und Erfüllungsmängeln, Zurich 2005.

Hedley Steve, The Empire Strikes Back? A Restatement of the Law of Unjust Enrichment [2004] Melbourne University Law Review 26.

Hellwege Philipp, Die Rückabwicklung gegenseitiger Verträge als einheitliches Problem, Tubingen 2004.

Hogg Martin A., Lowlands to Low Country: Perspectives on the Scottish and Dutch Law of Unjustified Enrichment, vol. 5.1 Electronic Journal of Comparative Law, (March 2001), <www.ejcl.org/ejcl/51/art51-1.html>.

Honorat Jean, Rôle effectif et rôle concevable des quasi-contrats en droit actuel, RTD civ. 1969, 653.

Huber Peter, Eigentumsschutz durch Deliktsrecht. Vergleichende Betrachtung zum englischen Recht der Wrongful Interference with Goods, RabelsZ 62 (1998), 59.

Huwiler Bruno, Zur Anspruchsgrundlage der Obligation aus ungerechtfertigter Bereicherung im Schweizerischen Obligationenrecht, Der Allgemeine Teil und das Ganze, Liber Amicorum für Herrmann Schulin, Basel 2002, 41.

Joerges Christian, Bereicherungsrecht als Wirtschaftsrecht, Cologne 1977.

Johnston David and Zimmermann Reinhard, Unjustified Enrichment: Surveying the Landscape, in: *id.* (eds.), Unjustified Enrichment—Key Issues in Comparative Perspective, Cambridge 2002, 3.

Krebs Thomas, Eingriffskondiktion und Restitution for Wrongs im englischen Recht, in: Reinhard Zimmermann and David Johnston (eds.), Unjustified Enrichment—Key Issues in Comparative Perspective, Cambridge 2002, 141.

Kupisch Berthold, Die Versionsklage, Heidelberg 1965.

Kupisch Berthold, Einheitliche Voraussetzungen des Bereicherungsanspruchs—ein Missgriff des Gesetzgebers?, in: Festgabe für U. v. Lübtow, Berlin 1980, 501.

Kupisch Berthold, Ungerechtfertigte Bereicherung, Geschichtliche Entwicklungen, Heidelberg 1987.

Larenz Karl/Canaris Claus-Wilhelm, Lehrbuch des Schuldrechts, vol. 2/2: Besonderer Teil, 13th ed. Munich 1994.

Maitland F.W., The Forms of Action at Common Law, A course of Lectures (eds. A.H. Chaytor and W.J. Whittaker), Cambridge 1976 (reprint).

Marty Gabriel/Raynaud Pierre, Droit civil, Les obligations, vol. 2: 2nd ed., Paris 1988.

Marx Astrid, Abschöpfung der Bereicherung aus Eingriff in fremde Rechtsgüter im französischen und deutschen Recht, Frankfurt am Main 1999.

Meier Sonja and Zimmerman Reinhard, Judicial Development of the Law, Error Iuris, and the Law of Unjustified Enrichment—a View from Germany, LQR 15 (1999), 556.

Meier Sonja, Irrtum und Zweckverfehlung: die Rolle der Unjust-Gründe bei rechtsgrundlosen Leistungen im englischen Recht, Tubingen 1999.

Millet P. J., Restitution and Constructive Trusts, LQR 114 (1998), 399.

Planiol Marcel/Ripert Georges/Esmein Paul, Traité pratique de droit civil, vol. VII: Obligations, 2nd ed., Paris 1954.

Reuter Dieter/Martinek Michael, Handbuch des Schuldrechts in Einzeldarstellungen: Ungerechtfertigte Bereicherung, Tubingen 1983.

Rouast André, L'enrichissement sans cause et la jurisprudence civile, RTD civ. 1922, 35.

Roubier Paul, La position française en matière de droit d'enrichissement sans cause, in: Travaux de l'Association Henri Capitant pour la culture juridique française, Journées de droit civil de La Haye et de Leyde, vol. IV, Paris 1949, 38.

Sage Yves-Louis and Angelo Anthony H., Some Reflections on the Economic Consequences of the Cancellation of a Contract in French Law, (2000) 31 Victoria University of Wellington Law Review.

Samuel Geoffrey, English Private Law: Old and New Thinking in the Taxonomy Debate, OJLS 2004, 335.

Savigny Friedrich Carl von, System des heutigen Römischen Rechts, vol. 5, Berlin 1841.

Schlechtriem Peter, Coen Christoph and Hornung Rainer, Restitution and Unjust Enrichment in Europe, European Review of Private Law 2001, 377.

Schlechtriem Peter, Europäisierung des Bereicherungsrechts, vol. 7.4 Electronic Journal of Comparative Law (November 2003), <www.ejcl.org/74/art74-3.html>.

Schlechtriem Peter, Privacy, Publicity and Restitution of Wrongful Gains: Another New Economy?, (2001) Oxford U Comparative L Forum 3 at <www.ouclf.iuscomp.org>.

Schlechtriem Peter, Restitution und Bereicherungsausgleich in Europa, vols. I and II, Tubingen 2000/2001.

Schluep Walter R., Über Eingriffskondiktionen, in: Mélanges Piotet, Berne 1990, 173.

Schrage Eltjo, Contract and Restitution: A Few Comparative Remarks, in: Francis D. Rose (ed.), Failure of Contracts, Contractual, Restitutionary and Proprietary Consequences, Oxford 1997, 231.

Sharpe Robert J. and Waddams S.M., Damages for lost opportunity to bargain, OJLS 1982, 290.

Simpson A.W.B., A History of the Common Law of Contract. The Rise of the Action of Assumpsit, Oxford 1975.

Smith Lionel, Property, Subsidiarity, and Unjust Enrichment, in: Reinhard Zimmermann and David Johnston (eds.), Unjustified Enrichment—Key Issues in Comparative Perspective, Cambridge 2002, 588.

Smits Jan M. Smits, A European Law on Unjustified Enrichment? A Critical View of the Law of Restitution in the Draft Common Frame of Reference, in: Antoni Vaquer (ed.), European Private Law Beyond the Common Frame of Reference, Groningen 2008, 153.

Swadling William, Property: General Principles, in: Peter Birks (ed.), English Private Law, vol. 1, Oxford 2000, 203.

Swann Stephen, The Structure of Liability for Unjustified Enrichment: First Proposals of the Study Group on a European Civil Code, in: Reinhard Zimmermann (ed.), Grundstrukturen eines europäischen Bereicherungsrechts, Tubingen 2005, 265.

Van Caenegem Raoul C., An Historical Introduction to Private Law, Cambridge 1992.

Virgo Graham, Failure of Consideration: Myth and Meaning in the English Law of Restitution, in: Reinhard Zimmermann and David Johnston (eds.),

Unjustified Enrichment—Key Issues in Comparative Perspective, Cambridge 2002, 103.

Von Caemmerer Ernst and Schlechtriem Peter (eds.), International Encyclopedia of Comparative Law, vol. X: Restitution, Unjust Enrichment and Negotiorum Gestio, Tubingen, Leiden, Boston 2007.

Waddams Stephen, Dimensions of Private Law: Categories and Concepts in Anglo-American Reasoning, Cambridge 2003.

Wendehorst Christiane C., Die Leistungskondiktion und ihre Binnenstruktur in rechtsvergleichender Perspektive, in: Reinhard Zimmermann (ed.), Grundstrukturen eines europäischen Bereicherungsrechts, Tubingen 2005, 47.

Werro Franz, Faut-il renforcer la protection de la personnalité? La tentation des dommages-intérêts punitifs en droit des médias, Medialex 2002, 81.

Wilburg Walter, Die Lehre von der ungerechtfertigten Bereicherung nach österreichischem und deutschem Recht, Graz 1934.

Wittmann Roland, Commentary to §§652–704 BGB, in: von Staudinger Julius, Kommentar zum Bürgerlichen Gesetzbuch mit Einführungsgesetz und Nebengesetzen, Zweites Buch: Recht der Schuldverhältnisse, 13th ed., Berlin 1995.

Worthington Sarah, Reconsidering Disgorgement for Wrongs, MLR 62 (1999), 218.

Zimmermann Reinhard, Bereicherungsrecht in Europa: Eine Einführung, in: *id.* (ed.), Grundstrukturen eines europäischen Bereicherungsrechts, Tubingen 2005, 17.

Zimmermann Reinhard, The Law of Obligations: Roman Foundations of the Civilian Tradition, Oxford 1996.

12

# Proprietary Security Rights in the Western European Countries

Francesca Fiorentini*

## Summary



## 1. Taxonomy

In the field of security rights, as in any other area of private law, the task of elaborating taxonomy has been undertaken by legal scholars and almost everywhere in Europe, legislators adhere to scholarly classifications when es-

* Ph.D., University of Trento, Italy; Assistant Professor at the Faculty of Law of the University of Trieste, Italy.

tablishing rules.[1] European legal thinking agrees on a basic, general notion of 'security right' intended as a protected right conferred upon the creditor for the purpose of strengthening its claim towards the debtor.[2]

On the basis of this general notion, a unanimously-recognized distinction is drawn between Proprietary Security Rights and Personal Security Rights.[3]

The category of Personal Security Rights comprises a variety of contractual relationships creating a personal obligation of a third party (security provider) towards the creditor. The personal security provider has an obligation to pay, or to render another performance, assumed to secure the exact fulfilment of the debtor's obligation owed to the creditor. Therefore, the typical feature of personal security contracts is that they create a personal liability of the security provider, which reinforces the debtor's liability.

Proprietary Security Rights are security devices which have a wholly different structure. This category comprises rights '*in rem,*' which are conferred upon the creditor in order to secure the debtor's obligation. A common feature of these rights is that, in the case of default by the debtor, they confer the creditor with the right to preferential satisfaction (i.e., the right to prior payment) from the encumbered assets *vis-à-vis* other (unsecured) creditors.[4] A

---

1. Legislative definitions of 'security right' are not usually found in the European Codes. However, definitions of the relevant elements of secured transactions are becoming common in international conventions on the matter: see, for instance, OHADA, art. 1 para. 1 of the *Acte uniforme portant organisation des sûretés*, of 17 Apr. 1997, OJ Ohada of 1st Oct. 1997; art. 1 lit. ii) and jj) of the Unidroit *Cape Town Convention on International Interests in Mobile Equipment* (2001), http://www.unidroit.org/english/conventions/mobile-equipment/main.htm. For an overview of the legal integration of secured transactions see *infra*, n. 7.5 and 8.2.

2. For the common law countries see, e.g., R. Goode, *Legal Problems of Credit and Security*, 3rd ed. (London 2003), 3 ff.; P. Ali, *The Law of Secured Finance. An International Survey of Security Interests over Personal Property* (Oxford 2002), 16; and for the civil law side see, e.g., M. Grégoire, *Le présent et l'avenir des sûretés réelles mobilières et des sûretés personelles*, in *The Belgian Reports at the Congress of Brisbane of the International Academy of Comparative Law* (Brussels 2002) 177.

3. This chapter adopts the terminology elaborated by the Study Group on a European Civil Code—Working Team on Personal and Proprietary Security Rights on which see *infra*, n. 8.2, fn. 133 and 134.

4. For the distinction between personal and proprietary security see R. Goode, *Legal Problems of Credit and Security*, cit., 5 f.; U. Drobnig, *Present and Future of Real and Personal Security*, in ERPL, 5, 2003, 623 ff., 625. For recent European developments in the law of personal security contracts see the special issue of the *European Review of Private Law* no. 3, 2005 and the essays by A. Colombi Ciacchi, S. van Erp, L. Kähler, R. Parry, P. Rott published therein, as well as U. Drobnig, *Neuere Entwicklungen im Recht der persönlichen Kreditsicherheiten in Deutschland und in den Niederlanden* (Munich 2003). The Rules

brief account of the latter term in the above distinction is provided by this chapter.

## 2. Security Rights' Efficiency

Empirical data show that recourse to proprietary security has been widespread and constant in the western countries, and that it is increasing.[5]

---

on *Personal Security Contracts* elaborated within the research conducted by the 'Study Group on a European Civil Code' have been recently published: U. Drobnig, *Principles of European Law. Personal Security* (Munich 2007).

5. Statistical data on the economic importance of proprietary security rights in the U.S. as well as in the world capital market can be found in H. Fleisig, *The proposed Unidroit Convention on mobile equipment: economic consequences and issues*, in Uniform Law Rev. 1999, 2, 253 ff.; Id., *Secured Transactions: The Power of Collateral*, in Finance & Development, June 1996, 44, according to which half of U.S. financing is secured by movable property; see also, more recently, but with the same data, N. de la Peña, H. Fleisig, *SMEs and Collateral*, in Centre for the Economic Analysis of Law (CEAL Issues Brief, n. 3), October 2002, 1 ff. See also the World Bank study *Law and Policy Reform at the Asian Development Bank 2000*, vol. II, v ff., at http://adb.org/Documents/Others/LAw_ADB/lpr_2000_2.asp?p=lawdevt#contents.

Data show that security over immovables offers even more advantages than security over movable assets. In the U.S. market, loans secured by immovables are 10 times larger than unsecured loans and loans secured by movable property only 4 time larger; moreover, loans secured by immovable property can be repaid over a period 5 time as long as that for an unsecured loan: H.W. Fleisig, N. de la Peña & M. Safavian, *Reforming collateral laws to expand access to finance*, The World Bank (Washington 2006) 1 ff.

Differently, in transitions economies where titling to immovable property is scarce and land registration system are not (efficiently) developed, security over immovables is more expensive and less efficient: Commission on Legal Empowerment of the Poor, *Making the Law Work for Everyone*, Somerset, NJ: Toppan Printing, 2008, vol II, Ch. 2, 63 ff., 77, 82 ff., 100 ff. and Ch. 4, 195 ff., available at: http://www.undp.org/legalempowerment/docs/ReportVolumeII/making_the_law_work_II.pdf; The International Bank for Reconstruction and Development/The World Bank, *Land Policies for Growth and Poverty Reduction* (Oxford 2003) 1 ss.; 3 ss.; 17 ss.; 27 ss.; 32 ss.; 44 ss. (Asia); 46 s. (Africa); 47 (Latin America Latina); 48 ff. for the interconnections between formalization of property rights and access to credit. As well-known, the thesis of the centrality of land registration systems to foster economic development has been promoted by H. De Soto, *The Mistery of Capital: Why Capitalism Triumphs in the West and Fails Everywhere Else* (London 2001), *passim*. In this vein, see *Celebrating Reform 2008, Doing Business Case Studies* (World Bank & International Finance Corporation, Washington 2008), 34 ff. for the case of the 2006 Egyptian land registration reform; and p. 47 ff. for the 2004 reform in Honduras; see also P. Machoka, *The Need for Efficient and Effective Secured Transactions Regimes in Sub-Saharan Africa: The Case for Kenya*, in 20(8)*J.I.B.L.R.*, 2005, 395; P. Larmur, *Policy Transfer and Re-*

It is widely believed internationally that the phenomenon is of such magnitude because security for credit has some sort of intrinsic efficiency.[6] Therefore, the reasons why banks pursue "the taking of security with apostolic zeal,"[7] as well as the efficiency of security rights, have been subject to close analysis conducted by a large body of literature.[8] In the same vein, one observes that

---

*versal: Customary Land Registration from Africa to Melanesia*, in 22 *Public Admin. Dev.* (2002), 151.

6. A functioning system of security rights is considered one of the most important requirements for an economy to develop: F. Modigliani & E. Perotti, *Security versus Bank Finance: The Importance of Proper Enforcement of Legal Rules* (FEEM Working Paper no. 37.99 2000), for a general frame of reference; S. Djankov, C. McLiesh & A. Shleifer, *Private Credit in 129 Countries*, January 2005, NBER Working Paper No. W11078, in http://www.nber/org/papers/w11078; The International Bank for Reconstruction and Development/The World Bank, *Land Policies for Growth and Poverty Reduction* (Oxford 2003); H. Fleisig, *Integrating the Legal Regimes for Secured Transactions and Bankruptcy: Economic Issues*, CEAL Issues Brief, 1, Oct. 2000:http://www.ceal.org/ceal-org/publications/Bankruptcy_Issues_Brief.pdf; U. Drobnig, A. Flessner, R. Goode, J. Kleinemann, J. Westbrook & J. Ziegel, *Building Effective Insolvency Systems. Debtor-Creditor Regimes* (Washington, D.C. 1999); R. Goode, *Security in Cross Border Transactions* (1998) 33 Tex Int'l L.J., 47 and U. Drobnig, *Secured Credit in International Insolvency Proceedings* (1998) 33 Tex Int'l L.J., 54. The recent law reforms in the matter of secured transactions regimes enacted on a massive scale in the Eastern European countries with the support of the European Bank of Reconstruction and Development (EBRD) demonstrate the point clearly: see in general T. Tajti, *Comparative Secured Transactions Law*, Budapest, 2002, and *infra* in this book, Chapter no. 13, by T. Tajti. For the projects recently implemented or planned by the EBRD suffice it here to cite the following: the new Serbian pledge law of 15 August 2005; the Mortgage Transactions Law Reform of Moldova of July 2005; the new Secured Transactions Regime of Georgia of July 2005; the publication in 2005 of the EBRD Report for the reform of pledge and mortgage law in Poland, commissioned to the EBRD by the National Bank of Poland; the publication of the Guiding Principles for the Development of a Charges Registry for Securities over Movable Assets of December 2004; all these texts and more are available at http://www.ebrd.com/country/sector/law/st/index.htm.

7. This being the expression used by G. McCormack in *Secured Credit under English and American Law* (Cambridge 2004), 4; see also J. White, *The Politics of Article 9: Work and Play in Revising Article 9*, (1994) 80 Va. L. Rev., 2089 ff., 2091.

8. H. Fleisig, *Economic Functions of Security in a Market Economy*, in J. Norton & M. Andenas, *Emerging Financial Markets and Secured Transactions* (London, The Hague, Boston 1998), 15 ff.; G. McCormack, *Secured Credit under English and American Law*, 22 ff. and for a survey of the main efficiency-theories see P. Ali, *The Law of Secured Finance*, 34 ff.; J. Armour, *The Law and Economics Debate About Secured Lending: Lessons for European Lawmaking?*, in H. Eidenmüller & E.-M. Kineninger (eds.), The Future of Secured Credit in Europe, European Company and Financial Law Review, Special Volume 2, Berlin, 2008, 3 ff.

the 'justification' of security rights has become a 'topos' of every introductory chapter on the topic.[9]

It must be stressed, however, that it is not yet evident how the results of such studies should be used. They are very often mutually conflicting, so that the factors inducing the market to seek security rights still remain—to a certain extent—covered: rational EAL models are not always sufficient to explain decision-making processes in the credit sector.[10]

Carrying out an EAL analysis of security rights would be beyond the scope of this chapter. Nevertheless, it is worth providing a frame of reference for the possible economic meanings of such legal devices. To this end, I shall outline the two main points put forward in the specific literature and on which there is general consensus.

(a) Security rights maximize the creditor's expectation to be satisfied in all cases of inability to pay by the debtor. The empirical evidence shows that, in the event of debtor insolvency, unsecured creditors have very low expectations of receiving anything in satisfaction of their claims.[11] The secured creditor's position is also stronger where (e.g., in some common law jurisdictions), in the event of non-performance by the debtor, the former is entitled to take possession of the secured assets and to sell them out of court.[12]

---

9. See for instance G. McCormack, *Secured Credit under English and American Law*, 1 ff.; R. Good, *Legal Problems of Credit and Security*, 1 ff.; P. Ali, *The Law of Secured Finance*, 15 ff.

10. Indeed, there also seem to be psychological reasons that prompt creditors to take security over the assets of their debtors. These reasons are not dealt with by the efficiency literature to any great extent, but they are emphasised, for instance, by R. Goode, *Security: A Pragmatic or Conceptualist's Response*, (1989) 15 Mon ULR 361 ff., 363. The potential cost of subjective judgement and discretion in credit decisions is studied by R. Inderst & H.M. Möllers, *Credit Risk Analysis and Security Design* (London 2003), CEPR Discussion Paper No. 3686; A. Saunders & L. Allen, *Credit Risk Measurement*, 2nd ed. (N.Y. 2002). On all these aspects see also Alb. Candian, *Le garanzie mobiliari. Modelli e problemi nella prospettiva europea*, Milan 2001, 47 ff.

11. For England, see the data reported by G. McCormack, *Secured Credit under English and American Law*, 7. The problem of the insufficiency of the insolvency asset for the satisfaction of unsecured creditors (the so-called *Massenarmut*) was at the basis of the German insolvency law reform of 5.10.1994 (*Insolvenzordnung*, in force since 1.1.1999): W. Uhlenbruck, *Das neue Insolvenzrecht* (Herne 1994) Introduction.

12. This is the case of English law, according to the Law of Property Act 1925, sec. 101(1) (iii), the Insolvency Act 1986, sec. 29(2), the Enterprise Act 2002, sec. 248; Schedule 16. In the practice of larger quoted U.K. companies, the secured creditors' powers of control over the debtor's business have developed into very flexible informal procedures

(b) Security rights enable the creditor to control the debtor's behaviour and strategies during the credit relationship. The interest rate charged by the creditor to the debtor for a loan is affected by the creditor's evaluation, during the negotiation stage, of the probability of the debtor's misbehaviour. The problem is that, after signature of the loan agreement, the creditor has no means with which to compel the debtor to behave in a manner consistent with that agreement. Moreover, there is evidence that the debtor has an incentive to misbehave, i.e. undertake riskier activities, because in this way it can obviously obtain cheaper financing for risky activities.[13] By contrast, if the debtor is compelled to grant a proprietary security, it loses exclusive control over its assets and will therefore be more likely to act properly so that it can repay and thus avoid forfeiture of the secured assets.[14]

## 3. A Panorama of Western European Legal Systems

In western Europe, a multiplicity of legal devices exist that perform the function of proprietary security, or which are used by the parties for the purposes of security.[15]

Needless to say, this variety has historical origins: in particular, it is due to the intermingling of the Roman and Germanic traditions in the shaping of continental law and to the differences between civil law systems and common law ones.

The abundance of techniques has induced scholars to resort to conceptual oppositions in order to explain this area of law. The traditional distinction is between possessory and non-possessory security rights, the former being those where the secured asset is held by the creditor (creditor-held security

intended to avoid, or postpone, formal statutory insolvency procedures. The most important example of this is the so-called 'London Approach', which applies to multi-banked companies in financial difficulties: references in G. McCormack, *Secured Credit under English and American Law*, 11.

13. T. Jackson & A. Kronman, *Secured Financing and Priorities among Creditors*, 1149–50.

14. This may be the prime reason for a creditor to take security over the debtor's assets, in particular when those assets are necessary for the debtor's business: D. Baird, *Security Interests Reconsidered* (1994) Va. L. R. 2249 ff., 2252.

15. This multiplicity is reflected in the intricate terminology of the different legal systems: F. Dahan, *Secured Transactions Law in Western Advanced Economies: Exposing Myths* (2001) 16(2) Butterworths J. of Int'l Banking and Financial Law, 60 ff.

rights) and the latter those where it is held by the debtor (debtor-held security rights).[16]

There are at least two further classifications which facilitate the task of establishing order to this multiplicity of legal devices. One centres on the type of assets subject to security and distinguishes security rights between those which concern movable assets and those which concern immovable ones.[17] As pointed out below (n. 6), this is an opposition deeply rooted in legal theory, as well as in legislation, and as such it will be adopted here, as well.

The other classification depends on whether the legal device considered is recognized and regulated by the legal system as a right specifically designed to perform the function of security ('formal' security right) or whether it is another kind of proprietary right or relationship which is recognized and regulated by the legal system to serve other ends, but is used by the parties to perform a security function ('functional' security right).[18] This distinction is similar to that between 'typical' and 'atypical' security rights—a manner of qualifying legal devices which is very familiar to continental lawyers and, as well-known, is based on the existence of regulation by positive law of such devices as security rights in a technical sense.[19] As

---

16. For the historical development of non-possessory secured transaction in Anglo-American law see G.L. Flint jr., *Secured Transactions History: The Fraudulent Myth*, (1999) 29 N.M. L. R. 363; Id., *Secured Transactions History: The Northern Struggle to Defeat the Judgment Lien in the Pre-Chattel Mortgage Act Era* (2000) 20 N.Ill.U.L.R. 1.

17. Alb. Candian, *Le garanzie mobiliari*, 20.

18. In this chapter I choose the opposition between the 'formal' and 'functional' security right. Although reference to a 'formal' security right may seem something new to some reader, I chose it for clarity's sake because it refers to the form of security right which has been ultimately recognized in almost all western countries at least since modern time as a limited right *in rem* which allows the security provider to remain owner of the encumbered asset while conferring upon the creditor a limited right *in rem* over the same asset, formally designed by the legal system to have function of security. Here the security function is expressed in a specific form or structure of the right, and not in its function as performed according to the parties' intentions. The terminological choice of the opposition between 'formal' and 'functional' security rights aims to also recall to the well-known opposition existing in the realm of the ideologies living behind western security rights regimes, i.e. that between 'formalism' and 'functionalism': see for all A. Veneziano, *Le garanzie mobiliari non possessorie. Profili di diritto comparato e di diritto del commercio internazionale* (Milan 2000) 112 ff.; see also *infra* fn. 101.

The substance of this distinction has been the basis of analysis by the Research-Team on Security Rights over Movables coordinated by Prof. U. Drobnig at the Max Planck Institute for Comparative and International Private Law (Hamburg), within the Study Group on a European Civil Code: see *infra*, n. 8.2.

19. E.g., see, for Italy, F. Fiorentini, *Garanzie reali atipiche*, in *Riv. dir. civ.* 2000, 253 ff.

we shall see (n. 8.1), recourse is usually made to 'functional' or 'atypical' security rights in order to remedy certain inefficiencies which affect 'formal' security rights, given that the former normally prove to be more efficient than the latter for creditors.

Whereas the first two classifications are merely descriptive, the one that counter poses 'formal' and 'functional' security rights is more interesting, as it seems to contain the core of the challenges that Europe—indeed, all the western economies—will have to face in the near future, namely the limits to place on freedom of contract in the field of proprietary security rights.[20]

The crucial point is that, whereas 'formal' security rights are generally considered to be unproblematic as to their legal discipline, there are differences among legal systems to the extent to which they recognize 'functional' or 'atypical' security rights. Below is a brief discussion for the reasons of this phenomenon.

## 4. Techniques of Regulation

When investigating the grounds for these differences, one must necessarily consider the ways in which the various legal systems approach the problem of the conflicting interests underlying the law of proprietary security rights.

As is well known, the rules governing proprietary security rights aim to resolve the conflicting interests of (a) the debtor (and its stakeholders), (b) the secured creditor (and its stakeholders), but also (c) third parties, like the debtor's other creditors, or the purchasers of the secured assets.[21] From this point of view, secured credit regimes govern not only private interests but public and general ones as well.

To be noted is that continental jurisdictions tend to control such conflicts by resorting to a strict system of mandatory rules that restrict the parties' autonomy in governing their secured transactions, the purpose being to prevent detriments to the general interests involved.[22] A series of prohibitions have

20. As to the relations between contract and property in European law: see Ch. von Bar & U. Drobnig (eds.), *The interaction of contract law and tort and property law in Europe* (Munich 2004), 322 ff. for analysis of proprietary security rights.

21. On the interactions between those conflicts and the policy choices behind the different models of regulation of proprietary security rights see Alb. Candian, *Le garanzie mobiliari*, 53 ff., 68.

22. Scholarly descriptions of the law of secured transactions in most civil law countries show that the system is organized on the principles of 'universal patrimonial liability' and *par condicio creditorum*, according to which the preference accorded to some of the debtor's creditors through rights of preferential satisfaction is considered an exception to the gen-

thus been established that tend to ban any kind of security right other than 'formal' ones, or any kind of enforcement of security rights other than public enforcement.[23]

The same ends are pursued in a different manner by the English common law. Proprietary rules developed over the centuries by the courts, mostly by courts of equity, have imposed upon the parties a series of duties intended to deter fraud and deception with regard to the general interests mentioned above.[24] Thus, the parties are granted greater freedom to regulate their interests, and judicial 'corrections' are imposed *ex post* and ban only individual transactions or individual clauses in light of specific circumstances.

The different approaches to the control issue referred to above—a public and centralized approach (*ex ante*) versus a private and diffused one (*ex post*)—impact the amount of private autonomy granted to the parties in the settlement of their transactions. Indeed, it has been noted that in common law jurisdictions broader recognition of the freedom of the parties to self-regulate their credit relationships generates a flexible system considered to be 'credit-friendly.'[25] By contrast, the civil law jurisdictions have often been regarded as rigid and, therefore, as tending to be inefficient.[26]

These different styles may also reflect the prevailing patterns of economic policy in each of the systems considered. In other words, where the legal regime is credit-friendly, a liberal attitude is taken to the problem of credit. By contrast,

---

eral rule of equal position among creditors. This rigid, mandatory scheme makes it difficult to recognize new legal devices used by commercial practice for the purposes of security, and it is therefore supported, in every system, by the idea of the *numerus clausus* of proprietary security rights. This is the case, for instance, of France: c.c., art. 2093, H. et L. Mazeaud, J. Mazeaud, F. Chabas, *Leçons de droit civil*, III, t. 1, *Sûretés. Publicité foncière*, 7th ed., (Paris 1999), 11; and Italy: L. Barbiera, *Responsabilità patrimoniale. Disposizioni generali, Artt. 2740–2744*, in *Il Codice Civile. Commentario* diretto da P. Schlesinger (Milano 1991); G. Tucci, *Garanzia*, in *Dig. IV, Disc. priv.*, Sez. civ., VIII (Torino 1991) 579.

23. The main example is the prohibition of forfeiture clauses in security agreements and its broad interpretation by courts and jurists in some civil law countries: M. Bussani, *Il problema del patto commissorio* (Turin 2000).

24. See Cousins, *The Law of Mortgages*, 2nd ed. (London 2001) 13 and Turner R.W., *The Equity of Redemption. Its Nature, History and Connection with Equitable Estates Generally* (Cambridge 1931).

25. M. Bridge, *The English Law of Real Security* (2002) 10(4) ERPL, 483 ff.

26. P.R. Wood, *Comparative Law of Security and Guarantees* (London 1995) 5 ff., 7 ff. distinguishes among world regimes of secured credit according to the concepts of *sympathy* and *hostility* towards security rights; the common law jurisdictions are among the more 'sympathetic' regimes.

a paternalistic approach to credit predominates where the rigidity of public control prevents the parties from finding new, flexible solutions to their interests.

However, I shall demonstrate that there are also differences among civil law jurisdictions as to the flexibility of legal regimes, so that any strict opposition between civil law and common law in this regard is to be considered an over-generalization.

## 5. Assessment of Legal Regimes' Flexibility

In every legal system, the link between freedom of contract and the efficiency of security rights law is the key criterion with which to assess the regime's ability to meet the security needs of all law users, including the main market actors.

Such assessment usually proceeds as follows:

(i) Examination of whether the parties are able to mitigate the rigidity, typical of 'formal' security rights, which requires a strict connection between the security right and the encumbered asset, on the one hand, and between the security right and the secured claim, on the other (rule of specificity). In the former case, the mitigation should allow for so-called real subrogation[27] for the encumbered asset, i.e. the possibility of replacing the asset originally subject to security with a different asset of the same value or an asset subsequently acquired by the security giver (revolving security rights). The occurrence of real subrogation in any case of fungible assets subject to security would highlight the fact that security encumbers specific assets considered in their value rather than in their specific individuality. In the latter case, the mitigation involves acknowledgment of so-called 'global security rights,' i.e. rights securing not only a claim which is determined in its existence and amount from the outset, but also future claims which may arise in the relationships between the creditor and the debtor and whose amount cannot be specified at the time when the security is created—of course, within the limits of a maximum amount of liability of the immovable which must be fixed by registration.

Needless to say, any weakening of the rule of specificity should not be prejudicial to the priority given to the security at the time of its creation.

(ii) Assessment of the mobility of the security, given that the creditor is able to transfer its security separately from the secured claim to other creditors of the debtor, enhances the economic value of the security as a fully disposable

27. V. Ranouil, *La subrogation réelle en droit civil français* (Paris 1985) 79 ff., 94 ff., 216 ff.

right of its owner. Therefore, the extent to which security rights are mobile seems to be a factor that influences the cost of access to credit.

(iii) Investigation of the extent to which a legal regime is open or closed to functional security rights alternative to (or merely concurrent with) 'formal' ones.

(iv) Evaluation of the efficiency of national enforcement procedures for security rights over immovable assets, also taking into account whether there exist 'self-help' procedures enabling creditors to gain out-of-court satisfaction from the secured asset.

These four points provide the basis for the following brief account of the current situation of proprietary security rights in the western European legal systems.

## 6. Movables and Immovables: Distinct Paths

As mentioned above (n. 3), a common feature of security rights regimes in all European systems is the tendency, rooted in the historical development of this province of the law,[28] for rules and problems concerning security rights over movables to be treated separately from those concerning security over immovables. Since the two sectors have developed different problems—mainly related to (or a consequence of) the differing physical natures of the assets—and because the efforts of law reform and/or legal integration in recent decades tend to affect them separately, distinct analysis of immovables and movables is nowadays common and justifiable.

28. Historical accounts of the law of proprietary security rights in the European context can be found, e.g., in M. Kaser, *Studien zum römischen Pfandrecht* (Neaples repr.: 1982); O von Gierke, *Deutsches Privatrecht* II (Leipzig 1905) 809 ff.; G. Gorla, *Le garanzie reali dell'obbligazione* (Milan 1935); H.D. Hazeltine, *Die Geschichte des englischen Pfandrechts*, in O. Gierke (Hersg.), *Untersuchungen zur Deutschen Staats-und Rechtsgeschichte*, 91. Heft (Breslau 1907), 147 ff.; K. von Amira, *Nordgermanisches Obligationenrecht* II (Leipzig 1882) 223 ff.; R.W. Turner, *The Equity of Redemption. Its Nature, History and Connection with Equitable Estates Generally* (Cambridge 1931); Ph.A. Merlin, *Répertoire universel et raisonné de la jurisprudence* (Paris 1812–1825) v. *Devoirs de loi*, VIII, 35; and v. *Nantissement*, XXI, 68 ff.; R.P. Troplong, *Priviléges et hypothèques: commentaire de la loi du 23 mars 1855 sur la transcription en matière hypothècaire* (Paris 1856); J.W. Hedemann, *Die Fortschritte des Zivilrechts im XIX. Jahrhundert* (Frankfurt/Main 1968) II/2.

## 7. Security Rights over Immovable Assets

The classic form of security over immovables is the hypothec/mortgage. It is regulated by positive law not only in all the continental codes[29] but, since 1925, in England as well.[30]

In very general terms, despite the different historical origins and paths of development of the continental devices with respect to the common law ones, the outcome has been the same almost everywhere: that of a limited right *in rem* whereby possession of the encumbered assets remains in the hands of the debtor and which confers on the creditor, in the event of the debtor's default, a right to preferential satisfaction from the encumbered assets.

A survey of the main features of the law of security rights over immovable assets follows in Western Europe.

### *7.1. The Rule of Accessority*

A feature shared by common and civil law is the special link that they establish between a security right and a secured credit (accessority rule). This bond signifies that a security right can only exist if a secured credit (or, once certain requirements are met, a future credit to be secured) exists, and with the extinction of the latter, the former is also extinguished. In reality, however, the rule is applied with differing degrees of rigidity among countries.

It is evident that the degree of rigidity of the accessority rule also affects the extent to which the security can be transferred to other creditors of the debtor, independently of the original, secured obligation.

Italy is an example of a system where only one single type of security right is regulated and is largely considered to be rigidly accessory to a secured obligation: that is, its existence is regarded as depending on the existence of the original secured obligation. Therefore, the transferability of the security separately from the (original) secured obligation is generally not allowed.[31]

---

29. Dutch c.c., art. 3:260 ff. (*hypotheek*); English common law (*mortgage*); German c.c., §1113 ff.; 1191 ff. (*Hypothek*, *Grundschuld*); Greek c.c., art. 1257 ff.; French cc., art. 2393 ff. (*hypothèque*); Italian c.c., art. 2808 ff. (*ipoteca*); Portuguese c.c., art. 686 ff. (*hipoteca*); Spanish c.c., art. 1874 ff. (*hipoteca*).

30. The 1925 Law of Property Act, in force since 01.01.1926, is considered to mark the beginning of the modern era of the English law on mortgage: Cheshire and Burns, *Modern Law of Real Property*, 16th ed. (London 2000) 8.

31. G. Tamburrino, *Della tutela dei diritti. (Delle ipoteche)*, in *Commentario del codice civile*, 2a edn. (Turin 1976), 250. Greek law (cc., art. 1258) adopts the same rule.

Conversely, the German BGB codifies a plurality of types of security rights, differentiating them in terms of different degrees of accessority. Thus, besides the *Sicherungshypothek*, which is a strictly accessory security device,[32] there exists a *Verkehrshypothek*, whereby the bond with the secured obligation is relaxed: the link with the credit is not regarded as being a necessary connection with the original secured obligation, so that the security right can be straightforwardly transferred to other creditors of the debtor and therefore connected with other secured obligations.[33] German law also regulates the *Grundschuld*, which is a proprietary right completely independent from a secured obligation, but that in practice is connected to an obligation to be secured by means of a contractual agreement between the parties (in this case it is called *Sicherungsgrundschuld*).[34]

These different situations can be regarded as indicating the prevalence in Italy, at the time of the civil codification of 1942 as well as today, of a paternalistic approach to secured credit. The impossibility of dissolving the bond between a security and a secured obligation reflected (and reflects) a protective function for the debtor, who is mainly regarded as a person in need of special protection. In Germany, by contrast, the legislature has been much readier to provide different solutions to different needs: market actors are free to choose riskier security devices if they deem them suitable, and the fact that the debtor is not always a subject in need of special protection is overtly recognized.[35]

---

32. German c.c., § 1184.

33. German c.c., § 1113 ff.

34. German c.c., § 1191 ff. for the *Grundschuld*. The *Sicherungsgrundschuld* is a legal device created by commercial practice and regulated by case law: U. Huber, *Die Sicherungsgrundschuld* (Heidelberg 1965, Nachdruck 1995). The Swiss equivalent to the German *Grundschuld* is the *Gült* (c.c. art. 847 ff.), and the Swiss *cédule hypothécaire* (c.c., art. 842 ss.) is the equivalent to the German *Sicherungsgrundschuld*. To be noted is that only recently the German *Sicherungsgrundschuld* has been statutorily regulated (although in a single detailed aspect). This has happened by way of *Risikobegrenzungsgesetz* of 18.08.2008 (BGBl. I, 1666), which introduced in the German civil code a new para 1(a) in § 1192. The new provision introduces a limit to the independence of this security from the secured obligations. Indeed it states that in case of assignment of the *Sicherungsgrundschuld* to a third party, the security provider can raise against the assignee the exceptions to which it is entitled towards the secured creditor assignor and deriving from the secured obligations as well as from the security. See R.-R. Bachner, *Notarrelevante Änderungen durch das Risikobegrenzungsgesetz—Schutz des grundpfandrechtlich gesicherten Darlehensnehmers bei Forderungsabtretung*, in *DNotZ* 2008, Heft 9, 644 ff., 647.

35. *Motive zu dem Entwurfe eines Bürgerlichen Gesetzbuches für das Deutsche Reich* (Berlin, Leipzig 1888) III, 611; *Protokolle der Kommission für die zweite Lesung des Entwurfes des Bürgerlichen Gesetzbuches* (Auftrage des Reichs—Justizamts, I–VI (VII: Register) Berlin

Towards modernization, some civil law countries have now remarkably weakened the rule of accessority of security rights over immovables. The 2006 French reform[36] has introduced the so-called 'rechargeable hypothec' (c.c. new art. 2422). This security is created for a maximum amount of liability of the encumbered asset. Within this limit it can be used several times by the security provider to secure either new credits provided by the same initial creditor, or new credits provided by different, successive creditors. The advantage from the borrower's point of view is obvious, since s/he no longer has the burden of paying off the old security set up in favour of the original creditor, in order to be able to set up another in favour of the later lenders. The lender under this type of arrangement, on his part, benefits by enjoying the same position of priority as under the original security, thereby being able to take priority over all the creditors who have provided credit secured on the same property after the creation of the rechargeable security, but before its 'recharging.'

In the same direction goes Spanish Law no. 41/2007, reforming the national mortgage market.[37] This law regulates an *hipoteca de máximo* (new art. 153 *bis Ley Hipotecaria*), i.e. a security that can secure present or future obligations within a maximum amount resulting from the registration of the security and that can be created only in favour of banks and credit institutions subject to banking supervision.[38]

Owing to the empirical nature of the English law of mortgage, which was developed by courts and not by legal scholars or by statutory rules, across the English Channel there has been little discussion of theoretical issues like the accessority of a security. However, in general the English mortgage can secure also obligations different from the original one, and future, if that results from

1897–1899) III, 515; E. Müll, *Die Interessenjurisprudenz im Hypothekenrecht* (Rheinfelden 1988) 43 f.

36. For the French reform of proprietary security rights, both over movables and immovables, see, e.g., P. Crocq, *La future réforme du droit français des sûretés réelles*, 20 Rev. Lamy Droit Civil, 2005, 1 ff. The reform has been enacted by *ordonnance* of 23 March 2006 n. 346, in J.O. of 24 March 2006. The result of the reform has been the introduction into the French civil code of a new Book IV on security rights.

37. *Ley 41/2007, de 7 de diciembre, por la que se modifica la Ley 2/1981, de 25 de marzo, Regulación del Mercado Hipotecario y otras normas del sistema ipotecario y financero, de regulación de las hipotecas inversas y el seguro de dependencia y por la que se establece determinada norma tributaria*, in BOE núm. 299, de 8 de diciembre de 2007, in force since 9 December 2007.

38. See, for all, Á. Carrasco Perera y E. Cordero Lobato, *El doble filo de la hipoteca global: caveat creditor!*, in Diario La Ley, 2008, n. 6988.

registration.[39] Furthermore, the value incorporated in the mortgage acquires a high degree of mobility from the possibility granted to the mortgagee to create sub-mortgages: the sub-security confers on its owner the same rights to which the mortgagee is entitled.[40]

The positive value of a flexible notion of accessority of the security seems to be confirmed by the facts that the German model has been followed by the secured transactions law reforms of several Eastern European countries in recent years[41] and that the same pattern is proposed for a possible 'Eurohypothec' (see n. 7.4 below).

## 7.2. The Rule of Publicity

One of the main differences that persisted until quite recently between common and civil law is the effect of registration for the creation of security rights over immovable assets.[42]

On the continent, as is said, general systems of registration have developed mainly since the national civil codifications, but the legal effect produced by the registration requirement differs among countries. In France, Belgium and Luxembourg the security arises between the parties at the moment when the notary records the document creating the security: here registration (only) affects the outcome in regard to third parties and establishes the security's order of priority. In Austria, Germany, Greece, Italy, Spain, Switzerland and the Netherlands registration is necessary for the existence itself of the security between the parties.

Another solution used to operate in the English common law. Here, the historical existence of broad territories without a (compulsory) land registration system,[43] as well as the dichotomy between common law and equity, for

---

39. This is achieved with an institution called *tacking of further advances*, regulated by LRA 2002, s. 49.

40. In areas of *registered land*, a *sub-charge* is created by registration: LRA 2002, s. 23(2)(b); *Fisher and Lightwood's Law of Mortgage*, 11th ed. (London 2002) 391.

41. See *infra* in this book, Chapter no. 13, by T. Tajti. See also some examples in H.G. Wehrens, *Real Security regarding Immovable Objects—Reflections on a Euro-Mortgage*, in H.S. Hartkamp a.o., *Towards a European Civil Code*, 3rd ed. (Nijmegen 2004) 769 ff., 781 f.

42. The following considerations are limited to the so called voluntary hypothec/mortgage, i.e. the security created by the contractual autonomy of the parties, leaving aside the security devices created by the courts or arising by operation of law.

43. The English Land Registration Act of 1925 introduced a system of voluntary land registration for certain territories. However, since 1 Dec. 1990 (S.I. 1989, n. 1347), all land

a long time hindered land registration as a general requirement for the creation of a mortgage. Only in some territories was registration necessary for the effectiveness of the security to all purposes, but not for its validity between the parties. This system obviously influenced the certainty of land transactions and introduced an element of irrationality into the English system—otherwise quite flexible—which called for legal reform. Yet legal reform has taken place with the enactment of the Land Registration Act of 2002,[44] intended to complete the institution of a compulsory land registration system in England and Wales and foster development of fully electronic conveyancing. The full implementation of the electronic conveyance will also impact the relationship between a mortgage and the publicity of its creation, for it will no longer be possible to create a valid mortgage without simultaneously registering it.[45] Hence, the present and future direction of English law seems to be towards the recognition of the 'constitutive' effects of registration, i.e. registration is going to be the requirement necessary to create a mortgage also *inter partes.*

## *7.3. Enforcement*

I have already mentioned, in regard to the crucial aspect of the enforcement of a security, that security rights in continental Europe have been traditionally governed by mandatory rules requiring public proceedings usually regulated by judicial orders. By contrast, in English legal practice, where a proceeding before the courts (the foreclosure) is possible, recourse to private enforcement techniques prevails, in that it is more rapid and therefore better suited to the needs of creditors.[46]

---

in England and Wales has been subject to compulsory registration. A joint publication by the Law Commission and the HM Land Registry in 1995, Law Comm., n. 235 made recommendations concerning *land registration* which were included in and developed by the Land Registration Act of 1997, in force since 1st April 1998, modifying the LRA 1925.

44. In force since 13 October 2003. The LRA 2002 (and its implementing legislation lastly completed by the Land Registration (Amendments) Rules 2008) is the last stage in a slow legislative process which began with the Land Registry Act of 1862; the basic guidelines for this statute were laid down in 1844 by a *solicitor*, Robert Wilson: J.S. Anderson, *Lawyers and the Making of English Land Law 1832–1940* (Oxford 1992), 58 ff., 63 ff.

45. LRA 2002, s. 27. It is no longer generally true that if a legal mortgage has been created but not registered it takes effect only in equity. Moreover, the role of equitable mortgages, which in theory can still be voluntarily created, will decrease more and more: P. Birks (ed.), *English Private Law*, L. Smith in *Supplement* (Oxford 2004), 44.

46. Nicholls V.-C. in *Palk* v. *Mortgage Services Funding Plc* [1993] Ch. 330, 336: "So far as I am aware, foreclosure actions are almost unheard of today and have been so for many

Widespread delays in rendering civil justice[47] have forced the civil law countries to introduce legislative reforms which shift control over enforcement proceedings from the courts to different subjects or institutions,[48] so that a cau-

---

years. Mortgagees prefer to exercise other remedies. They usually appoint a receiver or exercise their powers of sale. Take the present case: the security is inadequate, but Mortgage Services is not seeking to foreclose, nor is it seeking to sell at once. It is seeking to hold on to the house, preferably without becoming accountable as a mortgagee in possession, with a view to exercising its own power of sale at some future date". To be noted is that the General Report of the Law Commission n. 204, "*Transfer of Land—Land Mortgages*" of 13.11.1991, n. 7.26 f. suggested the abolition of foreclosure actions. On the power to appoint a receiver see LPA 1925, sec. 101 ff. The power to appoint a receiver for company floating charge holders has undergone some changes by the Enterprise Act 2002: G. McCormack, *Secured Credit under English and American Law*, 62 f.

However, also in Dutch law, in the event of of debtor's default, the mortgagee may assume management of the property, if expressly agreed in the deed of mortgage and with the authorisation of the President of the District Court: J.H.M. van Erp, L.P.W. van Vliet, *Real and Personal Security*, in 2002 6.4 EJCL, 121: http://www.ejcl.org/64/art64-7.doc.

Also in Swedish law, private sale is admitted in certain cases if there is a significant possibility of obtaining a better purchase price: Swedish Enforcement Code, Chap. 12, sec. 57.

47. The time taken by court proceedings has become one of the key issues regarding the efficiency of justice. It has been a major concern for the the European Commission for the Efficiency of Justice (CEPEJ), which has adopted a Framework Programme on this issue: Framework Programme—"A new objective for judicial systems: the processing of each case within an optimum and foreseeable timeframe" (CEPEJ(2004)19 Rev). Data concerning the evaluation of European judicial systems in general, including the time-issue, can be found in the Report: Council of Europe (ed.), „ *Systèmes judiciaires européens, 8.10.2008 (données 2006): Efficacité et qualité de la justice*, available at http://www.coe.int/t/dg1/legal-cooperation/cepej/default_FR.asp?.

As well-known, the enforcement of court decisions, in particular within a reasonable elapse of time, is regarded as an integral part of the right to a fair trial under Article 6 of the ECHR. For this reason, following proposals made by the European Ministers of Justice, two recommendations have been prepared on the execution of decisions in the administrative field and on enforcement in all other matters (except concerning deprivation of liberty). These texts were adopted by the Committee of Ministers of the Council of Europe on 9 September 2003 and are available, with an explanatory memorandum, at: http://www.coe.int/t/e/legal%5Faffairs/legal%5Fco%2Doperation/operation%5Fof%5Fjustice/Enforcement%5Fof%5Fjudgments.

Statistical data on foreclosure proceedings in the EU member states can be found in the Report of the Mortgage funding Expert Group of 22.12.2006, p. 22, available at: http://ec.europa.eu/internal_market/finservices-retail/home-loans/integration_en.htm. According to the Report, in the average foreclosures take 6–12 months in Germany, 8–12 months in U.K., 8–18 months in France, 5–7 years in Italy.

48. Notaries, for instance, as in Italy, according to law 03.08.1998, n. 302, in G.U. 24.08.1998, n. 169; in Italy law no. 80/2005 introduced a new art. 591-*bis* in the code of civil procedure to enlarge the delegation of enforcement power to other professionals than

tious trend towards alternatives to the traditional judicial enforcement procedures—though not yet the introduction of genuine 'self-help' arrangements—can also be identified in the civil law countries of Europe.

The efficiency of enforcement procedures is especially crucial in the debtor's insolvency. Empirical research shows that defective bankruptcy procedures can destroy the beneficial effects of substantive laws governing security rights.[49]

## *7.4. Security Rights over Immovables and European Legal Integration*

The field of security rights over immovable assets has attracted less interest than security over movables for legal integration purposes. The reasons for this difference reside in the idea—deeply-rooted in the western legal tradition—that real property law is the sector of private law most closely connected to the *lex rei sitae*, and therefore to the local dimension.[50] This idea has always been backed by emphasis on the technical obstacles against legal integration in this area, such as the differences among land registra-

---

notaries, notably to lawyers and accountants. In Germany the entire enforcement procedure is governed by the *Rechtspfleger*, according to § 20 nr. 17 and § 3 nr. 1(i) of the *Rechtspflegergesetz* of 05.11.1969 (BGBl. I, 2065). The *Rechtspfleger* is not a judge: O. Jauering, *Zivilprozessrecht*, 24. Aufl. (Munich 1993), 42 f. In Sweden, enforcement is a function of the Enforcement Service and is implemented by officers (enforcement administrators), not by judges (Enf. code, Chap. 1, sec. 3). Appeals against decisions by the Enforcement Service can be lodged with district courts (Enf. Code, Chap. 18, sec. 1).

49. B. Schäfer, *The Law and Economic Debate About Secured Lending: Lessons for European Lawmaking? Commentary*, in H. Eidenmüller & E.-M. Kineninger (eds.), The Future of Secured Credit in Europe, 30 ff.; the Author shows (at p. 32) that, according to world Bank data of 2007, recovery rates in insolvency proceedings are the following: Netherlands 86.3%; U.K. 85.2%; Germany 53.1%, France 48.0%, Italy 39.7%, just to take a few examples. Among the analyzed countries that have been classified as high income countries Japan has the highest recover rate: 92.7% and Italy the lowest.

50. The local dimension of the law of property in general has been made official by art. 295 EC Treaty and it receives further support from the subsidiarity principle set out in art. 5 of the same text. The problem of the tension between global and local in the field of property law is addressed, e.g., by U. Mattei, *I diritti reali. 1, La proprietà*, in *Tratt. dir. civ.* edited by R. Sacco (Turin 2001) 37 f.; A. Gambaro, *European Aspects of Property Law*, in F. Werro (ed.) *New Perspectives on European Private Law*, (Friburg 1998), 75 ff. On the diversities of property laws in Europe see, in this book, the Chapter on Western Property Law by A. Gambaro.

tion systems or among enforcement and bankruptcy procedures found in Europe.[51]

However, it is difficult to deny that also immovable assets as means to secure credit have economic weight. Indeed, in the advanced market economies, it is security over immovables that enables the creditor to obtain the best financing conditions, even in comparison with security over movables.[52]

This is why the European Community has not been insensitive to the issue of legal integration in the field of mortgage credit. The first approach of the EU Institutions to the issue has been discussion of the possible introduction a so-called Eurohypothek in the substantive law of the member states. This was envisaged as a security over immovables to be used in EU cross-border transactions and, therefore, as a device to be developed besides—and not in substitution for—the already-existing national institutions.[53] However, excessive divergences among the various national laws (not yet mitigated by sufficient comparative law knowledge about the subject) were considered a major obstacle to the legal integration in this field and the project was soon suspended. Subsequently, concerns about legal integration in European mortgage law has shifted from the perspective of intervention in substantive law to that of the EC Institutions as mechanisms to create an internal capital market including trans-border mortgage lending. Use was made of the mutual recognition technique, but this soon proved markedly inadequate.[54] Therefore, EC institutions sought to promote this sector by resorting to devices other than "legislative" integration. In 2001, the EU Commission consequently approved a Self-Conduct Code intended to standardize the pre-contractual

---

51. B. Foëx, *L'eurohypothèque*, in F. Werro (ed.) *L'européanisation du droit privé. Vers un code civil européen?* (Fribourg 1998) 481 ff.; H. Wehrens, *Real Security Regarding Immovable Objects—Reflections on a Euro-Mortgage*, in A. Hartkamp a.o. (eds.), *Towards a European Civil Code*, 2nd ed. (Nijmegen, The Hague, London, Boston 1998) 554 f.; F. Fiorentini, *Appunti sull'integrazione giuridica europea in materia di garanzie immobiliari*, in M. Bussani & F. Fiorentini (eds.), *Financial Contracts and Secured Transactions in the European Perspective* (Trieste 2003) 149 ff.

52. See data reported *supra*, fn. 5.

53. For an account of the Eurohypothek-debate since the time of the Segré-Commission of 1966 see: O. Stöcker, *Die Eurohypothek* (Berlin 1992); B. Foëx, *L'eurohypothèque*, in F. Werro (ed.) *L'européanisation du droit privé. Vers un code civil européen?* (Fribourg 1998) 481; H. Wirner, *Die Eurohypothek*, in *DNotZ*, 1994, 421.

54. First and Second Banking Directive of the EC (17 Dec. 1988, OJ L 322/30); H.G. Wehrens, *Real Security regarding Immovable Objects—Reflections on a Euro-Mortgage*, in H.S. Hartkamp a.o., *Towards a European Civil Code*, 3rd ed., 770.

duties of information incumbent upon banks and credit institutions towards 'consumers' of mortgage credit. The inadequacy of this scheme, too, soon became evident.[55]

A subsequent trend in EU strategy has therefore been developed, aiming at evaluating the opportunity to return to the idea of "legislative" integration in substantive law. Thus, in 2003 the EU Commission established the Forum Group on Mortgage Credit, which in 2004 published guidelines for a Eurohypothek.[56] Set up in 2004, under a Spanish initiative, was an international research group called "The Eurohypothek: A Common Mortgage for Europe". This, too, has elaborated guidelines for a Eurohypothek.[57]

In July 2005, the EU Commission published a Green Paper on Mortgage Credit with the purpose to begin evaluation of whether EU "legislative" intervention in this sector would be advisable.[58] Pursuant to this document, in August 2005 the EU Commission commissioned a study from the London Economics consultancies on costs and benefits of EU integration of the mortgage market.[59] Following the Commission's evaluation of this study, a White

---

55. The code was applicable only to residential lending for the purchase of the first home: http://europa.eu.int/comm/internal_market/finservices-retail/home-loans/index_en.htm#code. See also the results of the Second Report on Implementation of the said Code in the European Union, issued by the European Banking Industry Committee in December 2005, available at the same webpage.

56. *The Integration of the EU Mortgage Credit Markets*, 2004: http://europa.eu.int/comm/internal_market/finservices-retail/docs/home-loans/2004-report-integration_en.pdf: esp. 4 ff.; 30, point 117.

57. For the working papers of the group see www.eurohypothec.com and for the guidelines on the Eurohypothek see A. Drewicz-Tułodziecka (ed.), *Basic Guidelines for a Eurohypothek* (Warsaw 2005) in Mortgage Bulletin, 21/2005). As a result of this institutional input, academic studies in recent years have analyzed mortgage law in Europe, not necessarily with a view to legal integration, but mainly in order to acquire greater knowledge of the operational rules existent in the various jurisdictions. In 2004, a research group on Security Rights over Immovable Assets was established within the "The Common Core of European Private Law"; the coordinators of the research group are Prof. C. van der Merwe (Aberdeen), G. Watt (Warwick) and the author of this Chapter. The results will be published by Cambridge University Press; see www.jus.unitn.it/dsg/common-core/questionnaires.html. Comparative research on Real Property Law and Procedure in the European Union, concerning also mortgages/hypothecs, is ongoing at the European Institute of Florence and its results have already been published: http://www.iue.it/LAW/ResearchTeaching/EuropeanPrivateLAw/ProjectRealPropertyLaw.shtml.

58. COM(2005) 327, of 19 July 2005 (according to the Green Paper, possible interventions by the EU should be restricted to residential mortgage lending).

59. *The Costs and Benefits of Integration in the EU Mortgage Market*: http://europa.eu.int/comm/internal_market/finservices-retail/index_en.htm.

Paper has been published in December 2007,[60] setting out new EU's strategies, goals and measures to promote efficiency and competitiveness in the European mortgage market.

The White Paper shows that the future orientation of the EU Institutions will be no more focused on the introduction of a "Europhypothek" as the primary means to enhance legal integration in Europe, but will adopt a multi-level approach to the issues at stake. Therefore, the EU Commission intends to achieve an efficient single mortgage market by removing, by means of "legislative" instruments, relevant legal and economic obstacles to its growth. These obstacles are identified in national divergences on consumer protection standards in the mortgage credit; in a still lacking diversity of mortgage products; in insufficient infrastructures supporting the mortgage credit (like credit reporting systems); in the existence of different domestic legislations on land registration and enforcement of security rights over immovables.[61] Especially the opportunity to increase diversity in the supply of mortgage credit is connected to the target of enhancing consumers' trust *vis-à-vis* the new products. To this aim the Commission supports the prospective introduction of "legislative" innovations in the contractual terms of mortgage loans that should sound very similar to those contained in the new Directive on Consumer Credit Agreements.[62] In this direction the White Paper promotes a *responsible lending*, i.e. a lending system based on a series of measures, like a detailed assessment, in the pre-contractual stage, of the creditworthiness of the devised borrower[63] and the institution of independent legal advice for consumers seeking access to mortgage credit.[64] These measures are regarded as essential not only to the integration of the EU mortgage market but also to the protection of the latter from the spreading of dangerous phenomena like the U.S.A. *sub-prime* turmoil.[65]

---

60. COM(2007)807 final, 18th December 2007, *White Paper on the Integration of EU Mortgage Markets*, available at http://ec.europa.eu/internal_market/finservices-retail/home-loans/integration_en.htm#whitepaper.

61. *White Paper*, quoted *supra*, fn. 60, pt. 3.

62. Directive 2008/48/EC, of 23.4.2008 (in O.J. L 133, 22.5.2008, 66 ff.), on credit agreements for consumers, repealing Council Directive 87/102/EEC.

63. See, for all, T. Jappelli & M. Pagano, *The Role and Effects of Credit Information Sharing*, in G. Bertola, R. Disney & C. Grant (eds.), *The Economics of Consumer Credit* (Cambridge, Mass., London, 2006) 347 ff.

64. *White Paper*, quoted *supra*, fn. 60, pt. 3.3.

65. *White Paper*, quoted *supra*, fn. 60, pt. 3.1 and see *infra*, n. 7.6.

### *7.5. The Economic Reasons Behind Legal Integration in the EU Mortgage Market*

The content of the White Paper shows very clearly what are the reasons behind the actual interest of the EU Institutions for "legislative" interventions in the field of security over immovable assets. These are economic reasons, strictly connected to the needs of expansion of banking and financial markets, as they were perceived by the relevant industries before the explosion of the international credit crunch triggered by the failure of *sub-prime* securitizations in the United States.[66]

The strategic role of mortgage credit in the building of a common financial market is repeated in many passages of the EU documents mentioned above. They all point out that this common financial market shall be grounded on the value of immovable property as leverage of wealth for land owners, banks and financial institutions, as well as for the real economy of the European countries.[67] According to EU data, mortgage markets—that are largely still domestic—build a significant part of the EU economy: the outstanding residential mortgage loans amount approximately to the 47% of the EU's GDP.[68] The same sources underline that the trans-national mortgage credit

66. As well-known by this time, the so called *sub-prime* mortgage loans are loans granted by banks to borrowers who do not possess an adequate creditworthiness to get access to traditional mortgage loans. This is usually due to low income capacity, or to the filing against such borrower of previous defaults *vis-à-vis* banks. The U.S.A. credit reporting system for consumers is based on statistical analysis provided by few agencies, such as Equifax, Experian, TransUnion e Innovis: R.M. Hunt, *A Century of Consumer Credit Reporting in America*, June 2005, FRB Philadelphia Working Paper No. 05-13, available at: SSRN: http://ssrn.com/abstract=757929; Id., *Development and Regulation of Consumer Credit Reporting in the United States*, in G. Bertola, R. Disney & C. Grant (eds.), *The Economics of Consumer Credit*, 301 ff. In 2007 *sub-prime* mortgage loans in U.S.A. have reached the 20% of all outstanding loans. The price fall in the real estate sector and the raising of interest rates determined an increased number of insolvencies. This originated a liquidity crisis for banks that could not buy and sell financial instruments without high oscillations in prices. Financial instruments derived from securitizations of *sub-prime* mortgage loans remained immobilized in the originator's balance sheets. For details see, e.g., Y. Demyanyk & O. van Hemert, *Understanding the Subprime Mortgage Crisis*, Feb. 29, 2008, SSNR Working Paper Series, available at: http://ssrn.com/abstract=1020396; C.M. Reinhart & K.S. Rogoff, *Is the 2007 U.S. sub-prime financial crisis so different? An international comparison*, Working Paper N. 13761, Jan. 2008, National Bureau of Economic Research, Cambridge, Ma, available at: http://www.nber.org/papers/w13761;

67. E.g., *White Paper*, quoted *supra*, fn. 60, pt. 1.

68. HYPOSTAT 2005: *A review of Europe's Mortgage and Housing Markets, European Mortgage Federation*, November 2006, 140.

market developed slowly, to increase to a certain significance only in the last decade, and still presents wide possibilities of growth which have been quantified as amounting to the 0,7% of the EU's GDP and the 0,5% of private consumption for the next 10 years.[69]

The European Union has made of the exploitation of the above margins of growth one of the symbols of its economic and financial policy.[70] In this perspective, the project of the integration of the EU mortgage market is based on two interconnected pillars. The first one aims at promoting the widest access to mortgage credit for consumers; the second combines banking with finance markets and focuses on the strengthening of the securitizations of mortgage loans as an indispensible liquidity source for credit institutions.[71] This last point, however, is problematic today, since the still ongoing global financial crisis, and therefore deserves further examination.

## *7.6. Mortgage Securitizations in Europe after the* Sub-Prime *Crisis*

That security rights over immovables are particularly suitable asset for structured finance operations targeted to refinance credit institutions is widely demonstrated by the spreading of securitizations based on mortgage loans, be these techniques based on the U.S.A. model,[72] or inspired to the German pat-

---

69. *The Costs and Benefits of Integration of EU Mortgage Markets*, London Economics, Aug. 2005, quoted above, fn. 59, at p. 5.

70. *E.g.*, EU Commission's Communication *A single market for 21st century Europe*, COM(2007)724 of the 20th November 2007, at p. 6.

71. See., e.g., Y. Altunbas, L. Gambacorta & D. Marqués, *Securitisation and the bank lending channel*, (Working Papers), Bank of Italy, November 2007, 20 ff., available at: www.bancaditalia.it.

72. Briefly, this is a technique of structured finance aiming at mobilizing a pool of (present or future) credits owned by a bank or other financial institution called *originator*. The pool of credits of the originator must be sold or otherwise assigned to another entity called *special purpose vehicle*. The latter will, directly or through another *vehicle*, issue on the capital market tranches of bonds (generally called asset backed securities) incorporating the value of the sold credits. The liquidity gained by the investors in those bonds will be utilized by the *vehicle* to pay the credit pool to the originator. For an overview of national legal regimes on securitization in Europe and North America see International Financial Law Review, *Structured Finance Yearbook 2003*, 50 ff.; D.G. Glennie & E.C. de Bouter, R.D. Luke (eds.), *Securitization* (The Hague, London, Boston 1998); focusing on Europe: S. Nasarre-Aznar, *Securitisation & mortgage bonds: legal aspects and harmonisation* (Saffron Walden 2004).

tern of the issuance of *Pfandbriefe*.[73] Suffice here to recall that the German model of the so-called *covered bonds* has been successfully copied overall through Europe,[74] although not so in U.K. nor in the U.S.A.[75]

Up to the international financial crisis of September–October 2008 the policy of the European Institutions was centered in fostering legal integration of security rights over immovables precisely in order to promote the widest possible recourse to the refinancing techniques based on the so-called *originate-to-distribuite* model. This means originating credits as an asset deemed to be

---

73. The issuance of *Pfandbriefe* does not depend to an assignment or sale of the pool of credits to a vehicle. The mortgage loans remain on the balance sheet of the originator, but form a segregated asset, separate from the whole asset of the originator itself. The segregation of the mortgage loans is purported through a registration of them in a special register of the originator (*Deckungsregister*), held by a trustee (*Treuhändler*). Mortgage and loan are registered together in this register, *ex* § 18 para. 2 *Pfandbriefgesetz*. On the basis of the value of the mortgage loans that are registered, the originator issues covered bonds called *Pfandbriefe*, incorporating the right of its holder to reimbursement in a certain time which is determined in accordance with the date of maturity of the mortgage loans. In case of insolvency of the originator/issuer of the bonds, the bonds holders have a right to preferential satisfaction over the asset registered in the *Deckungsregister* (*ex* § 30 para. 1 *Pfandbriefgesetz*). The combination between a bond (*Pfandbrief*) that is standardized by statute and the security of a mortgage (within the maximum limit of the 60% of the value of the immovable, *ex* § 14 del *Pfandbriefgesetz*) allows the produce a bond extremely reliable for investors. The issuance of *Pfandbriefe* was regulated since 1900 by *Hypothekenbankgesetz*, today substituted by *Gesetz zur Neuordnung des Pfandbriefrechts*, 22.5.2005 (BGBl. Nr. 29 of 27.5.2005, S. 1373). The replacement of the older law was necessary since the abrogation of the state guarantee for German banks in 2005. Cp. Deutsche Bundesbank, *New Legal and Regulatory Framework for the German Securitisation and Pfandbrief Market*, in *Monthly Report*, March 2006, 37 ff.

74. The success of the German mortgage credit market fostered an "internationalization" process of the *Pfandbriefe*. In 1995 a new version of *Pfandbrief* was introduced, called *Jumbo Pfandbrief* and destined to the wholesale market. Its characteristics in comparison to the normal *Pfandbrief* are a higher liquidity and a stronger standardization of the modalities of its issuance. Since 2000, and even during the actual global crisis, the *Jumbo* covered bond has maintained a sufficient return on investment ratio. This is why the International Monetary Fund has proposed this type of covered bond as an alternative to the U.S.A. securitizations affected by the crisis: IMF, *Regional Economic Outlook, Europe Dealing With Shocks*, October 2008, 41 f.

Since the Nineties, the German *Pfandbriefe* system has been emulated by several western and eastern European countries that promulgated new legislations to regulate German style issuance of covered bonds. These national legislations are available at the website of the European Covered Bond Council: http://ecbc.hypo.org/content/default.asp?PageID=318. See also ECBC, *European Covered Bond Factbook*, Bruxelles, September 2008.

75. S. Nasarre Aznar, *Securitisation & mortgage bonds, Legal aspects and harmonisation in Europe* (Cambridge 2004) 37 ff., 75 ff.

immediately assigned (and sold) to an entity different from the originator, and therefore to be immediately canceled from the balance sheets of the originator.[76] The need to expand such funding model derives from the unsuitability of the classic method of financing mortgage loans based on retail deposits by bank clients. The latter show today a higher propensity to invest in financial products, relying less on saving deposits.[77] Moreover, retail deposits are insufficient means to fund mortgage loans, being they a source of liquidity potentially subject to a short-term reimbursement, while mortgage credits typically produce gradual reimbursement of the credit in the long-term. This obviously creates difficulties for banks in the asset-risk management.[78]

The need to overcome the classic funding system also results from the implementation of the EU Banking Directives. These aimed at introducing the universal banking model as opposite to the specialized banking system that was widespread throughout Europe.[79] This evolution imposed on banks the need—in order to successfully compete in the market—to add to traditional banking activities all other activities that allow funding through the financial market conduit, thereby opening the gates to complex asset management operations, such as structured finance techniques.

Another factor that pushed banks towards securitizations in the *originate-to-distribute* form has been the implementation of the Basel Accords on capital adequacy requirements for banks as established by the Basel Committee on Banking Supervision.[80]

---

76. On structure and problematic issues of this technique see European Central Bank, *EU Banking Structures*, October 2008, 18 ff, available at: http://www.ecb.int/pub/pub/prud/html/index.en.html?skey=+07%2F10%2F2005.

77. P. Branthomme, *Savings and the Financial Behaviour of European Households Between 1996 and 2000*, in *Banque de France Bulletin Digest*, n. 105, September 2002, 23 ff.; Unicredit Group, *CEE Households' Wealth and Debt Monitor*, November 2007, 4 ff., 8 ff., 12, ff., available at: http://www.bankaustria.at/en/19752.html. This document shows that in Europe the propensity to invest in financial markets is generalized and is connected to the weaknesses of public pension systems as well as to other faults of the *welfare system*.

78. *Report of The Mortgage Funding Expert Group*, 22.12.2006, 2 f., available at: http://ec.europa.eu/internal_market/finservices-retail/home-loans/integration_en.htm.

79. On EU banking legislation see http://ec.europa.eu/internal_market/bank/legislation/index_en.htm. *E multis*, J. Ernoult, W. Hemetsberger, H. Schoppmann & C. Wengler, *European Banking and Financial Services Law* (3rd edn, Brussels 2008).

80. On the Basel Accords, I and II, see www.bis.org. Basel II has been implemented into community law by EU Directives 2006/48/EC and 2006/49/EC of 14 June 2006 (both in O.J. L 177 of 30.6.2006, respectively p. 1 ff. and 201 ff.), relating to the taking up and pursuit of the business of credit institutions (recast) and to the capital adequacy of investment firms and credit institutions (recast).

According to Basel I of 1988—which has been implemented by more than a hundred of countries in the world including U.S.A.—to each lending activity a quote of capital (so-called regulatory capital) must be retained by the bank to cover the default risk connected to the loan. Basel I fixed this quote in the 8% of the risk-weighted credit activities. To assure stability and confidence in the banking systems this regulatory capital cannot be re-invested in other credit or financial activities. The point is that Basel I is now considered as one of the contributing elements to the springing up of the innovative structured finance that lead to the north American crisis of the securitizations market. This is because, first, Basel I provides that the quote of regulatory capital be the same, irrespective of the default risk of the borrower, thereby incentivizing investments in riskier activities.[81] Second, banks intensified recourse to the *originate-to-distribute* model of securitization, that enables banks to escape from the mandatory rule of retaining a quote of regulatory capital. Indeed, the credit pools are transferred—usually by means of a true sale—to entities different from the originator and therefore do not result from the balance sheets of the latter. It has been noted how this phenomenon lead to the formation of a "shadow banking system", living outside the capital adequacy regulations.

To correct these distortions in the development of international banking a new Accord known as Basel II has been elaborated and finalized in 2004.[82] This Accord maintains the quote of the 8% of regulatory capital for banking activities, but improves the techniques of risk measurement, imposing to banks a stricter control over the creditworthiness of the borrower.[83] However, the operative success of Basel II is hindered by the high implementation costs attached to it: the new standards and methods of risk-weighting are complex and require careful and time-consuming training for banks' operators. It is also for this reason that Basel II has remained almost not implemented in the

81. Basel Committee on Banking Supervision, *Capital requirements and bank behaviour: the impact of the Basel Accord*, Publication No. 1, April 1999, at p. 20 ff., available at: http://www.bis.org/publ/bcbs_wp1.htm; H. Price Tarbert, *Are International Capital Adequacy Rules Adequate? The Basel Accord and Beyond*, 148 U. Pa. L. Rev. (2000) 1771 ff., 1803.

82. See *supra*, fn. 80.

83. The risks that must be covered by the regulatory capital are divided in three types: credit risks, market risks and operative risks. Three methods to calculate these risks are introduced: Standard, IRB Foundation, IRB Advanced. See Basel Committee on Banking Supervision, *International Convergence of Capital Measurement and Capital Standards: a Revised Framework*, June 2004, http://www.bis.org/publ/bcbs107.htm.

U.S.A.,[84] this being an element that contributed to the degeneration of U.S. securitizations towards always riskier schemes.[85]

The American *sub-prime* phenomenon clearly demonstrates that the interaction between credit risks, market risks and liquidity risks can produce a dangerous trans-national domino effect, facilitated by the growing integration of financial markets around the globe. In this context, the open challenge for (not only) European financing is now to rebuild, or strengthen, a regulation framework suitable to recover market confidence in relation to securitizations of mortgage loans. It cannot be a task for these pages to show the path to be followed for such an ambitious, and dramatically necessary, enterprise. To be stressed here are rather the limits of the EU institutional project regarding the integration of the EU mortgage market as set out the White Paper.[86]

The EU is indeed focusing in the production and implementation of new rules deemed to standardize in Europe some contractual and procedural aspects of mortgage loans. The *sub-prime* crisis, however, shows that among the technical difficulties surrounding securitizations many other factors are relevant. Reference must be made to the unsuitability of supervisory authorities on financial markets and the imperfections of regulations governing rating procedures and companies—in the U.S.A. the existing regulation allowed rating activities to be remunerated by the subjects who commissioned them[87]—; in the same vein, the lack of transparency regarding financial instruments hindered to investors an easy evaluation of profitability and risks connected to

84. See United States Government Accountability Office, *Risk-Based Capital: New Basel II Rules Reduced Certain Competitive Concerns, but Bank Regulators Should Address Remaining Uncertainties*; GAO-08-953, September 12, 2008, available at: http://www.gao.gov/docsearch/repandtest.html.

85. See Basel Committee on Banking Supervision, *Liquidity Risk: Management and Supervisory Challenges*, February 2008, available at: http://www.bis.org/publ/bcbs136.htm. This document highlights that many banks had failed to take account of a number of basic principles of liquidity risk management when liquidity was plentiful. Many of the most exposed banks did not have an adequate framework that satisfactorily accounted for the liquidity risks posed by individual products and business lines, and therefore incentives at the business level were misaligned with the overall risk tolerance of the bank. Many banks had not considered the amount of liquidity they might need to satisfy contingent obligations, either contractual or non-contractual, as they viewed funding of these obligations to be highly unlikely.

86. See *supra*, n. 7.4.

87. A.B. Ashcraft & T. Schuermann, *Understanding the Securitization of Subprime Mortgage Credit*, (March 2008) Wharton Financial Institutions Center Working Paper No. 07-43, available at: SSRN: http://ssrn.com/abstract=1071189.

such products.[88] The frontline on financial battle will be world-wide regulation of supervisory systems on banks and financial institutions, improvement of risk measurement techniques to be applied to financial operations and instruments, and transparency of the financial system more in general.[89] After the global financial crisis, "legislative" EU action on the substantive laws of European member states, aiming at modifying selected aspects of the mortgage loans, or of the security rights attached to them, will never suffice to assure the economic splendors envisaged by the EU Institutions as direct consequence of the expansion of the European mortgage market.

## 8. Security Rights over Movable Assets: 'Formal' Security Rights

As mentioned above, each European system recognizes the pledge as a traditional 'formal' security over movable assets, the creation of which depends on delivery of possession to the creditor or to a third person,[90] in order to prevent the impression of false wealth being given. Although at the time of the continental codifications of private law the market demanded non-possessory security devices (given that in most cases it is highly undesirable, if not impossible, for a debtor to give up possession of its inventory or equipment), the possessory pledge was the main form of security over tangible movables cho-

88. On these aspects see also European Central Bank, *EU Banking Structures*, October 2008, quoted *supra*, fn. 76, 19–21.

89. The possible impact of this financial crisis on future behavior of the market actors, together with a list of advisable regulations to be implemented can be found in European Central Bank: *EU Banking Structures*, October 2008, quoted *supra*, fn. 76, 24 ff.

90. Dutch c.c., art. 3:236 (*pand*); English common law (*pledge*, *pawn*): L. Smith, *Security*, in P. Birks (ed.), *English Private Law*, I (Oxford 2000) 411; French c.c. old arts. 2071, 2076 (after the 2006 reform, the new arts. 2333 ff. concerning the *gage* for tangible movable assets and 2355 ff. on the *nantissement* for intangible movable assets no longer consider the delivery of possession as a requisite for the creation of the security); Belgian c.c., art. 2071 (*nantissement*); 2073 (*gage*) and art. 1 Law of 5 May 1872 for the commercial pledge (*gage*); German c.c., § 1205, 1206 (*Faustpfand*); Greek c.c., art. 1211; Italian c.c., art. 2786 (*pegno*); Portuguese c.c., art. 669 para. 1 (*penhor*); Spanish c.c., art. 1863 (*prenda*). Sometimes other formalities are required for the right of preferential satisfaction of the creditor to be valid: in Italy, art. 2787, para. 2 requires possession of the encumbered asset by the creditor or the third person, and para. 3 requires, in the case of a secured credit to the amount of Euro 2.58, evidence of the pledge deriving from a document with a 'certain date' and sufficiently stating the pledged asset and the secured credit.

sen and regulated by the civil codes from 1804 to 1992. Consequently, as far as movables are concerned, the codes were 'born old.'

As to the enforcement of pledges, generally the continental countries regulate public auctions, which are usually authorized by a judge. The reason for the introduction of public procedures is that creditors are not normally deemed to be the proper subjects to obtain a fair price from the purchase of pledge. If the secured asset has an official market price, it can in most instances be sold by a broker. The automatic transfer of ownership to the creditor in the event of debtor's default is forbidden in almost all countries by the prohibition of forfeiture clause (*lex commissoria*).[91] In England, by contrast, the creditor is allowed to arrange the private sale of the secured assets after maturity, and it is bound by case law to set a reasonable price.[92]

Although all European countries have shaped the pledge as an accessory proprietary right in the terms above mentioned in n. 7.1 (i.e., strictly dependent for its creation and extinction on a principal obligation), economic needs have sometimes led to mitigation of the consequences ensuing from overly strict accessority of the pledge, with greater ease than could have been possible in the field of security over immovables. In some countries, especially in the commercial and bank credit sector, the rule that the security must be specific to the secured credit, as well as to the secured assets, has been attenuated. In this way, the practice seeks to get global security rights (i.e. pledges securing all future undetermined credits arising from any contractual relationship between the same creditor and debtor)[93] mostly on the pattern of per-

---

91. Dutch c.c., art. 3:235; see French c.c., former art. 2078, para. 2 (the prohibition has now been strongly weakened by the reform of 2006: see new arts. 2347, 2348 for the *gage* and 2365 for the *nantissement*; French c. comm., art. L521-3 para. 4 as amended by the reform; note however that the prohibition of forfeiture clauses is still existent for the *gage de stocks*: French c.comm. art. L527-2); German c.c., §1229; Greek c.c., art. 1239; Italian c.c., art. 2744; Spanish c.c., art. 1859.

92. *Ex p Hubbard* (1886) 17 QBD 699; Consumer Credit Act 1974, s. 121; M. Bridge, *Personal Property Law*, 3rd ed. (Oxford 2002), 175 ff.

93. In Italy, the creation of pledges securing future credits is allowed if the future credits are to arise from a contractual relationship already existing between the parties. The problem of the *omnibus* clause is different, because in this clause not only the (exact amount of) the secured credit is not determined at the time of the creation of the security, but also the relationship from which the credits to be secured are to arise is not determined: E. Gabrielli, *Pegno*, in *Tratt. dir. civ.* edited by R. Sacco (Turin 2005), 138 ff. However, opinions differ greatly as to the full validity of this device, and Italian case law restricts the validity of the *omnibus* clause to the *inter partes* relationship between creditor and debtor, not to the effects concerning third persons: Cass. 5.7.2000, n. 8970, in BBTC, 2000, II, 606; Cass. 28.10.2005 n. 21084, Foro. It. Mass., 2005, 1631. In Dutch law, pledges secur-

sonal security contracts. 'Revolving' pledges have also been accepted: that is, security rights over movable assets that may be substituted by other assets of the same value during the secured relationship.[94] This has proved useful in the case of assets to be manufactured, or in the financial sector.[95]

The pledge as the central device for security over movables can be created over movable tangible assets, but also over intangibles. This concerns the case of claims to payments of money,[96] for which the legal scheme of the pledge over tangibles has been applied more recently, so that publicity of the creation of the security is performed through notice to the account debtor.[97] Owing to

---

ing credits on current accounts are made possible by an interpretation of art. 3:231 c.c. that allows pledges on future claims: J.H.M. van Erp & L.P.W. van Vliet, *Real and Personal Security*, 119. The Catalonian law, n. 19 of 5 July 2002 (*Llei de drets reals de garantia*), art. 13 para 2 states that the pledge can secure obligations whose amount is not known at the time of the creation of the security if a maximum amount has been agreed; para. 3 of the same article states that the pledge can secure different present or future obligations arising between debtor and creditor within an agreed time limit and for an agreed maximum amount.

94. New rules on the *gage de stocks* as revolving proprietary security have been introduced in the French commercial code by the French reform of security rights of 2006: c.comm. arts. L527-1 to L527-11. For the so-called *pegno rotativo* in Italy see E. Gabrielli, *Il pegno "anomalo"* (Padua 1990)181 ff., 216 ff.; Id., *Sulle garanzie rotative* (Neaples 1998) 87 ff.; Cass. 28.5.1998, n. 5264, in GC 1998, I, 2159. The Dutch Supreme Court has ruled that in the case of pledges on large amounts of claims the principle of specificity is applied leniently because the pledge does not require a full list of all claims (subject to security) to be registered. A shortened list suffices as long as it enables determination of the exact security objects, e.g. references to detailed computer lists which are not themselves registered (HR 14 October 1994, NJ 1995/447). The Supreme Court has extended the pledge on claims in an unusual way by stating that, according to art. 3:246(5) CC, a pledgee who demands payment of the claim himself will not lose his right of pledge: because of real subrogation it will subsist on the money as the new security object (HR 17 February 1995, NJ 1996/471; HR 23 April 1999, NJ 2000/30): cp. J.H.M. van Erp, L.P.W. van Vliet, *Real and Personal Security*, 120. In Spain, Catalonian law n. 19 of 5 July 2002, art. 16 and 17, recognizes real subrogation as to the object of the security.

95. EU Directive on Financial Collateral Arrangements 47/2002/CE art. 5 para. 3; EU Regulation on Insolvency Procedures, n. 1346/2000 of 29.5.2000, art. 5 para. 1. See the report on national implementations of the Financial Collateral Directive by the EU Commission, COM(2006)833fin. of 20.12.2006, available at: http://ec.europa.eu/internal_market/financial-markets/collateral/index_en.htm

96. Most codes expressly regulate the pledge over claims. When this option is not recognized by positive law, it is admitted by the interpretive formants, as in Spain: A. Carrasco, E. Cordero y M. Marín, *Tratado de los Derechos de Garantías* (Cizur Menor 2002), 862.

97. German c.c., § 1280, Italy, cc. art. 2800, Greece, art. 1248 c.c.; Portuguese c.c., art. 681, para. 2.

the burden of this notice requirement, and often also owing to a desire for discretion on debtor's side in commercial transactions, the tendency soon developed to use other means of creating security over receivables, like the assignment to security purposes. This 'functional' form of security is today the most common form of proprietary security over claims (see *infra*, n. 8.1.a).

Where registration systems have taken the place of delivery of possession by the debtor, specific laws (usually covering credit to enterprise only) have been enacted to regulate non-possessory pledges or hypothecs over movable assets.[98]

English case law has developed the floating charge as a non-possessory security for corporate financing.[99] In this case, the security does not encumber the assets in their individuality but rather in the universality of present and future assets of the company. The latter is free to dispose of the assets until the time of the so-called 'crystallization' of the charge from a floating into a fixed one. This is because of the occurrence of an event that is agreed upon by the parties to effect crystallization—usually the default of the company,

---

98. This is the case of Spain: *Ley sobre hipotheca mobiliaria y prenda sin desplazamiento de posesión*, of 18th Dec. 1954, BOE n. 352; and of the registered pledge introduced in Poland by the Act on Registered Pledges and the Register of Pledges adopted on 6 Dec. 1996, in force since 1st Jan. 1998: Gdansk Academy of Banking, *Analysis of the Economic Impact of the Registered Pledge System in Poland*, (Gdansk Nov. 2003). Also to be mentioned is the Italian 'contractual privilege' for banks: this is regulated by decree-law 1.9.1993, n. 385 (Italian Bank Law) art. 46; Although termed a 'privilege', it seems more like a proprietary security right (G. Tucci, *I privilegi*, in *Trattato di diritto privato* diretto da P. Rescigno, 19, 2nd edn., Turin 1997, 717). Swedish law regulates enterprise mortgages with the Enterprise Mortgage of Act 1984. However, as to the extent and effect of registration the various countries offer very different solutions: U. Drobnig, *Present and Future of Real and Personal Security*, 643 f. In the Netherlands, the '*fiducia*' banned by the new civil code of 1992 has been replaced by the 'silent' pledge on movables (art. 3:237 CC) or claims (art. 3:239 CC). By means of the 'silent' pledge, the pledgor remains in actual possession of the movables, or, in the case of a claim, the pledge will not be notified to the account debtor. A silent pledge requires a private deed registered with the tax department or, alternatively, a notarial deed. These formalities prevent antedating but are not intended to make the security interests public. The register at the tax department is not a public register: J.H.M. van Erp & L.P.W. van Vliet, *Real and Personal Security*, 119. The French reform provides for a pledge with delivery of possession and a non-possessory pledge with registration (new art. 2337 c.c.); consequently, the notion of *gage* itself has changed. It has become a consensual contract, because delivery of possession is no longer a requisite for the existence of the security (art. 2333): L. Aynès y P. Crocq, *Les sûretés, La publicité foncière*, 3e éd., Paris, 2008, no. 500, p. 214.

99. The first recognition of this legal device is in *Re Panama* v. *New Zealand and Australian Royal Mail Co.* (1870) 5 Ch App 318.

the opening of an enforcement procedure against it, or the interruption of its activity, etc.[100]

## 8.1. 'Functional' Security Rights: Ownership and Ownership-Related Contractual Arrangements

Recourse to 'functional' security rights has been made by commercial practice especially in countries where non-possessory 'formal' security rights have not been regulated, or have been so only fragmentarily—and, therefore, insufficiently. However, the outcomes of such recourse have differed greatly among countries.

The expression 'functional security rights' denotes various forms of recourse to ownership as security, in particular the transfer of ownership to the creditor for security purposes, or the retention of ownership by the creditor for security purposes. Other contractual arrangements—like financial leasing or sale and lease-back transactions—producing proprietary effects may also be regarded as performing a security function. A feature common to 'functional security rights' is that physical control over the assets serving as security remains with the security provider.

The widespread recourse to these arrangements for security purposes highlights another crucial issue of the law of secured transactions: the formalism as opposed to the functionalism existing in each national legal regime.

Put it briefly, where hostility is expressed against 'functional' security rights, a formal or structural approach to the topic prevails, because only rights with a specific structure are considered to be security rights ('formal' ones). Here,

---

100. M. Bridge, *Personal Property Law*, 188 ff. The difficulty with this device has been the weak priority which it gives to the secured creditor: the priority of a subsequent fixed charge, in fact, prevails over a previous floating charge; moreover, certain unsecured creditors with a preference ranking, such as employees for back wages, are given a special statutory priority that places them after fixed charges but before floating ones (Insolvency Act 1986, s. 386 and Schedule 6). In England, the registration and priority of floating charges, as well as of company security rights in general, are currently being reformed: G. McCormack, *The Floating Charge in England and Canada*, in J. De Lacy (ed.) The Reform of UK Company Law (London 2002) 389–414 and the last Law Commission Paper of 31 Aug. 2005, *Company Security Interests* (Law Com N. 296): http://www.lawcom.gov.uk/docs/lc296.pdf. More in general, on the risks of enterprise mortgages for the debtor's other creditors and the consequent statutory limitations existing in the European countries, see U. Drobnig, *Present and Future of Real and Personal Security*, 648.

the focus is on the structure, or form, of the security rights: a limited right *in rem* is a valid security; transfer of absolute title or retention of title is not.

By contrast, where the legal regime is open to 'functional' security rights, a pragmatic approach to security prevails: when the security purpose is proven, every legal device or arrangement between the parties is considered a valid security right—and is therefore legally treated as such—without any reference made to the form of the transaction. Needless to say, the prime example of this system in the sector of security over movables is the U.S. system set out in Art. 9 U.C.C. In addition, it is precisely the influence of this model that impacts the current European debate concerning legal reform in this field (see *infra*, n. 8.2). Moreover, the prevalence of formalism is a feature common to the laws of the western European countries, and in this respect, the English common law is perfectly aligned with the civil law.[101]

Because 'functional' security rights are arrangements quite different from each other, they warrant brief, separate consideration.

(a) *Transfer of Ownership*: Economic demand for non-possessory security devices has induced recourse to the (fiduciary) transfer of ownership over movables,[102] this being the very first method of creating real security to appear in legal history. The use of ownership for security purposes brings advantages, but also some disadvantages. As to the former, not only does transfer of title give rise to a non-possessory security, but it enables publicity of the burden on the security provider asset to be avoided, and also the costs of creating/registering a 'formal' security. Moreover, in the event of the debtor's default, more effective satisfaction is achieved because transfer of title to the creditor becomes final. This gives rise to the principal problem with these devices, namely the

101. The orthodox definition of a security right under English law is, in fact, that of the 'grant of an interest less than absolute ownership by a person who already has or will obtain an interest in property': L. Gullifer, *Quasi-security Interests: Functionalism and the Incidents of Security*, in I. Davies (ed.), *Issues in International Commercial Law* (Aldershot, Burlington 2005), 3 ff., 5; therefore, a retention of title is not a security right. The English law on company security rights is undergoing reform; the most recent Consultation Paper of the Law Commission, n. 296 of 31 Aug. 2005 (see *supra*, fn. 100) proposes the introduction of a functionalist approach to company security rights so that also quasi-securities, including the assignment of claims within factoring transactions, will be considered security and treated as such. For the civil law side of the problem see A. Veneziano, *Le garanzie mobiliari non possessorie*, 112 ff.

102. The phenomenon also exists in the case of immovable assets, but here it is of sometimes lesser magnitude, because of the costs of land transactions, and also because in some jurisdictions the needs of the market are covered by mortgages/hypothecs. This is the case of Germany or France for instance: M. Cabrillac, C. Mouly, *Droit des sûretés*, 452.

fact that they transfer to the creditor "more title" than the latter needs for security purposes, and this fact—mainly by reason of historical path dependency—is often considered dangerous for the debtor. I now provide a brief overview of the legal treatment of ownership as security in western Europe.

In most continental countries with prevalent Roman-law traditions, such security transfers of ownership tend to be banned for a variety of theoretical reasons, such as the existence of a *numerus clausus* of proprietary rights, or the unsuitability of the security purpose as the legal *causa* of a transfer of ownership.[103] However, the essential reason for this ban seems to be the deeply-rooted idea of debtor protection against usury—and it is this that constitutes the rationale for the prohibition of the *lex commissoria* in the mentality of the interpretive formants. In Italy, the *lex commissoria* ban is often applied by courts in order to declare the nullity of security transfers of ownership.[104] Substantially, the same ban can be observed in Spain[105] and in the Netherlands.[106]

By contrast, German law is well-known for its liberality in the development of fiduciary transfers of ownership or assignment of claims for security purposes (*Sicherungsübereignung, Sicherungsabtertung*), also in broader forms whereby the security also covers processing assets.[107] Here, prohibition of the *lex commissoria*—although it exists in the code—does not have operational relevance, in that it has almost never been applied by courts in cases concerning (the validity of)

103. F. Anelli, *L'alienazione in funzione di garanzia* (Milan 1996).

104. For a comparative analysis: M. Bussani, *Il problema del patto commissorio*; for Italy: F. Fiorentini, *Garanzie reali atipiche*, 253 ff.

105. In Spain, the problem is not the validity of the transfer of ownership for security purposes but its limits and effects towards third persons, also in consideration of the par *condicio creditorum* and the prohibition of the forfeiture clause: A. Carrasco, E. Cordero y M. Marín, *Tratado de los Derechos de Garantías*, 1058 ff. However, the ban of the *lex commissoria* has a more limited scope of application in Spain than in Italy (Id., 1064). The *Fuero Nuevo de Navarra*, Law n. 466 expressly regulates the *fiducia de garantía*.

106. To be noted is the recession of Dutch law on the subject. Security ownership was recognized by the Dutch Supreme Court in 1929 (HR 25 January 1929, NJ 1929, 616; HR 21 June 1929, NJ 1929, 1096) because a non-possessory security right over movables was needed. Gradually, over many decades following recognition of security ownership in 1929, the Supreme Court reduced the security owner's rights to the rights of a pledgee, maintaining that the owner is under a duty to sell the security object in execution and satisfy himself from the proceeds of sale. Any surplus money must be given to the debtor. It was thus accepted that security ownership is different from normal ownership. The 1992 Civil Code abolished *fiducia* at art. 3:84(3), mainly on the ground that security ownership gives the creditor more than is needed: ownership rather than a limited real right: J.H.M. van Erp & L.P.W. van Vliet, *Real and Personal Security*.

107. R. Serick, *Securities in Movables in German law. An Outline* (Den Haag 1990), 47 ff.

security transfers of ownership. Control over the proportionality of the security to the amount of the credit to be secured is exerted in Germany through an *ex-post* judicial assessment based on general clauses (esp. § 138 German c.c.).

The hostility shown by some European systems towards security ownership is difficult to understand if we bear in mind that where it is fully recognized, security ownership is also treated as a 'formal' security, and not as an absolute ownership, for instance in the debtor's insolvency, so that any danger of disproportion in the enforcement of the security is easily averted.[108]

A slightly different path has been followed by English law, for which a mortgage over movables has always been essentially a transfer of ownership to the creditor, where the proportionality of the transaction has always been checked by the rules of equity.[109]

Security ownership is generally valid even in the jurisdictions (like Italy) most adverse to it when the asset to be transferred for security purposes is a claim (security assignment). Two meta-positive reasons for this notable exception to the ban on security ownership may be identified where claims are concerned: (a) it is easier to check the proportionality of the secured relationship at the time of the enforcement—set-off often operates between the parties; (b) dogmatic objections may not stop actual bank practices worldwide in the sector of commercial lending.

(b) *Retention of Title (RoT):* The RoT is the classic security for credit granted by suppliers of goods, who sell the goods to the purchaser but grant him delayed payment of the purchase price, usually in instalments. In these cases, title passes to the purchaser only with full payment of the price (suspensive condition), so that the retention of the title by the seller/creditor has an evident function of security. The legal regimes on the validity and effects of RoT vary significantly among the European countries.

In general, validity of a RoT requires an express contract term which states the particular effect of the RoT, i.e. the transfer of title in the sold goods only at the time of the full payment of the purchase price.[110]

---

108. This is the legal treatment of the security ownership in Germany (*Insolvenzordnung*, § 50 and 51), but it is also the legal treatment of the 'irregular pledge' of money or fungible assets in Italian law, which evades the ban of forfeiture clause because it is expressly regulated by the code (art. 1851): S. Palummo, *Pegno irregolare e fallimento*, Fall. 2004, 383 ff.

109. Cousins, *The Law of Mortgages*, 2nd ed. (London 2001), 141.

110. An express contract term is usually necessary also in order to extend the effects of the RoT to the proceeds deriving from the sale of the goods. An exception is represented by French law: M. Cabrillac, C. Mouly, *Droit des sûretés*, 7th edn., (Paris 2004), 609 ff. For the legal regime of RoT in French law see c.c. new arts. 2329 n. 4, 2367–2372.

In England, Germany, and Sweden there is no registration requirement for the RoT to be valid between the parties, as well as *erga omnes*, and the security is treated as ownership in the case of the debtor's insolvency so that the supplier can reclaim the sold goods as its own.[111] In Spain, RoT produces effects against third persons if it is registered, and in the case of the debtor's insolvency it is regarded as full ownership.[112] In Italy, a 'certain date prior to the time of the attachment' is required for the validity of the RoT against third persons. In the case of machinery, when the price exceeds Euro 15.49, the RoT is effective against third persons provided that it has been entered on a special register kept at the Tribunal with jurisdiction in the place where the machinery is located.[113]

Finally, in England, Germany, Ireland, and Scotland, a RoT can secure not only payment of the purchase price but also any other obligation of the buyer towards the seller.[114] In Germany, the RoT extends not only to the goods sold but also to the products resulting from their manufacture or to proceeds deriving from their sale, whereas such cases are regarded as creation of a new security the Netherlands.[115] In England and Scotland, proceeds clauses are not favourably regarded by case law.[116]

---

111. U. Drobnig, *Present and Future of Real and Personal Security*, 649. In Greece, formalities are also not required for the ROT (art. 532 c.c.) to be valid even between the parties, where movables are concerned, unless statutory law expressly provides otherwise: C. Vainanidis, *Greece*, in I. Davies (ed.), *Retention of Title Clauses in Sale of Goods Contracts in Europe* (Aldershot, Brookfield 1999), 51. As to England, see however the ongoing reform process and the suggested registration of quasi-security in the area of company law: Law Comm. Cons. Rep. n. 296, 31 Aug. 2005 (see *supra*, fn. 100).

112. The *Ley de venta a Plazos de Bienes Muobles* (Law n. 28 of 13 July 1998, art. 15) creates a register of movables on which the RoT must be registered in order to produce its effects: A. Carrasco, E. Cordero, M. Marín, *Tratado de los Derechos de Garantías*, 967 ff., 981 ff.; Spanish c.c., arts. 1922 para. 2, 1926 para. 1; *Ley de venta a Plazos de Bienes Muobles* art. 16 para. 5.

113. Italian c.c., art. 1524. In addition to that requirement, and as concerns newly manufactured goods and machines with a value of at least euro 516,45, the Law of 28.11.1965, n. 1329 (so-called *legge Sabatini*) provides that the asset must bear a plate in a prominent position with the name of the seller as owner and information identifying the machine for a RoT to produce effects against third parties (see also decree of 21 February 1973 for the implementation of the *legge Sabatini*). Moreover, the contract containing the RoT clause must be registered on a special register kept at the Tribunal with jurisdiction in the place where the contract has been concluded.

114. These are called 'all money clauses'; Ireland: *Frigoscandia Ltd* v. *Continental Irish Meat Ltd*, [1982] ILRM 396; England and Scotland: *Armour* v. *Thyssen Edelstahlwerke AG*, [1991] 2 AC 339 (House of Lords decision on Scots law).

115. U. Drobnig, *Present and Future of Real and Personal Security*, 651.

116. References in I. Davies, *United Kingdom*, in I. Davies (ed.), *Retention of Title Clauses in Sale of Goods Contracts in Europe*, 101 ff., 110 ff.; 112 ff.

The main issues treated differently by national jurisdictions are (i) the effectiveness of the RoT against a good faith purchaser from the buyer; (ii) the requirements of validity of the RoT against the buyer's creditors, especially in the case of the buyer's insolvency; and (iii) the possibility to qualify the buyer's expectancy as a proprietary right. In this way, the buyer may be entitled to dispose of it (also as security), because the expectancy may have a substantial economic value depending upon the outstanding amount of the purchase price.[117] It is evident that these divergences may obstruct recognition of foreign RoT clauses in cross-border transactions among European countries.[118]

(c) *Financial leasing and lease-back*: In financial leasing and sale and lease-back transactions, contract and property law are inextricably bound up together to produce arrangements which may (but not always) have purposes of security.

Financial leasing usually involves a three-party situation in which the lessor purchases assets from the producer and leases them to the lessee. The economic purpose of this arrangement is to enable the entrepreneur (lessee) to use specific assets—especially machinery—without disbursing the amount of money necessary to purchase full ownership of those assets. In fact, the lessee is bound to pay (only) a periodic rent which reflects the discounted value of the goods and the finance charges of the operation until termination of the contract, when, in some countries,[119] he will have the option (a) to purchase the full ownership of the leased assets, (b) to renew the leasing contract, or (c) to return the assets to the lessor. To be qualified as such, a finance leasing must transfer substantially all the risks and rewards of ownership (except legal title) to the lessee.[120]

---

117. As is well-known, this is the German practice: R. Serick, *Securities in Movables in German law*, 61 ff.; U. Drobnig, *Present and Future of Real and Personal Security*, 651.

118. Only some fragmented aspects of RoT clauses have been object of European 'legislation': EC Directive 2000/35 of 29 June 2000, on combating late payments in commercial transactions: EC O. J. L 200 of 8.8.2000, 35 ff., see particularly arts. 2, 3 and 4; and see also arts. 7 and 41 of EC Regulation n. 1346/2000 on insolvency proceedings, in EC O.J. L 160 of 30.6.2000, 1 ff.

119. The inclusion in the leasing contract of an option to purchase is a necessary condition for a transaction to be regarded as a leasing arrangement, for instance, in France (art. 1 law n. 455 of 2 July 1966, modified by ordinance n. 837 of 28 Sept. 1967; now in art. L. 313-1 *code monetaire et financier*; Cass. com. 30 May 1989, Bull. civ. IV, n. 167; RTDCom. 1990, 93), in Italy (M. Bussani, *I contratti moderni*, in *Tratt. dir. civ.* edited by R. Sacco (Torino 2004) 267); but not in England (R. Goode, *Commercial Law*, 2nd edn (London 1995) 777: indeed, the option converts the transaction into a hire-purchase agreement).

120. See, for all, R. Goode, *Commercial Law*, 777.

The sale and lease-back schema is a unique version of the financial leasing transaction mentioned above. It is normally based on a bilateral transaction in which the entrepreneur sells the ownership of his assets to the lessor but continues to use it in his business on the basis of a lease contract. It is evident that this arrangement gives the lessee access to financing, which is alternative to the traditional bank loan.

Because of the strict factual connection of those transactions with financial strategies of the enterprise, it is sometimes difficult to distinguish them from transfers of ownership for security purposes. However, despite the economic framework in which leasing contracts are placed, in Western Europe such arrangements are normally classified not as 'security rights' but as 'business contracts,' as far as dogmatic classifications are concerned.[121] It is thus possible to discern a trend towards the development of a legal regime for such devices which differs from that of 'formal' security rights, at least when it is necessary to ensure market access to such arrangements. Exemplifying this trend is the relationship between leasing contracts and the prohibition of the *lex commissioria* in those legal systems that prohibit the security-ownership, such as those of Italy, Portugal, or the Netherlands. In these countries, the problem of saving such devices (particularly lease-back) from applicability of the *lex commissoria* ban has been solved by differentiating leasing arrangements from security rights and legitimating the former.[122] By contrast, some issues concerning the regulation of leasing transactions could be treated in a similar way to retention of title arrangements, as in the case of the formal requirements necessary to oppose the lessor's ownership to third parties.[123]

---

121. For the qualification of financial leasing as an "atypical contract" or a contract *sui generis*, also on the basis of the Unidroit Convention on International Financial Leasing of Ottawa, 28 May 1988, see, for Germany, M. Stoffels, *Leasing*, in *Staudinger Kommentar zum BGB*, II, *§§433–487 Leasing* (Berlin 2004), 956 n. 76; for Italy, M. Bussani, *I contratti moderni*, 268; for Spain A. Carrasco, E. Cordero y M. Marín, *Tratado de los Derechos de Garantías*, 1027. According to Austrian scholars, leasing contracts are mixed contracts where elements of sale are combined with elements of lease: C. Fischer-Czermak, *Mobilienleasing, Rechtsnatur, Gewährleistung und Gefahrtragung*, Wien, 1995, 161. For the Dutch differentiation of financial leasing from security arrangements, like the RoT, see S. Bartles & J. Smits, The Netherlands, in E.-M. Kieninger (ed.), *Security Rights in Movable Property in European Private Law*, 608.

122. Netherlands: HR 19 May 1995, NJ 1996/119; Italy: Cass. 16 Oct. 1995, n. 10805, in *Giur. it.*, I, 1, 1996, cc. 1382; the same is true for Spain: A. Carrasco, E. Cordero y M. Marín, *Tratado de los Derechos de Garantías*, 1043, 1052; for an account on the issue in Portugal, see L. Menezes Leitão, Portugal, in E.-M. Kieninger (ed.), *Security Rights in Movable Property in European Private Law*, 603.

123. In Italy, despite the fact that no formal requirements are established by the civil code for leasing transactions, the lessor's rights will be protected in case of execution only

## *8.2. Security Rights over Movable Assets and Legal Integration*

As mentioned above, the engine of the legal integration began to operate much earlier, and with much more intensity, in the field of security over movables than it did in that of security over immovables. The need to remove the most evident divergences among the legal regimes of the various jurisdictions, which hindered the recognition of foreign security devices and techniques in international commercial transactions, very soon stimulated international efforts for legal integration.[124]

In this respect, however, the first results have only been achieved in recent years, and mostly at regional level: the International Institute for the Unification of Private Law (UNIDROIT), the Organization of American States (OAS), the European Bank of Reconstruction and Development (EBRD), the Organisation pour l'Harmonisation en Afrique du Droit des Affaires (OHADA), the United Nations Commission on International Trade Law (UNCITRAL) have accomplished 'legislative' integration by means of model laws or international conventions.[125]

---

if the formal requirements provided by art. 1524 para. 1 for RoT clauses are fulfilled (documentary evidence with certain date: M. Bussani, *I contratti moderni*, 322 ff. In France and Greece, leasing contracts must be registered to render the lessor's ownership of the leased assets enforceable against third parties: for France see art. 8 of decree n. 72-665 of 4 July 1972; Code com. art. L. 621-116; for Greece see art. 4 law n. 1665/1986, modified by law n. 2367/1995.

124. U. Drobnig, Report of the Secretary-General: *International Payments. Study on Security Interests*, (1977) 8 U.N. Comm'n on Int'l Trade L.Y.B., 171–221, U.N.Doc.A/CN.9/SER.A; Id., *Empfehlen sich gesetzlichen Maßnahmen zur Reform der Mobiliarsicherheiten?*, Gutachten F zum 51. Deutschen Juristentag, München, 1976, 98.

125. The text of the UNIDROIT Convention on International Interests in Mobile Equipment (2001) is available at www.unidroit.org with bibliographical references; see the special issue of the *European Review of Private Law*, n. 12(1) 2004. More generally, on the role of the UNIDROIT in the harmonization of the law on secured transactions see M. Stanford, *From Ottawa to Cape Town: Unidroit's Role in the Modernisation of the Law Governing Leasing and the Taking of Security*, in I. Davies (ed.), *Security Interests in Mobile Equipment* (Aldershot 2002) 397.

The Inter-American Model Law on Secured Transactions (2002) is available at www.oas.org/; see also J.M. Wilson, *La nueva ley modelo interamericana sobre garantías mobiliarias*, in Rev. Mex. Der. Int. Priv., 2003, 33; L.P. Castro, *La ley modelo interamericana sobre garantías mobiliarias*, ivi, 2002, 31; A.M. Garro, *Security interests in Personal Property in Latin America: A Comparison with Artiche 9 and a Model Reform*, in (1987) 9 Houston J. Of Int'l L., 157; Id., *The Reform and Harmonization of Personal Property Security Law in Latin America*, in (1990) 59 Rev. Jur. Univ. Puerto Rico, 1; Id., *Difficulties in Obtaining*

Of course, not even the EU Institutions have been indifferent to the issue, particularly since they openly acknowledged that the existing divergences are a *de facto* obstacle to full implementation of the internal market.[126]

The European legal integration of security rights regimes has two aspects, one 'legislative', the other 'cultural'.

---

*Secured Landing in Latin America: Why Law Reform Really Matters*, in J.J. Norton, M. Andenas (eds.), *Emerging financial Markets and Secured Transactions*, 251.

For the EBRD Model Law on Secured Transactions (1994) see ZEuP, 1998, 766; and J.-H. Röver, *Vergleichenden Prinzipien dinglicher Sicherheiten* (München 1999) (with a German translation of the law); J. Simpson, J. Menze, *Ten Years of Secured Transactions Reform*, in (2001) 16(1) B.J.I.B. & F.L., 5; J.A. Spanogle, *A Functional Analysis of the EBRD Model Law on Secured Transactions*, in (1997) 3-spg NAFTA: Law & Business Rev. of the Americas, 82.

The Organisation pour l'Harmonisation en Afrique du Droit des Affaires (OHADA) has enacted a uniform law regulating personal and proprietary security and, among the latter, security rights over both movables and immovables, the Act Uniforme Portant Organisation des Sûretés, see J.O. OHADA, n. 3 of 1 Oct. 1997 and www.ohada.com; J. Issa-Sayegh, *Présentation générale de l'Acte Uniforme de l'OHADA sur les sûretés*, in (2003) Unif. L. Rev., 364; F. Anoukaha, *Le droit des sûretés dans l'Acte uniforme de l'OHADA* (Yaoundé 1998).

The United Nations Commission on International Trade Law (UNCITRAL) in 2001 has elaborated the United Nations Convention on the Assignment of Receivables in International Trade, introducing uniform rules on assignment of receivables also to security purposes (see Explanatory Notes, p. 29, par. 7; text and materials available at: http://www.uncitral.org/uncitral/en/uncitral_texts/payments/2001Convention_receivables.html); this Convention, however, has not yet entered into force. In December 2007 the UNCITRAL has also completed the Draft Legislative Guide on Secured Transactions (text and materials available at: http://www.uncitral.org/uncitral/en/uncitral_texts/payments/Guide_securedtrans.html).

Details on international integration projects concerning security over movable assets can be obtained from C. Bourbon-Seclet, *Cross-Border Security Interests in Movable Property: An Attempt at Rationalising the International Patchwork*, Part 1, (2005) 20(9) J.I.B.L.R. 419 ff; Part 2 (2005) 20(10) J.I.B.L.R., 501 ff.; M. Bussani, *Il diritto delle garanzie reali nella prospettiva transnazionale*, in Studi in onore di Piero Schlesinger, Milano, 2004, 849 and D.P. Fernández Arroyo, *Las garantías mobiliarias en el derecho del commercio internacional de nuestros días*, in 10 Rev. Mex. Der. Int. Priv., 2001, 11.

126. Communication from the Commission to the European Parliament and Council of 12 Feb. 2003, *A More Coherent European Contract Law. An Action Plan*, COM(2003) 68 fin. (in O.J. C 63, 15.3.2003, 1 ff.), expressly for the security for credit see points 41–43, 63, 67. The mandate of the EU to approximate rules concerning security rights and/or to create a European security right on its own is discussed by W.-H. Roth, *Secured Credit and the Internal Market: The Fundamental Freedoms and the EU' Mandate for Legislation*, in H. Eidenmüller & E.-M. Kineninger (eds.), The Future of Secured Credit in Europe, 36 ff.

Regarding the 'legislative' actions taken by the EU Institutions, the main results have been achieved by the financial collateral arrangements envisaged by Directive 2002/47/EC.[127] Notwithstanding the limits of any integration brought about by means of a directive, national implementation of this directive has been an important step towards convergence of legal rules in Europe: traditional principles of proprietary security rights, such as the rule of accessority, the rule of specificity, the prohibition of forfeiture clauses, have been eroded by the directive, so that exceptions to such principles have increased homogeneously. Nevertheless, it can also be noted that European legal integration through directives can also produce 'disintegrative' impacts.[128] In fact, traditional presentations of security rights national regimes may not correspond to the operational level of the empirical solutions developed by the interaction between European and national law. All of this also explains the increasingly urgent need for national legal reform. Of course, it is also because of the inputs from 'top down' EU actions that national legislators are undertaking reforms of their legal regimes of security for credit. The main example is France, which has reformed in quite a uniform manner the broad sector of security for credit, including personal and proprietary security over movables and immovables.[129]

'Cultural' integration is represented by academic activity, which is also, in most cases, a consequence of the EU's interest in the matter, given that the EU Commission is financing an ambitious research network on private law, which includes the law of security for credit.[130]

Two main approaches can be identified among research projects. One can be termed the 'cultural approach' and is the path chosen by the "The Common Core of the European Private Law" of Trento, directed by M. Bussani and U. Mattei.[131] This project aims to deepen comparative law knowledge in Eu-

---

127. EU Financial collateral directive 2002/47/CE, in O.J. L 168 of 27.6.2002, 43 ff. For the regulation of some aspects of RoT clauses by EU directives see *supra*, fn. 118.

128. For the essential terms of this paradox see, for all, Ch. Joerges, *The Impact of European Integration on Private Law: Reductionist Perceptions, True Conflicts and a New Constitutional Perspective*, (1997) European Law Journal (ELJ), 378; Id., *Disintegrative Effects of Legislative Harmonization: A Complex Issue and a Small Example*, in M. Bussani, U. Mattei (eds.), *The Common Core of European Private Law*, Den Haag, 2003, 105 ff.

129. See *supra*, fn. 36.

130. Since May 2005, the 'Study Group on a European Civil Code' has been part of the Joint Network on European Private Law, a Network of Excellence funded by the European Commission under the Sixth Framework Programme for Research: www.copelc.org.

131. M. Bussani & U. Mattei, *The Common Core Approach to the European Private Law*, in (1997/98) 3(3) Col. J. E. L., 339 ff.

rope in order to promote the formation of a truly European legal culture, a feature which seems necessary if any 'legislative' legal integration is to be successfully applied throughout Europe. It is well known that any 'top down' intervention will be fruitless if national traditions, interpretive usages and mentalities are not nourished and assisted by a European common culture. The factual approach developed by R. B. Schlesinger in the 1950s and 1960s for study of the "common core" in the formation of contracts and the dissociation of legal formants developed by R. Sacco are applied in comparative analysis which measures the degree of convergence or divergence among different legal systems. The main advantage of this technique is that it removes false analogies and false differences produced by merely formal descriptions deriving from the juxtaposition of analyses of individual legal systems made by municipal scholarship. The Common Core research project on security rights over movable assets has been carried out by a group of international researchers directed by Prof. E.-M. Kieninger, which has published its results in 2004.[132]

A different approach is taken by the Research Team working on Security Rights under the direction of Prof. U. Drobnig (Max Planck Institute for Comparative and International Private Law—Hamburg), within the European network known as the 'Study Group on a European Civil Code.'[133] The aim of this comparative inquiry into the national laws of the member states of the EU is to develop a complete set of rules governing the law of security over movables (as well as personal security contracts). Hence, in this case, the research work is based on a 'legislative' approach. Interestingly, the Study Group on the Proprietary Security Rights over Movables seems to have adopted the functional approach, although to an extent and with a meaning not equal to the functionalism of the U.S. Art. 9 U.C.C. Indeed, the provisional text of the black letter rules defines a 'Proprietary Security Right' as a category including both 'formal' and 'functional' security rights. However, a certain degree of differentiation between the legal regime of financial leasing and that of other functional security rights like RoT is still under discussion. A system of registration will be established for all the various domestic security rights—which in a distant future will probably lose their original, national names and become just 'security rights'—but

132. E.-M. Kieninger (ed.), *Security Rights over Movable Property in European Private Law* (Cambridge 2004).

133. Ch. v. Bar, *The Study Group on a European Civil Code*, in *The private law systems in the EU: discrimination on grounds of nationality and the need for a European Civil Code*, Directorate-General for Research of the European Parliament (DG IV): Legal Affairs Series, W.P. JURI 103, 06/1999: http://www.europarl.eu.int/workingpapers/juri/default_en.htm.

what features and effects this registration will have is also still under discussion.[134]

What the future of Study Group-Rules will be is not easy to predict, for it will mainly depend on the political aims of the EU—as well as of the member states—once the rules have been completed. Of course, any national implementation of such rules will require national legislative intervention, together with legislative reforms of many sectors of the national private law in general, because any instrument of soft law harmonization will have no impact on property law.

## References

Ali P., *The Law of Secured Finance. An International Survey of Security Interests over Personal Property* (Oxford 2002).

Altunbas Y., Gambacorta L. & Marqués D., *Securitisation and the bank lending channel*, (Working Papers), Bank of Italy, November 2007, 20 ff., available at: www.bancaditalia.it.

Amira K. von, *Nordgermanisches Obligationenrecht* II (Leipzig 1882).

Anderson J.S., *Lawyers and the Making of English Land Law 1832–1940* (Oxford 1992).

Anelli F., *L'alienazione in funzione di garanzia* (Milan 1996).

Anoukaha F., *Le droit des sûretés dans l'Acte uniforme de l'OHADA* (Yaoundé 1998).

Armour J., *The Law and Economics Debate About Secured Lending: Lessons for European Lawmaking?*, in H. Eidenmüller & E.-M. Kieninger (eds.), The Future of Secured Credit in Europe, European Company and Financial Law Review, Special Volume 2, Berlin, 2008, 3 ff.

Ashcraft A.B. & Schuermann T., *Understanding the Securitization of Subprime Mortgage Credit*, (March 2008) Wharton Financial Institutions Center Working Paper No. 07-43, available at: SSRN: http://ssrn.com/abstract=1071189.

Aynès L. y Crocq P., *Les sûretés, La publicité foncière*, 3e éd., Paris, 2008.

Baird D., *Security Interests Reconsidered* (1994) Va. L. R. 2249.

Bar Ch. von, *The Study Group on a European Civil Code*, in *The private law systems in the EU: discrimination on grounds of nationality and the need for a European Civil Code*, Directorate-General for Research of the European

134. The provisional text of the black letter rules is available at: www.sgecc.net.

Parliament (DG IV): Legal Affairs Series, Working Paper JURI 103, 06/1999: http://www.europarl.eu.int/workingpapers/juri/default_en.htm.

Bar Ch. von & Drobnig U., *The interaction of contract law and tort and property law in Europe* (Munich 2004).

Barbiera L., *Responsabilità patrimoniale. Disposizioni generali, Artt. 2740-2744*, in *Il Codice Civile. Commentario* diretto da P. Schlesinger (Milan 1991) Basel Committee on Banking Supervision, *Capital requirements and bank behaviour: the impact of the Basel Accord*, Publication No. 1, April 1999, available at: http://www.bis.org/publ/bcbs_wp1.htm.

Basel Committee on Banking Supervision, *International Convergence of Capital Measurement and Capital Standards: a Revised Framework*, June 2004, http://www.bis.org/publ/bcbs107.htm.

Basel Committee on Banking Supervision, *Liquidity Risk: Management and Supervisory Challenges*, February 2008, available at: http://www.bis.org/publ/bcbs136.htm.

Bourbon-Seclet C., *Cross-Border Security Interests in Movable Property: An Attempt at Rationalising the International Patchwork*, Part 1, (2005) 20(9) J.I.B.L.R. 419; Part 2 (2005) 20(10) J.I.B.L.R., 501.

Branthomme P., *Savings and the Financial Behaviour of European Households Between 1996 and 2000*, in *Banque de France Bulletin Digest*, n. 105, September 2002, 23 ff.

Bridge M., *Personal Property Law*, 3rd ed. (Oxford 2002).

Bridge M., *The English Law of Real Security* (2002) 10(4) ERPL, 483.

Burkhart A.M., *Lenders and Law* (1999) 64 *Missouri Law Review*, 249.

Bussani M., *I contratti moderni*, in *Tratt. dir. civ.* diretto da R. Sacco (Torino 2004).

Bussani M., *Il diritto delle garanzie reali nella prospettiva transnazionale*, in Studi in onore di Piero Schlesinger, Milan, 2004, 849.

Bussani M., *Le présent et l'avenir des sûretés réelles*, in *Italian National Reports to the XVIth International Congress of Comparative Law Brisbane 2002* (Milan 2002), 245.

Bussani M., *Il problema del patto commissorio* (Turin 2000).

Bussani M. & Mattei U., *The Common Core Approach to the European Private Law*, in (1997/98) 3(3) Col. J. E. L., 339.

Cabrillac M. et Mouly C., *Droit des sûretés*, 7th edn. (Paris 2004).

Candian Alb., *Le garanzie mobiliari. Modelli e problemi nella prospettiva europea*, Milan 2001.

Carrasco A., Cordero E. y Marín M., *Tratado de los Derechos de Garantías* (Cizur Menor 2002).

Castro L.P., *La ley modelo interamericana sobre garantías mobiliarias*, in Rev. Mex. Der. Int. Priv., 2002, 31.

Cheshire and Burn's, *Modern Law of Real Property*, 16th ed. (London 2000)
Chiquier L., Hassler O. & Lea M., *Mortgage Securities in Emerging Markets* (World Bank 2004): http://econ.worldbank.org/view.php?type=5&id=37706.
Commission on Legal Empowerment of the Poor, *Making the Law Work for Everyone*, Somerset, NJ: Toppan Printing, 2008, vol II, available at: http://www.undp.org/legalempowerment/docs/ReportVolumeII/making_the_law_work_II.pdf.
Cousins, *The Law of Mortgages*, 2nd ed. (London 2001).
Crocq P., *La future réforme du droit français des sûretés réelles*, 20 Rev. Lamy Droit Civil, 2005, 1.
Dahan F., *Secured Transactions Law in Western Advanced Economies: Exposing Myths* (2001) 16(2) Butterworths J. of Int'l Banking and Financial Law, 60.
Davies I. (ed.), *Retention of Title Clauses in Sale of Goods Contracts in Europe* (Aldershot, Brookfield 1999).
de la Peña N. & Fleisig H., *SMEs and Collateral*, in Centre for the Economic Analysis of Law (CEAL Issues Brief, n. 3), October 2002, 1.
De Soto H., *The Mistery of Capital: Why Capitalism Triumphs in the West and Fails Everywhere Else* (London 2001).
Demyanyk Y. & van Hemert O., *Understanding the Subprime Mortgage Crisis*, Feb. 29, 2008, SSNR Working Paper Series, available at: http://ssrn.com/abstract=1020396.
Deutsche Bundesbank, *New Legal and Regulatory Framework for the German Securitisation and Pfandbrief Market*, in *Monthly Report*, March 2006, 37 ff.
Djankov S., McLiesh C. & Shleifer A., *Private Credit in 129 Countries*, January 2005, NBER Working Paper No. W11078: http://www.nber/org/papers/w11078.
Drewicz-Tułodziecka A. (ed.), *Basic Guidelines for a Eurohypothek* (Warsaw 2005) in Mortgage Bulletin, 21/2005.
Drobnig U., *Principles of European Law. Personal Security Contracts* (Munich 2007).
Drobnig U., *Neuere Entwicklungen im Recht der persönlichen Kreditsicherheiten in Deutschland und in den Niederlanden*, (Munich 2003).
Drobnig U., *Present and Future of Real and Personal Security*, in ERPL, 5, 2003, 623.
Drobnig U., *Secured Credit in International Insolvency Proceedings* (1998) 33 Tex Int'l L.J., 54.
Drobnig U., Report of the Secretary-General: *International Payments. Study on Security Interests*, (1977) 8 U.N. Comm'n on Int'l Trade L.Y.B., 171–221, U.N.Doc.A/CN.9/SER.A.

Drobnig U., Empfehlen sich gesetzlichen Maßnahmen zur Reform der Mobiliarsicherheiten?, Gutachten F zum 51. Deutschen Juristentag, München, 1976.

Drobnig U. & Flessner A., Goode R., Kleinemann J., Westbrook J., Ziegel J., *Building Effective Insolvency Systems. Debtor-Creditor Regimes* (Washington, D.C. 1999).

Ernoult J., Hemetsberger W., Schoppmann H. & Wengler C., *European Banking and Financial Services Law* (3rd edn, Brussels 2008).

European Covered Bond Council, *European Covered Bond Factbook* (Bruxelles, September 2008).

Fernández Arroyo D.P., *Las garantías mobiliarias en el derecho del commercio internacional de nuestros días*, in 10 Rev. Mex. Der. Int. Priv., 2001, 11.

Fiorentini F., *Appunti sull'integrazione giuridica europea in materia di garanzie immobiliari*, in M. Bussani & F. Fiorentini (eds.), *Financial Contracts and Secured Transactions in the European Perspective* (Trieste 2003) 149.

Fiorentini F., *Garanzie reali atipiche*, in *Riv. dir. civ.* 2000, 253.

*Fisher and Lightwood's Law of Mortgage*, 11th ed. (London 2002).

Fleisig H., *Integrating the Legal Regimes for Secured Transactions and Bankruptcy: Economic Issues*, CEAL Issues Brief, 1, Oct. 2000: http://www.ceal.org/ceal-org/publications/Bankruptcy_Issues_Brief.pdf.

Fleisig H., *The proposed Unidroit Convention on mobile equipment: economic consequences and issues*, in Uniform Law Rev. 1999, 2, 253.

Fleisig H., *Secured Transactions: The Power of Collateral*, in Finance & Development, June 1996, 44.

Fleisig H.W., de la Peña N. & Safavian M., *Reforming collateral laws to expand access to finance*, The World Bank (Washington 2006).

Flint Jr. G.L., *Secured Transactions History: The Northern Struggle to Defeat the Judgment Lien in the Pre-Chattel Mortgage Act Era* (2000) 20 N.Ill.U.L.R. 1.

Flint Jr. G.L., *Secured Transactions History: The Fraudulent Myth*, (1999) 29 N.M. L. R. 363.

Foëx B., *L'eurohypothèque*, in F. Werro (ed.) *L'européanisation du droit privé. Vers un code civil européen?* (Fribourg 1998) 481.

Gabrielli E., *Pegno*, in *Tratt. dir. civ.* diretto da R. Sacco (Turin 2005).

Gambaro A., *European Aspects of Property Law*, in F. Werro (ed.) *New Perspectives on European Private Law*, (Friburg 1998), 75.

Garro A.M., *Difficulties in Obtaining Secured Landing in Latin America: Why Law Reform Really Matters*, in J.J. Norton & M. Andenas (eds.), *Emerging financial Markets and Secured Transactions* (The Hague 1998) 251.

Garro A.M., *The Reform and Harmonization of Personal Property Security Law in Latin America*, in (1990) 59 Rev. Jur. Univ. Puerto Rico, 1.

Garro A.M., *Security interests in Personal Property in Latin America: A Comparison with Artiche 9 and a Model Reform*, in (1987) 9 Houston J. Of Int'l L., 157.

Gdansk Academy of Banking, *Analysis of the Economic Impact of the Registered Pledge System in Poland*, (Gdansk Nov. 2003).

Gierke O. von, *Deutsches Privatrecht* II (Leipzig 1905).

Glennie D.G., de Bouter E.C. & Luke R.D. (eds.), *Securitization* (The Hague, London, Boston 1998).

Goode R., *Legal Problems of Credit and Security*, 3rd ed. (London 2003).

Goode R., *Security in Cross Border Transactions* (1998) 33 Tex Int'l L.J., 47.

Goode R., *Security: A Pragmatic or Conceptualist's Response*, (1989) 15 Mon ULR 361.

Gorla G., *Le garanzie reali dell'obbligazione* (Milan 1935).

Grégoire M., *Le présent et l'avenir des sûretés réelles mobilières et des sûretés personelles*, in *The Belgian Reports at the Congress of Brisbane of the International Academy of Comparative Law* (Brussels 2002) 177.

Gullifer L., *Quasi-security Interests: Functionalism and the Incidents of Security*, in I. Davies (ed.), *Issues in International Commercial Law* (Aldershot, Burlington 2005), 3.

Hazeltine H.D., *Die Geschichte des englischen Pfandrechts*, in O. Gierke (ed.), *Untersuchungen zur Deutschen Staats-und Rechtsgeschichte*, 91. Heft (Breslau 1907).

Hedemann J.W., *Die Fortschritte des Zivilrechts im XIX. Jahrhundert* (Frankfurt/Main 1968).

Huber U., *Die Sicherungsgrundschuld* (Heidelberg 1965, Nachdruck 1995).

Hunt R.M., *A Century of Consumer Credit Reporting in America*, June 2005, FRB Philadelphia Working Paper No. 05-13, available at: SSRN: http://ssrn.com/abstract=757929.

Hunt R.M., *Development and Regulation of Consumer Credit Reporting in the United States*, in G. Bertola, R. Disney & C. Grant (eds.), *The Economics of Consumer Credit*, (Cambridge, Mass., London, 2006) 301 ff.

Inderst R. & Möllers H.M., *Credit Risk Analysis and Security Design* (London 2003), CEPR Discussion Paper No. 3686.

International Bank for Reconstruction and Development/World Bank, *Land Policies for Growth and Poverty Reduction* (Oxford 2003).

International Monetary Funf, *Regional Economic Outlook, Europe Dealing With Shocks*, October 2008, available at: http://www.imf.org/external/pubs/ft/reo/2008/eur/eng/ereo1008.htm.

Issa-Sayegh J., *Présentation générale de l'Acte Uniforme de l'OHADA sur les sûretés*, in (2003) Unif. L. Rev., 364.

Italian Bar Association, *Atti del Convegno "Delegabilità ai notai delle operazioni di incanto nelle espropriazioni immobiliari, Roma, 23 e 24 maggio 1993* (Milan 1994).
Jappelli T. & Pagano M., *The Role and Effects of Credit Information Sharing*, in G. Bertola, R. Disney & C. Grant (eds.), *The Economics of Consumer Credit* (Cambridge, Mass., London, 2006) 347 ff.
Jauering O., *Zivilprozessrecht*, 24th ed. (Munich 1993).
Kaser M., *Studien zum römischen Pfandrecht* (Neaples repr.: 1982).
Kieninger E.-M. (ed.), *Security Rights over Movable Property in European Private Law* (Cambridge 2004).
Larmur P., *Policy Transfer and Reversal: Customary Land Registration from Africa to Melanesia*, in (2002) 22 Public Admin. Dev., 151.
Machoka P., *The Need for Efficient and Effective Secured Transactions Regimes in Sub-Saharan Africa: The Case for Kenya* (2005) 20(8) J.I.B.L.R., 395.
Mattei U., *I diritti reali. 1, La proprietà*, in Tratt. Dir. Civ. diretto da R. Sacco (Turin 2001).
Mazeaud H. et L., Mazeaud J., Chabas F., *Leçons de droit civil*, III, t. 1, *Sûretés. Publicité foncière*, 7th ed., (Paris 1999).
McCormack G., *Secured Credit under English and American Law* (Cambridge 2004).
McCormack G., *The Floating Charge in England and Canada*, in J. De Lacy (ed.) The Reform of UK Company Law (London 2002) 389–414.
Merlin Ph.A., *Répertoire universel et raisonné de la jurisprudence* (Paris 1812–1825).
Modigliani F. & Perotti E., *Security versus Bank Finance: The Importance of Proper Enforcement of Legal Rules* (FEEM Working Paper no. 37.99 2000).
*Motive zu dem Entwurfe eines Bürgerlichen Gesetzbuches für das Deutsche Reich*, III (Berlin, Leipzig 1888).
Müll E., *Die Interessenjurisprudenz im Hypothekenrecht* (Rheinfelden 1988).
Nasarre-Aznar S., *Securitisation & mortgage bonds: legal aspects and harmonisation* (Saffron Walden 2004).
Oditah F., *Legal Aspects of Receivables Financing* (London 1990).
Ploeger H. & van Loenen B., *EULIS-At the Beginning of the Road to Harmonisation of Land Registry in Europe*, in 12 ERPL, 3, 2004, 379.
Price Tarbert H., *Are International Capital Adequacy Rules Adequate? The Basel Accord and Beyond*, 148 U. Pa. L. Rev. (2000) 1771 ff.
*Protokolle der Kommission für die zweite Lesung des Entwurfes des Bürgerlichen Gesetzbuches* (Auftrage des Reichs—Justizamts, I–VI (VII: Register) III (Berlin 1897–1899).
Ranouil V., *La subrogation réelle en droit civil français* (Paris 1985).

Reinhart C.M. & Rogoff K.S., *Is the 2007 U.S. sub-prime financial crisis so different? An international comparison*, Working Paper N. 13761, Jan. 2008, National Bureau of Economic Research, Cambridge, Ma, available at: http://www.nber.org/papers/w13761.

Röver J.-H., *Vergleichenden Prinzipien dinglicher Sicherheiten* (München 1999).

Roth W.-H., *Secured Credit and the Internal Market: The Fundamental Freedoms and the EU' Mandate for Legislation*, in H. Eidenmüller & E.-M. Kieninger (eds.), The Future of Secured Credit in Europe, European Company and Financial Law Review, Special Volume 2, Berlin, 2008, 36 ff.

Saunders A., Allen L., *Credit Risk Measurement*, 2nd ed. (N.Y. 2002).

Schäfer B., *The Law and Economics Debate About Secured Lending: Lessons for European Lawmaking? Commentary*, in H. Eidenmüller & E.-M. Kieninger (eds.), The Future of Secured Credit in Europe, European Company and Financial Law Review, Special Volume 2, Berlin, 2008, 30 ff.

Scott H. (ed.), *Capital Adequacy Beyond Basel: Banking, Securities, and Insurance* (Oxford 2005).

Serick R., *Securities in Movables in German law. An Outline* (Den Haag 1990).

Simpson J. & Menze J.-H., *Ten Years of Secured Transactions Reform*, in (2001) 16(1) B.J.I.B. & F.L., 5.

Smith L., *Security*, in P. Birks (ed.), *English Private Law*, I (Oxford 2000).

Spanogle J.A., *A Functional Analysis of the EBRD Model Law on Secured Transactions*, in (1997) 3-spg NAFTA: Law & Business Rev. of the Americas, 82.

Stanford M., *From Ottawa to Cape Town: Unidroit's Role in the Modernisation of the Law Governing Leasing and the Taking of Security*, in I. Davies (ed.), *Security Interests in Mobile Equipment* (Aldershot 2002) 397.

Stöcker O.M., *Die Eurohypothek* (Berlin 1992).

Stoffels M., *Leasing*, in *Staudinger Kommentar zum BGB*, II, *§§433–487 Leasing* (Berlin 2004).

Tajti T., *Comparative Secured Transactions Law* (Budapest 2002).

Tamburrino G., *Della tutela dei diritti. (Delle ipoteche)*, in *Commentario del codice civile*, 2a edn. (Turin 1976).

The International Bank for Reconstruction and Development & The World Bank, *Land Policies for Growth and Poverty Reduction* (Oxford 2003).

The World Bank & International Finance Corporation, *Celebrating Reform 2008, Doing Business Case Studies* (Washington 2008).

Troplong R.P., *Privilèges et hypothèques: commentaire de la loi du 23 mars 1855 sur la transcription en matière hypothècaire* (Paris 1856).

Tucci G., *I privilegi*, in *Trattato di diritto privato* diretto da P. Rescigno, 19, 2nd edn., Turin 1997, 575–793.

Tucci G., *Garanzia*, in *Dig. IV, Disc. priv.*, Sez. civ., VIII (Torino 1991) 579.

Turner R.W., *The Equity of Redemption. Its Nature, History and Connection with Equitable Estates Generally* (Cambridge 1931).

United States Government Accountability Office, *Risk-Based Capital: New Basel II Rules Reduced Certain Competitive Concerns, but Bank Regulators Should Address Remaining Uncertainties*, GAO-08-953, September 12, 2008, available at: http://www.gao.gov/docsearch/repandtest.html.

van Erp J.H.M. & van Vliet L.P.W., *Real and Personal Security*, in 2002 6.4 EJCL: http://www.ejcl.org/64/art64-7.doc.

Veneziano A., *Le garanzie mobiliari non possessorie. Profili di diritto comparato e di diritto del commercio internazionale* (Milan 2000).

Wehrens H.G., *Real Security regarding Immovable Objects—Reflections on a Euro-Mortgage*, in H.S. Hartkamp a.o., *Towards a European Civil Code*, 3rd ed. (Nijmegen 2004) 769.

Wehrens H.G., *Real Security Regarding Immovable Objects—Reflections on a Euro-Mortgage*, in A. Hartkamp a.o. (eds.), *Towards a European Civil Code*, 2nd ed. (Nijmegen, The Hague, London, Boston 1998) 554.

White J., *The Politics of Article 9: Work and Play in Revising Article 9*, (1994) 80 Va. L. Rev., 2089.

Wilson J.M., *La nueva ley modelo interamericana sobre garantías mobiliarias*, in Rev. Mex. Der. Int. Priv., 2003, 33.

Wood P.R., *Comparative Law of Security and Guarantees* (London 1995).

World Bank, *Law and Policy Reform at the Asian Development Bank 2000*, vol. II: http://adb.org/Documents/Others/LAw_ADB/lpr_2000_2.asp?p=law devt#contents.

# 13

# Security Rights in Central and Eastern Europe in the First Decade of the New Millennium: Where Do We Go from Here?

Tibor Tajti[1]

## Summary

1. Introduction, 1.1. The Legal and Economic Environment, 1.2. Real and Personal Property Security: Distinct Paths of Development?—2. Real Property Security, 2.1. Common Legacies from the Socialist Past, 2.2. Variations on the Theme of the Tragedy of the Commons and Their Impact on the Development of the Security System, 2.3. Synopsis of the CEE Land Registry Systems, 2.4. Pathological Phenomena and Predatory Lending—3. Personal Property Security, 3.1. The Socialist Legacies and the Personal Property Security Law Reforms of the Transitory Period, 3.2. The Focal Points: Retention of Title, Assignment of Intangibles, Floating Security and Efficient Enforcement, 3.3. Persisting Problems and the Partial Success of the Reforms—4. In Lieu of Conclusions: Some Speculations on the Future Course of Events—References—List of Legislation

---

1. Associate professor of law; LL.M. and S.J.D. from the Central European University New York/Budapest, joint-appointment with the CEU Legal Studies Department (http://www.ceu.hu) and the CEU Business School (http://www.gsb.ceu.hu), both institutions located in Budapest, Hungary. Contact: email: tajtit@ceu.hu—telephone: + (361) 327 3275. The author would like to express its thankfulness for the invaluable comments of Prof. Stefan Messmann and for the kind help of Prof. Bernadett Bordás, Lina Aleknaite, Pilt Kerstin, Yuliya Gusseva and Krzysztof Kazmierczyk. The views expressed in this chapter are entirely those of the author.

# 1. Introduction

The first decade and half of security law[2] reforms is over in Central and Eastern Europe (hereinafter: CEE). Yet, considerable disparities persist between aspirations and achievements in creating a legal environment that would boost the local credit markets. Some level of skepticism is justified even with respect to the most successful jurisdictions, as numerous indicia show that the materialization of the fixed goals is many years ahead now. This claim is true irrespective that many—not only positivists—believe the contrary seeing in the reform of security law(s)—especially personal property collateral law—a one-shot type task; mistakenly finding analogy with the earlier successful international harmonization efforts, especially the Vienna International Sales Convention of 1980 (hereinafter: CISG).[3]

Apparently, yet with less hype, the age of the modernization of real property collateral law has also begun in the region[4]—partly because of the drive

2. This article is about *security law*, or the use of both, real (immovables) and personal property (all assets excluding immovables, like movables, rights and claims) as collateral to secure performance and payment as well as to get credit. The expressions 'secured transactions law', 'mortgage law' or 'collateral law' will be also employed to refer to this specific branch of law in this chapter. If anything said refers solely to either real property—or personal property collateral law, that will be stressed specifically.

3. A full account of the fundamental differences inherent to the harmonization of 'international sales laws' and 'domestic and transnational personal property security laws' would require a separate chapter. Hence, let me jot down just a few related thoughts. *First* of all, in the perception of the overwhelming part of CEE lawyers (at least before getting sufficiently acquainted with the security law reform project) the common-law inspired initiatives related to the introduction of modern personal property security law were invariably conceived as something essentially equal with the tasks that had awaited the domestic legislators with respect to the Vienna Sales Convention roughly a decade and half earlier. Yet the crucial difference is that while the unification of international sales law presupposed nothing else but passing the necessary legislation by national states and taking the steps to become signatories of the CISG, the creation of a working security law requires much more than 'merely' passing of legal acts. The most important such additional 'building blocks of the system' are, on one hand, the 'physical' installation and the mastering of proper maintenance of before non-existent registries for security interests on movables (or personal property), and, on the other hand, the dissemination of the practices and knowledge necessary—among others—to allow the emergence of local professionalized industries "exploiting secured transactions", from pawnshops through factoring companies. In Fleising's formulation, the reform of secured transactions law is "*a legal problem with a technical aspect.*" *See* H. Fleisig, *World Bank Financial Sector Reform: The Unfinished Legal Agenda*, CEAL Issue, Sept. 2004, at http://www.ceal.org <(visited on October 27, 2005)>.

4. As Sandeep put it "*[ ... ] [o]nly a decade ago, it would have been unimaginable that it would ever be possible to have international conventions in areas under the remit of prop-*

to eliminate the serious, endogenous deficiencies inherited from the past and partly under the impact of developments coming from outside of the region—often proceeding on a distinct track from its twin brother, personal property security law.

In some of the countries, the achievements with respect to the upgrading of both real and personal property security law cannot be described as more than modest. In others, certain concrete—measurable economic benefits generating—developments are readily identifiable, though clearly in none of them is this process over.[5] For one thing, unfortunately, there still remain black spots on the map of this part of Europe (though, occasionally also in Western Europe) where it has not been given proper attention even to the very *idea* that credit and security are unavoidable prerequisites of market economies. This is so irrespective that the 'social market economy' model known in Western Europe has become the unanimously embraced market economy model in CEE; even if not directly proclaiming that in any legal act. Consequently—though also due to the failure of law schools to adjust the curricula to the reforms and a noticeable level of hostility toward the flood of transplants of 1990s—the number of those who naively believe that viable market economies could be created without fundamentally reshaping this field of law—and who would like to make a virtue out of the imperfections of the inherited or more or less reshaped law—is not negligible. Hence, security law, in conjunction with the broader field of *financial law*, still awaits the ultimate task to usher these economies into a never-before-experienced era of credit economy-based prosperity.

---

*erty law or civil procedure. This was the product of a belief that these areas of the law embody aspects of national socio-political history and culture and that national sensibility may be so strong as to render any attempt at harmonization unsuccessful.*" The developments in the areas of property—especially collateral law—in CEE clearly corroborate "*[ ... ] [t]hat belief has given way today [and numerous] [a]spects of property law are being attacked with great vigor [ ... ].*" *See* G. Sandeep, *New Trends in the Making of International Commercial Law, Journal of Law and Commerce* 23 (2004) 117, 118–119.

5. A recent study has concluded on the basis of available preliminary data from Romania (data from local filing archives) that "*the outcome of the [secured transactions] reform appears to be billions of dollars in additional credit [ ... ] delivered through sustainable private channels.*" While in the lack of tested empirical data some level of cautiousness would be needed, indeed, it goes uncontested in CEE that "*[t]he benefits from a well-designed reform of the law of secured transactions [are] indisputable.*" *See* Heywood Fleisig, Nuria de la Peña, & Rodrigo Chaves, *Secured Transactions Reform: Early Results from Romania,* CEAL Issues Brief, Sept. 2004, at http://www.ceal.org.

To make things more complicated (because of influences coming predominantly from outside the region, additional—though often only epiphenomenal—tasks have emerged during the last few years), while in the 1990s it had been presumed that the secured transactions law reform could be safely restricted to personal property collateral and the existent mortgage law was sufficient to satisfy the economic expectations, nowadays it is getting crystallized that the burning problems of '*housing*'[6] or the wider-scale exploitation of '*mortgage- or asset-backed securitization*'[7] cannot be satisfactorily dealt with without fundamentally reshaping the contours of the law of real property security law; in addition to the mere 'revitalization' of the real property registry systems. Moreover, the steady growth of local mortgage markets both prompted for and was the catalyst of changes and adjustments of many segments of the capital markets and the related regulatory frameworks. However, as hinted at earlier, practical reasons were the main driving force behind these thoroughgoing changes, like the transplantation of '*securitization,*' a structured financing technique unknown essentially until the later part of the 1990s in the region.[8]

Similarly, significant changes are under way in the context of investment property,[9] as a peculiar type of collateral, which is in the process of not just

6. A recent study undertaken under the auspices of the United Nations succinctly states "*[a]fter more than fifteen years of transition, many countries still experience only sluggish development of market-based housing finance, due to legislative hurdles as well as to low levels of financial affordability, especially on the part of lower and middle income groups. [ … ].*" *See* United Nations, Economic Commission for Europe—Geneva, *Housing Finance Systems for Countries in Transition—Principles and Examples*—(United Nations, 2005).

7. The term 'securitization' is used in a variety of senses. Here it is applied to denote all forms of raising money on the capital market by way of issuing securities (mainly debt instruments) based on such a long term, constant flow of receivables, like the flow of installments in case of real estate mortgages-backed credits. In Hungary until the stepping into force of the Act No. L of year 2001 on the Amendment of the Act XXX of year 1997 on the Mortgage Credit Institution and on Mortgage-Backed Bonds, only the financial institution named the Mortgage Credit Institution had the right both, to extend real property mortgage backed credits and to issue bonds on the strength of these. After 2001—when the German law based '*independent charge*' ("*Grundschuld*") was introduced—commercial banks have also begun to extend mortgage-backed credits, in exponentially growing numbers, which were then sold to and securitized by the Mortgage Credit Institution.

8. A well-functioning mortgage system and a mortgaged-backed securitization are, in a sense, the two interdependent sides of the same coin as the "*[s]ecuritization systems that sit on top of such a mortgage system can provide some liquidity to bank holdings of large mortgages [however, they] cannot make the underlying 'securitized' assets less risky.*" *See* H. Fleisig *et al., supra,* note 3.

9. 'Investment property' is a *terminus technicus* borrowed from Article 8 of the U.S. Uniform Commercial Code (hereinafter: UCC) as it appropriately expresses the undeni-

becoming '*dematerialized*'[10] but also something held and handled completely differently than in the not so distant 'certificated-securities' era. The process of 'dematerialization' and the creation of a functioning 'indirect holding' system of investment property, in and of itself, forced these emerging economies to make quite serious efforts, as these novelties were expected to be appropriately placed in the context of capital market and banking laws virtually continuously undergoing changes.[11] Finally, it would be mistake to disregard that collateral laws are also part of financial laws in a broader sense and thus they are inevitably exposed to all the pathological phenomena emerging on capital markets and in the underworld of finances, the number of which has been meaningful virtually in each of the CEE countries.[12] This peculiar, yet unexplored, connection makes the successfulness of collateral and property law re-

---

ably *sui generis* character of this asset. Note, however, that in Hungary and much of CEE the utilization of this asset as collateral—especially in its dematerialized form—is rare and the pertaining regulation is not subject to the extensive technical detail as in the mentioned Article of the UCC. Yet, under the impact of the gradual opening of local capital markets, both—the volume and the sophistication of related laws and regulations—is increasing.

10. For example, Hungary has completely parted with 'certificated securities' and required 'dematerialization' of stock-exchange listed securities by the end of year 2004. *See* s. 408 (1) (the transitory provisions) of the Act CXX of year 2001 ("*2001. évi CXX. törvény a tőkepiacról*"). Furthermore, from the entry into the force of the Act (January 1, 2002) all securities—meant to be publicly marketed—in Hungary are to be *issued* in 'non-certificated' (dematerialized) form, with the exception of governmental securities (s. 6 (3) of the Capital Market Act). The matter of fact is that it seems the connected legal framework on some points has not been adjusted adequately at the same time. As a consequence inconsistencies do exist and they create dilemmas especially with respect to the utilization of dematerialized (electronic) securities as collateral. For example, it appears that dematerialized securities are inadequately protected from the potential adverse rights of third parties, or good faith creditors of intermediaries with whom the securities accounts are held. The act was substantially amended, for example, in 2005 primarily to implement the European Union's legislation on insider trading and prospectus requrements. *See 2005. évi LXII. Törvény a tőkepiacról szóló 2001. évi CXX. Törvény módosításáról.*

11. Suffice to mention the European Union level activities triggered by the 2001 Lamfalussy Report (the so-called Lamfalussy Directives) or the expectations brought about by 'Basle II and III'. *See* Ellinger, E.P., Lomnicka, E. & Hooley, R.J.A., *Ellinger's Modern Banking Law* (Oxford Univ. Press, 4th ed., 2006) at 55 and 61. Though, the Unidroit Draft Convention on Substantive Rules regarding Securities Held with an Intermediary is a document, which attempts to deal exactly with the problems corollary to the use of dematerialized investment property as collateral.

12. For a description and analysis of the fiasco of the Hungarian real estate investment cooperatives *see* Tajti, Tibor, Central European Contribution to the American Debate on the Definition of "Securities" or Why does the Definition of "Security" Matter?: The Fiasco of the Hungarian Real Estate Investment Cooperatives, Pyramiding, and Why Emerging

forms partly dependent on capital market laws, where the rapidity of changes is unprecedented. No better example could be served than the [in 2008 still unfoulding] global financial crisis; essentially triggered by the collapse of the American subprime market and thus by the technique of mortgage-backed off-balance sheet securitization. The exact repercussions of the 'new Great Depression' are still far from being known. As a first visible result, credits have become already significantly more expensive and less accessible virtually in all niches of the world; yet to what extent will the process of the further improvement of local security laws in CEE slow down because of that and to what extent and how will the connected CEE industries be affected—remains to be seen.

As the confines of this chapter do not allow for a full-scale exploration of each of the CEE systems, the ensuing eclectic elaboration will try to provide the reader with an insight into the security laws of this part of the world, by taking Hungary as the central model. Though, the reader will be given the opportunity to learn about some, more or less peculiar, developments from other CEE jurisdictions. It is hoped that this 'eclectic' methodology is appropriate to provide a fair insight into security law related, post-1990, developments in this distinct corner of Europe.[13]

## *1.1. The Legal and Economic Environment*

Every generalization is inevitably incorrect to certain extent; especially if one would like to find the common denominators of such a large number of countries as we are trying to do here.[14] The diversity is undeniably given and hence every attempt to place all these countries into a single absolutely homogenous basket is erroneous. Thus, the caveat is that the importance of local

---

Capital Markets Should be Equipped to "Act" Rather than "React", 15 Transnat'l L. & Contemp. Probs. 111, 216 (2005).

13. For an insight into the legal environment—including also collateral and leasing laws—of the Stability Pact countries *see* Messmann, Stefan & Tajti, Tibor (eds.), Investing in South Eastern Europe—Foreign Direct Investment in the Stability Pact Countries (European University Press, Bochum-Germany, 2005) as well as Messmann, Stefan & Tajti, Tibor (eds.), the Case Law of Central and Eastern Europe—Leasing, Piercing the Corporate Veil and the Liability of Managers & Controlling Shareholders, Privatization, Takeovers and the Problems with Collateral Laws (European Univesity Press, Bochum, Germany, 2007).

14. For the purposes of this chapter 'CEE' encompasses the countries of Central and Eastern Europe, including the Commonwealth of Independent States (CIS) and the ten countries that acceded to the European Union on May 1st, 2004.

idiosyncratic variants should never be completely put aside irrespective of the myriad, common features of CEE countries, which clearly do exist.

To start with, these countries form a distinct corner of Europe because of their common history: they have all been 'socialist' countries for a significant part of the 20th century. This is important, as one of the basic features of socialism was the preeminence given to public law at the detriment of private law.[15] The consequent 'degradation' of private law meant, for example, that 'credit'—one of the ideological enemies of the system—and the corollary security law were treated both, in theory and practice, as 'stepchildren,' to say the least. On the theoretical level this resulted in the 'vegetation' of socialist security laws on the level of pre-II World War capitalist laws. On the practical level, such 'hostility' has produced very visible results. For example, the maintenance of real estate registries and the cadastre systems (where existent) have not been financed appropriately all over the socialist period, which was the main cause behind the chaotic conditions that awaited the enthusiastic reformers in the 1990s.

Another common feature of the region's jurisdictions was their heavy reliance on leading civilian systems both, in the pre-II World War and—to a lesser extent—also in the socialist period. The resulting transplants were then more or less successfully accommodated in a single civil code or in more pieces of legislation.[16] Therefore, the big picture view has been and remains that the basic structure and principles of property—and security law—of CEE coun-

15. Admittedly there are views that deny the existence (now or in the past) of *socialist private law*. Undoubtedly, there is some level of truth in such contentions because each of these countries has had during most of their 'socialist existence' civil laws, which were modeled after Western European civilian systems. To be precise, the process of the creation of local civil laws has begun in most of these states already somewhere in the second half of the 19th century or at the outset of the 20th century, though in many this process has failed to produce a civil code until some later part of the 20th century. For example, Hungary has managed to enact her first Civil Code only in 1959. The former Yugoslavia, on the other hand, not opting for a 'single comprehensive code-regime', has reached this phase of development solely around the end of the 1970s and has enacted the Act on Obligations in 1978 and the 'Property Law Act' in 1980. Nevertheless, it should not be contested that the private law existent during socialism has undergone meaningful alterations on many points for ideological reasons.

16. Thus, it is pretty commonplace—at least among CEE lawyers themselves—to refer to Romania as the country that has in the region relied on French civil law presumably the most. As opposed to that, all countries once being part of the Austro-Hungarian Empire (roughly until the end of the World War I and the subsequent peace treaties) were primarily influenced by German and Austrian civil and commercial laws. These still continue to influence the CEE countries. Thus, the central question today is rather to what extent have these countries changed their attitudes in that respect?

tries, in essence, to a great extent resemble the laws of their western civilian kindred. Irrespective of the resemblance, however, in CEE even the—formally known yet rudimentary—'possessory pledge plus real estate mortgage' security system did not function properly. Moreover, one could claim that non-possessory security on personal property was in essence unknown in the region. Likewise, although the real property security system seemed to have existed formally and indeed mortgages were recorded to get credits (primarily in the westernmost socialist countries and only during the latter decades of socialism), in reality one could hardly find traces of court-orchestrated foreclosures.[17] This fact should be indicative as to the true efficiency of socialist mortgage laws and the surrounding enforcement systems, given that in CEE self-help enforcement was everywhere prohibited and the only avenue for satisfaction was through courts.

To illustrate the close ties with western systems let us highlight a few shared property law features. *First,* as in the western [Continental] part of Europe, CEE is also dominated by the 'unitary concept of ownership' and the *numerus clausus* of proprietary rights. *Furthermore,* in the context of immovables one can safely presume that the overwhelming part of the region is covered by land title registration systems, where entries into the registry are deemed to have constitutive effect. Moreover, right after the fall of the Berlin Wall, the types and forms of known security devices were all over the region similar to those in Germany; except perhaps the 'land charge' ("*Grundschuld*") and the so called "*kautelarische Sicherheiten.*"[18] Unfortunately, unlike in much of the West, prob-

---

17. Empirical data is, as a rule, not available and court decisions on foreclosures are non-public all over the region; especially as far as the socialist period was concerned. Consequently, besides 'anecdotal evidences', every piece of paper providing some insight into the region should be welcomed. Exactly because of that a short account of a former judge of a town-court from Hungary might tell us more about the past and partly the present than what one could presume. Namely, in the words of Judge Tímár—who spent more decades working as a judge dealing with mortgages—the inherited enforcement system from socialism was completely inappropriate to satisfy the demands of market economy. Partly because courts did not have experience with the enforcement of mortgages as actually rarely, if ever, were there court foreclosures in the socialist period. *See* Tímár, Sándor, *Enforcement of Real Property Mortgages filled with Question Marks*, in the Hungarian language law journal '*Magyar Jog*', No. 6 (1999) 344.

Obviously, 'maintenance of the social peace' was more important to the socialist regimes than pressing for the enforcement of mortgages. This officially unpronounced policy was just the other side of the same coin, which saw the solution of the housing problem in state subsidies and not in market mechanisms.

18. These 'contract-based' security devices were invented and later expanded and extended by businessmen and have eventually become recognized by courts in Germany. As

lems with the maintenance of the registries and the ensuing risks were also a common feature of CEE countries. Though, as a rule of thumb, the systems of the new European Union accessory countries are undoubtedly much better functioning than that of their easternmost neighbors.

These observations cannot be left out of sight when talking about security laws in contemporary CEE. The experiences with the security law reforms in CEE, indeed, confirm that one of the tokens of success is in parallel adjustment of the functionally connected fields of law, in particular bankruptcy, consumer protection and enforcement laws. The reforming of security laws with the aim of creating a maximally credit friendly legal and economic environment ('credit economy'), however, required in the 1990s resort [also] to the leading Anglo-Saxon legal systems to a heretofore unprecedented extent; partly it has become known that these systems had proved to be more suc-

---

they are not subject to any kind of registration it was relatively easy and cheap for CEE businessmen to transplant them, consequently they were readily available on the wake of the turn towards credit economies. These devices could be seen as the proof that the German Civil Code's *numerus clausus* principle of *in rem* rights is ill-suited to satisfy the needs of modern business. *See, e.g.*, T. Tajti, *Comparative Secured Transactions Law*, chapter on Germany (Akadémiai kiadó, Budapest, 2002).

Moreover, in at least two countries, Poland and Hungary, a *sui generis* conflict has arisen between the German non-registrable transplants—widely used by local banks (especially the local subsidiaries of German and Austrian banks)—and the newly introduced, common law-inspired and registrable security interests (in Poland named as "registered pledge"). The gist of the problem was that as the German transplants (especially security transfers and security assignments) were not subject to registration, hence, it was easier and cheaper to establish them than the "registered pledges" and were therefore favored by banks; what raised the issue whether and how to reconcile the two systems and consequently whether it made any sense to introduce the common law variant? On the dilemmas and solutions faced in Poland *see Krzysztof Kazmierczyk & Filip Kijowski, the* chapter on *Enforcement of Contracts in Poland, in:* Messmann, Stefan, & Tajti, Tibor, Case Law of Central and Eastern Europe, Enforcement of Contracts (European University Press, Bochum, Germany, publication expected in winter 2009). It must be added that both countries had introduced quite forward looking laws on security interests on movables and on enterprises—i.e., "registered pledges"—already prior to World Was II, but the then introduced devices could not have been fully exploited because of the turbulent 1930s and the war; only the fall of socialism gave these countries the chance to revive these important institutions of market economy once again and to "enrich" as well as "update" the inherited device with elements coming from the leading common law systems. Thus, some authors speak of these devices as 'common law transplants' and yet others as 'revived' local security devices. At any event, a closer look at comparative law might have helped prevent the described conflict of 'security laws being based on diametrically opposite philosophies' to arise.

cessful in creating efficient security laws than their developed civilian counterparts.[19] Though, admittedly the dominance of institutions promulgating common law-inspired models was of no less importance.

Yet it would be extremely naïve to think that the impact—initially quite limited, later expanding—of common laws boosted the CEE collateral regimes overnight. The complete revamping of the first reform laws in a number of countries—like Lithuania and Ukraine—is the best example of that. Thus, on the whole, the amelioration or even the *de novo* regulation of numerous property and security law issues remains an imminent task in the region. Albeit we are here concerned with security laws it should go uncontested that without clear, stable and predictable property laws the success of the new security laws will be doomed to failure. The graveness of this problem, though, differs from jurisdiction to jurisdiction. In its extreme version, like in Russia, often it is still not clear who owns what land or how a plot can be sold and thus whether it makes sense to accept it as collateral.[20] On the other hand, in Hungary, dilemmas of another sort exist, like whether a *lex specialis* should be passed to regulate and thus bolster the American (off balance sheet) type of mortgage-backed securitization, whether there is a need for a special more detailed law on condominiums in addition to the relatively general language of the Civil Code, or whether and what should be transplanted from the Cana-

---

19. This claim needs qualifications as, for example, Montenegro, Croatia and Slovenia have been almost exclusively interested in German security law so far and law reforms inspired by UCC Article 9 have largely bypassed them. Thus, in these countries the 1990s saw ever closer reliance on the German "*kautelarische Sicherheiten*" led by the famous 'security transfer' ("*Sicherungsübereignung*") and 'retention of title' ("*Eigentumvorbehalt*"). A corollary of this approach is that no registry for non-possessory securities has been created in these countries and the newly spreading advanced transaction normally known, as 'leasing' is not thought of as a security interest. Though, it has to be added that the winds seem to have changed even in these countries. In case of Serbia, for example, 2005 saw the beginning of the work of the central, computerized registry of both, security interests on movables and financial leasing contracts. See the website of the Serbian Agency for Business Registries (*Agencija za privredne registre*) at http://www.apr.sr.gov.yu (visited on October 28, 2005). Croatia has also stepped on this path of development by the enactment of its brand new *Law on the Register for the Registration of Court and Public Notarial Security Interests Established on Movables and Rights* in 2005.

20. *See in general,* D. Tumenova, *Evolution of Land Reform in Russia: the 2001 Land Code and its Impact on the Commercial Real Estate Market and Direct Foreign Investment, Pacific Rim Law and Policy Journal* 11 (2002) 769 (arguing that the 2001 Land Code represent a fundamental shift in Russia's attitude to land ownership, among others, by fostering foreign investment into land, irrespective of the new system's incompleteness).

dian[21] mortgage law and housing model. Though, one can find examples of remarkably successful efforts like the efficient completion of the make-up work on the land registries of the capital Budapest.

---

21. The Canadian model has been mentioned by media in Hungary—though without causing much upheaval—as a model that might fundamentally help to reach to point where the average wage-earner could move into his/her house with a down payment of 25% or less (with the application of a Canadian invention of 'registered retirement savings plan') paying 'decent' interests on the basis of mortgage & credit arrangements for a 25 or 30 years. At the moment, the Hungarian landscape—irrespective of the undeniable results available thanks to the present and the earlier governments' back up in some forms of credit arrangements—resemble the pre-Great Depression conditions of the U.S. when "[ ... ] home loans had short terms and were used primarily by the wealthy, because one was require to put down 50% of the purchase price in order to get a home loan. As a result of these conditions, only about 45% of the homes in the United States were owner-occupied. [ ... ]." *See* Martin, Nathalie, *The Role of History and Culture in Developing Bankruptcy and Insolvency Systems: the Perils of Legal Transplantation, Boston College International and Comparative Law Review* 28 (2005) 1, 15. The situation is not much different in the other jurisdictions of the region.

The Hungarian landscape is, thus, virtually equal with that existing Germany as far as the crucial elements of commercial mortgage arrangements are concerned. For example, as far as down-payments are concerned the standard rule is that loans are available solely with a 40%–50% down-payment (i.e., financing possible maximally up to 60% of the purchase price in case of acquisition of a new housing). It seems that this debilitating, generally accepted, down-payment standard is due to a more or less automatic and uncritical transplantation of German financing patterns into Hungary (and into other Central European countries as well) for what one could hardly find any explanation. *See* the study of the Hungarian Financial Supervisory Agency *A bankok ingatlanfedezetű devizahiteleinek összehasonlító elemzése* [A Comparative Study of the Foreign Currency Credits of Banks Secured by Mortgage of Immovables], electronically available in Hungarian language at <http://www.pszaf.hu> page on publications and studies; last visited on October 27, 2006.

For a synopsis of the lending practices of banks with respect to home acquisitions *see, e.g.*, the Report of the [Hungarian] Parliamentary Commissioner (i.e., Ombudsman) in the case No. OBH 4999/2003 on the Protection of the Right to Property in the Context of the Mortgage Financing Practices of some Banks (*Jelentés az OBH 4999/2003. sz. ügyben A tulajdonhoz való jog védelméről egyes bankok jelzáloghitelezési gyakorlatával kapcsolatban*) available in Hungarian language at the http//www.obh.hu, last visited on May 25th, 2005. The Ombudsman found the general practice of "unilateral double-reduction" ("*egyoldalúan elvégzett kétszeres leértékelés*") of the immovables' value by banks problematic and contrary to the good faith principle enshrined into the Civil Code. Namely, "the banks first fix the value of the immovable [i.e., house or an apartment] serving as collateral below its actual market value. Then such a reduced value is reduced for the second time. This second reduction in case of mortgage banks results in a figure that cannot exceed 70% [of the immovable's once reduced value], whereas in case of other commercial banks that value may be even less."

True, due to the increased competition on the housing market in 2006, banks (and to

The arrival of common law meant also the confrontation of the inherent functional approach with 'system thinking,' the idiosyncrasy of civilian laws; especially the ones modeling themselves after German law. A glance at the experiences with the personal property security reform in the region could easily show that this basic difference has not been given proper consideration. It has not been clarified at the outset of the drafting process what should enjoy priority: dogmatic requirements (e.g., finding the appropriate place in the system of the code) or, rather, the new solutions should yield to pragmatic considerations and efficiency? This fundamental dilemma is partly about the conflict of systemic versus functional thinking.[22] Or, more precisely, to what extent

---

a lesser also other financial organizations) extending mortgage-backed housing credits have been forced to attract riskier segments of the society by loosening the security requirements. Moreover, this year meant the employment of 'leasing' and title retention in the housing sector with the aim of bypassing the extremely onerous down payment requirements. Still, the home finance system with a 20% down payment as the rule is only a plan for some future times. Needless to say, the global financial crisis of 2008 has made the banks once again much more risk averse and reversion back to more conservative and cautious lending policies.

22. The experiences with the collateral law reform in Hungary are a perfect source of examples of the unsatisfactory consequences of the uncritical priority given to dogmatic considerations. For example, it was clear to the author of this chapter that the property encumbering charge ("*vagyont terhelő zálogjog*") introduced into the system in 1996—which was foreseen to be the local variant of the English floating charge—cannot really work in reality because the conditions for the enforcement of the charge (i.e., the crystallization) were unclearly formulated by the law, to say the least. *See*, the section on this topic in the Chapter devoted to Hungary in TAJTI, *supra note* # 15. On the problem in general *see also* Tajti, Tibor, *Viehweg's Topics, Article 9 UCC, the 'kautelarische Sicherheiten' and the Hungarian Secured Transactions Law Reform*, 6 Vindobona J. Int'l L & Com. Arb., 93 (2002).

Unfortunately, a few years were needed for this particular question to surface in practice and the concomitant dilemmas to reach high courts. Essentially only the 2005 decision of the Supreme Court has clarified the true legal nature (and thus the ranking position) of this peculiar security variant. The irony is that—irrespective that the property encumbering charge was placed in the section on security interests (i.e., *in rem rights)* and thus dogmatic expectations have been entertained—the Supreme Court was forced to proclaim that "*the property encumbering charge is a sub-type of security interests [ ... ] which comes into being through registration in the public notary registry of charges and which has equal proprietary and effects as any other form of security interests, including a priority position [ ... ]. The concretization of the property encumbering charge does not create a new security interest, rather only the type of the security interest will be changed [ ... ].*" *See* decision of the Hungarian Supreme Court in case Gfv. IX.30.247/2005/5 (as of November 24, 2005).

The question that lends itself to be formulated quite legitimately, and because of why this particular discrepancy between 'dogmatic' and 'pragmatic' considerations should be pointed at, is the hardly measurable price which must have been paid for this "experiment" these diverging policy choices are reconcilable. This is the point where comparative law and legal theory in conjunction should have provided the drafters of new laws with a better guidance.

### 1.2. Real and Personal Property Security: Distinct Paths of Development?

Another perplexing systemic dilemma created some uneasiness during the reform process. Namely, it has not been properly analyzed whether the reform of personal property security law is to be undertaken separately from its real property brethren. In case of Hungary, as per the view embraced during the first round of reforms in 1996, all types of collateral were to remain subject to a single legal regime and were to be placed into the same subchapter of the code. By such an account, the requirements of the abstract system of the code and civil law were clearly fully satisfied. Such a position fails, however, to take into account the degree to which the two types of property behave physically differently. In Hungary, it took roughly a decade, not just to see[23] but to admit that the traditional principles of real estate security law, based occasionally on preconceptions as old as a century, do not function properly when applied to the less venerable property types, movables and—in particular—intangibles, not necessarily because of a mysterious metaphysical explanation, but simply due to the physical differences of these distinct asset groups.[24]

---

by businesspeople. *See also*, Bodzási, Balázs, *Néhány szó a keretbiztosítéki vagyont terhelő jelzálogjogról* [Few Words about the Property Encumbering Charge Securing a Revolving Credit], *in:* Themis (the Electronic Journal of the ELTE Law School, Budapest), 2004 December issue.

23. The Official Preparatory Works for s. 252 of *the 2nd Hungarian Secured Transactions Reform Act from 2000*, noted quite shyly, and yet without introducing a clear change of policy, that, for example, it has been only subsequently found out that it is not possible to create a future or conditional charge on real property because the real property registry maintenance rules do not allow that. In the lack of an explicitly formulated policy choice it is still hard to determine in what respect and to what extent do the rules differ with respect to real versus personal property in Hungary.

24. As eventually the efficiency of enforcement is the important point on the basis of what everything is measured, one should mention here that while a secured creditor (mortgagee) having a duly registered mortgage on a piece of land does not have to rush to protect his interests, a secured creditor having a security interest on a car or a machine—as movables—must act *promptly* upon default of the debtor possessing the collateral otherwise the collateral might easily get out of sight and reach of both creditor(s) and courts/bailiffs. This problem is of heightened relevance in the fledgling markets of CEE.

This conceptual shift should be welcomed, as clearly the goals and expectations imposed on the reformers with respect to the reform of these two large fields are fundamentally different. Legal history might also corroborate that. Namely, as opposed to non-possessory security on personal property that was unknown—let alone widely utilized—prior to the 1990s, mortgage of immovables has been known since the 19th or early 20th century on in the region. As the story goes, while most countries of the region have striven to introduce land registries beginning already somewhere in the 19th century, no registries of *in rem* rights were envisaged by any of the systems with respect to most other types of assets.[25]

Still, connecting points between the two fields, naturally, do exist. At least two such important and practical instances must be mentioned: floating security and mortgage backed securitization. Both of these newcomers require the tackling of both, real and personal property security law. The floating security because it requires an answer to the question whether it should extend also to immovables, and if yes how? On the other hand, mortgage-backed securitization is impossible without crystal-clear and compatible rules on both, real property mortgages and the assignment of receivables as well as various credit enhancement methods (the latter two categories belonging to personal property security law).

As functionalism was not a key feature of the laws of the region insufficient attention has been given to the mentioned pragmatic considerations. Though, admittedly, time constraints, lack of expertise and fear from truly sophisticated novelties of the sort have also contributed to shying away from opting for more business-friendly, yet radical, innovations. It ought to be expected, however, that the mismatch and largely isolated development of the two fields will lessen over time, simply because that will be dictated by the constantly increasing transnational movement of capital, which does not know and does not tolerate theoretical divisions, ill-suited to modern business.

## 2. Real Property Security

According to traditional wisdom prevalent in the region, immovables have always been looked upon as the most important type of assets and, hence, col-

25. Naturally, we have to disregard at this point that registries for the registration of some intellectual property rights, ships, aircraft and encumbrances on them, which have been introduced in the CEE countries roughly simultaneously with the introduction of their counterparts in western jurisdictions many decades ago.

lateral. Moreover, mortgage of real property was not unheard of even during socialism irrespective that, as a rule, enforcement was extremely problematic. Such a state of affairs could not have been substantially changed overnight and thus the number of existent problems, dilemmas and pathological phenomena surviving up until today is far from negligible. Curiously enough, reforms aiming at the amelioration of the laws and legal system to entertain the strict expectations of credit economy have primarily been undertaken in relation to personal property in the overwhelming part of the region's countries.[26] However, changes are occurring also with respect to laws affecting real property: from the programs attempting to ameliorate the burning housing problems of the region through the appearance of the securitization of mortgages. The element that connects all these real social and economic problems is that none of them could be solved without the reform of real property security law; what in and of itself should be sufficient to take a closer look at the pertaining developments in the region.

## 2.1. Common Legacies from the Socialist Past

Obviously an entire book could be written about the socialist legacies affecting immovables; yet three of them need to be mentioned here briefly. *First,* a major break has begun in the development of property law right at after the end of World War II, in addition to the wide-ranging expropriations (especially of arable land and corporate property) because of the commonly known ideological dictates of those times. The property laws of the region have survived the non-market economy period without being in the position to adopt much from contemporaneous, market-friendly developments in western market economies. As a result, the other concomitant task imposed on the drafters of new laws in the reform years of the 1990s was to catch up with the developments of post-World War II market economies and to upgrade the system to satisfy the expectations of modern times.

*Secondly,* understandably subject to variations, it was a common feature all over the block that property law in its socialist variant has become "invaded

26. It is fair to claim that in CEE real property law has been a 'sacred cow'—partly because of the identical treatment in the leading western civilian jurisdictions. Real property law was in particular thought of as being so 'local and parochial' that no harmonization was deemed to be rational. *See generally* A. Douglas, *Emerging Market Economies and Government Promotion of Securitization, Duke Journal of Comparative and International Law* 12 (2002) 505, 515.

by public law."[27] This concretely meant that the ideological aims of socialism —maximal strengthening of state and other types of quasi-state property[28] at the detriment of all imaginable forms of private property—have been achieved to a great extent by heavy reliance on public law. As a corollary, private property with all of its traditional concomitants—including security interests—as well as credits, being among the most despised 'enemies' of the regime, have been degraded to the maximum extent. While in *Central* Europe private property has not been completely debilitated, the Soviet Union was much more successful in that respect. Consequently, with the fall of the Berlin Wall and rerouting of the direction of development towards market economy, one of the central aims has become to 'reprivatise' property law and to find the proper balance between private and public law elements in this sphere.

*Finally,* having in mind the realities of socialist times, conceptually it is justified to talk about a peculiar 'socialist degraded-ownership.' Namely, the hinted-at degradation of private property and the intrusion of public law has gradually deprived all forms of non-state ownership of everything but 'bare title' (*nuda proprietas*). Even if named as 'property' or 'ownership,' the entitlements inherent to these legal categories have become divested of their essence; this has also reduced their ready use for security purposes. For example, in the former Czechoslovakia, through public law three major rights were vested in the state to exploit privately owned assets for the sake of achieving the ideologically dictated ends: (1) the right to impose cooperative utilization, (2) the right of utilization in support of production, and (3) the right to impose substitute utilization.[29]

---

27. For example, it was a common characteristic in the region (though, subject to variations) that housing was "*orchestrated and financed directly or indirectly*" by the state or various state-connected entities (e.g., socialist variants of cooperatives) on a deeply subsidized basis.

28. For example, cooperative-property could be comfortably enlisted under this peculiar category. Yet, the *sui generis* 'societal ownership/property' ("*društvena svojina*") of the former Yugoslavia could be also easily put under this heading.

29. By way of cooperative utilization the state has forced individual landowners to transfer ownership on means for production other than land (i.e., buildings, livestock, inventory and supplies) to the cooperative. While the members of the cooperatives have retained ownership on the land plots, the rights based on ownership were so restricted that ownership virtually meant nothing. Those who escaped from becoming cooperatives members were, however, prevented from the enjoyment of their proprietary rights through the state's right of utilization in support of production, which essentially meant the transfer of the land for cultivation and harnessing to state agricultural enterprises. Substitute utilization, on the other hand, has subjected privately owned land plots to the interests of cooperatives and agricultural organizations under the excuse of the centralization of agricultural land

## 2.2. *Variations on the Theme of* the Tragedy of the Commons *and Their Impact on the Development of the Security System*

Besides many of the pathological phenomena known also in the West, real property law is plagued with other peculiar local problems. No elaboration of real property security could be understood without taking a glance on them as they prevent the ready exploitation of immovables for security purposes. The number of the local phenomena that could be safely brought under the heading of 'the tragedy of the commons' or 'anticommons' is not negligible. They represent a grave problem because predictably decades will be needed to oust these maladies. Two such examples peculiar to the region deserve mentioning.

Walking around the main streets of larger cities of the region one could easily notice that ideally located stores or even whole buildings remain non-exploited; moreover they physically deteriorate.[30] The failure of their utilization for business purposes normally implies also that they are improper objects for use as collateral. Albeit as a rule more than a single factor could be listed as a cause of such state of affairs and variations do exist from one jurisdiction to another, yet it is absolutely proper to refer to these as 'the tragedy of the commons (i.e., if they are owned, e.g., by a municipality) or anti-commons (i.e., when they are owned by several private owners whose property rights—in a shorthand manner—conflict or overlap).'[31]

---

for the sake of more efficient exploitation. *See* B. Donovan, *Argument for the Allocation of Resources to the Development of a Well-Defined System of Real Property Law in the Czech Republic, Vanderbilt Journal of Transnational Law* 29 (1996) 661, 665–667.

30. The process of the redefining of property rights to make the engine of market economy work efficiently in the post-socialism period has been an extremely complex and daunting task. Reality has proven that no ready-made recipes exist and many of the neglected but crucial elements of the process have only gradually been recognized. Similarly, no single factor could be attributed the many persisting problems. Heller has rightly noted, for example, that the storefronts in Moscow are empty while street kiosks in front are full of goods because the transitory governments have failed "*[ ... ] to endow any individual with a bundle of rights that represents full ownership of storefronts or other scarce resources [ ... ]*"and this form of the tragedy of the commons cannot be solely ascribed to the high level of corruption, lack of the rule of law and the failure to clearly define property rights. *See* M.A. Heller, *The Tragedy of the Anticommons: Property in the Transition from Marx to Markets, Harvard Law Review*, 111 (1998) 621, 623.

31. According to Heller '*anticommons*' exist when "*multiple owners are each endowed with the right to exclude others from a scarce resource, and no one has an effective privilege of*

Another set of problems causes major concerns in the capital of Budapest. Namely, more than half of the residential buildings had been built prior to World War II and a substantial portion even before World War I. Most of these buildings have become state property somewhere at the outset of socialism, during which period, neither the state, nor the tenants have invested enough into the maintenance of these buildings. As a result, the physical stature of the substantial portion of these realties has become hazardous to life by the 1990s.

The so-created variant of the tragedy of the commons has been then boldly resolved by the new democratic government: the immovables have been sold to the tenants at extremely lowered prices. However, the shortsightedness of the state has proved fatal, as clearly most of the tenants were either financially incapable to invest for maintenance, or because of the unclear legal ambient, they were not willing to do that. In other words, all the maintenance and other problems caused by aging have not been solved but rather only transferred onto the new citizen-owners. Thus, the resolution of these problems has been essentially only postponed. This is absolutely visible now when people live in or pass by these buildings at their own peril.[32]

True, the poor conditions of these immovables *per se* are not prohibitive in accepting them as collateral. Still, the process of the rehabilitation of this segment of the real property pool is far too slow and it is questionable whether it could be solved at all without a new major governmental program, presupposing also governmental financial support, irrespective that strictly *de jure* speaking these properties are privately owned.

Problems of this sort are preventing and delaying the full-scale development of the mortgage-market, let alone the other political and sociological negative corollaries. Similarly, huge funds and governmental involvement is needed for the rehabilitation of the hundreds of so-called 'panel buildings' which were built during socialism from the 1960s on and which occupy an equally large portion of the realties market. In their case, at least, centrally orchestrated governmental programs are already in place, irrespective of the modest results, that could be ascribed to the disproportion in the needed versus the available governmental funds.

---

*use*." Predictably '*anticommons*' lead to *underuse*, as opposed to *overuse* arising in the context of 'commons'. *Id.*, at 622.

32. To illustrate how serious this problem is, it suffices to cite the title of a recent article from the Hungarian daily *Népszabadság*, which should be self-explanatory: *A bérházak zöme veszélyforrás* [The Majority of Apartment Houses is Hazardous], by I. Schwartzenberger, in the June 14, 2005's issue of the daily *Népszabadság* at 7.

Needless to say, variants of these problems do exist also in the successor countries of the former Yugoslavia where during socialism, though through differently structured housing programs, often the best located apartments were given and then acquired by the socially most disadvantaged part of the populace, which is now also incapable to invest into maintenance. In sum, a large portion of the residency immovables market is not just in extremely bad shape, but also is outside of the reach of market forces. Thus, the healthy economic exploitation of huge portions of the CEE immovables markets—if appropriately reformed and consolidated—still wait for some better times.

## *2.3. Synopsis of the CEE Land Registry Systems*

Clearly, without a properly functioning registry of immovables and readily ascertainable proprietary rights, no security system could work. Exactly because of that, we cannot bypass this topic. Unfortunately, again one cannot really understand the contemporary landscape without turning back to the past. Actually the central deficiencies—lag of entries, discrepancies between the factual and the legal state of affairs, and on top of that, forms of corruption—could be ascribed to a large extent to the previous regime. Consequently, nowadays, especially in the early transition countries, a parallel double-track reform process is unfolding: one aiming at the creation and/or normalization of the functioning of the land registry system and the other focusing on drafting modern mortgage-laws.[33]

To start with, the whole region could be roughly divided into three major groups of jurisdictions[34] from the point of view of the employed land regis-

33. A good example is Serbia in which the German Organization for Technical Cooperation (GTZ) (financed by the German government) is assisting the Serbian government in both drafting a new Law on the Cadastre of Land and a modern Law on Mortgages ("*hipoteka*"), and revitalizing the registry and cadastre systems, since 2001. It is illustrative that Serbia had had altogether seven provisions on real property mortgages prior to 2001 what was clearly insufficient to support the emergence of a mortgage market. The former Yugoslav republic of Slovenia has, for example, enacted a brand new *Act on Land Registers* in 2003, which contains altogether 250 sections (*Uradni list Republike Slovenije* No. 58/2003 [Official Gazette of the Republic of Slovenia No. 58/2003).

34. No classification is perfect; the above one is not an exception. Thus, one of the central problems of Serbia at the moment is exactly that it still accommodates three immovables registry systems. Albeit the remnants of the Ottoman *tapi* system are clearly doomed to disappear for good, the views have not become crystallized whether a German-Austrian type of land registry system should be introduced on the whole territory of the country or rather a peculiar, locally invented 'unitary registry of immovables' should prevail. The unitary system has been introduced somewhere by the end of the 1980s and its maintenance has been entrusted to the cadastre offices. It has been primarily criticized because it is a

tration system. The loosely defined territory of Central Europe that had been under strong influence of German or Austrian law during the 19th and the beginning of the 20th century with respect to land registry systems now have a German-Austrian type of land title registry system. Another group could be formed from those southeastern European territories where the Ottoman "*tapi*" system of title deed registration persists,[35] or from the countries where some more or less peculiar mixture of known systems is at place. Worse yet, in some —primarily eastern parts of the region[36]—either no registry system has been installed so far, or large tracks of land, forests and even entire settlements exist without being [properly] registered. Naturally, in the case of the last two groups it is hard to imagine any modern mortgage based utilization of immovables.

In the newly acceded EU countries, registries do exist and thus the work does not have to start with building up the system from scratch. Yet on the questionable side other types of problems persist, like the negative consequences of the degradation of private property during socialism or the neglect of appropriate maintenance of the registries. Thousands of production facilities and even more dwelling houses were built, without proper entries having been made. As a consequence, nowadays it is quite common to find 'agricultural land or grassland' recorded at the places where buildings, occasionally with tens of apartments, have been located for many years.

Still, one may safely assume that the overwhelming part of *Central* Europe is covered by land registries,[37] yet with substantial differences in the efficiency

---

system maintained by an administrative body (i.e., cadastral offices) and because of the fact that it represents a mixed, factual & legal, registry system. For an overview of recent debates in Serbia *see* R. Cvetič, *Evidencija nepokretnosti* [The Registry of Immovables] *in:* the *Collected Papers of the Novi Sad Faculty of Law* XXXVIII—3/2004, at 327–344.

35. Originally the physical transfer of the document called '*tapi*'—a document to a great extent resembling a common law 'deed'—with witnesses present was adequate evidence of land transfer. This system has survived on the Balkans on the territories that had been part of the Ottoman Empire until the beginning of the 20th century, like the southern part of Serbia and Kosovo. Given that at the moment a German/Austrian type of registry system is being installed on the whole territory of Serbia—including Kosovo—most presumably *tapis* will disappear even from these territories very soon.

36. Especially a large portion of the territory of the former Soviet Union (e.g., Siberia).

37. As opposed to the deed registration systems—widely known in the U.S.—under the CEE systems entries into the registry have a 'constitutive force', meaning that the proprietary rights are created by the entry itself. Thus, in principle, the data in the registry is authentic proof on the actual state of ownership and on the existence of any encumbrances. However, because of the many problems surrounding the operation of registries (e.g., delays in effectuating entries, corruption) significant discrepancies do exist between what the books contain and the reality. Consequently, irrespective that 'title insurance' has not be-

of their operation.[38] Nonetheless, some commonly known general value judgments of the sort that the enforcement of real property mortgages (foreclosure) is everywhere a problem in the region, are definitively valid; though, subject to variation from country to country or even from region to region.

The high esteem of German real property security law is due that some central institutions have been transplanted exactly from this system by many of the region's countries, though no laundry list of such borrowings is available. Yet the influence of the German land charge ("*Grundschuld*"),[39] as a non-accessory security device—what is the *sine qua non* of securitization of mortgages—is undoubtedly indicative in that respect. In Hungary, for example, both the non-accessory land charge and the connected "*Pfandbrief*"-type securitization is already part of the business practices of local land-credit organizations.[40] A further step is planned to enact a special law that would allow

---

come domesticated in the region, it is prudent to rely on the services of public notaries and legal counsels whenever dealing with immovables even if that is not dictated by the law (e.g., Serbia does not have a system of public notaries). In Russia, for example, property rights acquired before the effective date of the Registration Law (January 31, 1998) have not been made subject to mandatory registration with the new land registries, thus, careful examination of all the documents, visual inspection of the objects themselves and prompt registration are strongly recommended. *See* L.S. Batalov, *The Russian Title Registration System for Realty and its Effect on Foreign Investors, Washburn Law Review* 73 (1998) 989, 1015. According to my personal experiences in case of Hungary and Serbia one has to be especially cautious in case of immovables located in larger settlements.

38. For example, Slovenia, Croatia, Bosnia and Herzegovina—former parts of the Austria-Hungary and nowadays the successor countries of the former Yugoslavia—and Serbia's northern province, *Vojvodina,* have had for more than a century an almost identical system of land registry and to a great extent resembling mortgage laws. Still, by now meaningful differences have been created due to various formants of law; among others, because of taking of differing paths of development since the dissolution of the former Yugoslavia. Though such factors as the war in Bosnia and Herzegovina and Croatia, and the economic decline in Vojvodina (caused also by the Balkan wars, though, also by the United Nation's embargo against the rump-Yugoslavia), were undoubtedly also of impact. Slovenia, on the other hand, has become an EU member state on May 1, 2004, what is a crucial factor in directing the further development of this country, even though, property and security law has not ranked high on the agenda of the EU so far.

39. As in Germany, in Hungary the main difference between the two devices is that the "*Hypothek*" is accessory whereas the land charge is not. *See, e.g.,* Strothmann, Chapter on Germany in W.E. Moojen & M. ph. van sint Truiden (eds.), *A Practical Guide on Security Devices available to Banks in Thirty Countries Throughout the World* (Kluwer Law International, the Hague, 1999).

40. As far as Hungary is concerned, albeit there is no law generally allowing 'securitization' (though there are opinions vouching for that), a separate act has been passed in 1997 on land-credit organizations ("*jelzálog-hitelintézet*") and on mortgage-bonds

securitization not just to the few land-credit organizations but also to a larger group of qualified commercial banks, which would denote the arrival of the American, off-balance sheet, type of asset securitization.[41] To wit, there is a natural and gradual line of development, a process that begins with the creation of a properly maintained land registry system and that ends with variants of mortgage- and asset-backed securitization. However, it is far from unusual that there are crucial differences in the level of related developments, even among very neighbors.

---

("*jelzáloglevél*"), whereby securitization has become possible, however, just to the land-credit financial organizations, specifically founded for this purpose. *See*, the *1997. évi XXX. törvény a jelzálog-hitelintézetről és a jelzáloglevélről* [Act No. XXX. of year 1997 on the Mortgage Loan Institution and on Mortgage-bonds]. The essence of the 'Hungarian model' is that securitization is limited to the [initially] government-supported land-credit financial organization and commercial banks are prohibited from engaging directly into securitization.

This system was inspired by German patterns as until 2001 exclusively these specialized entities were entitled to issue mortgage-bonds. With the Act No. L of year 2001, however, these credit institutions got permission to extend credits also on the basis of 'land charges' (i.e., independent, non-accessory mortgages). This possibility has opened new horizons for these businesses as from this moment on they have been given the right to purchase from banks and other financial organizations 'independent charges/mortgages' (s. the amended 3 (1) of the Act). The act subjects these entities to strict prudential rules and special administrative controls. Moreover, it also establishes that in case of the insolvency of these institutions special priority rules apply: only the costs of the liquidation procedure enjoy priority over the rights of the holder of the mortgage-bonds. At the moment three such mortgage-credit institutions function in Hungary quite successfully. One among them, the FHB Land Credit and Mortgage Bank Co. Plc,—whose shares are among the best performing ones on the Budapest Stock Exchange ever since the foundation in 1997—has been awarded also the title of 'Best Growth Company' by the Swedish 'East Capital' fund in 2004. See http://www.fhb.hu (also in English language).

41. Under the American model of securitization here we mean raising of money by way of selling securities through a '*special purpose vehicle*' (i.e., a legal entity or trust distinct from the mortgage bank) on the strength of a constant flow of receivables from a pool of mortgages (or other kinds of debts). As opposed to that under the German system no such special purpose vehicle is normally being created that would be from the mortgage bank distinct legal entity. Thus, the main difference is that under the American system in case of default in the payment of securities the security holder can resort to the special purpose vehicle only, which is 'bankruptcy remote' from the mortgage bank. As opposed to that, under the German "*Pfandbrief*—based" system the security holder has recourse directly against the mortgage bank and the banks' other (i.e., unrelated to the mortgage arrangements) assets. *See* Scott, Hal S. & Wellons, Philip A., International Finance—Transactions, Policy, and Regulation (Foundation Press, 10th ed., 2003) at 768.

## 2.4. Pathological Phenomena and Predatory Lending

No collateral law-related discussion would be complete without at least a cursory view on the numerous pathological phenomena corollary to contemporary CEE mortgage markets. In the lack of in-depth research and reliable empirical data, however, one can only speculate to what extent these are negatively affecting the overall picture.

To start with, typically mortgage-loans are protected by more kinds of security devices and creditors' position enhancing devices, including the ones made in government-sponsored housing programs; though, in that case, the government's back-up in the form of joint and several liability allows the banks to disregard some of the security devices normally exploited in purely commercial lending practices. This is so irrespective that by now a relatively strong mortgage market has evolved in Hungary[42] and the other Central European countries. True, credit transactions are inevitably riskier in the region than in most of the West and it seems to a great extent justified for lenders to protect themselves by a host of extra shields on the market. The problem is that (some) banks do misuse their powerful—according to some opinions, oligopolistic—position on the still vulnerable markets of the region.[43] The problems with the lending practices of banks (and to a lesser extent other financial organizations) have, interestingly, only recently noted in the European Union and, while the phenomenon of 'unfair consumer suretyships' is now being studied,[44] the concerns with 'over-securing' remain unnoticed (though, Germany

42. The Hungarian mortgage system and market resembles according to many parameters those of Germany and Austria. This applies with equal force also to the very concrete conditions of getting housing finance. The German/Austrian "*Bauspar housing finance system*" has become also such a common feature, though Hungary has opened its doors to this system a bit later and with less enthusiasm than its northern neighbors. See, e.g., D.B. Diamond, *Comment on the Bauspar System and Proposal for Lithuania*, a paper presented at a round table discussion in Vilnius, Lithuania, July 5, 2002; available electronically at <http://www.freema.org/Events/Papers/Bauspar.phtml> last visited on September 15, 2005.

43. According to some studies the 'return on assets' is the highest exactly in Hungary because of the oligopolistic position of banks; though, the data on the performance of banks in other CEE countries is very similar. In 2004, for example, (the year for which the data are available), while the return on equity rate in Hungary was 23.39%, in the Eurozone countries that was solely 12.8595. *See* the study of Rácz István, *Development of the Financial Sector after the EU Accession (June 2006)*, available electronically at the website of the Hungarian Financial Supervisory Agency at http://www.pszaf.hu last visited on October 27, 2006.

44. *See* the research project on 'unfair suretyships' run by the Centre of European Law and Politics at the University of Bremen (ZERP) in co-operation with the University of Ox-

does have a developed law on this issue).[45] In any event, the very fact that the Hungarian Parliamentary Commissioner (Ombudsman) for Civil Rights[46] was 'forced' to specifically deal with the anomalies in the real estate mortgage market related practices of banks is the best proof that it is legitimate to refer to these practices as 'problems.'

In the context of the analyzed cases, the crucial problems have revolved around the banks' reservation of the purchase option on the mortgaged immovable in case of default. The purchase option in combination with the banks' right to have a determinative say in fixing and determining the value of the collateral both at the time of contracting and foreclosure, and hence having the right to underrate the value of the collateral two times, creates then a situation which could be easily—and seemingly legitimately—exploited by the banks to make extra profits.

As mortgages are often sold by the banks to private factoring or enforcement agencies, it is easy to see that these practices essentially *drive* creditors to foreclose rather than to renegotiate the credit and mortgage arrangements. All in all, the newly-fledged mortgage industry is in serious need of adequate consumer protection mechanisms, what most presumably cannot be provided except by way of special legislation designed specifically to deal with these kinds of problems.[47] It is highly questionable whether the EU-dictated methods of

---

ford, at http://www.zerp.uni-bremen.de. *See also,* Ciacchi, Aurelia Colombi, *Non-Legislative Harmonisation of Private Law under the European Constitution: The Case of Unfair Suretyships,* Eur. Rev. Priv. L. 3-2005 (285–308).

45. *See* the decision of the German Supreme Court NJW 1998, 671 ff, which decision has harmonized the different approaches of the chambers of the civil Senate of the Court on this question.

46. Report in the case No. OBH 4999/2003 on the Protection of the Right to Property in the Context of the Mortgage Financing Practices of some Banks (*Jelentés az OBH 4999/2003. sz. ügyben A tulajdonhoz való jog védelméről egyes bankok jelzáloghitelezési gyakorlatával kapcsolatban*) available in Hungarian language at <http//www.obh.hu>; last visited on May 25th, 2005.

47. As the Ombudsman's Report is a 35 pages long document only a snapshot could be provided here. It is indicative that in the opinion of the ombudsman virtually all the gear wheels of the system have failed to fulfill their legislative mandates in the context of these mortgage-financing practices. The list includes the Hungarian Securities and Exchange Commission ("Pszáf") responsible for the monitoring of financial institutions; the system of public notaries (that has failed to fulfill their statutory duty to check the actual intents of the contracting parties and whether their intentions are adequately enshrined into their respective contracts); the National Antitrust Agency (that has failed to analyze whether the banks have misused their dominant position when engaging into the mentioned practices). Mention has been made also of the unethical practices of some attorneys at law (e.g., purchasing the claims against former clients by having knowledge

limited reach are sufficient to adequately deal with the pathological phenomena[48] or rather the US/Canadian experiences should be also consulted.

# 3. Personal Property Security

The fall of the Berlin Wall meant also the dawn of a new era for personal property security law. While it was easy to proclaim a shift of interest toward market economy, it was far from being clear what areas of law needed to be reformed and how. The many international organizations prompting and assisting the reforms have likewise only after a few years of experimentation realized that it is the rudimentary or non-existent personal property security law that has to enjoy priority.[49] In the hindsight, it is easily visible that serious mistakes have also been made in the reform process in some of the countries, among others, because of the neglect of comparative law and blind realiance on a single model.

## *3.1. The Socialist Legacies and the Personal Property Security Law Reforms of the Transitory Period*

The content of the collateral laws of the region could have been depicted at the time of the outset of transition with a very simple formula: rudimentary variations of 'rarely used possessory pledges' plus 'hard to enforce mortgage

---

about the complete financial affairs of such debtors). *See* the respective parts of the Report, *Id.*

48. For example, the so called 'total loan charge index' ("*teljes hiteldíj mutató—abbreviated as THM*") was introduced in Hungary in 2004 with the Governmental Decree No. 324/2004 as of December 6 amending the Governmental Decree No. 41/1997 as of March 5 on the Calculation and Publication of the Index on Deposit Interests, Yield of Securities and Total Loan Charge ("*41/1997 [III.5.] Kormány rendelet a betéti kamat, az értékpapírok hozama és a teljes hiteldíj mutató számításáról és közzétételéről*") following the impetus coming from the EU. While this novelty should be wholeheartedly welcomed, it has proved to be insufficient to change the problematic patterns of doing business as of yet.

49. Perhaps it was the Round Table discussion in Budapest in 1992 under the auspices of the European Bank for Reconstruction and Development (hereinafter: EBRD), which has set the ball rolling and where it has been recognized that most countries of the region simply do not have appropriate laws on personal property security law. As a follow-up, a secured transactions project team was set up at the EBRD and the final draft of the EBRD Model Law on Secured Transactions was presented already at the 3rd Annual Meeting in St. Petersburg in 1994. The Model Law has then served to many (e.g., Hungary) of the CEE governments in reforming the local laws.

of immovables.' Needless to say, even these formally existent *in rem* security devices had survived the forty-some years of socialism amidst of a legal environment having serious problems with their enforcement. Thus, it would not be a mistake to claim that the level of development of this field of law resembled the circumstances existent in western leading economies somewhere by the end of the 19th century or the beginning of the 20th century. The fact that these systems all had a few decades of lagging behind western legal systems already during their capitalist periods was then just further exacerbated with the arrival of socialism; one of the main ideological premises of which was its hostility towards everything connected to credits, as one of the paradigm institution of capitalism.

As a consequence, meager attention was given to credits and securities in law schools and, therefore, generations of lawyers have practiced without being aware of the importance security plays and without utilizing them. Unfortunately, one may only speculate on aggregate how much of value has been lost by CEE businesses because of the failure to protect their interest by some kind of security; be it personal or real. Simply, the 'security idea' was not present in the entire region, with the exception of some rudimentary security devices, like the penalty.[50]

Then, no wonder, almost all countries of the region have begun the transition towards market economy with the reform of personal property security law. Thus, we have not only systems which are on the verge of a third wave of reforms (e.g., Hungary), but there are also others where nothing meaningful has been undertaken so far (e.g., Bosnia and Herzegovina). These extremes prove our claim that in none of the region's countries is the reform process over. Rather, one can speak only of a formal conclusion of the process. Likewise, it would be hardly proper to claim that the reforms have boosted the market in any of the region's countries at this point in time. Though, the data of some of the westernmost CEE countries do resemble those of some of the older Member States of the European Union.

---

50. While in the former Yugoslavia the insertion of penalty clauses was not mandatory (Art. 270 of the 1978 Statute on Obligations), in the other socialist systems of CEE "*[ … ] where the attention of lawyers and economists center[ed] primarily on contracts among state-owned enterprises, the penalty [was] in practice the most important remedy for breach of contract [ … ]*" and a kind of security device. *See* Schlesinger, R., Baade, H., Damaska, M. & Herzog, P., *Comparative Law* (1978) at 682.

### *3.2. The Focal Points: Retention of Title, Assignment of Intangibles, Floating Security and Efficient Enforcement*

As understandably the transplantation of *chattel mortgage* law (i.e., security interests restricted to movables as tangible collateral but not extending to intangible types of personal property) has caused the least foreseeable problems, the most thoroughgoing novelties have been introduced exactly related to this subtype of personal property security law. Another reason for such a limited reach of reforms was dictated by the fact that all the more complex financing devices relying on personal property collateral law—in particular, title financing devices, receivables financing forms and the variants of the floating security—were almost completely unknown in the region prior to the 1990s. As a result, one could safely presume that virtually all the reform countries of the region now have, at least, brand new laws on chattel mortgages.[51] However, the regulation of the exploitation of all the other personal property types that do not have such an obvious 'tangible existence' as collateral is still a headache for the drafters. In their case one could hardly be satisfied with the heretofore achievements.

In case of the use of intangibles as collateral—given that all systems seem to be or have been strongly based on the notification [of the obligor] concept—few, if any, changes have been effectuated so far. Hence, the use of receivables for security purposes remains in essence restricted to one-shot type transactions and the use of a *constant inflow of receivables* as collateral is questionable. Likewise, often it is not possible to determine whether receivables could be used "*merely*" as collateral without being sold (discounted) and thus receivables financing is still, as a rule, clothed in quite a deep mystery. No wonder that the few local fledgling factoring companies—or rather, private

51. For example, the Polish reform act's security interest is normally translated as 'registered pledge'. I.e., the Act on Registered Pledge and Register of Pledges (*Ustawa o zastawie rejestrowym i rejestrze zastawów*) of December 6, 1996, as amended. The act governs a special type of security interest, which differs from civil code pledge in particular because it is created by an agreement between parties and entry into the Register of Pledges. This might be misleading given that in English legal terminology 'pledge' is per definition restricted to 'possessory security.' It is noteworthy to bear always in mind when dealing with this field of law that inconsistent use of terminology is an omnipresent problem seriously undermining communication. Actually, every discussion about security laws with CEE lawyers should start with clarifying the terminology. Moreover, it is fair to claim that in addition to the American/Canadian secured transactions law vocabulary and their distinct, yet substantially differing, English counterpart, a third English language idiosyncratic collateral law terminology is also distinguishable. The third variant is used by civilian lawyers communicating in English.

enforcement companies that engage also into the purchase of receivables—have hard times finding their way of prospering on the local markets. Yet their very existence, where they do exist, is the best proof that the security law reform has been successfully set into motion.

Likewise, without a credit-friendly receivables financing ambient it is hard, if not impossible, to create an efficient legal environment for floating securities; especially given that hardly has any of the CEE systems known of this kind of security device up until the reforms of our times.[52] As additionally this device is extremely complex, it is far from being easy to conceive appropriate rules. As it is most visible in case of such complex security devices that the token of successful reforms is a mind-shift not just on the side of the drafters but—more importantly—on the side of the addressees of the new law, a more detailed drafting language is needed. Though, admittedly to drafters to whom only dogmatic considerations deserve merit, such a shift would not only be foreign but also unacceptable.

Besides the obvious fact that the floating security's complexity and inexperience with it *per se* are prohibitive, the banks being active in the region pursue quite conservative business policies and refrain from taking the lead in applying such novelties. As all the CEE countries are bank-based systems—dominated by universal banks—and thus virtually all segments of the economy having a connection with finances is heavily controlled by banks, this is an important disincentive on the domestication of the floating security.[53]

---

52. As it is widely known it is still not possible to create a floating lien on the entirety of an enterprise' assets under German law and thus simply there is not German counterpart for the US floating lien or for the English 'floating plus fixed charge'. *See, e.g., Wenckstern, von Manfred, Die englische Floating Charge im deutschen Internationalen Privatrecht,56 Rabels Zeitschrift für auslandisches und internationales Privatrecht, 624 (1992); Bütter, Michael, English Fixed and Floating Charges in German Insolvency Proceedings: Unsolved Problems under the New European Regulation on Insolvency Proceedings,* 2002 Sing. J. Legal Stud., 271 (2002). *But see Hausmann, Jensen, The Value of Public-Notice Filing under UCC Article 9: A Comparison with the German Legal System of Securities in Personal Property,* 25 GA.J.INT'L & COMP. L. 427, 476 (1996).

The lack of this particular device from German law—the model followed by many of the CEE countries—could be partly ascribed that most of the CEE systems had not known for this security device either up to the outset of the reforms in the 1990s. It is interesting, though, that CEE systems that had more closely relied on French law—which knows for such a comprehensive collateral ("*nantissements des fonds de commerce*")—have likewise failed to borrow. Though, exceptions exist as, for example, Poland had passed an Act on Registered Pledge on Machines and Devices in 1939, what seems to be a rightful predecessor of the floating charge.

53. Interestingly enough, for example, Hungarian banks are quite venturous in applying some other common law-inspired, newcomer devices, like the negative pledge and *pari*

Perhaps the most important reason for the very cautious acceptance of this device lies with the fact that there is no experience with monitoring the business of debtors by creditors for the sake of acting promptly whenever needed to protect the creditor's interests. If this inexperience is added to the lack of private enforcement and the many problems with court enforcement, one could easily comprehend the cautiousness of the otherwise powerful banking sector.[54]

Retention of title (hereinafter: ROT) as a distinct type of security has proved to be yet another hurdle. This is another instance where the CEE reformers seem to be torn between the German (ROT as a full title or ownership) and American treatment (ROT being 'degraded' from title to the status of a 'mere' security interest') of this device.[55] It is, however, a matter of fact that these financing devices have remained almost invariably outside of the new collateral laws, with the notable exception of Romania, which introduced a system for security interests on motor vehicles to a great extent resembling French and American patterns. The dilemma what to do with these financial transactions might look of lesser importance. Moreover, the inattentive observer might easily vouch for leaving the resolution of the destiny of title financing devices for some happier future times wouldn't it be for the geometrically growing 'leasing' and relative industries in the region. At the moment, the subjection of

*passu* covenants. Banks exploit these without being absolutely sure whether courts would recognize them in case of disputes.

54. Understandably banks of the region are reluctant to admit and make public information about mass-scale problems and therefore it is very hard to detect exactly on what point(s) is the applicable law and legal system deficient. Some data have, however, become public. In Hungary, for example, the mid-1990s saw an avalanche of debtor-defaults. This forced banks to shift from the earlier, relatively liberal crediting policies, to a much conservative stance. As a result today it is still not easy to get credit from banks, neither by the citizenry nor by business entities. Additionally the price and the security requirements have become quite burdensome.

55. UCC Article 9 was criticized even by its ardent supporters because of the 'reconceptualization' needed to fit the title financing transactions into the system. As Cuming put it "*[t]here are two features of the U.C.C. Article 9 approach that appear to be troublesome even to those who are attracted to it. The first is the total reconceptualization that it requires in the context of types of transactions that traditionally are not viewed as secured financing devices and [ ... ] secondly, [ ... ] the bifurcated approach to the characterization of certain types of transaction. Since a title retention sales contract or a lease falls within a secured financing regime because it functions as a security device, it follows that the seller or lessor is not the owner of the goods sold or leased [ ... ].*" See Cuming, Ronald, Internationalization of Secured Financing Law, *in:* Cranston, Ross (ed.), Making Commercial Law: Essays in Honour of Roy Goode (Oxford University Press, 1999), at 522–23.

motor vehicle leasing transactions[56] (containing ROT clauses and performing security functions) to a local version of 'certificate of title-registration' by Romania following the system known in U.S. seems to be the better, yet more expensive, solution than the complete failure to regulate this area, which is a "model" applied by most other CEE jurisdictions.

Finally, a word needs to be cast on enforcement related problems. Namely, very soon after 1990 two things had to be realized virtually everywhere in the region. *First,* the often only formally existent bailiff or court enforcement system inherited from the socialist period is incapable of ensuring efficient enforcement of security interests, especially those being constituted on personal property. This state of affairs had not changed much even after the introduction of the collateral reform laws as the reforms were not necessarily paralleled with the upgrading of the enforcement laws. *Secondly,* private enforcement agencies have appeared in reality—many of them duly registered with company registries—and a private enforcement industry has begun to grow very soon after the turn towards market economy. Moreover, these agencies have over time begun to offer also the service of private repossession of collateral, what in and of itself should not be a reason for worry in a legal system where the myriad mechanisms of the rule of law would adequately monitor these novel enterprises. However, in the fledgling and unstable milieu of the CEE countries these businesses have been inclined to deviate gradually towards organized crime. Thus, at the present day the new enforcement services are now being

---

56. The fate of 'leasing' and retention of title (ROT) in the region is as important as the fact that 'leasing' or its variants were the main legal mechanisms used by the booming CEE motor vehicles markets during the last fifteen years. Especially in those jurisdictions where 'leasing' and ROT has not become subject of special regulation, lessors are often forced to make use of the formally not regulated emerging private enforcement industry to adequately protect their interests from a sizeable number of defaulting lessees.

In Hungary at the moment the work on a new civil code is well under way and besides the 'recognition' of leasing (transformation of the 'leasing' from an innominate to a nominate contract by inclusion into the code) the treatment of ROT is also debated. Most indicia seem to show that the pendulum has swung in the direction of not subjecting leasing or ROT to registration and rather the German non-public ROT system will be enshrined eventually into the code. In the light of the serious problems that are due to the deficiencies of the applicable law and enforcement system it is highly questionable whether this is the right solution. Unfortunately, the exact data on the number of leasing-related defaults is publicly not available in Hungary, yet the media are constantly reporting on the problems.

As a crucial result in Hungary today ROT is not sufficient to secure the risks of lessors and (one or more) additional security devices are asked as a rule (e.g., immovables as collateral, deposit of governmental securities, joint and several liability, bank guarantees).

provided in the twilight zone between legality and illegality, as self-help repossession is nowhere in the region given explicitly green light, albeit admittedly a detailed regulation of private enforcement would be the perfect solution.

There is no doubt, however, that numerous positive changes have also been implemented in some of the countries of the region. For example, in Hungary, besides the introduction of the category of private bailiffs, the new security laws have embraced—with the exception of self-help repossession—some other 'non-violent' forms of self-help. Thus, it would be improper to say that things have not changed for the better at all. The problem is rather that the system, together with the novelties in aggregate, still fails to protect the interests of the secured creditors appropriately and efficiently (i.e., if necessary, even promptly and *ex parte*). As a result resort to private enforcement agencies is something known by many but hardly, if ever, publicly debated. Moreover, the blindness of the legislator and the myriad of deficiencies of the court enforcement systems have, indeed, been the main reasons behind the appearance of organized crime in this domain.[57] On the other hand, the emergence and gradual growth of collection agencies (i.e., agencies not specialized solely to self-help repossession but rather providing other collection-related services) has become a fact in the last few years; though, considerable variations from country to country do exist.[58]

---

57. Unfortunately, the issue of private enforcement has remained outside of the reformers' purview in Hungary. Or, more precisely, *private repossession* as such has been completely left out from the reform of personal property law, inevitably pushing this 'business' into the hands of mushrooming private claim-enforcement organizations the legality of the activity of which is, in case of many, absolutely questionable—to say the least—in the light of the lack of a regulatory framework addressing exactly this set of problems. The situation is no better in the other countries of the region.

The prevailing concern and explanation behind such a neglect of the problem is partly the lack of pertaining information (in particular, the experiences of common law systems with self-help) partly the hesitation to depart from Central European traditions, but most importantly, because there is a fear that the outright introduction of self-help repossession might cause more harm than benefit. In any event, the findings of F. Modigliano and E.C. Perotti in *Security versus Bank Finance: the Importance of a Proper Enforcement of Legal Rules* (February 2, 2000/available electronically at http://www.SSRN.org) that "in an unreliable enforcement regime, transactions tend to be intermediated through institutions or concentrated among agents bound by some form of private enforcement [ … ]" seem to have been materialized in the region. It is a fundamental mistake attributable to all shaping the contours of laws in CEE—from scholars through legislators—that this particular question has not been given proper attention and hence obscurity persists.

58. Based on the available information, for example, no such agency has emerged in Albania until 2008. As opposed to that the international *Intrum Iustitia* agency has become

### 3.3. *Persisting Problems and the Partial Success of the Reforms*

It is important to underline that besides the above, other factors have contributed to the partial success of the security law reforms. One may legitimately object to this claim by pointing to those other areas of law, which have also been subject to fundamental changes and which have proved to be equally incapable to achieve much more in such a short period of time, in case of security laws this argument is unacceptable as in this domain the primary motivation behind the reforms was exactly the boosting of the local credit markets.[59] The planned or ongoing second or occasionally third waves of reforms in many of the region's countries nowadays are just one of the appropriate proofs of the correctness of this view. In case of Hungary, it is relieving to see that the mistakes made during the formulation of the first and second amendments of this area of law have been admitted, at least, by a narrower circle of reformers, who are now behind the third planned wave of reform.[60] Based on the already circulated *traveaux preparatoire*, the central aim is to

---

welknown in many other CEE countries. For the list of countries *see* <http://www.intrumjustitia.com>; last visited on October 16th, 2008.

59. It is part of the story that in many of the CEE countries the introduction of personal property security laws was undertaken simply to comply with the firm dictates of international banks conditioning financing of local governments or major project with the passing of these laws. Thus, some of the countries did not really do anything else but have enacted laws not wanting to go any further but to formally satisfy the demands of the foreign banks. In other words, the mere existence of a black-letter security law should not be determinative and a shrewd businessmen/investor should pay equal attention to the other formants of law. It is also indicative that in many parts of CEE it is essentially "expected" from local scholars to talk about the newly enacted security laws only in an uncritical manner.

60. *See* I. Gárdos, *A zálogjog felülvizsgálata a polgári kodifikáció keretében (vitaanyag)* [The Revision of Security Law within the Civil Law Codification Process—Material for Discussion] (2005). This problem was appropriately described by Mistelis, who has correctly noted that "*[r]egrettably [ ... ] many emerging states have occasionally experiences the services of opinionated and expensive foreign experts who attempted to export their legal system or their understanding of it without any concerns as to its compatibility with the system of the host country. Incidents of competition between foreign experts from different countries [ ... ] due to lack of international or local coordination [often resulted] in confusion of the host country experts [ ... ]. [As a result of that and in addition] lack of knowledge, or academic arrogance, voices against reform were strengthened [ ... ].*" *See* Mistelis, Loukas, A., *Regulatory Aspects: Globalization, Harmonization. Legal Transplants, and Law Reform: Some Fundamental Observations,* 34 INT'L LAW. 1055, 1064 (1999).

transplant much more from UCC Article 9 and, thus, the pivotal questions revolve around the problems that were raised in this chapter as well. However, due to the political and economic problems the entire project has been brought to stop.

To start with, the registration system is the building block of the new security regime that also suffers from some deficiencies. It has been noted recently that "*[i]f [registries are] not carefully designed and efficiently run, the whole framework for security over movables can be incapacitated.*"[61] In Hungary, numerous legal and technical dilemmas continue to arise related to the operation of the registry for movables—the effectuation of entries into which is entrusted to public notaries—albeit eight years have passed since the creation of the registry itself. That is, the physical erection, maintenance and the operation of registries is only seemingly an easy task.

It is a distinguishing feature of the region that significantly differing sets of problems subsist with respect to real as opposed to personal property security systems. Thus, while the lack of knowledge by local judges is omnipresent and it is of relevance in both contexts, clearly the brand new personal property security law causes bigger problems. Not necessarily only to judges but essentially to all the other addressees. That added up with the extraordinary pace and growing sophistication of changes in many other branches of law—let alone the challenges brought about with the need to apply the *acquis communautaire* in the new accessory countries—and one can easily see how serious impediment the lack of expertise is with respect to the domestication of the new laws.[62] The introversion, conservatism and inability to adequately follow the new developments of many of the CEE law schools just further aggravate the problems.

It was also a mistake to think that the personal property security law reforms could be finalized through a one-shot type reform effort. That could be partly explained by the pitfalls inherent to modern political systems: every government is keen to support primarily projects the beginning and completion of which do not last more than (in case of Hungary) four years, or even less, due to the instability of governments in many of the countries of the re-

61. *See* F. Dahan & J. Simpson, *Publicity of Security Rights: Setting Standards for Charges Registries, Law in Transition* (EBRD publication, 2005), at 26.

62. In a recent EBRD survey the following problems persist with respect to the judicial capacity of the commercial law sector: (1) lack of technical skills, esp. of the judges trained under the old regime; (2) scarce financial resources; (3) interference of the executive power; (4) unethical practices (esp. corruption); and (5) low prestige of judges in the society. See M. Nussbaumer, *Building Judicial Capacity in the Commercial Law Sector of Early Transition Countries, Law in Transition* (EBRD publication, 2005) at 39.

gion. Overambitiousness, system thinking, academic stubbornness, a degree of anti-Americanism[63] or lack of interest for doing anything more than passing a blackletter law to formally satisfy western expectations, on the side of the drafters and promoters of the reforms, have all contributed to some extent to the partial successfulness of the efforts. Though, the last few years have clearly proved also that the faith of purely private and commercial law projects may be equally doomed to failure because of the economic and democratic deficiencies of the CEE countries.[64]

The western advisors assisting the secured transactions reforms in CEE have also departed from the position that these systems could be efficiently reformed during a few years. At least, this is what one must conclude from the fact that none of the western reform-driving institutions has promulgated a program or project lasting more than a few years. Admittedly albeit each of these institutions has designed some kind of loose monitoring post-reform program, none of them has vouched initially for a more-stage reform process.[65]

---

63. In the hindsight, it seems to be also a mistake that the western promoters of personal property security laws have all brought with themselves only the models of their own countries, what essentially meant English, German and U.S. laws. True, with some delay the Canadians have also appeared on the 'personal property law market' (e.g., Ukraine). Still, the experiences of such mixed markets as Scotland or South Africa have been largely left out, albeit the CEE jurisdictions could have learned much exactly from these on the transplantation and subsequent reconciliation of common law and civilian law elements. See, e.g., G.L. Gretton, *Reception without Integration? Tulane Law Review* 78 (2003) 307; C.G. van der Merwe, *Interpenetration of Common Law and Civil Law as Experiences in the South African and Scottish Law of Property, Tulane Law Review* 78 (2003) 257.

64. As Osiatynski's noted "*[t]he possibility of simultaneous triple transition was first questioned by Jon Elster at the conference in Pecs, Hungary, in 1990. The essence of his argument was, that since the high costs of economic transition would be distributed unequally, the majority, which in the short run would be worse off, would use its newly won democratic powers to stop reforms.*" *See* Osiatynski, Wiktor, The Constitutional Honeymoon is Over. The Paradoxes of Post-Communist Constitution Making, *in:* Dahrendorf, Lord; Elkana, Yehuda; Aryeh, Neier, Newton-Smith, William & Rev, Istvan, the Paradoxes of Unintended Consequences, (CEU Press1999), at 143–44.

65. Even if not admitted, the matter of fact is that the reform process is, indeed, made of more segments. For example, the creation and operation of the registries of movables seems to be a sufficiently distinct set of problems from the drafting and enactment of the new security laws. This could be concluded also from the analyses made by EBRD—being at the forefront of the reform movement in CEE in the 1990s—which in the new Millennium is primarily focusing on the analysis of the available data and assisting of the still non-reformed jurisdictions. Thus, EBRD has only in 2004 developed a set of guiding principles for the efficient and effective development of charge registries, albeit its Model Law on Secured Transactions was published already in 1994. *See, e.g.*, F. Dahan & J. Simpson,

One of the most fundamental misunderstandings was the failure to recognize that our present knowledge base is deficient and incomplete on many points and, consequently, these prevent the comprehension of what is exactly behind a well-functioning security system. The easterners with their 'possessory pledge plus mortgage of immovables' simplified and extremely limited mind setting actually cannot be blamed for this. Their primary understanding was that the new system is nothing else but a somewhat-enriched pledge law together with subjection of pledges to registration and, therefore, that these are those elements that make the system work efficiently in common laws. Needless to say, one of the crucial misunderstandings lies exactly in this fact: Article 9 and its relatives are extremely well performing among others because they have managed to bring under the penumbras of the system an unprecedentedly varied number of transactions.[66] In the CEE countries, many of these fields remain scattered and subject to differing laws. The additional economic value produced by the synergy of the individual security devices brought under the same roof hardly if ever arises in jurisdictions with fragmented security laws. *To wit*, where assignment law (i.e., laws allowing for use of receivables as collateral) are obsolete and obscure—what is the case in virtually all CEE countries—a floating security device cannot work appropriately either as they presuppose each other.[67]

---

*Publicity of Security Rights: Setting Standards for Charges Registries, Law in Transition* (publication of the EBRD) 17. Serbia has, for example, enacted its 'Act on Registered Charges Constituted on Movables' already in 2003 (*Zakon o založnom pravu na pokretnim stvarima upisanim u registar*, Official Gazette No. 57/2003), yet the registry has begun with almost a two-years delay.

66. As the official comment to section 9-101 of the pre-Revised Version of UCC Article 9 provides "*[t]he aim of [the] Article is to provide a simple and unified structure within which the immense variety of present-day secured financing transactions can go forward with less cost and with greater certainty*." The impressive list of security devices that had long been known prior to the completion of UCC—each essentially serving also as a basis for self-standing industries—is in no other country so varied as it encompasses "*pledge, assignment, chattel mortgage, chattel trust, trust deed, factor's lien, equipment trust, conditional sale, trust receipt, other lien or title retention contract and lease or consignment intended as security*." (*See* s. 9-102 (2) of the pre-Revised Version of UCC Article 9). In other words, as it has been proven in the common law provinces of Canada by now, the mere systemic approach, i.e., "*unified conceptual and legislative structure [ ... ] permitted the flexibility, [ ... ] dramatic [ ... ] simplification of the law [and] the use of computer technology in a new, single registry system for all security devices*." Cuming, C.C. Ronald, Article 9 North of 49º: The Canadian PPS Acts and the Quebec Civil Code, 29 Loyola L.A. L. Rev. 971, 972 (1996).

67. The contest of developed security systems in our globalized world is given and emerging market should note that. For example, they may want to learn from the experi-

On the other hand, a typical CEE reform system limited to a simple chattel mortgage and a simple form floating security can produce no more than a meager portion of the additional economic value generated by a comprehensive system. In addition, in skeleton systems "synthetic" financing schemes (like securitization or mezzanine financing) cannot be employed simply because of the deficiencies of the legal system.[68] Similarly, without the coverage of all functionally equivalent transactions, there would be all the time an incentive to resort to that transaction that would be left out from under the system. One of the fallacies of the 'retention of title' and 'leasing' puzzle—posing one of the biggest challenges to the CEE reformers—lies exactly in this fact.

Little importance has been given also to the fact that Article 9 is *industry based*. The strong industrial underpinning of Article 9 as the ultimate model is crucial because of the following main reasons. In locating the reasons we have to resort to pre-UCC American legal history from where at least two important things could be learned.

*First,* Article 9 is actually similar to a carefully put together mosaic where each of the constituent-stones is based on a more or less differing subset of rules. Without a pretension of completeness, hence, we could identify a number of distinct security devices—each with its own distinct subset of legal rules—from possessory pledge, through chattel mortgage ending with assignment of receivables. Each of these devices had prior to being enlisted under Article 9 been a peculiar and normally distinct legal institution. The *other* essential lesson to be learned from legal history is that virtually each of the se-

---

ences of Singapore, one of the economically most successful systems of the late 20th century, which has also found it important to revamp its collateral law. In the rivalry of the English and the UCC Article 9 models it seems that the latter has prevailed there irrespective that "*Singapore has a body of British precedents that, over the years, have fostered economic activity. [I]t has, however, come under criticism for being fragmented and conceptually incoherent [ … ]. Article 9 of the U.S. Commercial Code, on the other hand, is [ … ] arguably more responsive to commercial needs [ … ].*" *See* McCormack, Gerard, Reforming the Law of Security Interests: National and International Perspectives, 2003 Sing. J. Legal Stud. 1, 2, (2003).

68. Suffice to point to one such complex financial method to prove the point made. As Bazinas put it related to receivables financing "*[m]obilizing receivables for financing purposes is inevitable since receivables are often the main or the only asset a company may have at its disposal. In addition, future receivables, the future cash flow of a business, often provide the most inexpensive basis for financing. In view of this reality, any difficulties in transferring receivables may negatively impact the availability and cost of credit, [and] the ability of a company to compete in the global marketplace [ … ].*" *See* Bazinas, Spiros, Lowering the Cost of Credit: The Promise in the Future UNCITRAL Convention on Assignment of Receivables in International Trade, 9 Tulane J. Int'l & Comp. L. 259, 261 (2001).

curity devices rests on a peculiar 'industry,' which had been in existence for decades; some of them even for a century or more. Suffice it to mention the thousands of pawnshops, or hundreds of 'leasing' and 'factoring' companies. In other words, by the time when the drafting of Article 9 had begun, these industries were already made of mature businesses with their more or less unique patterns of doing business (i.e., the "know how"). For one thing, Gilmore and his companions could have readily relied on the business practices and experiences of these in formulating the rules of Article 9. More importantly, however, these industries have at that time been made of mature and not fledgling enterprises. To them Article 9 meant a significant improvement of the earlier legal framework that had been often plagued with unnecessary gaps and inconsistencies. In other words, they were absolutely prepared and mature enough to readily apply the new system because of their long business past and gained expertise.

As opposed to that in CEE these industries were—and many of them are still—non-existent; or are in the process of development.[69] Actually, the newly introduced laws were expected to set the ball rolling. They were thought of as being capable to form a basis for a number of new industries. Unfortunately, all the potential implications of the 'industrial-foundations' of personal property security law have been only indirectly reckoned with, if at all. Thus, taking Hungary again as example, while a nationwide functioning pawnshop system has re-emerged very soon after 1990, the first factoring company attempting to thrive solely from factoring of receivables has appeared only at the beginning of the Millennium.[70] More precisely, the completely neglected fact is that the provisions of Article 9 are directly based on the business prac-

69. Hungary may serve as an appropriate example on the point, where pawnshops have a history going back at least to the 19th century, as opposed to the first quasi-factoring companies that had emerged solely around the end of the 1990s. Consequently, now in Hungary there is an economically relatively strong company the most profitable activity of which is, indeed, pledge-based crediting with a nationwide system of pawnshops. (*See* the website of the company at http://www.bav.hu). On the other hand, albeit more than hundred entities have a permission from the local Financial Supervisory Authority ("*Pszáf*") to get engaged in factoring, most of the entities actually making use of receivables on a larger scale are primarily enforcement agencies rather than 'pure' factoring companies. The situation is similar in all the CEE countries. *See* the website of the Hungarian Factoring Association at http://www.faktoringszovetseg.hu.

70. The 'inauguration' of factoring in Hungary was paralleled by the publication of the —also inaugural—monograph by K. Martinkó, *Faktoring—A vállalatfinanszírozás hamupipőkéje* [Factoring—the Cinderella of Business Financing] (Saldo Rt, Budapest, 2002).

tices of distinct mature industries, something that has not been and it is to a large extent still non-existent in the region's countries.[71]

In other words, the ingeniousness of the drafters and the system of Article 9 superbly connecting all the constituent industries are only partially responsible for the success story of secured transactions law in America.[72] One cannot disregard that the system functions so well—among others—because the industries that profit from this peculiar legal framework had existed together with their sophisticated, professionalized and expert patterns of doing business already prior to the enactment of UCC.[73] This 'unwritten part' of Article 9—I am tempted to identify it as a distinct formant of law—is what has been largely bypassed in the reform process in CEE.[74] Had this fact been fully understood, most presumably somebody would have definitively proposed a more-stage lasting reform process in which the more sophisticated areas (e.g., receivables financing) of personal property security law would have been postponed to later stages of the process.[75]

---

71. Gilmore described this facet of the UCC Article 9 the following way. "*[ ... ] Only professionals could accomplish the tricky rituals of field-warehousing or comply with the rule of Benedict or cope with the almost incomprehensible metaphysics of trust receipt financing. Widows, orphans and country bankers would be well advised to stay away from such mysteries.*" *See* Gilmore, Grant, Security Law, Formalism and Article 9, 47 Nebr. L. Rev. 659, 665 (1968).

72. Naturally, we should not forget that much of UCC Article 9 has been transplanted also by the Canadian common law provinces and this Article influenced also the reforms in New Zealand which Australia is about to follow. It would have been interesting to see to what extent and in respect of what have the existence or non-existence of local industries influenced the formulation of the pertaining sections of security laws in these recipient countries.

73. To make another example: private enforcement of secured creditors' rights functions well in the U.S. not just because of the qualities of Article 9 but because there has been a professionalized business of private enforcement for many decades.

74. Many things guaranteeing the efficient functioning of UCC Article 9 could be comprehended solely by taking a look at Gilmore's two volume work *Security Interests in Personal Property* (1965) describing not just the preparatory and drafting process of the Article, but also the pre-UCC history of American personal property security law. It is indicative that in CEE hardly if any author has referred to this work in the otherwise very limited number of publications related to collateral laws.

75. This claim requires some qualification. Namely, admittedly some level of concern was definitively felt by local experts, some of whom has correctly concluded that it was too early to introduce right at the beginning of the reform most of the more sophisticated industry-related rules (e.g., receivables financing in Hungary). However, this was primarily because of a 'natural fear from the unknown and extremely sophisticated' rather than because of a deliberate choice. In other words, all the other formants of law have been neglected but the black-letter law of the models relied on.

Likewise, it is worthwhile to mention here that the role of the various purely contractual devices that allow the secured creditor to monitor the debtor's affairs and the handling of the collateral—and to react promptly if needed to protect its security interest—has been also left out from sight in the reform processes. This could be ascribed to the fact that the models relied on normally also fail to deal with these devices (in common laws often known as 'covenants', like the negative-pledge covenant) for a simple reason: these devices do not create security interests but are only personal security devices.

## 4. In Lieu of Conclusions: Some Speculations on the Future Course of Events

One has a feeling that after the first waves of reforms the collateral systems of CEE countries resemble more the problems and dilemmas that have arisen in the context of some western civilian systems[76] and a radical shift towards security law of leading common law systems is a story for some future times. As in other fields of law and as an unwritten rule, these systems are still more willing to follow the lead of the leading civilian legal systems.[77] Thus, the fate of security laws in this niche of the world depends to a great extent also on the attitude western civilian systems will take in this respect.

As one could see from the preceding cursory exposition, significant changes have occurred in the context of both real and personal property security roughly since 1990 in most of the CEE countries.[78] Interestingly enough, how-

76. For an insightful discussion of the dilemmas that have emerged related to Italian collateral law *see* Bussani, Mauro, *Le présent et l'avenir des sûretés réelles, in Italian National Reports to the XVIth International Congress of Comparative Law*, Brisbane 2002 (Giuffrè Editore, Milano, 2002) 245. For example, it seems that all the CEE systems have faced the identical initial problem, which was that the inherited code provisions on real estate mortgages were absolutely inappropriate for developing a business-friendly system of non-possessory security devices on personal property. This seems to have been the case also in Italy.

77. Though, CEE countries should be also aware of the fundamental differences that exist exactly in the context of personal property security law between the leading legal systems of the world, the concrete consequences of what may be detrimental to businessmen. The best illustration of this threat is the *Hong Kong and Shanghai Banking Corp., Ltd. v. HFH USA Corporation* [805 F.Supp. 133, 19 UCC Rep. Serv.2d 885], the potential repercussions of which for emerging markets and in the context of international commercial arbitration *see* Tajti, Tibor, Secured Transactions under Article 9 of the Uniform Commercial Code: A Role for International Arbitration?, Journal of Int'l Arb. 20(2), 131–151 (2003).

78. On a very practical level, for example, quite a lot has been achieved with respect to the launching of new housing financing systems. Still, it remains true that "[d]espite the

ever, this period was primarily devoted to the traditionally less venerable of the twin brothers: to creating of brand new systems allowing for ready use of personalties as collateral. Some believed naively that this process could be finalized in a matter of a few years. However, by now it has become crystal clear that decades of painstaking work and learning from mistakes will be needed to achieve that end.[79] Consequently, the upcoming years should be expected to see the tackling of those black spots on the European map that have so far escaped the winds of change.[80]

On the other hand, almost completely detached from the developments in the sphere of personal property security law, we are witnessing the unfolding of a region-wide movement aiming at the modernization of property laws and especially real property security laws. Still, the heat of the realties mortgage law reforms is about to come, partly due to the changes caused by the newly introduced personal property security systems, and partly because of the con-

---

major progress in recent years, the housing finance systems of the accession countries [let alone the other countries of CEE that are still waiting at the gates of the EU] remain small, heavily subsidized and relatively inefficient." *See* M. Lea, *Housing Finance in the Accession Countries, Mortgage Finance Gazette* (April 2004) 36.

79. In April 2004—on the eve of the official accession to the EU—quite optimistic predictions thought that the "*[e]ntry to the European Union [would] likely to be quite beneficial for these countries as the combination of fiscal discipline, lower interest rates and increased competition become evident.*" In the hindsight, these predictions do not seem to have become fully true. It could be that simply too little time has passed since May 1, 2004; during that period of time nothing meaningful could have been changed. Though, it is more realistic to claim that the overall housing and mortgage market is such a distinct world of its own in which in-depth changes cannot occur solely due to the indirect, yet beneficial impacts coming from the EU.

This is so to a great extent because the EU has produced very little in these domains so far; in a sense the incapability of the EU even to minimally harmonize collateral laws is the best proof of the fundamental differences existing among the laws of the Member States. Essentially only the efforts related financial collateral are the ones that could be listed as [partial] success. In Estonia, for example, the Directive 2002/47/EC of the European Parliament and Council on Financial Collateral Arrangements (OJ L 1168, 27.06.2002, p. 43-50) was implemented by the Act to Amend the Law of Property Act, the Estonian Central Register of Securities Act, the Credit Institutions Act, the Insurance Activities Act, the Bankruptcy Act, the Law of Obligations Act, the Private International Law Act and the Securities Market Act. The English text of the act is available electronically at <http://www.legaltext.ee/text/en/X80030.htm>; last visited on October 22, 2008.

80. A hopefully realistic herald of the future is the recent *Green Paper* of the EU Commission on *Mortgage Credit in the EU* (as of 17.6.2005) 3, which realizes that "*[a] more efficient and competitive mortgage credit market that could result through greater integration could contribute to the growth of the EU economy.*"

stant growth of domestic and especially cross-border securitizations; remains to be seen to what extent and in what form will the 2008 credit crunch affect all that. In the modest estimate of the author of this chapter, except for the increased regulatory powers of the state and a much higher level of governmental control of the banking sector coupled with measures aimed at curbing taking excessive risks in the world of finances, little will change as far as collateral law is concerned. Businesses will need credit in the future as well and the citizenry's housing problems will continue to be burning problems; the resolution of what will hardly be imaginable without resort to real and personal property security laws. It would be mistaken to believe that the cyclical nature of the economy and especially of the capital markets coupled with the continuously increasing interlinking of modern economies will not cause newer problems in the future; the question is rather when and in what form and not whether a crisis-proof model can be invented. Unfortunately, one cannot but agree with those views,[81] which warn about the myriad political, economic and social problems that may destabilize the financial markets [for the umpteenth time] in the years to come, seeing perhaps once again—as it seems to have occurred during the 2008 credit crunch—in credits and collateral law the scapegoats.

It could be also predicted that the clarification and resolution of the dilemmas related to the connecting points of the realty and personalty securities is another task awaiting international scholarship. At any event, the seemingly narrow underworld of security (collateral) law will predictably remain an important and challenging item on the agenda of private and comparative lawyers for many years to come;[82] though, from now on in closer cooperation with

81. *See, e.g.*, Mattei, Ugo & Nader, Laura, Plunder—When the Rule of Law is Illegal (Blackwell, 2008), who succinctly point to the essence of the problem when stating that "[ … ] *the problem is not with the creation of rules on paper but with patterns of enforcement. Today, in the USA, the Securities and Exchange Commission…, as for all administrative agencies in times of neo-liberalism, is still underfunded and understaffed, so it is unrealistic to think that it can handle the tremendous workload of a monitoring and control agency in a complex market. [ … ].*" *Id.*, at 175.

82. Let us mention two examples to corroborate the above claim that the reform of secured transactions law is a process. Poland has, for example, passed the Amendment of the Registered Pledge and Register of Pledges Act and Amendment of other Statutes ("*Ustawa o zmianie ustawy o zastawie rejestrowym i rejestrze zastawów oraz o zmienic innych ustaw*") on September 5th, 2008, published in Journal of Laws 2008, No. 180, item 1113 (as the vacatio legis is three months, the amendment will enter into effect on 11 January 2009). On the other hand, the World Bank has likewise quite recently released a related major publication—what in and of itself is telling about the importance and the nature of se-

scholars in the cognate disciplines of economics, political sciences and sociology.[83] In fact, while at the outset of the reforms and harmonization efforts in the 1990s nobody really thought that these efforts will affect more than collateral law, now it should be clear that the launched projects are leading to a new era where the very basics of property law come into the focus; let alone the connecting points to the world of capital markets, finances and banking, as well as the impact of the fact that credits and securities are part of these economy segments.[84]

## References

András, Jakab, Péter Takács and Allan F. Tatham, the Transformation of the Hungarian Legal Order 1985–2005 (Kluwer Law International, 2007).

Batalov, S. Lev, *The Russian Title Registration System for Realty and its Effect on Foreign Investors, Washburn Law Journal* 73 (1998) 989.

Bazinas, Spiros, Lowering the Cost of Credit: The Promise in the Future UNCITRAL Convention on Assignment of Receivables in International Trade, 9 Tulene J. Int'l & Comp. L. 259, 261 (2001).

Bodzási, Balázs, *Néhány szó a keretbiztosítéki vagyont terhelő jelzálogjogról* [Few Words about the Property Encumbering Charge Securing a Revolving Credit], *in:* Themis (the Electronic Journal of the ELTE Law School, Budapest), 2004 December issue.

Burke, Donovan, *Argument for the Allocation of Resources to the Development of a Well-Defined System of Real Property Law in the Czech Republic,* Vanderbilt Journal of Transnational Law 29 (1996) 661.

---

cured transactions law and its reform—; *to wit,* Fleisig, Heywood, Safavian, Mehnaz & Nuria de la Peňa, Reforming Collateral Laws to Expand Access to Finance (World Bank publication, 2006).

83. The reform of secured transactions law has already become an important item on the agenda of contemporary political scientists. *See generally* Edward S. Cohen, *The Diffusion of Legal Models for Financial Governance: The Case of Secured Finance,* a paper presented at the 3rd Conference of the European Consortium of Political Research, Budapest, Hungary, 8 September, 2005.

84. Harmathy has reached a similar conclusion, though departing from a different starting point: the implications of the great divide between the civilian concept of unitary ownership versus the common law concept of divided ownership. *See* A. Harmathy, *Dologi jog —Kötelmi jog* [Property Law—Law of Obligations] in *Liber Amicorum Lajos Vékás Dedicata* (published by the ELTE Law School, Budapest, 1999), at 119.

Bussani, M., *Le présent et l'avenir des sûretés réelles,* in *Italian National Reports to the XVIth International Congress of Comparative Law,* Brisbane 2002 (Giuffrè Editore, Milano, 2002) 245.

Cohen, Edward S., *The Diffusion of Legal Models for Financial Governance: The Case of Secured Finance,* paper presented at the 3rd Conference of the European Consortium of Political Research, Budapest, Hungary, 8 September, 2005.

Commission of the European Communities, *Green Paper—Mortgage Credit in the European Union* (Brussels, 17.6.2005).

Csiby, A., Chapter on Hungary in Kälin, H. Christian, *International Real Estate Handbook* (John Wiley & Sons, UK, 2005) 311.

Cuming, Ronald, Internationalization of Secured Financing Law, *in:* Cranston, Ross (ed.), Making Commercial Law: Essays in Honour of Roy Goode (Oxford University Press, 1999), at 522–23.

Cvetič, R., *Evidencija nepokretnosti* [Registry of Immovables], *in:* Collected Papers of the Novi Sad Faculty of Law, No. XXXVIII—3/2004 (in Serbian).

Dahan, F. & Simpson, J., *Publicity of Security Rights: Setting Standards for Charges Registries, law in Transition* (EBRD publication, 2005) 17.

Diamond, B. Douglas, *Comment on the Bauspar System and Proposal for Lithuania,* a paper presented at a round table discussion in Vilnius, Lithuania, July 5, 2002.

Douglas, A., *Emerging Market Economies and Government Promotion of Securitization, Duke Journal of Comparative & International Law* 12 (2002) 505.

Ellinger, E.P., Lomnicka, E. & Hooley, R.J.A., *Ellinger's Modern Banking Law* (Oxford Univ. Press, 4th ed., 2006).

Fleisig, Heywood, *World Bank Financial Sector Reform: The Unfinished Legal Agenda,* CEAL Issue, Sept. 2004.

Fleisig, de la Peňa, Chaves, *Secured Transactions Reform: Early Results from Romania,* CEAL Issues Brief, Sept. 2004.

Fleisig, Safavian, & de la Peňa, *Reforming Collateral Laws to Expand Access to Finance* (World Bank publication, 2006).

Gárdos, I., *A zálogjog felölvizsgálata a polgári kodifikáció keretében (vitaanyag)* [The Revision of Security Law within the Civil Law Codification Process—Material for Discussion] (2005).

Gilmore, Grant, Security Interests in Personal Property (Little, Brown & Co., 1965).

Gilmore, Grant, Security Law, Formalism and Article 9, 47 Nebr. L. Rev. 659, 665 (1968).

Gopalan, S., *New Trends in Making of International Commercial Law, Journal of Law and Commerce* 23 (2004) 117.

Gretton, L., *Reception without Integration?* Tulane Law Review 78 (2003) 307.

Harmathy, A., *Dologi jog—Kötelmi jog* [Property Law—Law of Obligations] in: LIBER AMICORUM *LAJOS VÉKÁS* DEDICATA, at 119 (published by the ELTE Law School, Budapest, 1999).

Heller, A. Michael, *The Tragedy of the Anticommons: Property in the Transition from Marx to Markets, Harvard Law Review* 111 (1998) 621.

The Hungarian Financial Supervisory Agency *A bankok ingatlanfedezetű devizahiteleinek összehasonlító elemzése* [A Comparative Study of the Foreign Currency Credits of Banks Secured by Mortgage of Immovables].

The Hungarian Parliamentary Commissioner (Ombudsman) for Civil Rights, *Report in the case No. OBH 4999/2003 on the Protection of the Rights to Property in the Context of the Mortgage Financing Practices of some Banks.*

Lea, Michael, *Housing Finance in the Accession States,* Mortgage Finance Gazette (April 2004) 36.

Lenkovics, Barnabás, *Magyar Polgári Jog—A dologi jog vázlata* [Hungarian Civil Law—An Outline of Hungarian Property Law] (Eötvös József Publisher, Budapest, 1999).

Martin, Nathalie, *The Role of History and Culture in Developing Bankruptcy and Insolvency Systems: the Perils of Legal Transplantation, Boston College International and Comparative Law Review* 28 (2005) 1.

Martinkó, Károly, *Faktoring—A vállalatfinanszírozás hamupipőkéje* [Factoring—the Cinderella of Business Financing] (Saldo Rt, Budapest, 2002).

Mattei, Ugo & Nader, Laura, Plunder—When the Rule of Law is Illegal (Blackwell, 2008).

McCormack, Gerard, Reforming the Law of Security Interests: National and International Perspectives, 2003 Sing. J. Legal Stud. 1, 2, (2003).

Merwe, van der C.G., *Interpenetration of Common Law and Civil Law as Experiences in the South African and Scottish Law of Property,* Tulane Law Review 78 (2003) 257.

Messmann, Stefan & Tajti, Tibor (eds.), Investing in South Eastern Europe—Foreign Direct Investment in the Stability Pact Countries (European University Press, Bochum-Germany, 2005).

Messmann, Stefan & Tibor Tajti (eds.), The Case Law of Central and Eastern Europe—Leasing, Piercing the Corporate Veil and the Liability of Managers & Controlling Shareholders, Privatization, Takeovers and the Problems with Collaterla Laws (European University Press, Bochum, Germany, 2007).

Messmann, Stefan, & Tajti, Tibor, Case Law of Central and Eastern Europe—Enforcement of Contracts (European University Press, Bochum, Germany, publication expected in winter 2009).

Modigliano, F. Franco and Perotti, C. Enrico, *Security versus Bank Finance: the Importance of a Proper Enforcement of Legal Rules* (February 2, 2000/available electronically at http://www.SSRN.org.

Moojen, Winnibald, W. & Truiden, Ph. van Sint (eds.), *A Practical Guide on Security Devices available to Banks in Thirty Countries throughout the World* (Kluwer Law International, the Hague, 1999).

Nussbaumer, Michel, *Building Judicial Capacity in the Commercial Law Sector of early Transition Countries, Law in Transition* (EBRD publication, 2005) 39.

Osiatynski, Wiktor, *The Constitutional Honeymoon is Over. The Paradoxes of Post-Communist Constitution Making, in:* Dahrendorf, Lord; Elkana, Yehuda; Aryeh, Neier, Newton-Smith, William & Rév, István, The Paradoxes of Unintended Consequences, (CEU Press 1999.

Rácz István, *Development of the Financial Sector after the EU Accession* (June 2006).

Schlesinger, R., Baade, H., Damaska, M. & Herzog, P., *Comparative Law* (1978).

Schwartzenberger, István, *A bérházak zöme veszélyforrás* [The Majority of Apartment Houses is Hazardous] the Hungarian daily *Népszabadság*, June 14, 2005's issue 7.

Scott, Hal S. & Wellons, Philip A., International Finance—Transactions, Policy, and Regulation (Foundation Press, 10th ed., 2003).

Tajti, Tibor, *Central European Contribution to the American Debate on the Definition of "Securities" or Why does the Definition of "Security" Matter?: The Fiasco of the Hungarian Real Estate Investment Cooperatives, Pyramiding, and Why Emerging Capital Markets Should be Equipped to "Act" Rather than "React"*, 15 Transnat'l L. & Contemp. Probs. 111, 216 (2005).

Tajti, Tibor, *Comparative Secured Transactions Law*, chapter on Germany (Akadémiai kiadó, Budapest, 2002).

Tajti, Tibor, Secured Transactions under Article 9 of the Uniform Commercial Code: A Role for International Arbitration?, Journal of Int'l Arb. 20(2), 131–151 (2003).

Tajti, Tibor, *Viehweg's Topics, Article 9 UCC, the 'kautelarische Sicherheiten' and the Hungarian Secured Transactions Law Reform*, 6 Vindobona J. Int'l L & Com. Arb., 93 (2002).

Tímár, Sándor, *Enforcement of Real Property Mortgages full with Questions Marks*, in the Hungarian language law journal '*Magyar Jog*', No. 6 (1999) 344.

Tumenova, Dana, *Evolution of Land Reform in Russia: the 2001 Land Code and its Impact on the Commercial Real Estate Market and Direct Foreign Investment, Pacific Rim Law and Policy Journal* 11 (2002) 769.

Unidroit Draft Convention on Substantive Rules regarding Securities Held with an Intermediary (2004).

United Nations, Economic Commission for Europe—Geneva, *Housing Finance Systems for Countries in Transition—Principles and Examples—* (United Nations, 2005).

## List of Legislation[85]

**Hungary**

1927: *XXXV. Törvény cikkely a jelzálogjogról* [Law Number 35 on Mortgages]

1959: *IV. Törvény a Magyar Köztársaság Polgári Törvénykönyvéről* [The 4th Act of year 1959 on the Hungarian Civil Code]

1990: *VII. Törvény az Állami Vagyonügynökségről és a hozzá tartozó vagyon kezeléséről és hasznosításáról* [The 7th Act of year 1990 on the State Property Agency and on the Handling and Exploiting of the Property Entrusted to the Agency]

1991: *XXV. Törvény a tulajdonviszonyok rendezése érdekében, az állam által az állampolgárok tulajdonában igazságtalanul okozott károk részleges kárpótlásáról* [The 25th Act on the Partial Compensation for Damages Unlawfully Caused by the State to Properties Owned by Citizens in the Interest of Setlling Property Relations]

1991: *XXXII. Törvény a volt egyházi ingatlanok tulajdoni helyzetének rendezéséről* [The 32nd Act on the Return of Former-Church Properties]

1991: *XXXIII. Törvény egyes állami tulajdonban lévő vagyontárgyak önkormányzatok tulajdonába adásáról* [The 33rd Act on the Transfer of certain Assets in State Ownership to Local Governmental Units]

1992: *IL. Törvény a kárpótlási jegy termőföldtulajdon megszerzésére történő felhasználásának egyes krédéseiről* [The 49th Act on some Questions Related to the Use of Indemnification Coupons for Acquisition of Agricultural Land]

1992: *LIII. Törvény a tartósan állami tulajdonban maradó vállalkozói vagyon kezeléséről és hasznosításáról* [The 53rd Act on the Handling and Exploitation of Enterprise Property left in Permanent Ownership of the State]

---

85. Note that due to space constraints the full list of all amendments of the above acts has not been provided. Thus, the reader is advised to consult local counsel to determine exactly what version of the acts is in force whenever a precise account of the law in force would be needed. Local counseling is a must also because the laws of all the countries of the region are frequently subject to various types of amendments, modifications and changes.

1992: *LIV. Törvény az időleges állami tulajdonban levő vagyon értékesítéséről, hasznosításáról és védelméről* [The 54th Act on the Sale, Exploitation and Protection of the Property left Temporarily in the Ownership of the State]

1993: *LXXVIII törvény a lakások és helyiségek bérletére, valamint az elidegenítésükre vonatkozó egyes szabályokról* [The 78th Act on some Rules Related to the Renting and Sale of Appartments and other Premises]

1994: *XL. Törvény a termőföldről* [The 40th Act on the Agriculatural Land]

1995: *XXXIX. Törvény az állam tulajdonában lévő vállakozói vagyon értékesítéséről* ("privatizációs törvény"/unofficially known as the 'privatization law') [The 39th Act on the Sale of the Enterprise Property in State Ownership]

1996: *7/1996 (I. 18.) Kormányrendelet a külföldiek ingatlanszerzéséről* [Governmental Decree No. 7/1996 as of January 18th on the Acquisition of Immovables by Foreigners]

1996: 1996. évi *XXVI. Törvény a Polgári törvénykönyv egyes rendelkezéseinek módosításáról* (első zálogjogi reformtörvény/first charge law reform act) [The 26th Act of year 1996 on the Amendment of some Provisions of the Civil Code]

1997: *7/1997 (I. 22.) Kormányrendelet az ingó dolgokat terhelő jelzálogjog és a vagyont terhelő zálogjog nyilvántartásáról* [Governmentla Decree No. 7/1997 as of January 22nd on the Registry of Chattel Mortgages and Property Encumbering Charges]

1997: *CXLI. Törvény az ingatlan-nyilvántartásról* [The 161th Act on the Immovables Registry]

1997: *CXLII. Törvény a társadalmi szervezetek által használt állami tulajdonú ingatlanok jogi helyzetének rendezéséről* [The 162th Act on the Regulation of the Legal Status of State Owned Immovables in Use by Social Organizations]

2000: *CXXXVII. Törvény a Polgári törvénykönyv zálogjogi szabályainak módosításáról* [The 137th Act of year 2000 on the Amendment of the Law On Charges; known also as the 2nd charge reform act].

2004: Governmental Decree No. 324/2004 as of December 6 amending the Governmental Decree No. 41/1997 as of March 5 on the Calculation and Publication of the Index on Deposit Interests, Yield of Securities and Total Loan Charge ("*41/1997 [III.5.] Kormányrendelet a betéti kamat, az értékpapírok hozama és a teljes hiteldíj mutató számításáról és közzétételéről*")

**The United States**

1999 The Revised Version of Article 9 of the Uniform Commercial Code.

Selected personal property security reform laws of CEE:

**Croatia**

2005 Law on the Register for the Registration of Court and Public Notarial Security Interests Established on Movables and Rights.

2006 *Zakon of Leasingu* (Leasing Law).

**Estonia**

2004 Act to Amend the Law on Property Act, the Estonian Central Register of Securities Act, the Credit Institutions Act, the Insurance Activities Act, the Bankruptcy Act, the Law of Obligations Act, the Private International Law Act and the Securities Market Act (entered into force on May 1st, 2004).

**Lithuania**

1997 Law on Charges on Movable Property (not in force since December 31, 2002). It has been replaced by the Amendment of Chapter XII of the Civil Code (2002).

**Moldova**

2001 Law on Pledge (entered into force in November 2001).

**Poland**

1996 Act on Registered Pledge and Register of Pledges (*Ustawa o zastawie rejestrowym i rejestrze zastawów*) of December 6, 1996, as amended.

2008 Amendment of the Registered Pledge and Register of Pledges Act and Amendment of other Statutes ("*Ustawa o zmianie ustawy o zastawie rejestrowym i rejestrze zastawów oraz o zmienie innych ustaw*"), September 5th, 2008, published in Journal of Laws 2008, No. 180, item 1113.

**Romania**

1997 Ordinance No. 51/1997 on Leasing Transactions and Leasing Companies.

1999 Law no. 99/1999 on the Acceleration of the Economic Reform ["*Legea nr. 99/1999 privind accelerarea reformei economice*"].

**Russia**

1994 The Civil Code of the Russian Federation, Chapter 17 on the Rights of Ownership and other Rights in Land.

1997 The Federal Statute "On Public Registration of the Rights in Immovable Property and Transactions with Immovable Property __ of July 21, 1997; _________ [**missing text ???**].

1998 The Federal Statute __ On Hypothec (Pledge of Immovable Property) ______ [**missing text ???**].

2001 The [new] Land Code.

**Serbia**

2003 The Act on Registered Charges Constituted on Movables (*Zakon o založnom pravu na pokretnim stvarima upisanim u registar,* Official Gazette No. 57/2003).

**Slovakia**

2003 Law Amending the Civil Code, Notarial Law and Other Laws (in force since July 1, 2003).

**Slovenia**

2003 The [new] Act on Land Registers (*Uradni list Republike Slovenije* No. 58/2003 [Official Gazette of the Republic of Slovenia No. 58/2003).

**Ukraine**

2003 Law of Ukraine on Mortgage Credit Lending, Operatins with Consolidated Mortgage Debt and Hypothecation Certificates.

2003 Law of Ukraine on Hypothecation.

2004 Law of Ukraine on Securing Creditors' Claims and Registration of Encumbrances.

# 14

# Family Law

Esin Örücü*

## Summary



## 1. Introduction

Family law has experienced considerable changes over the last four decades. Its purposes have been re-examined under changing social and economic conditions. For instance, traditionally regarded solely as a branch of private law, it is no more so regarded. Furthermore, its protective, adjustive, and supportive functions have been challenged. Yet everyone seems to want to support the family, as social reality becomes more and more disconnected.

---

* Professor Emeritus of Comparative Law, University of Glasgow and Erasmus University Rotterdam.

Once the link of family law to human rights is established—not only concerning the right to family life and the right to privacy, but also related to non-discrimination, equality, the rights of the child and the right to a personal life-style—the place of family law in public law and political economy becomes unquestionable. To see family law in the context of political economy points to its complimentarity with taxation, social and labour market policies, income and class equality, social welfare, provisions of social security, fiscal policies and welfare models. There has indeed been cross-fertilization between human rights law, European Union law, tax and social security law, immigration, employment law, property law, and family law. Moreover, we see internationalization of family law in areas such as maintenance orders, parental responsibility and child abduction cases.[1]

1. See for example, Brussels Convention on the Jurisdiction and the Enforcement of Judgments in Civil and Commercial Matters, 1968; Brussels Convention on Jurisdiction and the Recognition and Enforcement of Judgments in Matrimonial Matters (Brussels II), 1998—incorporated into the Council Regulation on Jurisdiction and the Recognition and Enforcement of Judgments in Matrimonial Matters and in Matters of Parental Responsibility for Children of both Spouses, 2000, making Brussels II part of the domestic law of EU states, other than Denmark; European Convention on the Adoption of Children and on the Status of Children Born out of Wedlock; European Convention on the Adoption of Minors, 1967; European Convention for the Protection of Human Rights and Fundamental Freedoms, 1953; European Convention for the Exercise of Children's Rights, 1994; European Convention on the Recognition and Enforcement of decisions relating to Custody of Children and Restoration of Custody of Children, Luxembourg, 1980; European Convention on the Repatriation of Minors, 1970; Hague Convention on the Celebration and Recognition of the Validity of Marriages, 1978; Hague Convention on the Protection of Children and Co-operation in respect of Inter-Country Adoptions, 1993; Hague Convention on the Law Applicable to Matrimonial Property, 1978; Hague Convention on the Recognition and Enforcement of Decisions relating to Maintenance Obligations, 1958, 1973; Hague Convention relating to the Recognition of Divorces and Judicial Separation, 1970; Hague Convention on Jurisdiction, Applicable Law, Recognition, Enforcement and Cooperation in Respect of Parental Responsibility and Measures for the Protection of Children, provided that the child concerned is habitually resident in a member state, 1996; Luxembourg Convention on the Recognition of Decisions Relating to the Validity of Marriages, 1967; Rome Convention on the Simplification of Procedures for the Recovery of Maintenance Payments, 1990; UN Convention concerning Consent to Minimum Age for and Registration of Marriages; UN Convention on the Recovery Abroad of Maintenance, 1956; UN Convention on the Rights of the Child, 1989.

## *1.1. Conceptual Frameworks*

Family law is undergoing profound transformation. Even the term 'family' needs re-definition to cater for diverse new family forms. Thus, the first conceptual question to be tackled becomes: what is a family? Family is a site and law ultimately draws the boundaries of this site, be it domestic, European or international. Although the family is universally valued as 'the chief locus of social contacts' and 'the repository of traditional virtues', it is seldom defined—the definition of the family is an important political issue. Clashes between the left and the right, the progressive and the conservative, the libertarian and the egalitarian, and the religious and the secular are reflected in the various approaches to the concept. Even Article 8 of the European Convention on Human Rights, which guarantees for everyone the right to respect for privacy and family life, leaves the door open to interpretation and does not resolve the question of how a family should be defined, showing the indeterminancy of the provision. Pluralism, which seems to be a mark of modern family life, also makes it difficult to provide unambiguous rules and settled definitions.[2] So it appears that family becomes a matter of conscience and the right to a family can be taken as the right to lead a family life as one personally understands it,[3] though we see three models of 'family', the statist, the religious and the liberal.

Problematic as a classification may seem, it is possible in our day to talk of the extended family (household), traditional or nuclear family (with marriage as the starting point), reconstituted family (new family after divorce), post-nuclear or modern families such as one-parent family (lone-parent family or incomplete family), same-sex family, imperfect family (where both natural parents are dead and children have social and legal parents), and the family of unmarried cohabitees. Notwithstanding the practical difficulties caused by such a wide approach, putting forward a prototype of what is meant by 'a family' would hamper future developments and the basic principles of freedom, security, and choice covering rights and liberties in relation to family life today. These issues become more pressing in the multicultural and multi-faith societies that European states have become, where the very nature of the family is diverse.

Within the context of the European Union for instance, for the purposes of free movement of persons and sex equality law, the family is understood as

---

2. See J. Kurczewski & M. Maclean, *Introduction: The Two Europes*, in J. Kurczewski & M. Maclean (eds), *Family Law and Family Policy in the New Europe* (Aldershot 1997), xv.

3. Kurczewski & Maclean, *Introduction: The Two Europes*, in Kurczewski & Macleans, (eds) *Family Law and Family Policy in the New Europe*, xxv.

the traditional 'nuclear' family, that of a married heterosexual union, in which the husband is the head and principal breadwinner and the wife the primary carer; children being dependants and appendages.[4] This understanding appears to be out of step with the empirical realities of family life in the European Union. However, recently the European Court of Justice treated a cohabitee as a 'spouse' within the ambit of a 'member of the family', taking the lead from the European Court of Human Rights.[5] Later, step-children were also so treated.[6] Nevertheless, neither the European Court of Human Rights nor the European Court of Justice regard gay or lesbian couples as having 'family life' for the purposes of Article 8. Yet, the European Court of Human Rights protects access to information about identity (*Gaskin v UK* 1989), the private lives of gay men (*Dudgeon v UK* 1981, *Norris v Ireland* 1991, *Modinos v Cyprus* 1993) and of transsexuals (*B v France* 1993, *Van Oosterwijck v Belgium* 1981, *Rees v UK* 1986, *Cossey v UK* 1991), and regards children of unmarried parents (*Johnston v Ireland* 1986), children of single mothers (*Marckx v Belgium* 1979), couples in common households (*Johnston v Ireland* 1976), couples who wish to choose their family name as a combination of both names (*Burghartz v Switzerland* 1994), the rights of unmarried fathers to be informed of the adoption of their children (*Keegan v Ireland* 1994), the right of gay fathers to have custody of or access to children (*Salgueiro da Mouta v Portugal* 1999), the right to 'family life' for couples with one transsexual partner (*X, Y and Z v United Kingdom* 1997) and immigrant families (*Berrehab v Netherlands* 1988), as included in 'respect for family life'.[7] Thus, we can see that there is no correspondence between 'family law' and 'family life'. We also see that case law can shift the meaning of legal rules.[8]

---

4. See for examples of cases, C. McGlynn, *Challenging the European Harmonisation of Family Law: Perspectives on "The Family"*, in K. Boele-Woelki (ed.) *Perspectives for the Unification and Harmonisation of Family Law in Europe*, European Family Law Series, volume 4, (Antwerp-Oxford-New York 2003), 221–227. Also see, for the impact of European Community law on family law, C. Hamilton, L. Woods, *Europe*, in C. Hamilton & A. Perry (eds), *Family Law in Europe*, 2nd edn (London 2002), 206–228.

5. Case C-65/98 *Eyüp*, judgment of 22 June 2000.

6. Case C-60/00 *Carpenter v Secretary of State for the Home Department*, judgment of 11 July 2002.

7. See K. O'Donovan, *Family Definitions and Human Rights: Rights to Respect for Private and Family Life under the European Convention on Human Rights*, in Kurczewski & Maclean (eds), *Family Law and Family Policy in the New Europe*, 33–34.

8. See for example, the English case *Fitzpatrick v Sterling Housing Association Ltd.* [1999] 3 W.L.R. 1113, where three of the five Law Lords held that, though the terms 'spouse', and 'husband and wife' were gender specific and therefore could not apply to a homosexual couple, the purpose of the Schedule 1 of the Rent Act 1977 as amended by the Housing Act

'Law and the family' has become a highly sensitive political issue given the importance of family life and family values. To be meaningful any research into family law today must take into account current legal developments and policy considerations as well as social and economic developments, that is socio-legal research and contextual analysis well beyond normative analysis, and show their impact on family law.

## *1.2. Current Directions*

Family law has become a challenging area of study, covering matters as diverse as rights of the child, child support, surrogate parenthood, IVF treatment and medical reproductive techniques, cross-border adoption, adoption by same-sex couples, child abduction, domestic violence, financial consequences of divorce, protecting the rights of the individual family members, parental responsibility, custody, abortion, informal cohabitation, same-sex partnerships and marriage, and rights of transsexuals. These areas are in addition to areas of general concern in all jurisdictions during the 1970s and 80s: the status of illegitimate children, rules on divorce, maintenance and matrimonial property.

Law can be regarded as one of the most important factors in shaping and regulating contemporary family life. However, what part law should play in family life is not a resolved question. For example, should law enforce religious codes of behaviour or give secular guidance only, or manage the outcomes of individual actions, or proactively protect the vulnerable, or only protect individual members of the family from physical harm?[9] In addition, to what extent can private law "regulate the excesses of the liberal society and offer protection to the individual, and at what cost?"[10]

It is true that changing social, religious and economic conditions give rise to principles in family law that apply to divergent societies. Emancipation of

---

1988, was to protect those who shared their lives, and therefore, the concept of 'family' was not confined to relationships based on consanguinity or affinity but could include "a stable, loving and caring relationship which is not intended to be merely temporary and where the couple live together broadly as they would if they were married." (*per* Lord Slynn, 1122H-1123A.)

9. See M. Maclean & J. Kurczewski, *Introduction: The Issues in Context*, in M. Maclean & J. Kurczewski (eds) *Families, Politics and the Law: Perspectives for East and West Europe* (Oxford, 1994) 11–12.

10. Maclean & Kurczewski, *Introduction: The Issues in Context* in Maclean & Kurczewski (eds) *Families, Politics and the Law*, 23.

women, equalization of the rights of the illegitimate child, the child as a legal subject, liberalization of divorce, joint custody of children after divorce and giving legal recognition to factual relationships are among the many changes. Many of these developments transcend the so-called 'civil law-common law divide' and defy the notion of 'cultural identity'. The more important divide of religious affiliation has been affected, though not totally resolved, by secularization, which is a contemporary value alongside equality, freedom, security and justice in Europe. These values on the whole tend to override traditional values.[11] Additionally, many contemporary principles have universality and therefore transferability. Inevitably, there is convergence in the family laws of the European states. Moreover, European Union citizenship and human rights also have a standardizing impact on family law.

Nevertheless, it must also be noted that the dichotomy between liberty and equality has created another question: How far should family law be left to individuals to organize and how far should the law intervene to protect at least the vulnerable family members? State withdrawal increases individual liberty but it fails to protect. In such choices, the boundaries between public and private interests should be taken into account. This issue is of particular concern to the states of Eastern Europe some of which have now joined or are poised to join the European Union.

For instance, in Western Europe, family life is increasingly becoming a matter for individuals to decide, this being described sometimes as the 'privatization' of the family, the state placing less emphasis on equality and narrowing the focus to the protection of the rights of vulnerable family members. In Western Europe 'privatization' also means reduction of public expenditure. However, there is an ongoing clash of policies here between progressive liberals and conservative traditionalists. In Eastern Europe, the emphasis was on equality of gender, civil status and freedom for the individual to end marriage and pregnancy. These pre-1989 Family Law Codes are now undergoing revision, reducing state interference in the family. Thus in Eastern Europe also, 'privatization' means increased personal freedom. However, this 'privatization' has also been described as 'desecularization'. For instance, in Poland, "the law reform policies which aim to move towards the rule of law in democracy are now subject to the influence of the Church, which sees marriage as a sacrament and

---

11. But see, D. Bradley, *Convergence in Family Law: Mirrors, Transplants and Political Economy*, *Maastricht Journal of European and Comparative Law*, 6 (1999), 127–150; and D. Bradley, *A Family Law for Europe? Sovereignty, Political Economy and Legitimation*, in Beole-Woelki (ed.) *Perspectives for the Unification and Harmonisation of Family Law in Europe*, 65–104.

abortion as a sin."[12] Thus we see a reduction of individual liberty, though the goal was to turn away from collective regulation of family obligations by rejecting state involvement and embracing liberal values of respect for individual liberty rather than equality as the primary objective.[13] In both settings, West and East, 'privatization' seems to sit well with a free market economy.

However, can it be said that the ideological dimension of family law is one and the same throughout Europe? If not, what is the impact of this dimension on how family law is regulated in individual jurisdictions? Since family laws form parts of integrated political designs, there will always remain differences in spite of convergence. In many areas covered by family law, individual jurisdictions can still be placed at points on a spectrum from canon law at one end to Enlightenment values at the other, with the 'common core' representing a basic threshold or mid-point and 'the better law' representing modernity, with intermediate points along the way.[14]

## *1.3. The Scope of the Survey*

Within the confines of this work, it is not possible to cover all the current topics of interest cited above. Choices had to be made. First, as this work appears in a volume entitled 'European Private Law', family law is here approached solely in its private law aspects. Second, the concern of this work is to present to readers what they expect to find from a chapter entitled 'Family Law'. As a consequence, instead of assuming that what falls traditionally within the area of family law is known, and concentrating on new developments, I will concentrate on two areas impacted by marriage: status and property. Marriage can be seen as the starting point in family law and its first outcome is that it creates legal status. This status can be contrasted and compared to factual relationships. Marriage has an impact on status in the sense of who can marry and what impact it has on the individual. Marriage also has an impact on property entitlements. The termination of marriage has similar impact on both status and property. At the conclusion of this survey, the most recent trends will be revisited.

Having selected the subjects for extended treatment, I must indicate the selection of the systems to be covered. In this survey I cover Austria, Belgium,

---

12. Maclean & Kurczewski, *Introduction: The Issues in Context*, in Maclean & Kurczewski (eds), *Families, Politics and the Law*, 3.

13. See Maclean & Kurczewski, *Introduction : The Issues in Context*, in Maclean & Kurczewski (eds) *Families, Politics and the Law*, 4.

14. E. Örücü, *A Family Law for Europe: Necessary, Feasible, Desirable?*, in Beole-Woelki (ed.) *Perspectives for the Unification and Harmonisation of Family Law in Europe*, 557.

Denmark, England and Wales, Finland, France, Germany, Greece, the Republic of Ireland, Italy, the Netherlands, Northern Ireland, Norway, Portugal, Scotland, Spain, Sweden, and Switzerland.[15] In addition, wherever possible, some recently joined members of the European Union and Turkey have also been looked at. However, by necessity, this can only be an overview.

## *1.4. Sources of Family Law*

All the legal systems under this survey deal with family law by legislative Acts. Some, such as Belgium, France, Greece, Lithuania, the Netherlands, and Turkey do this by Civil Codes alone; some such as Germany, Italy, Malta, Sweden and Spain by Civil Codes and additional legislative Acts; some such as Hungary, Denmark, Finland, Norway, and Sweden by legislative acts alone with court practice playing an important role, and some such as England and Wales, the Republic of Ireland, Northern Ireland, and Scotland, by legislative Acts and case law.[16] It is possible to envisage legal systems on a spectrum with strictly applied legislation at one end and unconstrained discretion of the judiciary at the other, with a number of intermediary points, where there are guidelines, principles, analogies, checklists of factors and presumptions along the way. The shift everywhere is towards the 'rule end of the spectrum.'[17]

Some legal systems have fundamental family law principles in their constitutions. For instance, the 1976 Portuguese Constitution contains a number of principles related to the family: an equal right to constitute a family and to contract a marriage; the primary right of the family in educational matters; equal capacity of husband and wife and equal capacity of both parents towards

---

15. These are systems covered by C. Hamilton & A. Perry (eds), *Family Law in Europe*, 2nd edn (London 2002), with contributions from European practitioners: A. Kriegler (Austria), J. Sosson (Belgium), L. Nielsen (Denmark), C. Hamilton (England and Wales), R-L. Luomaranta (Finland), V. Chauveau & A. Cornec (France), K. Schweppe (Germany), E. Kounougeri-Manoledaki (Greece), P. Ward (Republic of Ireland), R. Ceschini (Italy), B.E. Reinhartz (The Netherlands), L. Stevenson (Northern Ireland), P. Lodrup (Norway), A. de Sousa Machado (Portugal), K.B. Lockhart (Scotland), E. Roca (Spain), A. Saldeen (Sweden), B. Graham-Siegenthaler (Switzerland).

16. Many authors refer to systems as 'codified' where the Civil Codes are centre stage. Common law systems, giving extensive discretion to the judiciary are referred to as non-codified and therefore represented as based on case law. This view omits the importance attached to Acts of Parliament in the field of Family Law in common law jurisdictions.

17. See J. Dewar, *Reducing Discretion in Family Law*, in J. Eekelaar & T. Nhlapo (eds), *The Changing Family: Family Forms and Family Law* (Oxford 1998), 235.

their children; the protection of paternity and maternity; and non-discrimination between children born into and out of wedlock. The German Basic Law (*Grundgesetz*) of 1949 gives special protection to marriage and family (Art 6) alongside values such as human dignity, liberty, and equality. The 1937 Constitution of the Republic of Ireland contains provisions relating to family, marriage, parents, and children it its Articles 41 and 42. The 1978 Spanish Constitution lays down guarantees such as non-discrimination between spouses (Art 32) and children (Art 39), and the protection of the family (Art 39), on which family law must be based. The 1982 Turkish Constitution states in Article 41 that the family is the foundation of Turkish society and is based on equality between the spouses, that the peace and the welfare of the family will be ensured by the state, and the mother and the children will be protected. The 1997 Polish Constitution cites in Article 18, marriage, as a union between a man and a woman, the family (also in Art 4, 47 and 71), maternity (also Art 33), and parenthood (also Art 48, 53 and 70) as institutions to be protected.

### 1.5. Meaning of Marriage

The nuclear family is the essential family unit in Europe, though for purposes of maintenance, a form of extended family is also apparent. The nuclear family comprises a man and a woman in a sexual relationship and their children. Some legal systems consider marriage as a 'union', and therefore an institution, while others accentuate the contractual element of marriage.[18] As a general rule, a couple have to marry before they acquire mutual legal rights and obligations, and it is only then that their income and capital are regulated by law when the relationship breaks down, in the form of financial provisions on divorce.

However, in most legal systems a large number of couples live in stable sexual relationships outside marriage. Some legislators have provided cohabitees with certain rights related to certain matters, such as the occupation of the home in which the cohabitees live, or have been living, as we see in Scotland. In this jurisdiction, there was until recently also a distinction between formal marriage and irregular or informal marriage called 'marriage by cohabitation

18. For example, the Civil Code of Lithuania, which came into force on 1 January 2001, shifted the emphasis from 'union' to 'contract'. See S., Keserauskas, *Moving in the same Direction? Presentation of Family Law Reforms in Lithuania*, in A. Bainham (ed) *The International Survey of Family Law, 2004 Edition*, published on behalf of The International Society of Family Law (Bristol 2004), 319.

with habit and repute' with its own requirements.[19] Some jurisdictions such as Belgium and the Netherlands allow marriage for same-sex partners.[20]

Most jurisdictions treat marriage as civic marriage and some do not mention religious marriage at all, such as Austria and Sweden. Some accept that religious marriage, with no legal consequences, can be concluded following the civic marriage. Such is the case in Belgium, the Netherlands, France, Switzerland, Turkey, and Germany. However, in Germany for instance, though only the civil registrar has exclusive authority to solemnize a marriage, if neither party is a German national, the marriage may be solemnized by a Catholic, Protestant, or Orthodox clergyman, by a rabbi or imam subject to authorization of the person to perform the marriage ceremony by the national government of one of the parties and the Minister of the Interior of the German State (*Land*). In France, a marriage, whether civil or religious, must be solemnized in accordance with prescribed formalities in front of the appropriate civil authorities.

Some jurisdictions however, such as Denmark, England and Wales, Finland, Greece (since 1982), the Republic of Ireland, Italy, Latvia, Lithuania,[21] Northern Ireland, Norway, Poland, Portugal, Sweden, Spain, and Scotland give equal weight to civil and religious marriages. Denmark has a most tolerant approach to religious marriage in that it can be performed within the Danish Established Church, a recognized religious community, an unrecognized religious community or a religious community in another country placed on an equal footing with the Danish Established Church. In the case of Finland, a religious marriage must be performed either in the official state church or in another religious community, granted permission by the Ministry of Education to perform marriage ceremonies. In Italy, civil marriages are governed by the Civil Code and celebrated before a state official, Catholic marriages are governed by Canon law and celebrated before a Catholic priest, and though members of other religions can also have marriages according to their religious rites, the marriage is regulated by the Civil Code. Since 2001, the scope of the recognized religions for the purposes of religious marriage has been

19. See J.M. Thomson, *Family Law in Scotland*, 4th edn (Edinburgh 2002), 16–20. However, this institution has been abolished by the Family Law (Scotland) Act 2006 on 4 May 2006.

20. It is worth noting that in Belgium, France, Hungary, the Netherlands and Portugal opposite sex couples can also enter civil partnerships.

21. In Lithuania, the 1992 Constitution specifically provides for unconditional recognition of religious marriages (Art 38). However the 2001 Civil Code states that religious marriages must be registered in the public register within 10 days (Art 3).

widened in Portugal, and though Roman Catholic marriages still remain under a set of special rules, all religious marriages celebrated under any recognized religion are effective. In Spain, a religious marriage—and only those celebrated according to the Catholic Church, the Evangelical Church, and the Jewish and Muslim faiths are recognized—will only have legal effect in respect of third parties if it is officially registered. In Scotland also, all marriages (except 'irregular marriages'[22]) whether civil or religious, must comply with certain complicated preliminary formalities, thereafter the solemnization would differ. Similarly, in England and Wales all marriages, civil or religious, except for Church of England marriages, must comply with prescribed civil formalities before the marriage can be solemnized. However, the religions mentioned in the Marriage Act 1949 are Church of England, other non-Church of England Christian denominations, Jewish, and Quaker.

In many societies, couples become engaged (unenforceable contract) for a period before they marry. Some legal systems, such as the Austrian, Latvian, Lithuanian, and Turkish, attach legal consequences to the breaking of the engagement such as return of gifts, compensation for pecuniary loss and *solatium* for the innocent party's injured feelings, though the incidence of these is now very rare. In Finland, although engagement is now a purely traditional custom with no legal effects, the Marriage Act 1987 states that a woman and a man who have agreed to marry each other shall be engaged and further mentions 'engaged persons' in the section which sets out the requirements for a valid marriage ceremony.

Although this survey considers marriage in a legal context, its religious and social meanings must also be borne in mind.

## 2. Status

### *2.1. Legal Requirements of a Valid Marriage*

#### 2.1.1. Age

In most legal systems under review, as in the Republic of Ireland, the minimum age for marriage is 18 for both sexes. In Switzerland the minimum age for marriage is 18; however, if persons below that age marry, the marriage would still be considered valid provided the persons were of sound mind and mentally capable of understanding the significance of marriage. In France,

22. See *Petrie v Petrie* 1911 SC 360, *Cunninghams v Cunninghams* (1814) 2 Dow 482, and *Donnelly v Donnelly's Executor* 1992 SLT 13.

until 5th April 2006 a man must have been at least 18, but a woman 15 to marry. LOI no 2006-399 has amended Article 144 of the Code and now the minimum age for marriage is 18 for both sexes. In some jurisdictions such as Scotland and Portugal, 16 is the norm for both parties; in Turkey, parties can marry at 17, this to be lowered in exceptional circumstances to 16 for both; while in some others 18 can be lowered to 16 in certain circumstances for one of the parties (Austria, England and Wales, Germany, Poland, Italy, the Netherlands), or dispensation given to depart from this rule (Belgium, Denmark, Finland, Greece). In Norway, Sweden, and Lithuania for instance, it is only stated that "if a person under 18 wishes to marry ..." but no absolute minimum age is mentioned, it being left to the courts to decide.

### 2.1.2. Not to Be within the Prohibited Degrees of Relationship

In all legal systems under review, this prohibition covers ascendants and descendants in a direct line. Greek law applies this rule also to collateral affinity up to the fourth degree. Austrian law and Lithuanian law for instance, also include full and half-brothers and sisters and adopter and adoptee. However, in Finland, Sweden, and Germany, dispensation may be given for this last category. Aunts, nephews, uncles, and nieces can marry under Dutch law, as can they in Belgium if permitted by the King, and in France, if permitted by the President; in Belgium brothers, sisters, and their spouses can marry after the death of one. In England and Wales, step-daughter, step-mother and mother-in-law do not fall into the prohibition; marriage with the step-daughter is also allowed in Germany; in France the President may give permission for marriage to a mother-in-law.

### 2.1.3. Not to Be Already Married

This legal requirement is without exception. Europe believes in monogamy, and bigamy is a criminal offence in most legal systems.[23]

---

23. But see H. Willekens, *Long-term Developments in Family Law in Western Europe: an Explanation*, in Eekelaar & Nhlapo (eds), *The Changing Family: Family Forms and Family Law*, 57, 67. Willekens claims that while the principle of monogamy has been maintained, polygamy has been introduced into family law in Europe, first, as serial polygamy, with the possibility of remarriage and second, simultaneous polygamy, with acceptance of some of the consequences of marriages entered into in other legal systems where this form is recognized, combining remarriage with sometimes life long subsistence of some economic rights and duties of former marriages, institutionalized unmarried cohabitation giving rise to rights and duties in relation to two partners, and the possibility for a man to have children with the same legal status by more than one woman.

### 2.1.4. Be Respectively Male and Female

This is the general rule. However, some legislators, such as in Denmark (1989), Norway (1993), Sweden (1994), Iceland (1996), Hungary (1996), the Netherlands (1998), Spain (1998), France (1999), Belgium (2000), Portugal (2001), Finland (2001), Germany (2001), Switzerland (2002), Slovenia (2005) and, as recently as December 2005, in England and Wales, Northern Ireland, and Scotland,[24] have created marriage-like status for same-sex couples, providing for civil partnerships, registered partnerships or civil unions.[25] Even the possibility of marriage between same-sex couples exists in Belgium (2002), Spain and the Netherlands, where since 1 April 2001 'being one male and one female' is not a legal requirement for a valid marriage. In Sweden, Switzerland and in the Norwegian Marriage Act 1991, this requirement is not mentioned explicitly, though it is implicit and is said to follow from legal tradition. Transsexuals can now marry the opposite sex partners in many jurisdictions including Turkey, and most recently England and Wales, and Scotland.

### 2.1.5. Additional Conditions

Some jurisdictions, such as France, Belgium and Italy, mention as a separate requirement 'free consent'; others such as Scotland and Switzerland, 'being capable of understanding the nature of a marriage ceremony'. In Greece, the law states that both parties must have the capacity to enter into juridical acts (not be under the age of 10, mentally ill, or under judicial protection.)

In Norway, suffering from a contagious disease transmittable by sexual contact is a bar to marriage. Moreover, since 1994, an addition to the 1991 Act Section 16 states that a party may have the marriage declared void if he/she has been forced into it; this being introduced as a measure against arranged marriages common in some traditions of certain religions.

In the Republic of Ireland, where marriage by civil ceremony has been possible since 1844, another requirement is to notify the Registrar of Marriages in writing of the intention to marry not less than three months prior to the date on which the marriage is to be solemnized. In addition there are special

---

24. The Civil Partnership Act 2004 (for England and Wales, Northern Ireland and Scotland) came into effect on 5 December 2005.

25. Forty-seven jurisdictions world-wide recognize registered partnerships for same-sex couples. For a recent and thorough analysis see I. Curry-Sumner, *All's well that ends registered? The Substantive and Private International Law Aspects of Non-Marital Registered Relationships in Europe*, European Family Law Series, volume 11, (Mortsel, 2005).

arrangements for marriages according to the rites of the Roman Catholic Church, for other Christian marriages and for Jewish marriages.

In Spain, Portugal, and Italy, a person must not have been condemned for murder or attempted murder of his/her spouse or the previous spouse of the other party to the marriage. In addition in Portugal, a woman may not marry before a period of 300 days and a man for 180 days has passed after the dissolution of a previous marriage, conditions now removed from other legal systems.

Some of the jurisdictions under survey have extensive treatment of lack of valid consent, void marriages, 'sham' marriages, putative marriages, voidable marriages, and the effects of these.

## *2.2. Legal Consequences of Marriage*

### 2.2.1. Personal Relations

In general, spouses have equal rights and duties in relation to each other. They have to reach agreement on organizing their conjugal life, that is, housekeeping, employment, mutual support, parental authority taking into account the welfare of the children, and equality of contributions. Some legal systems mention these principles in their Constitutions. For example, under the Italian Constitution of 1948, spouses have a duty to provide each other with moral and material care and parents have a duty to support, rear and educate their children (Art 30). It is also stated that marriage is based on the moral and legal equality of the spouses, with limits established by law to guarantee the family unity (Art 29). Mutual duties include: faithfulness, provision of help and assistance, and, in some legal systems such as the French, living together is additionally mentioned. In Greece, the right to consortium cannot be surrendered by agreement; the spouses also have a mutual right to sexual intercourse.

In most of the legal systems under survey, spouses take a mutual surname on marriage. If they do not do so, they may choose one of their surnames for the children. In Germany and Switzerland, for instance, that choice is still called 'the family name', and in Germany since 1991, if the spouses have made no choice recorded by the registrar, each will continue to keep the family name he/she had at the time of the marriage ceremony. In Poland, also, if there is no spousal declaration concerning the surname, each retains his/her previous surname. In Sweden, if the spouses fail to choose a surname, the child is registered under the mother's name. In Switzerland, the wife adopts her husband's family name unless the spouses have been authorized, for legitimate interests, to adopt the wife's maiden name as their family name. A wife may also retain her own maiden name and add the husband's to it, this intention to be declared at the time of the wedding before the registrar of civil status. Similarly since 1994, a husband may also carry a combined name, adding the wife's name to his pre-marriage name.[26] In Turkey, although normally a woman acquires the surname of her husband upon marriage, since an amendment to the Civil Code in 1997 and now in the new Civil Code of 2002, her surname can be added before that of her husband's, upon her written request.

An extreme position is portrayed in England and Wales where a person's name is a matter of usage and therefore adults may call themselves by any name without any legal procedure to effect a lawful change. This means that a married woman may call herself by her maiden name, a divorced woman may retain her married name and an unmarried woman may adopt her partner's surname. However, once a child's name is registered at birth it cannot be changed subsequently by the wish of either parent. The possibility of a unilateral change, especially in cases of one parent with parental responsibility, proved to be a problematic area in view of the Children Act 1989. It was held in *Re PC (Change of Surname)*[27] that a unilateral change cannot be made, as the change of name is a matter subject to agreement or court order.

### 2.2.2. Citizenship

In all the systems under survey, foreigners do not acquire citizenship automatically on marrying a national. In Switzerland, until 1990, marriage to a Swiss man automatically conferred Swiss citizenship upon a non-Swiss wife, but since the 1990 revision of the Nationality Law, the process of naturalization, though facilitated, has a period of residence requirement coupled with being integrated into the country and not posing a threat to internal and external security. Many jurisdictions such as Austria, Belgium, Denmark, France, the Netherlands, and Spain have residence requirements for certain periods. For instance, in England and Wales, and Northern Ireland a person who marries a British citizen may apply for naturalization after three years of residence in the country. In Norway, however, there is no requirement to be resident in Norway as long as the other spouse is Norwegian. In France, an additional negative condition is that the French government can oppose the acquisition of French nationality on the ground that the foreign spouse is 'unworthy' of French nationality or proved to be unable to adapt to France or French society. In a similar vein, in Germany 'adjusting to the German

26. Following the decision of the European Court of Human Rights: *Burghartz v Switzerland* (1994) 18 EHRR 101.

27. [1997] 2 FLR 730.

way of life' and naturalization 'not running counter to essential interests of the Federal Republic such as external and internal security and international relations' are mentioned as conditions additional to standard conditions related to naturalization.

Separate rules apply to children, such as a child is deemed to be a national of a country if at the time of birth one of the parents is a national (such is the case in Denmark, England and Wales, France and the Netherlands).

### 2.2.3. Property

Marriage confers rights to a share in property. This topic is dealt with below under the general heading of Property: during marriage and after divorce (3.), where I look at property regimes (3.1.), and the matrimonial home (3.2.).

### 2.2.4. Financial Obligations

Here, obligations of the spouses to each other and to children will be covered. Other financial provisions during marriage such as financial provisions from the courts, family allowance, health insurance, accidents at work, unemployment benefits, survivor's pension, inheritance law and taxation will not be tackled. Most disputes concerning property and finance occur on the termination of marriage.

Spouses have a mutual duty to maintain each other and their children during marriage, contributing to the cost of living according to their means. Similar to most legal systems, in Greece, for instance, until 1983, the husband was considered by law as the main supporter of the family. Today equality prevails. In addition, in most legal systems under review such as the Austrian, Danish, Finnish, German, Greek, Dutch, and Turkish, 'work in the home' is cited as a contribution in the same way as making financial contribution. Generally if one spouse neglects his or her maintenance obligations, the court, upon request, may order this spouse to pay maintenance to the other.

In some legal systems such as the Belgian one, children may also be obliged to support their parents. In Italy, financial obligations extend further: spouses and other family members have a duty to provide financial assistance, in cash or in kind such as expenses for food, housing, clothing, medical care, and for the upbringing and education of minors to members of the nuclear and extended family in need, for instance, due to lack of income and/or incapacity to work. The order of priority in this kind of assistance is: spouse, children, parents, grandparents, sons and daughters-in-law, fathers and mothers-in-law, and brothers and sisters. Where more than one person is liable to provide this aid, provision is shared according to each provider's economic circumstances.

### 2.2.5. Parental Authority

Married persons living together share parental responsibility equally and have a duty to exercise joint custody over minor children and maintain them (Examples are Austria, Belgium, Denmark, England and Wales, France, Scotland, Sweden, and Turkey). Maintenance is understood to mean giving children sufficient physical and moral care, choosing how they should be educated, and preparing them for life. In Portugal, the term used for parental authority is '*poder paternal*' though used jointly by married parents. In Turkey, the new Civil Code of 2002 also cites the right of the parents to determine the religious education of the child.

In most legal systems under review, parental authority lasts until the child reaches majority at the age of 18. For children in full-time education, this is extended to 21. In Germany to support the child is a lifelong duty as a matter of principle and so is the duty of a child to support his or her parents. However, to share income and property with children only applies to unmarried children. So is this the case in the Netherlands in theory; however, as every person aged 21 and over is entitled to state benefits, in practice parents are not called upon to support such persons.

## *2.3. Divorce*

Changes in the field of divorce began after the 1960s for most legal systems and are continuing. Laws have responded to demands for easier divorce with systems based on the non-fault principle of breakdown of marriage. The spectrum of divorce has at one end 'no divorce' and at the other, divorce by unilateral application, granted administratively. Although I will not be considering 'separation', which merely suspends the marriage whereas divorce terminates it, a number of legal systems still have this option.

Courts have jurisdiction to hear applications for divorce if one of the spouses is a national or if the plaintiff is resident in the country. Generally these would be courts of the spouses' common habitual residence and divorce by mutual consent could be heard in non-contentious proceedings.

Divorce will be covered under the following sub-headings: time bars, mediation/reconciliation, grounds, legal effect and maintenance. The impact of divorce on property will be discussed under property regimes (3.1) and the matrimonial home (3.2).

### 2.3.1. Time Bars

In some jurisdictions such as Scotland, France (since 1 January 2005), the Republic of Ireland, Italy (except where brought on the three years separation ground), and Portugal, a petition for judicial separation or divorce can be lodged at any time after the celebration of a marriage. In some legal systems there is a time bar on divorce in the first year of marriage (England and Wales, Latvia and Lithuania, Greece and Turkey, in divorce by mutual consent). In Northern Ireland, this is a two-year period. In Spain, there is a bar on divorce, if by mutual consent, for two years from the marriage, and three or five years in contentious divorces depending on the ground.

### 2.3.2. Mediation/Reconciliation

Conciliatory hearings are compulsory in Poland as the opening stage of divorce litigation. In Scotland, reconciliation is encouraged by periods of resumed cohabitation: in adultery, cohabitation up to three months after knowledge of adultery, cohabitation up to six months after one or two years in separation. In Italy, the judge must attempt to reconcile the parties at the initial hearing. In Switzerland, mediation proceedings initiated orally or in writing by a spouse with a justice of the peace is the first step in contested divorces. In Norway, if there are children under the age of 16, mediation to reach agreement on parental responsibility and arrangements for children must take place before the decree on divorce or separation can be granted by the county governor. In France the *juge aux affaires familiales* must seek to reconcile the spouses as an initial procedure with the aim of encouraging them to regulate the consequences of divorce amicably, and reach and draft an agreement.

### 2.3.3. Grounds

Malta is a case apart in Europe. Although since December 1993 there is equality between the spouses to a large extent, divorce has not entered the legal system. Yet, divorce obtained abroad is given recognition and such judgments can be registered in Malta. It is possible to request personal separation before a civil court however, on the grounds of adultery, excesses, cruelty, threats or grievous injury, or desertion for two years. Since 1981 the spouses can also plead that they 'cannot reasonably be expected to live together as the marriage has irretrievably broken down.' This ground can only be raised if the spouses have been married for four years. Separation is possible by litigation or 'effected by mutual consent of the parties by means of a public deed'.

The Republic of Ireland is a late-comer to the divorce scene by accepting divorce by the Family Law (Divorce) Act 1996 which came into force in 1997 following a referendum in 1995. There is only one ground of no-fault divorce: at the date of the institution of the proceedings, the spouses must have lived apart for at least four years during the previous five years. They could be living in the same house.[28] The court must be assured that there is no reasonable prospect of reconciliation and that divorce would not have any adverse effects on dependent members of the family. Other options are nullity (for impotence and inability to enter into or sustain a normal marriage relationship), and judicial separation (the respondent has committed adultery, acted in such a way that the applicant cannot reasonable be expected to live with the respondent, desertion by the respondent for at least one year, the spouses have lived apart for at least one year and the respondent consents to the decree or they have lived apart for at least three years without this consent, or that the court is convinced that the marriage has broken down and that for at least one year normal marital relationship has not existed). The position of couples divorced abroad, prior to and after 2 October 1986, have also been equalized. As the 'dependent domicile' principle was found unconstitutional by the Supreme Court, it is now the case that a divorce granted abroad is recognized if either party was domiciled in the divorce jurisdiction at the commencement of the proceedings.[29]

Austria is a good example of a modernized traditional system in the area of divorce. It distinguishes between divorce by mutual consent, divorce on the basis of fault, and divorce for other reasons. Divorce by mutual consent has five conditions: (1) six months separation, (2) irretrievable breakdown, (3) a deed of arrangement of custody and maintenance of children, (4) partition of property, and (5) a joint application for divorce. The requirement for divorce for fault is grave misconduct of a spouse such as adultery, violence, infliction of severe mental harm, and serious breaches of spousal obligations, leading to irretrievable breakdown. Here, the spouse suing for divorce needs 'clean hands' and the claim has to be brought within six months of the knowledge of the misconduct or within ten years of its occurrence. There are additional grounds such as separation for at least three years and irretrievable breakdown of marriage, the conduct of a mentally deranged spouse, insanity of a spouse, the contagious disease of a spouse. These last three instances are subject to a special 'hardship clause'; thus if there is hardship, divorce can only be granted after a separation of six years, after which the other spouse cannot object to divorce.

Turkey is also in this category, where the grounds are adultery, threat to life, extreme cruelty or serious insult, committing a humiliating crime, leading a dishonourable life, desertion to last for six months, incurable mental ill-

28. *MMcA v XMcA* [2000] 1 IR 457.
29. *W v W* [1993] ILRM 294.

ness, and irretrievable breakdown of marriage, where mutual consent or one spouse accepting the petition of the other for divorce and the condition that 'it cannot be expected that they live together' are sought. However, three years after an unsuccessful divorce case, divorce is granted upon the application of either spouse.

Since I January 2005, France, though in the same category as Austria, moved still further along the spectrum. For instance, the grounds are now: mutual consent, acceptance of the breakdown of the marriage (claimed by one spouse and accepted by the other), irretrievable breakdown of the marital relationship, and fault. Divorce by mutual consent is usually petitioned by a joint request of the spouses and there is no longer need for the six months waiting period. Divorce can now be granted at the first hearing and the three months deliberation or 'cooling down' period has been repealed. There is no longer need to show the court that life in common has become intolerable. In contentious divorce—that is, if one of the spouses opposes the divorce—the following apply: a separation for at least two years or the commission of a serious and repeated violation of the obligations of marriage (fidelity, support and assistance, supporting and educating the children, contribution to marriage expenses, and living together as a couple) making living together intolerable. Mental illness has been abandoned as a ground, and the six years separation period has been reduced to two. The procedure for the evaluation of financial provisions have been separated from the attribution of fault and the party at fault is not any more deprived of a compensatory payment. Duty of support is no more and an abandoned spouse cannot oppose divorce by using the 'hardship clause'.

The 2001 Civil Code of Lithuania introduced the institution of separation and made divorce possible through judgment of a court rather than maintaining the old 'administrative divorce'. One ground of divorce is mutual consent, possible only after one year of marriage, accompanied by an agreement on the consequences of divorce, stating also the reasons of the breakdown of marriage. Courts have discretion in accepting the reasons. The other grounds are the fault of one or both of the spouses (breaching spousal duties of loyalty, respect, and support which includes desertion for over a year) or the application of one of the spouses for divorce in cases following a judicial separation of at least one year, or exceptionally, where the other is legally incapacitated, declared missing, or serving a term of imprisonment for over a year. The guilty party loses maintenance rights and suffers other serious financial consequences. Yet, the Civil Code of Latvia of 1 September 1993 accepts as the main ground of divorce, 'disruption of family' when the spouses have lived apart for three years. Additional proof is where one spouse exposes the other to danger, is absent for at least one year, has a serious mental illness or an infectious disease or has committed felony or leads a dishonourable life, when the other can claim divorce. There is also the possibility of divorce by mutual consent.

Scotland, England and Wales, and Northern Ireland are examples of a modern approach hiding the traditional approach, which is in the background. This may be seen as a transitional stage in the development of divorce law. The only ground for divorce is seemingly irretrievable breakdown. However, this is to be established on proof of one or more of five facts: adultery, unreasonable behaviour where the petitioner/pursuer cannot reasonably be expected to live with the respondent, desertion followed by two years non-cohabitation, two years separation with consent to divorce, or five years separation without such consent.[30] Separation is possible in the same house. For adultery, *lenocinium* and condonance prevent relying on this proof. After the five years separation, the court still has discretion to refuse divorce if the pursuer can show that he/she would suffer grave financial hardship if divorce were granted, a rarely used defence. However, in Scotland, there is also the do-it-yourself divorce where divorce can be sought under a cheap and simple procedure by filling a form and submitting it to the court if the divorce is based on separation (one or two years), there are no minor children, neither party seeks an order for financial provisions, there are no other pending proceedings, and neither party suffers from a mental disorder. Another option is 'undefended divorce' which goes through an affidavit procedure and neither parties nor witnesses have to appear in court. This can be used for any of the grounds for divorce. In England and Wales, an 'undefended divorce' can be obtained by an administrative procedure.

In Poland also, divorce is granted only on the ground of complete and permanent breakdown of marriage—however, if the best interests of the children would suffer, if the petitioner is 'solely guilty' of the breakdown, or if divorce would be contrary to the principle of social co-existence, divorce is not granted.

At the other end of the spectrum, we see Finland, where each spouse has the right to divorce by unilateral application, no grounds being needed. Divorce is granted after a consideration period of six months and usually before the expiry of this period. There is no need for a consideration period if spouses have been separated for at least two years. Similarly, in Sweden, the legislature allows those who do not want to remain in a marriage union to be released from it as easily and painlessly as possible. Thus all grounds have been abolished. When spouses agree, they have the right to an immediate divorce.

30. Note that Family Law (Scotland) Act 2006 came into force on 4th May 2006 and reduced 2 years separation to 1, and 5 years to 2. Also desertion is no longer a ground, and in non-cohabitation without consent there is no bar to divorce, neither is collusion a bar.

There is no reconsideration period if the spouses have lived apart for at least two years. However, if a spouse has custody or is living with a minor child, if both spouses request it, or if only one spouse wants divorce, then there must be a six month period of reconsideration running from the time of the divorce application before the divorce is granted. There is no requirement of living apart during this period. The aim is to prevent too-hasty divorces. If both parties are in agreement on obtaining the divorce and the ancillary issues, the court may enter judgment based on documents as parties are not required to attend the court. The Marriage Act also abolished grounds for divorce in Norway in 1991. Each spouse may unilaterally claim a separation or divorce decree that is generally granted administratively. Normally a divorce can be obtained after a period of separation of one year, sought jointly or unilaterally. If cohabitation has ceased for two years, either spouse can apply for divorce. A spouse may also obtain divorce, if the other spouse has attempted to kill him/her or the children, or has wilfully maltreated them. A demand for divorce has to be submitted within six months of the knowledge of the act and not later than two years from the act. Ancillary issues are dealt with separately from the divorce.

Germany is another example at this end of the spectrum. Divorce is pronounced by the judgment of the family court, attached to each local court. In 1977, all grounds were abolished and replaced by breakdown (*scheitern*), conceived as totally objective and to be assumed where matrimonial cohabitation has terminated and is not expected to resume. After one year of separation, divorce is granted if sought and agreed upon by both spouses. If one spouse terminates cohabitation and refuses to resume it, the period of separation extends to three years. However, divorce may be refused in cases of extensive hardship or in the interests of minor children. The Netherlands is another example: here, a divorce decree to legally terminate divorce must be registered with the registrar by either spouse within six months of the judgment. This procedure also applies to termination of registered partnerships. For a decree of judicial separation to have any effect, it must be registered at the matrimonial property register. The only ground is irretrievable breakdown of marriage and if there is a joint application such breakdown is assumed. Moreover, if only one party asserts that the marriage is broken down, then as long as this belief is sustained throughout the proceedings, the divorce will be granted even if the other party fails to accept this fact.

There are intermediary positions along the spectrum upon which many legal systems sit. For instance in Belgium, a petition for divorce can be brought to court on specific facts (fault based), after two years separation or by mutual consent together with details of the agreement on ancillary matters. In

Denmark, divorce can be granted when a legal separation lasts at least one year or if parties agree to divorce, after six months separation, if the parties have lived apart for more than two years, and for adultery, bigamy or gross ill treatment of spouse or children. A court can grant separation and divorce or the country governor can grant it administratively when spouses agree on separation or divorce and all related matters.

The law relating to divorce was revised in Greece in 1983 and non-fault divorce and divorce by mutual consent were introduced. If the spouses agree to divorce (consensual or uncontested), then they must petition together. They must have been married for at least one year and they or their representatives must consent to divorce before the court. There is a six-month waiting period for reflection and reconsideration after which they return to court. If there are minor children, the spouses must also submit an agreement on custody and access, which the judge scrutinizes in the best interests of the children. Another ground is irretrievable breakdown to be shown by evidence relating to behaviour with four rebuttable presumptions: bigamy, adultery, desertion, and an attempt on the life of the spouse. Other grounds are separation for four years and absence. The divorce may not be granted however, if this would create grave hardship for the respondent. Contested cases are adjudicated within the adversarial system, non-contested ones within the inquisitorial system.

The main ground for divorce in Italy is that 'the spiritual and material communion' between the spouses no longer exists or cannot be recreated. A spouse can petition for divorce after three years separation, where the other spouse committed certain crimes, the marriage has not been consummated or a party is a transsexual. If spouses make a joint application, the decree of divorce is granted immediately, as long as the judge is satisfied with the agreed ancillary matters such as child custody, access, and maintenance. If not, 'normal procedure' applies where, similar to one spouse making the application, the judge attempts reconciliation. The judge has discretion in divorce cases. Upon the request of a spouse, the judge can name the spouse responsible for the breakdown of marriage. However, the responsible spouse may also be entitled to alimony.

In Portugal, it is the civil courts that grant divorce in both civil and Catholic or other religious marriages. An 'amicable divorce' can be presented at the registration office. A judicial separation can be converted to a decree of divorce after two years. In divorce by mutual consent where both spouses petition for divorce, there is no need to prove any grounds and a decree is granted if the parties agree on the future of minor children, the matrimonial home, and alimony. Reconciliation must be attempted, but if this fails, the registration officer approves the agreement and terminates the marriage. However, when only one spouse petitions for divorce, the grounds are: serious violation of any marital obligation making living together intolerable, three years of separation, absence for two years, and change in mental health for at least three years making living together intolerable.

Separation is the main ground for divorce in Spain. The rule is: after one year of separation where there is mutual consent, after two years' separation on application of either spouse, and after five years' separation where there is desertion or no communal marital life. Since the Civil Code was amended in 1981, a divorce can be sought by mutual consent or in contentious proceedings. In consent divorce, parties must agree to divorce and ancillary matters. A decree of judicial separation makes it easier to obtain divorce. The judge must be satisfied with the arrangements of ancillary matters. Divorce can be granted at any time with or without separation if one spouse has been convicted of an attack on the applicant spouse or his/her progeny or relatives.

In Switzerland, the provisions of the Civil Code on divorce were amended in 1998 and came into force on 1 January 2000. There are three grounds for divorce: joint application with a comprehensive or partial agreement on ancillary matters to be confirmed by the judge, petition by one spouse after living separately for four years, and petition for divorce due to grave conditions not attributed to the petitioner because of which he/she cannot be expected to remain in the marriage. Fault has been abolished. Children affected by divorce have the right to be heard by the court. The law stipulates a two months reflection period after the first hearing.

### 2.3.4. Legal Effects

Joint custody, maintenance, division of gains, splitting of pensions or loss of pension rights, allocation of the matrimonial home, freedom to remarry, orders for periodical payments, property division, lapse of a will making a bequest to a former spouse, each party losing the right to use the name of the other unless permitted to retain it, and dissolution of matrimonial regimes are the legal effects to be seen in the legal systems under survey. In a few legal systems, such as the Spanish, Portuguese, Italian, Belgian, and Greek, fault, or 'guilt', still plays a part in financial allocations. It was only on 1 January 2000 that the concept of fault/guilt was eliminated from Swiss family law in relation to financial provisions, and on 1 January 2005 from the French; thus if one party cannot be expected to maintain him or herself, the other is required to make an adequate contribution as alimony, regardless of the fault of the parties while the court considers various other conditions.

### 2.3.5. Maintenance

In some legal systems such as the Austrian, divorce by mutual consent is only granted if the spouses have concluded a maintenance agreement. Following the 1999 family law reform, maintenance can be granted irrespective of fault in a divorce if, due to child care duties, a spouse cannot be expected to take up employment or if one spouse, as mutually agreed, had undertaken childcare, housekeeping or care of relatives during marriage and therefore has a low earning potential. In England and Wales, the respondent may ask the court not to make the decree nisi absolute unless the court is satisfied that adequate financial arrangements have been made. Some legal systems such as the Belgian, though still using guilt as a measure for financial support of the innocent spouse after divorce, overlooks this if the latter has not sufficient income to meet living expenses according to circumstances. The maintenance payment can be an equitable amount if it were to endanger the debtor's own living. In the calculation, other maintenance duties such as for minor children or other former spouses are taken into account. Maintenance claims can be time-limited.

In most legal systems under review, either spouse can claim interim relief during the divorce proceedings in respect of child maintenance, payment of debts such as rent or mortgage and spousal maintenance. In England and Wales, for instance, the court has broad discretion in these matters. Exercising its power to make financial provision in favour of a party, the court frequently decides on 'clean break' provisions and orders periodical payments for a limited time, orders that a spouse cannot make a maintenance application in the future, or orders a lump sum payment in order to terminate a relationship as soon as is just and reasonable and perhaps even immediately upon divorce. A court can alter any maintenance agreement by the parties. 'Clean break' settlements are also encouraged in France, where since 1 January 2005 duty for support has been abolished. Compensatory benefits have a new content in that the spouse at fault does not automatically lose his/her entitlement. The court weighs the needs and means of the parties, the age and health of the spouses, the duration of the marriage, the time devoted to the care of the children and professional qualifications and opportunities and then decides on the compensatory benefit as a lump sum payment, sometimes supplemented by an annuity or periodic payments.

In Sweden, obligation to maintain ceases upon divorce, except where one spouse cannot find work, or the ability and opportunity to support him/herself is reduced as a result of caring for children (for a transitional period) or old age and illness (beyond the transitional period). The situation is similar in Norway, where the transitional period cannot exceed three years; if the marriage has lasted for more than twenty years there is no time limit however. In the Republic of Ireland, on the other hand, periodic payment orders are potentially indefinite.

In some legal systems such as the Danish, maintenance is not common and, if granted, is usually of limited duration and never for more than ten years. What is taken into consideration is the needs of the applicant, the defendant's ability to pay, the duration of the marriage and the applicant's need for financial support for education and training. In Germany also, a divorced spouse is expected to be self-supporting. A maintenance payment can be ordered for taking care of or educating a child, old age, illness, handicap or shortage of adequate job opportunities. In deciding, the court has to give proper weight to the needs of the child living with such a spouse.

In Greece since the revision of family law in 1983, the principle is also self-sufficiency, and the right to maintenance is only granted when the former spouse is destitute and the other spouse has sufficient means. Then the payment can either be a lump sum or periodical. Again, length of marriage, the fault of the claimant or willingly causing destitution, the age and health of the claimant spouse, and care of minor children are taken into account. Similar conditions apply in Turkey and, in addition, material damages are awarded for existing or expected interests.

In Finland, spouses may enter into a 'divorce contract' under general contract law concerning the distribution of matrimonial assets and the quality and quantity of any compensation to be paid. When divorce is granted, if a spouse is in need of maintenance, the court may order such payments as periodic instalments or as a lump sum.

In Spain, either the parties make an agreement on ancillary matters, which the judge may amend, or the judge makes an order for financial provisions for the spouse economically disadvantaged by the divorce and for the children. The court cannot make a lump sum order. Alimony is a periodic payment and depends on fault, but factors such as age, health, professional qualifications and employment opportunities, duration of marriage, and past dedication to the marriage are also considered. The situation in Portugal is similar.

Under the Family Law (Scotland) Act 1985, the court has wide powers to make orders for financial provisions. The principle of 'clean break' is preferred and capital is preferred to income. Parties can reach their own agreement but the court can set aside or vary that agreement if terms are not fair or reasonable, or if the debtor becomes bankrupt. The court can order payment of a capital sum, transfer of property, periodical allowances, pension sharing, looking at the age, health and earning capacity of the claimant, the duration of the marriage, the standard of living and the needs and resources of the parties.

In the Netherlands, financial provisions are also in the form of periodic payments and lump sums. If the duration of the marriage has been short, the order is for a short fixed term, the limit being twelve years. If the marriage has lasted for less than five years and there are no children, then the duration is the same as that of the marriage. When the recipient spouse earns sufficient income, maintenance orders cease.

In Italy, maintenance is only paid when the payee has inadequate means and the criteria taken into consideration are support (economic circumstances of the spouses), reparation (responsibility for the divorce) and compensation (contribution of each spouse to family life and family property). A one-off lump sum payment may be made.

## 3. Property: During Marriage and after Divorce

In most jurisdictions, legal equality between spouses has been achieved and spouses are treated as independent persons with equal rights by law, except in respect of tax, pensions and social security provisions. In this survey, the topics of state benefits, family allowances, unemployment benefits, pension rights, and taxation including inheritance and donations taxes are not considered, extremely important though they are for European families.

Today, marriage may have little legal significance for the property of the spouses during marriage However, in historic terms, the impact of marriage on property relationships was immense, with total control on property, even when separate, being vested in the husband during marriage. Now, there is diversity in the way legal systems regulate property rights of the spouses, with three main groups: legal systems with no community property of any kind (except the matrimonial home), community property regimes during the marriage, and community property regimes coming into effect when the marriage terminates. The spectrum has at one end sharing, that is total community property, and at the other formal equality, that is total separation of property, with most legal systems moving towards the mean, some sort of deferred community, with additional protection being attached to the matrimonial home. In this survey I will be specifically looking at the property regimes, the status of matrimonial property during marriage, the rights on the matrimonial home and division of property upon divorce. It is important to remember at this point that the term 'matrimonial property' and 'matrimonial home' may soon become inappropriate as the same or very similar rules apply to the assets of cohabitees and registered partners in those jurisdictions—whose numbers are on the increase—where these relationships are legally recognized.

### 3.1. Property Regimes

One end of the spectrum is stated in the Family Law (Scotland) Act 1985 Section 24: '... marriage shall not of itself affect—(a) the respective rights of the parties to the marriage in relation to their property.' Thus, ordinary rules of property apply to spouses as though they were unmarried. This achieves formal equality but does not consider the position of the woman in a classical household who is the child-rearer with little opportunity to acquire property. True, she can obtain compensation for economic disadvantages suffered as a result of marriage in the form of financial provisions on divorce, but is the 'family' element of property such as the home, furniture, and car to be ignored? In Scotland, special property rules have been introduced to alleviate the injustice of the strict application of a separate property system. In movables these rules relate to wedding presents, gifts between spouses, household goods, furniture and 'plenishings' of the matrimonial home, money, securities and savings from housekeeping.[31] Movables will not be considered in this survey. As far as immovables are concerned, special status is attributed to the matrimonial home, which will be dealt with below. There are, however, guiding principles that the Scottish courts will apply when using their discretion to justify their orders:[32] the net value of the matrimonial property is to be shared equally between the spouses; fair account should be taken of any economic advantage derived by one party from the contributions of the other or any disadvantage suffered by either party in the interests of the other; after divorce, any economic burden of caring for a child under 16 must be shared fairly between the spouses; a party who has been dependent to a substantial degree on the financial support of the other should be awarded reasonable financial provision over a period of not more than three years from the date of the divorce decree, to enable that party to adjust to the loss of that support on divorce; and a party who at the time of the divorce seems likely to suffer serious financial hardship as a result of the divorce should be awarded reasonable financial provision to relieve him/her of hardship over a reasonable period (no longer than three years). On divorce, the court gains wide discretionary powers to distribute and allocate property irrespective of strict prop-

31. See, Thomson, *Family Law in Scotland*, 61–72.
32. Family Law (Scotland) Act 1985, s.9.

erty rights. The system for England and Wales is similar. In the Republic of Ireland, also, the general principle is that of separate property. However, again, an equitable interest arises for the spouse who has directly or indirectly contributed to the purchase of the property of the other, and the court has wide discretionary powers upon divorce or judicial separation in the reallocation of property regardless of ownership.

Similarly, in Finland, marriage has no effect on the property of the spouses. However, according to the Marriage Act of 1929 as amended in 1987, if circumstances are not conclusive, the spouses are deemed to have acquired property jointly. In addition, one spouse cannot dispose of the matrimonial home and objects related to it without the consent of the other. To avoid the potential injustice of the separation of property regime, each spouse has at the end of the marriage a 'marital right' (*avio-oikeus*) to the property of the other, which is half of the spouses' net property. Variations may be introduced by marriage settlement agreements.

In Codal systems, we encounter legal or statutory regimes (the preferred regime of the legal system), with the possibility of opting, normally pre-nuptially, for other regimes by notarial agreement to replace or modify the legal regime. Thus for example, the legal regime in Austria is separation of property, other options being community property, community property during marriage, community property deferred on death, and marriage portion.

In Greece since 1983, the legal regime is also separation of property. However, there is the possibility of sharing the profits and gains. When the marriage is dissolved, annulled, or marital life is interrupted for three years, each spouse has the 'right to profits and gains', whereby each can make a claim for a distribution of profits and gains arising from the property of the other to which he or she has contributed. This right exists unless the spouses have opted for community of acquisitions.

In Denmark, the legal regime is deferred community, which applies upon divorce, legal separation, or death. This system covers all goods acquired during marriage and goods each spouse has brought into marriage. During marriage, the system is similar to separation of property, though the spouses cannot misuse the right to dispose of property to the detriment of the other. The spouses can opt for total or partial separate property regime.

Although in Norway, spouses are regarded as independent in law with equal rights and the Marriage Act 1991 states that each spouse has the right to dispose of his or her property whether the assets form part of the community property (*felleseie*) or separate property (*saereie*), and therefore, during marriage there is no difference between the two forms of property, all property is treated as community property unless there is a prior agreement in a marriage settlement that property shall be treated as separate property, or a donor or testator expressly provides for this. At the termination of marriage, assets in the community are divided equally. This community property system has therefore been referred to as a deferred community property system. Spouses may agree by a marriage settlement that assets in separate property also become community property at the termination of marriage.

In Belgium, on the other hand, the legal regime is one of community of acquisitions, which means that all assets acquired after marriage are owned in common and will be shared equally on divorce or death. The spouses retain individual ownership of assets owned before marriage and those acquired through gift or inheritance at any time. Two alternative regimes are total community and separation of property.

In the absence of a pre-nuptial agreement, the French Civil Code also opts for community of acquisitions. Property belonging to this community is deemed to belong to spouses jointly and is administered on equal terms. Other regimes spouses can opt for are: separation of property, deferred community and universal community. Spouses cannot make an agreement to avoid the '*régime primaire*' which confers on them the duty to make financial contributions to household expenses, upbringing of children and the family home.

The 2001 Civil Code of Lithuania also accepts community of acquisitions (limited community) as the statutory regime where both spouses own the entire property jointly. By a marriage contract however, spouses can define their property rights during marriage, on divorce or on separation (Art 3.101). Spouses can opt for total separation of property, total community, or community of acquisitions (or limited community) where spouses share the acquisitions by owning a definitive part of the property. Different combinations are also possible.

Since 1 January 2002 the legal regime in the Turkish Civil Code is 'participation in acquisitions'. The other regimes, separation of property (the previous Codal regime), community of property (in two forms of limited community and community of acquisitions), and shared separation can be opted for by notarial contract either before or after the marriage. In exceptional circumstances or bankruptcy the judge can decide on a return to 'separation of property'.

Germany follows a model borrowed from Swedish Law of 1920, the 'gain-sharing community' (*Zugewinngemeinschaft*) as the preferred statutory regime under which each spouse's property remains separate throughout the marriage subject to certain restrictions imposed upon each, and the gains are divided upon its termination. The regime makes its full impact on the termination of marriage. Net increases are split upon divorce and the spouse whose property has increased to a lesser extent is entitled to gain one half of the difference. Other options are: total separation and total merger. In Sweden today, deferred community is the legal regime. Each spouse on division of property has the right to one-half of the aggregate value of the spouses' marital property after deduction of debts. Spouses may also hold separate property which is not divided.

Switzerland also has deferred community of acquisitions as the statutory regime. Spouses enjoy their property during the marriage, but the value of their acquisitions is divided upon the dissolution of marriage. Spouses can also opt for community of property or separation of property regimes.

In Italy, the legal regime is community property on all property, movable and immovable, acquired during marriage. The spouses own the property jointly, regardless of whether it was bought jointly or severally. The consent of both spouses is needed for extraordinary, important transactions on the common property.[33] On termination of marriage, property held personally by each spouse such as rents and dividends from property and income from separate professions also falls into this community. Spouses can opt for other regimes under contract law during or after marriage: separation of property and community of property for certain items.

Portugal also has a legal regime of community property if spouses do not by pre-nuptial agreement opt for separation of property or another system they can create within the limits of the law. The legal regime regards assets acquired during marriage, whether purchased jointly or severally, and income from work or investment as communal assets. However, where one or both spouses are sixty years of age or more at the time of the marriage, mandatory separation of property applies. The situation is similar in Spain where the community property regime is both in the Civil Code and under the laws of certain autonomous communities. The regime of the Civil Code applies unless there is a marital property agreement or if autonomous community laws provide otherwise. Under the Codal regime (*gananciales*) property purchased during marriage, property acquired by the labour of either spouse, profits, rents and interests belonging to either spouse and business established during marriage fall into the community. Spouses can opt for community of gains or separation of property. In some communities such as Catalonia, Navarre, Aragon, and the Basque Country different regimes apply.

The Netherlands is at the extreme end of the spectrum with a universal community regime. Following on from the Act on Rights and Duties of

33. Extraordinary and ordinary transactions are defined by the courts. See for example, Cass no 592 of 21 February 1969.

Spouses and Registered Partners, which came into force on 22 June 2001, the Act on Contractual Participation Clauses was passed on 14 March 2002. However, the universal community system of 1838 still applies to marriages and registered partnerships alike. Even when spouses opt for separation of property, they often make an exception for the matrimonial home, which is jointly owned. The move today is towards limiting the extent of the community to assets acquired during the marriage, which is already a widely used contractual option in the Netherlands. In addition, contrary to what is now the case, property received by inheritance or gift may not in future fall into the community and the courts may have increased discretionary powers to adjust property rights. These reforms are under discussion.

Similarly, Poland has a community property regime comprising the acquisitions of both spouses and the income from the common and separate property of each. By contracting out, the other option is separation of property. However, community property in the family home is compulsory.

### *3.2. Matrimonial Home*

One of the innovative developments of recent times has been the special status and protection allocated to the matrimonial or family home. We see this special status in most of the systems under survey from Scotland to Turkey, from Finland to the Republic of Ireland, from Lithuania to Malta. The matrimonial home has a special status during marriage and upon divorce. For example, during marriage spouses have restricted rights to dispose of the matrimonial home and the house contents (Austria, Belgium, Denmark, Finland, France, Germany, Greece, Scotland, and Turkey), if the non-owner spouse has a housing need, the other cannot dispose of it and cannot limit the right of occupation of the needy spouse (Austria, Denmark, and Greece). Such rules apply whether the spouse is the owner, the mortgage payer or the tenant, and whether the matrimonial regime is one of separation of property or some form of community property. Given that the family home is usually the most substantial asset of the family, the question of ownership of the home and entitlement to interests in it by the respective spouses, including occupation, vest in each spouse, especially in systems that opt for separation of property.

In Finland, where there is no community of property upon marriage, and Norway, where there is no provision with gives the non-owner spouse the right to occupy the matrimonial home, the spouse who owns 'the real property which is solely or mainly used as the common home of the spouses' cannot sell, give away, lease, or mortgage the matrimonial home without the written consent of the other. The Family Home Protection Act 1976 in the Republic of Ireland also requires the prior written consent of a spouse if the other wishes to sell or pass on any interest in the family home. The case is similar in the Netherlands.

In England and Wales, spouses have statutory rights of occupation (Family Law Act, 1996). If one of the spouses has the right of occupation, then the other has statutory 'matrimonial home rights', which include the right not to be evicted or excluded from the home if in occupation and, if not in occupation, then with the leave of the court, to enter and occupy the home. Though the case is similar in Scotland, this right does end at the termination of marriage, but the house will be part of financial provision on divorce. The court has discretion but must at all times consider whether a spouse or a child would suffer significant harm. The case is similar in Northern Ireland.

In France, if the matrimonial home is rented the presumption is that the lease is vested in both spouses. In the Republic of Ireland, practice shows that spouses usually arrange for joint ownership or ownership in common of the matrimonial home. If one spouse is the owner, the other may claim equitable or beneficial interest by virtue of direct or indirect contributions made to the purchase. Courts have discretion to make necessary adjustments. Similarly, in Scotland most couples take the title to the matrimonial home in joint names. However, each spouse has the right to live in the matrimonial home regardless of ownership. These rights need no registration but can be enforced by court order. For example, where one spouse is a tenant the court can transfer the tenancy to the other.

In Malta, following a judgment of separation, the court, if asked to do so by either spouse, decides according to the circumstances whether one of them shall be entitled to reside in the matrimonial home.

Upon divorce, even in legal systems where the matrimonial home may be included in the partition though bought by one of the spouses, if the other spouse needs to continue to use it or is caring for children, then the court can order that the non-owner spouse be entitled to remain in the matrimonial home, order the transfer of ownership or order that spouse to take-over the contract, such as a lease agreement governing the use of the matrimonial home (Austria, Denmark, France, Germany, Greece, and Turkey). The court may even have the power to seal off the matrimonial home and matrimonial property or freeze all assets (Belgium, England and Wales).

If the matrimonial home is the only asset of significant value, then the non-occupying spouse must be provided with his/her half share of the asset. In Denmark for instance, it is possible to make only a part payment initially to help the custodial spouse to remain in the home. In France, if the matrimonial home has been purchased jointly, it must be sold and the proceeds equally divided upon divorce, regardless of whether there are children or not. However, the judge can order that co-ownership should continue for up to five years, at the end of which period he can order the transfer of the home to one of the spouses and the transferee to pay the transferor's share in the property. If, however, the home is owned by one of the spouses, he/she remains the sole owner upon divorce, though the judge can order the owner to let the home to the other spouse for rent where the non-owner has custody of the children. This is also the case in Greece. Similarly, in the Netherlands, the non-owner spouse may remain in the family home for up to six months and thereafter, by showing 'a greater interest' and by paying rent. Looking after the children or having no other accommodation are signs of 'greater interest'.

As seen earlier, in Finland, each spouse has a 'marital right' on the property of the other which means retaining half of the other's net property, unless decided otherwise by a marriage settlement. Even when there is no such right, the spouse caring for the children is entitled to keep the former matrimonial home and the movable property related to it, undivided. Under Irish law, a court may transfer to a spouse the right to reside in the family home for life or such other period as is prescribed. In Italy, the spouse who is without title but has custody of the children remains in the family home upon separation or divorce. If there are no children, the judge gives preference to the economically weaker spouse.

According to Scots law, the net value of the matrimonial property is to be shared fairly between the spouses upon divorce. This is property acquired during the marriage; the family home, its furnishings, and 'plenishings' can be included even if they were acquired prior to marriage. Where there are children of the family needing a home, the court can order that the matrimonial home be transferred to the spouse looking after the children. This spouse's share of the rest of the matrimonial property can then be reduced proportionately. In Spain also, if there are children subject to '*patria potestas*', the matrimonial home will be allocated to the spouse with custody and care and control. If both parents have children living with them, the court decides who shall remain in occupation of the home depending on which of the spouses is in most need of protection. A rent may be paid. Even when there are no children, the court may order that the non-owning spouse may occupy the family home for as long as necessary.

Under the separation of property regime in Switzerland, when the property is divided on divorce according to the rules of the deferred community system, a spouse has a right to be allocated his or her own property. However, the joint dwelling and the household goods will be allocated to the spouse who has the greater need, understood to mean the one who has custody of the children or the actual care of the children in case of joint custody. This spouse may take over the matrimonial home even when that property is the separate property of the other spouse. This spouse's share will be deducted from his/her portion of the marital property.

The concept of matrimonial home entered Turkish law in 2002 with the new Civil Code. One spouse cannot end a lease contract, or transfer the home, or limit the rights on it without the overt consent of the other. The judge can intervene when there is no agreement. The owner-spouse can ask for an 'entry of interest' into the land register that the house be designated as a 'family home'. If the 'family home' is rented, this fact can be written into the lease contract. In this way, the spouse party to the contract cannot cause the eviction of the other by not paying the rent, as long as the other pays the rent. The old regime of separation of property continues to apply to marriages concluded before 1 January 2002 unless those spouses had drawn up a contract before 1 January 2003 and decided that 'participation of acquisitions' would apply to their property from the beginning of their marriage. Only property acquired after the latter date will be covered by the new regime.

## 4. Concluding Remarks

From the foregoing survey a number of general questions arise. For instance, does the content of current family laws mirror changes in the economic, political and social structures and political ideologies of different European states? What about social acceptance? How desirable or possible is it for legal norms to guide social behaviour? Do the legislators strike an acceptable balance between individualism and 'traditional' familial ideologies? Can we discern convergence here? Can we say that a pluralist society, which more and more of the jurisdictions under survey claim to have become, necessitates a pro-active role for family law and the recognition of support for a variety of different family forms? Is there a future for 'monolithic cultural insularity' in European family law preventing recognition of the 'different others'? How easy would it be to change deeply ingrained social habits in family matters? Could adopting neutral solutions, where there is a lack of family policy consensus, do this? Is family policy a product of social change or can it be a creator of social change? What is the place and role of 'legal transplants' in this field? What about a harmonized 'Family Law for Europe'?

In one sense, it would not be an exaggeration to talk of the transformation of family law in Europe in recent decades. The authority structure of the marriage has been altered, the economic content of marriage has changed, the role of the family as a safety-net has been weakened, disadvantages attaching to children born out of wedlock have been removed, rules on occupation of the family home have been developed, divorce laws have tended to abolish fault and see the traditional categories of offences as symptomatic of the breakdown of marriage, not its cause, mediation is becoming an alternative to court action, concepts such as adultery have been more or less abandoned, novel statutory concepts such as 'children's rights', 'parental responsibility' and 'joint custody' after separation, have been adopted, and individualism has replaced familialism as a cultural value.

As stated by Willekens, some changes point to a deinstitutionalization of marriage, such as the breakdown of the distinction between legitimate and illegitimate children and relaxation of the conditions for divorce. Some changes such as the partial survival of the dissolved relationship because of the economic consequences of divorce, and a modest convergence of marriage and unmarried cohabitation point to a measure of reinstitutionalization. Other such developments are a fundamental shift regarding "marriage as a set of rules organising social security and material solidarity within the nuclear group;" a change in the pattern of legal authority in the family by both an equalization of the husband and wife and the limitation of parental rights; the recent exceptions, though rare, to the principles of gender difference between the partners; and one and the same person having simultaneous institutional relations with two or more partners and children therefrom.[34]

In another sense, much remains unchanged. Marriage is still central to family law: it is the way to acquire access to various legal consequences, being privileged as a form of familial living, and it is on the whole envisaged to be between members of different sexes; so even when alternative life styles are recognized this has not meant the deinstitutionalization of marriage, but the extending of its boundaries as an institution.

The family is still the smallest social and multi-functional unit in society, but is undergoing continuous modernization, dubbed by Rottenbacher 'unfinished modernity'.[35] However, to a certain extent, differences in Eastern and Western Europe and the South and the North of Europe persist. In many of the jurisdictions under survey, the family faces rising secularization, declining familialism, with comprehensive social security systems replacing its func-

34. See H. Willekens, *Long-term Developments in Family Law in Western Europe: an Explanation*, in J. Eekelaar & T. Nhlapo (eds), *The Changing Family: Family Forms and Family Law* (Oxford, 1998), 58–59.

35. F. Rothenbacher, *Social Change in Europe and its Impact on Family Structures*, in Eekelaar & Nhlapo (eds), *The Changing Family: Family Forms and Family Law*, 9.

tion and easing the development of new family forms, different household and family forms co-existing both within individual countries and within Europe. Yet, in a small number of jurisdictions, mostly under post-socialist regimes, there is also a movement backwards.

Legislators are interested in strengthening parental stability by, for instance, regulating joint custody both for married and cohabiting parents upon divorce and breakdown, and redressing inequality. They do not seem to be overly interested in family or marriage stability. Legislators provide rules for solving social problems and aim to influence the behaviour of people by laying down principles to indicate 'appropriate family values': 'pro-marriage', 'pro-children' and 'anti-violence'. They are also 'pro non-adversarial divorce', and at times 'pro cost-cutting'.[36] Rather than relying on judicial discretion (technocratic liberalism), legislators also become involved in adjusting the economic consequences of family breakdown by sponsoring 'adjustive financial regimes' in, for instance, spouse maintenance and property division.

Considering the above survey, can the last word be that "the general direction of the change is the same in all legal systems under review, but there are substantial differences in both the pace and the extent of the change?"[37]

## References

Agell, A., *Should and Can Family Law Influence Social Behaviour?*, in J. Eekelaar, & T. Nhlapo, (eds), *The Changing Family: Family Forms and Family Law* (Oxford 1998), 125–137.

Antokolskaia, M. (ed) *Convergence and Divergence of Family Law in Europe* (Antwerp, 2007).

Antokolskaia, M., *Harmonisation of Family Law in Europe: A Historical Perspective. A Tale of Two Millennia* (Antwerp 2006).

Antokolskaia, M., *Comparative Family Law: Moving with the times* in E. Örücü and A. Harding (eds) Comparative Law: A Handbook, (Oxford, 2007), 241–262.

36. A. Bainham, *Changing Families and Changing Concepts. Reforming the Language of Family Law*, in Eekelaar & Nhlapo (eds), *The Changing Family: Family Forms and Family Law*, 116.

37. Willekens, *Long-term Developments in Family Law in Western Europe: an Explanation*, in Eekelaar & Nhlapo (eds), *The Changing Family: Family Forms and Family Law*, 47.

Bainham, A., *Changing Families and Changing Concepts: Reforming the Language of Family Law*, in J. Eekelaar & T. Nhlapo (eds), *The Changing Family: Family Forms and Family Law* (Oxford 1998), 153–171.

Bercovitz, R., *Comentarios a las Reformas del Codigo Civil* (Madrid 1993).

Boele-Woelki, K. & Sverdrup, T. (eds) European Challenges in Contemporary Family Law (Antwerp, 2008)

Bradley, D., *Convergence in Family Law: Mirrors, Transplants and Political Economy*, *Maastricht Journal of European and Comparative Law*, 6 (1999), 127–150.

Bradley, D., *A Family Law for Europe? Sovereignty, Political Economy and Legitimation*, in K. Beole-Woelki (ed.) *Perspectives for the Unification and Harmonisation of Family Law in Europe*, European Family Law Series, volume 4, (Antwerp-Oxford-New York 2003), 65–104.

Chaveau, V. & Poivey-Leclercq, H., *Le Droit de la Famille*, Collections guides pratiques (Le seuil 2001).

Cian, G., Oppo, G. & Trabucchi, A., *Commentario al Diritto Italiano della Famiglia* (Padova 1992).

Cretney, S., *Family Law in the Twentieth Century* (Oxford 2003).

Curry-Sumner, I., *All's well that ends registered? The Substantive and Private International Law Aspects of Non-Marital Registered Relationships in Europe*, European Family Law Series, volume 11, (Mortsel, 2005).

Deschenaux, H., Tercier, P. & Werro, F., *Le marriage et le divorce*, 4th edn (Berne 1995).

Dewar, J., *Reducing Discretion in Family Law*, in J. Eekelaar & T. Nhlapo (eds), *The Changing Family: Family Forms and Family Law* (Oxford 1998), 231–250.

Eekelaar, J. & Nhlapo, T. (eds), *The Changing Family: Family Forms and Family Law* (Oxford 1998).

Eriksson, A., *Den nya familjerätten*, 5th edn (Stockholm 1997).

Farrugia, R., *Malta: The Impact of CEDAW and the Aftermath*, A. Bainham (ed) *The International Survey of Family Law, 1994*, published on behalf of The International Society of Family Law (The Hague 1996), 329–343.

Ferrari, S. & Hopf, G., *Eherechtsreform in Österreich* (Vienna 2000).

Freeman,M. (ed), *The Family, Law and Society* (London 2008).

Fulchiron, H., Ferre-André, S. & Gouttenoire, A., *A Pause in the Reform of French Family Law*, in A. Bainham (ed) *The International Survey of Family Law, 2004 Edition*, published on behalf of The International Society of Family Law (Bristol 2004), 181–191.

Graham-Siegenthaler, B. & Siehr, K, *Swiss law of marriage, marital relations and divorce*, in M. Rotondi (ed), *The marriage*, Inchieste di diritto comparato Vol 11, (Milano 1998).

Hamilton, C. & Perry, A., (eds), *Family Law in Europe*, 2nd edn (London 2002).

Hamilton, C. & Woods, L., *Europe*, in C. Hamilton & A. Perry (eds), *Family Law in Europe*, 2nd edn (London 2002), 163–229.

Keserauskas, S., *Moving in the same Direction? Presentation of Family Law Reforms in Lithuania*, A. Bainham (ed) *The International Survey of Family Law, 2004 Edition*, published on behalf of The International Society of Family Law (Bristol 2004), 315–334.

Kurczewski, J., *Privatizing the Polish Family after Communism*, in M. Maclean & J. Kurczewski (eds) *Families, Politics and the Law: Perspectives for East and West Europe* (Oxford 1994), 25–52.

Kurczewski, J. & Maclean, M. (eds), *Family Law and Family Policy in the New Europe* Onati International Series in Law and Society, (Aldershot 1997).

Kurczewski, J. & Maclean, M., *Introduction: The Two Europes*, in J. Kurczewski & M. Maclean (eds), *Family Law and Family Policy in the New Europe* Onati International Series in Law and Society, (Aldershot 1997), ix–xxvii.

Lowe, N. & Douglas, G., *Bromley's Family Law*, 9th edn (London 1998).

Maclean, M. & Kurczewski, J., *Introduction: The Issues in Context*, in M. Maclean & J. Kurczewski (eds) *Families, Politics and the Law: Perspectives for East and West Europe* (Oxford 1994), 1–23.

McGlynn, C., *Challenging the European Harmonisation of Family Law: Perspectives on "The Family"*, in K. Boele-Woelki (ed.) *Perspectives for the Unification and Harmonisation of Family Law in Europe*, European Family Law Series, volume 4, (Antwerp-Oxford-New York 2003), 219–238.

Nielsen, L. & Vorstrup Ramussen, J., *FamilieRetten* (Gads Forlag 2001).

O'Donovan, K., *Family Definitions and Human Rights: Rights to Respect for Private and Family Life under the European Convention on Human Rights*, in J. Kurczewski & M. Maclean (eds) *Family Law and Family Policy in the New Europe* Onati International Series in Law and Society, (Aldershot 1997), 27–42.

Örücü, E., *A Family Law for Europe: Necessary, Feasible, Desirable?*, in K. Beole-Woelki (ed.) *Perspectives for the Unification and Harmonisation of Family Law in Europe*, European Family Law Series, volume 4, (Antwerp-Oxford-New York 2003), 551–572.

Örücü, E., *Turkey: Family Law Enters the New Century*, in A. Bainham (ed) *The International Survey of Family Law, 2004 Edition*, published on behalf of The International Society of Family Law (Bristol 2004), 469–482.

Piconto-Novales, T., *Family Law and Family Policy in Spain*, in J. Kurczewski & M. Maclean (eds), *Family Law and Family Policy in the New Europe* Onati International Series in Law and Society, (Aldershot 1997), 109–127.

Pöyhönen, J. (ed), *An introduction to Finnish law* (Helsinki 2002).
Roca, E., *Derecho de Familiard*, 3rd edn (Valencia 1997).
Rothenbacher, F., *Social Change in Europe and its Impact on Family Structures*, in J. Eekelaar & T. Nhlapo (eds), *The Changing Family: Family Forms and Family Law* (Oxford 1998), 3–31.
Rymsza, M., Socio-Cultural and Ideological Aspects of the Evolution of Family Policies in Liberal Societies, in J. Kurczewski & M. Maclean (eds) *Family Law and Family Policy in the New Europe* Onati International Series in Law and Society, (Aldershot 1997), 221–246.
Shatter, A.J., *Shatter's Family Law*, 4th edn (London 1997).
Schwab, D., *Familienrecht*, 11th edn (Munich 2001).
Schwimann, M., *Familienrecht* (Vienna, 1999).
Sosson, J. & Demars, S., *Tout savoir sur le Divorce*, Editions Juridiques, (Brussels 2000).
Thomson, J. M., *Family Law in Scotland*, 4th edn (Edinburgh 2002).
Varela, A., Direito da Familia, 3rd edn (Lisbon, 1993).
Vathrakokoilis, V., *The New Family Law*, 2nd edn (Athens 2000).
Vlaardingerbroek, P (ed), Het hedendaagse personen—en familierecht, 3rd edn (Deventer 2002).
Willekens, H., *Long-term Developments in Family Law in Western Europe: an Explanation*, in J. Eekelaar & T. Nhlapo (eds), *The Changing Family: Family Forms and Family Law* (Oxford 1998), 47–71.

# 15

# The Law of Successions

Antoni Vaquer*

## Summary



## 1. Preliminary Remarks

Within the context of the harmonization of private law in Europe, the law of succession still occupies the role of Cinderella. Whilst the Europeanization of family law has reached an interesting stage[1] and even a Commission on Eu-

---

* Professor of civil law, Universitat de Lleida. The author is indebted to professors Shael Herman and Sergio Cámara Lapuente for valuable remarks to a previous draft of this chapter and to Ms Rosa Miquel for assistance in editing the typescript. All errors, however, are the author's fault. The author tries to include references to as much European legal systems as possible, which requires the availability of materials at least in English or German. But, in order not to burden too much the reader, references to Spain are mainly limited to the *Código Civil* and the civil law of Catalonia and usually do not cover all the regional legal systems in force within Spain.

1. See now the landmark achievements in D. Martiny, *Is Unification of Family Law Feasible or even Desirable?*, in A. Hartkamp *et al* (eds.), *Towards a European Civil Code. Third fully revised and expanded edition* (Nijmegen 2004), 307.

ropean Family Law has been established,[2] there have been no comparable steps in the field of inheritance law and legal literature on successions is still scarce.[3] In the previously mentioned reference textbook on European private law only one chapter among forty-four is devoted to the law of succession—that is to say, 16 out of 831 pages.[4] This handbook has a similar allocation of attention. However, two recent facts may pave the way for further developments. On the one hand, the European Commission has adopted a Green Paper on transnational successions which, although from an international private law perspective, faces some of the core questions of the law of successions such as form of wills, compulsory share, fideicommissary substitutions and so forth.[5] On the other hand, the XVIIth Congress of the International Academy of Comparative Law (2006) held sessions on "new developments in succession law."[6]

---

2. All details are available at http://www2.law.uu.nl/priv/cefl/.

3. Y.-H. Leleu, *Nécessité et moyens d'une harmonisation des règles de transmission successorale en Europe, ERPL* 159 (1998); C. Pamplona Corte-Real, *Um código civil para a Europa. Necessidade e interesse de uma unificação no âmbito do direito das successões*, unpublished paper delivered at the Conference held in Coimbra (2000) on a European Civil Code organised by the Portuguese Government; K. Kuchinke, *Über die Notwendigkeit, ein gemeineuropäisches Familien—und Erbrecht zu schaffen*, in *Europas universale reschtsordungspolitische Aufgabe im Recht des dritten Jahrtausends. Festschrift für Alfred Söllner* (München 2000), 589; D. Leipold, *Europa und das Erbrecht*, in *Festschrift für Alfred Söllner*, 647; W. Pintens, *Die Europäisierung des Erbrechts, ZeuP* 628 (2001); S. Edenfeld, *Europäische Entwicklungen im Erbrecht, Zeitschrift für Erbrecht und Vermögensnachfolge (ZEV)* 457 (2001); M. Puelinckx-Coene, *La protection de la famille dans le domaine des successions, rapport général de la 6e Conférence Européene sur le droit de la famille* (available at http://www.coe.int/T/E/Legal_Affairs/Legal_co-operation/Family_law_and_children's_rights/Documents/CONF%20FA%20_2002_%20RAP%20GEN%20E%20-%20Rapport%20Puelinckx-Coene.asp); *Le droit de successions en Europe. Actes du Colloque du 21 Février 2003* (2003); W. Pintens, *Grundgedanken und Perspektiven einer Europäisierung des-Familien und Erbrechts, Fam RZ* 329 417, 499 (2003).

4. A. Verbeke, Y.H. Leleu, *Harmonisation of the Law of Succession in Europe*, in A. Hartkamp *et al* (eds.), *Towards a European Civil Code*, 335–350. The same can be said of the Spanish textbook on European Private Law [S. Cámara Lapuente (ed.), *Derecho privado europeo* (Madrid 2003)], where the chapter on the law of succession [(S. Cámara Lapuente, *¿Derecho europeo de sucesiones? Un apunte*] takes up 48 of the 1233 pages.

5. Brussels, 1.3.2005, COM(2005) 65 final. See H. Dörner, Ch. Hertel, P. Lagarde, W. Riering, *Auf dem Weg zu einem europäischen Internationalen Erb-und Erbverfahrensrech, Praxis des internationalen Privat-und Verfahrensrechts (IPRax)* (2005) 1; B. Jud, *Rechtswahl im Erbrecht: Das Grünbuch der Europäischen Kommission zum Erb-und Testamentsrecht, Zeitschrift für Gemeinschaftsprivatrecht* (2005) 133.

6. Further information at http://www2.law.uu.nl/priv/AIDC/index1.asp.

I will not deal with the feasibility of a unified European law of succession.[7] Succession law is deeply rooted in the fundamental social and cultural values of a society, and the main European research groups concerned with the issue of harmonization have consciously sidestepped inheritance law.[8] Nonetheless, some common trends can be outlined in the European national—and regional —laws of succession. Some legal writers speak of a "spontaneous harmonisation" affecting the law of succession as a consequence of common features in recent developments of family law that have had a marked impact on succession law.[9] The following pages sketch some areas where spontaneous harmonization is becoming evident. Whether spontaneous harmonization could be a sufficient basis for a "Europeanised law of succession" will remain an open question.

## 2. Freedom of Testation

Freedom of testation means that every *competent* person has the right to nominate his/her heirs at his/her own discretion and thus to decide the destiny of his/her property after his/her death. Freedom of testation is acknowledged in all European national laws,[10] although its extent may differ slightly in relation to the legal rights of inheritance of certain persons.[11]

7. The lack of competence of the EU is one of the hindrances. See J. Basedow, *Das BGB in künftigen europäischen Privatrecht. Der hybride Kodex, Archiv für die civilistiche Praxis* (2000) 445, 483; C. Schmid, *Legitimitätsbedingungen eines Europaischen Zivilgesetzbuchs, Juristenzeitung (JZ)* 674, 675 (2001); Pintens, *Die Europäisierung* 646 (2001); Pintens, *Grundgedanken* 502. See now art. I-13.b), I-14.2.b), f) and j) of the Project of a European Constitution.

8. See e.g. C. von Bar, *Le group d'éstudes sur un Code civil européen, Revue Internationale de Droit Comparé* 127, 131 (2001).

9. Cámara Lapuente, *¿Derecho europeo de sucesiones?* 1199; Puelinckx-Coene, *La protection* 18; Pintens *Die Europäisierung* 648; Pintens, *Grundgedanken* 330; Verbeke/Leleu, *Harmonisation* 336–338, 347–348 (under the expression "spontaneous convergence").

10. Kuchinke, *Über die Notwendigkeit, ein gemeineuropäisches Familien—und Erbrecht zu schaffen*, in *Europas universale reschtsordungspolitische Aufgabe im Recht des dritten Jahrtausends. Festschrift für Alfred Söllner*, 604; Edenfeld, *Europäische Entwicklungen* 457. M.J. De Waal, "A Comparative Overview", in K.G.C. Reid, M.J. De Waal, R. Zimmermann, *Exploring the Law of Succession* 14 (Edinbutgh 2007): "There can be no doubt that all developed systems of testate succession are based on the premise of freedom of testation". One of the aims of the last legal reform in France was to "give more freedom in order to organise one's succession". See the "exposé des motifs" at http://www.lexisnexis.fr/do/documents_utiles_DO.htm.

11. See *infra sub* 4.

The legal instrument that makes freedom of testation possible is the will. All the European laws in force admit more than one type of will. Therefore, it is possible to say that the legislator facilitates making a will. As further evidence of the legislator's policy favouring wills, an international trend seeks to avoid the nullity of a will based exclusively on formal reasons. Art. 1 of The Hague Convention on the Conflicts of Laws relating to the Form of Testamentary Dispositions establishes a set of alternatives that in practice make it very difficult to nullify a will based on formal grounds.[12] However, nullity is still possible, since not all types of wills are valid for nationals making a will in their home countries according to their national laws.[13] Consequently, the proposal of admissibility of as many types of will as possible in a comparative perspective deserves consideration.[14]

Freedom of testation does not refer exclusively to the freedom of disposal of the testator's property. Wills may include clauses without patrimonial character, such as the appointment of guardians for minors and the disabled.[15] Hence, a will is the best expression of the testator's autonomy, since he/she

---

12. "A testamentary disposition shall be valid as regards form if its form complies with the internal law:

a) of the place where the testator made it, or

b) of a nationality possessed by the testator, either at the time when he made the disposition, or at the time of his death, or

c) of a place in which the testator had his domicile either at the time when he made the disposition, or at the time of his death, or

d) of the place in which the testator had his habitual residence either at the time when he made the disposition, or at the time of his death, or

e) so far as immovables are concerned, of the place where they are situated."

13. For example, the (unattested) holograph will does not exist in the Netherlands (D. Hayton, *European Succession Laws* 2nd ed. [Bristol, 2002], 15.1), Ireland (J.C. Brady, *Succession Law in Ireland*, 2nd ed. [Dublin 1995], 2.32 ff) or England (C.H. Sherrin *et al*, *Williams on Wills*, vol. 1 8th ed. [London-Dublin-Edinburgh 2002], 10.18). See further the detailed classifications of the types of wills given by Cámara Lapuente, *¿Derecho europeo de sucesiones?*, 1227–1229, and Verbeke/Leleu, *Harmonisation* 342.

14. Cámara Lapuente, *¿Derecho europeo de sucesiones?* 1231.

15. For example, Catalonia: art. 171.a) and 173 Family Code, on which J. Marsal Guillamet, in F. Badosa Coll (dir.), *Manual de dret civil català* (Madrid-Barcelona 2003), 661; England: s. 5(5) Children Act 1989, on which *Williams on Wills* 28.4 ff; Germany: §1777 BGB, on which Palandt/U. Diederichsen 62nd ed. (München, 2003), Rn 1, 2; Ireland: Brady, *Succession Law in Ireland* 4.01; Italy: art. 348 *Codice Civile*, on which P. Rescigno, *Manuale di diritto privato* (Milano 2000), 371; Luxembourg: art. 398 Civil Code; Malta: art. 159 Civil Code; Spain: art. 223 *Código civil*, on which C. Rogel Vide, in *Comentario del Código civil* I (Madrid 1991), 698 ff.

can express his/her last intention concerning his/her property and other non-patrimonial interests.

Freedom of testation also implies the testator's free revocation of his/her will. A will is ambulatory; it can be revoked at any time, regardless of the testator having stated that the will cannot be revoked.[16] To make or revoke a will the testator must be of sound mind and of legal age. Legal age varies by legal system, although it is normally related to the age of majority.[17] Testamentary capacity is presumed, so that whoever seeks to nullify a will must prove the incapacity of the testator. The increasing longevity of men and women can make it very difficult in practice for the courts to assess testamentary capacity, but if any doubt arises, it should be resolved in favor of upholding the will.[18]

---

16. Austria: §716 ABGB; Catalonia: art. 422-8.1 Civil Code; Czech Republic: M. Hrušáková, in IEL vol. 1, p. 198, para 518; England: Caroline Sawyer, *Principles of Succession, Wills and Probate* 2nd ed. (London-Sydney 1998), 35; Estonia: §86 Law of Succession Act; Finland: art. 10:5 *Perintökaari;* France: art. 895 *Code Civil;* Italy: art. 587.1, 679 *Codice Civile;* Germany: §2253 BGB; Portugal: art. 2311 *Código civil;* Scotland: Hilary Hiram, *The Scots Law of Succession* (Edinburgh 2002), 6.27; Spain: art. 737 *Código civil.*

17. Austria: §591 ABGB; Belgium: art. 904 *Code civil* (over 16 under limitations); Denmark: §39 *Arveloven*; England: *Williams on Wills*, 4.7; Ireland: s. 77(1) Succession Act; Italy: art. 591.1 *Codice civile;* Finland: art. 9:1 *Perintökaari*; Greece: art. 1719 *Astikos Kodikas*; Sweden: 9:1 *Ärvdabalke*; Switzerland: art. 467 Civil Code. Nevertheless, limitedly in Malta (art. 597.a, 598 Civil Code), in Spain (art. 663.1 *Código civil*) and Catalonia (art. 421-4 Civil Code) a notarial will is valid if the testator is over 14, although the holographic will requires majority of age (art. 688 *Código civil* and 421-17.1 Civil Code, respectively); in Scotland in theory the testator must be over 12 (Hiram, *Scots Law of Succession* 9.5 and 9.6); in the Czech Republic, a minor over 15 can make a notarial will [§476d(2)]; in France (art. 903, 904 *Code civil*), Germany (§2229(1) BGB) and the Netherlands (art. 4:55(1) BW) the legal age is 16. In Portugal, emancipated minors are capable of testation (art. 2189.a *Código civil*); emancipation results from marriage (art. 132 *Código civil*), and a valid marriage requires to be 16 years old (art. 1601.a *Código civil*). Additionally, some systems of law allow married minor testators to dispose partially of their assets (Sweden, Finland); in Luxembourg, the testator must be 18 years old, but minors of 16 years can dispose of half of their patrimony by will (art. 904 Civil Code; see Monique and Raymond Wagen, *Successions et donations* (3rd. ed., Luxembourg 2006) 356–357, nº 318).

18. Such tendency can be observed in Germany [Palandt/W. Edenhofer, *BGB*, §2229, Rn 10-11; H.G. Bamberger, H. Roth/W. Litzenburger, *BGB*, Band 3 (München 2003), §2229, Rn 11], Italy [Guido Capozzi, *Successioni e donazioni* 2nd ed. (Milano 2002), t. 1, 378–379], Scotland (Hiram, *Scots Law of Succession* 9.10 ff), Spain [J.L. Lacruz Berdejo *et al, Elementos de derecho civil V. Sucesiones* (Madrid 2004), 161–163], Catalonia [A. Vaquer, *La capacitat per a testar en la jurisprudència del Tribunal Superior de Justícia de Catalunya, Revista Catalana de Dret Privat* 173 (2002)]; a more nuanced approach is the English one (*Williams on Wills* 4.12).

## 3. Pre-Eminence of Testator's Intention

The will expresses the testator's intention, but sometimes it can be difficult to know exactly what the testator intended to mean when he/she—or the notary—employed specific words in drawing up the will. Here it seems necessary to distinguish interpretation from construction. "Interpretation" refers to the ascertainment of the meaning of the testator's words, whereas "construction" consists in filling gaps in the testator's expressed intention. Interpretation and construction of the will are very delicate tasks. The interpreter not only risks creating an intention alien to that of the testator. Even if the interpreter were able to ascertain the testator's truest intention, that intention must find some support in the words of the will. Wills are formal, the testamentary intention has to be declared under strict formalities—as said above, each system of law admits only certain types of will, and the wills that do not fulfil the formal requirements are void. Therefore, giving effect to an intention expressed without such formalities would breach the essential formal character of wills.

That tension between form and intention may explain the success of literalism. "There is ( … ) one rule of construction, of universal application, which admits of no exception, and which ought never under any circumstances, to be departed from, viz. that if any term is used by a testator which has a primary and ordinary legal meaning, *that* is the sense in which it ought to be construed, unless the Court is reasonably satisfied, by evidence to be collected from the will itself, of the testator's intention to use it, not in that sense, but in some different sense."[19] This fragment reflects the pre-eminent opinion of John Wigram in the English courts,[20] which led to increasingly vocal complaints when judges were compelled, for example, to interpret "money" as "cash" although the testatrix had invested the money in shares or whatever.[21] Needless to say, that construction was unfair to the testator's intention. It is not surprising, therefore, that when the literal interpretation of "money" was finally set aside, Lord Atkin could "anticipate with satisfaction that henceforth

19. *In re Crawford's Trusts* (1854) 61 ER 707.

20. John Wigram, *An Examination of the Rules of Law, respecting the Admission of Extrinsic Evidence in aid of the Interpretation of Wills* (London 1831), on which R. Kerridge, *Hawkins on the Construction of Wills* (London 2000), and R. Kerridge, J. Rivers, *The Construction of Wills, Law Quarterly Review* 287 (2000).

21. "I have reluctantly come to the conclusion that we are bound to apply a rule which it has been said more than once by judges, members of the profession and laymen, that it defeats the intention of the testatrix", confessed Lord Greene MR in *In re Morgan* [1942] 1 Ch 345, 346.

the group of ghosts of dissatisfied testators who, according to a late Chancery judge, wait on the other bank of the Styx to receive the judicial personages who have misconstrued their wills, may be considerably diminished."[22] However, this tendency toward literalism was not unique either to English law or common law.[23] On the contrary, similar principles can be found on the Continent. "Soll man deutliche und klare Dispositionen niemal auszulegen, oder zu verbrechen suchen," the *Codex Maximilianus Bavaricus* proclaimed solemnly (III,2,§12). Clear words need not to be interpreted in order to avoid misconstructions, only obscure terms deserve a construction, explained the authoritative commentator of the Bavarian *Codex*.[24] But what result when are the words not clear enough?

The Digest contained two apparently irreconcilable fragments of Paulus. The first one seems to anticipate the English literalism and the Bavarian prohibition of interpretation: "cum in verbis nulla ambiguitas est, non debet admitti voluntatis quaestio" (D. 33, 25, 1). The second one invites us to seek the true intention of the testator: "in testamentis plenius voluntates testantium interpretamur." Steadily the centre of gravity moved to the testator's intention, but without disregarding the words employed by the testator, since they were used to express such intention.[25] The standard book of Mantica summarizes the evolution in the ius commune: "optimum est, non propriam verborum significationem scrutari, sed in primis, quid testator senserit, & demonstrare, seu significare, voluerit," because "calumniatoris officium est, verba & litera sequi, & negligere voluntatem testatoris."[26]

---

22. *Perrin v Morgan* [1943] AC 399, at 415.

23. The Irish case *In re Julian* [1950] Irish Reports 57 shows the unfair result of a literal interpretation of the words used by the testatrix, who bequeathed a certain sum to the "Seaman's Institute", without taking into account that there were two institutes under that name, one catholic and the other protestant. No evidence of the testatrix religion was admitted. Kingsmill Moore J. had to accept that it was "by no means the first—and equally certain will not be the last-case in which a judge ha[d] been forced to give a decision on the construction of a will which he believed to be contrary to the intentions of the testator".

24. W.X.V. von Kreittmayr, *Anmerkungen über den Codicem Maxilianeum Bavaricum Civilem* (München 1821), 217–218.

25. E. Schanze, *Interpretation of Wills—an Essay Critical and Comparative*, in D.L. Carey Miller and D.W. Mayers (ed.), *Comparative and Historical Essays in Scots Law: A Tribute to Professor Sir Thomas Smith QC* (Edinburgh 1992), 112–113; G. Chiodi, *L'interpretazione del testamento nei glossatori* (Milano 1997); H.J. Wieling, *Testamentsauslegung im römischen Recht* (München 1972).

26. Franciscus Mantica, *De coniecturis ultimarum voluntarum* (Lugduni 1581), lib. III, tit. III, 1.

In fact, even English courts resorted to the armchair principle[27] and the dictionary principle in order to avoid complete misconstructions where the testator had not used the words in their ordinary sense. The famous will whose only clause was "*all for mother*" evidences the limitations of literalism: the testator's "mother" was in fact his wife.[28] Lord Denning here is noteworthy: "The object of the Court in construing a will is to discover the intention of the testator. I do not think his intention is to be discovered looking at the literal meaning of the words alone. That has led, times out of number, to the frustration of his intentions. ( ... ) Eschewing technical rules and literal interpretation, you must look to see simply what the testator intended."[29]

The search for the true intention of the testator entails the admission of extrinsic evidence because in many cases the will itself does not offer all the clues needed to construe the clauses. Of course, using extrinsic evidence risks creating a new intention absent from the will. But this peril can be avoided if a support in the words of the will is required. Ireland and England amended the law under a much more intentionalist approach. According to s. 90 of the Succession Act (1965), "extrinsic evidence shall be admissible to show the intention of the testator and to assist in the construction of, or to explain any contradiction in a will," although the Irish courts have been cautious in the application of this provision.[30] As for English law, s. 21 of the Administration of Justice Act provides:

---

27. "You must put yourself so to speak, in [the testator's] armchair and consider the circumstances by which he was surrounded, when he made his will to assist you in arriving at his intention", stated James LJ in *Boyes v Cook* (1880) 14 Ch. D. 53, 56. See further J.B. Clark, J.G.R. Martin, *Theobald on Wills* (London 1993), 215–216; Sawyer, *Principles of Succession* 240–242.

28. *Thorn v Dickens* (1906) Weekly Notes 54. See also *Re Lynch* [1943] All ER 168 (the testator appointed "my wife Annie Ethel Lynch", although they were not married and could not marry because of being uncle and niece] or *In re Davidson* [1949] Ch 670 (the testatrix referred to "my son" and "my granddaughter", but the son was in fact of her sister, marrying after her death with his brother-in-law).

29. *In Re Allsopp* [1968] 1 Ch 39, 47.

30. Brady, *Succession Law in Ireland* 138 ff. In *Lynch v Burke* (1999) IEHC 22, Mr Justice McCracken ruled that extrinsic evidence was admissible to explain a contradiction in the will, stating that "the primary rule [is] that the last Will must be construed according to the intention of the Testator having regard to the actual terms thereof, and it would ultimately be a matter for me in the light of this primary rule, to determine what regard could be had to the extrinsic evidence".

"(1) This section applies to a will
(a) In so far as any part of it is meaningless;
(b) In so far as the language used in any part of it is ambiguous on the face of it;
(c) In so far as evidence, other than evidence of the testator's intention, shows that the language used in any part of it is ambiguous in the light of surrounding circumstances.
(2) In so far as this section applies to a will extrinsic evidence, including evidence of the testator's intention, may be admitted to assist in its interpretation."

Although there are limits on the admission of extrinsic evidence, the legal reform has broadened its scope on the basis of an ambiguity in the text of the will.[31] If this is understood to mean that "it does not enable the court to give effect to the testator's intention if the words used are not capable of bearing the meaning he intended, or if he has failed to put his intentions into writing at all,"[32] the situation is quite similar to that on the Continent. Most of the European legal systems admit the use of extrinsic evidence,[33] but the Por-

31. See the recent case *Ross v Perrin-Hughes and others* [2004] All ER (D) 159, concerning the interpretation of the clause "I leave devise and bequeath my apartment and contents thereof to my friend Irene", where at the date of his death the principal assets of the deceased comprised within his estate were (a) the freehold reversion of 96 Wrentham Avenue, Kensal Rise, London NW10 3HG, which was a building comprising two purpose built maisonettes, and (b) the Lease of the first floor maisonette known as 96A Wrentham Avenue. Leslie Kosmin QC considered the will ambiguous, and decided that Irene was entitled to take the Lease of 96A Wrentham Avenue free of the mortgage, and that the gift to Irene of "my apartment" under the Will included the Lease of 96A Wrentham Avenue and the freehold reversion to the building at 96 Wrentham Avenue.

32. *Williams on Wills*, 57.26.

33. Austria: R. Welser, §552, in P. Rummel (ed.), *Kommentar zum Allgemeinen Bürgerliches Gesetzbuch*, t. I 3rd ed. (Wien 2000), Rn 2; Catalonia: A. Vaquer, *La interpretación del testamento* (Madrid 2008), 74–75; Italy: A. Palazzo, *Le successioni* II, 2nd ed. (Milano 2000), 632; Spain: J.B. Jordano Barea, *El testamento y su interpretación* (Granada 1999), 65 ff, 100 ff; Sweden: V. Boström, *Hereditary relations and testament law in Finland and Sweden*, unpublished paper delivered at the conference "Hereditary relations in Europe" held in Athens on 8–9 February 2001, 16; Switzerland: J.N. Druey, *Grundriss des Erbrechts* 5th ed. (Bern 2002), 155. More cautious is the French approach, since the extrinsic evidence is deemed to be a subsidiary means of interpretation; courts may only resort to it where the intrinsic evidence is insufficient to clarify the testator's intention (P. Malaurie, *Les successions. Les liberalités* (Paris 2006), n° 504-505). Only Scotland seems to be more anchored to literalism; see D.R. Macdonald, *Succession*, 2nd ed. (1994), 10.02 and 03; M.C. Meston, *Meston's Succession Opinions, ed by D. O'Donell* (Edinburgh 2000), 83, 459; Hiram, *Scots Law of Succession* 6.43 ff.

tuguese and the German codes are especially noteworthy in their search for a balance between intention and form. Art. 2187.2 of the Portuguese Civil Code admits extrinsic evidence, but it stresses that "a testator's intention without a minimum of correspondence in the context, although imperfectly, has no effect". The court can resort to extrinsic evidences, but the words of the will must be capable of bearing the interpretation attained.[34] The German authors have coined the *Andeutungstheorie*, according to which the interpretative result must in some way have been manifested in the will by the testator.[35] Thus, the search for the true intention of the testator, including the extrinsic evidence, is compatible with the strict formal requirements of a will: only what is included in the form can be interpreted,[36] and only a testamentary intention governs the succession.[37] However, this testamentary intention can be construed by extrinsic means, if necessary.

## 4. The Steady Weakness of Legitim

Freedom of testation is limited by the hereditary rights legally conferred on some relatives or quasi-relatives of the testator. The character, extent, and even the subsistence of the compulsory portion or legitim are controversial. In some countries, the controversy has even accrued a constitutional dimension. Be-

---

34. See J. de Oliveira Ascensão, *Direito civil. Successões* 5th ed. (Coimbra 2000), 76, 294–295; F.A. Pires de Lima, J. Antunes Varela, *Código civil comentado,* vol. VI (Coimbra 1998), *sub* art. 2187, 303.

35. G. Otte, vor §2064, in *J. von Staudingers Kommentar zum BGB,* 13th ed. (Berlin 1996), Rn 28 ff; Palandt/Edenhofer, *BGB* §2084, Rn 4; Bamberger/Roth/Litzenburger, *BGB* §2084, Rn 2; D. Leipold, *Erbrecht,* 15th ed. (München 2004), 123, Rn 364; W. Schlüter, *Erbrecht,* 15th ed. (München 2004), 91–92, Rn 192; J.F. Stagl, *Der Wortlaut als Grenze der Auslegung von testamenten,* 2nd ed. (Wien, 2005).

36. U. Foerster, *Die Form des Testaments als Grenze seiner Auslegung, Deutsche Notar Zeitschrift* 84 (1993).

37. Similar results are achieved in Austria [Welser/Rummel, *Kommentar* I, §552 330; B. Eccher, *Bürgerliches Recht VI. Erbrecht* (Wien 2000), 46]; Belgium [P. Delnoy, *Les libéralités et les successions* 98 (Bruxelles 2004), 132–133]; the Czech Republic [Hrušáková, in IEL vol. 1, 198, para. 536]; Denmark [H.V. Godsk Peddersen, *Denmark,* in IEL vol. 2, 167, para. 191]; Italy [G. Bonilini, *Diritto delle successioni* (Roma-Bari 2004), 169–171; S. Belloni, *Nota di comento a Cass. Civ. II sez. 18.9.1998, Nuova Giurisprudenza Civile Commentata* 110 (2000)], Catalonia and Spain (Vaquer, *La interpretación* 97–103], Portugal (Ascensão, *Successões* 294–296); Sweden [Boström, *Hereditary relations* 16; J. Schiratzki, *Sweden,* in IEL vol. 4, 150, para. 241]; Switzerland [Druey *Grundriss* 153 ff].

cause legitim is among the most disparately regulated subjects in the European laws of successions, only the main comparative trends can be here outlined.

## *4.1. Two Political Decisions*

The restriction of freedom of testation on the basis of an acknowledgment of a right in favor of certain relatives and eventually the spouse to a share of the inheritance, either as an entitlement to assets or to a value, is primarily a political decision. This was true, for example, in England, where the complete freedom of testation was only limited in 1938 with the Inheritance (Family Provision) Act.[38] Today, within Europe, an absolute freedom of testation exists only in some Spanish regions.[39] Even the countries whose succession law has been recently amended have maintained the legitim, although in some cases the reform has been substantive. Therefore, despite the increasing longevity of testators and their descendants, with the consequence that legitim is deferred usually when the descendant has already settled down, the legislator seems wedded to the principle of intergenerational family solidarity.[40] In Germany, there is even discussion about whether the compulsory portion is constitutionally guaranteed; most of the authors think it is, on the basis of Arts. 14 (right of inheritance) and 6.1 (protection of family) of the Constitution.[41] However, it is not the same to say that legitim conforms to the Constitution that it is a compulsory institution as a consequence of the constitutional rules. This last statement has been only recently affirmed by the German Constitutional Court: the compulsory share is the indefeasible children's minimum share in their parents' estate which does not depend on any necessity, has the same rank and constitutional guarantee as freedom of testation, and fulfils the function of realizing the continuation of the ideal and economic

38. See R. Kerridge, *Perry and Clark The Law of Succession*, 11th ed. (London 2002), 8–01.

39. Thus, in a small part of the Basque Country (north of the province of Alava) where the so-called *Fuero de Ayala* is in force (art. 131 Act on the Foral Civil Law of the Basque Country); and Navarre, where the compulsory portion is merely formal (*ley* 267 Compilation of the Foral Civil Law of Navarre), although the surviving spouse is entitled to a legal right of usufruct (*ley* 253 ff). See J.M. Hernández Hierro, *La sucesión forzosa* (Granada 2004), 114 ff., 138 ff. See also Fn 55 in relation to the Isle of Man.

40. For a very suggestive and acute analysis, G. Otte, *Das Pflichtteilsrecht—Verfassungsrechtssprechung und Rechtspolitik*, *AcP* 317 (2002).

41. Otte, *Das Pflichtteilsrecht* 317 ff; J. Mayer, §2303 BGB, in Bamberger/Roth, *BGB*, Rn 2; Palandt/Edenhofer, *BGB* §2303, Rn 6, all with further references.

connection between property and family beyond the *de cujus*' death.[42] In truth, the arguments of the German Constitutional Court are far from convincing, since the German legal tradition and a comparative survey are the main foundations of the decision.

Taking into account that freedom of testation deserves, at least, the same legal standing as its restriction, the national legislature is not neutral in its shaping of the legitimate portion. This is the second political decision: either to strengthen freedom of testation without ignoring the right to the legitimate portion, or to further restrict the testator's power of disposal by giving the beneficiaries a right to the assets. Later, we will consider this second political decision.

To sum up, as to the first political decision, legitim may be a relic,[43] but it is still brimming with health.

## *4.2. A Fixed Portion or an Alimony-Based Portion*

The great majority of the European succession laws establish a system of fixed compulsory portion. Legitim is always granted to descendants.[44] Parents, and eventually other ascendants,[45] can also be beneficiaries, as can be the sur-

---

42. BverG 19.4.2005, *Neue Juristische Wochenschrift (NJW)* 1561 (2005). Critical comments by S. Stüber in *NJW* 2122 (2005); Kleensang, *Familienerbrecht versus Testierfreiheit —Das Pflichtteilsentziehungsrecht auf dem Prüfstand des Bundesverfassungsgerichts, ZEV* 277 (2005).

43. J.C. Sonnekus, *The New Dutch Code on Succession as Evaluated Through the Eyes of a Hybrid Legal System, ZEuP* 71, 84 (2005). In the author's opinion, "the continental systems that still retain a form of legitimate portion or reserve will most probably be compelled, by virtue of the movement towards a unification of European law, to abandon this relic", whilst the family provision systems are much closer to the ideal of freedom of testation.

44. In the following legislations descendants are the only beneficiaries: the Czech Republic (see M. Hrušáková, in *Familienerbrecht und Testierfreiheit*, 344–345; id., in IEL, 195, Rn 527; R. Süß, in J. Mayer et al, *Handbuch Pflichtteilsrecht* (Angelbachtal 2003), 869, Rn 395); Finland (see M. Savolainen, in IEL, 120–121; R. Süß, in *Handbuch Pflichtteilsrecht*, 893, Rn 481; K.F. von Knorre, W. Mincke, in R. Süß, *Erbrecht in Europa* (2nd ed., Angelbachtal 2008), 600, Rn 83), Luxembourg (S. Frank, in *Erbrecht in Europa*, 1005, Rn 107), Sweden (R. Süß, in *Handbuch Pflichtteilsrecht*, 848, Rn 312; E. Johansson, in *Erbrecht in Europa*, 1302–1303, Rn 105).

45. In Portugal the share of asdentants it is reduced to one-third (art. 2161.2 *Código civil*). In Spain the share is the same for other ascendants than parents, but they are only entitled to the share when the latter are lacking (art. 810 *Código civil*). In Belgium the compulsory share is split up between the two ascendants lines, so that the *réserve* corresponding to each line is one-quarter; but if there is no ascendant in one line, the *quotité disponible* raises to three-quarters (art. 915 *Code Civil*).

viving spouse;[46] nevertheless, usually ascendants have only a right to the compulsory portion where descendants or, exceptionally, the surviving spouse[47] are absent.[48] Fixing the portion admits different mechanisms. Thus, the legitimate portion can be a share of the intestate inheritance that would devolve to the beneficiary[49] or a share of the estate to be equally divided among the

---

46. Austria (§762 ABGB), Belgium (art. 915*bis Code civil*), Denmark (§25 *Arveloven*), Germany (§2303.III(1) BGB), Greece (art. 1825(1) *Astikos Kodikas*), Hungary (art. 615 Civil Code), Italy (art. 540 ff *Codice Civile*), Malta (art. 615, 631 and 632 Civil Code), Norway (R. Süß, in *Handbuch Pflichtteilsrecht*, 698), Poland (art. 991 Civil Code), Portugal (art. 2157, 2158 *Código civil*), Spain (art. 834 ff *Código civil*), Switzerland (art. 471.3 ZGB).

47. In Belgium, ascendants are not entitled to a *réserve* against the surviving spouse (art. 915 *Code civil*). See Delnoy, *Les liberalités* 222–223; A. Verbeke, A. van Zantbeek, *Belgium*, in Hayton, *European Succession Laws* 3.124.

48. Austria (§762 ABGB), Belgium (art. 915 *Code Civil*), Catalonia (art. 451-4 Civil Code), Germany (§2309 BGB), Greece (art. 1825(1) *Astikos Kodikas*), Hungary (§661 Civil Code), Italy (art. 538.1° *Codice civile*), Latvia (art. 423 *Civillikums*), Poland (art. 991 Civil Code), Portugal (art. 2142.1, 2157 and 2161 *Código civil*), Spain (art. 807.2° *Código civil*), Switzerland (art. 471.2 ZGB). In Scotland the right of the surviving spouse is known as *ius relicti* or *ius relictae*; if there is no issue, the spouse receives one-half of the value of the movable estate after payments of the debts; jointly with descendants, the spouse receives one-third (see Hiram, *Scots Law of Succession* 4.7). In France the *réserve* of ascendants has been suppressed in 2006; see Alain Delfosse, Jean-François Peniguel, *La réforme des successions et des liberalités* (Paris 2006) 145 ff.

49. One-half of the intestate share is the amount of legitim in Denmark (R. Süß, in *Handbuch Pflichtteilsrecht* 764, Rn 22, H.V.G. Pedersen, in IEL, 164, para 188), Estonia (§105 Law of Succession Act), Finland (*Savolainen*, in IEL, 120, para 297; von Knorre/Mincke, in *Erbrecht in Europa* 600, Rn 83), Germany (§2303 BGB, although concerning the spouse it may vary depending on the matrimonial property regime; see Bamberger/Roth/Mayer, *BGB* §2303, Rn 15 ff), Greece (art. 1825(1) *Astikos Kodikas*), Hungary (§665 Civil Code; see E. Weiss, *Familien Erbrecht und Testierfreiheit im ungarischen Recht*, in D. Henrich, D. Schwab (ed.), *Familienerbrecht und Testierfreiheit im europäischen Vergleich* (Bielefeld 2001), 367; R. Süß, in *Handbuch Pflichtteilsrecht*, 876, Rn 421), Latvia (art. 425 *Civillikums*), the Netherlands (A.R. van Maas de Bie, in *Erbrecht in Europa*, 1073, Rn 89), Sweden (R. Süß, in *Handbuch Pflichtteilsrecht*, 848, Rn 312; V. Boström, *Familienerbrecht und Testierfreiheit in Schweden und anderen skandinavischen Ländern*, in Henrich/Schwab, 259). In the Czech Republic, descendants minors of age receive the full intestate share, while the compulsory share of descendants of full age is one-half of the intestate share (Hrušáková, in IEL vol. 1, 195, para 527; R. Süß, in *Handbuch Pflichtteilsrecht*, 869, Rn 395). In Austrian law, the compulsory share of descendants and spouse is one-half of the intestate share too (§765 ABGB), but the one of ascendants is reduced to one-third of the intestate share (§766 ABGB); the same happens in Slovenia in relation to descendants and spouse (K. Zupančič, B. Novak, *Slovénie*, in *Jurisclasseur de droit comparé*, para. 137; R. Süß, in *Erbrecht in Europa*, 1406, Rn 19). In Poland, the ordinary compulsory share is one-half of the intestate share, but the share increases to one-third in case of beneficiar-

beneficiaries.[50] However, the amount of the share may vary depending on the number of beneficiaries, the class of beneficiaries,[51] or a combination of both factors.[52] A unique solution is found in Norwegian law: the compulsory share

---

ies under age or lasting incapacitated for work (A. Mączyński, in Henrich/Schwab, *Familienerbrecht* 200–201; R. Süß, in *Handbuch Pflichtteilsrecht*, 843, Rn 289). In Switzerland, the compulsory share of descendants is three-quarters of the intestate share, and that of the spouse and of parents one-half (art. 471 ZGB); but where the deceased is survived by descendants and spouse, the compulsory share of descendants is 3/8 of the intestate share, whilst that of the spouse is one-quarter [see Druey, *Grundriss* 61; R. Süß, in *Handbuch Pflichtteilsrecht*, p. 854, Rn 854, Rn 332].

50. Catalonia: one-fourth of the value of the estate (art. 451-5 Civil Code).

51. Spain: two-thirds of the estate for descendants, although one-third *(tercio de mejora)* can be distributed unequally by the *de cujus* among the beneficiaries (art. 808 *Código civil*); ascendants are entitled to one-third. As mentioned above, Fn. 49, in Austria and Slovenia the compulsory share of ascendants is reduced from one-half to one-third.

52. In Belgian law, the *quotité disponible* is one-half of the estate where there is only one child or one branch of descendants, one-third if they are two, and one-fourth if they are three or more (art. 913, 914 *Code Civil);* concerning ascendants, the *quotité disponible* is one-half where the *de cujus* has relatives in the paternal and the maternal line, and one-fourth where there are only beneficiaries in one line (art. 915 *Code Civil).* In French law, the shares are the same as in Belgium (see art. 913, 914 *Code Civil*), but there are some differences in relation to the spouse where he/she is beneficiary jointly with ascendants: the *quotité disponible* by the deceased in favour of the spouse is enlarged, since the spouse may receive not only one-half or three-quarters of the inheritance in full property, but also another moiety or the remainder quarter in usufruct (art. 1094 *Code Civil).* In Italy, the surviving spouse is entitled to one-half of the estate (art. 540 *Codice Civile*), but if the deceased leaves also one child, the compulsory share of the spouse is reduced to one-third and the child is entitled to another third; if the deceased leaves two or more children, the spouse in entitled to one-quarter and the children to one-half (art. 542 *Codice Civile);* where the deceased is survived by ascendants and spouse, the spouse is still entitled to one-half, whilst the legitim of ascendants is one-quarter (art. 544 *Codice Civile*; see M.C. Tatarano, "La successione necessaria",·in R. Calvo, G. Perlingieri (ed.), *Diritto delle successioni* (Napoli 2008), 454 ff). In Malta, the compulsory share of descendants varies depending on the number of children: if they are four or less, the share is one-third, if they are five or more, one-half (art. 616 Civil Code); the spouse is entitled to one-fourth in case there are children, otherwise to one-third (art. 631, 632 Civil Code). In Portuguese law, if the beneficiaries are jointly descendants and the spouse, the compulsory share is two-thirds of the estate; if there is no spouse, the compulsory share is one-half when there is only one child, and two-thirds when there are two or more children (art. 2159 *Código civil).* If the beneficiaries are jointly ascendants and the spouse, the compulsory share is two-thirds of the estate; if there is no spouse, the compulsory share of parents is one-half, whilst the share of other ascendants is reduced to one-third (art. 2161 *Código civil*). In Scotland, legal rights to inherit a share of the deceased is given to spouse and children; legal rights consists of *jus relictae* in favour of the surviving spouse (one-half of the movable estate if no children or issue survive, one-third in they do) and legitim in favour of the children (one-half if there

of the decedent's children is two-thirds of the inheritance, but a descendant—or his/her branch—can neither claim more than NOK 1,000.000 nor receive less than NOK 200.0000 in respect of legitim.[53] A few legal systems grant the surviving spouse, unlike descendants and ascendants, a right of usufruct instead of a share of the inheritance in full property.[54]

English law has a completely different approach. It denies every beneficiary compulsory rights, but allows certain persons to apply for family provision provided the disposition of the decedent's estate effected by will or intestacy has not made reasonable financial provision for the applicant.[55] Family provisions are not, strictly speaking, based on alimony, since it does not depend on the applicant's necessity; its amount is not decided upon the applicant's future necessities, either. A standard of reasonable financial provision is maintenance, which means neither merely the provision of bare necessities of life nor anything desirable for welfare.[56] The court has discretion to decide whether to award a family provision and, if so, its amount. The court should consider the applicant's financial resources and needs, the obligations and responsibilities of the decedent, the size and nature of the estate, the disability of any applicant or beneficiary, the conduct of the applicant or any other person, and the decedent's reasons and state of mind. In addition, particular guidelines are provided for the persons who may apply for a family provision. The following survivors of the testator may apply to the court: the decedent's wife or husband, the decedent's former wife or husband if he or she has not remarried, cohabitants, children of the decedent, persons treated by the dece-

---

is no spouse, one-third if there is) (R. Macdonald, "Scotland", in Hayton, *European Succession Laws* 4.220-222). The Swiss solution must also be taken into account here (see *retro* Fn. 49).

53. About € 126.000 as a maximum and € 25.200 as a minimum. As for the spouse, he/she is entitled to one-fourth again with a variable minimum that, lacking descendants, amounts to € 49.000. See V. Lange, in *Jurisclasseur de droit comparé*, para. 357; Boström, in Henrich/Schwab, *Familienerbrecht* 259; R. Süß, in *Erbrecht in Europa*, 1085, Rn 17; T. Frantzen, *Die Stellung des überleben Ehegatten im norwegischen Ehegüter-und Erbrecht: Auswirkungen auf deutsch-norwegische Sachverhalte, Zeitschrift für die vergleichende Rechtswissenschaft* 482 (2002).

54. See *infra sub* 6.

55. s. 1(1) Inheritance (Provision for Family and Dependants) Act 1975, amended by the Law Reform (Succession) Act 1995. A similar system of family provision is in force in the Isle of Man (N. Morris, in Hayton, *European Succession Laws*, 4.402), so that there is no absolute freedom of testation in the same sense as in English law.

56. Kerridge, *Perry and Clark The Law of Succession* 8–13. See, for a comparison with the German *Pflichtteilsrecht*, M. Trulsen, *Pflichtteilsrecht und englische family provision im Vergleich* (Tübingen 2004).

dent as children of the family, and dependents of the decedent.[57] Although the core requirement is the maintenance standard, not the applicant's necessity,[58] family provisions are like alimony rights in practice. Not every descendant or relative of the deceased may successfully apply for provision; persons who do not belong to the deceased's family may obtain an order from the court. The relationship of maintenance, the conduct of the applicant, and of the deceased must be taken into account. Yet, a family provision is similar to a legitim, since it entails a restriction of freedom of disposal, insofar as a part of the decedent's estate is attributed to someone that he/she did not want to favour.[59] Hence, family provisions achieve an interesting balance between freedom of testation and the hereditary expectations of persons closely linked to the testator, although the regulation may be considered from a continental point of view as too vague and imprecise.[60]

There is a third solution that combines elements of the two previous ones. A beneficiary has a right to a fixed portion of an estate or of its value, but only if he/she is in a necessity situation. This situation appears where the descendants are minors or where ancestrors are disabled or incapable of working. For example, Estonia's law provides that "if a bequeather has by a will or succession contract disinherited an ascendant, descendant or his or her spouse who are incapacitated for work and are entitled to succeed in intestacy, or has reduced their shares of the estate as compared to their shares according to intestate succession, the relatives and spouse have the right to succeed to the compulsory portion" (§ 104 Law of Succession Act).[61] The compulsory portion consists of one-half of the intestate share (§ 105). Similarly, in Lithuania, children, parents and the spouse of the decedent are entitled to the compulsory share provided that "they need to be maintained" at the moment of the decedent's death; the amount of the share is also one-half of the intestate share.[62] In Slovenia, grandparents, brothers, and sisters of the deceased are entitled to the compulsory portion only if they are incapable of working and have no economic means for their necessities.[63] In 2001, Art. 13 of the Suc-

57. For further details, Kerridge, *Perry and Clark The Law of Succession* 8–30 ff.

58. Trulsen, *Pflichtteilsrecht* 119–120.

59. This is the conclusion reached by Trulsen, *Pflichtteilsrecht* 192.

60. Otte, *Das Pflichtteilsrecht*, 348–351.

61. See R. Hausmann, U. Liin, *Grundzüge des neuen estnichen Erbrechts*, *Jahrbuch für Ostrecht* 261, 277 (2000).

62. M. Michalauskas, *Lituanie*, in *Jurisclasseur de droit comparé*, para. 128.

63. Zupančič/Novak, in *Jurisclasseur de droit comparé*, para. 135; M. Geč-Korošec, S. Kraljič, *Familienerbrecht und Testierfreiheit im slowenischen Recht*, in Henrich/Schwab, *Familienerbrecht* 290.

cession Act was amended so that the spouse or heirs who lack the necessary means for living may go before the court and request an increase of their shares at the other heirs' or the spouse's expense.[64] Lastly, in Poland, the amount of the compulsory share is increased to two-thirds if the beneficiaries are underage or incapable of working.[65]

Even a strict system of fixed compulsory share that, like the Spanish one, grants a right over the assets has been tempered in favour in disabled persons. The new articles 808.3 and 813.2 *Código civil,* introduced by Act 41/2003 of 18 November, allow exceptionally the imposition of a fideicommissary substitution over the compulsory shares in favor of the judicially incapacitated descendants of the testator, who become fiduciary heirs, while the other descendants entitled to the legitim become fideicommissary heirs and will receive their shares only after their incapacitated brother's death.[66]

## *4.3. A Right to the Assets or a Credit Right*

The compulsory share may take shape in two distinct ways. On the one hand, it can turn into a forced heirship, in the sense that the beneficiaries are entitled to a share of the assets (a *pars bonorum*).[67] On the other hand, the

64. The Slovenian Courts may decide that the spouse inherits the whole estate, provided that its value is so low that he/she would suffer poverty in case of sharing it with other successors. The State can recoup against the estate the support given by the social security. I am much indebted to Ms. Suzana Kraljič, University of Maribor, for kindly providing me with this information.

65. S. Łakomy, *Polen,* in *Erbrecht in Europa* 1154, Rn 36; Mączyński, in Henrich/Schwab, *Familienerbrecht* 200.

66. See S. Díaz Alabart, *La sustitución fideicomisaria sobre el tercio de legítima estricta a favor de hijo o descendiente incapacitado judicialmente, Revista de Derecho Privado* 259 (2004).

67. Belgium: Delnoy, *Les liberalités* 231 ff. Czech Republic: C. Rombach, in *Erbrecht in Europa,* 1501, Rn 71. Estonia: § 105, 106(1) and (4) Law of Succession Act. Greece (although Greeks living for 25 years in a foreign country have an absolute freedom of testation over the assets located out of Greece): I. Vlassopolou, *Kein Noterbrecht für die Hinterbliebenden eines Auslandgriechen, IPRax* 61 (2005). Italy: Capozzi, *Successioni* 265–266 (at least when the deceased has not attributed the legitim in a certain way). Luxembourg: Frank, in *Erbrecht in Europa* 1005, Rn 105. Portugal: J.J. Gonçalves de Proença, *Direito das sucessões* 2nd ed. (Lisboa 2005), 118. Slovenia: Zupančič/Novak, in *Jurisclasseur de droit comparé* para. 134. Spain: art. 806, 808, 809 *Código Civil* (but the legitim of the spouse can be converted into money under the requirements established in art. 839 and the testator can lay *down that the portion* of descendants is paid in cash, art. 841 *Código Civil*). Sweden: Johansson, in *Erbrecht in Europa,* 869, Rn 89. In Finland the deceased can impose the payment of the compulsory share in money: von Knorre/Mincke, in *Erbrecht in Europa* 600, Rn 83. In France being the *réserve* a portion of the estate, it tends to adopt some char-

beneficiaries may be entitled only to a value of the estate, so that they have a right of credit against the heir or the representative of the estate in order to obtain their share in cash.[68] There is no dominant tendency in the European laws of succession, although the option for a personal right in the Netherlands could have been a model, since the latest States to reform their succession law, Malta[69] and Croatia,[70] have followed different patterns. However, the compulsory share as a credit right represents a better balance between freedom of testation and the acknowledgment of the right of the beneficiaries, because the testator can freely dispose *mortis causa* of the estate notwithstanding the compulsory share and the principle of intergenerational solidarity. By contrast, where the beneficiaries are entitled to a right *in rem* over the assets up to their share, freedom of disposal is more restricted and consequently most of the assets remain within the deceased's family.

## *4.4. Some Conclusions*

Although most of the European succession laws grant the spouse and close relatives a compulsory right over the estate, this right is qualified in different

---

acters of a right of credit; see M. Grimaldi, *Droit civil. Successions*, 6th ed. (Paris 2001), nº 283; Malaurie, *Les successions* nº 615, 619.

68. Austria: Eccher, *Erbrecht* 109. Catalonia: art. 451-1, 451-5 Civil Code. Germany: H. Brox, *Erbrecht*, 21th ed. (Köln 2004), 308, Rn 542; J. Mayer, in *Handbuch Pflichtteilsrecht*, 27, Rn 23, 29, Rn 36. Hungary: E. Weiss, *Hongrie*, in *Jurisclasseur de droit comparé*, para. 135; Á. Tóth, "Ungarn", in *Erbrecht in Europa*, 1590, Rn 83. Latvia: art. 425 *Civillikums* (but Dr. K. Balodis, University of Riga, has kindly drawn my attention to the fact that courts are still rooted in the soviet tradition and consider legitim a share to the assets). Netherlands: van Maas de Bie, in *Erbrecht in Europa* 1073, Rn 89. Poland: Łakomy, in *Erbrecht in Europa* 1154, Rn 36. The English family provision also consists in a right of credit; see Trulsen, *Pflichteilsrecht* 137. In Switzerland there is a trend toward the conception of legitim as a part of the value of the estate, at least where the deceased has attributed the compulsory share by means of a disposition in his/her will; see Druey, *Grundriss* 58; H. Hausheer, R. Aebi-Müller, *Familienerbrecht und Testierfreiheit in der Schweiz*, in Henrich/Schwab, *Familienerbrecht* 219–220.

69. After the reform carried out by Act No XVIII of 2004, art. 615 reads: "(1) The reserved portion is the right on the estate of the deceased reserved by law in favour of the descendants and the surviving spouse of the deceased. (2) The said right is *a credit of the value* of the reserved portion against the estate of the deceased". Former art. 615 said: "Legitim is *a portion of the property* of the deceased …". Emphasis added.

70. T. Pintarič, *Reform des kroatischen Erbrechts*, *ZEV* 498, 499 (2003). I. Gliha, *Croatia*, in IEL, 258, para 453, 455, points out that beneficiaries of the legal portion are "legitimate heirs", although they are entitled to a "corresponding portion of the value from the estate of inheritance".

ways. Firstly, it can be shaped as a credit right rather than as a right *in rem*. Secondly, the successors' personal characteristics can be taken into account, namely if they are disabled or need to be maintained. Perhaps legislators have in mind that the worst inequality is to treat different situations equally. Changes in families are not alien to this trend: the centre of gravity of society is the nuclear family and the increasing longevity of people dictates a compulsory share at a later age when a beneficiary is supposed to have already settled down. There are likely to be more reforms along these lines favouring freedom of testation.

## 5. Equality of Children

Equality of children in the law of succession has been stimulated by the case law of the European Court of Human Rights. A series of decisions has forced several EU Member States to amend their legislation and it has indirectly influenced other new member States of the EU.[71] This has led to a convergence of national legislations.[72] The landmark decisions have been:

> a) Marckx v. Belgium [1979] ECHR 2. The Court held contrary to Arts. 8 and 14 of the Convention for the Protection of Human Rights and Fundamental Freedoms the Belgian legislation on "illegitimate children", in the case the position and rights of the daughter of a single mother.
> b) Inze v. Austria [1987] ECHR 28. The case concerned discrimination against children born out of wedlock to inherit so-called "hereditary farms" according to the regional law of Carinthia, which was considered to entail a breach of Art. 14 of the Convention.
> c) Mazurek v. France [2000] ECHR 47. The Court held that the different treatment of adulterine children in the *Code civil* (art. 760) violated Art. 14 of the Convention.

The consequence of these decisions is a full equality of children whether born in or out of wedlock. However, all these decisions concerned discrim-

---

71. This is the case of Malta (Act N°. XVIII of 2004), which has suppressed the references to "legitimate" and "illegitimate children" aiming at the achievement of full equality among children irrespective of they having being conceived or born in or out of wedlock.

72. See with further details Cámara Lapuente, *¿Derecho europeo de sucesiones?*, 1207 ff. See also Verbeke/Leleu, *Harmonisation* 346–347; De Waal, "A Comparative Overwiew" 7.

inatory legal treatment of children, and therefore the State had set out an unjustifiable discrimination. The European Court has gone one step further—too far, probably—in the case Pla i Puncernau v. Andorra [2004].[73] An Andorran testatrix established a fideicomissary substitution in her will made in 1939 in favour of "a son or a grandson—of the fiduciary heir—born of a lawful and canonical marriage." The testatrix died in 1949. Her son in 1969 had adopted a child in Spain. Since Roman law was in force in Andorra, adoption was almost unknown both at the time the will was made and at the time the testatrix died, and adoption according to Spanish law, in force when the child was adopted, had limited effects. Kinship was only established with their adoptive parents, but not with their adoptive parents' families. According to the High Court of Andorra (18 June 2000), the applicant was not entitled to the testatrix's succession, taking into account the time when the will was made and the effects of adoption. In the Court's opinion, the will had to be construed as not including adoptive children in the substitution. The Constitutional Court of Andorra upheld the decision on the ground that there was no violation of the principle of equality of children irrespective of the kind of affiliation. By contrast, the application before the European Court of Human Rights was successful. According to the judgment, the interpretation given to the will by the Andorran High Court entailed discrimination contrary to Art. 14 of the Convention: "The High Court of Justice's interpretation of the testamentary disposition, which consisted in inferring a negative intention on the part of the testatrix and concluding that since she did not expressly state that she was not excluding adopted sons this meant that she did intend to exclude them, appears over contrived and contrary to the general legal principle that where a statement is unambiguous there is no need to examine the intention of the person who made it."[74] Leaving aside the literalist flavour of the European Court of Human Right's opinion and the fact that literalism is declining in the comparative landscape,[75] some of the Court's arguments are hard to follow. The European Court of Human Rights states that "the interpretation could not be made exclusively in the light of the social conditions existing when the will was made or at the time of the testatrix's death, namely in 1939 and 1949,

73. ECHR 13 July 2004. See E. Arroyo i Amayuelas, D. Bondia García, *¿Interpretación de testamento contraria a los derechos humanos? El caso Pla & Puncernau vs Andorra, Derecho Privado y Constitución* 7 (2004); J. Marsal Guillamet, *Els fills posats en condició: interpretació del testament i discriminació, Revista Jurídica de Catalunya* 477 (2005).

74. ECHR 13 July 2004, para. 58. See also specifically para. 57 and 60.

75. *Retro, sub* 3.

particularly where a period of fifty-seven years has elapsed between the date when the will was made and the date on which the estate passed to the heirs. Where such a long period has elapsed, during which profound social, economic and legal changes have occurred, the courts cannot ignore these new realities."[76] If these words were to be taken strictly, the testatrix's intention would not govern her succession, since that formally expressed intention could be overridden on the grounds of social changes occurring after the testatrix's death; the Court has ignored that the object of interpretation is the testator's intention, and that consequently the decisive moment is that of the expression of the intention. Freedom of testation would then play a secondary role. The Court not only gave a horizontal effect to the European Convention, as the dissenting opinions of the judgment stress, but also an absolutely retrospective effect. It is self-evident that testators are not obligated to treat their descendants equally, otherwise there would be no freedom of testation. Only the law must recognise their equality specifically in relation to intestate succession or legitim. Therefore, the interpretation given by the Andorran High Court could not have infringed the European Convention in relation to the principle of equality of rights.

Lastly, the judgment in the case Haas v. The Netherlands [2004] ECHR 13 deserves to be mentioned. The applicant considered himself an illegitimate son of a certain Dutch national who had died intestate, but no succession right was conferred on him by the Dutch courts. No violation of Art. 8 or Art. 13 of the Convention was considered, since no family relationship between the applicant and the deceased had been proved; in fact, the applicant had not sought a judicial declaration of affiliation. In the words of the European Court of Human Rights, "an applicant cannot derive from Article 8 a right to be recognised as the heir of a deceased for inheritance purposes."[77]

## 6. Strengthening the Spouse's Position

An apparent feature of legal reforms of the European law of successions has been the strengthening of the surviving spouse's rights. The strategies for achieving the result may be diverse and can be combined. A compulsory share is attributed to the spouse, the pre-existing share is increased, or specific rights are granted to him or her; for example, the spouse may

76. ECHR 13 July 2004, para. 62.
77. At para. 43.

be entitled to the family dwelling[78] or to its furnishings.[79] Of course, strengthening the position of the spouse implies a detriment in the position of other successors, specifically that of descendants.[80] In fact, the delay in enacting the book on succession law of the new Dutch Civil Code was due to the debate on ways to render a spouse's increased rights compatible with the rights of descendants.[81] Also complicated has been the reform of the succession rights of the spouse in France, which were enacted in Act 2001-1135, of 3 December 2001.

It is interesting to compare these two particular legal reforms, as they had the same goal. In the Netherlands, the surviving spouse receives all the deceased's property, while the children have only a right of credit against the estate to require the payment of their compulsory shares; this credit is payable only under certain circumstances, notably the death of the surviving spouse and his/her insolvency. However, in case the surviving spouse remarries, the right of credit turns into the naked ownership of assets corresponding to the value of their rights, and the spouse maintains the right of usufruct over those assets.[82] In France, the surviving spouse may now

78. s. 56(1) Irish Succession Act, on which Brady, *Succession Law in Ireland* 7.26 ff. In Scotland, the surviving spouse has in the intestate succession the so-called "prior rights", consisting of three categories: a right to the interest in the dwelling house, a right to its furniture, and a right to claim a sum of money (see Hiram, *Scots Law of Succession* 5.7 ff). In Luxembourg, the surviving spouse may opt for a right of usufruct over the dwelling [see Frank, in *Erbrecht in Europa* 997, Rn 59-60). A mere right of use is granted in Austria (§758 ABGB) or Catalonia (art. 36 Family Code, a right of use lasting one year); a right of habitation in Italy (art. 540 *Codice Civile;* see Bonilini, *Diritto delle successioni* 111 ff).

79. For example, §758 ABGB, art. 35 Catalan Family Code, §17 Estonian Law of Succession Act, §1932 BGB; see a comparative analysis by U. Liin, *Laws of Succession in Europe and Estonia: How We Got to Where We Are and Where We Should be Heading, Juridica International* 114, 119 ff (2001). (available at http://www.juridica.ee). In Belgium (Delnoy, *Les liberalités* 233) and Poland (Łakomy, in *Erbrecht in Europa* 1150, Rn 16), the spouse may require the inclusion of the family dwelling or of the dwelling's furnishing in his/her share. In Malta only the use of the furniture is granted (art. 635 Civil Code).

80. De Waal, "A Comparative Overwiew" 7. For example, in Norway the surviving spouse may opt for the undivision of the estate and become a joint owner together with the other heirs [see Lange, in *Jurisclasseur de droit comparé* para. 309 ff; R. Süß, in *Erbrecht in Europa,* 1083, Rn 9].

81. D. van Dijk, *Der Politische Werdergang des Niederländischen Bürgerlichen Gesetzbuches 1992,* in F, Bydlinski, T. Mayer-Maly, J.W. Pichler (ed.), *Renaissance der Idee der Kodifikation* (Wien-Köln-Weimar 1990), 31; E.H.J. Schrage, *Natura pater et filius eadem persona paene intelliguntur, Revista Catalana de Dret Privat* 41, 45–46 (2002).

82. See van Maas de Bie, in *Erbrecht in Europa* 1070–1071, Rn 74; A. Schimansky, *Reform des niederländischen Erbrechts, ZEV* 149, 150–151 (2003).

choose between a universal usufruct over the estate or one-fourth in full property.[83]

The position of the surviving spouse is stronger in the Netherlands than in France. Nevertheless, both legal systems resort—though only eventually in the Netherlands—to a right of usufruct. This solution is not widespread.[84] Granting rights of usufruct is not the most efficient solution, since it entails a division of the rights over the assets between the spouse and the naked owners; where the assets are unproductive, the situation is especially unsatisfactory. Not surprisingly, in most legal systems that grant a right of usufruct, several mechanisms of conversion into capital are provided.

In my opinion, granting a legal usufruct to a surviving spouse should be avoided, because it leads to inefficiency and impracticability. Only if the estate is very wealthy could a usufruct satisfy the spouse, but surely it would not satisfy the heirs. In addition, since conversion into capital is established in order to avoid the inconveniences, the door is open to further controversies. Strengthening the spouse's position must be welcome, but solutions based on full property should be preferred over solutions that split the rights over the estate.

---

83. See the details in Malaurie, *Les successions* nº 86 ff; W. Pintens, D. Pignolet, *Le nouveau droit successoral français et son positionnement dans l'européanisation du droit successoral, Familia* 451 (2003).

84. In Belgium, the compulsory share of the spouse consists in the usufruct over one-half of the estate (art. 915*bis Code civil*). In Catalonia, the surviving spouse has a right of usufruct over the estate where he/she is not universal intestate heir because descendants exist (art. 442-3, 442-4 Civil Code). In Hungarian law, the surviving spouse is granted as a legitim a right of usufruct over the estate where he/she would not be intestate heir because the deceased left issue; where the deceased leaves no issue, the spouse is entitled to one-half of the intestate share [Weiss, in Henrich/Schwab, *Familienerbrecht* 367; Süß, in *Handbuch Pflichtteilsrecht*, 876, Rn 421]. In Spain, the compulsory share of the spouse consists in a right of usufruct over one-third of the inheritance where the deceased leaves common descendants (art. 834 *Código Civil*), one-half if the deceased leaves ascendants or non-common descendants (art. 837 *Código Civil*), and two-thirds where there are neither descendants nor ascendants (art. 838 *Código Civil*); see J.A. Fernández Campos, *El pago de la legítima al cónyuge viudo* (Valencia 2005). The Swedish solution, although it has been presented as a right of usufruct [Schiratzki, in IEL 139, para. 221], resembles more a fideicomisssary substitution, since the issue's right to inherit is postponed until the surviving spouse dies and the powers of the spouse are wider than those of a mere usufructuary [see also Boström, in Henrich/Schwab, *Familienerbrecht* 254–255; Johansson, in *Erbrecht in Europa* 1289, Rn 48].

## 7. The Effect of Divorce on Wills

Legal inheritance rights of spouses usually depend on the continuation of the marriage until the deceased's death.[85] However, another issue related to divorce must be examined, namely that of the effect of divorce on the will, assuming that the testator has made a disposition in favour of the (former) spouse. A survey of some of the main European systems of law shows a common trend concerning the effect of a divorce on a will, although the approaches vary from country to country.[86]

In Germany, §2077 BGB establishes the *ineffectiveness* ("ist unwirksam") of a disposition in favour of the spouse in cases of annulment of the marriage and divorce, as well as in cases of judicial separation. German authors consider the rule as one of construction of wills.[87] The ordinary intention of the testator would be that the disposition in favour of the spouse is only effective if he or she is still the spouse when the succession is opened. Therefore, the ineffectiveness of the disposition is automatic.[88] The testator needs not revoke the will, nor must the successor who benefits from the ineffectiveness bring suit against the spouse. On the contrary, the spouse must prove that the in-

85. Austria: §757 ABGB; Eccher, *Erbrecht* 30. Belgium: art. 731 *Code civil*; see Delnoy, *Les liberalités* 213, 234. Catalonia: art. 442-6 Civil Code. Czech Republic: Rombach, in *Erbrecht in Europa* 1488, Rn 21; England: Kerridge, *Perry and Clark The Law of Succession* 2-09, although a claim for family provision may still be available; Finland: Z. Sundström, in Hayton, *European Succession Laws* 7.12; France: Malaurie, *Les successions* n° 87; Germany: Brox, *Erbrecht* 44, Rn 65; Palandt/Edenhofer, *BGB* §1931, Rn 2-5. Greece: K.D. Magliveras, in Hayton, *European Succession Laws* 10.63; Italy: separation reduces drastically the succession rights of spouses according to art. 548 and 585 *Codice Civile* (Capozzi, *Successioni* 335–336]; Latvia: art. 397 *Civillikums*; Scotland: Macdonald in Hayton, *European Succession Laws*, 4.228. Spain: art. 945 *Código civil;* Sweden: L. Herslow, P. Gellström, in Hayton, *European Succession Laws* 18.36.

86. Further details in A. Vaquer, *Wills, Divorce and the Fate of the Dispositions in Favour of the Spouse: a Common Trend in European Laws of Succession*, *ERPL* 782 (2003). For a convincing attempt in Italian law see F. Giardini, *Testamento e sopravvenienza* (Padova 2003).

87. Staudinger/Otte, *BGB* §2077, Rn 4; D. Leipold in *Münchener Kommentar zum Bürgerlichen Gesetzbuch* 4th ed., (München 2004), §2077, Rn 3; Brox, *Erbrecht* 135, Rn 219; Palandt/Edenhofer, *BGB* §2077, Rn 1; Schlüter, *Erbrecht* 100–101, Rn 211.

88. Staudinger/Otte, *BGB* §2077, Rn 5; *Münchener Kommentar*/Leipold, §2077, Rn 10. German authors emphasise the fact that during the BGB drafting process the non-automatic ineffectiveness but on demand of the successors was rejected by the Second Commission. See *Protokolle der Kommission für die zweite Lesung des Entwurfs des Bürgerlichen Gesetzbuchs*, V (Berlin 1899), 51.

tention of the testator was to make the disposition effective despite divorce. This intention to preserve the disposition even in case of divorce must derive from the will.[89]

According to Art. 11:6 Swedish *Ärvdabalken,* the dispositions made by the testator in favour of a spouse become ineffective if at the testator's death the marriage has already been dissolved or divorce has been judicially requested. The same applies to unmarried couples if they do not cohabit any more. Nevertheless, the spouse may prove that even in that event the testator would have made the disposition in order to save it.[90] According to Art. 4:52 of the New Dutch Civil Code, "a disposition made in favor of a person with whom, at the moment the last will was made, the testator was married or with whom he has exchanged wedding promises, is no longer effective in case of a later divorce or judicial separation, unless a contrary intention appears from the last will itself." A similar regulation, based on the failure of the reason underlying the disposition in favour of the spouse, is to be found in Art. 601 of the Hungarian Civil Code.[91] Art. 2317 Portuguese Civil Code, establishes as a ground for a will's lapse judicial separation, divorce, or annulment when the beneficiary of the disposition is the spouse. Lapse ("caducidade") means that the disposition becomes ineffective.[92]

As for Spain, Art. 132 of the Catalan Succession Code presumes the revocation of any disposition in favour of a surviving spouse in case of subsequent separation, divorce, or annulment, unless the surviving spouse proves that the testator would have made the disposition anyway.[93] This provision has inspired Article 123 of the Succession Act of Aragon, which uses the term "ineffectiveness" of the disposition rather than "presumption of revocation."

In Latvia, Art. 431 *Civillikums* states that a testator may exclude his or her spouse from the inheritance—the spouse in entitled to the compulsory share (Art. 423)—for causes that give a spouse the right to ask for a divorce.

---

89. *Münchener Kommentar*/Leipold, *BGB* §2077, Rn 18 ff; Palandt/Edenhofer, *BGB* §2077, Rn 6; Schlüter, *Erbrecht* 101, Rn 211; M. Rudolf, *Handbuch Testamentsauslegung und—anfechtung* (2000), 223 ff.

90. Boström, *Hereditary relations* 16–17.

91. Weiss, in *Jurisclasseur de droit comparé* para. 133; Tóth, in *Erbrecht in Europa* 1577–1578, Rn 25-26.

92. Pires de Lima/Antunes Varela, *Código civil comentado,* vol. VI, *sub* art. 2317, 501.

93. R. Casas Vallés, *Las disposiciones testamentarias a favor del cónyuge y las vicisitudes del matrimonio (Sobre el art. 132 del Código de Sucesiones de Cataluña), Anuario de Derecho Civil (ADC)* 1752 (1993); A. Vaquer, *Testamento, disposiciones a favor del cónyuge y crisis del matrimonio, ADC* 67 (2003).

In Croatia, the new Succession Act has introduced a provision according to which the will is revoked by virtue of the final judgment on divorce, unless the decedent has provided differently in the will.[94]

Finally, in England, according to s. 18A of the Wills Act as amended by the Law Reform (Succession) Act 1995, the spouse where there has been a divorce or an annulment, is deemed to have predeceased the testator unless the will discloses a contrary intention.[95]

Apparently, there are noteworthy differences among the provisions considered. Some of them use the term "revocation," while others refer to "ineffectiveness." In contrast, while English law does not qualify the effect, it prescribes that the spouse is deemed to have predeceased the testator. It is necessary to stress that the concept of "revocation" seems improperly employed in the corresponding succession laws. "Revocation" implies a later intention contrary to the effectiveness of the clause or of the whole will. However, a testamentary intention can only be revoked by another testamentary intention, and this implies a new will made under the formalities legally required. The testator has to fulfil all the formal requirements that every system of law establishes. Therefore, the case is not one of revocation, since a new will is not required. Although the expression is misleading, the use of the term "revocation" highlights the choice of the legislator. "Revocation" means that the previous will has no consequences. In that sense, "revocation" is a case of ineffectiveness. Furthermore, it denotes a link with the testator's intention. Revocation depends on the intention, either because the testator states expressly that the previous will regulates his/her succession, or because the new will is incompatible with the previous one. The same result occurs if the spouse is deemed to have pre-deceased the testator: as survivorship is a requirement to inherit, the disposition in favour of the spouse becomes ineffective.

The ineffectiveness of a disposition in favour of a surviving spouse that the legislator lays down in case of judicial separation, divorce, or annulment of marriage is, in fact, based on the testator's intention. It is a hypothetical intention, one has to admit, but an intention nevertheless that can be deduced

94. Gliha, in IEL 242, para 417.

95. *Williams on wills,* vol. 1, 504–505, vol. 2, 1483–1484; Kerridge, *Perry and Clark The Law of Succession,* 14–32 ff. The legal approach is thus quite similar to the American Uniform Probate Code, since according to § 2-508, "if after executing a will the testator is divorced or his marriage annulled, the divorce or annulment revokes any disposition or appointment of property made by the will to the former spouse ( … ) unless the will expressly provides otherwise ( … ). Property prevented from passing to a former spouse because of revocation by divorce or annulment passes as if the former spouse failed to survive the decedent". See L.H. Averill Jr, *Uniform Probate Code in a nutshell,* 5th ed. (St. Paul, Minn. 2001), 265–268.

from another intention expressed in the will. The testator does not insert in the will a clause stipulating the ineffectiveness of the disposition in favour of the spouse if they later divorce. This idea is implicit. A testator routinely wants to benefit the spouse only insofar as he or she is still the spouse at the moment of death. The disposition in favour of the spouse usually fulfils an objective function. Marriage presupposes the co-operation of the spouses in the multiple aspects of ordinary life, including the formation of their respective assets irrespective of whether they are married under a regime of separation of property. Therefore, a testator who makes a disposition in favour of the spouse wishes to recognise those facts and, consequently, he/she pursues the welfare of the surviving spouse. A subsequent judicial separation, divorce, or annulment causes the testator's purpose to vanish and the disposition to lose its reason.[96] The effectiveness is thus automatic. The testator needs not revoke his/her will, nor should any successor bring suit against the surviving spouse. The ineffectiveness is automatic, irrespective of the way the testator has appointed the spouse or the time elapsed since the marriage was dissolved or annulled. As this is a legal effect linked to the hypothetical intention of the testator, the legislator does not impose the ineffectiveness of the disposition. On the contrary, the legislator admits that the testator's intention can be to appoint the spouse as an heir or to bequeath him or her some assets in spite of the divorce. Hence, if the spouse succeeds in proving an intention contrary to the ineffectiveness of the disposition, the property will pass to him/her. However, all the provisions dealing with the effect of divorce on wills require that the intention negating the ineffectiveness of the will appear from the will. In other words, it has to be a testamentary intention, not an extrinsic intention, although extrinsic evidence of that testamentary intention should be admissible, since the purpose must always be to ascertain the true testator's intention. The proof of such contrary intention is quite difficult, apart from the case of the will made during the divorce process. A German case deserves citation: the testator gave part of his assets to his spouse, to his children and to his lover whom he later married.[97]

---

96. R. Battes, *Zur Unwirksamkeit von Testamenten und Erbverträgen nach der Ehescheidung*, *JZ* (1978) 735–736.

97. BGH 6.5.1959, *FamRZ* (1960) 28.

# 8. Concluding Remarks

This chapter shows that spontaneous harmonization becomes evident in core aspects of succession law. Longer life expectancy, reduction of nuclear family structures and changes in the pattern of transfer of property to descendants involve a tendency towards recognizing the prominent role of freedom of testation, though ensuring the protection of minor and disabled children, and strengthening the spouse's position.

# References

Arroyo i Amayuelas, E., Bondia García, D., *¿Interpretación de testamento contraria a los derechos humanos? El caso Pla & Puncernau vs Andorra*, *Derecho Privado y Constitución* (2004).

Ascensão, J. de Oliveira, *Direito civil. Successões* 5th ed. (Coimbra 2000).

Averill Jr, L.H., *Uniform Probate Code in a nutshell*, 5th ed. (St. Paul, Minn. 2001).

Badosa Coll, F., (dir.), *Manual de dret civil català* (Madrid-Barcelona 2003).

Bamberger, H. G., Roth H., *BGB*, Band 3 (München 2003).

Basedow, J., *Das BGB in künftigen europäischen Privatrecht. Der hybride Kodex*, *Archiv für die civilistiche Praxis* (2000).

Battes, R., *Zur Unwirksamkeit von Testamenten und Erbverträgen nach der Ehescheidung*, *Juristenzeitung* (1978).

Belloni, S., *Nota di comento a Cass. Civ. II sez. 18.9.1998*, *Nuova Giurisprudenza Civile Commentata* (2000).

Bonilini, G., *Diritto delle successioni* (Roma-Bari 2004).

Boström, V., *Hereditary relations and testament law in Finland and Sweden*, unpublished paper delivered at the conference "Hereditary relations in Europe" held in Athens on 8–9 February 2001.

Brady, J. C., *Succession Law in Ireland*, 2nd ed. (Dublin 1995).

Brox, H., *Erbrecht*, 21th ed. (Köln 2004).

Bydlinski, F., Mayer-Maly, T., Pichler, J.W., (ed.), *Renaissance der Idee der Kodifikation* (Wien-Köln-Weimar 1990).

Calvo, R., Perlingieri, G. (ed.), *Diritto delle successioni* (Napoli 2008).

Cámara Lapuente, S., *¿Derecho europeo de sucesiones?*, in Cámara Lapuente S., (ed.), *Derecho privado europeo* (Madrid 2003).

Capozzi, Guido, *Successioni e donazioni* 2nd ed. (Milano 2002).

Casas Vallés, R., *Las disposiciones testamentarias a favor del cónyuge y las vicisitudes del matrimonio (Sobre el art. 132 del Código de Sucesiones de Cataluña)*, *Anuario de Derecho Civil* (1993).

Chiodi, G., *L'interpretazione del testamento nei glossatori* (Milano 1997).

Clark, J.B., Martin, J.G.R., *Theobald on Wills* (London 1993).

*Comparative and Historical Essays in Scots Law: A Tribute to Professor Sir Thomas Smith QC* (Edinburgh 1992).

De Waal, M.J., "A comparative overview", in Reid, K.G.C., De Waal, M.J., Zimmermann, R., *Exploring the Law of Succession* (Edinburgh 2007).

Delnoy, P., *Les liberalités et les successions* (Bruxelles 2004).

Delfosse, A., Peniguel, J-F., *La réforme des successions et des liberalités* (Paris 2006).

Díaz Alabart, S., *La sustitución fideicomisaria sobre el tercio de legítima estricta a favor de hijo o descendiente incapacitado judicialmente, Revista de Derecho Privado* (2004).

Dörner, H., Hertel, Ch., Lagarde, P., Riering,W., *Auf dem Weg zu einem europäischen Internationalen Erb-und Erbverfahrensrech, Praxis des internationalen Privat-und Verfahrensrechts* (IPRax) (2005).

Druey, J. N., *Grundriss des Erbrechts,* 5th ed. (Bern 2002).

Eccher, B., *Bürgerliches Recht VI. Erbrecht* (Wien 2000).

Edenfeld, S., *Europäische Entwicklungen im Erbrecht, Zeitschrift für Erbrecht und Vermögensnachfolge* (2001).

Fernández Campos, J.A., *El pago de la legítima al cónyuge viudo* (Valencia 2005).

Foerster, U., *Die Form des Testaments als Grenze seiner Auslegung, Deutsche Notar Zeitschrift* (1993).

Frantzen, T., *Die Stellung des überleben Ehegatten im norwegischen Ehegüter- und Erbrecht: Auswirkungen auf deutsch-norwegische Sachverhalte, Zeitschrift für die vergleichende Rechtswissenschaft* (2002).

Giardini, F., *Testamento e sopravvenienza* (Padova 2003).

Gonçalves de Proença, J.J., *Direito das successões* 2nd ed. (Lisboa 2005).

Grimaldi, M., *Droit civil. Successions,* 6th ed. (Paris 2001).

Hausmann, R., Liin, U., *Grundzüge des neuen estnichen Erbrechts, Jahrbuch für Ostrecht* (2000).

Hartkamp, A. *et al* (eds.), *Towards a European Civil Code. Third fully revised and expanded edition* (2004).

Hayton, D., *European Succession Laws* 2nd ed. (Bristol, 2002).

Henrich, D., Schwab, D., (ed.), *Familienerbrecht und Testierfreiheit im europäischen Vergleich* (Bielefeld 2001).

Hernández Hierro, J. M., *La sucesión forzosa* (Granada 2004).

Hiram, Hilary, *The Scots Law of Succession* (Edinburgh 2002).

*International Encyclopaedia of Laws. Volume IV, Family and Succession Law.*

Jordano Barea, J. B., *El testamento y su interpretación* (Granada 1999).

Jud, B., *Rechtswahl im Erbrecht: Das Grünbuch der Europäischen Kommission zum Erb-und Testamentsrecht, Zeitschrift für Gemeinschaftsprivatrecht, IPRax* (2005).

Kerridge, R., *Hawkins on the Construction of Wills* (London 2000).

Kerridge, R., *Perry and Clark The Law of Succession,* 11th ed. (London 2002).

Kerridge, R., Rivers, J., *The Construction of Wills, Law Quarterly Review* 287 (2000).

Kleensang, *Familienerbrecht versus Testierfreiheit—Das Pflichtteilsentziehungsrecht auf dem Prüfstand des Bundesverfassungsgerichts, Zeitschrift für Erbrecht und Vermögensnachfolge* (2005).

Kuchinke, K., *Über die Notwendigkeit, ein gemeineuropäisches Familien—und Erbrecht zu schaffen,* in *Europas universale reschtsordungspolitische Aufgabe im Recht des dritten Jahrtausends. Festschrift für Alfred Söllner* (München 2000).

*Jurisclasseur de droit comparé.*

Lacruz Berdejo, J.L., *et al, Elementos de derecho civil V. Sucesiones* (Madrid 2004).

*Le droit de successions en Europe. Actes du Colloque du 21 Février 2003* (Genève 2003).

Leipold, D., *Europa und das Erbrecht,* in *Festschrift für Alfred Söllner* (München 2000).

Leipold, D., *Erbrecht,* 15th ed. (München 2004).

Leipold, D., in *Münchener Kommentar zum Bürgerlichen Gesetzbuch,* 4th ed. (München 2004).

Liin, U., *Laws of Succession in Europe and Estonia: How We Got to Where We Are and Where We Should be Heading, Juridica International* (2001) (available at http://www.judica.ee).

Macdonald, D. R., *Succession,* 2nd ed. (Edinburgh 1994).

Malaurie, P., *Les successions. Les liberalités* (Paris 2004).

Mantica, Franciscus, *De coniecturis ultimarum voluntarum* (Lugduni 1581).

Marsal Guillamet, J., *Els fills posats en condició: interpretació del testament i discriminació, Revista Jurídica de Catalunya* (2005).

Martiny, D. *Is Unification of Family Law Feasible or even Desirable?,* in A. Hartkamp *et al* (eds.), *Towards a European Civil Code. Third fully revised and expanded edition* (Nijmegen 2004).

Meston, M. C., *Meston's Succession Opinions, ed by D. O'Donell* (Edinburgh 2000).

Otte, G., *Das Pflichtteilsrecht—Verfassungsrechtssprechung und Rechtspolitik, Archiv für die civilistische Praxis* (2002).

Otte, G., vor. §2064, §2077, in *J. von Staudingers Kommentar zum BGB,* 13th ed. (Berlin 1996).

Palazzo, A., *Le successioni* II, 2nd ed. (Milano 2000).
Palandt/Diederichsen, U., 62nd ed. (München, 2003).
Palandt/Edenhofer, *Bürgerliches Gesetzbuch*, 64th ed. (München, 2003).
Pamplona Corte-Real, C., *Um código civil para a Europa. Necessidade e interesse de uma unificação no âmbito do direito das successões*, unpublished paper delivered at the Conference held in Coimbra (2000) on a European Civil Code organised by the Portuguese Government.
Pintarič, T., *Reform des kroatischen Erbrechts, Zeitschrift für Erbrecht und Vermögensnachfolge* (2003).
Pintens, W., *Grundgedanken und Perspektiven einer Europäisierung des-Familien und Erbrechts, Fam RZ* 329 (2003).
Pintens, W., *Die Europäisierung des Erbrechts, Zeitschrift für europäisches Privatrecht* 628 (2001).
Pintens, W., Pignolet, D., *Le nouveau droit successoral français et son positionnement dans l'européanisation du droit successoral, Familia* (2003).
Pires de Lima, F. A., Antunes Varela, J., *Código civil comentado,* vol. VI, (Coimbra 1998).
*Protokolle der Kommission für die zweite Lesung des Entwurfs des Bürgerlichen Gesetzbuchs,* V (Berlin 1899).
Puelinckx-Coene, M., *La protection de la famille dans le domaine des successions, rapport général de la 6e Conférence Européene sur le droit de la famille.*
Rescigno, P., *Manuale di diritto privato* (Milano 2000).
Rogel Vide, C., in *Comentario del Código civil* I (Madrid 1991).
Rudolf, M., *Handbuch Testamentsauslegung und—anfechtung* (Bonn 2000).
Sawyer, Caroline, *Principles of Succession, Wills and Probate* 2nd ed. (London-Sydney 1998).
Schanze, E., *Interpretation of Wills—an Essay Critical and Comparative*, in D.L. Carey Miller and D.W. Mayers (ed.).
Schimansky, A., *Reform des niederländischen Erbrechts, Zeitschrift für Erbrecht und Vermögensnachfolge* (2003).
Schlüter, W., *Erbrecht,* 15th ed. (München 2004).
Schmid, C., *Legitimitätsbedingungen eines Europäischen Zivilgesetzbuchs, Juristenzeitung* (2001).
Schrage, E.H.J., *Natura pater et filius eadem persona paene intelliguntur, Revista Catalana de Dret Privat* (2002).
Sherrin, C. H., *et al, Williams on Wills,* vol. 1 8th ed. (London-Dublin-Edinburgh 2002)
Sonnekus, J. C., *The New Dutch Code on Succession as Evaluated Through the Eyes of a Hybrid Legal System, Zeitschrift für europäisches Privatrecht* (2005).

Stagl, J.F. *Der Wortlaut als Grenze der Auslegung von testamenten,* 2nd ed. (Wien, 2005).

Stüber, S., comment to BverG 19.4.2005, *Neue Juristische Wochenschrift* 2122 (2005).

Süß, R., in J. Mayer et al, *Handbuch Pflichtteilsrecht* (Angelbachtal 2003).

Süß, R., (ed.), *Erbrecht in Europa* (2nd ed., Angelbachtal 2008).

Trulsen, M., *Pflichtteilsrecht und englische family provision im Vergleich* (Tübingen 2004).

van Dijk, D., *Der Politische Werdergang des Niederländischen Bürgerlichen Gesetzbuches,* in Franz Bydlinski, Theo Mayer-Maly, Johannes W. Pichler (eds.), *Renaissance der Idee der Kodifikation* (Wien-Köln-Weimar 1990).

Vaquer, A., *La capacitat per a testar en la jurisprudència del Tribunal Superior de Justícia de Catalunya, Revista Catalana de Dret Privat* 173 (2002).

Vaquer, A., *Wills, Divorce and the Fate of the Dispositions in Favour of the Spouse: a Common Trend in European Laws of Succession, European Review of Private Law* 782 (2003).

Vaquer, A., *Testamento, disposiciones a favor del cónyuge y crisis del matrimonio, Anuario de Derecho Civil* 67 (2003).

Vaquer, A., *La interpretación del testamento* (Madrid 2008).

Vlassopolou, I., *Kein Noterbrecht für die Hinterbliebenden eines Auslandgriechen, IPRax* 61 (2005).

von Bar, C., *Le group d'éstudes sur un Code civil européen, Revue Internationale de Droit Comparé* (2001).

von Kreittmayr, W. X. V., *Anmerkungen über den Codicem Maxilianeum Bavaricum Civilem* (München 1821).

Watgen, M. and R, *Successions et donations* (3rd ed., Luxembourg 2006).

Welser, R., §552, in Rummel, P., (ed.), *Kommentar zum Allgemeinen Bürgerliches Gesetzbuch,* t. I 3rd ed. (Wien 2000).

Wieling, H. J., *Testamentsauslegung im römischen Recht* (München 1972).

Wigram, John, *An Examination of the Rules of Law, respecting the Admission of Extrinsic Evidence in aid of the Interpretation of Wills* (London 1831).